PROFESSIONAL
WINDOWS® EMBEDDED COMPACT 7

Continues

PROFESSIONAL

Windows® Embedded Compact 7

PROFESSIONAL

Windows® Embedded Compact 7

Samuel Phung
David Jones
Thierry Joubert

WILEY

John Wiley & Sons, Inc.

Professional Windows® Embedded Compact 7

Published by
John Wiley & Sons, Inc.
10475 Crosspoint Boulevard
Indianapolis, IN 46256
www.wiley.com

Copyright © 2011 by John Wiley & Sons, Inc., Indianapolis, Indiana

Published simultaneously in Canada

ISBN: 978-1-118-05046-0
ISBN: 978-1-118-16750-2
ISBN: 978-1-118-16748-9
ISBN: 978-1-118-16747-2

Manufactured in the United States of America

10 9 8 7 6 5 4 3 2 1

For general information on our other products and services please contact our Customer Care Department within the United States at (877) 762-2974, outside the United States at (317) 572-3993 or fax (317) 572-4002.

Wiley also publishes its books in a variety of electronic formats and by print-on-demand. Not all content that is available in standard print versions of this book may appear or be packaged in all book formats. If you have purchased a version of this book that did not include media that is referenced by or accompanies a standard print version, you may request this media by visiting http://booksupport.wiley.com. For more information about Wiley products, visit us at www.wiley.com.

Library of Congress Control Number: 2011934627

ABOUT THE AUTHORS

 SAMUEL PHUNG has worked in the technology field for more than 20 years. In the early 1990s, he led a financial database software development team, developing software for the banking industry. Later he led a software team developing Windows-Based telephony applications for a venture capital-funded startup. He started to work in the embedded computing field in the late 1990s and engaged with the Windows Embedded product team, starting with Windows NT 4.0 Embedded. He has been working with Windows Embedded Compact since version 2.12 was introduced.

As the VP of sales and marketing for ICOP Technology, a hardware manufacturer headquartered in Taiwan with a branch office in the United States and a manufacturing facility in China, Samuel is responsible for strategic business development for ICOP in the North America region. In 2003, he created the Vortex86 branding and started an initiative focused on developing business around Windows Embedded technology for ICOP.

In 2009, he wrote *Professional Microsoft Windows Embedded CE 6.0*.

Samuel enjoys working with technology, actively engages with the academic community, and received the Windows Embedded MVP recognition from Microsoft since 2005. As part of his involvement in the academic community, Samuel actively works with university teaching professionals in the United States, China, and Taiwan and other regions to adopt Windows Embedded technology as part of their teaching curriculum.

As part of his Windows Embedded community activities, Samuel maintains a personal website: www.embeddedpc.net, to provide information resources related to Windows Embedded. In 2010, he initiated the Embedded101 Windows Embedded community portal, www.embedded101.com.

 **DAVID JONES** has a Master of Engineering degree from RMIT University and BSc(Hon) from Melbourne University. David has been actively engaged in Embedded Systems and Computing Technologies for more than twenty years. From 1990 to 2006, he was a University Lecturer in Computer Engineering at RMIT University in Melbourne, Australia. After leaving his university teaching role in late 2006, he joined the Victorian Partnership for Advanced Computing (www.vpac.org) to provide embedded system training, consulting, and development services with a focus on modern Embedded-system technologies. VPAC is a non-profit research agency established in 2000 by a consortium of Victorian Universities to provide advanced computing expertise, training, and support to academia, industry, and government.

While teaching at RMIT, he mentored student teams participating in the Windows Embedded Student Challenge competition sponsored by Microsoft. One of the student teams he mentored won first place during the 2005 worldwide final competition. David actively engages in the Windows Embedded community. He has delivered presentations on behalf of Microsoft in the Asia Pacific region, covering Windows Embedded and .NET technologies. In 2010, he initiated the effort to develop a Device-Driver Wizard and a Component Wizard, both for Windows Embedded CE 6.0 and Windows Embedded Compact 7. He released community versions for both. David is a certified Windows Embedded trainer.

 THIERRY JOUBERT is the CTO and co-founder for THEORIS, a technology company in France that provides project management, software consulting, outsourcing, and training services with focus on modern embedded technology. He graduated from the Ecole Centrale de Nantes in France with an engineering degree in computer science. Thierry has been actively engaged in Embedded-system design and real-time application development for over 25 years.

In addition to his responsibility working on commercial projects, Thierry is actively involved in the academic community, delivering Windows Embedded trainings and technical seminars for engineering schools and universities. In 2004, Thierry developed a case study on Windows CE for Microsoft's MSDN Academic Alliance curriculum, and published multiple technical papers to help teach Windows Embedded technology on the Microsoft Faculty Resource site. To recognize Thierry's effort and contribution to the Windows Embedded developer community, Microsoft has awarded the Windows Embedded MVP status to Thierry since 2007.

ABOUT THE TECHNICAL EDITOR

 **DOUG LOYD** first learned to write code on his parents' Commodore 64, drawing inspiration from the pages of BYTE magazine. He earned his degree in Computer and Information Sciences from the University of Delaware and has spent the last 10 years working on Windows CE devices. He lives in rural Maryland with his wife and daughter. You can contact Doug at douglas.loyd@gmail.com.

CREDITS

ACQUISITIONS EDITOR
Paul Reese

PROJECT EDITOR
Ed Connor

TECHNICAL EDITOR
Doug Loyd

PRODUCTION EDITOR
Daniel Scribner

COPY EDITOR
San Dee Phillips

EDITORIAL MANAGER
Mary Beth Wakefield

FREELANCER EDITORIAL MANAGER
Rosemarie Graham

ASSOCIATE DIRECTOR OF MARKETING
David Mayhew

MARKETING MANAGER
Ashley Zurcher

BUSINESS MANAGER
Amy Knies

PRODUCTION MANAGER
Tim Tate

VICE PRESIDENT AND EXECUTIVE GROUP PUBLISHER
Richard Swadley

VICE PRESIDENT AND EXECUTIVE PUBLISHER
Neil Edde

ASSOCIATE PUBLISHER
Jim Minatel

PROJECT COORDINATOR, COVER
Katie Crocker

PROOFREADER
Jen Larsen, Word One

INDEXER
Robert Swanson

COVER DESIGNER
LeAndra Young

COVER IMAGE
©Aleksandr Volkov/iStockPhoto

ACKNOWLEDGMENTS

FIRST, I WANT TO RECOGNIZE the Windows Embedded Compact development team's effort. Without their hard work, the Windows Embedded Compact product would not be where it is today.

As I went through the process to learn Windows Embedded Compact, I found many information resources on the news group and forum, which helped me learn and resolved problems. I want to thank the developers in the community who helped answer questions on the news group, shared their knowledge, and posted valuable application notes online to help others.

Thanks to David and Thierry for participating in this book project and helping to expand the contents. Throughout the book project, I gained valuable knowledge from David and Thierry.

I want to recognize the following individuals for their helpfulness:

➤ Michael Fosmire with the MVP team. He is always accommodating and willing to listen. I want to thank Michael for the resources he provided to help the Windows Embedded community.

➤ Olivier Bloch with the Windows Embedded team. I could count on Olivier to be responsive and help provide answers to the questions we had throughout the book project.

➤ D'Arcy Salzmann with the Windows Embedded team. D'Arcy initiated the dialog about the book project and motivated us to move forward with this book.

➤ James Y. Wilson, one of the authors of the *Building Powerful Platforms with Windows CE (version 3.0)* book. James helped me to get over the initial hurdle to learn and engage in Windows Embedded Compact development. For the more than 7 years that I have known James, he has provided valuable resources and contributions to both the professional and academic developer communities.

As an amateur writer, with English as my second language, writing is not an easy task. I want to thank Ed Connor and San Dee Phillips, editors for the book project, for reviewing my writing, correcting many mistakes that I made, and providing valuable input.

Most of all, I want to thank my wife, Ann, and my children, Aaron, Narissa and Nathan for their understanding and patience while I took time away from the family to work on the book.

—SAM PHUNG

I WOULD LIKE TO ACKNOWLEDGE the support and assistance I have previously received from Microsoft staff in past, particularly when I was an academic. People in Australia such as Nigel Watson, John Warren, Don Kerr, Tim Schroeder and others have assisted me in many ways. At

Redmond I'd also like to thank Mike Hall, Stewart Tansley, Lindsay Kane, and Sondra Weber. Thanks also to Nelson Lin for your assistance and friendship.

I would like to thank the many students who have worked on Windows Embedded projects with me; especially those who competed in Microsoft Windows Embedded Student Challenges. It has been great to act a facilitator of those projects. I am always amazed at the way students can take nebulous ideas and turn them into something substantial and useful.

The current Windows Embedded team at Microsoft have been timely and constructive with their support during this activity. Thanks to Olivier Bloch, D'Arcy Salzmann, and others. They have been busy with the release of Compact 7 but found the time to support us.

I would also like to thank all of those Embedded MVPs and others who have contributed to my understanding of Windows Embedded though books, presentations, newsgroups, forums, and blogs. There are many of you. ("Standing on the shoulders of giants" — Isaac Newton.)

Thanks Sam and Thierry for input to this activity as co-authors. I have known Sam for a number of years through the Windows Embedded forum. His contribution to Windows Embedded through such things as student and Embedded Spark competitions is invaluable. Sam has been at the helm of this project and without his effort it would not have come to fruition. Thierry has been a great help on the technical side. He has much experience with commercial development with Windows Embedded. His feedback has been precise and constructive.

Thanks also to Ed Connor and San Dee Phillips for their reviews and feedback of my chapters. As a first-time author this has been a big learning curve for me. Their assistance is greatly appreciated.

I'd like to finish with a big thank you to my wife Wendy who has had to put up with my long hours working at this project. Thanks Wendy.

—DAVID JONES

I STARTED WORKING WITH Windows CE 3.0 when Microsoft released it in 2000 and the product has come a long way since then to reach Windows Embedded Compact 7. All these years the Windows Embedded development and marketing teams have made sustained efforts to improve their products. I thank Lorraine Bardeen, Myriam Semery, Sondra Webber, Kevin Dallas, Olivier Bloch, Mike Hall, and D'Arcy Salzmann for their availability and openness when we make suggestions.

A special thanks to Samuel, who invited me as a co-author of this book, and to David who contributed to make the writing task enjoyable. I also thank my colleague Vincent Cruz, who gave me the image transformation code in Chapter 41, and our reviewers Ed Connor and San Dee Phillips.

Most of all I want to thank my family for their patience during this long period where I rarely left my desk.

—THIERRY JOUBERT

CONTENTS

FOREWORD

It's July 2011, I'm in New York judging the Embedded competition at the Imagine Cup (www.imaginecup.com), Samuel Phung and Thierry Joubert (two of the authors of this book) are also embedded judges. I've known Sam, Thierry and David Jones for a number of years and consider them to be good friends. They have been involved with Windows Embedded as MVPs, through the community, the Windows Embedded Student Challenge and Imagine Cup. Each has extensive knowledge of Windows Embedded technologies and is able to provide experience-based insight into building and deploying embedded systems.

Imagine Cup is a worldwide competition that challenges students to solve big problems through innovative use of technology. The theme for the competition this year is, "Imagine a world where technology helps solve the toughest problems." Students are given an embedded hardware reference board and a copy of the Windows Embedded Compact 7 development tools and are then let loose on building something cool that also solves real world problems. Projects range from smart control of street lights, controlling the growth of Algae (for use in bio fuels), self-guiding robots, patient monitoring systems, self-navigating helicopters for use in disasters, harmonica-based lung function training device, smart baby monitoring, intelligent fire escape systems, and TV-based social/communication systems for the elderly.

Now think about all the embedded devices you touch in a single day. This might include a Set Top Box, Digital Picture Frame, Automotive Infotainment device, smart traffic light systems, home automation, thin client devices, conference room projectors, video conference device, ATMs, Point of Sale systems, medical monitoring devices, etc ... Embedded systems are all around us. These devices are smart, connected, and are able to consume and share data across the internet. Conservative estimates predict billions of devices being connected to the internet by 2014, and we've already passed the point where more *devices* are connected to the internet than people.

Windows Embedded Compact 7 is a small footprint, componentized, real-time embedded operating system that runs on ARM, x86, and MIPS processor architectures. The embedded development tools integrate into Visual Studio and enable rapid prototyping of operating system images, user experiences and applications on physical hardware or desktop based emulators. Whether you are building a consumer device that requires a web browser, Flash, and media playback, or an enterprise device that provides a task-based user experience, local database and data sync capabilities, or industrial device that requires hard real-time capabilities, Compact 7 has the tools and technologies you need to bring a smart, connected device to market quickly.

Building an embedded system requires skills ranging from hardware design, driver development, operating system configuration/build, debugging, testing, performance analysis, user interface design and application development — a very diverse set of skills! This book provides novice and experienced embedded developers with practical and hands-on working examples of building embedded devices using Windows Embedded Compact 7.

Now the challenge! Given your newly acquired Windows Embedded Compact 7 skills, and seeing some of the amazing projects students are working on for the Imagine Cup 2011 competition, how do you imagine a world where technology helps solve the toughest problems?

—MIKE HALL
Principal Software Architect
Windows Embedded Business
Microsoft Corporation

INTRODUCTION

WINDOWS EMBEDDED Compact 7 (Compact 7) is a 32-bit, small-footprint, hard real-time operating system (OS) with great graphics and multimedia support, developed by Microsoft to support handheld, mobile, automotive, multimedia, retail, medical, industrial, robotics, and other embedded devices. It's designed to support multiple processor architectures, including ARM, MIPS, and x86.

Windows Embedded Compact development supports subsets of Win32, .NET Framework, and Silverlight and uses the popular Visual Studio integrated development environment to provide a developer-friendly environment to develop embedded applications.

The first version initially released to the public in 1996 as Windows CE; Microsoft subsequently changed the product name to Windows Embedded Compact for the current release. This OS platform has cumulated more than 15 years of continuous development and improvement and evolved to become a mature and robust OS platform. Along with the efficient and developer-friendly environment, Windows Embedded Compact provides the latest networking, multimedia, Silverlight for Windows Embedded, and application development framework that enables the product development team to rapidly develop smart, connected, and service-oriented devices with an exciting and visually compelling user interface.

New Generation of Embedded Devices

During the past three decades, technology has been through a phenomenal growth and is one of the key contributing factors that helped to improve our lives. As technology evolves, new generations of System-on-Chip (SoC) are being built with faster and more powerful processors. Each new generation of SoC is designed with additional integrated peripherals in a smaller package with more built-in features. Although the SoC becomes faster, more powerful, and has more built-in features, the increased demand in the market helps lower the cost. As a new generation of SoC evolves, it enables developers to design and deliver to consumers a new generation of embedded devices with far more capability, at a lower cost than its predecessors. Computers, smartphones, media players, navigation devices, and game consoles are just some of the prime examples.

Aside from the consumer market, a new generation of SoC provides the core engine that enables developers to create a new generation of medical, retail, industrial, robotic, and communication devices that are the critical building blocks to help shape the living environment around us.

Embedded devices are everywhere. Knowingly and unknowingly, we use and interact with embedded devices throughout our daily living, as we travel, work, and go about our everyday life. Think about the ATM, gas pump, ticketing machine, credit card terminal, vending machine, digital camera, remote control, security alarm system, mobile phone, GPS navigation device, and more.

New Generation of Development Platform

As the evolving technology enables a new generation of embedded devices to be built with more functions and features, it also raises consumers' expectation for better products. To keep up with customers' demands and remain competitive in the market, many legacy device manufacturers have to find an efficient and effective development platform to redesign their product with new technology to incorporate additional features and functions, to meet their customers' expectations.

Different development environments require different tools. The environment needed to develop aerospace technology has a different focus than the environment needed to develop general consumer devices. Like an ancient saying in Asia, you do not use a butcher knife to kill a mosquito. To be an efficient and productive developer, you need to identify and select the right development tools for the project.

The Windows Embedded Compact development platform provides the proper balance between the need for a small-footprint OS with hard real-time capability and ease of development, where you can use native code to develop highly efficient applications to meet hard real-time requirements as well as a high-level language such as Visual Basic and C# to rapidly develop applications for different types of devices, servicing the following markets:

- Automotive
- Consumer and entertainment
- Engineering and scientific instrument
- Home and building automation
- Industrial automation, process control, and manufacturing
- Information kiosk and self-serve terminal
- Medical
- Mobile phone and communication
- Office equipment
- Retail and hospitality
- Robotics

In the fast-paced and unforgiving technology market, rapid application development, fast time-to-market, and the ability to manage development risk and minimize cost are key factors contributing to a successful project.

Windows Embedded Compact provides an efficient and effective development environment that helps developers simplify complicated tasks and enables project managers to establish a manageable development plan and schedule.

WHO THIS BOOK IS FOR

This book is written for system integrators who need to create the operating system for a new hardware platform and for application developers who need to develop software for a device. No specific knowledge of Windows Embedded Compact or operating systems is required to understand the content of the book.

Whether you have experience with managed code using C# and Visual Basic or native code using C and C++, the information in this book can help establish the foundation for you to engage in Windows Embedded Compact development.

WHAT THIS BOOK COVERS

Embedded development involves tinkering with hardware, developing interesting devices and writing codes to control and interact with the device. Windows Embedded Compact provides a development environment that enables serious developers to develop highly efficient hard real-time applications using native code to access low-level system resources and hardware. At the same time, entry-level developers can take advantage of the .NET Compact Framework that supports managed code development using the developer-friendly programming languages such as Visual Basic and C# to develop real-life embedded applications.

The Windows Embedded Compact development environment involves multiple development disciplines that cover a broad range of technologies and development expertise. It's not within this book's objectives to cover application development concepts and how to write code.

One of the keys to learn and engage in Windows Embedded Compact development is to know your way around the tools and what they can do for you. This book is written to provide practical information about the Windows Embedded Compact development environment, showing how to use the tools and the debugging and testing facilities.

This book talks about the development environment for Windows Embedded Compact and provides simple exercises, when applicable, to demonstrate how to perform different development tasks. Following is a list of the covered subjects:

- ➤ Windows Embedded Compact operating system overview
- ➤ Development environment overview and required software
- ➤ Board support package, OAL, and bootloader
- ➤ Windows Embedded Compact OS design
- ➤ Target device connectivity using KITL and CoreCon
- ➤ Debugging and debugging tools
- ➤ Developing managed code applications for Windows Embedded Compact devices using Visual Studio
- ➤ Developing native code applications for Windows Embedded Compact devices using Visual Studio
- ➤ Windows Embedded Compact system registry
- ➤ Deployment of Windows Embedded Compact OS and auto-launch application during startup
- ➤ DiskPrep power toy and BIOSLoader
- ➤ Developing stream interface drivers
- ➤ Real-time application

➤ Extending low-level system access to managed code applications with messages

➤ Web service applications for Windows Embedded Compact

HOW THIS BOOK IS STRUCTURED

The content for each chapter is written with minimal dependency on the other chapters. The book contents are organized in seven parts.

Part I: Introducing Embedded Development

➤ **Chapter 1, "Embedded Development"** — This chapter talks about embedded development in general, covering hardware, software, and development considerations for embedded devices.

➤ **Chapter 2, "Windows Embedded Compact 7"** — This chapter introduces Windows Embedded Compact 7 and talks about its features and a little bit of history.

➤ **Chapter 3, "Development Station Preparation"** — This chapter talks about the development station requirements and required software and development station setup.

➤ **Chapter 4, "Development Process"** — This chapter talks about the process to develop a Windows Embedded Compact 7 device.

➤ **Chapter 5, "Development Environment and Tools"** — This chapter talks about the Platform Builder development environment, target device connectivity, and Compact Test Kit.

Part II: Platform Builder and OS Design

➤ **Chapter 6, "BSP Introduction"** — This chapter talks about the board support package and works through the exercise to clone and customize a board support package.

➤ **Chapter 7, "OS Design"** — This chapter talks about Windows Embedded Compact 7 OS design and works through the exercises to develop an OS design and generate an SDK from the OS design.

➤ **Chapter 8, "Target Device Connectivity and Download"** — This chapter talks about target device connectivity and downloading an OS runtime image to the target device.

➤ **Chapter 9, "Debug and Remote Tools"** — This chapter talks about debugging a Compact 7 OS design, debugging the build process, and using remote tools.

➤ **Chapter 10, "The Registry"** — This chapter talks about the Windows Embedded Compact system registry.

➤ **Chapter 11, "The Build System"** — This chapter talks about the build process that compiles and generates the OS run-time image.

➤ **Chapter 12, "Remote Display Application"** — This chapter talks about the remote display application, a useful utility to access a Compact 7 device's desktop remotely.

➤ **Chapter 13, "Testing with Compact Test Kit"** — This chapter talks about the Compact Test Kit and works through the exercises showing the steps to configure and use the test kit.

Part III: Application Development

➤ **Chapter 14, "Application Development"** — This chapter talks about the general environment to develop an application for Windows Embedded Compact.

➤ **Chapter 15, "NET Compact Framework"** — This chapter talks about application development consideration using the .NET Compact Framework.

➤ **Chapter 16, "CoreCon Connectivity"** — This chapter talks about CoreCon and connectivity between the development station and target device to deploy the Visual Studio 2008 application for testing and debugging.

➤ **Chapter 17, "Visual Studio Native Code Application Example"** — This chapter works through an exercise showing the steps to develop a Visual Studio 2008 C++ native code application.

➤ **Chapter 18, "Managed Code Application Example"** — This chapter works through an exercise showing the steps to develop a managed code application using C#.

➤ **Chapter 19, "Platform Builder Native Code Application Example"** — This chapter works through an exercise showing the steps to develop a native code application as a subproject to an OS design in Platform Builder.

➤ **Chapter 20, "Developing Embedded Database Applications"** — This chapter talks about database applications for Compact 7 devices.

➤ **Chapter 21, "Silverlight for Windows Embedded"** — This chapter talks about Silverlight for Windows Embedded, a user interface development framework.

➤ **Chapter 22, "Silverlight for Windows Embedded Application Examples"** — This chapter works through multiple exercises showing the steps to create a Silverlight for Windows Embedded application.

➤ **Chapter 23, "Auto Launching Applications"** — This chapter talks about different options to automatically launch one or more applications during startup.

➤ **Chapter 24, "Application Deployment Options"** — This chapter talks about the different options to deploy Compact 7 applications.

Part IV: Deploy Windows Embedded Compact 7 Devices

➤ **Chapter 25, "Deploy OS Run-time Images"** — This chapter talks about the options and considerations for deploying a Compact 7 OS runtime image to a device.

➤ **Chapter 26, "Bootloader"** — This chapter talks about the bootloader for Compact 7.

➤ **Chapter 27, "BIOSLoader"** — This chapter talks about the BIOSLoader, a bootloader for x86 devices.

➤ **Chapter 28, "The DiskPrep Power Toy"** — This chapter talks about the DiskPrep power toy, a utility that helps simplify the effort to deploy a Compact 7 OS run-time image onto bootable flash media.

Part V: Device Drivers, Bootloader, BSP, and OAL Development

➤ **Chapter 29, "An Overview of Device Drivers"** — This chapter introduces device drivers for the Windows Embedded Compact environment.

➤ **Chapter 30, "Device Driver Architectures"** — This chapter talks about device driver architectures for Windows Embedded Compact.

➤ **Chapter 31, "Interrupts"** — This chapter talks about interrupts in Windows Embedded Compact.

➤ **Chapter 32, "Stream Interface Drivers"** — This chapter talks about stream interface drivers for Windows Embedded Compact.

➤ **Chapter 33, "Developing a Stream Interface Driver"** — This chapter works through an exercise showing the steps to develop a stream interface driver.

➤ **Chapter 34, "Stream Driver API and Device Driver Testing"** — This chapter talks about debugging and testing stream interface drivers.

➤ **Chapter 35, "The Target System"** — This chapter talks about the board support package and OEM adaptation layer development and the required Kernel Independent Transport Layer to support debugging.

Part VI: Advanced Application Development

➤ **Chapter 36, "Introduction to Real-Time Applications"** — This chapter describes the notion of time determinism for embedded systems, and lists the OS-dependent items. It explains why and how Compact 7 can be used for real-time applications.

➤ **Chapter 37, "A Simple Real-Time Application"** — This chapter works through an exercise to create a simple real-time application in order to measure the determinism of Windows Embedded Compact 7 timer drivers.

➤ **Chapter 38, "Extending Low-level Access to Managed Code"** — This chapter talks about accessing low-level system resources from managed code, and focuses on P/invoking the stream driver interface from applications in C-Sharp.

➤ **Chapter 39, "Extending Low-Level Access to Managed Code with Messages"** — This chapter talks about accessing a managed application from native code, it explains how low-level code as a device driver can notify a managed code application with messages.

➤ **Chapter 40, "A Web Server Application"** — This chapter talks about using the HTTP protocol to provide an interface to access a headless device, and works through an exercise to develop a web server application that enables you to access a Compact 7 device's registry remotely from a web browser.

➤ **Chapter 41, "A USB Camera Application"** — Due to the nonstandard hardware environment, the Windows Embedded Compact driver for USB camera is still not readily available. This chapter talks about the USB camera driver project on Codeplex, the Windows CE Webcam project, and works through an exercise showing the steps to use this driver with Compact 7.

Part VII: Sample Projects

➤ **Chapter 42, "Develop a Windows Network Projector"** — This chapter talks about the Windows network projector sample application provided as part of the Windows Embedded Compact to enable the OEM and system integrator to rapidly develop a network-enabled projector device that supports the Connect to Network Project Wizard, available as part of the Windows Vista and Windows 7 OS, and works through an exercise to create a Windows Network Project device.

➤ **Chapter 43, "Phidgets Devices"** — This chapter talks about interfacing a Windows Embedded Compact device to external peripherals. Using the RFID reader module from Phidgets, this chapter works through an exercise showing the steps to develop a simple Compact 7 application to capture data from RFID tags.

➤ **Chapter 44, "FTDI Devices"** — This chapter talks about interfacing a Compact 7 device to FTDI peripherals through an USB interface.

➤ **Chapter 45, "Integrating Managed Code Projects"** — This chapter provides information showing what is needed to include a managed code application project as a subproject to a Compact 7 OS design and to debug the application, as it runs on the target device, using a Kernel Independent Transport Layer (KITL).

In addition to the above chapters, the following appendixes provide additional information resources:

➤ **Appendix A, "Virtual PC Connectivity"** — This appendix provides information about using a Virtual PC as the target device to support Windows Embedded Compact development.

➤ **Appendix B, "Microsoft Resources"** — This appendix provides information about Windows Embedded Compact resources available from Microsoft.

➤ **Appendix C, "Community Resources"** — This appendix provides information about Windows Embedded Compact community resources independent of Microsoft.

➤ **Appendix D, "Embedded Hardware"** — This appendix provides information about embedded hardware.

WHAT YOU NEED TO USE THIS BOOK

To work through the sample code and exercises provided as part of this book, you need a development station and a target device configured to support the Windows Embedded Compact 7 development environment.

Development Station

The development station needs to have the following software installed:

➤ Windows 7, Windows Vista with service pack 2, or Windows XP with service pack 3 and later

➤ Visual Studio 2008

➤ Visual Studio 2008 service pack 1

➤ Microsoft .NET Framework 3.5

➤ Microsoft Expression Blend 3 (needed for the Silverlight for Windows Embedded exercise)

➤ Platform Builder for Windows Embedded Compact 7

Target Device

A target device is needed for the exercises to deploy the Compact 7 OS runtime image and application.

The eBox-3310A-MSJK is used as the target device for the exercises in the book, as shown in Figure I-1.

FIGURE I-1

More information about the eBox-3310A-MSJK is available in Appendix D, "Embedded Hardware."

You can use a Virtual PC machine as the target device. To use an alternative hardware platform as the target device, you need the following resources to work through the exercises in this book:

➤ Board support package for Compact 7

➤ Ethernet connectivity

➤ Ethernet driver for Compact 7 that is able to support Compact 7's Kernel Independent Transport Layer (KITL)

➤ Bootloader to launch Compact 7 OS run-time image from local storage

➤ Bootloader to download Compact 7 OS runtime image from development station

CONVENTIONS

To help you get the most from the text and keep track of what's happening, we've used a number of conventions throughout the book.

 Notes, tips, hints, tricks, and asides to the current discussion are offset and placed in italics like this.

For styles in the text:

➤ We *italicize* new terms and important words when we introduce them.

➤ We show keyboard strokes like this: **Ctrl+A**.

➤ We show filenames, URLs, and code within the text like so: `persistence.properties`.

➤ We present code in two different ways:

```
We use a monofont type with no highlighting for most code examples.
We use bold to emphasize code that's particularly important in the present
context.
```

SOURCE CODE

As you work through the examples in this book, you may choose either to type in all the code manually or to use the source code files that accompany the book. All the source code used in this book is available for download at www.wrox.com. When at the site, simply locate the book's title (either by using the Search box or by using one of the title lists) and click the Download Code link on the book's detail page to obtain all the source code for the book. Code that is included on the Web site is highlighted by the following icon:

Available for
download on
Wrox.com

Listings include the filename in the title. If it is just a code snippet, you'll find the filename in a code note such as this:

Code snippet filename

 Because many books have similar titles, you may find it easiest to search by ISBN; this book's ISBN is 978-1-118-05046-0.

After you download the code, just decompress it with your favorite compression tool. Alternatively, you can go to the main Wrox code download page at www.wrox.com/dynamic/books/download .aspx to see the code available for this book and all other Wrox books.

ERRATA

We make every effort to ensure that there are no errors in the text or in the code. However, no one is perfect, and mistakes do occur. If you find an error in one of our books, like a spelling mistake or faulty piece of code, we would be grateful for your feedback. By sending in errata you may save another reader hours of frustration, and at the same time you can help us provide even higher quality information.

To find the errata page for this book, go to www.wrox.com and locate the title using the Search box or one of the title lists. Then, on the book details page, click the Book Errata link. On this page you can view all errata that has been submitted for this book and posted by Wrox editors. A complete book list including links to each book's errata is also available at www.wrox.com/misc-pages/booklist.shtml.

If you don't spot "your" error on the Book Errata page, go to www.wrox.com/contact/techsupport.shtml and complete the form there to send us the error you have found. We'll check the information and, if appropriate, post a message to the book's errata page and fix the problem in subsequent editions of the book.

P2P.WROX.COM

For author and peer discussion, join the P2P forums at p2p.wrox.com. The forums are a Web-based system for you to post messages relating to Wrox books and related technologies and interact with other readers and technology users. The forums offer a subscription feature to e-mail you topics of interest of your choosing when new posts are made to the forums. Wrox authors, editors, other industry experts, and your fellow readers are present on these forums.

At p2p.wrox.com you can find a number of different forums to help you not only as you read this book, but also as you develop your own applications. To join the forums, just follow these steps:

1. Go to p2p.wrox.com and click the Register link.

2. Read the terms of use and click Agree.

3. Complete the required information to join as well as any optional information you want to provide, and click Submit.

4. You will receive an e-mail with information describing how to verify your account and complete the joining process.

 You can read messages in the forums without joining P2P but to post your own messages, you must join.

After you join, you can post new messages and respond to messages other users post. You can read messages at any time on the Web. If you would like to have new messages from a particular forum e-mailed to you, click the Subscribe to This Forum icon by the forum name in the forum listing.

For more information about how to use the Wrox P2P, be sure to read the P2P FAQs for answers to questions about how the forum software works as well as many common questions specific to P2P and Wrox books. To read the FAQs, click the FAQ link on any P2P page.

PART I
Introducing Embedded Development

1

Embedded Development

WHAT'S IN THIS CHAPTER?

- ➤ Defining an embedded device
- ➤ Using software for an embedded device
- ➤ Establishing key elements for embedded development

Embedded development has been around for decades. The terms such as *embedded system* and *embedded computer* are widely used by marketing professionals across multiple industries. However, the actual meaning and representation for the term *embedded* is still vague.

Although it's not within this book's objective to delve into the definition for the term embedded, you need to understand a general boundary for the embedded device, embedded software, and development environment relevant to Windows Embedded contents in this book.

WHAT IS AN EMBEDDED DEVICE?

When referring to an embedded device, some of you may still think of the small devices, typically built with a microcontroller with limited processing capability and memory. Contrary to this thinking, many embedded devices in today's market are built with a powerful processor, abundant memory, and storage.

Some of the current embedded devices are built with computing technology that can rival an enterprise class server from just a few years ago. Not too long ago, enterprise servers were built with processors that operate in the sub gigahertz (GHz) range, with system memory in the 100 megabyte (MB) range and storage in the gigabyte (GB) range.

Today, many of you use smartphones built with a GHz processor, 512MB or more system memory, and 8GB to 32GB of storage.

As technology rapidly advances and enables more powerful processor modules with more integrated features to be built in a smaller footprint at a lower cost, it enables a new generation of consumer, industrial, medical, robotics, education, and other devices to be built with better and innovative features that can deliver these devices to the market with a higher perceived value at a lower cost.

Today, using available technology, embedded devices can be built with a broad range of capabilities, with processors ranging from low-power, 8-bit microcontrollers with limited memory to powerful processors with CPU clocks operating in the GHz, memory in the GB, and storage in the 100-GB range. With some imagination and creativity, the possibilities for embedded devices are endless.

Similarity to Personal Computer

From a general architecture point of view, an embedded device has many similarities to a typical personal computer (PC).

➤   It has a processor.

➤   It has system memory.

➤   It has storage to store software.

➤   It requires software applications to be useful.

Difference from Personal Computer

Although a general purpose PC is designed to enable the user to install different operating systems and software applications to perform different tasks, an embedded device is built with preconfigured software, designed to perform a specific set of tasks and functions.

Table 1-1 shows some of the differences between the PC and embedded device.

TABLE 1-1: Personal Computer and Embedded Device Comparison

PERSONAL COMPUTER	EMBEDDED DEVICE
Support 1024x768 or better display resolution	Headless (does not support displays) Smaller displays that support limited resolution LCD modules that display ASCII text.
Keyboard and mouse to capture user input	Handful of hardware buttons and touch screens to capture user input
Abundant system memory, common for PC to equip with 2GB or more RAM	Limited system memory
Abundant storage, common for PC to equip with 300GB or larger hard disk for storage	Flash storage with limited storage capacity

Specialized Purpose Device

An embedded device is a specialized purpose device designed to serve a specific purpose and built to meet designated specifications and cost objectives.

For some markets, the same hardware used to build a general purpose PC can be used to build a specialized purpose embedded device; therefore, making the distinction between an embedded device and personal computer vague.

Following are two separate application scenarios that use similar hardware. One of them is categorized as a general purpose computer and the other as a specialized purpose device:

➤ A small retail store owner uses a computer as a point-of-sale terminal. In addition, this store owner uses the same computer to send and receive e-mail using Outlook, to write business letters using Word, and to install additional software onto the PC to perform accounting and record keeping-related tasks.

➤ A major department chain store uses computers as point-of-sale terminals for each of its branch locations. To minimize service and support issues and to simplify management tasks, the computers are configured to perform only point-of-sale-related tasks. The computers are also configured to not enable additional software to be installed and limit access to its system to prevent existing software accidentally being removed.

In the first preceding scenario, the store owner uses the computer as a general-purpose PC. In the second scenario, the department chain store uses the computer as a specialized-purpose device.

Example of Embedded Devices

Embedded devices are all around you. Think about your daily living, when you travel, visit a theme park, interact with a financial institution, use entertainment devices in your home, drive your automobile, and so on.

Following are examples of some of the embedded devices in today's market:

➤ Mobile phone
➤ Set-top-box
➤ Television
➤ Media entertainment system
➤ Printer
➤ Portable media player
➤ GPS navigation device
➤ Credit card processing terminal
➤ Automated ticketing machine
➤ Digital camera
➤ Medical instrument
➤ Engineering instrument

➤ Network router

➤ Information kiosk

➤ Automated teller machine

➤ Video projector

➤ Self-serve checkout station at your local super market

WHAT IS EMBEDDED SOFTWARE?

While software applications for general purpose PCs are designed to function on a broad range of computers, built by different manufacturers that meet general requirements (such as processor speed, available memory, and storage), software developed for the embedded device is intended for one specific model or category of devices.

Comparing to software for general purpose PCs, following are the main differences for embedded software:

➤ Designed to operate on hardware with limited resources.

➤ Application codes are tightly coupled with hardware.

➤ Errors and exceptions can't be thrown to the user.

Programming Languages and Principles

Other than the different development considerations, which will be explored later in this chapter, similar programming languages and principles apply to developing Windows applications for a desktop PC and embedded applications for a Windows Embedded Compact device.

If you are developing desktop PC applications using Visual Studio 2005 and 2008, you are already familiar with the Visual Studio application development environment for Windows Embedded Compact. With little more effort, you can easily adapt existing Visual Studio experience to develop Windows Embedded Compact applications.

Programming Discipline

When developing applications for a general-purpose desktop PC, you can make the following assumptions about the PC, without considering the end user's environment in detail:

➤ It's equipped with a 1.0 GHz or faster processor.

➤ It has at least 1GB or more of system memory.

➤ It has a hard disk with abundant storage space, in the 100GB range.

➤ The video output is capable of supporting a 1024x768 or better display resolution.

➤ A keyboard and mouse are used to capture user input.

➤ A network connection is available.

When developing applications for an embedded device, you cannot make any of the preceding general assumptions and must have details and accurate information about the device's features and capability. You also need to have a clear understanding about the device's operating environment and how the end users interact with the device. The embedded device may be built with the following features:

- ➤ Headless without a user interface
- ➤ Limited system memory and storage
- ➤ Battery powered
- ➤ A few hardware buttons to capture user input

You also may be required to develop applications for an embedded device to meet one or more of the following design objectives:

- ➤ Minimize power consumption to extend operating time for battery-powered devices.
- ➤ Minimize memory and resources leakage for devices that operate 24/7.
- ➤ Meet the hard real-time characteristic for the timing critical device that requires the application to perform required tasks within a specified time slot.
- ➤ Prevent file corruption resulting from unexpected loss of power to the device.
- ➤ Develop applications to directly access and control the device's hardware.
- ➤ Develop applications to access a headless device (built without a user interface) remotely for service and maintenance purposes.
- ➤ Develop applications to perform self-diagnostic functions and implement automated routines to correct errors found.

Seasoned embedded developers develop the discipline to account for additional design considerations from their experience, which may include technical issues, user interactions, and an operating environment related to the final product. Often, these additional design considerations are not part of the specifications and requirements; however, in many cases, these additional design considerations are critical to the project's success.

Specialized Purpose Application

Although software for the PC is designed to operate on all desktop and portable notebook computers that meet a general technical specification, embedded software is a specialized-purpose application designed to run on one particular class or category of specialized-purpose device.

Software for the PC is designed to enable the end user to install and remove the application at will. However, embedded software is usually shipped as a preinstalled component on the device and is designed to limit the end user's ability to remove the software from the device or to make changes.

DEVELOPMENT CONSIDERATIONS

Embedded development skill is a discipline that cumulates and improves over time, with active engagement and hands-on involvement in the actual embedded development projects.

Operating systems, programming languages, and the hardware platforms are tools used by the developer to design, compose, and build embedded devices.

Whether working on a PC or an embedded device development project, you can have similar development concerns and needs, such as the following:

➤ Firmware

➤ Operating system

➤ Hardware adaptation codes

➤ Device drivers for peripherals

➤ File system

➤ Network protocol stack

➤ Codecs

➤ Support libraries

➤ Application

An embedded device development project can involve any or all these concerns. To be effective, an embedded developer needs to have a good understanding about the device's operating environment, how the user uses the device, the hardware platform, and design objectives.

Different categories of embedded device design objectives are quite different, such as the following:

➤ A consumer-oriented device needs to meet the targeted performance at the least cost, sufficient for the device to meet the 1-year to 3-year warranty period.

➤ In addition to meeting the targeted function requirements, many embedded devices designed for industrial applications need to meet strict quality requirements, operate 24/7, and survive a harsh operating environment that involves a wide operating temperature range from −40°C to +85°C and exposure to high humidity and chemical conditions.

In general, when working on an embedded development project, in addition to the design specification, the development team needs to consider the following:

➤ Hardware

➤ Operating environment

➤ User environment

Hardware

In addition to the direct impact to the cost of manufacturing, the selected hardware can affect the development schedule and engineering cost. When selecting the hardware, you need to consider the following:

➤ Is the required hardware readily available in the market?

➤ Are there sufficient components available in the market and engineering resources to develop customized hardware for the project?

➤ Is the selected hardware's processor architecture supported by the selected operating system?

➤ Can the hardware vendor provide support for the selected operating system?

➤ Does the selected hardware provide the best value from an overall project perspective? (Lower-cost hardware may require additional development, have limitations that create other cost centers, raise the overall project cost, and significantly impact the project's time-to-market schedule.)

Operating Environment

To develop a good product, you need to understand how the product is used and the environment the product needs to operate in. You need to take into account the following considerations, which may impact the hardware requirements:

➤ How can the embedded device be used?

➤ What temperature range is the device expected to operate in?

➤ Can the device operate 24/7?

➤ Can the device be deployed on an automobile, a vessel, or an airplane?

➤ Can the device be subjected to vibration and shock during operation?

➤ Can the device be subjected to strong electrostatic shock during operation?

➤ Can the device be placed in an outdoor environment?

User Environment

User expectation is one of the most important factors. If the embedded device does not meet user expectation, the user is not likely to purchase or use the device.

Feasibility

From an engineering perspective, with sufficient resources and time, the development team can engineer a perfect device. In real life, all development projects are bounded by the following:

➤ Limited development resources and budget.

➤ Development must be completed within a predetermined schedule.

After all the technical, environment, and user requirements are met, the product development team also needs to consider the required resources and time needed to successfully complete all required development tasks. These considerations can have a strong impact on the business' cost, profit, and time-to-market and can influence whether to move the project forward.

SUMMARY

Embedded development is an engineering discipline that involves multiple technical skills, covering both hardware and software. As technology rapidly changes and evolves, the embedded development environment will continue to change, adopt new technology, and create new ways to do things.

A career in the embedded development field can be challenging and rewarding at the same time. It's a challenge to learn and adapt rapidly to changing technologies. It's also rewarding to work with a broad range of technology to create cool devices that can help solve challenging problems.

Windows Embedded Compact 7

WHAT'S IN THIS CHAPTER?

➤ Introducing Windows Embedded Compact

➤ Exploring new features in Windows Embedded Compact 7

➤ Understanding a little bit of history

➤ Seeing what you do with Windows Embedded Compact

➤ Choosing Windows Embedded Compact

With the first version released in 1996, the Windows Embedded Compact family of technology has been through more than 15 years in the making. Evolving through seven major versions, with countless hours of development, bug fixes, improvements, and enhancements, this latest version is solid, packed with features, and optimized to enhance performance and security.

To help you better understand Windows Embedded Compact, this chapter provides a brief overview of Windows Embedded Compact 7, the market it serves, and some of the key features.

WHAT IS WINDOWS EMBEDDED COMPACT?

Windows Embedded Compact is not binary-compatible with any version of the desktop Windows operating system (OS) and is not a scaled-down version of a desktop Windows OS. Windows Embedded Compact was created initially to service the handheld portable computing device market and was developed from the ground up to support multiple processor architectures.

It is a small-footprint, highly customizable, 32-bit OS with hard real-time capabilities, developed to support multiple processor architectures, including ARM, MIPS, and x86.

Windows Embedded Compact is a multithreaded, multitasking, and preemptive OS. It can handle up to 32,000 concurrent processes. Each process can access up to 2GB of virtual memory.

Compact 7 is designed to support a new generation of small-footprint, smart, connected, and service-oriented embedded devices, built with limited system memory, storage, and processing resources.

Since its inception in 1996, each new version of this product has been improved with added features while maintaining the following design criteria:

- **Small footprint** — Depends on selected components.

- **Modular architecture** — Componentized OS enables the OEM to make decisions about components to include in the final runtime image.

- **Real-time support** — Provides bounded, deterministic response times.

- **Support of broad range of hardware** — ARM, MIPS, and x86.

- **Efficient power management** — Provides uniform power management libraries.

- **Efficient development tools** — Applications can be developed with C, C++, C#, and Visual Basic using the Visual Studio integrated development environment.

- **Efficient debugging and testing tools** — The Compact 7 development environment provides efficient connectivity to enable Real Time debugging, as the OS image and application execute on the target device. A full-featured Windows Embedded Compact Test Kit includes a board-support-package, device driver, and memory leak and stress tests.

Windows Embedded Compact 7 Features

Windows Embedded Compact is optimized for devices built with minimal memory and storage and processing resources. Windows Embedded Compact provides the flexibility for you to build and configure a device with just the required components, as a closed system that does not enable an end user to add or modify an application, or as an open system that enables the end user to enhance the system with additional applications.

Without being redundant to the product information provided as part of the product documentation and on Microsoft's MSDN site, following are some of the key features for the Windows Embedded Compact product family:

- Deterministic hard real-time operating system

- Separate kernel-mode and user-mode spaces, keeping critical codes separate from noncritical codes to enhance system security and stability

- FAT12, FAT16, FAT32, and exFAT file systems

- UDF and UDFS v2.5 file systems to support CD, DVD, and HDDVD

- Graphic and multimedia core components

- Touch and Gesture user interface

- Silverlight for Windows Embedded

- Digital Rights Management (DRM) technology
- Video and audio capture pipeline
- Voice over IP (VoIP)
- Web, FTP, and file servers
- DirectDraw, DirectShow, and DirectX
- Networking with Bluetooth, NDIS, Remote Desktop Protocol (RDP), TCP/IP, and Wi-Fi
- USB host and device
- Cellcore component to access mobile communication resources
- Internet Explorer, Windows Media player
- Microsoft Office application viewers
- Win32 API and .NET Compact Framework
- SQL Compact and EDB (a lightweight and efficient database engine)
- International languages support

The latest version, Windows Embedded Compact 7, is a continuing development from the Windows Embedded CE 6.0 (CE 6.0) OS kernel. Prior to CE 6.0 release, the OS kernel was limited to 32 concurrent running processes with each process accessing 32MB of virtual memory. Major redevelopment effort was invested in CE 6.0 to enable the kernel to support up to 32,000 concurrent processes with 2GB of accessible virtual memory per process. For Compact 7, the kernel is further enhanced with additional features and optimized to improve performance and stability.

In addition to the large collection of components already available as part of the previous version, following are some of the new features added to the Compact 7 release:

- Multicore processor support.
- Supports up to 3GB of physical memory (up from 512MB in CE 6.0).
- Silverlight for Windows Embedded, a user interface (UI) development framework that enables developers to create visually compelling UI for embedded devices.
- Digital Living Network Alliance (DLNA) support, as digital media renderer, server, and controller.
- Media Transfer Protocol (MTP) support.
- Internet Explorer for Embedded, based on IE 7 with some performance updates from IE 8 added.
- Flash 10.1 renderer included without the need to pay additional license fee.
- Updated to use NDIS 6.1 network stack.
- Updated Microsoft Office application and PDF viewers.
- Better touch and gesture support.

➤ New remote tools framework with updated remote tools for debugging.

➤ Windows Embedded Compact test kit. This test kit replaces the CE Test Kit (CETK) for CE 6.0 and prior, with significant improvement and added features. This new test kit has a completely new graphical user interface to help simplify the tasks needed to test board support packages, device drivers, and application components.

In addition to the new features mentioned, a lot of effort has been invested to improve and optimize the network stack, file system, USB stack, and other system components to enhance system performance, security, and stability.

Modular and Compact Operating System

Compact 7 is a highly modular OS. Each Compact 7 OS runtime image is composed of a collection of components, which include the OS, programming library, hardware interface, device driver, application, and other software components.

Using Platform Builder, a plug-in to the Visual Studio 2008 integrated development environment, you can create and configure a customized Compact 7 OS design and include only the needed components to generate an OS runtime image with the smallest possible footprint.

A device built with smaller footprint OS runtime image requires less system memory, storage, and processing resources to run.

A device built with a smaller footprint OS image takes less time to boot up. By minimizing the OS footprint, you can build the device with lesser-cost hardware, which helps improve the device's value and competitiveness.

Real-Time Operating System

There are soft real-time and hard real-time systems. A soft real-time system can miss its bounded time response once in a while and still maintain a reasonable level of acceptable performance, such as when a Voice over IP device may delay, or skip, the delivery of voice packets and still provide acceptable service to the user.

A hard real-time system cannot miss any of its bounded time responses. When a hard real-time system misses a bounded time response, it can cause catastrophic system failure. Imagine what happens when an automobile's electronic brake system fails to engage in a timely manner, while the automobile travels at a high speed and needs to make an urgent stop to avoid a collision.

Compact 7 is a hard real-time OS that provides reliable core services to support embedded system design that demands low-latency, deterministic real-time system performance. Compact 7 has the following features required by a real-time system.

➤ Multithreaded and preemptive

➤ Prioritized thread scheduling

➤ Priority inversion prevention using priority inheritance to dynamically adjust thread priorities

➤ Predictable thread synchronization

Support Broad Range of Hardware

Compact 7 supports hardware built with ARM, MIPS, and x86 processors. The Compact 7 OS provides the platform to support multiple families of a processor by abstracting the hardware features with hardware adaptation layer codes unique to each processor family, referred to as the OEM Adaptation Layer (OAL).

By abstracting hardware-specific features to provide a uniform application programming interface across multiple families of a processor, Compact 7 provides a uniform development environment that helps simplify development project management effort and minimize development cost.

With a quality board support package (BSP was developed to support the target device), you can create a customized Compact 7 OS runtime image for the target device, with minimum knowledge about the device's hardware, and include the necessary OS components to support your application.

History

With the initial version released in November 1996, Compact 7 reaches its 15th birthday in November 2011. Following is a list of the major releases for the Windows Embedded Compact product family:

- ➤ 1996 — Windows CE 1.0
- ➤ 1997 — Windows CE 2.0
- ➤ 1998 — Windows CE 2.11
- ➤ 1999 — Windows CE 2.12
- ➤ 2000 — Windows CE 3.0
- ➤ 2002 — Windows CE .NET 4.0
- ➤ 2002 — Windows CE .NET 4.1
- ➤ 2003 — Windows CE .NET 4.2
- ➤ 2004 — Windows CE 5.0
- ➤ 2006 — Windows Embedded CE 6.0
- ➤ 2007 — Windows Embedded CE 6.0 R2
- ➤ 2009 — Windows Embedded CE 6.0 R3
- ➤ 2011 — Windows Embedded Compact 7

Windows CE was the initial product name. With version 4.0, released in 2002, the name changed to Windows CE .NET, as part of Microsoft's .NET evolution. When version 6.0 was released in 2006, the name changed to Windows Embedded CE 6.0. As Microsoft releases the latest version, the name has been changed to Windows Embedded Compact 7.

In addition to the major version releases listed, the Windows Embedded Compact core technology has also been adopted by other product groups within Microsoft, such as Pocket PC, Windows

Mobile, Windows Automotive, Zune, and Windows Phone. Following is a list showing some of these products:

➤ Pocket PC 2000

➤ Pocket PC 2002

➤ Windows Automotive

➤ Windows Embedded Automotive /

➤ Windows Smartphone 2002

➤ Windows Smartphone 2003

➤ Windows Mobile 2003

➤ Windows Mobile 5.0

➤ Windows Mobile 6.0

➤ Windows Mobile 6.5

➤ Windows Embedded Handheld

➤ Windows Phone 7

In addition to the general product releases, as part of Microsoft's support effort, countless number of fixes, enhancements, and updates, known as Quick Fix Engineering (QFE), are released monthly to help resolve problems that arise in the field.

If you want to know more about Windows Embedded Compact's history, the following page on the Wikipedia site, `http://en.wikipedia.org/wiki/Windows_CE`, *has a good collection of information.*

Targeted Market

The first version of Windows Embedded Compact, Windows CE 1.0, released in 1996, was created for the Handheld PC.

With Windows CE 2.0 released in 1997, this version found its way into the PDA market. Auto PC 1.0 was born from Windows CE 2.01. As version 2.10, 2.11, and 2.12 evolved, developers started to adopt Windows CE to develop applications for a variety of vertical markets.

With Windows CE 3.0 released in 2000, Microsoft started to dominate the PDA market with PocketPC and began to engage in the mobile smartphone market.

As the Windows Embedded Compact technology evolved with improvements and enhancements added to each new version, more developers adopted the technology to develop a broad range of applications for a different vertical market, including the following:

➤ Automotive

➤ Consumer device

➤ Home and building automation

➤ Industrial automation and control

➤ Instruments

➤ Medical device

➤ Mobile phone

➤ Portable GPS Navigation

➤ Retail and hospitality

➤ RFID

➤ Robotics

➤ Security and access control

➤ Telematics

WHY WINDOWS EMBEDDED COMPACT?

With more than 15 years in the making, continuous development, enhancement, and improvement, the Windows Embedded Compact product is feature-rich, mature, and stable with a strong proven track record. Windows Embedded Compact has been adopted by hundreds of key companies worldwide with tens of millions of devices shipped.

The OS is one of the critical components for your project. With Windows Embedded Compact, you have the assurance the underlying operating system technology is supported by the largest software company on the planet, with the sole interest to help you complete your development project quickly and efficiently to ship your product.

Microsoft cannot receive license revenue from your product until you successfully complete the development, release the design to production, and ship the product to the end user.

With Windows Embedded Compact, you don't need to worry about potential intellectual property licensing conflicts associated with components you use as part of the OS. Microsoft provides the license to use the components, available as part of the Windows Embedded Compact to support your product. Microsoft is responsible for handling any legal complications that arise from the use of these components.

Developer-Friendly Tools

Platform Builder for Windows Embedded Compact 7 is a plug-in to the Visual Studio 2008 integrated development environment (VS2008 IDE). With VS2008 IDE, Windows Embedded Compact provides an efficient and developer-friendly environment that helps simplify complicated development tasks. With Visual Studio 2008 as the primary development environment, you can develop a broad range of Windows Embedded Compact applications using C, C++, C#, and Visual Basic.

If you currently use VS2008 for PC-related development tasks, you can find a lot of similarities when developing Compact 7 applications. If you are new to VS2008, you can find the graphical user interface is easy to use and learn.

Debug, Testing, and Quality Control

Debugging and testing consume a large portion of a development project's resources. During the planning stage, it's difficult to accurately estimate resources and efforts needed to resolve bugs and development mishaps during the development process.

A development team with an efficient and effective debugging and testing environment can help minimize the impact associated with bugs and development mishaps.

Windows Embedded Compact provides efficient debugging and testing facilities, which include Kernel Independent Transport Layer (KITL) and CoreCon connectivity to support the included remote tools' framework, which enable you to trace and debug OS design, device driver, programming library, and application codes as they execute on the target device.

Windows Embedded Compact also includes the Compact Test Kit, which enables you to perform compatibility and quality control tests related to the BSP, device drivers, and application.

SUMMARY

Windows Embedded Compact is a mature, real-time capable, small-footprint embedded operating system with features to support a new generation of media-rich, smart, connected, and service-oriented devices.

With its well-established code base, efficient development environment, and large pool of hardware and technical support resources, Windows Embedded Compact is an attractive development platform that can minimize development cost and risk and help the product development team to shorten development schedules and gain a critical time-to-market advantage.

3

Development Station Preparation

WHAT'S IN THIS CHAPTER?

➤ Introducing development computer requirements

➤ Defining the required software and installation

➤ Exploring the development environment

A properly configured development station helps minimize problems caused by inadequate software installation and improper setup, which can be difficult to identify and can waste unnecessary development resources. This chapter provides information about requirements for the development computer and best practices to set up an effective development environment to work with Windows Embedded Compact.

DEVELOPMENT COMPUTER REQUIREMENTS

It's a common practice for a software provider to specify the minimum system requirements needed for the software to function. In the actual working environment, it's good to invest a little more to get a better development computer with a faster processor and more system memory and storage. The return on investment, in terms of time-saving and increased efficiency, is much greater than the cost.

Hardware

Platform Builder for Compact 7 documentation states the following minimum development computer requirements:

➤ 2.4GHz or faster CPU

➤ 1024MB or more system memory (RAM)

➤ 1280x1024 or better display resolution

➤ 7200RPM or faster hard disk

As PC technology rapidly advanced in recent years, a PC is no longer privileged equipment for the IT professional and becomes a consumer device that many people simply cannot live without. The PC market's exponential growth and enormous market size make it possible for PC manufacturers to produce higher performance PCs at a much lower cost.

It's best to get the highest performance computer with the most system memory and storage you can afford. If you work in the computer software development and consulting field, you can recover the additional investment within 1 to 3 months in time-saving and added efficiency with a higher performance development computer. For this book, the following minimum is recommended for the development computer:

➤ Quad cores CPU

➤ 4GB or more RAM

➤ 7200RPM or faster hard disk with much more than 100GB of available space

Platform Builder for Compact 7 requires more than 50GB of storage space for a full install. Each OS design project can take as much as 1GB to well over 3GB of storage. If you need to save and maintain OS design projects that you develop, you need a lot of storage space.

In addition to the above recommendation, it's good to have a second monitor to display multiple screens simultaneously. As part of the OS design and application development process for Windows Embedded Compact, you need to view and refer to information from multiple program screens. Two display monitors provide more display space, enable you to view multiple screens simultaneously, and minimize the need to switch from one screen to another, which helps increase your efficiency and save time.

Software

Platform Builder for Windows Embedded Compact 7 is a plug-in for Visual Studio 2008 and requires the following to function:

➤ Visual Studio 2008

➤ Visual Studio 2008 Service Pack 1

➤ .NET Compact Framework 3.5

➤ Expression Blend 3 (needed to support Windows Embedded Silverlight tools)

You can set up a Windows Embedded Compact 7 development computer with any one of the following Windows desktop operating systems:

➤ Windows XP with Service Pack 3

➤ Windows Vista with Service Pack 2

➤ Any version of Windows 7, including both 32-bit and 64-bit

WINDOWS EMBEDDED COMPACT 7 SOFTWARE

Platform Builder is the primary development tool for Windows Embedded Compact 7 to develop a customized OS runtime image, device driver, BSP, and OAL codes. Instead of referring to the full product name, most developers use the abbreviated versions such as Platform Builder for Compact 7, Platform Builder 7, or just Platform Builder.

Following are the two available versions of Windows Embedded Compact 7 software, the evaluation version and full version:

➤ **Full version in retail package** — This version includes Platform Builder for Windows Embedded Compact 7, Visual Studio 2008 Professional edition, and Expression Blend 3. To purchase the retail package, locate a distributor in your region from the following URL:

```
http://www.microsoft.com/windowsembedded/en-us/partners/find-microsoft-
authorized-embedded-distributor.aspx
```

The full version is available for download as part of MSDN Embedded, Visual Studio Premium with MSDN, or Visual Studio Ultimate with MSDN subscription.

➤ **180-day evaluation version on DVD software package** — This version includes the 180-day evaluation version of Platform Builder for Compact 7 and 90-day evaluation version of Visual Studio 2008 Professional Edition. You can order this software package from the following URL:

```
https://ms.kpcorp.com/WinEmbedded/AspxFiles/Home.aspx
```

The 180-day evaluation version is available for download from the Microsoft website.

Other than the 180-day usage limit, the evaluation version is fully functional, which provides a good environment for you to fully evaluate and try Windows Embedded Compact 7 before making a financial commitment to purchase the full version. You can download the evaluation version, without cost, from the following URL:

```
http://www.microsoft.com/windowsembedded/en-us/downloads/download-windows-
embedded-compact-ce.aspx
```

Recommended Installation Steps

When the required software is not properly installed to the development computer, you may not correctly identity whether the problem you have is caused by the codes you develop or improper software setup. You need to install the required software in a proper sequence to minimize problems.

Following are recommended steps to install Compact 7 and related software:

Windows Embedded Compact 7 does not support a side-by-side install with the earlier version, Windows Embedded CE 6.0. If you have a previous version, uninstall the previous version before installing Compact 7.

1. Visual Studio 2008.

Visual Studio 2008 Express edition does not support Platform Builder for Compact 7. It's recommended that you use the Visual Studio 2008 Professional edition. A full version of Visual Studio 2008 Professional edition is included as part of the retail package version of Windows Embedded Compact 7 software.

A 90-day evaluation version of the Visual Studio 2008 Professional edition is included as part of the evaluation version of Windows Embedded Compact 7 DVD.

The 90-day evaluation version of Visual Studio 2008 Professional edition is available for download from the following URL:

```
http://www.microsoft.com/downloads/en/details.aspx?FamilyID=83c3a1ec-ed72-
4a79-8961-25635db0192b&displaylang=en
```

2. Visual Studio 2008 Service Pack 1.

You need Visual Studio 2008 Service Pack 1 to support Platform Builder for Compact 7, which is available for download from the following URL:

```
http://www.microsoft.com/downloads/en/details.aspx?FamilyID=27673C47-
B3B5-4C67-BD99-84E525B5CE61
```

3. Expression Blend 3.

Expression Blend 3 is the tool you need to create XAML codes for Silverlight project. If you plan to use Silverlight for Windows Embedded, you need to install Expression Blend 3 prior to installing Platform Builder. Otherwise, the Silverlight for Windows Embedded template will not be installed.

4. Platform Builder for Windows Embedded Compact 7.

Platform Builder for Compact 7 software requires a large amount of storage space. Full installation with support for all processor architectures selected occupies more than 50GB of space. It's best to select the processor you work with and exclude the others. The target device used for the sample exercises in this book is built with an x86 processor. You need support for an x86 processor to work through the exercises.

5. BSPs and third-party components for Windows Embedded Compact 7.

It takes quite a bit of time to install all the required software components. Be patient, install each software component in sequence, and wait for the current installation to complete before attempting to install the next component.

Quick Fix Engineering Updates

Microsoft releases Quick Fix Engineering (QFE) updates routinely as part of its ongoing support for Compact 7. QFEs are released to address and resolve issues discovered after Compact 7 was released to the public.

Unless you work on projects with strict revision controls that prevent you from installing QFEs, you should keep your Compact 7 development environment updated with the latest QFEs. Often, installing updated QFEs can help resolve problems.

For the previous versions, you need to manually search for QFEs from the Microsoft website. Compact 7 implemented a push model, similar to Windows Updates, where it automatically checks and notifies you when new QFEs are available and enables you to decide whether to install the QFEs. You can still manually search the Microsoft website for QFEs.

 Install QFEs in chronological order, based on the QFE's release date.

DEVELOPMENT ENVIRONMENT SETUP

In order to develop Windows Embedded Compact application for an embedded device, you need to set up a development environment that enables you to deploy application from the development computer to the device for testing and debug.

Target Device

A Windows Embedded Compact development environment is not complete without a target device. Whether developing a custom OS design, device driver, programming library, or application, you develop Compact 7 software components for a target device, or family of devices.

If you don't have access to a real target device, you can use Virtual PC as a Compact 7 target device to test a software function that is not hardware-specific.

Virtual PC is great for learning how to use Platform Builder. Platform Builder for Compact 7 provides the necessary resources, including Virtual PC BSP and a sample virtual machine, needed to work through OS design project and application development exercises. Using Virtual PC, you can work through the exercises to download an OS runtime image to the virtual machine and deploy an application to the virtual machine with Compact 7 OS launched.

The target device, whether real hardware or virtual machine, needs to establish connectivity to the development computer to download an OS runtime image and deploy an application, from the development computer to the device. Depending on the device's design and available features, it can connect to the development computer via an Ethernet, Serial, USB, and other connection.

It's common for consumer portable devices to use the USB interface to establish connectivity with the development computer. A low cost and headless device built with limited peripherals can use the serial port to establish connectivity. For industrial embedded devices, it's common to use the Ethernet interface as the connection between the development computer and target device.

For the exercises in this book, the target device, an eBox-3310A, is built with an Ethernet interface and uses this Ethernet interface to establish connection to the development computer.

To use an Ethernet interface to establish connectivity, both the development computer and target device must connect to the same LAN. In addition, both the development computer and target device must be configured with IP addresses within the same segment.

To develop the Compact 7 OS design, device driver, support library, and application for a target device, you need a Compact 7 board support package for the target device, with the necessary device drivers and bootloader. In addition, the target device must include the necessary bootable storage preconfigured with a Compact 7 bootloader.

Virtual PC as Target Device

If you don't have access to a real target device with Compact 7 support, using a Virtual PC as the target device is a good alternative.

Platform Builder for Compact 7 includes a Virtual PC board support package, which you can use to develop a Compact 7 OS runtime image to deploy to a Virtual PC. A sample Virtual PC image, preconfigured with the necessary Compact 7 bootloader, is provided as part of the Virtual PC board support package.

LAN with DHCP

With both the development computer and target device attached to the same LAN with DHCP service, both of them can receive IP address assignments within the same subnet, from the DHCP service.

With DHCP service to provide IP addresses dynamically, it minimizes the need to configure IP addresses and the network-related configuration needed to establish connectivity between the development computer and target device.

Most of the LANs, in large enterprise and small business, are set up with a DHCP service to assign IP addresses dynamically. For some of the large enterprises, as part of their IT security implementation, both the development computer and target device need to be approved by the IT department and register the associated MAC address with the DHCP server, to access the system's DHCP service to acquire IP addresses.

If you set up the development environment at home, as part of the resources to connect to the Internet via a DSL or cable, you may already have a router or wireless-access-point-router, which is equipped with a DHCP service to provide IP addresses dynamically. You can use this environment and attach your target device to the existing network to establish your Compact 7 development environment.

LAN without DHCP

When working in an environment without DHCP service, you need to configure the development computer and target device with appropriate static IP addresses. You must configure both the development computer and target device with IP addresses in the same subnet to establish the connectivity needed to transfer the OS runtime image and deploy the application to the target device.

Connectivity for Debugging and Testing

Debugging and testing are critical parts of a product development lifecycle to help improve the product's quality. Efficient debugging tools help identify and locate bugs quickly. A testing facility is necessary to validate that the product meets the design specifications.

Platform Builder provides the facilities to simplify the debugging and testing effort, which include remote tools for debugging and a Compact Test kit to perform various functions' compatibility and stress tests. To use these tools the target device needs to establish connectivity to the development computer, with the necessary transport to support these tools.

Following are some of the common connections used for debugging and testing:

➤ Ethernet

➤ Serial port

➤ USB via RNDIS

➤ JTAG

These connection methods are hardware-specific and require additional driver and software support components unique to each target device to function.

Ethernet

Developed during the 1970s, Ethernet has been around for more than 30 years. Ethernet is part of the Internet's explosive growth that drives the need for efficient network connectivity and provides the catalysts to motivate network technology companies to develop better solutions.

As networking technology evolved, Ethernet has grown into a mature and stable connectivity option adopted as a de facto connectivity option for computers, servers, and all types of devices.

With communication speed ranging from 10 to 100 to 1000 Mbps, Ethernet connectivity can support communication with high bandwidth requirements. Even at its lowest range, 10 Mbps, Ethernet can support much higher data throughput compared to some of the older legacy connectivity options used in embedded devices, such as parallel and serial ports.

With a well-established presence in the market, and stable and matured technical support resources across multiple hardware and software platforms, Ethernet is an attractive and practical connectivity option for many types of devices.

In many cases, although a finished device for distribution is designed without Ethernet connectivity, to ease testing and debug efforts, a special version of the device is created with Ethernet connectivity to help minimize the development team's testing and debug efforts, and improve development efficiency.

Ethernet connectivity is the preferred option for the Platform Builder development environment to transfer an OS runtime image, deploy an application to the target device, debug, and test.

Serial

Serial port is a half-century-old legacy technology initially created in the early 1960s, which is still one of the common connectivity options used by a broad range of products.

Whether you work on an embedded device built with an 8-bit microcontroller, or a new generation of an embedded system built with the latest high performance processor, the device is likely to have one or more RS-232 serial interfaces available.

The serial port was used to output debug messages from the target device in the previous versions of Windows Embedded Compact and is still in use to serve the same purpose for this latest version, Windows Embedded Compact 7.

You can configure a Compact 7 target device to send debug messages in ASCII text through one of the available serial ports. These debug messages can easily be captured using a terminal program such as HyperTerminal, available as part of the Windows XP OS.

Typical Development Environment

The development environment with both the development computer and target device connected to a Local Area Network with DHCP service to provide IP addresses dynamically is a common setup for Platform Builder for Compact 7 development, as shown in Figure 3-1.

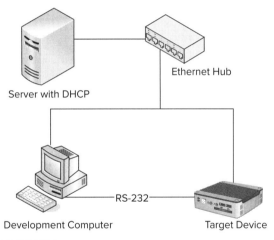

As shown in Figure 3-1, a null RS-232 serial modem cable connects a serial port on the development computer to an available serial port on the target device, configured to output debug messages. The development computer is configured with a terminal program to capture these debug messages.

FIGURE 3-1

For the preceding setup to function, you must configure the target device with an appropriate bootloader, which is needed to establish connectivity with the Platform Builder development computer to download an OS runtime image and application.

To capture serial debug messages from the target device, the development computer needs to launch a terminal emulation program, with a function similar to the HyperTerminal.

HyperTerminal is no longer available as part of Windows Vista and Windows 7. You can use HyperTerminal from Windows XP under Windows Vista and Windows 7. Alternatively, you can use programs such as TeraTerm and PuTTY; both are open-source.

SUMMARY

A properly configured development computer and target device with proper connectivity resources are important elements to establish an efficient environment for Windows Embedded Compact 7 development.

It is well worth the extra time and effort invested to research and figure out the best setup for your development environment. In most cases, the technology vendor that provided the target device and Compact 7 board support package is the best source to provide information and recommendations about setting up an efficient development environment.

Development Process

WHAT'S IN THIS CHAPTER?

➤ Developing a Compact 7 device

➤ Selecting the hardware

➤ Understanding the steps to develop a Compact 7 device

Developing a Compact 7 device involves multiple tasks, with different phases, and requires both hardware and software development resources. To learn about Windows Embedded Compact, you need to understand the overall development process and establish the initial learning focus that is relevant to your immediate needs. This chapter provides an overview of the steps and process to develop an embedded device using Windows Embedded Compact 7.

PLANNING

Planning is important. A development project starts with proper planning has better chance to accomplish designated objectives. A design and development project should start with a plan that takes into account all relevant components to minimize problems, reduce costs, and shorten the development schedule.

After you establish the product functions and features, a typical embedded device project development plan should include the following:

➤ Hardware requirements

➤ Required hardware development resources

➤ Operating system and other software requirements

➤ Required software development resources

➤ Regulatory certification requirements

➤ Expected life for the device's marketability

➤ Expected life for the device's serviceability

➤ Licensing and intellectual property concerns

HARDWARE SELECTION

With the right hardware platform from a vendor with the necessary resources to support the platform, Windows Embedded Compact 7 can help ease quite a number of development challenges for the project.

When selecting the hardware platform, in addition to the features and specifications, the following considerations should be taken into account:

➤ **Standard off-the-shelf hardware** — Often, an off-the-shelf hardware platform may not meet all the project's design specifications. If you can find off-the-shelf hardware that meets all the core requirements with the exception of certain nice-to-have features, this may be a good, safe, and predictable option.

➤ **Design custom hardware internally** — Although the plan to design custom hardware internally seems to provide better control, unless your team has strong hardware experience and development resources, this option may trigger unpredictable costs and can seriously impact your development schedule.

➤ **Design custom hardware through outsourcing** — When the need to develop custom hardware for your project is obvious, hiring an experienced hardware design service provider can be a good option, especially when your team does not have strong hardware development resources. When choosing this option, be sure to account for the required device drivers and operating system components.

➤ **Hardware support** — A hardware platform with the lowest price tag does not necessarily mean it's the most economical. The following considerations should be taken into account as part of the hardware platform selection:

  ➤ Does the hardware vendor provide the necessary board support package and device drivers to support Compact 7?

  ➤ Does the hardware vendor have a competent technical team to support Compact 7-related hardware issue?

➤ **Hardware life cycle** — It takes significant time and effort to develop a product. After the development process is successfully completed, the product needs to go through different required regulatory certifications, depending on the type of device and the market it serves. In addition to the huge costs associated with the development and regulatory certifications, it requires lots of time to accomplish. When selecting hardware, it's critical for the selected hardware to be readily available throughout the product's expected service life.

➤ **Hardware design for evaluation** — Many hardware technology companies provide evaluation hardware to help potential customers evaluate and test the technology. Often, the evaluation hardware is not designed with the quality needed for production. To use this type of hardware requires additional effort and resources to design a production version, which introduces additional costs and requires a longer development schedule and additional testing to validate the new design's function and performance.

 Within the Windows Embedded Compact environment, the term target device *represents the selected hardware platform.*

SOFTWARE SELECTION

The software technology field is dynamic and evolving continuously. Although newly evolved technology is exciting and attractive, when adapting new technology to your product, you need to question whether the technology is stable enough for the type of product and market you serve.

Although it may seem safe to continue to use legacy software to develop the same type of application, unless your company has certain patents and trade secrets that provide strong competitive advantage and prevent your competitors from entering the market, it's naïve to think that a product built with outdated technology can gain strong market share.

Following are some of the things to consider when selecting the software:

➤ Has the selected software been proven?

➤ Is the selected software adopted by other key companies in the market?

➤ Is there a large developer base using the selected software?

➤ Does it have a productive, robust, and easy-to-learn development environment?

➤ Is there a steep learning curve for your development team to become proficient with the software?

➤ Are there existing development resources you can tap into?

➤ Is the selected software manageable and predictable?

➤ Is there a creditable and reliable entity supporting the selected software?

➤ Are there business concerns related to intellectual property, copyright, and patents?

➤ Does the selected software force your company to expose sensitive intellectual property and trade secrets?

TYPICAL DEVELOPMENT PROCESSES

With Windows Embedded Compact 7 devices ranging from small head-less devices with minimal processing requirements for automation and control application, to sophisticated medical instruments with high-performance processing requirements to capture complex inputs and support high-resolution display, there isn't a set of detailed processes or steps that are generally applicable to all these devices.

The information in this section covers some of the typical Windows Embedded Compact development steps to help you better understand the environment.

With the assumption that a hardware platform for the development project has been selected, following are some of the typical steps needed to develop a Compact 7 device:

➤ Board Support Package (BSP)

➤ OS design

➤ Application

➤ Debugging and testing

➤ Deployment

➤ Post-deployment support and update

Board Support Package (BSP)

After you select the hardware platform, if it does not include a Compact 7 BSP, developing the BSP is the next major hurdle.

BSP is a software package that contains the necessary components needed to generate the OS run-time image for the target device, typically including the following:

➤ OEM adaptation layer (OAL) codes

➤ Device drivers for the target device's peripherals

➤ File system support unique to the target device

➤ Bootloader or bootstrap codes needed to launch Compact 7 OS run-time image on the target device

➤ Bootloader with connectivity codes to establish connection and download OS run-time image from the development station to the target device

➤ Kernel Independent Transport Layer (KITL) or other form of connectivity component to provide the function and connection needed to support debugging and testing

Not all BSPs are equal. Although some hardware vendors provide a BSP that fully supports the intended target device's features as part of their product offering, there are hardware vendors that provide a reference BSP from the silicon vendor, a company that designs and manufactures the processor for the hardware, as part of their support, which may not include all the components needed to support the intended target device.

A high-quality BSP that includes proper components to support the target device and connectivity components to link the development station and target device for debugging, testing, and application deployment can help streamline the overall development process.

A quality BSP is one of the important components needed to establish an efficient development environment. An efficient and effective development environment can help eliminate unnecessary aggravation among the development team, minimize development costs, and shorten the development schedule.

OS Design

With the hardware option selected and a quality BSP in place, the next step is to develop an OS design project to generate the OS run-time image for the target device. Typically for a Compact 7 device, the OS run-time image is generated with the application compiled as part of the image.

Following are some of the development tasks that can impact the OS design:

> ➤ A software development kit (SDK), generated from the OS design, is needed to develop an application for the device.

> ➤ When the application, to be compiled as part of the OS run-time image, is modified, the OS design needs to be updated and recompiled to generate a new OS run-time image with the updated application.

> ➤ When any one of the device drivers for the target devices is modified, the OS design needs to be updated and recompiled to generate the new SDK and OS run-time image to reflect the changes.

Application Development

With an SDK generated from the OS design, you and your team can start the application development process. To shorten the development schedule, you can start the application development process in parallel with hardware, BSP, and OS design development, by using a reference SDK from the hardware vendor or a generic SDK from Microsoft that supports the same processor family as the target device for your project.

Changes to the hardware, device drivers, BSP, and OS design may impact the application's function and require an additional development effort to modify the application to address these changes.

Debugging and Testing

Debugging is an ongoing part of every development process. Debugging is the action of identifying, understanding, and resolving issues. Testing is necessary to validate whether each development step delivers the required components that meet the specification. Structured debugging and testing steps should be implemented as part of every development process. From the surface, it seems like these efforts introduce additional costs and may impact the overall development schedule. On the contrary, without structured testing processes to identify problems earlier in the development cycle, your project will likely have to deal with unexpected problems later in the cycle where both costs and impact to the schedule are more significant.

Deployment

After the OS run-time image, application development, debugging, and testing steps are completed, you need to compose the final software package to be deployed with the target device for distribution.

As part of the process to develop the final software package to deploy to the target device, you need to take into account the following considerations:

➤ Simplifying the initial setup needed to start using the device.

➤ Providing the mechanisms needed to back up device configuration and restore the device to an archived configuration.

➤ Reset and recover the device to the default factory settings.

Post-Deployment Support and Updates

Although post-deployment support and updates do not directly impact the development process, these are important business concerns that you need to address as part of the development efforts.

The technology world is not perfect. As new improvements become available, a product with an effective way to enable the customer to gain access to these new improvements can be an important key to help capture more customers and increase market share.

You need to consider resources for post-deployment support and updates as part of the development process and include them as part of the product design. These resources should address the following:

➤ Connectivity for the device to access the update and new software

➤ Mechanism needed to update the applications for the device

➤ Mechanism needed to update the OS components for the device

SUMMARY

Embarking on a new project to develop an embedded device for an evolving market, using new technology, can take you into unfamiliar and uncharted territories. To be prepared for the unexpected, you need to arm yourself with knowledge and develop a plan to deal with both the expected and unexpected.

From a project management perspective, thorough knowledge about the development process and required steps can help you put together a development plan that anticipates and addresses the unexpected, with minimal impact to the project's budget and schedule, as these unexpected challenges happen.

5

Development Environment and Tools

WHAT'S IN THIS CHAPTER?

➤ Reviewing the Platform Builder environment

➤ Reviewing target device connectivity options

➤ Reviewing the Windows Embedded Compact Test Kit

As part of the Windows Embedded Compact learning process, the first step is to get to know the development environment and tools. This chapter is not intended to be a complete reference for the Compact 7 development tools. The information in this chapter provides an overview about the development environment and reviews some of the commonly used tools and wizards to help you explore the development environment, including connectivity and transport options needed to connect the target device to the development station for testing and debugging.

DEVELOPMENT ENVIRONMENT

The primary development environment for Compact 7 is the Visual Studio 2008 integrated development environment (VS2008 IDE). From the VS2008 IDE, you can perform the following development tasks for Compact 7:

➤ Create an OS design

➤ Develop a device driver

➤ Clone and develop board support package

➤ Develop native code applications

➤ Develop managed code applications

To develop a Compact 7 OS design and generate a custom OS run-time image for a device, you need Platform Builder for Windows Embedded Compact 7 (Platform Builder).

For Compact 7, Platform Builder is a plug-in to the VS2008 IDE and requires the professional or a higher version to function. Figure 5-1 provides a visual view to the Windows Embedded Compact 7 development environment.

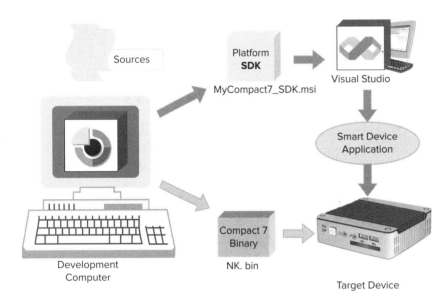

FIGURE 5-1

Compact 7 Terminology

Every development environment has a set of commonly used terms, jargon, and abbreviated key words, which are used as part of the documentation, application notes, and marketing purposes. Table 5-1 lists some of the terms and abbreviated key words commonly used in the Windows Embedded Compact environment, which may not be common in other environments.

TABLE 5-1: Compact 7 Terminology

TERMINOLOGY	DESCRIPTION
BSP	Board Support Package is a set of software components that include OEM adaptation layer codes, device drivers, and configuration files for a specific target device.
Build release directory	Refers to the directory where the active OS design places files and components during the build and compilation process.
Catalog	A container for Compact 7 OS features, modules, device drivers, BSPs, and application components.

TERMINOLOGY	DESCRIPTION
CE	Windows CE is still a common term many veteran developers in the Windows Embedded Compact community use to refer to the product.
CoreCon	Short for Core Connectivity, used to establish connectivity between the development station and target device.
KITL	Kernel Independent Transport Layer is a communication protocol used for debugging for Windows Embedded Compact devices.
OAL	OEM Adaptation Layer is a low-level code acting as the interface between the hardware and Compact 7.
OS design	A VS2008 project that contains a selection of Windows Embedded Compact catalog items and subproject and configuration files to build a custom OS run-time image.
OS run-time image	The binary image file generated from an OS design project. The default filename for the OS run-time image is NK.BIN. After a successful compilation of the OS design project, the NK.BIN run-time image is generated in the OS design project's build release directory.
Release directory	Same as build release directory. Refers to the directory that the active OS design uses to place files and components during the build and compilation process.
Target device	The hardware platform used in the Windows Embedded Compact development environment. When using Virtual PC as an alternative to launch Compact 7 OS as part of the development setup, the Virtual PC is the target device.

PLATFORM BUILDER FOR WINDOWS EMBEDDED COMPACT 7

The primary development tool for Windows Embedded Compact 7 is Platform Builder, which provides all the tools needed to develop Compact 7 OS design and components to support an embedded device based on the Compact 7 OS.

You can perform the following Compact 7 development tasks using Platform Builder:

➤ Develop a Board Support Package.

➤ Develop a bootloader.

➤ Develop a device driver.

➤ Develop a custom OS run-time image.

➤ Develop a native code application.

➤ Debug an OS run-time image, a device driver, and an application.

Prior to Windows Embedded CE 6.0(CE 6.0), Platform Builder was a standalone development tool. When CE 6.0 released, it became a plug-in to the Visual Studio 2005 IDE.

For the latest version, Windows Embedded Compact 7, Platform Builder is a plug-in to the VS2008 IDE. As a plug-in to the VS2008 IDE, Platform Builder can take advantage of VS2008's context-sensitive graphical user interface.

As part of the context-sensitive behavior, the VS2008 IDE shows different features on the menu that are relevant to the current development environment. With limited display space, the context-sensitive user interface scheme provides an efficient method to present relevant and easily accessible features dynamically to the developer, based on the current active development project and tasks. Features not shown on the immediate user interface, in the form of buttons or icons, are accessible from the VS2008 menu. Figure 5-2 shows the VS2008 IDE with an OS design project open.

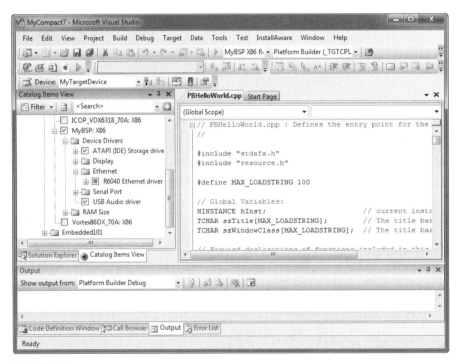

FIGURE 5-2

The VS2008 IDE is flexible and provides the option for you to change the IDE layout. As a result, your VS2008 IDE can look completely different from someone else's.

What's New in Compact 7

As part of the ongoing development efforts, new features and improvements are added to the Platform Builder development environment for each new version. With more than 15 years of development efforts, Platform Builder cumulated an impressive collection of development resources. To learn the full spectrum of Platform Builder resources, refer to the product documentation.

Table 5-2 lists some of the new features available as part of the Compact 7 release that deserves attention.

TABLE 5-2: New Compact 7 Features

NEW FEATURE	DESCRIPTION
SMP (Symmetric Multiprocessing Support)	Added to support multicore processors.
Adobe Flash Player 10.1	Supports playback of flash video and animation embedded in Internet Explorer. No additional license fee to Adobe is required to include this feature as part of a Compact 7 OS run-time image.
DLNA (Digital Living Network Alliance)	Enables Compact 7 device to interact with DLNA devices. A DLNA-enabled Compact 7 device can be a digital media renderer, server, or controller.
Internet Explorer 7	Compact 7's Internet Explorer for Embedded is based on IE 7, with some performance updates from IE 8 added.
Silverlight 3	Silverlight for Windows Embedded is updated to Silverlight 3 and Expression Blend 3.
Windows Embedded Silverlight Tools	Windows Embedded Silverlight Tools convert Expression Blend 3 XAML code project into a C++ native code subproject for a Compact 7 OS design.
3GB physical memory support	Compact 7 raised the 512MB physical memory support limit to 3GB.
Remote Tool	A new Remote Tools Framework is added to support the remote tools.
Compact Test Kit	A new testing suite that replaces the old Windows CE Test Kit (CETK), with more features added and a completely new graphical user interface.
Virtual PC BSP	Develops Compact 7 OS run-time image for Virtual PC, which can be used as a target device to support application development exercises without the need to have real hardware.
Application notes and white papers	More than 30 well-written and informative application notes and white papers are included, as part of the Compact 7 installation, to provide information resources showing how to use some of the new features. These resources are separate from the product documentation.

In addition to the features in Table 5-2, many other new features, improvements, and information resources have been added to make Compact 7 more efficient and developer-friendly.

As part of the effort to help developers to learn, engage, and use Compact 7, a series of application notes and white papers covering different aspects of Compact 7 were created. Thirty-one application notes and white papers, provided in PDF format separate from the product documentation, were released as part of the Platform Builder for the Compact 7 installation. You can find these PDF documents in the Windows Embedded Compact 7 installation folder under Documentation.

Take time to read the Windows Embedded Compact 7 Release Notes, which contain detailed information covering what's new with Compact 7 and other important information.

Environment Variables

Platform Builder uses different groups of environment variables to configure the OS design and provides uniform vocabularies that represent the drive path and configuration string. These environment variables are separated into the following groups:

- ➤ BSP environment variables
- ➤ IMG environment variables
- ➤ PRJ environment variables
- ➤ Miscellaneous environment variables

BSP Environment Variables

The BSP environment variables are related to the BSP, to provide additional options to configure the OS design. Following are two categories of BSP environment variables:

- ➤ BSP environment variables
- ➤ BSP_NO environment variables

BSP environment variables define optional components that you can include in the OS design. These components can be part of the BSP or other components available from the Platform Builder catalog.

Use BSP_NO environment variables to define options not supported by the BSP or target device.

In addition to the BSP environment variables available as part of Platform Builder, you can create additional BSP environment variables unique to your target device.

Table 5-3 lists a few examples of the BSP environment variables with descriptions to explain their purpose.

TABLE 5-3: BSP Environment Variables

ENVIRONMENT VARIABLE	DESCRIPTION
BSP_DISPLAY_NOP	When set, the stub display driver (also referred to as a null display driver), DDI_NOP.DLL, is included in the OS design.
BSP_NIC_RTL8139	When set, the OS design is configured to include the device driver for the RTL-8139 Network interface.
BSP_NOAUDIO	When set, the OS design is configured to exclude audio support.
BSP_NOUSB	When set, the OS design is configured to exclude support for USB.
BSP_VORTEX86DX_9120A	This BSP environment variable is unique to BSP, to support hardware built with the Vortex86DX SOC. When this variable is set, the OS design is configured to support the 9120A IDE storage controller.

You can find more detailed information and a full listing of BSP environment variables from the Compact 7 product documentation, or from the following URL: `http://msdn.microsoft.com/en-us/library/ee478674.aspx`.

IMG Environment Variables

You can use the IMG environment variables to remove modules from the OS design while leaving the associated registry entries intact. IMG variables can be used to configure the memory footprint for the OS run-time image.

When setting an IMG environment variable to alter an OS design's configuration, after the OS design has been through the build process and successfully generated an OS run-time image, you can use the Make Run-time Image to generate a new OS image without the need to perform a full rebuild of the OS design.

The IMG environment variables are intended for the development environment and not to be used in a shipped product.

Table 5-4 lists a few examples of IMG environment variables with descriptions to explain their purpose.

TABLE 5-4: IMG Environment Variables

ENVIRONMENT VARIABLE	DESCRIPTION
IMGNOKITL	Configures the OS design to generate an OS run-time image with KILT disabled.
IMGRAM256	Configures the OS design to generate an OS run-time image to support a target device with 256MB of system memory. In addition to setting this variable, the BSP must be configured to support 256MB of system memory.

You can find more detailed information and a full listing of IMG environment variables from the Compact 7 product documentation, or from the following URL: `http://msdn.microsoft.com/en-us/library/ee479025.aspx`.

PRJ Environment Variables

Use the PRJ environment variables to enable project-specific functionality in the OS design. Table 5-5 lists a few examples of the PRJ environment variables with descriptions to explain their purpose.

TABLE 5-5: PRJ Environment Variables

ENVIRONMENT VARIABLE	DESCRIPTION
PRJ_ENABLE_FSREGHIVE	Configures the OS design to generate an OS run-time image with hive-based registry enabled. In addition to setting this environment variable, the BSP must include the necessary components to support the hive-based registry feature.
PRJ_BOOTDEVICE_ATAPI	Configures the OS design to enable ATAPI as the boot device.

You can find more detailed information and a listing of PRJ environment variables from the Compact 7 product documentation, or from the following URL: `http://msdn.microsoft.com/en-us/library/ee479112.aspx`.

Miscellaneous Environment Variables

Platform Builder uses different variables to specify directory paths and configure the build environment. Table 5-6 lists a few examples of these miscellaneous environment variables with descriptions to explain their purpose.

TABLE 5-6: Miscellaneous Environment Variables

ENVIRONMENT VARIABLE	DESCRIPTION
_FLATRELEASEDIR	Represents the build release directory for the OS design, where OS components and configuration files are placed during the build process.
_OSDESIGNROOT	Represents the current OS design project's root directory: `C:\WINCE700\OSDesigns\<project name>\<project name>`.
_PLATFORMROOT	Represents the platform directory. By default, it's `C:\WINCE700\PLATFORM`.
_PUBLICROOT	Represents the public directory. By default, it's `C:\WINCE700\PUBLIC`.
_TGTPLAT	Defines the name of the BSP for the active OS design project.
_WINCEROOT	Represents the root directory where Platform Builder's OS component files are installed. By default, it's `C:\WINCE700`.

You can find more detailed information and a listing of the miscellaneous environment variables from the Compact 7 product documentation, or from the following URL: `http://msdn.microsoft.com/enus/library/ee479008.aspx`.

You can review all environment variables configured for an OS design project as follows:

➤ From the VS2008 Build menu, click on Open Release Directory in Build Window to launch the Command Prompt build window for the OS design.

➤ From the Command Prompt window enter the `SET` command to list the environment variables configured for the active OS design project.

Board Support Package (BSP)

Platform Builder includes a number of reference BSPs that support difference processors. Table 5-7 lists the reference BSPs available as part of the Platform Builder installation.

TABLE 5-7: Reference BSPs

SUPPORTED PROCESSOR	BSP NAME
ARMv5	Freescale i.MX27
ARMv6	Freescale i.MX31
ARMv6	NEC NE1TB
ARMv6	Samsung SMDK6410
ARMv7	TI OMAP 3530
MIPS	Sigma Designs Vantage 8654
x86	Generic CEPC
x86	ICOP eBox-3300
x86	Virtual PC

These BSPs provide technical references and function as the starting point to develop a custom BSP to support your project's hardware platform.

BSP Cloning Wizard

A Compact 7 BSP is a software package containing the necessary device drivers, hardware adaptation codes, and support library for a target device needed to develop custom OS design.

Developing a BSP from the ground up is a complex and challenging process. To ease the process, it's a common practice to clone an existing BSP, supporting similar hardware, and use the cloned BSP as a starting point to develop a customized BSP to support the intended target device.

To access the BSP Cloning Wizard, from the VS2008 Tools menu, select Platform Builder, and click Clone BSP to bring up the wizard, as shown in Figure 5-3.

The BSP Cloning Wizard greatly simplifies the tasks needed to duplicate BSP. The exercise in Chapter 6, "BSP Introduction," steps you through the process to clone an existing BSP and how to use the cloned BSP for the exercises in the subsequent chapters.

As part of the process to develop a custom OS design, you may need to make changes to the BSP. It's a good practice to clone the BSP and use the cloned BSP to develop the custom OS design. If you need to modify the cloned BSP while developing a custom OS design,

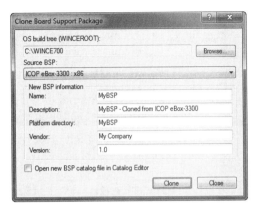

FIGURE 5-3

it does not impact the original BSP. This way, you can keep the original BSP intact and can refer back to the original codes and settings when needed.

OS Design Wizard

A Compact 7 OS design is a VS2008 project, a workspace to develop a custom Compact 7 OS run-time image.

When creating a new OS design project from the VS2008 IDE, the OS Design Wizard springs into action and steps through the process to help you create the initial project workspace. As part of the process, the wizard provides multiple OS design templates, BSPs, drivers, applications, and OS components that you can select and include in the project. At the conclusion of the OS Design Wizard process, it includes all the selected components to the project.

The OS Design Wizard is automatically triggered as part of the process to create a new OS design project from the VS2008 IDE. Chapter 7, "OS Design," covers the initial section of the OS design exercise steps through the OS Design Wizard steps to create an OS design project.

OS Design Templates

Platform Builder includes a number of OS design templates that you can use as the starting point for a new OS design project. Use the following OS design templates.

Customer Device

The Customer Device template provides the options to select Compact 7 components during the OS Design Wizard steps so that you can create the initial project workspace to develop a Compact 7 OS design for a custom device.

Embedded Device with Silverlight XAML

The Embedded Device with Silverlight XAML template includes selected components, with additional selectable components during the OS Design Wizard steps so that you can create the initial project workspace to develop a Compact 7 OS design for an embedded device that supports Silverlight for Windows Embedded.

Handheld

The Handheld template includes components so that you can create the initial project workspace, with features such as stylus and touch, to develop a Compact 7 OS design for a handheld device.

Industrial Controller

The Industrial Controller template includes components so that you can create the initial project workspace to develop a Compact 7 OS design for industrial-automation, process-control, human-machine interface, and other industrial devices.

Network Projector

The Network Projector template includes components so that you can create the initial project workspace to develop a Compact 7 OS design for a network-enabled projector device, which works seamlessly with the Windows-based computer to display content to the device using Remote Desktop Connection, as part of the Connect to Network Projector feature available with the Windows 7 and Vista operating systems.

Portable Media Player

The Portable Media Player template includes components so that you can create the initial project workspace to develop a Compact 7 OS design for a consumer device that plays and stores digital media.

Small Footprint Device

The Small Footprint Device template includes a minimum set of components so that you can create the initial project workspace to develop a Compact 7 OS design for an embedded device with limited memory and resources.

Thin Client

The Thin Client template includes components so that you can create the initial project workspace to develop a Compact 7 OS design for a Windows Embedded Compact 7-powered thin client device.

Catalog Items

The Catalog Item View window contains all the installed Compact 7 components, provided by Microsoft or third-party companies, which include the following:

- ➤ BSP
- ➤ Device drivers
- ➤ Networking
- ➤ Multimedia

➤ Codecs

➤ Application and utility

➤ Programming library

As part of the Platform Builder IDE, the Catalog Items View windows provides the user interface so that you can select and remove components for the OS design, as shown in Figure 5-4.

From this window, you can review which components are selected for the OS design.

FIGURE 5-4

SDK Wizard

With an SDK generated from the OS design project, an application developer using VS2008, without Platform Builder, can develop native and managed code applications for the target device.

Platform Builder includes an SDK Wizard to simplify the tasks to generate an SDK from the OS design. The OS design must be compiled to generate an OS run-time image prior to launching the SDK Wizard to generate the SDK.

To launch the SDK Wizard, with the OS design project open, from the VS2008 Project menu, click Add New SDK to bring up the SDK Wizard, as shown in Figure 5-5.

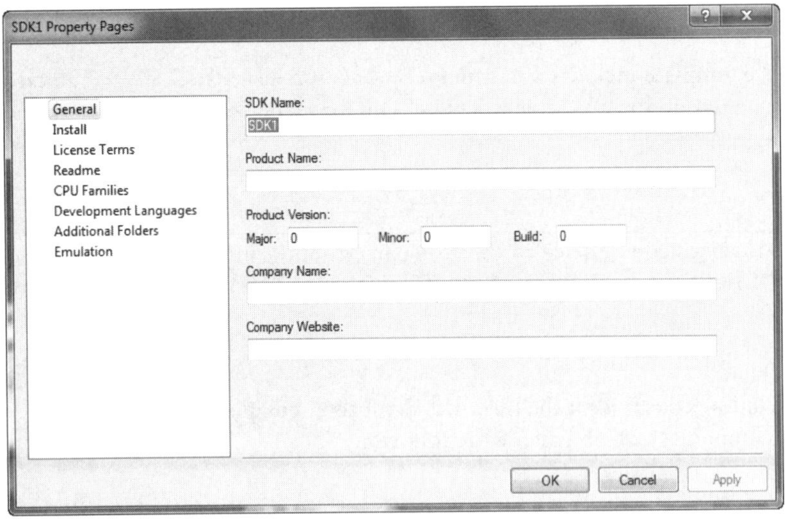

FIGURE 5-5

Remote Tools

Platform Builder for Compact 7 includes a set of remote tools that enable the development station to debug Compact 7 OS run-time on the target device remotely.

Table 5-8 lists the included remote tools.

TABLE 5-8: Remote Tools

REMOTE TOOL	DESCRIPTION
Remote File Viewer	Accesses the target device's file system remotely, copies files to and from the device, renames files and folders, and deletes files and folders on the device.
Remote Heap Walker	Views heap identifiers and flags for running processes on the target device, and system memory use by the process. Reviews heap usage, detects memory leaks, and locates heap fragmentation.
Remote Process Viewer	Views running processes on the target device, showing threads and modules associated with each process.
Remote Profiler	Diagnoses performance-related issues.
Remote Registry Editor	Accesses registry on the target device, to view, add, edit, and delete registry entries.
Remote Resource Consumer	Imposes a simulated condition for the target device to consume CPU, memory, and storage, processes resources, and creates a condition to test how an application behaves when the system runs out of resources.
Remote Resource Leak Detector	Tracks handle usage and detects memory leaks and heap corruption.
Remote System Information	Views system information, settings, and properties for the target device.
Remote Timeline Viewer	Viewing utility provides graphical presentation for data from Kernel Tracker, Performance Monitor, and Power Monitor.
Remote Zoom	Displays the target device's current screen image.

Windows Embedded Silverlight Tool

The Windows Embedded Silverlight Tool differs from the desktop version, which runs within a browser. Silverlight for Windows Embedded Compact is a native code application that can be launched as the primary user interface for a Compact 7 device.

The Windows Embedded Silverlight tool, included as part of Platform Builder for Compact 7, can convert a XAML project, created in the Expression Blend 3 development environment, into a C++ native code subproject for Compact 7.

TARGET DEVICE CONNECTIVITY

To set up a proper development environment to perform Compact 7 development, the development station needs to establish connectivity to the target device to perform the following tasks:

➤   Download the OS run-time image to the target device for testing and debugging.

➤   Deploy an application to the target device for testing and debugging.

Depending on the device's hardware architecture and included features, it may connect to the development station through an Ethernet, Serial, or USB connection. Some hardware platforms use a JTAG interface for debugging and testing purposes, which requires specialized software.

Kernel Independent Transport Layer (KITL)

Kernel Independent Transport Layer (KITL) is a debugging protocol for Windows Embedded Compact devices, which can be implemented over an Ethernet, Serial, or USB connection.

KITL is a critical component needed to debug the OS design and is included as part of the BSP for the target device, provided by the hardware vendor. KITL over Ethernet is the most common implementation. Most of the Platform Builder training materials and learning references are based on KITL over an Ethernet connection.

Core Connectivity

The Platform Builder development environment uses Core Connectivity (CoreCon), which is a communication infrastructure to establish connectivity between the development station and target device.

CoreCon provides the infrastructure to support the following:

➤   Download of an application or a set of files to the target device.

➤   Connectivity between the development station and target device to support remote tools.

➤   Kernel-level connectivity stream between the development station and target device, which can be used by Platform Builder, such as KITL transport.

➤   Flashing a run-time image onto the target device.

➤   Connectivity stream that can be used by the OEM to develop proprietary OS image download services.

For an application developer, CoreCon is a transport mechanism to deploy applications from the VS2008 IDE to the target device for testing and debugging.

As an application developer, you can establish CoreCon connectivity between the development station and target device to perform the following:

➤ Deploy a VS2008 application to the target device.

➤ Launch the application on the target device.

➤ Remotely debug an application executing on the target device.

APPLICATION FOR COMPACT 7

Developing a native code application using Visual C++ or managed code application using C# or Visual Basic for Compact 7 does not require Platform Builder. All you need is the SDK generated from the Platform Builder OS design that generated the Compact 7 OS run-time image for the target device.

WINDOWS EMBEDDED COMPACT TEST KIT

Windows Embedded Compact Test Kit, also referred to as Compact Test Kit (CTK), is a test suite provided as part of the Compact 7 software suite. The CTK's user interface is a completely new design from the previous version, CE Test Kit (CETK).

CTK is designed to test BSP, OAL, and device driver functionality to ensure these components include the required function to support Compact 7 and meet the performance requirements. The Compact Test Kit also provides the facility to develop custom tests by the OEM to test hardware.

The previous version, CE Test Kit (CETK), has been around for quite some time. As a result, when searching for information resources related to CTK, whether on MSDN or via the Web, you can run across quite a few articles referring to CETK.

SUMMARY

The Windows Embedded Compact 7 development environment has many components; each requires different resources and involves different knowledge.

Although the Visual Studio 2008 and Platform Builder combination provides an efficient and developer-friendly environment, this environment involves multiple layers of technical knowledge that requires time and effort to master.

Familiarizing yourself with the development environment, terminology, and where to locate resources is important to speed up your learning process.

PART II
Platform Builder and OS Design

BSP Introduction

➤ Introducing BSP

➤ Cloning an existing BSP to create a new BSP

➤ Customizing the cloned BSP

A Board Support Package (BSP) is one of the essential components needed to develop Windows Embedded Compact 7 operating system (OS) design and generate the operating system run-time image for the target device. This chapter provides an overview of BSP and works through the exercises to create a new BSP for the OS design project in this book by cloning an existing BSP and modifying the cloned BSP. Chapter 35, "The Target System," offers more detailed BSP development-related subjects.

BSP is a software package that contains hardware-dependent codes, developed to support designated hardware platforms. In general, the BSP is provided by the hardware manufacturer or the hardware development team.

Typically, an application developer does not need to be concerned about BSP development. However, knowing the BSP structure and how it's developed can be helpful to develop applications to control hardware and access low-level system resources.

Windows Embedded Compact is designed to support multiple processor architectures, including ARM, MIPS, and x86. Support libraries for the supported processors are provided as part of the Platform Builder for Windows Embedded Compact software. All BSP references make use of these processor support libraries. These libraries are installed as part of the Windows Embedded Compact software in the following directory: $(_WINCEROOT)\PLATFORM\COMMON.

The _WINCEROOT variable is used to represent the directory where Windows Embedded Compact OS file components are installed to the development station. When installed to the default location, this variable represents the C:\WINCE700 directory.

BSP PROVIDED BY PLATFORM BUILDER

As part of the support resources, the Platform Builder for Windows Embedded Compact software suite provides a number of BSPs that support different processor architectures. You can use one of these BSPs, which supports the same processor architecture as the target device you work with, as a starting point to develop a new BSP, customized to support your target device.

Table 6-1 lists the BSPs provided as part of the Platform Builder for Compact 7 software suite.

TABLE 6-1: BSPs for Platform Builder

PROCESSOR	BSP NAME
ARMv5	Freescale i.MX27 3DS : ARMv5
ARMv6	Freescale i.MX31 3DS : ARMv6
ARMv6	NEC NE1-TB : ARMv6
ARMv6	Samsung SMDK6410 : ARMv6
ARMv7	Texas Inst. OMAP 3530 EVM : ARMv7
MIPSII	Sigma Designs SMP865X : MIPSII
MIPSII_FP	Sigma Designs SMP865X : MIPSII_FP
x86	Generic CEPC : x86
x86	ICOP eBox-3300 : x86
x86	Virtual PC : x86

BSP COMPONENTS, FILES, AND FOLDERS

A Windows Embedded Compact 7 BSP includes the following components:

- ➤ OEM Adaptation Layer (OAL) codes
- ➤ Boot loader
- ➤ Device drivers to support peripherals on the target device
- ➤ System configuration files

Typically, BSP components and configuration files are organized in one main folder, under the _PLATFORMROOT directory, with subdirectories, as shown in Table 6-2, for the BSP named MyBSP.

TABLE 6-2: BSP Directory Structure

DIRECTORY	DESCRIPTION
$(_PLATFORMROOT)\MyBSP	BSP's main directory.
$(_PLATFORMROOT)\MyBSP\Bins	Precompiled BSP components provided in binary are placed in this directory.
$(_PLATFORMROOT)\MyBSP\Catalog	The BSP catalog file is in this directory.
$(_PLATFORMROOT)\MyBSP\Cesysgen	The makefile in this directory can be configured to perform certain tasks during the build process.
$(_PLATFORMROOT)\MyBSP\Files	Registry and system configuration files are placed in this directory.
$(_PLATFORMROOT)\MyBSP\Src	Source code for the bootloader, device driver, OAL, and KITL are placed in this directory.

In addition to the codes and libraries that reside within the BSP folder, the BSP also references and uses common codes, libraries, and header files, located in the following directory: $(_PLATFORMROOT)\Common\SRC\.

There are multiple folders under this directory; each contains a different set of common codes for a different processor, as shown in Table 6-3.

TABLE 6-3: Common Codes for BSP Provided by Microsoft

DIRECTORY	DESCRIPTION
$(_PLATFORMROOT)\Common\SRC\ARM	Common codes to support ARM processors.
$(_PLATFORMROOT)\Common\SRC\Common	Common codes for all processors.
$(_PLATFORMROOT)\Common\SRC\INC	Header files common to all processors.
$(_PLATFORMROOT)\Common\SRC\MIPS	Common codes to support MIPS processors.
$(_PLATFORMROOT)\Common\SRC\SOC	Common codes to support System-On-Chip. (There are multiple subfolders; each support a different SOC.)
$(_PLATFORMROOT)\Common\SRC\x86	Common codes to support x86 processors.

CLONE AN EXISTING BSP

The Compact 7 Platform Builder software suite provides a wizard to clone an existing BSP and modify the cloned BSP without affecting the original BSP. The exercise in this section works through the steps to clone an existing BSP.

Launch VS2008 on your development workstation and work through the following steps to create a new BSP by cloning the existing ICOP eBox3300 BSP, which will be used for the OS design project exercise in the next chapter:

1. From the VS2008 Tools menu, select Platform Builder, and click Clone BSP to bring up the Clone Board Support Package screen, as shown in Figure 6-1.

2. From the Source BSP selection, select the ICOP eBox-3300 : x86 BSP.

3. For the Name, type **MyBSP** as the BSP name.

4. For the Description, type **BSP cloned from the ICOP eBox-3300 BSP**.

5. For the Platform directory, type **MyBSP** as the main BSP directory.

6. For the Vendor, type **Embedded101** to identify the company that created the BSP.

7. For the Version, type **1.0** to provide version control information.

8. Enable the Open New BSP Catalog File in Catalog Editor check box, and click Clone to clone the BSP.

9. When the cloning process is successful, the Clone BSP screen displays with the message Board Support Package Cloned Successfully, as shown in Figure 6-2.

FIGURE 6-1

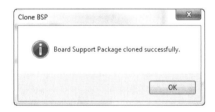

FIGURE 6-2

10. Click OK to close the Clone BSP screen. After the Clone BSP screen is closed, the cloned BSP, MyBSP, opens in the VS2008 IDE, as shown in Figure 6-3.

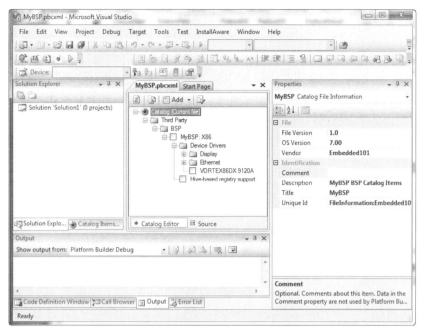

FIGURE 6-3

11. From the VS2008 File menu, select Exit to close the MyBSP project and exit VS2008.

After the wizard finishes the cloning process, it creates a directory for the BSP and places all the cloned files for the newly created BSP, MyBSP, in the following directory: $(_PLATFORMROOT)\MyBSP.

CUSTOMIZE THE CLONED BSP

In the previous section, you worked through the exercise to clone and create a new BSP. Although the cloned BSP, MyBSP, contains all the core components needed to develop an OS design and generate a run-time image for the intended target device, it does not include a device driver for the storage device and file system and does not provide an easy access to configure display and other system parameters.

In this section, you work through additional exercises to customize MyBSP and add the following components to make this BSP more developer-friendly:

➤ ATAPI device driver to support the IDE storage controller and associated file-system components.

➤ Hive-based registry support component to persist Registry settings between power reset.

➤ Additional display component to configure the target device's display resolution.

➤ System memory component to support target device equipped with a different system memory size.

➤ Serial port components and the option to enable serial debug message output.

➤ Device driver for the USB audio controller.

➤ USB mass storage class driver to support external USB flash and USB storage devices.

First, you need to open the MyBSP's catalog file, MyBSP.pbcxml, to make the changes. Following are two different methods to open the MyBSP BSP for editing within the VS2008 IDE:

1. From the Windows Explorer screen, navigate to the _PLATFORMROOT\MyBSP\Catalog folder, right-click the MyBSP.pbcxml file, select Open with, and click on Microsoft Visual Studio 2008, as shown in Figure 6-4.

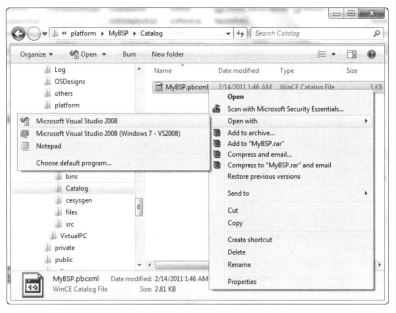

FIGURE 6-4

2. Launch VS2008. From the VS2008 File menu, select Open, and click File to bring up the Open File screen. From the Open File screen, navigate to the $(_PLATFORMROOT)\MyBSP\Catalog folder, select the MyBSP.pbcxml file, and click Open.

Add an ATAPI Driver Component to MyBSP

The ATAPI component is needed to support the storage device, which is an essential component for the target device. When working with multiple OS design projects with this BSP, adding this component to the BSP can help simplify the effort to include this component to the OS design projects.

The ATAPI storage block driver component is provided as part of the Platform Builder, under the \Core OS\Windows Embedded Compact\Device Drivers\Storage Devices node.

With the MyBSP.pbcxml catalog file open within the VS2008 IDE, work through the following steps to add the ATAPI driver and associated components:

1. From the Catalog Editor window, expand Catalog ⇨ Third Party ⇨ BSP ⇨ MyBSP: x86 to get to the Device Drivers folder.

2. Right-click the Device Drivers folder, and click Add Catalog Item to add a new catalog item entry. The new catalog item, Item:DefaulVendor:DefaultCatalogItemName, is created, as shown in Figure 6-5.

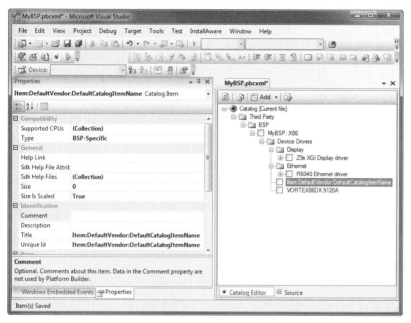

FIGURE 6-5

3. From the Properties window, type **ATAPI (IDE) Storage driver** for the Title.

4. For the Unique ID, type **ATAPI: Embedded101:MyBSP**.

5. For the Description, type **ATAPI device driver to support IDE storage** to provide information about this component, as shown in Figure 6-6.

The ATAPI component is provided as one of the components within the Platform Builder component catalog and is associated with the SYSGEN_ATAPI variable. Continue with the next step to add the SYSGEN_ATAPI variable to the component.

6. From the Properties tab, when you click the Additional Variable entry, a button displays

FIGURE 6-6

to the right. Click this button to bring up the String Collection Editor; then type the **SYSGEN_ATAPI** variable, as shown in Figure 6-7. Then, click OK to close the String Collection Editor screen.

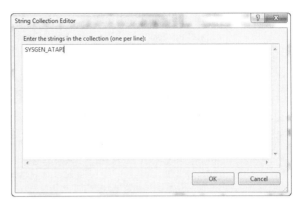

In addition to the ATAPI driver, the FAT file system driver component is needed to provide file system services. This component can be included in the OS design via the SYSGEN_FATFS variable. Continue with the next step to add this variable to the component.

FIGURE 6-7

7. From the Properties tab, for the Sysgen Variable, type **SYSGEN_FATFS**, as shown in Figure 6-8.

You have successfully completed the steps to add the ATAPI driver component to MyBSP. From the VS2008 File menu, click on Save All to save the changes.

Add a Hive-Based Registry Component to MyBSP

The system registry contains critical system configuration parameters. To save changes to the system registry between power reset, the hive-based registry support component is needed. Because the hive-based registry component is dependent on the ATAPI component, you should add this component as a subcomponent to the ATAPI component.

FIGURE 6-8

Delete the Existing Hive-Based Registry Component

The existing hive-based registry support component, cloned from the source BSP, located at the root of the BSP, is in the wrong place. Work through the following step to delete this component:

➤ From the Catalog Editor tab, right-click the hive-based registry support component, and click Remove to delete this component.

Create a Hive-Based Registry Subcomponent

Work through the following steps to create the hive-based registry support component, as a subcomponent to the ATAPI (IDE) Storage driver component:

1. Right-click the ATAPI (IDE) Storage driver component, and click Add Catalog Item to create a new item under this node.

2. For the title, type **Hive-based registry support**.

3. For the Unique ID, type **HiveBased: Embedded101:MyBSP**.

4. For the Additional Variable, via the String Collection Editor screen type **SYSGEN_ATAPI, PRJ_ ENABLE_FSREGHIVE** and **PRJ_ BOOTDEVICE_ATAPI** variables, as shown in Figure 6-9.

5. For the Sysgen Variable, type **SYSGEN_FATFS, SYSGEN_ FSREGHIVE**, and **SYSGEN_ FSRAMROM**, as shown in Figure 6-10.

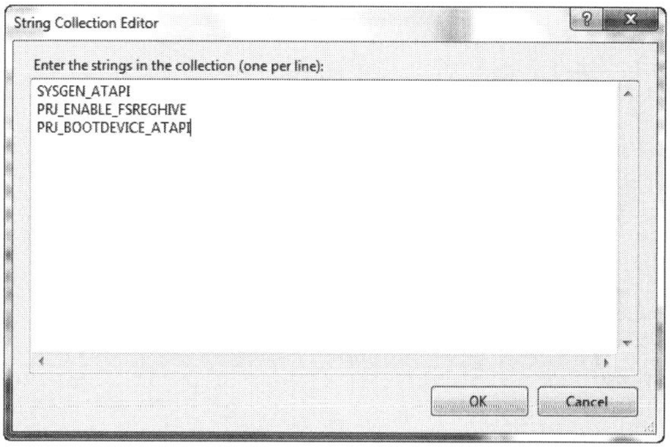

You have successfully completed the steps to create the hive-based registry support subcomponent. From the VS2008 File menu, click on Save All to save the changes.

Add a Display Configuration Component to MyBSP

Although the BSP provides the option to select the display driver component, it does not provide an easy way to configure the display resolution.

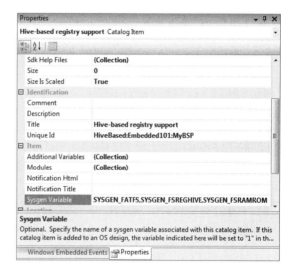

FIGURE 6-9

FIGURE 6-10

Subcomponent to Configure 640x480 Display Resolution

Work through the following exercise to create a subcomponent for the Z9s XGI Display driver component, to configure the display to support 640x480 with 16-bit color and 60Hz refresh rate:

1. From the Catalog Editor tab, right-click the Z9s XGI Display driver component, and click Add Catalog Item to create a new item under this node.

2. From the Properties tab, for the Title, type **VGA-00 640x480x16 @ 60Hz**.

3. For the Unique ID, type **VGA640x480x16x60:Embedded101:MyBSP**.

4. For the Additional Variables, type the **BSP_DISPLAY_Z9s_640x480x16x60** variable, via the String Collection Editor screen.

5. From the Properties tab, change the Choose One Group selection from False to **True**.

6. Open the following Registry file with a text editor, such as Notepad:

   `$(_PLATFORMROOT)\MyBSP\Files\PLATFORM.REG`

7. Append the following entries to the PLATFORM.REG file:

```
IF BSP_DISPLAY_Z9s_640x480x16x60
[HKEY_LOCAL_MACHINE\Drivers\Display]
    "ModeNumber"=dword:0
ENDIF BSP_DISPLAY_Z9s_640x480x16x60
```

Code snippet is from platform.reg

Subcomponent to Configure 800x600 Display Resolution

Repeat the previous steps to create an additional subcomponent for the Z9s XGI Display driver component, to configure the display to support 800x600 with 16-bit color and 60Hz refresh rate:

1. From the Catalog Editor tab, right-click the Z9s XGI Display driver component, and click Add Catalog Item to create a new item under this node.

2. From the Properties tab, for the Title, type **VGA-03 800x600x16 @ 60Hz.**

3. For the Unique ID, type **VGA800x600x16x60:Embedded101:MyBSP.**

4. For the Additional Variables, type the **BSP_DISPLAY_Z9s_800x600x16x60** variable, via the String Collection Editor screen.

5. From the Properties tab, change the Choose One Group selection from False to **True**.

6. Open the following Registry file with a text editor, such as Notepad:

   `$(_PLATFORMROOT)\MyBSP\Files\PLATFORM.REG`

7. Append the following entries to the PLATFROM.REG file:

```
IF BSP_DISPLAY_Z9s_800x600x16x60
[HKEY_LOCAL_MACHINE\Drivers\Display]
    "ModeNumber"=dword:3
ENDIF BSP_DISPLAY_Z9s_800x600x16x60
```

Code snippet is from platform.reg

Subcomponent to Configure 1024x768 Display Resolution

Repeat the previous steps to create an additional subcomponent for the Z9s XGI Display driver component, to configure the display to support 1024x768 with 16-bit color and 60Hz refresh rate:

1. From the Catalog Editor tab, right-click the Z9s XGI Display driver component, and click Add Catalog Item to create a new item under this node.

2. From the Properties tab, for the Title, type **VGA-06 1024x768x16 @ 60Hz.**

3. For the Unique ID, type **VGA1024x768x16x60:Embedded101:MyBSP.**

4. For the Additional Variables, type the **BSP_DISPLAY_Z9s_1024x768x16x60**, via the String Collection Editor screen.

5. From the Properties tab, change the Choose One Group selection from False to **True**.

6. Open the following Registry file with a text editor, such as Notepad:

```
$(_PLATFORMROOT)\MyBSP\Files\PLATFORM.REG
```

7. Append the following entries to the PLATFROM.REG file:

Available for download on Wrox.com

```
IF BSP_DISPLAY_Z9s_1024x768x16x60
[HKEY_LOCAL_MACHINE\Drivers\Display]
    "ModeNumber"=dword:6
ENDIF BSP_DISPLAY_Z9s_1024x768x16x60
```

Code snippet is from platform.reg

You can configure the Z9s display driver to support more than 20 different display configurations. The three subcomponents created in the previous exercises provide enough information to show the steps needed to create additional subcomponents to configure display settings.

Subcomponent to Include DirectDraw Support

For some conditions, you need the DirectDraw component for the Z9s display to function. Work through the following steps to create a DirectDraw subcomponent for the Z9s XGI Display driver:

1. From the Catalog Editor tab, right-click the Z9s XGI Display driver component, and click Add Catalog Item to create a new item under this node.

2. From the Properties tab, for the Title, type **DirectDraw**.

3. For the Unique ID, type **DirectDraw:Embedded101:MyBSP.**

4. For the Sysgen Variable, type **SYSGEN_DDRAW**.

You have successfully completed the steps to add a subcomponent to the Z9s XGI Display driver component to configure the display resolution and add DirectDraw support.

Add Files to the BSP

The ICOP eBox-3300 BSP does not include a device driver to support the USB audio. As the result, the clone BSP, MyBSP, does not have USB audio support.

The exercise in this section works through the steps to add an USB audio driver component to the BSP and includes the CMUAD.DLL driver. For this to work, you need to add the CMUAD.DLL file to the BSP.

The CMUAD.DLL file is provided as part of the software accompanying this book and is available for download from the following URL: www.embeddedpc.net/Compact7Book/.

After you acquire the CMUAD.DLL file, place a copy of this file in the following directory: $(_PLATFORMROOT)\MyBSP\Files.

All files in the preceding directory will be copied to the build release directory during build time. You can configure the BSP to include files from the build release directory to the compiled OS run-time image.

Work through the following steps to create the USB audio driver component for the BSP:

1. From the Catalog Editor tab, right-click the Device Drivers folder, and click Add Catalog Item to add a new catalog item to the BSP.

2. From the Properties tab, for the Title, type **USB Audio driver.**

3. For the Unique ID, type **USBAudio:Embedded101:.**

4. For the Additional Variables, type the **BSP_VORTEX86DX_USB_AUDIO** variable, via the String Collection Editor screen.

5. For the Sysgen Variable, type the **SYSGEN_USB** variable.

6. Open the following Registry file with a text editor, such as Notepad:
   $(_PLATFORMROOT)\MyBSP\Files\PLATFORM.REG

7. Append the following Registry entries for the driver to the PLATFROM.REG Registry file, to be included to the OS run-time image:

```
; @CESYSGEN IF CE_MODULES_USBD
    IF BSP_NOUSB !
        IF BSP_VORTEX86DX_USB_AUDIO
            [HKEY_LOCAL_MACHINE\Drivers\USB\LoadClients\Default\Default\1\Audio_Class]
                "Prefix"="WAV"
                "Dll"="CMUAD.DLL"
            [HKEY_LOCAL_MACHINE\Drivers\USB\ClientDrivers\Audio_Class]
                "Prefix"="WAV"
                "Dll"="CMUAD.DLL"
        ENDIF BSP_VORTEX86DX_USB_AUDIO
    ENDIF BSP_NOUSB !
; @CESYSGEN ENDIF CE_MODULES_USBD
```

Code snippet is from platform.reg

8. Open the following Binary-Image-Builder (BIB) file with a text editor, such as Notepad:
   $(_PLATFORMROOT)\MyBSP\Files\PLATFORM.BIB.

9. The PLATFORM.BIB file contains command scripts configured to include the intended files in the OS run-time image. Append the following entries to the PLATFROM.BIB file to add the CMUAD.DLL file to the OS run-time image.

```
FILES
;  Name              Path                                               Memory Type
;  -------------     ------------------------------------------------   -----------
;  @CESYSGEN IF CE_MODULES_USBD
      IF BSP_NOUSB !
          IF BSP_VORTEX86DX_USB_AUDIO
              CMUAD.dll      $(_FLATRELEASEDIR)\CMUAD.dll      NK   SH
          ENDIF BSP_VORTEX86DX_USB_AUDIO
      ENDIF BSP_NOUSB !
;  @CESYSGEN ENDIF CE_MODULES_USBD
```

Code snippet is from platform.bib

You have successfully completed the steps to add the USB Audio driver component to MyBSP.

Add a Component to Configure System Memory

It's common for a hardware vendor to provide the same hardware platform with a different amount of built-in system memory (RAM). The exercise in this section works through the steps to add a memory configuration component to the BSP to simplify the effort to support the same hardware built with a different amount of system memory.

Add a Component to Configure 128MB Support

Work through the following steps to create the memory configuration component to support a target device with 128MB RAM:

1. From the Catalog Editor tab, right-click the MyBSP: x86 node, and click Add Catalog Item in Subfolder to bring up the New Subfolder screen, as shown in Figure 6-11.

2. For the Subfolder name, type **RAM Size**, and click OK to close the New Subfolder screen. Under the newly created RAM Size subfolder, a new catalog item, Item: DefaulVendor:DefaultCatalogItemName, is created.

FIGURE 6-11

3. From the Properties tab, click the new catalog item; for the title, type **128MB RAM**.

4. For the Unique ID, type **RAM128:Embedded101:MyBSP**.

5. For the Additional Variables, type the **IMGRAM128** variable, via the String Collection Editor screen.

6. From the Properties tab, change the Choose One Group selection from False to **True**.

Add a Component to Configure 256MB Support

Work through the following steps to create the memory configuration component to support a target device with 256MB RAM:

1. From the Catalog Editor tab, right-click the RAM Size folder, and click Add Catalog Item to add a new catalog item.

2. From the Properties tab, for the Title, type **256MB RAM**.

3. For the Unique ID, type **RAM256:Embedded101:MyBSP**.

4. For the Additional Variables, type the **IMGRAM256** variable, via the String Collection Editor screen.

5. From the Properties tab, change the Choose One Group selection from False to **True**.

The ICOP eBox-3300 BSP, which the MyBSP is cloned from, is configured to support 128MB and 256MB RAM. Review the IMGRAM128 and IMGRAM256 codes in the CONFIG.BIB file, in the following directory: $(_PLATFORM)\MyBSP\Files\CONFIG.BIB.

In addition to the configuration entries to the CONFIG.BIB system configuration file, additional code modification to the OEM Adaptation Layer (OAL) is needed.

Add Serial Port Driver Components

Work through the following steps to add serial port driver components, to support COM1 (Serial1) and COM2 (Serial2), to the BSP:

1. From the Catalog Editor tab, right-click the Device Drivers folder, and click Add Catalog Item in Subfolder to bring up the New Subfolder screen, as shown in Figure 6-12.

FIGURE 6-12

2. For the Subfolder name, type **Serial Port**, and click OK to close the New Subfolder screen. A new catalog item, Item:DefaulVendor:DefaultCatalogItemName, is created under the newly created Serial Port subfolder.

3. Click the new catalog item, from the Properties tab; for the Title, type **COM1**.

4. For the Unique ID, type **COM1:Embedded101:MyBSP**.

5. For the Additional Variables, type the **BSP_SERIAL** variable, via the String Collection Editor screen.

6. For the Sysgen Variable, type the **SYSGEN_SERDEV** variable.

7. From the Catalog Editor tab, right-click the Serial Port folder, and to add a new catalog item, click Add Catalog Item.

8. From the Properties tab, for the Title, type **COM2**.

9. For the Unique ID, type **COM2:Embedded101:MyBSP**.

10. For the Additional Variables, type the **BSP_SERIAL2** variable, via the String Collection Editor screen.

11. For the Sysgen Variable, type the **SYSGEN_SERDEV** variable.

Registry entries, needed to support COM1 and COM2, are already included to the BSP, cloned from the ICOP eBox-3300 BSP. To review these Registry entries, use a text editor such as Notepad; open the following Registry file; and search for entries wrapped within the BSP_SERIAL and BSP_SERIAL2 variables: $(_PLATFORMROOT)\MyBSP\Files\PLATFORM.REG.

You have successfully created the driver components to support COM1 and COM2.

Add a Component to Enable Serial Debug Messages

The current BSP settings configure the serial port to output debug messages. This feature should be disabled on a device produced for distribution.

Modify System Registry to Disable Serial Debug by Default

Work through the following steps to modify the system Registry and wrap the serial debug port entries within the BSP_SERIAL_DEBUG environment variable to configure the BSP to disable serial debug by default:

1. Open the PLATFORM.REG Registry file, with a text editor such as Notepad, from the following directory: $(_PLATFORMROOT)\MyBSP\Files\.

2. Locate the following block of entries:

Available for
download on
Wrox.com

```
[HKEY_LOCAL_MACHINE\Drivers\BootArg]
    "SerialDbg1"="Drivers\\BuiltIn\\Serial1"
IF BSP_SERIAL2
    "SerialDbg2"="Drivers\\BuiltIn\\Serial2"
ENDIF BSP_SERIAL2
```

Code snippet is from platform.reg

3. Change the preceding block of entries to the following:

Available for
download on
Wrox.com

```
IF BSP_SERIAL_DEBUG
    [HKEY_LOCAL_MACHINE\Drivers\BootArg]
        "SerialDbg1"="Drivers\\BuiltIn\\Serial1"
ENDIF BSP_SERIAL_DEBUG
```

Code snippet is from platform.reg

The preceding modified Registry entries enable serial debug message output to COM1 when the BSP_SERIAL_DEBUG variable is set.

Add a Component to Enable a Serial Debug Message on COM1

Work through the following steps to add the Enable Serial Debug component to the BSP:

1. From the Catalog Editor tab, right-click the COM1 node, and click Add Catalog Item.

2. From the Properties tab, for the Title, type **Enable Serial Debug**.

3. For the Unique ID, type **SerialDebug:Embedded101:MyBSP**.

4. For the Additional Variables, type the **BSP_SERIAL_DEBUG** variable, via the String Collection Editor screen.

You have successfully cloned and customized the MyBSP BSP. With the customized and added components, MyBSP provides developer-friendly features that are not part of the original BSP, the ICOP eBox-3300 BSP, as shown in Figure 6-13.

This concludes the steps to customize MyBSP.

SUMMARY

BSP is one of the key ingredients needed to develop an OS design to generate OS run-time image for the target device. A BSP package contains hardware dependent codes, including low-level device driver and OAL codes that require a strong software development background and knowledge about the hardware. Developing a BSP from the ground up can be complex and may take weeks, or even months, to complete. With a quality BSP, the effort to develop a customized OS run-time image is greatly simplified. The exercises in this chapter, in addition to showing the steps to clone and customize BSP, provide information to help you understand the structure and inner components within the BSP, which is essential to perform BSP development work.

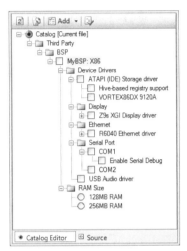

FIGURE 6-13

7

OS Design

WHAT'S IN THIS CHAPTER?

➤ Developing an OS design project

➤ Customizing the OS design and generating a run-time image

➤ Generating an SDK to support application development

Developing an OS design is an integral part of the Windows Embedded Compact development process. The OS run-time image for the target device is generated from an OS design. The SDK, needed to support application development, is also generated from an OS design.

This chapter provides information about the OS design and associated components. The exercises in this chapter show the steps to create an OS design project, compile an OS run-time image for a target device, and generate an SDK to support application development for the target device.

WHAT IS AN OS DESIGN?

An OS design is one of the Visual Studio 2008 project templates installed to the development station as part of the Platform Builder for Windows Embedded Compact 7 software.

OS design is an integral part of the Windows Embedded Compact development process, providing the workspace to develop customized OS images, device drivers, and a programming support library for the target device.

An SDK, generated from the same OS design that generated the OS run-time image for the target device, is needed to support application development for the target device.

Subprojects can be added to the OS design to provide the workspaces to develop device drivers, programming libraries, and applications for the target device.

DEVELOP AN OS DESIGN

This section works through the exercises to create an OS design project, stepping through the process to customize the OS design and generate a customized OS run-time image for the target device.

The OS design project is created with the cloned BSP from Chapter 6, "BSP Introduction," using an eBox-3310A as the target device.

To successfully complete the exercises in this chapter, the development station needs to have the following software installed:

➤   Visual Studio 2008 with Service Pack 1

➤   Platform Builder for Windows Embedded Compact 7

➤   BSP cloned from the previous chapter, MyBSP

➤   AutoLaunch_v200_Compact7 component

➤   CoreCon_v200_Compact7 component

> *You can download the* AutoLaunch_v200_Compact7 *and* CoreCon_v200_Compact7
> *components from the following Codeplex projects:*
>
>   http://AutoLaunch4CE.codeplex.com
>   http://CoreCon4CE.codeplex.com

OS Design Wizard

The Compact 7 development environment includes an OS Design Wizard that greatly simplifies the tasks you need to perform to create the initial OS design project workspace. When creating a new OS design project, VS2008 launches the OS Design Wizard, steps through the project creation process, and provides templates to use as the starting point to develop a customized OS image.

With help from the OS Design Wizard, work through the following steps to create a new OS design project:

1.   From the VS2008 File menu, select New, and click Project to bring up the new Project Wizard, as shown in Figure 7-1.

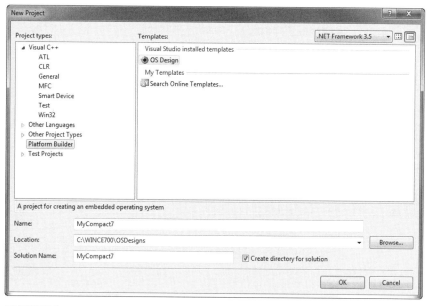

FIGURE 7-1

2. Select Platform Builder from the Project Types pane. Select OS Design from the Templates pane. Enter **MyCompact7** as the project name, and click OK to continue. At this point, VS2008 launches the OS Design Wizard and brings up the Create an OS Design screen, as shown in Figure 7-2.

3. Click Next to continue and bring up the OS Design Wizard's Board Support Packages selection screen, as shown in Figure 7-3.

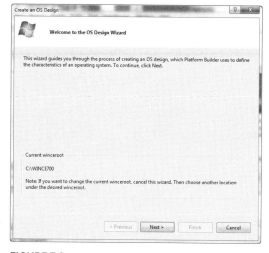

FIGURE 7-2

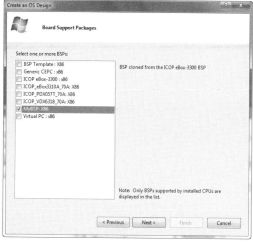

FIGURE 7-3

All installed BSPs, from Microsoft and third-party companies, are listed in the Board Support Packages selection screen. It's possible to select multiple BSPs to support the same OS design project and generate multiple OS run-time images, from the same OS design project, to support multiple target devices.

For each selected BSP, a separate group of build release folders are created to store OS design files for the selected BSP. The OS design needs to go through a separate build process to build the OS design project and generate an OS run-time image for each of the selected BSPs, to support the target device associated with the BSP.

4. Select MyBSP: X86 to support the eBox-3310A as the target device. Click Next to continue and bring up the OS Design Wizard's Design Templates selection screen, as shown in Figure 7-4.

FIGURE 7-4

If you don't have access to an eBox-3310A, you can use a Virtual PC as the target device. To support Virtual PC as the target device, select the Virtual PC: x86 BSP and ignore the steps that involve selecting a BSP component specific to the MyBSP BSP.

5. Expand the Enterprise Device folder, select Industrial Controller, and click Next to continue and bring up the OS Design wizard's Application and Media selection screen.

6. For the Applications and Media selection step, select the following components, as shown in Figure 7-5.

    ➤   .NET Compact Framework 3.5

    ➤   Console Window

    ➤   Internet Explorer 7.0

    ➤   Network User Interface

    ➤   Waveform Audio

    ➤   Windows Internet Services

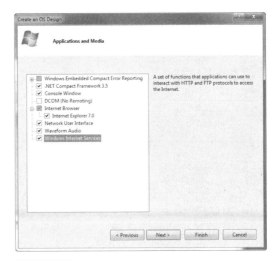

FIGURE 7-5

7. Click Next to continue to the Networking and Communication selection screen, as shown in Figure 7-6.

8. For the Network and Communication selection step, keep the default selection, and click Next to continue and bring up the final OS Design Project Wizard step, as shown in Figure 7-7.

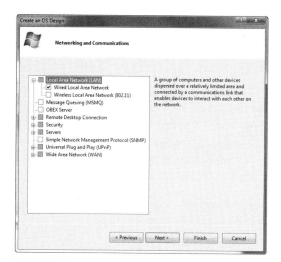

FIGURE 7-6

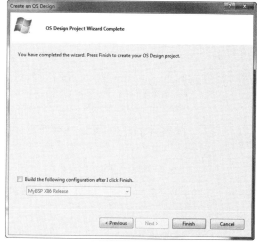

FIGURE 7-7

9. As you click on Finish, the Catalog Item Notification screen displays security warning messages to notify you that one or more of the catalog items included in the OS design may compromise system security, as shown in Figure 7-8.

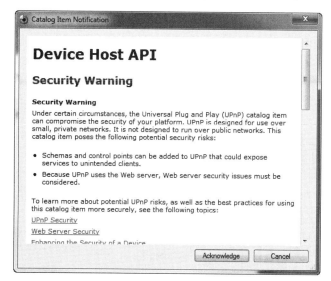

FIGURE 7-8

10. From the Catalog Item Notification screen, click Acknowledge to acknowledge the warning, and close the screen to complete the OS Design Wizard steps.

OS Design Project Files and Folders

After you complete the OS Design Wizard steps, Platform Builder creates and configures the initial workspace for the MyCompact7 OS design project, using the selected OS design template, BSPs, and components.

The following VS2008 solution folders were created for the project:

➤ `$(_WINCEROOT)\OSDesigns\MyCompact7`

This is the root folder for the MyCompact7 solution. VS2008 supports different project types. The MyCompact7 VS2008 solution provides a centralized workspace to store different project types supporting the same solution in one location.

For example, the MyCompact7 solution may include an OS design, a Visual Basic application, a C# application, and a Visual C++ application projects.

➤ `$(_WINCEROOT)\OSDesigns\MyCompact7\MyCompact7`

This is the folder where you can find the MyCompact7 OS design project files and Platform Builder subprojects. Platform Builder uses the `_OSDESIGNROOT` variable to represent this folder.

Catalog Item View

The Compact 7 OS design contains a collection of components, which may include BSP, file system, networking, media, Codecs, device driver, programming library, utility, and other third-party software components. The Catalog Item View window provides a graphical interface to view these components. It's also the interface used to add and remove components to and from the OS design.

The Catalog Item View window contains all the Platform Builder for Compact 7 components, including OS, programming libraries, device drivers, utilities, and third-party components installed to the development station and available to be included in the OS design.

To review components included in the MyCompact7 OS design project, from the Catalog Item View window, expand all folders and nodes to review the included components, as shown in Figure 7-9.

The Catalog Item View window provides the following visual indication to show components that are included in the OS design:

➤ A component with a check mark to the left indicates it's selected during the OS Design Wizard steps, or manually added afterward.

➤ A component with a solid green square to the left indicates the component is included in the OS design by Platform Builder because it is a dependency to another component included in the OS design.

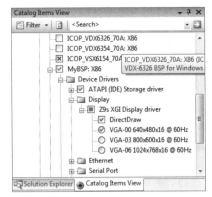

FIGURE 7-9

➤ A component with a red cross to the left indicates the selected component is not active and will not be included in the compiled OS run-time image due to one or more of the following reasons:

➤ This component requires another component to function, which is not available.

➤ The OS design's build configuration excluded this component from the current OS design project setting.

By default, the Catalog Item View window lists all components installed in the development station. You can enable a filter to exclude components not included in the OS design from showing. To enable the filter, from the Catalog Items View window's top-left part, click Filter, and select User-Selected Catalog Items and Dependencies. With this filter enabled, components not included in the MyCompact7 OS design are not displayed.

The component list can be further shortened by enabling the User-selected Catalog Items Only filter, which excludes components not included in the OS design. This filter also excludes component includes to the OS design because it's a dependency to another component that is selected for the OS design.

Customize the OS Design

You can further customize the MyCompact7 OS design project with the following:

➤ Add a component to the OS design.

➤ Remove a component from the OS design.

➤ Add an application and a library as a subproject to the OS design.

➤ Modify the system configuration and Registry file to customize system behavior.

This section offers additional exercises to customize the OS design.

Add Components from the Board Support Package

With MyCompact7 OS design active, from the Catalog Items View window, expand the \Third Party\BSP\MyBSP: X86 BSP node. Expand all folders and nodes under the MyBSP: X86 BSP node and include the following BSP components to the OS design, as shown in Figure 7-10.

➤ **MyBSP: X86/Device Drivers/ATAPI (IDE) Storage driver** — Sets the SYSGEN_ATAPI variable to include the ATAPI storage driver and the SYSGEN_FATFS variable to include FAT file system support in the OS design.

➤ **MyBSP: X86/Device Drivers/Display/Z9s XGI Display driver** — Enables the device driver for the Z9s XGI display controller to be included in the OS design.

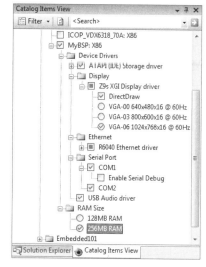

FIGURE 7-10

➤ **X86/Device Drivers/Display/Z9s XGI Display driver/VGA-06 1024x768x16 @ 60Hz** — the BSP environment variable, `BSP_DISPLAY_Z9s_1024x768x16x60`, which configures the display driver Registry to support 1024x768 display resolution with 16-bit color and 60Hz refresh rate.

➤ **MyBSP: X86/Device Drivers/Ethernet/R6040 Ethernet driver** — Sets the `BSP_NIC_R6040` environment variable, which configures the OS design to include the R6040 Ethernet device driver.

➤ **MyBSP: X86/Device Drivers/Serial Port/COM1** — Sets the `SYSGEN_SERDEV` and `BSP_SERIAL` environment variables to include the serial port support and configure the system Registry to enable a designated serial port as COM1.

➤ **MyBSP: X86/Device Drivers/Serial Port/COM2** — Sets the `SYSGEN_SERDEV` and `BSP_SERIAL2` environment variables to include the serial port support and configures the system Registry to enable a designated serial port as COM2.

➤ **MyBSP: X86/Device Drivers/USB Audio driver** — Sets the `SYSGEN_USB` and `BSP_VORTEX86DX_USB_AUDIO` environment variables to enable USB support and includes a USB audio device driver in the OS design.

➤ **MyBSP: X86/Device Drivers/256MB RAM** — Sets the `IMGRAM256` environment variable, which configures the OS design to generate an OS run-time image that supports 256MB of system memory.

 If you don't have access to an eBox-3310A, using Virtual PC as the target device and configuring the OS design to use the Virtual PC:x86 BSP, select and include the VCEPC keyboard driver (select the appropriate version) and DEC 21x40 Ethernet components in the OS design.

Add Other Compact 7 OS Components

In addition to the OS components included in the OS design as part of the selected template by the OS Design Wizard and the BSP components from the previous step, you need to add the following components to the OS design to support application development and other functions:

➤ **CAB file installer/uninstaller** — Needed to support application development and provide the function to deploy and remove an application, to and from the target device.

From the Catalog Items View window, expand the `\Core OS\Windows Embedded Compact\Applications - End User` folder and include this component in the OS design.

➤ **USB storage class driver** — Configures the OS design to include a USB storage class driver needed to support a USB storage device.

Expand the `\Core OS\Windows Embedded Compact\Device Drivers\USB\USB Host\USB Class Drivers` folder and include this component in the OS design.

➤ **USB HID keyboard and mouse** — Configures the OS design to include the necessary driver to support a USB keyboard and mouse.

Expand the `\Core OS\Windows Embedded Compact\Device Drivers\USB\USB Host\ USB Class Drivers\USB Human Input Device (HID) Class` node and include this component in the OS design.

➤ **8042 PS/2 keyboard/mouse** — Configures the OS design to include the necessary driver to support a PS/2 keyboard and mouse.

Expand the `\Core OS\Windows Embedded Compact\Device Drivers\Input Devices\ Keyboard/Mouse` folder and include this component in the OS design.

➤ **FTP server** — Configures the OS design to include the FTP Server component. An FTP server provides a convenient method to upload a file to the target device's local storage.

Expand the `\Core OS\Windows Embedded Compact\Communication Services and Networking\Servers` folder and include this component in the OS design.

For the FTP server to function, you need additional Registry entries to configure this component to function as intended, which the later step, in the OS Design Registry Configuration section, covers.

 Platform Builder components selected in this section are hardware-independent.

Use Search to Locate a Component from the Catalog

The Platform Builder IDE provides a search function to locate a component from the catalog by searching the catalog using a keyword or partial keyword associated with the component.

Following these steps to locate the Remote Display application by searching the catalog using the remote display keyword:

1. From the Catalog Item View window, enter the **remote display** keyword in the search textbox, and click the small green arrow in the upper-right corner (see Figure 7-11).

2. Select and include the Remote Display Application to the OS design.

The Remote Display Application provides the function to access the Compact 7 desktop remotely, from the development station. It's similar to the Remote Desktop feature for the Windows XP, Vista, and 7 OS.

With the Remote Display Application active on a Compact 7 device, to access the device's desktop remotely from the development station, launch the `CERHOST.EXE` executable from the `$(_WINCEROOT)\Public\Common\Oak\Bin\i386` folder.

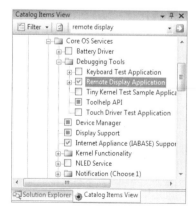

FIGURE 7-11

 The Remote Display application component is hardware-independent.

Add a Third-Party Component

To configure and prepare a Compact 7 OS image for application development, CoreCon connectivity files need to be included as part of the OS image or made accessible from the Compact 7 OS image's file system. In addition, the CoreCon connectivity service must be launched to establish connection from the VS2008 development IDE to the Compact 7 device.

To help simplify the tasks needed to include CoreCon files in the OS run-time image and automatically launch the necessary CoreCon service when the OS starts, add the following two components to the OS design:

➤ **AutoLaunch_v200_Compact7** — Adds the AUTOLAUNCH.EXE executable to the OS design and the necessary Registry entries to launch this executable when the OS starts. You can add Registry entries to the OS design's OSDESIGN.REG Registry file to configure the AUTOLAUNCH.EXE executable to launch designated application when the OS starts.

Expand the \Third Party\Embedded101 folder and include this component to the OS design.

➤ **CoreCon_v200_Compact7** — Includes the necessary CoreCon files to the OS design, needed to establish CoreCon connectivity between VS2008 IDE and the target device to download the application to the target device for testing and debugging.

Expand the \Third Party\Embedded101 folder and include this component to the OS design.

 The AutoLaunch and CoreCon components selected in this section are hardware-independent.

Edit Build Configuration

You can configure the OS design to build a run-time image in Checked, Debug, or Release mode. The OS design is configured to build in Release mode by default. To change the build configuration, from the VS2008 Build menu, click Configuration Manager and the Configuration Manager screen displays, as shown in Figure 7-12.

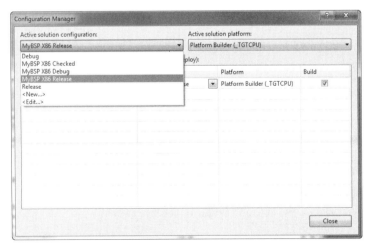

FIGURE 7-12

An OS design configured to build in Release mode enables compiler optimization and does not generate debugging information in object files and does not place object files in the build release directory, which is not recommended for use with the debugger.

A debug mode OS run-time image is significantly larger (approximately 50%) than a release mode image, which includes additional components to support debugging.

An OS design configured to build in checked mode results in a more compact OS run-time image, compared to Debug mode, and contains resources to provide debug information not available in Release mode.

For each build configuration, Platform Builder compiles and generates OS design files to a separate build release directory. For an OS design configured to Release mode, the OS design files are compiled and generated to the following build release directory: `$(_OSDESIGNROOT)\RelDir\MyBSP_x86_Release\`

Debug mode OS design files are compiled and generated to the following build release directory: `$(_OSDESIGNROOT)\RelDir\MyBSP_x86_Debug\`

Checked mode OS design files are compiled and generated to the following build release directory: `$(_OSDESIGNROOT)\RelDir\MyBSP_x86_Checked\`

For the exercise in this chapter, configure the OS design to build in Release mode, which is the default configuration.

Configure OS Design Build Options

The OS design build options provide different settings to configure the build process to generate an OS run-time image with different behaviors.

Following these steps to configure the OS design's build options:

1. From the VS2008 Project menu, click MyCompact7 Properties and the MyCompact7 Property Pages screen displays, as shown in Figure 7-13.

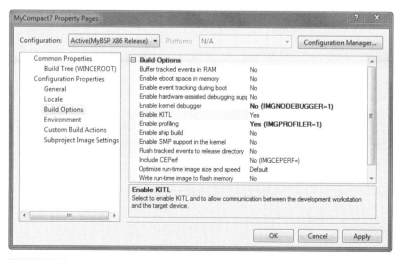

FIGURE 7-13

2. From the screen's left pane, expand the Configuration Properties node, and select Build Options.

3. From the screen's right pane, change the Enable profiling build option to Yes. In addition, check to confirm the Enable KITL option is configured to Yes. The KITL option is enabled by default. The KITL and profiling build options are needed to support the Platform Builder remote tools exercise in Chapter 9, "Debug and Remote Tools."

 To generate an OS run-time image to deploy to the target device's local flash storage, the KITL build option should be disabled. Otherwise, the image fails to boot.

4. Click Apply and OK to save the settings, and close the screen.

OS Design Environment Variables

The MyCompact7 OS design can be configured to include components, Registry entries, and files by setting the associated environment variables.

You can establish a customized environment variable to control whether a file or Registry entry is included in the OS design.

The environment variable for the OS design can be set from the MyCompact7 Property Pages screen, as shown in Figure 7-14.

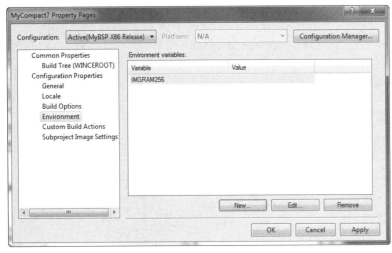

FIGURE 7-14

Work through the following steps to set the IMGRAM256 environment variable:

1. From the VS2008 Project menu, click MyCompact7 Properties to bring up the MyCompact7 Property Pages screen.

2. From the screen's left pane, expand the Configuration Properties node, and click the Environment node.

3. From the screen's right pane, click New and the Environment Variable screen displays, as shown in Figure 7-15.

4. For the Variable name, enter **IMGRAM256**.

5. Enter **1** for the Variable value entry; click OK to close the screen.

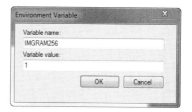

FIGURE 7-15

 The previous exercise shows the steps to set an environment variable, IMGRAM256, for an OS design, from the OS design property page, MyCompact7 Property.

The MyBSP includes two RAM Size components, "128MB RAM" and "256MB RAM". By including the "256MB RAM" component to the OS design, it configures the OS design to set the IMGRAM256 environment variable, which has the same effect as the setting this variable from the property page.

OS Design Registry Configuration

Windows Embedded Compact system Registry plays a key role in controlling how the OS run-time behaves, loads a driver, launches an application, and more.

In this chapter's earlier steps, as part of the process to customize the OS design, the FTP server, remote display application, CoreCon, and AutoLaunch components were added to the OS design. For these components to function as intended, appropriate Registry entries need to be added to the OS design's OSDESIGN.REG Registry file.

Work through the following steps to add the required Registry entries to the OS design:

1. From the VS2008 View menu, click Solution Explorer to bring up the Solution Explorer window, as shown in Figure 7-16.

FIGURE 7-16

➤ Expand the \Parameter Files folder.

➤ Double-click the OSDESIGN.REG Registry file to open this file in the code editor window, as shown in Figure 7-17.

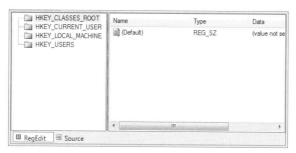

FIGURE 7-17

> On the code editor window's lower-left corner, click Source to view the `OSDESIGN.REG` file in source format and append the following Registry entries to the file:

```
; Registry for FTP server
[HKEY_LOCAL_MACHINE\COMM\FTPD]
    "IsEnabled"=dword:1
    "UseAuthentication"=dword:0
    "UserList"="@*;"
    "AllowAnonymous"=dword:1
    "AllowAnonymousUpload"=dword:1
    "AllowAnonymousVroots"=dword:1
    "DefaultDir"="\\"

; Registry for AutoLaunch
[HKEY_LOCAL_MACHINE\Startup]
    "Process0"="cerdisp -c"
    "Process0Delay"=dword:00001388
    "Process1"="ConmanClient2.exe"
    "Process1Delay"=dword:00002710
```

Code snippet is from OSDESIGN.REG

Compile and Generate OS Run-time Image

At this point, the MyCompact7 OS design is configured with the components needed for the exercise and is ready to be built to generate an OS run-time image from the project.

From the VS2008 Build menu, expand Advanced Build Commands, and click `Sysgen (blddemo -q)` to start the build.

As the MyCompact7 OS design project is being built, compilation activities are shown on the VS2008's Output window, as shown in Figure 7-18.

```
Output                                                              ▾ ₽ ×
Show output from: Build              ▾ | 🔊 | 🔊 🔊 | 🗟 | 🗟
------ Build started: Project: MyCompact7, Configuration: MyBSP X86 Release Platform Builder (_TGTCPU) ----- ▲
Starting Build: blddemo -q
===============
Wince x86 CEBASE MyBSP Development Environment for Samphung
"C:\Windows\system32\cmd.exe" /d /c "blddemo -q"
BuildLogs: BUILDMSG: Saving last successful log as "C:\WINCE700\build.lkg.log".
BuildLogs: BUILDMSG: Starting: BldDemo1.bat  -q
BuildLogs: BUILDMSG: Logs at "C:\WINCE700\build.*".
BLDDEMO: BUILDMSG: BldDemo started at 21:44:29 11 on Sat 02/19/2011
◄        III                                                       ►
🔲 Code Definition Window 🔩 Call Browser 🗟 Output 🔩 Error List
```

FIGURE 7-18

Depending on the development station's processing capabilities, such as the processor speed and available system memory, the build process may take anywhere from 10 minutes to well over 20 minutes. After the build process successfully completes, the VS2008 IDE's Output window shows a build succeeded message (see Figure 7-19).

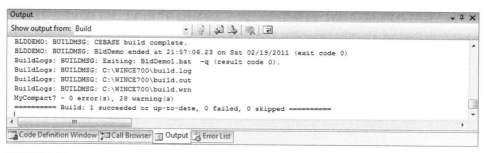

FIGURE 7-19

Upon a successful build, a Compact 7 OS run-time image file, NK.BIN, is generated in the following build release directory: $(_OSDESIGNROOT)\RelDir\MyBSP_x86_Release

Platform Builder uses the _FLATRELEASEDIR variable to represent the preceding active build release directory.

During the build process, Platform Builder logs build activities to the following files: $(_WINCEROOT)\ BUILD.LOG.

When the build process ends with any error, the build fails and does not generate an OS image. Platform Builder logs additional activities to the following error log file: $(_WINCEROOT)\BUILD.ERR.

In addition to the BUILD.LOG and BUILD.ERR log file, Platform Builder logs additional warning messages to the following file: $(_WINCEROOT)\BUILD.WRN.

The BUILD.LOG file contains detailed build and compilation information for the OS design, needed to analyze the build process, and helps identify problems related to the build process.

GENERATE SDK FROM THE OS DESIGN

You need a software development kit (SDK), generated from the MyCompact7 OS design, to support application development for the target device associated with the OS design.

Create a New SDK

With the MyCompact7 OS design project active, work through the exercise in this section to create and configure a new SDK:

1. From the VS2008 Project menu, click Add New SDK to bring up the new SDK Wizard, as shown in Figure 7-20.

2. For the SDK Name, enter **MyCompact7_SDK**.

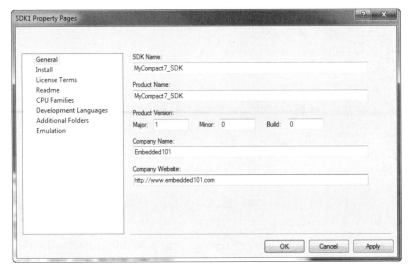

FIGURE 7-20

3. For the Product Name, enter **MyCompact7_SDK**.

4. For the Product Version, enter **1** for Major and keep the 0 entries for Minor and Build.

5. For the Company Name, enter **Embedded101**.

6. For the Company Website, enter **http://www.embedded101.com**.

7. From the left pane, click the Install node and enter **MyCompact7_SDK.msi** for the MSI File Name entry, as shown in Figure 7-21.

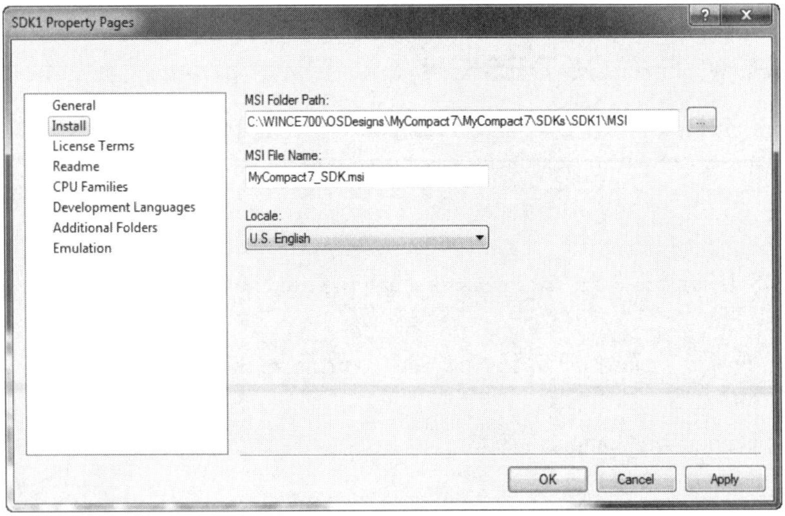

FIGURE 7-21

8. From the left pane, click the Development Languages node; on the right, click the check box to enable Managed Development Support, as shown in Figure 7-22.

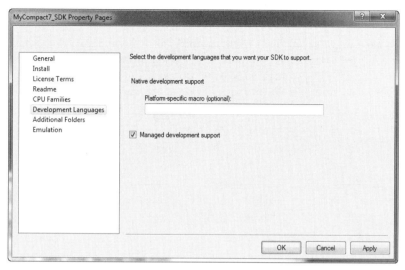

FIGURE 7-22

9. Click Apply and then OK to save and close the SDK Wizard screen.

After the new SDK is created, the newly created `MyCompact7_SDK` is listed under the SDK's node on the Solution Explorer window.

Build and Generate an SDK MSI File

With the SDK created and configured in the previous step, from the VS2008 Build menu, select Build All SDKs to build and generate a `MyCompact7_SDK.msi` file to distribute to the application developer to support application development for the MyCompact7 OS design.

After the build process completes, the `MyCompact7_SDK.msi` installation file generates in the following directory: `$(_OSDESIGNROOT)\RelDir\SDKs\SDK1\MSI`.

Launch the `MyCompact7_SDK.msi` to install this SDK to the development station to support application development for the MyCompact7 OS design.

Each time you create a new OS run-time image for the target device, the newly created OS image may have changes that affect the supported API, which can impact the application running on the device based on the older SDK. Generate a new SDK from the modified OS design to support application development to ensure the application is written to support the available API.

SUMMARY

Developing an OS design is one of the important steps in a Windows Embedded Compact device development project. Throughout the development process, the OS design needs to be changed and reconfigured to resolve problems and adopt new design changes.

Although a Compact 7 OS design involves many different components and complex codes, using a quality BSP with properly written device driver, support library, and application components that adhere to the Windows Embedded Compact's design, the process to develop an OS design and generate an OS run-time image for the intended target device can be fairly straightforward.

Target Device Connectivity and Download

WHAT'S IN THIS CHAPTER?

➤ Establishing connectivity to the target device

➤ Downloading the OS run-time image to the target device

As part of the Windows Embedded Compact OS design development process, the development station needs to establish connectivity to the target device, to download an OS run-time image to the target device for testing and debug.

This chapter includes exercises to show the steps needed to establish connectivity from the development station to the target device and download the OS run-time image generated in the previous chapter to the target device.

Following are the prerequisites needed to work through the exercises in this chapter, using an eBox-3310A or Virtual PC as the target device:

➤ Successfully create and build the MyCompact7 OS design project from Chapter 7, "OS Design"

➤ An eBox-3310A or Virtual PC virtual machine (VM) preconfigured with Compact 7 bootloader as the target device

➤ Both the development station and target device attached to the same Local Area Network (LAN)

TARGET DEVICE CONNECTIVITY

Depending on the target device's hardware architecture and connectivity built in to the design, the development station can be connected to the target device through one of the following types of connection:

➤ Ethernet

➤ Serial

➤ USB

To download an OS run-time image to the target device, you need a bootloader for the target device, with appropriate codes to establish connectivity and initiate the OS run-time image download, that supports one of the connectivity options above.

CONNECTING TO THE TARGET DEVICE

To work through the exercise in this section to establish connectivity between the development station and the target device for the image download, you need to meet the following conditions:

➤ Successfully create the MyCompact7 OS design, from the exercise in Chapter 7, and build the OS design to generate a Compact 7 OS run-time image for the intended target device.

➤ Both the development station and target device attach to the same LAN with DHCP service to provide a IP address dynamically. Or both the development station and target device attach to the same LAN without DHCP service, and both have been configured with the appropriate static IP address within the same subnet.

➤ The target device has the necessary bootable storage configured with an appropriate Compact 7 bootloader.

Establish Connection to Download Compact 7 Image to Target Device

After you complete the previous conditions, work through the following steps to establish connectivity from the development station to the target device, to download a Compact 7 OS run-time image to the device:

1. If the MyCompact7 OS design project is not active, open the project from VS2008 IDE.

2. From the VS2008 menu, check to make sure the (auto) Ether option is selected as the device setting, as shown in Figure 8-1.

3. From the VS2008 Target menu, click Attach Device to bring up the Ethernet Download Settings screen, as shown in Figure 8-2, waiting for the BOOTME messages from the target device.

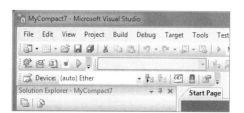

FIGURE 8-1

FIGURE 8-2

When establishing connectivity from a Windows 7 development station to a target device for the first time, the Windows Security Alert screen displays and prompts you to allow the Platform Builder CE Service Host through the firewall.

Click Allow Access to create an exception and allow the Platform Builder CE Service Host to communicate through the firewall.

4. Turn on the target device and launch the preconfigured bootloader.

If you use a Virtual PC VM as the target device, launch the VM, preconfigured with Compact 7 bootloader. You can use the VM provided as part of the Virtual PC BSP in the following directory: `$(_PLATFORMROOT)\VirtualPC\VM`.

From the preceding directory, double-click the `cevm.vmc` file to launch the virtual machine.

When working with a Windows XP or Vista development station, you need to install Virtual PC 2007 to use a Virtual PC VM as a target device. Refer to Chapter 3, "Development Station Preparation," for more information.

A new bootloader framework is released as part of Compact 7. For this exercise, use the new bootloader framework.

 A new bootloader framework, with a common code shared by all supported hardware platforms, is provided as part of the Compact 7 release. With this bootloader, the boot up behavior between the eBox-3310A and Virtual PC are identical.

5. When the bootloader is launching, the target device's screen shows a series of messages, as shown in Figure 8-3.

```
Microsoft Windows CE XLDR Version 1.0 (Built Feb  8 2010 01:19:43)
Microsoft Windows CE Boot Loader Version 1.3 (Built Feb  8 2010 01:19:42)
255MB, VRAM 4MB, PCI Extension 2.10, EDD Services 3.0, VESA 2.0, APM Services 1.
2

Hit space to enter configuration menu 5...
Hit space to enter configuration menu 4...
Hit space to enter configuration menu 3...
Hit space to enter configuration menu 2...
Hit space to enter configuration menu 1...
```

FIGURE 8-3

6. If the target device launches the bootloader for the first time, press the spacebar to enter configuration mode, as shown in Figure 8-4.

```
Microsoft Windows CE XLDR Version 1.0 (Built Feb  8 2010 01:19:43)
Microsoft Windows CE Boot Loader Version 1.3 (Built Feb  8 2010 01:19:42)
255MB, VRAM 4MB, PCI Extension 2.10, EDD Services 3.0, VESA 2.0, APM Services 1.
2

Hit space to enter configuration menu 5...
Hit space to enter configuration menu 4...
Hit space to enter configuration menu 3...
Hit space to enter configuration menu 2...
----------------------------------------------------------------------
Main Menu
----------------------------------------------------------------------

[1] Show Current Settings
[2] Select Boot Source
[3] Select KITL Device
[4] Network Settings
[5] Display Settings
[6] Debug Port Settings
[7] Save Settings
[0] Exit and Continue

Selection:
```

FIGURE 8-4

7. From the configuration main menu, press 2 (Select Boot Source) to enter the Select Boot Device menu.

8. From the Select Boot Device menu, press 2 (R6040 at PCI bus 0 dev 8 func 0) to select booting from Ethernet. After pressing 2, the screen goes back to the main menu.

 If you are using a Virtual PC VM as the target device, press 2 to select DEC21140 as the boot device.

9. From the main menu, press 7 (Save Settings) to save the newly configured setting. Then, press 0 to exit the Configuration mode.

At this point, the bootloader launches on the target device and broadcasts a series of BOOTME messages, as shown in Figure 8-5.

```
[0] Exit and Continue

Selection: 7
Current settings has been saved

Main Menu

[1] Show Current Settings
[2] Select Boot Source
[3] Select KITL Device
[4] Network Settings
[5] Display Settings
[6] Debug Port Settings
[7] Save Settings
[0] Exit and Continue

Selection: 0

Send BOOTME Message (device name PC-009909210147, attempt 1)
Send BOOTME Message (device name PC-009909210147, attempt 2)
Send BOOTME Message (device name PC-009909210147, attempt 3)
Send BOOTME Message (device name PC-009909210147, attempt 4)
```

FIGURE 8-5

If the target device is not broadcasting BOOTME messages, reset the device's power. As it boots up, the newly configured boot option takes effect.

10. As the target device broadcasts BOOTME messages, the Ethernet Download Settings screen on the development station detects the BOOTME message and lists the captured device information on the Active target device list box, as shown in Figure 8-6.

11. From the Active target devices list, click the device ID to select the device. As you click the device ID, the information expands to show the device's IP address and version of the bootloader in use.

12. Click Apply to complete this step.

FIGURE 8-6

DOWNLOAD OS RUN-TIME IMAGE TO TARGET DEVICE

Following up from the previous step, after you click Apply on the Ethernet Download Settings screen, connectivity is established between the development station and the target device. At this point, the process to download the OS run-time image to the target device is initiated. The Device Status screen, as shown in Figure 8-7, displays the download activities.

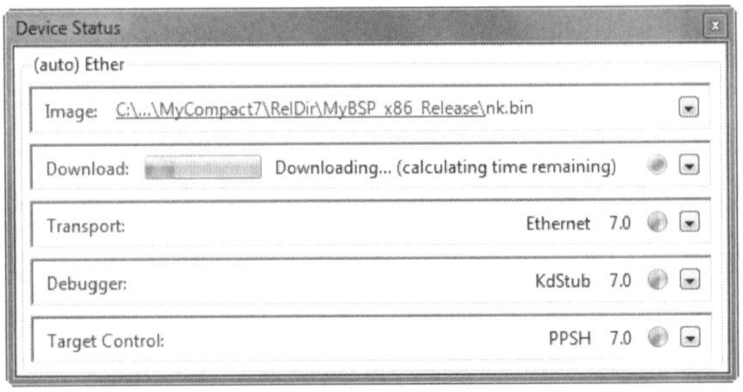

After the OS run-time image downloads, it is launched on the target device.

FIGURE 8-7

As the development station establishes connection and downloads the OS run-time image to the target device, the Platform Builder Debug output window on the VS2008 IDE displays debug messages, showing the download progress and activities as the image is launched on the target device, as shown in Figure 8-8.

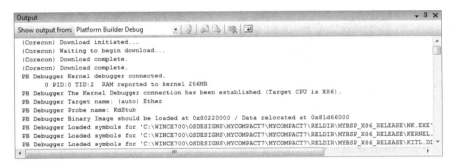

FIGURE 8-8

When downloading an OS run-time image built in Release mode with KITL disabled, the Platform Builder Debug output window does not display activities associated with the image launched on the target device. KITL is required to capture debug messages from the target device.

TARGET DEVICE CONNECTIVITY SETTING

In the previous section, you established the connection to the target device using the (auto) Ether device option, which does not require special settings. When you work on an OS design to support multiple target devices, after initiating the download to one device with the (auto) Ether option, you need to exit and restart the VS2008 IDE to connect to another device.

When working with multiple target devices, you can create multiple target device connectivity setting profiles, one for each target device. Work through the following steps to create a new profile:

1. From the VS2008 Target menu, click Connectivity Options to bring up the Target Device Connectivity Options screen, as shown in Figure 8-9.

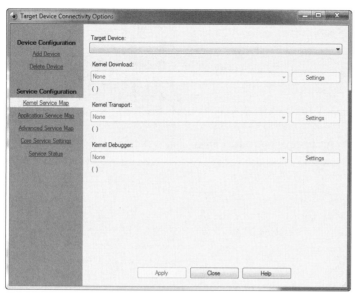

FIGURE 8-9

2. From the screen's top-left corner, click Add Device and enter **MyTargetDevice**, as the new profile name, to the new target device name entry on the right, and click Add to create the new profile, as shown in Figure 8-10.

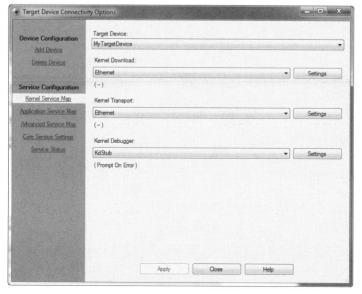

FIGURE 8-10

For the exercises in this book, the default settings for the kernel download, kernel transport, and kernel debugger are correct.

3. To associate a target device with the newly created MyTargetDevice connectivity profile, click the topmost Settings button to bring up the Ethernet Download Settings screen, similar to Figure 8-2.

4. Power on the target device to launch the bootloader and broadcast BOOTME messages.

5. As the target device broadcasts BOOTME messages, the BOOTME message is detected by the Ethernet Download Settings screen on the development station and lists the captured device information on the Active Target Device List box, similar to Figure 8-6.

6. From the Active Target Devices list, click the device ID to select the device. As you click the device ID, the information expands to show the device's IP address and version of the bootloader in use, as shown in Figure 8-11.

FIGURE 8-11

7. Click Apply to close the Ethernet Download Settings screen.

8. After the Ethernet Download Settings screen closes, the device settings are applied on the Target Device Connectivity Options screen, as shown in Figure 8-12.

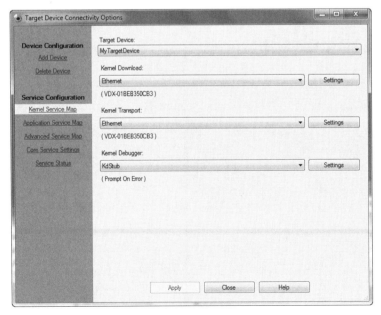

FIGURE 8-12

9. Click Close to save and close the screen.

To use the newly created MyTargetDevice setting, from the VS2008 menu, select MyTargetDevice as the device option, as shown in Figure 8-13.

To initiate the image download to the target device, from the VS2008 Target menu, click Attach Device, and power on the target device to launch the bootloader.

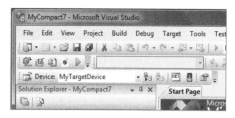

FIGURE 8-13

SUMMARY

During the process to develop a Compact 7 OS run-time image for a target device and download the image to the device, you need to establish connectivity between the development station and the intended target device.

With the target device properly configured with a Compact 7 bootloader and attached to the same LAN as the development station, you can establish connectivity between the development station and target device to download an OS run-time image to the device. With the KITL build option enabled, you can generate an OS run-time image with the necessary resources to support debugging from the development station, using remote tools.

Debug and Remote Tools

WHAT'S IN THIS CHAPTER?

➤ Debugging Windows Embedded Compact 7 OS design

➤ Debugging the build process

➤ Using Compact 7 remote tools

Even with the best engineering team, you are expected to spend a great deal of time and resources to identify elusive problems and look for alternative ways to improve system performance and stability.

Debugging and troubleshooting are integral parts of the development process. A productive debugging environment can help minimize the time and effort you need to spend for debugging, which can have a direct impact to the project's cost, schedule, and success.

The Platform Builder for Windows Embedded Compact 7 provides efficient tools and facilities to remotely debug an OS run-time image as it runs on the target device. This chapter provides information about the debugging facilities and remote tools available as part of the Compact 7 development environment, and works through multiple exercises showing the steps to use these tools.

DEBUGGING ENVIRONMENT

To take advantage of the debugging facilities and tools provided as part of the Platform Builder for Compact 7 development environment, you need to know which tools are available, how to use the tools, and the required connectivity.

You need to establish proper connectivity between the development station and target device, to capture debug information from the target device to help analyze the device's function and behavior. Proper connectivity is also needed for the development station to send commands to the target device to launch applications and utilities needed for testing and debugging.

Kernel Independent Transport Layer (KITL)

By now, you should have seen the KITL acronym many times and know that it's short for Kernel Independent Transport Layer. KITL is a communication protocol that abstracts the actual physical hardware layer to provide a hardware-independent communication interface to support Platform Builder debug facilities and remote tools. As an abstraction layer between the hardware and Windows Embedded Compact kernel, KITL provides uniform, hardware-independent interfaces to the debug facilities and remote tools provided by Platform Builder IDE. You can implement KITL over the Ethernet and Serial and USB interfaces.

To set up a proper Platform Builder development environment to develop a custom Compact 7 OS design efficiently, you must have KITL. Platform Builder debugging facilities and remote tools are dependent on KITL.

In general, KITL should be provided as part of the BSP for the target device by the hardware vendor. KITL is a must-have component for a quality BSP.

To enable KITL for an OS design, set the following environment variable: `IMGNOKITL=0`.

Alternatively, you select the KITL build option for an OS design from the OS design's property page, which sets the preceding environment variable.

Core Connectivity (CoreCon)

Core Connectivity is a unified communications infrastructure that provides the basic components needed to establish connectivity between a development station and a Compact 7 device to support the following:

➤ Downloading a collection of files to a target device

➤ Flashing a run-time image on a target device

➤ Launching an application on a target device

➤ Accessing resources on a target device

➤ Providing a connectivity framework for OEMs to develop customized remote tools to support their Compact 7 devices

To the Visual Studio application developer, CoreCon has been widely referred to as the connectivity framework to support Visual Studio application development, providing the transport between the Visual Studio IDE and the Windows Embedded Compact device to deploy, test, and debug applications.

With a CoreCon connection established between the VS2008 IDE and Compact 7 target device, you can deploy an application to the target device, from the VS2008 IDE. As the application executes on the target device, you can set a breakpoint to halt application execution, from the

VS2008 IDE, and step through the code, one line at a time, as the application executes on the target device.

The required CoreCon files to establish connectivity between the VS2008 IDE and a Compact 7 device to support VS2008 application development are installed to the development station, as part of the VS2008 software installation.

To establish CoreCon between the development station and Compact 7 target device to support remote application debugging, the required CoreCon files must be accessible from the target device's file system and launched from the device, using one of the following options:

- ➤ Include the required CoreCon files as part of the Compact 7 OS run-time image.
- ➤ Place the CoreCon files in the target device's local storage and generate an OS run-time image with the required file system driver to access the local storage.
- ➤ Place the CoreCon files on a Network share accessible by the target device after it boots up with the Compact 7 OS run-time image.

Chapter 16, "CoreCon Connectivity," provides more detailed coverage about CoreCon.

Serial Debug

Some Compact 7 devices are built without Ethernet, USB, and graphic display interfaces and use the serial port as the primary interface to interact with the development station and send debug messages.

For a Compact 7 device built with Ethernet, USB, and graphic display interfaces, the device cannot send debug messages from these interfaces until the Compact 7 OS run-time launches and loads the required device drivers. During the bootloader phase, while the device drivers for these interfaces are not loaded, it's common for developers to incorporate serial communication as part of the bootloader to utilize the serial port to send status and debug messages.

A Compact 7 OS run-time image can be configured to enable the serial debug port and send debug messages through one of the available serial ports. The following registry entries configure the OS run-time image to use the first serial port to send serial debug messages:

```
[HKEY_LOCAL_MACHINE\Drivers\BootArg]
    "SerialDbg1"="Drivers\\BuiltIn\\Serial1"
```

When a serial port is captured by the OS to send debug messages, the serial port is not accessible to other applications.

Serial Debug Connectivity

To establish serial debug connectivity between the development station and target device, you can use a serial cable with cross-over connections between the transmitting and receiving signals between the two endpoints.

There are ready-made serial debug cables you can purchase from most computer components retailers. Some common descriptions for this type of cable are as follows:

➤ RS-232 cross-over cable

➤ RS-232 null modem cable

➤ Serial null modem cable

Some of these commercially available cables are built without connecting the hardware handshake signal to save cost and may not work for certain types of target devices.

Serial Debug Messages

Serial debug messages are sent in ASCII text. With proper configuration, you can use any terminal program to capture serial debug messages from a Compact 7 device. The Hyper Terminal program that comes as part of the Windows XP OS has been deprecated from Windows Vista and is not available in Windows 7.

You can use a number of alternative terminal programs on Windows Vista and Windows 7 machines, such as the following:

➤ **Tera Term** — `http://ttssh2.sourceforge.jp/`

➤ **PuTTY** — `http://www.chiark.greenend.org.uk/~sgtatham/putty/`

If you still have a Windows XP machine around, you can copy the following two Hyper Terminal files from the Windows XP machine to your Windows Vista or Windows 7 machine; Hyper Terminal for XP does work under Windows Vista and 7:

➤ `Hypertrm.dll`

➤ `Hypertrm.exe`

Special setup is not needed to use Hyper Terminal on Windows Vista or 7 machines. You can simply copy both of these two files to the same directory and launch the `Hypertrm.exe` executable.

DEBUGGING THE OS DESIGN

After compilation, a Compact 7 OS design contains a large collection of files from different OS, programming support library, device driver, networking, media Codec, file system, and other application components.

It's common for a typical OS design project to cumulate in thousands of files that occupy well over 1 GB of storage during the build process to generate an OS run-time image. Without understanding how these files come together to form the final OS run-time image, searching for problems is often like looking for a needle in a haystack.

As part of the OS design development process, you are expected to carry out debugging tasks. Following are some examples:

➤ The OS design build process ended with an error and failed to generate an OS run-time image. You need to figure out what is causing the build error.

➤ The OS design build process completed successfully and generated an OS run-time image. However, the OS run-time image cannot boot. You need to figure out what is preventing the OS run-time image from completing the boot process.

➤ The OS design build process completed successfully and generated an OS run-time image. However, some of the features configured as part of the OS design cannot function. You need to figure out why these configured features failed to function as intended.

➤ The OS design build process completed successfully and generated an OS run-time image and included all the required files. However, the application configured to launch during startup failed to launch as expected. You need to figure out what is preventing the application to launch during startup.

An OS design includes many complex components, where some of the components are dependent on other components. In addition to including the required files to the OS design, proper configurations are important for the generated OS run-time image to perform the required functions and behave as intended.

To debug an OS design effectively, you need to understand the Compact 7 OS design build system. Chapter 11, "The Build System," provides more information about the Compact 7 build system.

Build Error

A Compact 7 OS design project contains many different pieces of components. When not properly configured, the OS design build process can end with errors and fail to generate the expected OS run-time image. There are many potential problems that can cause the build to fail. Following are some of the common causes:

➤ Missing file

➤ Incorrect directory reference to a needed file

➤ Typo in the OS design configuration files

➤ Improper memory configuration

➤ Incorrect registry value

➤ Subproject included in the OS design failure to generate the expected files

A typical OS design project includes an enormously large collection of files after compilation. Without knowing what to look for, it's difficult to locate and identify the problem.

As part of the OS design, there are project configuration files for the OS design, which provide helpful information about the OS design. During the build process, the build system logs compilation activities to a log file, which is helpful to identify build problems. Prior to compiling the OS run-time image, the build system combines all binary image builder configuration files into a single file. It also combines all Registry files into a single file to be compiled as part of the OS run-time image.

Although it's challenging to debug an OS design with thousands of files and complicated project settings, the OS design's project configuration files and build system's log files provide useful information to help you identify and resolve build errors quickly. Table 9-1 lists these files and describes how they can be helpful in debugging the OS design.

TABLE 9-1: Files with Helpful Information for Debugging

FILE NAME	DESCRIPTION
BUILD.LOG	All the activities during the build process to build an OS design project are recorded to this file, including any build errors.
	This is a long file with a lot of cryptic information. However, when the build process ends with an error, reviewing entries immediately before the error entry can provide helpful information about the potential problem.
BUILD.ERR	When the build process encounters any error during the build process, the error is recorded to this file.
	However, you need to refer back to the BUILD.LOG file to see more details.
CE.BIB	The BIB, short for Binary Image Builder, file contains build configuration information to assemble the OS run-time image, including memory layout, included files, and modules. During the build process, BIB file entries from all different OS, device driver, and application components are combined into this file.
	This file defines all the modules and files to be included in the final OS run-time image and contains memory configuration for the OS run-time image.
	If you need to check whether a file or module is included as part of the OS run-time image, CE.BIB is the file to check.
	If the build process ends with a memory error, such as Image Is Too Large for Current RAM and RAMIMAGE Settings, check the BIB file's MEMORY section.
REGINIT.INI	Most of the Compact 7 OS, device driver, and application components each have their own registry file, <component name>.REG.
	During the build process, entries from all registry files for the OS design are combined into this file.
	All the registry entries for the final OS run-time image are in this file.
	If you need to check whether a registry entry is properly set for the OS run-time image, REGINIT.INI is the file to check.
	This file may contain multiple entries for the same registry key. The value for the last entry is the one that takes effect.
	All registry files are combined in the REGINIT.INI file in the following order:
	1. COMMON.REG
	2. PLATFORM.REG
	3. <Subproject>.REG
	4. OSDESIGN.REG
	Registry values for duplicate registry keys entered last supersede the earlier entry.

FILE NAME	DESCRIPTION
CECONFIG.H	This file is created during the Sysgen phase and contains the complete list of Sysgen variables set for the OS design.
	This is the file to check whether a Compact 7 OS component is included to the OS design.
	This file contains the necessary information to check which Compact 7 OS license is required for the OS run-time image.
	If you have an OS run-time image without the associated OS design project and need to re-create an OS design project to generate an OS run-time image with the same OS components, review the CECONFIG.H file contents from the OS image's \WINDOWS folder.

REMOTE TOOLS

Platform Builder for Compact 7 includes the following suite of remote tools, which you can use to access the target device remotely to help with debugging the OS run-time image as it executes on the target device:

➤ Remote File Viewer

➤ Remote Process Viewer

➤ Remote Profiler

➤ Remote Registry Editor

➤ Remote Resource Consumer

➤ Remote Resource Leak Detector

➤ Remote System Information

➤ Remote Zoom

➤ Remote Timeline Viewer

➤ Remote Kernel Tracker

➤ Remote Performance Monitor

➤ Remote Power Monitor

To use these remote tools to debug a Compact 7 OS image on the target device remotely, the OS image must be generated with KITL enabled, and an established KITL connection between the Platform Builder development station and the target device.

A proper KITL connection between the Platform Builder development station and Compact 7 target device requires the following:

➤ KILT driver for the target device, which should be provided as part of the BSP

➤ Bootloader with KITL support, which should be provided as part of the BSP

➤ Connectivity between the development station and target device with KITL support, which can be an Ethernet, Serial, or USB interface supported by the target device's KITL driver

To support the exercises for the later section in this chapter, you need an OS run-time image with KITL and profiling enabled. If you did not work through the exercise in Chapter 7, "OS Design," to create the MyCompact7 OS design project, review Chapter 7 and create the OS design project.

Work through the following steps to configure the MyCompact7 OS design from Chapter 7, and generate an OS run-time image with the KITL and profiling build options enabled:

1. Launch VS2008 and MyCompact7 OS design project.

2. From the VS2008 Solution Explorer window, click to highlight MyCompact7 OS design project.

3. From the VS2008 Project menu, click Properties to bring up the MyComapct7 Property Pages screen.

4. From the left pane, expand the Configuration Properties node, and select Build Options to bring up the Build Options configuration pane on the right.

5. From the Build Options pane on the right, enable the following build options, as shown in Figure 9-1, and click OK:

➤ Enable KITL

➤ Enable Profiling

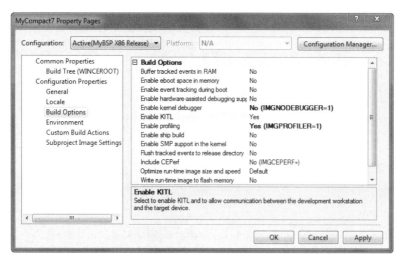

FIGURE 9-1

6. In addition to enabling the KITL and profiling build options, select and add the Windows Media Player from the component catalog to the OS design. This component is needed for the remote tools exercises later in this chapter.

7. From the VS2008 Build menu, click Build Solution to build the OS design and generate an OS run-time image.

8. After the build process finishes, download the OS run-time image to the target device.

After the OS run-time image is downloaded and launched on the target device with KITL connectivity to the development station established, the Device Status screen provides a visual indication to confirm the connection, as shown in Figure 9-2.

In Figure 9-2, there are four status indicators to the right. Before the OS run-time image is downloaded to the target device, these indicators should be half-green and half-yellow. After the image is downloaded, the Download indicator changes to full-green

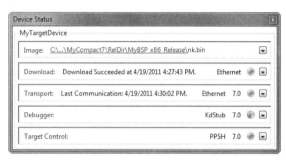

FIGURE 9-2

to indicate a successful download. The Transport indicator changed to full-green to indicate the transport connectivity is established. The Target Control indicator changed to full-green to indicate KITL connectivity is established. Because the image is built with the Kernel-debugger build option disabled, the Debugger indicator remains half-green and half-yellow.

Remote File Viewer

You can use the Remote File Viewer tool to view contents on the target device's file system, in much the same way as using Windows Explorer locally on the device. This tool also enables you to do the following from the development station:

➤ Export a file from the development station to the target device's file system.

➤ Import a file from the target device's file system to the development station.

➤ Delete a file from the target device's file system.

➤ Rename a file on the target device's file system.

➤ Create a new directory on the target device's file system.

To use the Remote File Viewer tool, work through the following steps, assuming a KITL-enabled OS run-time image is downloaded to the target device from the same VS2008 session:

1. From the VS2008 Tools menu, select Remote Tools, and click File Viewer to bring up the Select a Windows CE Device screen, as shown in Figure 9-3.

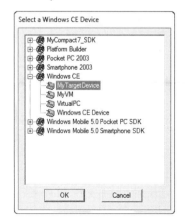

FIGURE 9-3

2. From the Windows CE Device screen, select MyTargetDevice or the device profile you use to download the OS run-time image to the target device, and click OK to bring up the Connecting to Device screen, as shown in Figure 9-4.

3. It takes a few seconds for the Remote File Viewer tool to connect to the target device and retrieve information from the device. After connection is established, the Windows CE Remote File Viewer screen displays the contents from the target device's file system, as shown in Figure 9-5.

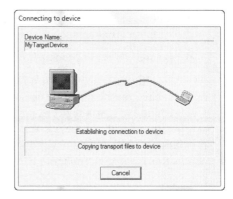

FIGURE 9-4

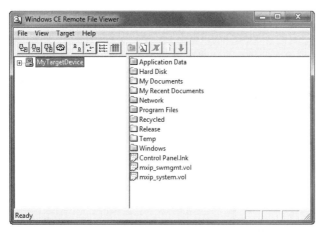

FIGURE 9-5

4. After you finish reviewing the Remote File Viewer's features, close the Windows CE Remote File Viewer screen to continue on to the next exercise.

Remote Heap Walker

The Remote Heap Walker is used to examine heaps and memory contents for each process running on the target device. You can use the Remote Heap Walker to detect memory leaks, estimate heap usage for an application, and identify heap fragmentation.

With a KITL-enabled OS run-time image downloaded to the target device from the same VS2008 session, work through the following steps to review the Remote Heap Walker remote tool's features:

1. From the VS2008 Tools menu, select Remote Tools, and click Heap Walker to bring up the Select a Windows CE Device screen, which is the same screen shown in Figure 9-3 for the Remote File Viewer exercise. Select MyTargetDevice or the device profile you use to download the OS run-time image to the target device, and click OK to bring up the Connecting to Device screen.

2. It takes a few seconds for the Remote Heap Walker to connect to the target device and retrieve information from the device. After connection is established, the Windows CE Remote Heap Walker screen appears, displaying the Process_List window, showing processes and associated heaps running on the target device.

3. From the Process_List window, you can double-click a process to bring up the Heap_List window, to show the heaps, block size, and flags for the process. From the Heap_List windows, you can double-click one of the heap addresses to bring up the Heap_Dump window to show the contents for the selected memory block, as shown in Figure 9-6.

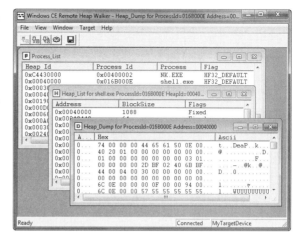

FIGURE 9-6

4. From the Remote Heap Walker's File menu, you can save the contents from the active window to a text file.

5. After you finish reviewing the Remote Heap Walker's features, close the Windows CE Remote Heap Walker screen to continue on to the next exercise.

Remote Process Viewer

The Remote Process Viewer enables you to view all running processes on the target device and shows the threads and modules within each process.

With a KITL-enabled OS run-time image downloaded to the target device from the same VS2008 session, work through the following steps to review the Remote Process Viewer remote tool's features:

1. From the VS2008 Tools menu, select Remote Tools, and click Process Viewer to bring up the Select a Windows CE Device screen, which is the same as the screen shown in Figure 9-3 for the Remote File Viewer exercise. Select MyTargetDevice or the device profile you use to download the OS run-time image to the target device, and click OK to bring up the Connecting to Device screen.

2. It takes a few seconds for the Remote Process Viewer to connect to the target device and retrieve information from the device. After connection is established, the Windows CE Remote Process Viewer screen appears, displaying the active processes, threads, and modules from the target device, as shown in Figure 9-7.

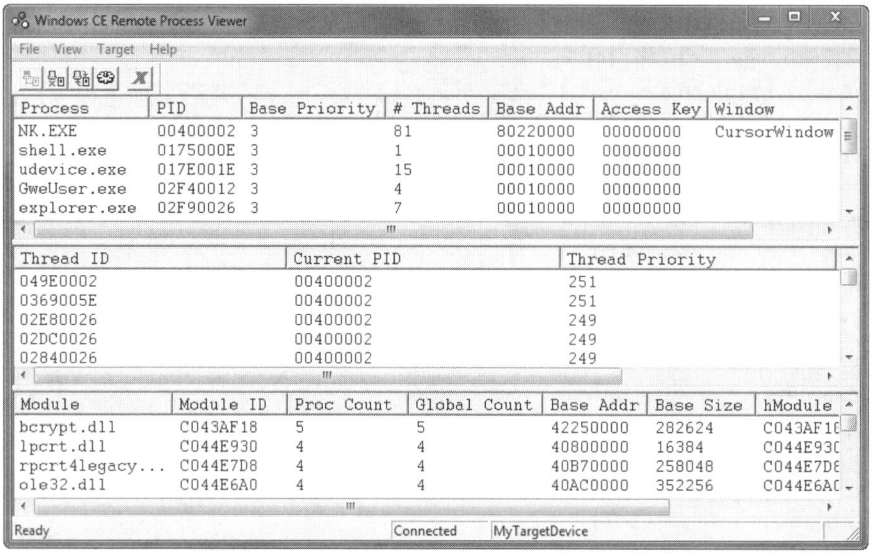

FIGURE 9-7

3. From the top pane, when you click one of the processes, the middle pane displays the threads, and the bottom pane displays the modules associated with the selected process.

4. Using the Remote Process Viewer, you can terminate a selected process running on the target device.

5. From the target device, launch the Music Player program. After the Music Player Program launches on the device, from the Windows CE Remote Process Viewer screen's Target menu, click Refresh to get updated information from the target device.

6. After the Windows CE Remote Process Viewer screen refreshes the display, from the top pane, scroll downward to locate the mplayer.exe process for the Music Player, just launched in the previous step. Click to select the mplayer.exe process.

7. From Windows CE Remote Process Viewer's File menu, click Terminate Process to terminate the mplayer.exe process. At this point, a warning dialog appears. Click Yes to acknowledge and terminate the mplayer.exe process. As the mplayer.exe process terminates, the Music Player program screen on the target device closes.

8. After you finish reviewing the Remote Process Viewer's features, close the Windows CE Remote Process Viewer screen to continue on to the next exercise.

Remote Profiler

The Remote Profiler tool is used to collect and analyze data from the target device to diagnose performance-related issues. The Remote Profiler supports two profiling modes:

➤ **Instrumented profiling** — In this mode, the profiler can capture every function entry and exit in your instrumented modules. It can tell you the exact timings and totals of calls, and complete call trees. This profiling mode records two data points for every function call and can be intrusive. You need to rebuild the modules you want to measure to use this profiling mode.

➤ **Monte Carlo profiling (Kernel-level sampling)** — In this mode, the profiler collects information by interrupting the system and checks the current state of the hardware register. This profiling mode does not require you to rebuild the profiled code.

With the KITL-enabled OS run-time image downloaded to the target device from the same VS2008 session, work through the following steps to review the Remote Profiler's features:

1. From the VS2008 Tools menu, select Remote Tools, and click Profiler to bring up the Connecting to Device screen to connect to the target device. After connection is established, the Remote Tools Shell screen displays with the Remote Profiler active, as shown in Figure 9-8.

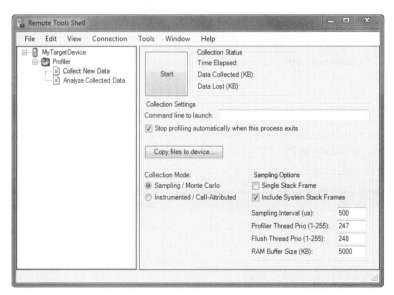

FIGURE 9-8

2. From the Remote Tools Shell screen, enter 500 for Sampling Interval, 247 for Profiler Thread Prio, 248 for Flush Thread Prio, and 5000 for RAM Buffer size; then click the big Start button on top to start collecting profiling data.

3. As the Remote Profiler remote tool starts to collect profiling data, launch the Music Player from the target device. Minimize the Music Player and launch Internet Explorer.

4. From the Remote Tools Shell, click Stop to stop the Profiler from collecting data. The Remote Tools Shell screen now displays the Performance Report Summary from the collected data, as shown in Figure 9-9.

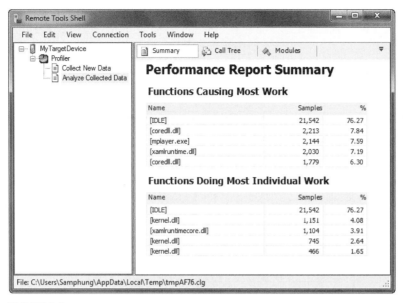

FIGURE 9-9

5. On the right pane, click Call Tree; from the Function Name column, expand the mplayer.exe node and all subnodes, as shown in Figure 9-10.

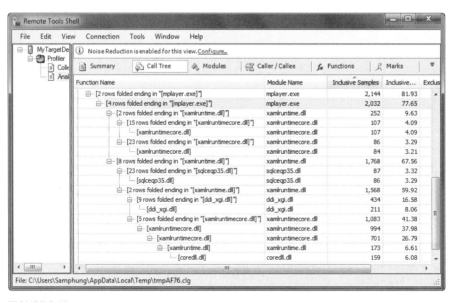

FIGURE 9-10

6. The Music Player program has a Silverlight skin that is dependent on the XAML. As you can see from the call tree, the `mplayer.exe` application calls the following modules:

   ➤ `Xamlrun-timecore.dll`

   ➤ `Xamlrun-time.dll`

   ➤ `Sqlceqp35.dll`

   ➤ `Ddi_xgi.dll`

   ➤ `Coredll.dll`

7. The Remote Profiler tool is a useful debug tool that requires some time and effort to learn and use. The time you invest to learn and become comfortable with this tool will pay back many times over.

8. After you finish reviewing the Remote Profiler's features, close the Remote Tools Shell screen to continue on to the next exercise.

Remote Registry Editor

The Remote Registry Editor enables you to view and edit the target device's registry data remotely, and enables you to extract registry entries from the target device and save these entries to a file.

With the KITL-enabled OS run-time image downloaded to the target device from the same VS2008 session, work through the following steps to review the Remote Registry Editor remote tool's features:

1. From the VS2008 Tools menu, select Remote Tools, and click Registry Editor to bring up the Connecting to Device screen to connect to the target device. After connection is established, the Remote Tools Shell screen displays with the Remote Registry Editor active, as shown in Figure 9-11.

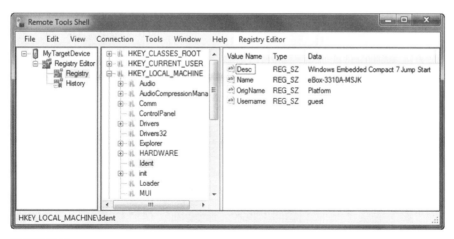

FIGURE 9-11

2. From the Remote Registry Editor interface, you can view, add, edit, and delete registry entries for the target device.

3. After you finish reviewing the Remote Registry Editor's features, close the Remote Tools Shell screen to continue on to the next exercise.

Remote Resource Consumer

The Remote Resource Consumer is used to consume memory and CPU resources on the target device to simulate low-resources conditions to test how the device and application on the device behave under these conditions.

Using the Remote Resource Consumer, you can adjust the amount of CPU, memory, and storage resources available on the target device.

With the KITL-enabled OS run-time image downloaded to the target device from the same VS2008 session, work through the following steps to review the Remote Resource Consumer remote tool's features:

1. From the VS2008 Tools menu, select Remote Tools, and click Resource Consumer to bring up the Connecting to Device screen to connect to the target device. After connection is established, the Remote Tools Shell screen displays with the Remote Resource Consumer active, as shown in Figure 9-12.

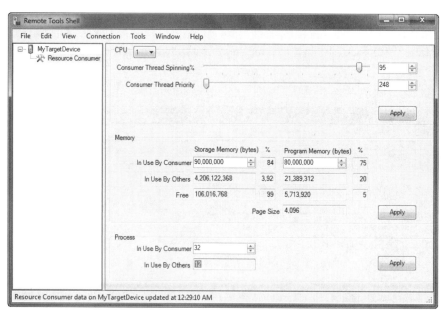

FIGURE 9-12

2. For the Consumer Thread Spinning, increase the loading to 95%. For the Consumer Thread Priority, set to 248, and click Apply.

3. For Storage Memory, enter **90,000,000**. For Program Memory, enter **80,000,000**, and click Apply.

4. In the Process pane, set the In Use by Consumer setting to 32, and click Apply.

5. With the Remote Resource Consumer occupying most of the target device's processing and memory resources, you can see the mouse cursor is not as responsive as it should be. If you attempt to launch a program from the target device at this point, the program cannot launch. The system simply does not have sufficient resources.

6. As soon as you close the Remote Tools Shell screen, which in turn shuts down the Remote Resource Consumer, releasing the resources it occupied on the target device, you can notice the mouse cursor becomes responsive almost instantly.

7. After you finish reviewing the Remote Resource Consumer's features, close the Remote Tools Shell screen to continue on to the next exercise.

 The Remote Resource Consumer exercise in this section uses an eBox-3310A as the target device. If you are using a Virtual PC as the target device, you may need to increase the resource consumption to see the performance degradation.

Remote Resource Leak Detector

The Remote Resource Leak Detector is designed to support native code application development to track handle usage, and detect memory leaks and heap corruption. It can capture snapshot information showing the resources in use by a running application.

With the KITL-enabled OS run-time image downloaded to the target device from the same VS2008 session, work through the following steps to review the Remote Resource Leak Detector remote tool's features:

1. From the VS2008 Tools menu, select Remote Tools, and click Resource Leak Detector to bring up the Connecting to Device screen to connect to the target device. After connection is established, the Remote Tools Shell screen displays with the Resource Leak Detector active, as shown in Figure 9-13.

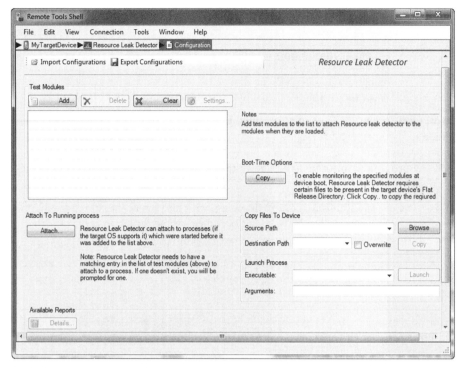

FIGURE 9-13

2. From the Test Modules pane, click Add to bring up the Test Settings screen, as shown in Figure 9-14.

3. From the Module pane on the Test Settings screen, select the Monitor Specific Module option. Click the file selection button to the right to select `mplayer.exe` from the MyCompact7 OS design's build release directory, and click OK to close the screen.

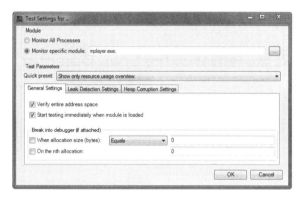

FIGURE 9-14

4. After the Test Settings screen closes, the `mplayer.exe` module is listed on the Test Modules pane on the Remote Tools Shell screen.

5. From the VS2008 Target menu, select Run Programs to bring up the Run Program screen.

6. From the Run Program screen, select `mplayer.exe` from the available program selection, and click Run to launch the music player program on the target device.

7. At this point the Available Reports pane on the Remote Tools Shell screen lists the `mplayer.exe` process as one of the available reports, as shown in Figure 9-15.

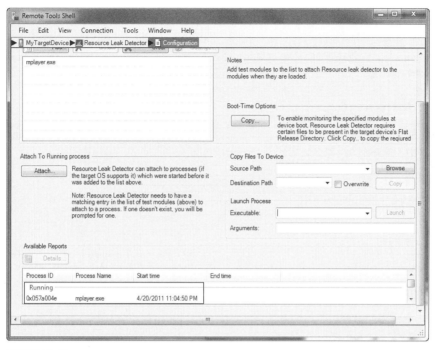

FIGURE 9-15

8. Double-click the `mplayer.exe` process to open the report in the analysis window, as shown in Figure 9-16.

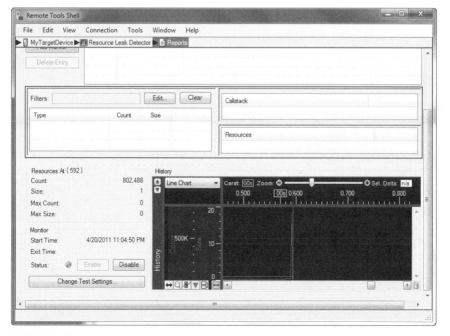

FIGURE 9-16

9. Any detected leaks appear in the middle pane, just above the Resources and History panes. Because the `mplayer.exe` process does not have any leak, nothing is shown.

10. After you finish reviewing the Remote Resource Leak Detector's features, close the Remote Tools Shell screen to continue on to the next exercise.

Remote System Information

The Remote System Information utility enables you to access the target device remotely to retrieve the following information from the device:

➤ System summary

➤ Physical and virtual memory usage

➤ Storage usage

➤ Active device drivers

➤ Battery information for battery-powered device with supported device driver

➤ Time zone settings

➤ User interface metrics and color scheme

➤ Security policies

With the KITL-enabled OS run-time image downloaded to the target device from the same VS2008 session, work through the following steps to review the Remote System Information remote tool's features:

1. From the VS2008 Tools menu, select Remote Tools, and click System Information to bring up the Connecting to Device screen to connect to the target device. After connection is established, the Remote Tools Shell screen displays with the System Information utility active, showing system summary information for the target device, as shown in Figure 9-17.

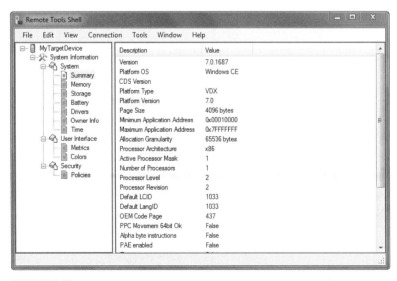

FIGURE 9-17

2. After you finish reviewing the Remote System Information utility's features, close the Remote Tools Shell screen to continue on to the next exercise.

Remote Zoom-In

The Remote Zoom-In utility enables you to capture the target device's desktop and display the capture screen graphic on the Remote Tools Shell. This remote tool is useful for documenting the target device's UI for debugging purposes or when you need screenshot to create user and support documentation.

With the KITL-enabled OS run-time image downloaded to the target device from the same VS2008 session, work through the following steps to review the Remote Zoom utility's features:

1. From the VS2008 Tools menu, select Remote Tools, and click Zoom to bring up the Select a Windows CE Device screen, which is the same as the screen shown in Figure 9-3, for the Remote File Viewer exercise. Select MyTargetDevice or the device profile you used to download the OS run-time image to the target device, and click OK to bring up the Connecting to Device screen.

2. It takes a few seconds for the Remote Zoom utility to connect to the target device. After the connection is established, the Windows CE Remote Zoom-In screen appears, displaying the current desktop from the target device, as shown in Figure 9-18.

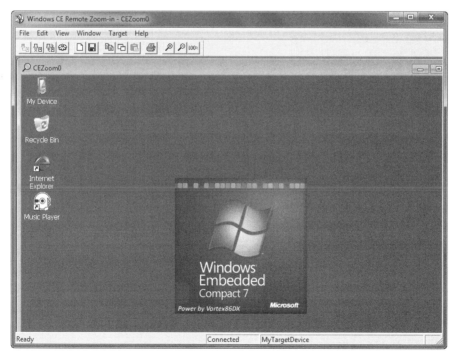

FIGURE 9-18

From the Windows CE Remote Zoom-In Target menu, you can click Refresh to capture an updated screen image from the target device.

After you finish reviewing the Remote Zoom-In utility's features, close the Windows CE Remote Zoom-In screen to continue on to the next exercise.

Remote Timeline Viewer

The Remote Timeline Viewer utility provides graphical presentation for the data from the following:

➤ Kernel Tracker

➤ Performance Monitor

➤ Power Monitor

To work through the exercises in this section, you need to configure the OS design and generate an OS run-time image to download to the target device, with the following build options enabled:

➤ Enable Eboot Space in Memory

➤ Enable Event Tracking During Boot

➤ Enable KITL

➤ Enable Profiling

➤ Flush Tracked Events to Release Directory

➤ Include CEPerf

Kernel Tracker

The Kernel Tracker utility is part of the Timeline Viewer remote tool that provides graphical presentation for event tracking data, which includes information about the target device's running processes, thread interactions, system events that mapped to running threads, system interrupts, and so on. When the OS run-time image, configured with the preceding build options, downloaded to the target device, events data are logged to the CELOG.CLG file in the build release directory.

Work through the following steps to review the Kernel Tracker's features:

1. Deploy the OS run-time image, configured with the required options, to the target device.

2. After the OS run-time image downloads and launches on the target device, shut down the target device.

3. From the VS2008 Target menu, click Detach Device.

4. From the VS2008 Tools menu, select Remote Tools and click Timeline Viewer to bring up the Remote Tools Shell screen.

5. From the Remote Tools Shell File menu, select Open Any and click Kernel Tracker (.clg) to bring up the Open Data File screen.

6. From the Open Data File screen, locate the CELOG.CLG file from the $(_FLATRELEASEDIR) build release directory, and click Open.

7. At this point, a second Open Data File screen is shown; locate the same CELOG.CLG file, as in step 5, and click Open.

8. The Remote Tools Shell screen, with Kernel Tracker utility active, display two instances of the events data from the CELOG.CLG file, as shown in Figure 9-19.

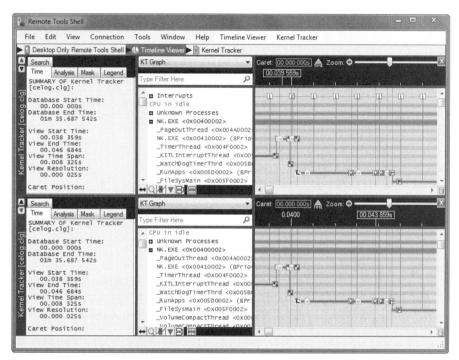

FIGURE 9-19

The time interval for the screen capture in Figure 9-19 has been adjusted to provide a better view.

9. The duplicated kernel tracker data display enables you to view two separate processes with activities from both processes shown within the same timeline. This is useful to track how one process can impact another process' performance.

10. After you finish reviewing the Kernel Tracker's features, close the Remote Tools Shell screen to continue on to the next exercise.

Performance Monitor

The Remote Performance Monitor utility provides performance information for the target device, which you can use to monitor resource usage and review the device's performance-related issues.

Work through the following steps to review the Remote Performance Monitor's features:

1. Download the same OS run-time image from the Kernel Tracker exercise to the target device. After the image boots up, launch Internet Explorer on the target device.

2. From the VS2008 Tools menu, select Remote Tools, and click Timeline Viewer to bring up the Remote Tools Shell screen.

3. From the Remote Tools Shell File menu, select Collect Live Data, and click Performance Monitor to bring up the Launch Performance Monitor Options screen, as shown in Figure 9-20.

4. From the Launch Performance Monitor Options screen, select MyTargetDevice, and click OK to bring up the Connecting to Device screen.

5. After the connection is established with the target device, the Remote Tools Shell screen displays the Timeline Viewer without data.

6. From the Remote Tools Shell screen's Configuration pane on the left, select the following from the Available Counters:

FIGURE 9-20

> ➤ CE Process Statistics object for the first selection

> ➤ iesample [PID:05DD000e] instance for the second selection

> ➤ % Processor Time counter for the third selection

7. Click Add to add the preceding selections to the Active Counters list, as shown in Figure 9-21.

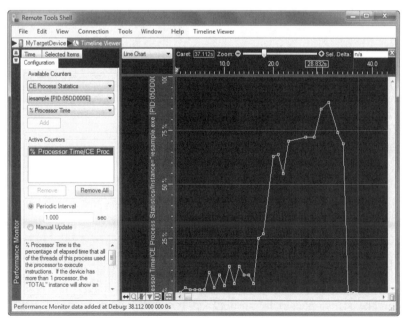

FIGURE 9-21

8. From the Internet Explorer already launched on the target device, navigate to view another URL. As the Internet Explorer is active, the Timeline display window shows different levels of processor activity.

9. After you finish reviewing the Performance Monitor's features, close the Remote Tools Shell screen to continue on to the next exercise.

Power Monitor

You can use the Power Monitor utility to analyze power consumption for the target device and use the information to optimize the device's power usage.

TARGET CONTROL

The remote Target Control is a useful tool that enables you to send commands to control the target device remotely, launch programs, view running processes, terminate a running process, display contents from memory block, and display memory usage from the target device.

To review the Target Control remote tool's features, download the KITL-enabled OS run-time image to the target device. After the image launches on the target device, from the VS2008 Target menu, click Target Control to bring up the Windows CE Command prompt window, as shown in Figure 9-22.

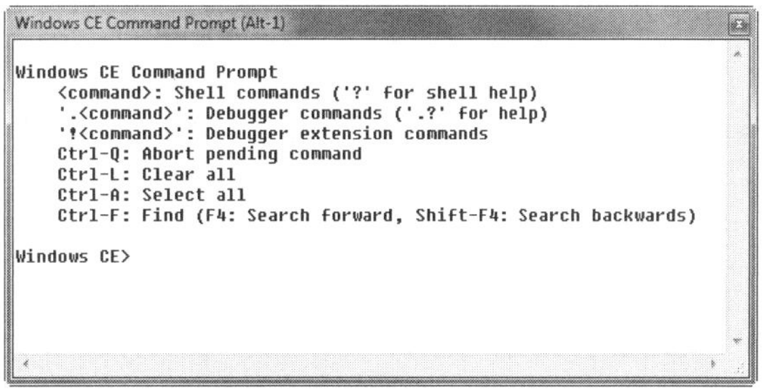

```
Windows CE Command Prompt (Alt-1)

Windows CE Command Prompt
    <command>: Shell commands ('?' for shell help)
    '.<command>': Debugger commands ('.?' for help)
    '!<command>': Debugger extension commands
    Ctrl-Q: Abort pending command
    Ctrl-L: Clear all
    Ctrl-A: Select all
    Ctrl-F: Find (F4: Search forward, Shift-F4: Search backwards)

Windows CE>
```

FIGURE 9-22

Display Target Device Running Processes

From the Windows CE Command Prompt window, you can enter the following Target Control command to show running processes from the target device: gi proc.

After this command executes, the Windows CE Command Prompt window displays all running processes from the target device, as shown in Figure 9-23.

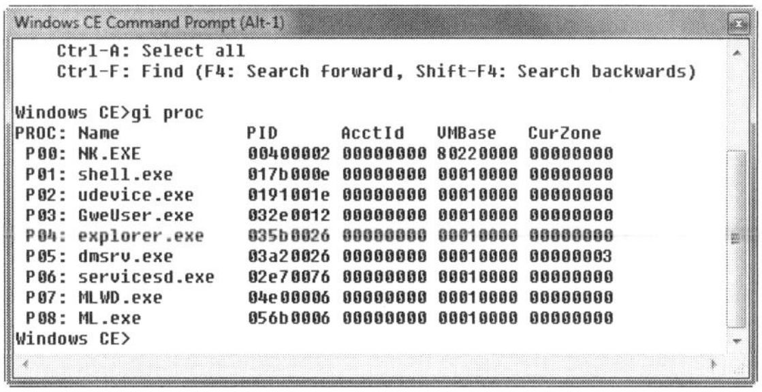

```
Windows CE Command Prompt (Alt-1)

    Ctrl-A: Select all
    Ctrl-F: Find (F4: Search forward, Shift-F4: Search backwards)

Windows CE>gi proc
PROC: Name            PID       AcctId    VMBase    CurZone
   P00: NK.EXE         00400002  00000000  80220000  00000000
   P01: shell.exe      017b000e  00000000  00010000  00000000
   P02: udevice.exe    0191001e  00000000  00010000  00000000
   P03: GweUser.exe    032e0012  00000000  00010000  00000000
   P04: explorer.exe   035b0026  00000000  00010000  00000000
   P05: dmsrv.exe      03a20026  00000000  00010000  00000003
   P06: servicesd.exe  02e70076  00000000  00010000  00000000
   P07: MLWD.exe       04e00006  00000000  00010000  00000000
   P08: ML.exe         056b0006  00000000  00010000  00000000
Windows CE>
```

FIGURE 9-23

Launch Internet Explorer with Target Control

From the Windows CE Command Prompt window, you can enter the following Target Control command to launch Internet Explorer on the target device: s iesample.

After this command executes, Internet Explorer launches on the target device.

Terminate Running Process with Target Control

From the Windows CE Command Prompt window, you can perform the following Target Control commands to terminate the Internet Explorer process:

1. Enter the following command to show running processes from the target device, as shown in Figure 9-24: gi proc.

2. The Internet Explorer process is shown as the last process, as follows:
   P09: iesample.exe.

FIGURE 9-24

3. To terminate the Internet Explorer process, enter the following Target Control command from the Windows CE Command Prompt window: kp 09.

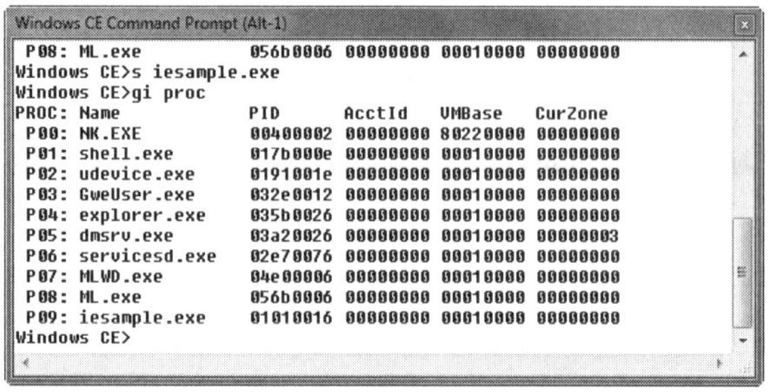

After this command is executes, the Internet Explorer process terminates.

Other Target Control Commands

In addition to the earlier exercises to review the Remote Target Control's features, Table 9-2 lists the commands you can use:

TABLE 9-2: Target Control Commands

COMMAND	DESCRIPTION
dev	Use this command to list all the loaded device drivers.
dd	Use this command to dump DWORD values from memory.
df	Use this command to dump DWORD values from memory to a designated file.
gi	Use this command to get information on processes, threads, and modules.
kp	Use this command to terminate a process.
log	Use this command to display or modify zones for the event-tracking subsystem, flush the existing CeLog buffer, and set the size of the buffer used to hold events captured by the event tracking engine. The event-tracking subsystem must be running for this command to function.
mi	Use this command to display memory usage information.
prof	Use this command to start and stop the kernel profiler. This command requires the OS image built with profiling support.
zo	Use this command to perform debugging zone operations.

Refer to the Compact 7 documentation or the following URL for more information about Target Control commands:

```
http://msdn.microsoft.com/en-us/library/ee479807.aspx
```

SUMMARY

For a typical developer, even with the best development plan and team support, problems and bugs are inevitable. Although you may be one of those special people who doesn't have to deal with bugs, for the typical developer, whether senior or entry level, dealing with bugs is just part of life.

The debug and remote tools provided as part of the Platform Builder for Compact 7 development environment are intended to help ease your headache in dealing with bugs, by providing easy-to-use and efficient tools that provide useful information to help identify, analyze, and resolve problems.

10

The Registry

WHAT'S IN THIS CHAPTER?

➤ Understanding the difference between hive-based and RAM-based registry

➤ Persisting changes to the registry between power reset

➤ Introducing examples of registry entries

➤ Accessing the registry

The registry is a critical part of the Windows Embedded Compact 7 OS. The registry is a collection of data containing configurations, settings, and usage parameters for the operating system, device drivers, and applications. The registry affects the system's boot process, device drivers, and applications' loading sequences.

Some device driver and applications have dependencies and must be configured to load after certain components are loaded before launching. When the registry is not configured correctly, the system cannot function as expected, exhibits unpredictable behavior, and can cause the device not to complete the boot process.

This chapter provides an overview of Compact 7 system registry, talks about different registry options, how the registry can affect the boot process, and sample registry entries for some of the commonly used components.

WINDOWS EMBEDDED COMPACT REGISTRY

Windows Embedded Compact registry stores configuration data and settings for the OS, device drivers, applications, and user preferences. The registry plays a key role in controlling a Compact 7 device's device drivers and applications' loading process during startup.

Compact 7 registry stores data in a tree structure. Each branch of the tree is called a registry key. Each registry key may contain other registry subkeys and entries. Each registry entry has a value, which can be a string or binary value. The registry data is stored in the registry entry. Think of the registry key and subkeys as the file folders for registry data, which also provide the marker and grouping to store and identify the registry entry.

Windows Embedded Compact registry contains the following four root keys:

➤ HKEY_CLASSES_ROOT stores information about file types.

➤ HKEY_CURRENT_USER stores user data for the current active user.

➤ HKEY_LOCAL_MACHINE stores data specific to the hardware platform, such as OS configuration, device drivers, and settings.

➤ HKEY_USERS stores data for all users including the default user.

Windows Embedded Compact supports two different types of registry implementation, RAM-based and hive-based registry.

RAM-Based Registry

The RAM-based registry implementation stores registry data within the objectstore. The objectstore functions similar to the hard drive for the desktop PC and provides storage support for the device's file system, databases, and system registry. During startup, the objectstore is created in RAM. A device that uses RAM-based registry typically has battery-backed RAM to keep the objectstore, and whatever data it holds, intact when the device is turned off. This is an efficient implementation for devices that rarely power off.

Many battery-powered devices are designed with battery-backed RAM. As part of the device's normal operation, during the power-off stage, the battery-backed RAM maintains the object store in the RAM, which also includes the registry data, to provide the "instant-on" feature.

Some of the older generation battery-powered devices were built with RAM-based registry, without the capability to persist registry data when the device completely loses power. With these types of devices, cold boot and power reset causes the device to lose configuration data and render the device back to the default factory state.

RAM-based registry data can be lost if the RAM loses power. For devices using RAM-based registry implementation and built without battery-backed RAM to maintain the object store during power-off, the device must be designed with the function to back up the registry during power-off and restore the registry when power is resumed.

RAM-based registry is designed to support devices that rarely need to cold boot.

Hive-Based Registry

The hive-based registry implementation stores registry data in files, or hives, which can be stored on any file system. With hive-based registry, the device does not need to have battery-backed RAM to maintain device configuration and other data during power-off.

Hive-based registry is designed to support devices built without battery backed RAM and devices that often cold boot.

For devices built with hive-based registry implementation, the registry data is broken into three different hives — the boot hive, system hive, and user hive. Table 10-1 provides description for these three hives.

TABLE 10-1: The Three Hives of Registry Data

REGISTRY HIVE	DESCRIPTION
BOOT.HV	The boot hive is compiled as part of the OS run-time image, which contains system settings that affect the first boot phase.
SYSTEM.HV	When in use, the system hive is stored on the target device's local storage.
USER.HV	When in use, the user hive is stored on the target device's local storage.

Hive-Based Registry Triggers Two Boot Phases

With hive-based registry implemented, a Compact 7 device goes through two boot phases during startup.

A Compact 7 OS run-time image is built with a set of default registry settings, configured as part of the OS design. When the Compact 7 image boots for the first time, the target device's local storage does not contain any registry data. During the initial boot, default SYSTEM.HV and USER.HV registry hives are created on the device's local storage.

During the first boot phase, based on the system configuration settings in the BOOT.HV, the system loads the kernel with minimum drivers to access the device's file system and to access registry data in SYSTEM.HV and USER.HV. After the registry data is read, the system continues with the second boot phase to load the remaining components based on the registry configuration data saved in the SYSTEM.HV and USER.HV registry hives.

 Improper hive-based implementation is a common cause for a system failing to complete the boot process.

Persistent Registry with Hive-Based Registry

To use hive-based registry implementation to persist changes to the registry between power reset, the OS design project needs to be configured with proper entries, which are unique to the hardware platform, for the hive-based registry feature to function.

Following are the general steps to implement a hive-based registry:

1. Add the hive-based registry catalog item to the OS design.

2. Wrap registry entries associated with the device driver that need to launch during the first boot phase within a HIVE BOOT SECTION, as follows:

```
; HIVE BOOT SECTION
< Entries for drivers that launch in the first boot phase>
; END HIVE BOOT SECTION
```

3. Set the following flag for each driver that needs to launch during the first boot phase to prevent the driver from launching again during the second phase:

```
[HKEY_LOCAL_MACHINE\Drivers\<driver name>]
    "Flags"=dword:1000
```

4. Add the following registry entries to the OS design's OSDESIGN.REG registry file:

```
[HKEY_LOCAL_MACHINE\init\BootVars]
    "SYSTEMHIVE"="\\Registry\\system.hv"
    "PROFILEDIR"="\\Registry"
    "Flags"=dword:3
    "DefaultUser"="User"
```

 Using a BSP designed to support hive-based registry implementation, you only need to perform step 1 above, adding the hive-based catalog item to the OS design. In step 4, the registry entries configure the OS run-time image to store the SYSTEM.HV to the REGISTRY folder at the target device's storage.

Hive-based registry support should be implemented as part of the BSP. You can review the PLATFORM.REG registry file for the ICOP eBox-3300 BSP to review hive-based registry implementation for this BSP, in the following directory: _PLATFORMROOT\eBox3300\Files

Registry Flushing with RegFlushKey()

With hive-based registry implementation, when there are changes to the device's registry, Windows Embedded Compact needs to flush and save these changes to the file system.

The device with hive-based registry implemented needs to have a mechanism to flush registry changes and store them to the file system. You can perform registry flushing programmatically by calling the RegFlushKey() function.

Following is the sample code for a simple program that calls the RegFlushKey() to flush and save the registry to the file system.

```
; Sample codes to flush the registry

#include "stdafx.h"

int WINAPI WinMain(HINSTANCE hInstance,
```

```
                HPINSTANCE hPrevInstance,
                LPTSTR lpCmdLine,
                int nCmdShow)
    {
        RegFlushKey(HKEY_LOCAL_MACHINE);
        RegFlushKey(HKEY_CLASSES_ROOT);
        RegFlushKey(HKEY_CURRENT_USER);
        RegFlushKey(HKEY_USERS);
    }
```

Code snippet is from Registry_Flush.CPP

Flush-On-Close Registry Flush

The Windows Embedded Compact OS run-time image can be configured to flush the registry automatically by setting the following registry:

```
[HKEY_LOCAL_MACHINE\init\BootVars]
    "RegistryFlags"=dword:1
```

Flush-on-close is also referred to as Aggressive Flushing in some documentation for the earlier version of Windows Embedded Compact. When this feature is enabled, it can cause performance degradation.

REGISTRY FOR WINDOWS EMBEDDED COMPACT COMPONENT

When adding a component from the component catalog to the OS design, the default registry entries may not be included or configured to launch the component.

For some OS components, in addition to adding the component from the catalog to the OS design, you need to include additional registry entries to the OS design, to the OSDESIGN.REG file, for the component to function as intended.

Registry for the Serial Port

Serial port is one of the legacy interfaces that has been around for a long time and is still a common interface for many devices in the market. After you configure the serial port with the correct parameters, accessing and using the serial port are simple and straight forward tasks.

An embedded device is built with different mixes of hardware and specifications. The serial ports on the device may not be configured with the same standardized parameters as the PC, and may use different interrupt and input-output (I/O) addresses.

If you experience problems accessing and using the serial ports on a Compact 7 device, review the device's hardware and firmware (BIOS) settings for the serial ports and compare these settings with the serial ports registry configurations for the device to ensure the registry configurations match the hardware settings.

Serial ports on some target devices are designed to be configurable to use different interrupt and I/O ports. Although this flexibility is helpful, it's also a source of problems some developers may overlook.

The following partial registry entries for the serial ports are extracted from the eBox-3300 BSP:

```
[HKEY_LOCAL_MACHINE\Drivers\BuiltIn\Serial1]
    "Flags"=dword:0010
    "Dll"="Com16550.Dll"
    "Prefix"="COM"
    "Order"=dword:0
    "Index"=dword:1            ; Driver index - COM1
    "SysIntr"=dword:14         ; IRQ-4
    "IoBase"=dword:03F8        ; I/O address
    "IoLen"=dword:8
    "DeviceArrayIndex"=dword:0 ; Hardware device index
    "IClass"="{CC5195AC-BA49-48a0-BE17-DF6D1B0173DD}"

[HKEY_LOCAL_MACHINE\Drivers\BuiltIn\Serial2]
    "Flags"=dword:0010
    "Dll"="Com16550.Dll"
    "Prefix"="COM"
    "Order"=dword:0
    "Index"=dword:2            ; Driver index - COM2
    "SysIntr"=dword:13         ; IRQ-3
    "IoBase"=dword:02F8        ; I/O address
    "IoLen"=dword:8
    "DeviceArrayIndex"=dword:1 ; Hardware device index
    "IClass"="{CC5195AC-BA49-48a0-BE17-DF6D1B0173DD}"
```

Code snippet is from Sample_Registry.txt

The preceding registry entries are configured to support two serial ports, COM1 and COM2, with the following hardware configuration:

➤ COM1 is configured to use IRQ-4 and 3F8 as the I/O address.

➤ COM2 is configured to use IRQ-3 and 2F8 as the I/O address.

When writing a native code application to access the serial port, the application accesses each port through file system functions such as CreateFile(), ReadFile(), WriteFile(), and so on.

Following is a sample code to access the first serial port, using "COM1:" as the file handle:

```
HANDLE hStr = CreateFile(_T("COM1:"), GENERIC_READ | GENERIC_WRITE, _
                    0, NULL, OPEN_EXISTING, 0, 0);
```

In the preceding example, the device filename, "COM1:", is a combination of the prefix "COM", defined by the "Prefix" registry entry, and the driver index, defined by the "Index" registry entry and a colon (:).

USEFUL REGISTRY REFERENCES

System registry is one of the key components to configure a Compact 7 OS run-time image's function and behavior. When a driver or application component is included in an OS design, you need to ensure the OS design includes appropriate registry entries for the component. Following are sample registry entries that can be useful for the development environment.

Registry for the FTP Server

When the FTP server component is added to the OS design, the following default entries are added to the project:

Available for download on Wrox.com

```
[HKEY_LOCAL_MACHINE\COMM\FTPD]
    "IsEnabled"=dword:0
    "UseAuthentication"=dword:1
    "AllowAnonymous"=dword:1
    "AllowAnonymousUpload"=dword:0
    "AllowAnonymousVroots"=dword:0
    "DefaultDir"="\\Temp\\"
    "IdleTimeout"=dword:12c
    "DebugOutputChannels"=dword:2
    "DebugOutputMask"=dword:17
    "BaseDir"="\\Windows"
    "LogSize"=dword:1000
```

Code snippet is from Sample_Registry.txt

The `IsEnable` entry is set to 0, which disables the FTP server and prevents it from running when the OS launches. With the default registry configuration, you need to manually launch the FTP server after the Compact 7 OS is launched on the target device.

To configure the FTP server to launch as part of the OS, enter the following entries to the OS design project's OSDESIGN.REG registry file:

Available for download on Wrox.com

```
[HKEY_LOCAL_MACHINE\COMM\FTPD]
    "IsEnabled"=dword:1
    "UseAuthentication"=dword:0
    "UserList"="@*;"
    "AllowAnonymous"=dword:1
    "AllowAnonymousUpload"=dword:1
    "AllowAnonymousVroots"=dword:1
    "DefaultDir"="\\"
```

Code snippet is from Sample_Registry.txt

The preceding registry entries configure the FTP server to launch with user authentication disabled and enable anonymous login and upload. These registry entries are provided as examples for the development environment, which impose serious security risks and should not be used on the device intended for distribution to the end user.

Registry for the Telnet Server

The Telnet server component enables remote terminal access to a Compact 7 device over TCP/IP, a useful tool to gain access to a headless device for testing and debugging and routine maintenance.

When the Telnet server component is added to the OS design, it does not include the needed registry entry to enable the Telnet server. Add the following registry entries to enable the Telnet server with user authentication disabled:

Available for
download on
Wrox.com

```
[HKEY_LOCAL_MACHINE\COMM\TELNETD]
    "IsEnabled"=dword:1
    "UseAuthentication"=dword:0
```

Code snippet is from Sample Registry.txt

The preceding registry entries configure the Compact 7 OS to launch the Telnet server with user authentication disabled. These registry entries are provided as examples for the development environment, which impose serious security risks and should not be used on devices intended for distribution to the end user.

Device Identification and Description

A Compact 7 device's name and device description can be configured by the registry, using the following entries:

Available for
download on
Wrox.com

```
[HKEY_LOCAL_MACHINE\Ident]
    "Name"="Compact7-device"
    "Desc"="Professional Windows Embedded Compact 7 device project."
```

Code snippet is from Sample_Registry.txt

Registry to Launch Application during Startup

A typical Compact 7 device is expected to deploy with an OS run-time image configured to launch one or more applications when the devices power up. More detail about automatically launching applications during startup is covered in Chapter 23, "Auto Launch Application."

A Compact 7 device can be configured to automatically launch an application during startup, with the following registry entries:

Available for
download on
Wrox.com

```
[HKEY_LOCAL_MACHINE\Init]
    "Depend90"=hex:14,00,1e,00,32,00
    "Launch90"="MYAPP.EXE"
```

Code snippet is from Sample_Registry.txt

Device Name for USB Removable Storage

USB removable storage is a common storage option that you can use for many purposes. Use the following registry key to configure a folder name for the removable USB storage with a more descriptive name.

Available for download on Wrox.com

```
[HKEY_LOCAL_MACHINE\System\StorageManager\Profiles\USBHDProfile]
    "Folder"="USB Storage"
```

Code snippet is from Sample_Registry.txt

Internet Explorer Startup Page

Accessing the Internet with a browser is an important feature for many devices. Configuring a Compact 7 device to visit a designated website, to provide additional product information and support resources, can be helpful to the end user and a good way for the company to establish a customer support program to develop future business.

The following registry entries configure the internet browser's startup page:

Available for download on Wrox.com

```
[HKEY_CURRENT_USER\Software\Microsoft\Internet Explorer\Main]
    "Start Page"="http://www.embedded101.com"
```

Code snippet is from Sample_Registry.txt

Auto Flush and Save Registry

For a Compact 7 device configured with hive-based registry implementation, one of the simplest methods to configure the device to save registry changes to the file system is to enable the flush-on-close, also referred to as aggressive flushing. With this feature enabled, the Compact 7 device automatically flushes registry changes and saves them to the file system.

The following registry entries enable the flush-on-close feature:

```
[HKEY_LOCAL_MACHINE\init\BootVars]
    "RegistryFlags"=dword:1
```

On the other hand, aggressive flushing can cause performance degradation. The following registry entries disable background flushing:

```
[HKEY_LOCAL_MACHINE\init\BootVars]
    "RegistryFlags"=dword:2
```

Disable Suspend Function on the Start Menu

Unless the BSP disabled this feature, the Suspend option on Windows Embedded Compact 7 desktop's Start menu is enabled by default. For target devices that do not support the Suspend option, you can suppress it by adding the following registry entries to the OS design:

```
[HKEY_LOCAL_MACHINE\Explorer]
    "Suspend"=dword:0
```

Static IP Address

To develop an OS design or application for a Compact 7 device, you need to establish connectivity between the development station and the target device. If you are connecting the target device to the development station through an Ethernet connection, both the development station and target device must be configured with proper IP addresses.

Although a Compact 7 OS run-time image is generated with DHCP enabled by default to acquire IP address dynamically, you need to configure the OS design to generate an OS run-time image with a static IP address, under the following conditions:

> ➤ DHCP server is not available to provide IP addresses dynamically.

> ➤ You are working on a head-less device (without user interface and display) and need to know the device's IP address to connect to the device to the development station.

To configure the OS design to generate a run-time image with a static IP address, include the following registry in the OS design:

Available for download on Wrox.com

```
[HKEY_LOCAL_MACHINE\Comm\PCI\R60401\Parms\TcpIp]
    "EnableDHCP"=dword:0
    "IpAddress"=multi_sz:"192.168.2.232"
    "Subnetmask"=multi_sz:"255.255.255.0"
    "DefaultGateway"=multi_sz:"192.168.2.1"
```

Code snippet is from Sample_Registry.txt

The preceding registry entries configure a static IP address for the R6040 Ethernet controller. This is the Ethernet controller on the eBox-3310A. When an OS design is configured to generate an OS run-time image with KITL enabled, it uses the VMINI driver. Use the following registry entries to configure a static IP address for the VMINI driver:

Available for download on Wrox.com

```
[HKEY_LOCAL_MACHINE\Comm\VMINI1\Parms\Tcpip]
    "EnableDHCP"=dword:0
    "IPAddress"="192.168.2.233"
    "SubnetMask"="255.255.255.0"
    "DefaultGateway"=multi_sz:"192.168.2.1"
```

Code snippet is from Sample_Registry.txt

WINDOWS EMBEDDED COMPACT REGISTRY FILES

In a Compact 7 OS design project, there are multiple registry files for different OS design components. During the build process, these registry files are copied to the build release directory where the registry entries from these files are combined into a single file, REGINIT.INI, to be included to the OS image during the make image phase.

COMMON.REG

The COMMON.REG registry file contains a large collection of default registry entries for OS components, which are included as part of the Platform Builder software. Registry entries for each OS component are wrapped between a SYSGEN variable, which Platform Builder uses to control whether to include the registry entries in the OS design.

The COMMON.REG file is in the following directory: $(_PUBLICROOT)\COMMON\OAK\FILES.

PLATFORM.REG

The PLATFORM.REG registry file is from the BSP for the current OS design, which includes all the required registry entries, to support device drivers and configuration settings for the target device. Registry entry in this file supersedes entry in the COMMON.REG file.

The PLATFORM.REG file is provided as part of the BSP, in the following directory: $(_PLATFORMROOT)\<BSP directory>\Files.

Catalog Item Registry

Some of the catalog components included in the OS design have associated registry files. During the build process, these registry files are copied to the build release directory, combined into REGINIT .INI, and compiled as part of the OS image.

These registry entries supersede the entries in COMMON.REG.

Subproject Registry

Each subproject created as part of the OS design has its own set of registry entries to support the software component generated from the subproject.

Registry entries in the subproject's registry file supersede the entries in COMMON.REG and PLATFORM.REG.

OSDESIGN.REG

The OSDESIGN.REG registry file is from the OS design project itself, which contains registry entries specific to the current OS design.

Registry entry in the OSDESIGN.REG file supersedes entry in the COMMON.REG, PLATFORM.REG, and subproject registry files.

REGINIT.INI

During the build process, registry entries from all registry files in the build release directory are combined into the REGINIT.INI file, before the make image phase. All the registry entries and the value for each entry that applies to the OS run-time image are from this file.

To check whether a registry entry is set and included in the OS run-time image as expected, review the REGINIT.INI registry file in the build release directory for the OS design project.

For a registry key with multiple values in the REGINIT.INI files, the value associated with the last entry found in the file is the one that takes effect.

ACCESSING THE REGISTRY

Windows Embedded Compact does not provide a registry editor that is accessible to the end user. During the development process, you can access the registry on a Compact 7 device as follows:

➤ Generate an OS run-time image with KITL enabled and download the image to the target device. From the development station, use the Remote Registry Editor tools to access the registry on the target device.

➤ Develop a custom application to programmatically access the Compact 7 device's registry.

Registry editors from third-party companies can support Windows Embedded Compact.

SUMMARY

Registry is an important part of a Compact 7 device, providing the parameters that control drivers loading, application startup, and the overall Compact 7 OS run-time behavior on the target device. Improper registry configuration can cause a Compact 7 device to have unpredictable behavior and failure to complete the boot process.

It's critical to review registry entries added to an OS design project and know the purpose these entries serve and how they impact the Compact 7 OS run-time on the target device.

11

The Build System

➤ Understanding Windows Embedded Compact 7 build system and process

Windows Embedded Compact OS design development tasks involve building and rebuilding the OS design project repeatedly, to generate an OS run-time image for testing and debugging, to resolve problems and ensure the run-time image includes the required components and delivers the expected function and performance.

Working on a preconfigured OS design project from the Platform Builder IDE, compiling and generating an OS run-time image from the project involves just a few simple clicks to launch the build and Sysgen command. The IDE shields much of the complexity and makes the process seem easy.

To be effective in the Windows Embedded Compact development environment, you need to understand how the build system works and the different phases within the build process. Understanding the Compact 7 build system can help improve your ability to quickly debug and identify OS design-related problems.

THE OS DESIGN BUILD PROCESS

The Windows Embedded Compact 7 build system is complex and involves multiple build steps. The build system generates an OS run-time image for a target device from the OS design project, which includes OS components, hardware adaptation code, device drivers, and application components developed to support the target device. To generate the OS run-time image, the build system goes through multiple build phases to compile, link, and assemble codes and modules for all the components included as part of the OS design to generate the OS run-time image.

Although the Platform Builder IDE shields the complicated build environment from you and provides a friendly graphical user interface to simplify the process, you need to include the necessary components to the OS design and apply the proper configuration for each component for the Platform Builder build system to successfully complete the build process and generate the desired OS run-time image.

Understanding the build system helps you to be more effective in developing Compact 7 OS design, avoiding redundant tasks, and shortening the time needed to develop and debug, which in turn minimizes the aggravation dealing with bugs and makes your life a little easier. Figure 11-1 provides a graphical representation of the build system.

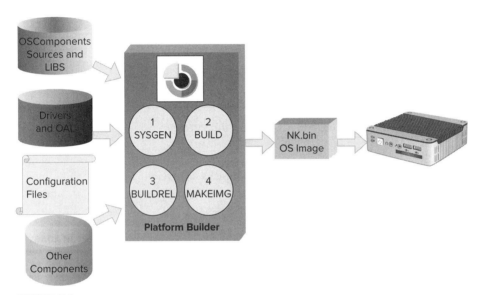

FIGURE 11-1

A Compact 7 OS design project goes through the following phases as part of the build process to generate an OS run-time image for the target device:

➤ Pre-Sysgen (Also referred to as the Build OS phase)

➤ Sysgen

➤ Build

➤ Build Release

➤ Make Image

You can configure the OS design project to generate OS run-time images in four different build configurations: debug, release, checked, and ship. All OS design build configurations go through the same build phases as part of the build process.

The checked build configuration is new for Compact 7 and not available in the previous version. The checked build configuration is a hybrid between the debug and release configurations. An OS run-time image built in a checked build configuration is built with compiler optimization and contains ASSERT, DEBUGMSG, and RETAILMSG to provide resources needed for debugging.

An OS run-time image built in a debug configuration is built without optimization, which makes it difficult to debug certain types of timing and performance-related problems. An optimized image built in a release configuration is built with the resources to output RETAILMSG, does not contain ASSERT, and cannot output DEBUGMSG needed to provide more debugging information. Compact 7 introduces the checked build configuration to fill the gap between debug and release configurations.

Table 11-1 shows the differences between the build configurations.

TABLE 11-1: OS Design Build Configurations

BUILD MODE	OPTIMIZED	CONTAINS RETAILMSGs	CONTAINS DEBUGMSGs	CONTAINS ASSERTS
Debug		X	X	X
Checked	X	X	X	X
Release	X	X		
Ship	X			

Pre-Sysgen Phase — Build OS

This is the first step in the build process and takes the longest time to perform. In this build phase, all the Compact 7 OS components, provided as part of the Platform Builder software in the $(_PUBLICROOT) and $(_PRIVATEROOT) folders, are built and compiled to generate the necessary .LIB and .DLL files needed for the later build steps. As part of the Platform Builder resources, Microsoft precompiled these Compact 7 OS components and provides all the necessary .LIB and .DLL files as part of the Platform Builder installation.

Working in a typical Compact 7 development environment, you don't need to build these OS components to generate the .LIB and .DLL files for the OS design. Changing the codes in the $(_PUBLICROOT) and $(_PRIVATEROOT) folders and rebuilding the Compact 7 OS components can cause serious build problems and is not recommended for an inexperienced Compact 7 OS design developer.

Even for a seasoned Compact 7 OS design developer, recompiling the Compact 7 OS components in the $(_PUBLICROOT) and $(_PRIVATEROOT) folders is not recommended. When you need to change the source code for a component in the $(_PUBLICROOT) folder, it's strongly recommended that you clone the component's source code to the OS design project folder, make changes to the code from the OS design project workspace, and leave the original code intact.

Sysgen Phase

In the Sysgen phase, Platform Builder links and copies all the OS components for the OS design and outputs them to the OS design's Sysgen output folder. Platform Builder uses the SYSGEN_XXX environment variables, from the OS design, to determine which OS components and their dependencies to include in the process. The resulting files are copied to the $(SG_OUTPUT_ROOT) directory.

An OS design must go through the Sysgen phase at least once. During the OS design development process, when the OS design's included catalog item is changed, it needs to repeat the Sysgen phase. Otherwise, the build process may encounter errors and fail to generate the expected OS run-time image.

Build Phase

In the build phase, components for the BSP and subprojects added to the OS design are built and copied to the $(SG_OUTPUT_ROOT) directory.

The build system builds the BSP components before building the subproject components. When multiple subprojects are in an OS design, the subprojects are built in alphabetical order, based on subproject name.

Each BSP is dependent on some common codes from the $(_PLATFORM\COMMON) directory for the processor or system-on-chip which the BSP supports. These common codes are built and copied to the $(SG_OUTPUT_ROOT) directory during this build phase.

To build the required codes, the build system scans through the folders in the $(_PLATFORM\COMMON), BSP, and subproject directories for DIRS and SOURCES files to compile and build designated components based on the macro in each component's SOURCES file.

DIRS File

A DIRS file contains a list of subdirectories, which the build system goes through to scan for additional DIRS and SOURCES files. The subdirectory is relative to the current directory where the DIRS file is located.

During the build process, the build system scans the root folder for each of the components included in the build process, looking for a DIRS file. If a DIRS file is present, the build system continues to scan the subdirectories listed in the DIRS file. When a DIRS file is not present, the build system searches for the SOURCES file and performs designated build tasks according to the SOURCES file macro set for the current folder.

For example, MyBSP has a DIRS file at the BSP's root folder, with the following entries:

```
DIRS=\
    src \
```

The build system continues to scan the SRC directory under the current directory for DIRS or SOURCES files. There is a DIRS file in the SRC directory, with the following contents:

```
DIRS= \
    common      \
    drivers     \
    oal         \
    kitl        \
    bootloader \
    boot \
```

Based on the preceding DIRS file entries, the build system continues to scan the COMMON, DRIVERS, OAL, KITL, BOOTLOADER, and BOOT folders.

Following the same process, the build system continues to scan for the DIRS file until it reaches a folder that does not have one. When the build system reaches the SRC\DRIVERS\EHCI folder, where it has a SOURCES file and does not have a DIRS file, the build system stops scanning for the DIRS file and processes the macro in the SOURCES file.

SOURCES File

The SOURCES file contains the macro and configuration for the build system to build the codes in the same folder where the file is located.

As part of the build system's tasks to scan and process the DIRS file, when it reaches a directory without a DIRS file, it searches for a SOURCES file. If a SOURCES file is present, the build system builds and compiles the code modules in the current folder based on the macro and configuration in the SOURCES file.

The following entries are from the SOURCES file for the EHCI USB driver from the MyBSP BSP, in the BSP's SRC\DRIVERS\EHCI folder:

The MyBSP BSP is from the cloning exercise in Chapter-6, "BSP Introduction."

Available for download on Wrox.com

```
TARGETNAME=ehci

TARGETTYPE=DYNLINK
RELEASETYPE=PLATFORM
SYNCHRONIZE_DRAIN=1

DLLENTRY=_DllMainCRTStartup

DEFFILE=$(_COMMONOAKROOT)\inc\ehcd.def

INCLUDES=$(INCLUDES);$(_PUBLICROOT)\common\oak\drivers\usb\hcd\usb20\ehci;\
    $(_PUBLICROOT)\common\oak\drivers\usb\hcd\usb20\usb2com

CDEFINES=$(CDEFINES) -DBSP_EHCI_MANUAL_DATATOGGLE

SOURCELIBS=\
    $(_COMMONOAKROOT)\lib\$(_CPUINDPATH)\hcd2lib.lib

TARGETLIBS=\
    $(_COMMONSDKROOT)\lib\$(_CPUINDPATH)\coredll.lib \
    $(_COMMONSDKROOT)\lib\$(_CPUINDPATH)\ceddk.lib \

SOURCES=\
    cpipe.cpp \
    chw.cpp    \
```

```
ctd.cpp     \
trans.cpp   \
system.c    \
cehcd.cpp   \
usb2lib.cpp
```

Code snippet is from Sample_Sources.txt

The preceding `TARGETNAME`, `TARGETTYPE`, and `RELEASETYPE` entries instruct the build system to build and compile the `cpipe.cpp`, `chw.cpp`, `ctd.cpp`, `trans.cpp`, `system.c`, `cehcd.cpp`, and `usb2lib.cpp` code modules to generate a DLL named `EHCI.DLL` for the current platform.

To learn more about SOURCES file macros, search MSDN using the "SOURCES file macro" keyword.

Build Release Phase

In the build release phase, all the files from the Sysgen and Build phases are copied to the OS design's build release directory, which also is referred to as the FLAT release directory, `$(_FLATRELEASEDIR)`. This directory contains all the final modules and configuration files for the Compact 7 OS run-time image.

Make Image Phase

Make image phase is the final step, where the contents from the build release directory, `$(_FLATRELEASEDIR)`, are assembled into a Compact 7 OS run-time image file, `NK.BIN`.

In this phase, all registry files for the OS, BSP, and subproject components combine into a single registry file, `REGINIT.INI`. All of the BIB (binary image builder) files for the OS, BSP, and subproject components combine into a single BIB file, `CE.BIB`. You can find both the `REGINIT.INI` and `CE.BIB` files in the `$(_FLATRELEASEDIR)` directory after the build process completes.

The `REGINIT.INI` registry file reflects all the registry entries for the OS run-time image. The `CE.BIB` file contains the configuration to instruct the build system which files and modules to include in the OS image and where to place these files and modules in the image.

To review and analyze an OS run-time, `REGINIT.INI` is the file you need to review to check whether the necessary registry entries are included or whether the values for the registry entries are set correctly for the OS image. `CE.BIB` is the file you need to review to check whether the required files and modules are included in the OS image and configured with the appropriate properties.

BUILD SYSTEM TOOLS

You can build a Compact 7 OS design project from the Platform Builder IDE, using the graphical user interface or command line.

Although the build system for Compact 7 has been through major improvements and it takes less time to build an OS design compared to the previous version, many veteran Windows Embedded Compact developers still prefer to build from the command line. Building from the command line provides more flexibility and control over the build process. The Platform Builder IDE is just a graphical shell that calls the command-line tools.

Learning to use the command-line tool to perform different OS design build steps helps you understand the underlying build system better than using the Platform Builder IDE.

Build from the Platform Builder IDE

The Platform Builder IDE (VS2008 IDE) is context-sensitive. The options available from the IDE change according to the environment you select. For example, with MyCompact7 OS design project open, when you select the Solution 'MyCompact7'(1 project) option from the Solution Explorer tab, the Build menu shows the build options to build the solution, as shown in Figure 11-2.

When you select MyCompact7, an OS design project, from the Solution Explorer tab, the Build menu shows additional build options, as shown in Figure 11-3.

FIGURE 11-2

FIGURE 11-3

From the Build menu (refer to Figure 11-3), you can select Advanced Build Commands to see additional build options.

When building the OS design for the first time, you can use any one of the following options, from the Platform Builder IDE Build menu:

➤ Build Solution

➤ Build MyCompact7 (Build <OS design name>)

➤ Advanced Build Commands | Sysgen (`blddemo -q`)

The preceding three options launch the build system and go through the complete process to build the OS design; you can use them to build the OS design under all conditions. For certain conditions, these build methods take longer than necessary, and you can use an alternative method that takes less time to complete.

When rebuilding a previously built OS design, the Build command you should use depends on what has been altered from the previous build.

Rebuild OS Design — Changes That Affect Sysgen

After creating a successful build that generated a working OS run-time image, you need to add or remove catalog items to further customize the OS design. Adding and removing catalog items affect the OS design's Sysgen. After adding or removing catalog items, the OS design needs to go through the complete build process to generate a new OS run-time image, using one of the following options:

➤ From the VS2008 Build menu, click Build Solution.

➤ From the VS2008 Build menu, select Advanced Build Commands and click Sysgen (`blddemo -q`)

Rebuild OS Design — Modified Registry Entries

After a successful build process that generates a working OS run-time image, you might need to change an entry in the OS design's `OSDESIGN.REG` registry file. For a condition like this, the OS design does not need to go through the complete build process. To build an OS run-time image with the updated registry entries, follow these steps:

1. From the VS2008 Build menu, click Copy Files to Release Directory.

2. From the VS2008 Build menu, click Make Run-Time Image.

The preceding two steps should take less than 3 minutes to perform, compared to 15 to 20 minutes for a full build.

Rebuild OS Design — Modified Build Options

After a successful build process that generates a working OS run-time image built in Release configuration, you need to generate a new image with the KITL and kernel debugger enabled to do some testing, which change the following two IMG environment variables for the OS design:

➤ IMGNODEBUGGER

➤ IMGNOKITL

When only the IMG environment variable for the OS design is changed, you can execute the Make Image command to generate an updated image without going through a full build, as follows:

From the Build menu, select Make Run-Time Image.

The Make Run-Time Image build command can take under 3 minutes to perform, compared to 15 to 20 minutes for a full build.

Rebuild OS Design — Modified Subprojects Codes

After a successful build process that generates a working OS run-time image, you might need to change some of the codes in one of the subproject within the OS design, which does not impact the Sysgen components. To generate an updated OS run-time image, launch the following build command:

1. From the Build menu, select Advanced Build Commands.

2. Click Build Current BSP and Subprojects (`blddemo -qbsp`).

The preceding advanced build command takes approximately half the time compared to the full build.

Build from the Command Line

The command-line build method provides more flexibility. With correct usage, the command-line build method is more efficient compared to using the Platform Builder IDE.

With the OS design project open, from the VS2008 Build menu, select Open Release Directory in Build Window to bring up a console command window, as shown in Figure 11-4.

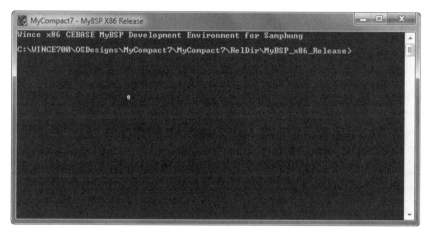

FIGURE 11-4

The console command window (refer to Figure 11-4) is launched with the appropriate environment variables set to support the build system for the active OS design project. From this window, you can set additional environment variables with the SET command, such as the following to disable the kernel debugger and KITL:

```
SET IMGNODEBUGGER=1
SET IMGNOKITL=1
```

Although the command-line build method is more flexible and efficient, it's not recommended for an inexperienced OS design developer. Improper use of the command-line build method can be unproductive.

Table 11-2 lists some of the build conditions and the command line to build the OS design.

TABLE 11-2: Command Line Build Commands

CONDITION	COMMAND LINE
Building the OS design for the first time	Blddemo -q
Rebuilding a previously built OS design, with changes that affect Sysgen components	Blddemo clean -q
Rebuilding a previously built OS design, with changes to the subproject that do not affect Sysgen components	Blddemo -qbsp Or Blddemo -c -qbsp
Rebuilding a previously built OS design, modifying registry entries in OSDESIGN.REG	Fmerge.exe and Makeimg.exe

Review the Windows Embedded Compact 7 product documentation to learn more about the build system and command-line tools.

BEST PRACTICE TO SAVE TIME AND MINIMIZE PROBLEMS

It's a simple task to launch the command to build an OS design from the Platform Builder IDE; just select and click a command. However, this single-click has the following cost in terms of time:

> ➤ Depending on the development station's performance, it takes anywhere from 10 to more than 20 minutes to build an OS design project to generate an OS run-time image.

> ➤ After an OS run-time image is generated, you and your team need to spend time to run tests and debug the image to see whether the OS image contains all the required components and is properly configured to meet the design specification, which may take hours, days, or even weeks.

It's a good practice to check and validate updates to the OS design to ensure the required features are included and changes to the project are as intended and properly implemented before releasing the OS image to the next development step.

Understand the Build Process

A typical Compact 7 OS design project includes hundreds of modules with multiple configuration files; it's not realistic to go through all files trying to debug and identify problems. With a good understanding about the build process and results generated by each build step, you are better equipped to identify build problems.

Table 11-3 lists some of the common problems related to building the OS design.

TABLE 11-3: Remedy for Common Build Problems

COMMON PROBLEM	REMEDY
The required file is not included in the final OS run-time image.	Check to see whether the file is in the build release directory and whether there is a proper entry in the `CE.BIB` file to include the file to the image. Check to see whether the environment variable to include the file to the image is set within the OS design.
The required file is not included in the final OS run-time image. The OS design is properly configured.	This problem may be caused by improper use of the build step. Launch the Clean Sysgen (`blddemo clean -q`) to clear files from the previous build. Then use Sysgen and build the OS design.
The required registry is not included in the final OS run-time image.	Check the `REGINIT.INI` file in the build release directory. Check to see whether the environment variable to include the registry entry to the image is set within the OS design.
The required registry entry included in the final OS run-time image has the wrong value.	Check the `REGINIT.INI` file in the build release directory for multiple instances of the same registry key. During the make image phase, all registry files are combined into the `REGINIT.INI` file. For a registry key with multiple instances, the last entry is the one that takes effect. Review Chapter 10, "The Registry," to understand the order where the value for a registry key in one file supersedes the value for the same registry key in another file.
The OS design is able to complete the build process without error. However, the binary file for the subproject is not included to the final OS run-time image and is not in the build release directory.	Check to see whether `DIRS` file is properly implemented and includes the subproject's folder. Check to see whether the subproject has a proper `SOURCES` file with the correct macro for the build system to compile the subproject as intended.
When downloaded from the development station, the OS Image is able to launch on the target device. When deployed to the target device's local storage, the image fails to boot.	Check to see whether the target device is properly configured to launch the OS run-time image from local storage. Check to see whether KITL and kernel debugger is disabled. Retail image with KITL and kernel debugger enabled cannot boot from local storage.

Project Documentation and Archive

A Compact 7 OS design project includes many different components with complicated configuration parameters. Developing Compact 7 OS design for a target device involves a lot of repetitive tasks. Proper project documentation is important to minimize redundant tasks, create an environment to track, and resolve bugs efficiently. Most important, it can make your life a lot easier.

From time to time, you may need to reverse back to an earlier OS design that works. Or a customer may come back to you looking for the project files you created for the project a few months back. Without documentation and archive, these situations cost unpredictable time and effort to fulfill.

Proper documentation for each OS design project and archives of the OS design project files are important to keep. If you are new to team development and version control, following are some of the development practices to consider, even when working solo:

➤ Invest some effort to learn about version control. It's a good way to establish a cumulative and structured environment to improve a software development project and resolve bugs and compatibility issues.

➤ Do not depend on your memory to remember which components are included in the project, what you did to generate a successful build to get the OS run-time image to boot up on the target device, and so on. A Compact 7 OS design project includes many components and variables. After a few weeks or months have lapsed, you will forget some of the details.

➤ Document each OS design project and keep cumulative project records with the following information:

   ➤ BSP selected for the OS design.

   ➤ OS design template selected for the OS design.

   ➤ Additional Compact 7 catalog items added to the OS design.

   ➤ Third-party components added to the OS design.

   ➤ Additional environment variables configured for the OS design.

   ➤ Registry and BIB file entries added to the OS design.

   ➤ Changes made to the OS design since the last build.

   ➤ Date and timestamp for the current build and result.

   ➤ Some comments about how the OS run-time image and associated application performed on the target device.

➤ Keep archives of working OS design projects along with the BSP and third-party components used for each OS design, to use in the event you need to reverse back to a previously working version. Although a compiled OS design can span well over 1GB of storage space, the precompiled version can be less than 1MB. Even with compiled SDK, BSP, and third-party components, the storage space needed to keep a copy of these components is manageable.

SUMMARY

When Platform Builder abstracted the complicated environment and minimized the need to dwell into Compact 7's build system, developers new to the Compact 7 OS design development may underestimate the level of difficulty involved in OS design development when a quality BSP for the target device is not available, and fail to invest sufficient effort to learn about the Compact 7 build system.

Understanding the build system provides one of the key puzzles to help you fully grasp the whole Windows Embedded Compact 7 development environment and advantages. With thorough understanding of the Compact 7 development environment, you are equipped with the proper knowledge to source the correct hardware platform for your target device, with the required software support components to minimize unexpected development challenges and to put together a more accurate and predictable project development plan.

12

Remote Display Application

WHAT'S IN THIS CHAPTER?

➤ Adding a remote display application to the OS design

➤ Using the remote display application

The Remote Display application provided as part of Windows Embedded Compact 7 is a useful utility, which provides remote access to the Compact 7 desktop. For many application developers, this application can help eliminate the need to have a separate display monitor for the target device, by routing the device's display, keyboard, and mouse interface to the desktop on the development station. It can even work with a headless Compact 7 device.

This chapter provides an overview of the Remote Display application and includes an exercise showing how to include this application in the OS run-time image and how to utilize this application.

ACCESS COMPACT 7 DESKTOP REMOTELY

The Remote Desktop application provides the support so that you can access the Windows Embedded Compact 7 desktop from a remote computer. With this application properly configured, you can access the Compact 7 desktop over a TCP/IP connection to view and interact with the desktop using a keyboard and mouse from the remote computer, similar to remote desktop.

ADD REMOTE DISPLAY APPLICATION TO AN OS DESIGN

The Remote Display application is provided as a catalog item available as part of the Platform builder's component catalog, which can be added to an OS design.

Add Remote Display Application from the Catalog

Open the MyCompact7 OS design project created in Chapter 7, "OS Design," and follow the steps to add the remote display application and configure the OS design to build a release mode image.

1. From the Catalog Items View tab, select and include the Remote Display Application item to the OS design, as shown in Figure 12-1.

2. From the VS2008 Build menu, click Configuration Manager to bring up the Configuration Manager screen.

3. From the Configuration Manager screen, select MyBSP X86 Release from the Active Solution Configuration selection options, as shown in Figure 12-2, and click Close.

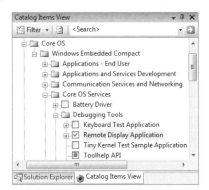

FIGURE 12-1

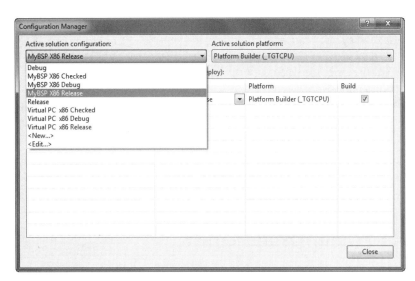

FIGURE 12-2

3. From the VS2008 Project menu, click MyCompact7 Properties to bring up the MyCompact7 Property Pages screen.

4. From the left pane, expand the Configuration Properties node and click the Build Options node to show available build options on the right pane.

5. Disable the kernel debugger and KITL build options, as shown in Figure 12-3.

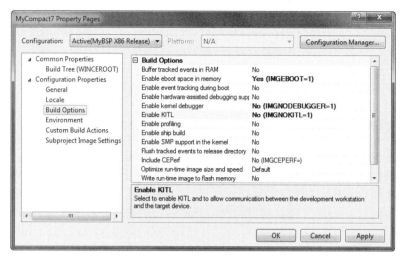

FIGURE 12-3

6. Click Apply; then click OK to save the setting and close.

Add Registry to Launch Remote Display Application

The preceding steps added the Remote Display application, CERDISP.EXE, to the OS design that will be compiled to be part of the OS run-time image. For this application to perform the function it serves, it needs to be launched on the target device. You can either manually launch the remote display application, CERDISP.EXE, or configure the OS design to automatically launch this application during startup.

As part of the exercise in Chapter 7 to create the MyCompact7 OS design project, the AutoLaunch component is included in the OS design, which can be used to launch the CERDISP.EXE executable when the Compact 7 OS starts. To accomplish this, add the following registry entries to the OS design project's OSDESIGN.REG registry file:

Available for
download on
Wrox.com

```
[HKEY_LOCAL_MACHINE\Startup]
    "Process0"="cerdisp -c"
    "Process0Delay"=dword:00002710
```

Code snippet is from OSDesign.reg

Generate OS Run-time Image with Remote Display Application

With the Remote Display application component and registry entries to launch the application added to the OS design, you can build and generate an OS run-time image for the next exercise.

From the VS2008 Build menu, select Advanced Build Commands, and click Sysgen (blddemo -q) to build the image. After the build process is completed without error, an OS run-time image is generated with the Remote Display application compiled as part of the image.

Follow the steps in Chapter 8, "Target Device Connectivity and Download," to download the image to the target device. After the image is launched on the target device, an additional icon, for the Remote Display application, is shown on the Compact 7 desktop's taskbar, to the left of the network icon, as shown in Figure 12-4.

FIGURE 12-4

HOW-TO: USE REMOTE DISPLAY APPLICATION

To access the Compact 7 target device's desktop, with the Remote Display application launched from the previous steps, you need to use the Platform Builder CE Remote Display Host application, CERHOST.EXE, from the development station.

The CERHOST.EXE application is included as part of the Platform Builder software, installed to the following directory: $(_WINCEROOT)\PUBLIC\COMMON\OAK\BIN\i386.

Work through the following steps to remotely access the Compact 7 target device's desktop from the development station:

1. From the development station, launch the CERHOST.EXE executable to bring up the Remote Display Control for Windows CE screen, as shown in Figure 12-5.

2. From the Remote Display Control for Windows CE File menu, click Connect to bring up the Connect screen, as shown in Figure 12-6.

FIGURE 12-5

FIGURE 12-6

3. After a few seconds, as the messages broadcasted by the Remote Display application from the Compact 7 target device are detected, the device ID, VDX, is listed on the Active target devices list.

4. Click the device ID to select the device. As you click the device ID, the target device's IP address is shown on the Connect screen.

5. Click OK to close the Connect screen, and launch the target device's Compact 7 desktop, as shown in Figure 12-7.

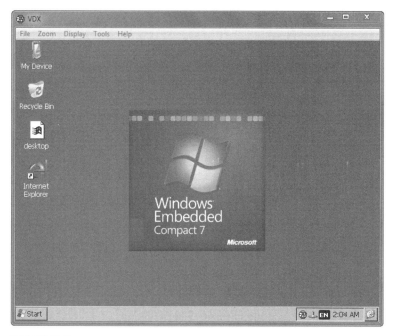

FIGURE 12-7

From the Remote Display Host application window on the development station, as shown in Figure 12-7, you can interact with the target device using the development station's keyboard and mouse, just as the keyboard and mouse are attached to the device directly.

USING REMOTE DISPLAY APPLICATION ON HEADLESS DEVICE

Working with a headless Compact 7 device, a device built without user interface, you can use the Remote Display application to access the Compact 7 desktop on device remotely, which is a useful development tool.

Using similar steps as the previous exercises in this chapter, you can configure the OS design, created to support a headless target device, to include the Remote Display application and enable access to the device's desktop remotely using the Platform Builder CE Remote Display Host application, CERHOST.EXE, from the development station.

Although a headless Compact 7 device does not have video display hardware, the headless Compact 7 OS run-time image for the device requires the NULL (Stub) display driver to function, like a virtual display.

SUMMARY

The Remote Display application is a useful tool to access a Compact 7 target device's desktop and interacts with the device remotely, without the need to have a dedicated display monitor. When working with a headless Compact 7 device, you can remotely access the headless Compact 7 device's desktop.

In addition to using the Remote Display application for testing and debugging purposes, this is a useful tool for the documentation team, enabling the team to capture screen images from the Compact 7 device, as the application executes on the device.

13

Testing with Compact Test Kit

WHAT'S IN THIS CHAPTER?

➤ Establishing connectivity for the Compact Test Kit

➤ Testing with the Compact Test Kit

The Compact Test Kit is part of the Windows Embedded Compact 7 software suite. This test kit is a complete makeover from the CE Test Kit (CETK) for the previous versions, with a new graphical user interface and added features.

The Compact Test Kit provides the facilities to test and validate whether a Compact 7 device driver, BSP, and OEM hardware adaptation code meet the design specification needed to support the Compact 7 OS kernel, and Microsoft's quality control guidelines.

The CTK is intended to help minimize the time and resources needed to perform testing to ensure the design meets a certain level of performance and quality.

The CTK's ease of use and setup does not mean that it's a lightweight testing environment. CTK tests are thorough and provide credible test data in a standardized report format that can meet rigid testing requirements and provide useful test data and documentation for the project. Microsoft's Windows Embedded Compact team uses the same CTK test to perform BSP and device driver testing for its BSP and device driver certification program.

COMPACT TEST KIT

The Compact Test Kit (CTK) provides an easy setup and easy-to-use environment, with a complete set of useful testing tools, provided as part of the Platform Builder for Compact 7 development environment, without additional cost. You can use the CTK tool to test functionality and performance for device driver and OAL components.

Although the CTK runs as a standalone application, it's tightly coupled with the VS2008 and Platform Builder IDE.

Following are the typical steps involved in running CTK tests:

1. Establish connectivity to the target device.

2. Select one or more tests to perform.

3. Run the test.

4. View the test result.

ESTABLISHING CONNECTIVITY FOR CTK

To use the CTK, you need to establish connectivity between the CTK IDE and the target device, using one of the following options:

➤ CoreCon

➤ KITL

Whether the connection between the development station and target device connects through KITL or CoreCon, the steps to perform CTK Tests are identical between the two connection methods, after you establish the connection.

Preparing an OS Run-time Image to Support CTK

To support CTK testing, the OS run-time image is not required to include any CTK-related files. After the CTK IDE establishes connectivity to the target device, it downloads the required files and launches the required CTK application on the target device.

All the components to be tested must be included in the OS run-time image and become active after the OS run-time image launches on the target device.

Connecting CTK to the Target Device with KITL

To establish connectivity with the target device using KITL, you need to configure the OS design to generate an OS run-time image with KITL enabled.

Work through the following steps to establish connectivity between the CTK IDE and target device:

1. Configure the MyCompact7 OS design from Chapter 7, "OS Design," to generate an OS run-time image with KITL enabled, and download the image to the target device.

2. With the KITL-enabled OS run-time image downloaded to the target device, from the development station's Start menu, click All Programs, and expand the WindowsEmbedded Compact7TestKit folder to launch the WindowsEmbeddedCompact7TestKit program, and bring up the Windows Embedded Compact Test Kit screen, as shown in Figure 13-1.

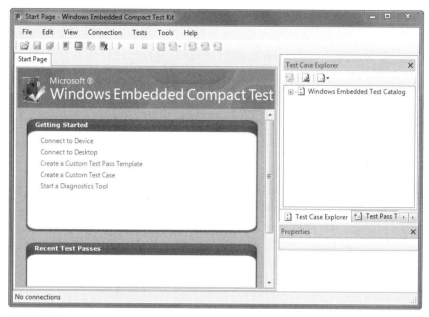

FIGURE 13-1

3. From the Windows Embedded Compact Test Kit screen's Connection menu, click Connect to Device to bring up the Select a Device screen, as shown in Figure 13-2.

4. From the Select a Device screen, expand the Platform Builder node to select MyTargetDevice, and click OK to bring up the Connecting to Device screen. It takes a little while to connect to the target device and transfer the necessary files to establish the needed connection.

5. After you establish the connection, the Windows Embedded Compact Test Kit program launches on the target device.

6. On the development station, the Windows Embedded Compact Test Kit screen displays updated information to indicate the IDE connected to the target device, as shown in Figure 13-3.

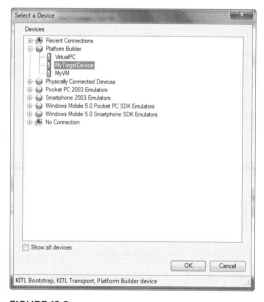

FIGURE 13-2

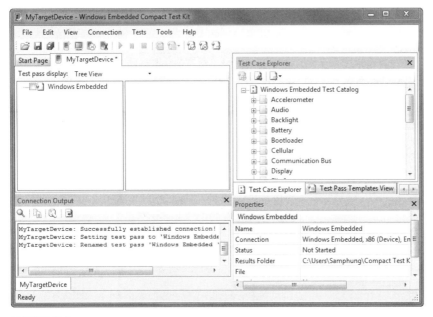

FIGURE 13-3

If you use the KITL connection to the target device to perform CTK tests, skip the next section and go to the CTK tests section.

Connecting CTK to a Target Device with CoreCon

To establish connectivity with the target device using CoreCon, you need to configure the OS design to generate an OS run-time image and download the image to the target device with the following configurations:

1. Configure to build in release mode.

2. KITL disabled.

3. Include the necessary files to establish the CoreCon connection to the development station.

4. Either manually launch CoreCon, or configure the OS to auto-launch CoreCon during startup.

5. Install `MyCompact7_SDK.msi`, generated from the MyCompact7 OS design project in Chapter 7, to the development station.

Basically, you need to deploy an OS run-time image to the target device, with the same CoreCon files and configurations to support VS2008 application development.

After the OS run-time image is launched on the target device, work through the following steps to establish connectivity between the CTK IDE and target device:

1. From the VS2008 Tools menu, click Options to bring up the Options screen.

2. From the left pane, expand the Device Tools node, and select the Devices node to bring up the device settings on the right.

3. From the Devices selection list, select MyCompact7_SDK x86 Device, as shown in Figure 13-4.

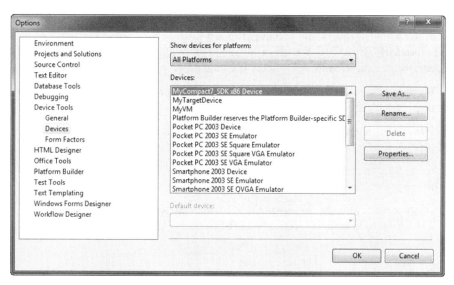

FIGURE 13-4

4. With MyCompact7_SDK x86 Device selected, click Properties to bring up the MyCompact7_SDK x86 Device Properties screen, as shown in Figure 13-5.

5. From the MyCompact7_SDK x86 Device Properties screen, click Configure to bring up the Configure TCP/IP Transport screen, as shown in Figure 13-6.

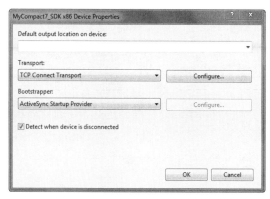

FIGURE 13-5

FIGURE 13-6

6.   From the Configure TCP/IP Transport screen, select Use Specific IP Address to enter the target device's IP address, and click OK to close the screen.

7.   Click OK to close the MyCompact7_SDK x86 Device Properties screen; then click OK on the Options screen.

8.   From the development station's Start menu, click All Programs, and expand the WindowsEmbeddedCompact7TestKit folder to launch the WindowsEmbeddedCompact7TestKit program, to bring up the Windows Embedded Compact Test Kit screen.

9.   From the Windows Embedded Compact Test Kit screen's Connection menu, click Connect to Device to bring up the Select a Device screen.

10.   From the Select a Device screen, expand the Physically Connected Devices node, and select MyCompact7_SDK x86 Device; click OK to connect to the device.

11.   After the connection is established, the Windows Embedded Compact Test Kit program launches on the target device.

12.   On the development station, the Windows Embedded Compact Test Kit screen displays updated information to indicate the IDE connected to the target device, similar to Figure 13-3 in the previous section.

TESTING COMPACT 7 DEVICE WITH CTK

The Compact Test Kit provides a large collection of test suites to test different type of components and devices, which include the following categories of components and devices:

➤   Accelerometer

➤   Audio

➤   Backlight

➤   Battery

➤   Bootloader

➤   Cellular

➤   Communication Bus

➤   Display

➤   File System

➤   Input

➤   Kernel

➤   Multimedia

- ➤ Networking
- ➤ NLED
- ➤ OAL
- ➤ Power Manager
- ➤ Security
- ➤ Shell
- ➤ Smart Card
- ➤ Storage Media
- ➤ USB

In addition to the tests provided as part of CTK, you can develop customized tests to support your device. Some of the CTK tests take a long time to run. For a device with a slow processor, some of the tests can take hours. You can select multiple tests that do not require user interaction and launch CTK to run these tests all at once unattended.

Although some of the CTK tests can run unattended after launch, there are some tests that require you to interact with the device throughout the testing process.

CTK Test with Manual Interaction: Input Device

This section works through an exercise to perform a CTK test for the target device's input device, the keyboard driver.

With a Compact 7 OS run-time image launched on the target device with connection to the CTK IDE established from the earlier exercise in this chapter, work through the following steps to perform the required CTK tests:

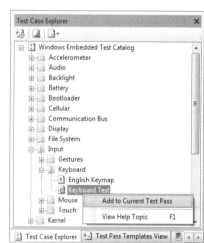

FIGURE 13-7

1. From the Test Case Explorer tab on the CTK application screen, expand the Input node by expanding the Keyboard node, as shown in Figure 13-7.

2. From the Test Case Explorer tab, right-mouse-click the Keyboard Test node, and click Add to Current Test Pass.

3. As the Keyboard Test is added to the current test pass, the middle context-sensitive window presents more information and links to additional references about the selected test, Keyboard Test, as shown in Figure 13-8.

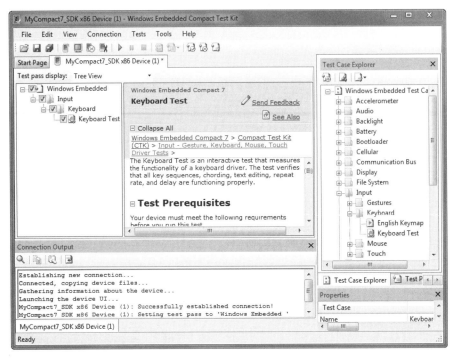

FIGURE 13-8

4. To start the test, from the Windows Embedded Compact Test Kit screen's Tests menu, click Run Test Pass to launch the test.

5. As the Keyboard Test launches, a test application launches on the target device and displays information and instructions about the test, as shown in Figure 13-9.

6. If you wait too long to interact with the target device, an Input Required dialog appears, giving you the opportunity to click Yes to continue or the No button to cancel the test.

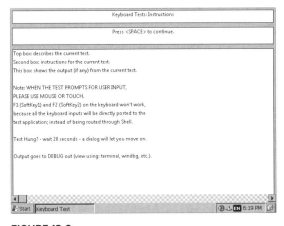

FIGURE 13-9

7. Follow the instruction and interact with the target device to run the test.

8. After the test finishes, the test program on the target device unloads.

9. On the development station, the Windows Embedded Compact Test Kit screen shows the summary for the test, on the Windows Embedded [Results] tab, as shown in Figure 13-10.

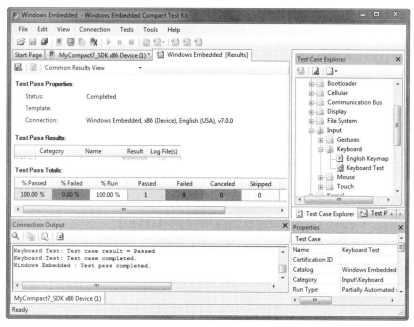

FIGURE 13-10

10. Each CTK test includes multiple testing routines for different features. The test summary provides information to indicate whether the test passed or failed. To view the detailed test result, click the Keyboard Test [Results] tab, as shown in Figure 13-11.

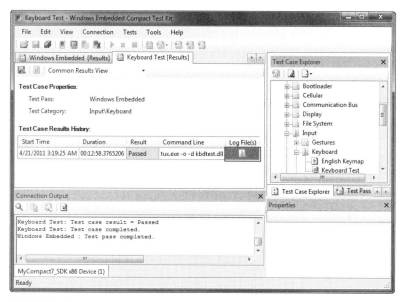

FIGURE 13-11

11. From the Keyboard Test [Results] tab, click the Folder icon just under the LogFile(s) column to bring up the File Explorer showing the `result.log` file.

12. Open the `result.log` file with a text editor such as Notepad to review the detailed test report.

The CTK keyboard test is a simple and short test to demonstrate the steps to run a CTK test that requires manual interaction.

Unattended CTK Test: Display Driver

This section works through an exercise to perform a CTK test for the target device's video, the display driver. After the initial setup, the display driver test does not require user interaction and can run unattended.

With a Compact 7 OS run-time image launched on the target device with connection to the CTK IDE established from the earlier exercise in this chapter, work through the following steps to perform the required CTK tests:

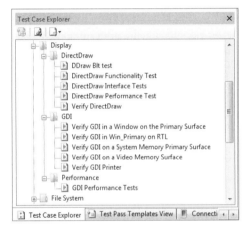

1. From the Test Case Explorer tab on the CTK application screen, expand the Display node and the three subnodes, as shown in Figure 13-12.

2. From the Test Case Explorer tab, right-mouse-click on each of the following tests, and click Add to Current Test Pass to include these tests in the current testing session:

FIGURE 13-12

➤ DDraw Blt Test

➤ DirectDraw Functionality Test

➤ DirectDraw Interface Tests

➤ DirectDraw Performance Test

➤ Verify DirectDraw

➤ Verify GDI in a Window on the Primary Surface

➤ Verify GDI on a System Memory Primary Surface

➤ Verify GDI on a Video Memory Surface

➤ Verify GDI Performance Tests

3. After the preceding selected tests are added, the Test pass display pane on the MyTargetDevice tab displays these tests with a check mark to indicate the tests are selected.

To launch all the selected tests, right-mouse-click the Windows Embedded node, and click Run Selected Tests to launch the tests, as shown in Figure 13-13.

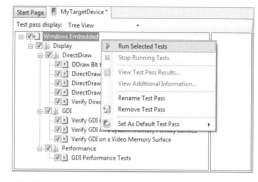

As the selected display driver tests launch on the target device, the device's screen actively displays different graphic patterns as part of the testing processes.

Depending on the target device's processing capability, the preceding selected tests can take a few hours to perform. However, it can be run unattended. To save time, you can launch this type of test just before the end of the day and let the tests run over night. This way, you will have the test results the following morning.

FIGURE 13-13

The display driver test suite includes a large collection of individual tests. Some of the display drivers will fail some of these tests. Failing the tests does not mean the driver is bad or not up to the quality standard. You need to identify the reason that caused the failed test.

When a CTK test is testing a feature that is not supported by the device driver, the test will fail. In this case, it's not the device driver's quality that causes the test to fail.

To fully take advantage of the CTK environment, you need to understand which function each of these tests are testing for, and the basic required set of specifications that must be passed to meet the quality design guidelines set by Microsoft.

BSP Test

Using CTK to test BSP is not the same among different devices. Testing a BSP involves the following group of tests:

- ➤ OAL - Cache
- ➤ OAL - Interrupt
- ➤ OAL - IOCTL
- ➤ OAL - KITL
- ➤ OAL - Memory
- ➤ OAL - RTC
- ➤ OAL - Timer
- ➤ Bootloader

In addition to the testing the preceding OAL and Bootloader components, BSP testing for a target device is required to test the device driver included as part of the BSP to support the target device's peripherals, which may include one or more of the following type of components:

- ➤ Audio
- ➤ Display

➤ I2C

➤ Network

➤ Storage

➤ Serial interface

➤ SPI

➤ Touch controller

➤ USB interface

➤ Etc.

CTK Test Pass

A typical CTK test session for a target device involves multiple tests. A CTK test pass is like a template, which you can create to run multiple selected CTK tests for one or more designated target devices.

Instead of selecting and launching multiple individual tests to fulfill the testing requirements for a target device, you can organize all the required tests into a single CTK Test Pass template and launch a single test pass to perform all the required tests.

With a Compact 7 OS run-time image launched on the target device with a connection to the CTK IDE established from the earlier exercise in this chapter, work through the following steps to create a CTK Test Pass template:

1. From the Windows Embedded Compact Test Kit screen's File menu, select New, and click Test Pass Template to bring up the Test Manager screen, as shown in Figure 13-14.

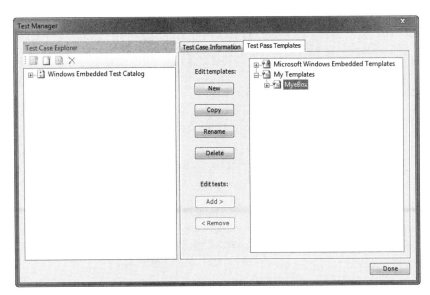

FIGURE 13-14

2. From the Test Pass Templates tab, click New, and enter **MyeBox** as the name for the new test pass.

3. From the Test Case Explorer pane on the left, expand the OAL folder to select the Cache folder, and click Add to add all tests under the Cache folder to the MyeBox test pass, as shown in Figure 13-15.

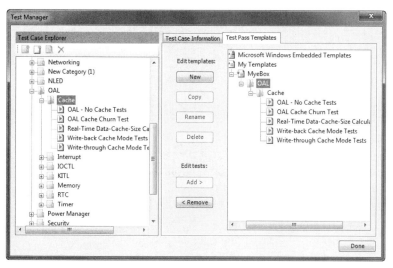

FIGURE 13-15

4. From the Test Case Explorer pane on the left, expand the Display folder followed by the Performance folder to select GDI Performance Tests, and click Add to add this test case to the MyeBox test pass, as shown in Figure 13-16.

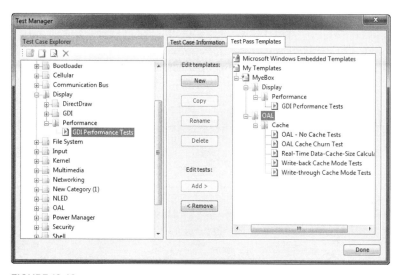

FIGURE 13-16

5. Following the procedure in steps 3 and 4, you can select a single test case to add to the MyeBox test pass. Or you can select a group of tests within one of the folders to add to the MyeBox test pass. After all the required test cases are added to the test pass, click Done to save and close the Test Manager screen.

6. To use the MyeBox test pass, from the Windows Embedded Compact Test Kit screen, click the Test Pass Templates View to show the available Test Pass templates.

7. From the Test Pass Templates View tab, expand all the folders, right-mouse-click the MyeBox template, and click Use as Current Test Pass to use this template for the current test pass, as shown in Figure 13-17.

8. After all the MyeBox Test Pass template is applied to the current test pass, you can press F5, or click Run Test Pass from the Tests menu, to launch CTK to run all the test cases in the current test pass.

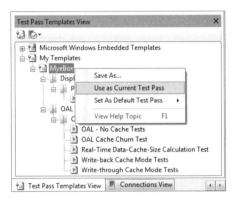

FIGURE 13-17

SUMMARY

A product with a good design but without adequate testing to ensure the final product can deliver the intended functions consistently with an acceptable quality to maintain a positive user experience is likely to fail in the marketplace.

Testing is an important part of the product development process. In addition to the loss of revenue and profit, a product with poor quality reflects poorly on the company's image, which can have long-term damaging impact.

The huge resources invested in the Compact Test Kit provide a much needed tool that functions as the gate keeper to help your development team ensure that the Windows Embedded Compact 7 product developed by your team can deliver the expected functions and meet the targeted quality expectations.

PART III
Application Development

14

Application Development

WHAT'S IN THIS CHAPTER?

➤ Understanding Compact 7 application development options

➤ Understanding the connectivity needed to support application development for Compact 7

You can do Windows Embedded Compact 7 application development in C, C++, C#, and Visual Basic from the Visual Studio 2008 IDE. This chapter talks about different options for Compact 7 applications development and connectivity between the development station and target device.

DEVELOPING COMPACT 7 APPLICATIONS

You can develop all Windows Embedded Compact 7 applications from the VS2008 IDE. Writing code for a Compact 7 application is not much different from writing code for an application for the desktop Windows OS. Whether you code in C++, C#, or Visual Basic, the fundamental coding practices and syntax are the same. If you already use the Visual Studio development IDE, your experience can help you quickly master Compact 7 application development.

The best approach to learn Compact 7 application development is to jump right in, start writing code, and learn as you move along. When creating a new application project, the VS2008 IDE has different wizards, each with multiple project templates, to help you establish the initial project workspace. With a Compact 7 application project workspace properly created by the wizard, all you need to do is to write code to add functionality.

To support Compact 7 application development, the following framework, library, and resources are available as part of the Platform Builder resources:

➤ .NET Compact Framework

➤ Active Template Library (ATL)

➤ C/C++ Libraries for Windows Embedded Compact

➤ COM and DCOM

➤ Internet Explorer Script Support

➤ Messaging API

➤ Pocket Outlook Object Model

➤ Silverlight for Windows Embedded

➤ XML

➤ XmlLite

In addition to the general application framework and library resources, a large collection of application-specific resources and sample application projects are provided as part of the Platform Builder installation, covering the following technologies:

➤ ActiveSync

➤ Internet Explorer Embedded

➤ Windows Embedded Compact Terminal Services Client

➤ FTP Server

➤ MSMQ Message Queuing

➤ RAS Server/PPTP Server

➤ Remote Desktop Connection

➤ Servicesd.exe

➤ Simple Network Time Protocol (SNTP)

➤ Telnet Server

➤ Universal Plug and Play (UPnP)

➤ User Help

➤ Web Server (HTTPD)

➤ Windows Media Player OCX Control version 6.4 and 7.0

➤ Windows Media Technologies

➤ MTP Responder

Differences When Developing Desktop Applications

Although similarities exist between developing applications for a Compact 7 device and a PC, applications for Compact 7 devices involve different design criteria and consideration from the PC.

Following are some of the design considerations and environments for Compact 7 that are different from the PC:

➤ Compact 7 devices can be built with different type of processors, including different derivatives of the ARM, MIPS, and x86 processors and System-On-Chip (SoC). Although x86-based devices have a lot of similarities to the PC hardware structure, ARM and MIPS devices are completely different.

➤ Although you can develop Compact 7 applications that can run on multiple processor platforms, most Compact 7 applications are developed for one particular device or family of devices with application codes tightly coupled with the devices' hardware architecture to achieve the highest level of performance.

➤ Compact 7 devices typically are built with much fewer system resources and with minimal memory, storage, and processing capability to keep the cost low while meeting the device's required function and performance. Unlike the PC environment, swap files that provide additional resources to extend available RAM are not supported in Compact 7 devices.

➤ Many Compact 7 devices are built with a low resolution display with a small screen size. Instead of using the typical PC video interface, such as VGA, many Compact 7 devices are designed to use different types of interfaces for display output, such as an LCD panel capable of displaying two to four lines of ASCII text.

➤ Some Compact 7 devices are headless, built without a display, keyboard, and mouse. Some may be built with buttons and sensor to capture inputs, with a few LEDs to provide on/off status or to blink in different frequencies to indicate the operating status.

➤ A Compact 7 OS run-time image can be customized by the OEM device makers to exclude certain unused OS components to minimize the OS image size, and to use a lower cost license from Microsoft, which can result in certain system resources and application programming interfaces not being available for the device.

➤ The Win32 API available for the Compact 7 device is a subset of the desktop Win32 API. The .NET Compact Framework 3.5 for Compact 7 device is a subset of the .NET Framework 3.5 for the desktop Windows. Not all the functions and features from the desktop versions of these are available in Compact 7.

➤ Many Compact 7 devices operate in an environment in which an unexpected loss of power to the device is a routine occurrence. To address unexpected loss of power, the application must be written with a provision to manage the loss of data and potential file system corruption that can render the device unable to boot.

Real-Time Application

There are misperceptions among some software developers about the Windows Embedded Compact's real-time capability. In general, you should look at the real-time behavior from a total system point of view, including the OS, hardware, BSP, device driver, and application that make up the complete system.

The Windows Embedded Compact 7 OS is developed to meet hard real-time requirements, and to support timing-critical applications. To take advantage of Compact 7's hard real-time capability, applications created for the Compact 7 device must be written to meet the requirements and adhere to the hard real-time development principle.

An embedded device built with Compact 7 OS, or any other real-time OS, does not automatically inherit the real-time behavior. A Compact 7 device can be rendered to lose its real-time behavior when the application or BSP for the device is poorly written, or not intended to be in real time.

Although you can find hacks from some managed code gurus that indicate it's possible to develop real-time managed code applications, adding a .NET Compact Framework and managed code application as part of a Compact 7 device can render the device to lose its real-time capability. One of the main causes for a Compact 7 to lose its real-time behavior with a managed code application is the .NET Compact Framework's garbage collector.

Chapter 36, "Introduction to Real-Time Applications," provides more coverage about real-time applications. You can find a simple real-time application exercise in Chapter 37, "A Simple Real-Time Application."

Managed-Code Applications Using Visual Studio

You can write a managed code application for Compact 7 using C# and Visual Basic with the .NET Compact Framework library within the VS2008 IDE. The managed code application development environment hides many of the lower-level complicated APIs from you and simplifies many of the coding tasks. Developing managed code applications for Compact 7 is quite similar to that for the desktop Windows OS.

Unless the managed code application uses P/Invoke to access a custom DLL that supports hardware unique to one particular family of target devices, the byte code assembly generated from a managed code application written with the standard .NET Compact Framework library is portable across different hardware platforms.

You can develop a headless application in managed code for Compact 7. A special version of .NET Compact Framework to support headless application is provided.

Other than having to consider the target device's constrained resources and differences in the hardware, user, and operating environment, writing managed code applications for Compact 7 is similar to the desktop Windows OS, using similar language syntax and programming principles.

If you have existing managed code application development experience, you can find writing managed code applications for Compact 7 is not much different from the desktop Windows OS. If you are new to the Visual Studio and managed code environment, you can find this development environment amazingly efficient and effective to develop a human-machine interface, a database, and a variety of Windows form applications.

The following chapters cover more content on managed code application development:

- ➤ Chapter 15, ".NET Compact Framework"
- ➤ Chapter 18, "Managed Code Application Example"
- ➤ Chapter 38, "Extending Low-Level Access to Managed Code"
- ➤ Chapter 39, "Extending Low-Level Access to Managed Code with Messages"

VS2008 IDE provides a New Project Wizard to help create the initial workspace for smart device managed code application projects. Table 14-1 lists the smart device project templates available from VS2008.

TABLE 14-1: Managed Code Project Templates for Compact 7

VS2008 SMART DEVICE PROJECT TEMPLATE FOR MANAGED CODE	DESCRIPTION
Device Application	Project workspace to develop a .NET Compact Framework Windows forms application
Class Library	Project workspace to develop a .NET Compact Framework class library
Console Application	Project workspace to develop a .NET Compact Framework headless console application, without graphical user interface
Control Library	Project workspace to develop a .NET Compact Framework controls
Empty Project	An empty project workspace to a develop .NET Compact Framework application

Native Code Application for Compact 7

A Windows Embedded Compact application written in native code, using C and C++, provides the highest performance with the smallest application footprint. A native code application for Compact 7 is the preferred development environment when performance is important.

You can develop a Compact 7 native code application from the VS2008 IDE or from the Platform Builder IDE.

Native Code Application from VS2008 IDE

With a Compact 7 SDK generated from the OS design for the target device installed to the development station, you can develop a native code application for Compact 7 using Visual C++ from the VS2008 IDE.

With the required software installed and properly configured to support Compact 7, the VS2008 IDE provides a Project Wizard to help create the initial smart device native code application project workspace for the following types of projects, as shown in Table 14-2, to support Compact 7 devices.

TABLE 14-2: Native Code Project Templates for Compact 7

VS2008 SMART DEVICE PROJECT TEMPLATE FOR NATIVE CODE	DESCRIPTION
ATL Smart Device Project	Project workspace to develop a Compact 7 application using the Active Template Library
MFC Smart Device ActiveX Control	Project workspace to develop a Compact 7 ActiveX control using the Microsoft Foundation Class (MFC) library
MFC Smart Device Application	Project workspace to develop a Compact 7 application using the MFC library
MFC Smart Device DLL	Project workspace to develop a Compact 7 dynamic-link library (DLL) using the MFC library
Win32 Smart Device Project	Project workspace to develop a Compact 7 Win32 application

Native Code Application from Platform Builder IDE

From the Platform Builder IDE, you can create a Compact 7 native code application for the active OS design, as a subproject to the OS design, and can easily include the application as part of the OS run-time image.

From the Platform Builder IDE, you can create different types of native code applications, as shown in Table 14-3.

TABLE 14-3: Platform Builder Native Code Project Templates

PLATFORM BUILDER NATIVE CODE PROJECT	DESCRIPTION
WCE Application	Provides the options to create an empty subproject, a simple application, or a typical hello-world native code application project
WCE Console Application	Provides the options to create an empty subproject, a simple application, or a typical hello-world native code console application project
WCE Dynamic-Link Library	Provides the options to create an empty subproject, a simple DLL, or a DLL that exports some symbols
WCE Static Library	Provides the option to create a Windows Embedded Compact static library project
WCE TUX Dynamic-Link Library	Provides the project framework to develop a custom Tux DLL for the Compact Test Kit

CONNECTIVITY TO DEPLOY AND DEBUG AN APPLICATION

To deploy an application for testing and debug, you need to establish connectivity between the development station and target device. Deploying a VS2008 application to the target device for testing and debug uses different connectivity from an application developed as a subproject to the OS design from the Platform Builder IDE. To deploy a VS2008 application to a Compact 7 target device, the development station needs to establish CoreCon connectivity to the device.

A native code application developed as a subproject to the OS design compiles as part of the OS run-time image and downloads to the target device as part of the image, which requires a KITL connection to debug.

CoreCon

To establish CoreCon connectivity, the Compact 7 device needs to have access to the CoreCon files, installed to the development station as part of the VS2008 installation, from the following directory:

```
$(PROGRAMFILES)\ Common Files\Microsoft Shared\CoreCon\1.0\Target\Wce400\
```

Under the preceding directory, there are multiple folders. Each of these folders contains a set of CoreCon files to support a designated processor, with a corresponding processor name as the folder name. You can make these CoreCon files accessible to the Compact 7 device with one of the following methods:

- ➤ Manually place these CoreCon files to the Compact 7 device's local file system.

- ➤ Add entries to the OS design's OSDESIGN.BIB to include CoreCon files as part of the OS run-time image.

- ➤ Include the CoreCon_v200_Compact7 component to the OS design to include CoreCon files to the OS run-time image.

Including the CoreCon_v200_Compact7 component to the OS design is probably the simplest method. This component is created with the appropriate script to include the required CoreCon files to the OS design. Using the AutoLaunch_v200_Compact7 component, you can configure the OS run-time image to automatically launch CoreCon during startup and simplify the task to establish connectivity between the development station and the Compact 7 device. Chapter 16, "CoreCon Connectivity," provides more coverage on CoreCon.

Kernel Independent Transport Layer (KITL)

KITL is the connectivity used to debug a Compact 7 OS run-time image on the target device. Because a native code application from the Platform Builder IDE is developed as a subproject to the OS design and compiled as part of the OS run-time image, you can configure the OS design to generate an OS run-time image with KITL enabled to debug the application, as it executes on the target device. Chapter 19, "Platform Builder Native Code Application Example," talks about Platform Builder native code applications and provides more coverage on using KITL to debug the applications.

SUMMARY

Developing an application for a Windows Embedded Compact device involves connectivity to the target device, design considerations, a development environment, and a user environment that are different from the desktop Windows OS.

To be efficient and effective in Compact 7 application development, you need to understand the following:

➤ The impact, benefits, and challenges associated with your project's selected application development option.

➤ The connectivity options between the development station and target device, which is crucial for testing and debugging the application as it executes on the target device.

➤ How to implement debug messages in your application to provide meaningful information to help identify bugs and resolve problems.

15
.NET Compact Framework

➤   Understanding .NET Compact Framework 3.5

➤   Considering .NET Compact Framework 3.5 development

As a subset to the .NET Framework for the Windows desktop OS, .NET Compact Framework (CF) encapsulates the efficient rapid application development environment from .NET Framework to support Windows Embedded Compact 7 application development.

To support the small footprint of the Compact 7 OS and resource-constrained target device, .NET CF is optimized to include key features from the full .NET Framework into a much smaller package with some modified features and behavior to support embedded devices.

To fully cover .NET CF's ins and outs could take a whole book, which is not within this book's objectives. This chapter provides a compressed view of the .NET CF environment to help you better understand and start with managed code application development for a Compact 7 device, learning as you move along.

To develop a .NET CF application for Compact 7, you need to understand the environment. If you are already developing managed code applications for the desktop using .NET Framework, .NET CF is similar to what you already know, with some minor differences. If you are new to managed code development and expect to do quite a bit of work in this environment, this environment is developer-friendly and easy to work with.

The information in this chapter, along with the managed code application exercise in Chapter 18, "Managed Code Application Example," helps you start to develop working managed code applications targeting the .NET CF and learn the environment using a hands-on approach.

.NET COMPACT FRAMEWORK APPLICATION

There are different versions of .NET Compact Framework: 1.0, 2.0, and 3.5. When developing a Compact 7 OS design from the Platform Builder IDE, .NET CF 3.5 is provided as one of the available catalog items, which you can select and include in the OS design project, to generate a Compact 7 OS run-time image with .NET CF 3.5 as part of the image, to support managed code application.

Required Compact 7 OS Components

You can develop managed code applications using C# or Visual Basic. To support managed code application development from the VS2008 IDE, you need to include .NET CF in the Compact 7 OS run-time image by configuring the OS design project to include the following components from the Platform Builder catalog:

➤   .NET Compact Framework 3.5

➤   OS Dependencies for .NET Compact Framework 3.5

➤   CAB File Installer/Uninstaller

If you develop a headless or console mode managed code application, instead of the preceding components, select and include the following components in the OS design:

➤   .NET Compact Framework 3.5 — Headless

➤   OS Dependencies for .NET Compact Framework 3.5 — Headless

➤   CAB File Installer/Uninstaller

Connectivity to Target Device

In addition to the required OS components, to establish an effective development environment that enables you to deploy applications directly from the VS2008 IDE to the Compact 7 target device, you need to configure the device with CoreCon connectivity components. With CoreCon enabled on the Compact 7 device, you can connect to the device from the VS2008 IDE, deploy applications directly to the device, and set breakpoints to step through the application code, one line at a time, as the application executes on the device. Chapter 16, "CoreCon Connectivity," provides more coverage about CoreCon connectivity.

Steps to Develop, Deploy, Test, and Debug

Following are the steps to develop, deploy, test, and debug a managed code application for a Compact 7 device:

1. Create and configure a Compact 7 OS design with the necessary .NET CF components to support managed code application.

2. Generate an OS run-time image from the OS design and deploy the image to the target device.

3. Launch another instance of VS2008 (or launch VS2008 from a different development station) to create a managed code smart device application project.

4. Develop codes for the managed code application project.

5. From the target device, with Compact 7 OS launched, launch the CoreCon component to enable connectivity from the managed code application development station. (Chapter 16 provides more coverage on CoreCon connectivity.)

6. From the managed code application development station, configure the VS2008 IDE's device properties with the target device's IP address, and establish connectivity to the target device.

7. With CoreCon connectivity established, deploy the managed code application to the target device for testing and debug.

These are really just the steps to deploy and debug a managed code application for a Compact 7 device. You can implement some of the steps in different sequences.

The .NET CF environment provides a rich set of Windows form components, database, file system, networking, multimedia, and other system resources in an easy-to-use format to help you rapidly develop a high-quality Compact 7 application in record time. If you are new to .NET CF and managed code application development, it's well worth your time to take a closer look. To learn more, pick up a book about .NET CF and visit the .NET CF portal at `http://msdn.microsoft.com/en-us/library/cc656764(v=VS.90).aspx`.

.NET CF APPLICATION CONSIDERATIONS

A Compact 7 device is typically built based on a resources constrained design specification to keep the cost low with just the sufficient processing, memory, and storage resources to serve the intended purpose. The .NET CF library is a miniature version of the .NET Framework from the desktop Windows OS, with some of the features and function removed and optimized to support resource-constrained devices. When developing a Compact 7 application, you need to be aware of the Compact 7 device's limited resources and nonstandard system architecture, compared to the desktop PC.

Similarity to Windows Phone 7

Although many similarities exist between the OS and .NET CF environment for the Windows Phone 7 and a custom designed Compact 7 device, they are not the same. Some of the Windows Phone features are unique to the Windows Phone platform and not available to Compact 7. For example, although Silverlight for Windows Phone 7 supports managed code, Silverlight for Windows Embedded is based on native code.

For .NET CF development, whether you develop a .NET CF application for Windows Phone or a customized Compact 7 device, the general programming principles and practices are the same.

As Windows Phone is gaining market share and momentum, there are more .NET CF application information resources related to the Windows Phone and Windows Mobile platform than the Compact 7 platform, which you can use and apply to the .NET CF development for the Compact 7 platform.

.NET Compact Framework Garbage Collector

One of the .NET CF's key advantages, the garbage collector, is designed to automatically clean up and release system resources no longer required by the application. Although the garbage collector is an advantage for the managed code development environment, it's one of the causes for a Compact 7 device to lose its hard real-time behavior. When the .NET CF garbage collector springs into action, it prevents the Compact 7 OS from responding to system events within the acceptable time delay to meet the hard real-time system requirements.

Platform Invoke (P/Invoke)

Often, an application for an embedded device involves interacting with the hardware and system resource that requires Win32 APIs, which are not directly accessible from the managed code environment. To access these hardware and system resources, you need to use P/Invoke to call unmanaged Win32 APIs from the managed code.

Separate Thread for Event Handler and GUI

When using .NET CF to develop applications involving event handling from an I/O peripheral, the code for the peripherals' event handler run on a separate thread from the application's GUI thread. To update the display data on the GUI to reflect up-to-date information from the peripheral, you need to use a delegate to invoke the GUI thread from the peripheral's event handler thread to update the displayed data.

Differences from the Full .NET Framework

As a subset to the .NET Framework, .NET CF contains only a fraction of the features from the full .NET Framework. Following are some of the differences between .NET CF and .NET Framework:

➤ Not all the class libraries from the .NET Framework are available in .NET CF.

➤ A Compact 7 device's file system is different from the desktop Windows OS. As the result, filenames and paths handling are different with a Compact 7 device. The `GetCurrentDirectory` and `SetCurrentDirectory` methods are not supported in .NET CF.

➤ Not all the Reflection features is supported in .NET CF.

➤ Remoting is not supported in .NET CF.

➤ Not all the Serialization features from the .NET Framework are supported.

➤ Not all the Socket features from the .NET Framework are supported.

The preceding list includes just some of the differences between the .NET CF and the full .NET Framework. The following URL on MSDN provides more detailed information about the differences between the .NET CF and .NET Framework: `http://msdn.microsoft.com/en-us/library/2weec7k5(v=VS.90).aspx`.

To learn more about supported members of the .NET CF in the class library, visit the following URL on MSDN at:

`http://msdn.microsoft.com/en-us/library/ms172548(v=VS.90).aspx`.

SUMMARY

.NET Compact Framework is a subset of the .NET Framework, designed to support the resource-constrained Windows Phone and mobile and Compact 7 devices. The .NET CF class libraries contain some of the same class libraries from the .NET Framework with some libraries developed specifically to support mobile and Windows Embedded Compact devices.

Combining .NET Compact Framework, VS2008, and Windows Embedded Compact 7, you have an effective and developer-friendly environment to rapidly create smart, connected, and service-oriented applications to support a new generation of embedded devices based on the Windows Embedded Compact 7 OS.

16

CoreCon Connectivity

WHAT'S IN THIS CHAPTER?

➤ Implementing CoreCon connectivity to support VS2008
   application development

You can use CoreCon to establish connectivity between the Visual Studio 2008 IDE and
Windows Embedded Compact 7 device to deploy an application for testing and debugging.
With CoreCon connectivity established, you can deploy applications directly from the VS2008
IDE to a Compact 7 device for testing and debugging, with the facility to halt the program
and step through the application codes line by line, as it executes on the device. This chapter
provides information about CoreCon and required components and steps to implement
CoreCon to support Compact 7 application development from the VS2008 IDE.

IMPLEMENTING CORECON FOR APPLICATION DEVELOPMENT

To implement CoreCon to support VS2008 application development for Compact 7, the
required CoreCon files need to be accessible within the Compact 7 target device's file system.
There are multiple methods to accomplish this, with varying complexities.

The CoreCon for Compact 7 component, from the CoreCon4CE project on the Codeplex
site, provides a simple method to include CoreCon to the OS design. With the CoreCon for
Compact 7 component installed in the Platform Builder component catalog, you can simply
select and include this component in the OS design and generate an OS run-time image with
the required CoreCon files included.

Although using the CoreCon4CE component from the Codeplex site greatly simplifies the process,
it keeps you from knowing the details. The manual process (the hard way) provides the best
information to show the required components and steps to implement CoreCon connectivity on a
Compact 7 target device. This chapter covers the following three methods:

➤ After a Compact 7 OS run-time image is deployed onto the target device, manually copy the required CoreCon files to the Compact 7 target device's file system, and launch CoreCon from the target device.

➤ Edit the OS design project's OSDESIGN.BIB file to include the required CoreCon files.

➤ Select and include the CoreCon_v200_Compact7 component from the Platform Builder to the OS design. This is the CoreCon4CE component.

Required CoreCon Files

The required CoreCon files are installed in the development station as part of the Visual Studio 2008 installation. On a development station with a 32-bit OS, you can find these CoreCon files in the following directory:

```
\Program Files\Common Files\Microsoft Shared\CoreCon\1.0\Target\WCE400\
```

On a development station with a 64-bit OS, you can find these CoreCon files in the following directory:

```
\Program Files (x86)\Common Files\Microsoft Shared\CoreCon\1.0\Target\WCE400\
```

Multiple subfolders are under the preceding directory. Each of these folders contains a set of CoreCon files to support one particular family of processor corresponding to the folder name. For example, the CoreCon files to support an x86 processor, on a development station with a 32-bit OS, are in the following folder:

```
\Program Files\Common Files\Microsoft Shared\CoreCon\1.0\Target\WCE400\x86
```

Copy CoreCon Files to Compact 7 Device's File System

Now that you know where to find the required CoreCon files, you can manually place these files in a location accessible from the Compact 7 target device's file system. You can copy the required files to the device's local storage or shared storage accessible from the device.

By configuring the OS design with USB mass storage support, you can generate an OS run-time image for the target device with support to access portable USB flash storage, and use an USB flash storage as the transport mechanism to copy CoreCon files to the device's local storage.

Using an x86 target device as an example, the following CoreCon files need to be accessible from the device's file system:

➤ Clientshutdown.exe

➤ CMAccept.exe

➤ ConmanClient2.exe

➤ DeviceAgentTransport.dll

➤ EDbgTL.dll

➤ TcpConnectionA.dll

After you copy these files to the target device's file system, or make them accessible from the device's file system, you need to launch the following CoreCon executables in sequence, from the target device, to enable the device to accept a connection from the development station:

1. `ConmanClient2.exe`

2. `CMAccept.exe`

When you launch either one of the two preceding executables on the target device, neither one of them trigger a display to indicate it has been launched. The only indication you can see is a file with a cryptic file name created in the same folder after you launched the `ConmanClient2.exe` executable.

When the `CMAccept.exe` executable is launched, it temporarily disables the target device's security to enable the development station to establish connection to the device. After launching, you have approximately 3 minutes to establish the connection. If you fail to establish the connection within this time frame, you need to launch `CMAccept.exe` again to make an additional connection attempt.

You don't need to launch the `CMAccept.exe` executable when the OS run-time image is generated with the following registry entries included:

Available for download on Wrox.com

```
[HKEY_LOCAL_MACHINE\System]
    "CoreConOverrideSecurity"=dword:1
```

Code snippet is from Chapter16_Snippet.txt

The above registry disables the Compact 7 device's security to enable the VS2008 development station to connect to the device and should not be included in a device intended for distribution.

Edit OSDesign.BIB to Include CoreCon Files in the OS Image

Another method to enable the target device to access the required CoreCon files is to include these files as part of the OS run-time image. To accomplish this, you need to add the following entries to the OS design project's `OSDESIGN.BIB` file:

Available for download on Wrox.com

```
; To make the entry easy to read, a directory variable is used.
;
; _CORECON = \Program Files\Common Files\Microsoft Shared_
;                    \CoreCon\1.0\Target\WCE400\x86
;

FILES
; ------------------------------------------------------------------
Clientshutdown.exe          $(_CORECON)\clientshutdown.exe          NK
CMAccept.exe                $(_CORECON)\CMAccept.exe                NK
ConmanClient2.exe           $(_CORECON)\ConmanClient2.exe           NK
DeviceAgentTransport.dll    $(_CORECON)\DeviceAgentTransport.dll    NK
eDbgTL.dll                  $(_CORECON)\eDbgTL.dll                  NK
TcpConnectionA.dll          $(_CORECON)\TcpConnectionA.dll          NK
```

Code snippet is from Chapter16_Snippet.txt

The OSDESIGN.BIB file, a Binary Image Builder file, contains the entries to instruct the build system to include designated files to the OS run-time image. The _CORECON variable is used for this book to keep each entry within one line to make it easier to read. An incorrect entry can cause the build system to not locate the file and to not complete the build.

The preceding code snippet, with a correct path to the CoreCon files, is provided for this chapter as part of the source code for this book.

To add the previous entries to the OS design project's OSDESIGN.BIB file, from the VS2008 Solution Explorer tab, under the Parameter Files folder, double-click OSDESIGN.BIB to open the file in the code editing window, as shown in Figure 16-1. (Make sure to substitute the _CORECON variable with the correct path to the files.)

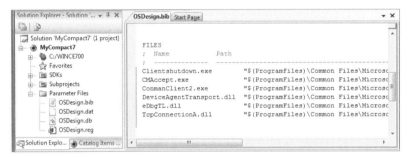

FIGURE 16-1

With the previous entries added to the OS design project's OSDESIGN.BIB file, the project can generate an OS run-time image with the required files to support CoreCon connectivity between the development station and target device, to support VS2008 application development.

After the OS run-time image is generated and deployed to the target device, you need to launch the following CoreCon executable, from the target device, to enable the device to accept connectivity from the development station:

1. ConmanClient2.exe

2. CMAccept.exe

Using a Third-Party CoreCon Component

A simple method to include the required CoreCon files to the OS run-time image is to use the CoreCon4CE component from the Codeplex site. You can download and install this component to the development station from the following site:

http://corecon4ce.codeplex.com

After you install the CoreCon4CE component, it appears on the Platform Builder's component catalog as CoreCon_v200_Compact7. To include the required CoreCon files in the OS run-time image, simply select and include the CoreCon_v200_Compact7 component in the OS design project, as shown in Figure 16-2.

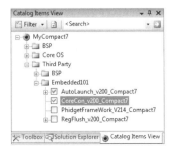

FIGURE 16-2

The CoreCon_v200_Compact7 component contains the necessary BIB file entries and settings to configure the OS design to include the required CoreCon files in the final OS run-time image. In addition, the CoreCon_v200_Compact7 component adds the following registry entries to the OS design:

Available for download on Wrox.com

```
[HKEY_LOCAL_MACHINE\System]
    "CoreConOverrideSecurity"=dword:1
```

Code snippet is from Chapter16_Snippet.txt

To configure the OS run-time image to automatically launch the required CoreCon executable when the OS starts, you can add the AutoLaunch4CE component from the Codeplex site to the OS design. You can download the AutoLaunch4CE component from the following Codeplex project:

```
http://autolaunch4ce.codeplex.com
```

After the AutoLaunch4CE component is installed, it shows up on the Platform Builder's component catalog as AutoLaunch_v200_Compact7. Select and include the AutoLaunch_v200_Compact7 component to the OS design. In addition, you need to add the following registry entries to the OS design's OSDESIGN.REG file to configure the AutoLaunch component to launch the required CoreCon executable during startup:

Available for download on Wrox.com

```
[HKEY_LOCAL_MACHINE\Startup]
    "Process0"="ConmanClient2.exe"
    "Process0Delay"=dword:00002710
```

Code snippet is from Chapter16_Snippet.txt

To add the preceding registry entries to the OS design project's OSDESIGN.REG file, from the VS2008 Solution Explorer tab, under the Parameter Files folder, click OSDESIGN.REG to open the file in the code editing window. From the code editing window's lower-left pane, click Source to view and edit the file in source format, as shown in Figure 16-3.

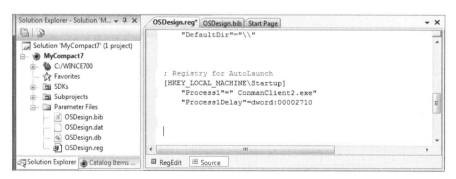

FIGURE 16-3

With CoreCon_v200_Compact7 and AutoLaunch_v200_Compact7 components added to the OS design, and the previous registry entries, the resulting OS run-time image from this OS design project can automatically launch the CoreCon executable during startup.

CONNECTING TO A TARGET DEVICE WITH CORECON

The previous section shows the steps and files needed to prepare and enable a Compact 7 target device to accept a CoreCon connection from the development station. With the Compact 7 target device able to access the required CoreCon files and launch the necessary CoreCon executable, you can initiate a CoreCon connection from the development station to the target device. For the connection to take place, both the development station and target device must be attached to the same Local Area Network and assigned with IP addresses for the same subnet.

A CoreCon connection to support VS2008 application development can be established only within an active VS2008 smart device application project. With a smart device application project open, from the VS2008 IDE, click the Device Options icon, as shown in Figure 16-4, to bring up the Options screen, as shown in Figure 16-5.

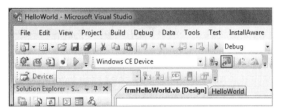

FIGURE 16-4

 Instead of clicking the Device Options button, you can bring up the Options screen from the VS2008 Tools menu. From the VS2008 Tools menu, click Options.

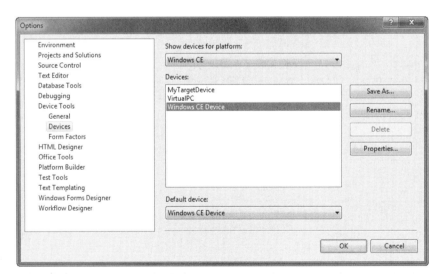

FIGURE 16-5

From the Options screen's left pane, expand the Device Tools node, and click Devices. From the right, select the device associated with the current active application project from the list, and click Properties to bring up the Windows CE Device Properties screen, as shown in Figure 16-6.

From the Windows CE Device Properties screen, click Configure to bring up the Configure TCP/IP Transport screen, as shown in Figure 16-7.

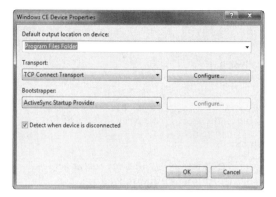

FIGURE 16-7

FIGURE 16-6

From the Configure TCP/IP Transport screen, select the Use Specific IP Address option, enter the target device's IP address, and click OK to close the screen.

 To get the target device's IP address, from the Compact 7 desktop's task bar, double-click the Network icon on the right to bring up the network information screen.

Click OK to close the device properties screen and options screen.

At this point, you can click the Connect to Device icon to connect to the target device, as shown in Figure 16-8.

FIGURE 16-8

 Instead of clicking the Connect to Device icon, you can initiate the connection from the VS2008 Tools menu. From the VS2008 Tools menu, click Connect to Device to bring up the Connect to Device screen; select the device, and click the Connect button.

If everything is properly configured, the Connecting screen shows the Connection Succeeded message, as shown in Figure 16-9.

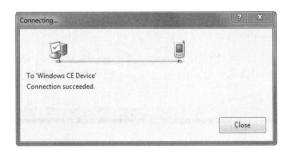

With the CoreCon connection established, you can deploy a VS2008 application to the target device. If the VS2008 IDE fails to establish connection to the target device, check the following:

FIGURE 16-9

➤ Make sure all the CoreCon files are accessible from the target device's file system.

➤ Make sure the `ConmanClient2.exe` executable launched.

➤ Make sure the `CMAccept.exe` executable launched.

   If the CoreCon files are included as part of the Compact 7 OS run-time image and configured to launch during startup, make sure the following registry entries are included as part of the OS.

Available for download on Wrox.com

```
[HKEY_LOCAL_MACHINE\System]
    "CoreConOverrideSecurity"=dword:1
```

Code snippet is from Chapter16_Snippet.txt

➤ Make sure both the development station and target device are attached to the same Local Area Network.

➤ Make sure both the development station and target device are assigned IP addresses within the same subnet.

SUMMARY

To take full advantage of the VS2008 and Compact 7 development environment, to enable you to establish an efficient environment to rapidly develop Compact 7 smart device applications, you need to be comfortable with setting up CoreCon connectivity between the development station and target device.

With CoreCon connectivity established between the VS2008 application development station and Compact 7 target device, you can deploy VS2008 applications from the VS2008 IDE to the target device for testing and debugging.

17

Visual Studio Native Code Application Example

WHAT'S IN THIS CHAPTER?

➤ Developing a native smart device application for a Compact 7 device

➤ Debugging a native smart device application on a Compact 7 device

A Windows Embedded Compact application in native code is preferred when performance is important, especially for an application that requires real-time behavior. From the VS2008 IDE, you can develop a native code application for a Compact 7 device using an Active Template Library (ATL), a Microsoft Foundation Class (MFC), or a Win32 library.

A native code binary executable is compiled with CPU instructions specific to the designated processor and cannot execute on a different type of processor. A native application compiled to run on an ARM processor-based device cannot run on an x86 processor-based device.

This chapter works through the exercises showing the steps to develop a Win32 native code application for Compact 7 using Visual C++ from the Visual Studio 2008 IDE and deploys the application to a Compact 7 target device for testing and debugging.

PREREQUISITES AND PREPARATION

To complete the native code application exercise in this chapter, you need to have the following:

➤ A Compact 7 OS run-time image, generated from MyCompact7 OS design from Chapter 7, "OS Design," launched on a target device with the following components:

➤ CAB File Installer/Uninstaller

➤ CoreCon_v200_Compact7

➤ AutoLaunch_v200_Compact7

➤ The Compact 7 OS run-time image configured with the following registry to launch a CoreCon executable during startup:

```
[HKEY_LOCAL_MACHINE\Startup]
    "Process0"="ConmanClient2.exe"
    "Process0Delay"=dword:00002710
```

➤ Installed MyCompact7_SDK, generated from a MyCompact7 OS design in Chapter 7, to the development station.

➤ Both the development station and target device attached to the same Local Area Network, with DHCP service to provide IP addresses dynamically. Or the development station and target device are configured with different IP addresses within the same subnet.

DEVELOP A NATIVE CODE APPLICATION FOR COMPACT 7

With the prerequisites and preparations out of the way, developing a native code application from the VS2008 IDE is straightforward. When you create a new project from the VS2008 IDE, it automatically launches a New Project Wizard to step through the new project creation process and provides different project templates and options for you to choose from to create the initial workspace for the project.

Creating a Win32 Smart Device Application Project

The exercise in this section creates a Win32 smart device application project. Work through the following steps to create the Win32 smart device application project:

1. From the VS2008 IDE File menu, select New, and click Project to bring up the New Project Wizard screen, as shown in Figure 17-1.

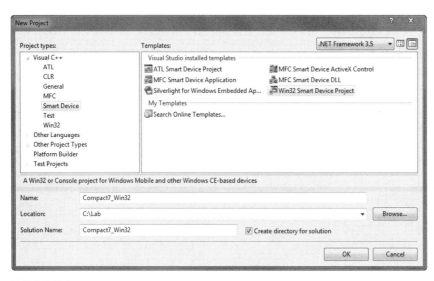

FIGURE 17-1

2. From the left pane, expand the Visual C++ node, and select Smart Device.

3. From the right pane, select Win32 Smart Device Project.

4. Enter `Compact7_Win32` as the project name, and click OK to bring up the Win32 Smart Device Project Wizard screen.

5. From the Win32 Smart Device Project Wizard screen, click Next to bring up the Platforms selection screen, as shown in Figure 17-2.

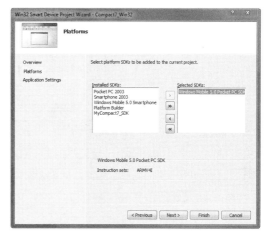

FIGURE 17-2

6. The Windows Mobile 5.0 Pocket PC SDK is selected by default. You need to remove this SDK and add MyCompact7_SDK as the selected SDK. From the Selected SDK's pane, select the Windows Mobile 5.0 Pocket PC SDK, and click the single left-pointing arrow to remove this SDK.

7. From the Installed SDKs pane on the left, select MyCompact7_SDK, and click the right-pointing arrow to add MyCompact7_SDK to the Selected SDKs pane, as shown in Figure 17-3.

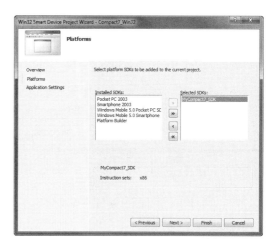

8. Click Next to bring up the Project Settings screen.

FIGURE 17-3

9. Keep the default project setting, and click Finish to complete the New Project Wizard steps. At this point, the wizard creates the project workspace with an initial set of project files. From the project's Solution Explorer tab, you can see the initial set of project files, as shown in Figure 17-4.

Add Code to a Win32 Smart Device Application

With the Win32 smart device native code application project created in the previous section, the exercise in this section adds some code

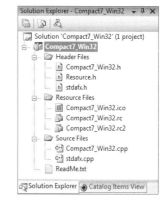

FIGURE 17-4

to the application project. Continue from the exercise in the previous section and work through the following steps to add code to the project:

10. From the Solution Explorer tab, in the Source Files folder, double-click the `Compact7_Win32` `.cpp` file to open this file for editing in the code editor window, as shown in Figure 17-5.

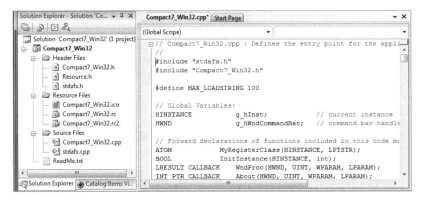

FIGURE 17-5

11. From the code editor window, locate the following block of code:

```
case WM_PAINT:
hdc = BeginPaint(hWnd, &ps);

// TODO: Add any drawing code here...

    EndPaint(hWnd, &ps);
    break;
```

12. Replace the preceding codes with the following code:

Available for
download on
Wrox.com

```
case WM_PAINT:
    // Codes added for Chapter-17
    RECT rect;
    GetClientRect (hWnd, &rect);
    hdc = BeginPaint(hWnd, &ps);
        DrawText(hdc, TEXT("Compact 7 Win32 Native Application!"),-1,
        &rect, DT_CENTER|DT_VCENTER|DT_SINGLELINE);
    EndPaint(hWnd, &ps);
    break;
```

Code snippet is from Chapter17_Snippet.txt

13. From the VS2008 Build menu, click Build Solution to build the project and generate the executable binary, `Compact7_Win32.exe`.

Connecting to a Target Device

With the binary executable generated for the Win32 smart device application project, you can work through the exercise in this section to deploy the application to the target device.

To work through the exercise in this section, a Compact 7 OS run-time image needs to be launched on the target device. The Compact 7 target device needs to access the required CoreCon files and launch the necessary CoreCon executable to enable the device to accept the connection from the development station.

Work through the following steps to connect the development station to the target device:

14. With the Compact7_Win32 application project open, from the VS2008 Tools menu, click Options to bring up the Options screen.

15. From the Options screen's left pane, expand the Device Tools node, and click Devices to bring up the device configuration screen, as shown in Figure 17-6.

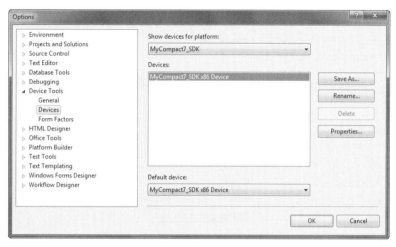

FIGURE 17-6

16. If MyCompact7_SDK x86 Device is not already selected, select this device, and click Properties to bring up the MyCompact7_SDK x86 Device Properties screen, as shown in Figure 17-7.

17. From the MyCompact7_SDK x86 Device Properties screen, click Configure to bring up the Configure TCP/IP Transport screen, as shown in Figure 17-8.

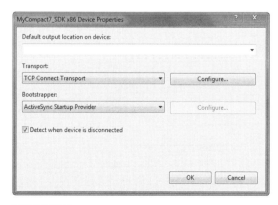

FIGURE 17-7

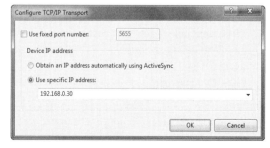

FIGURE 17-8

18. Select the Use Specific IP Address option, and enter the target device's IP address. Then, click OK to close the screen.

19. Click OK to close the MyCompact7_ SDK x86 Device Properties screen.

20. From the Options screen, click OK to close this screen.

21. From the VS2008 Tools menu, click Connect to Device to bring up the Connect to Device screen, as shown in Figure 17-9.

22. If the MyCompact7_SDK x86 Device is not already selected, select this device, and click Connect to establish the connection and bring up the Connecting screen.

23. Upon a successful connection, the Connecting screen displays the Connection Succeeded message, as shown in Figure 17-10.

After connection to the target device is established, you can click Close to close the Connecting screen.

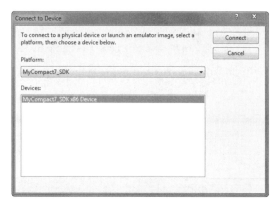

FIGURE 17-9

FIGURE 17-10

Deploy an Application to a Target Device for Testing

With CoreCon connectivity established between the development station and the Compact 7 target device, you can deploy the application directly from the VS2008 IDE to the target device.

From the VS2008 Debug menu, click one of the following options to deploy the application:

> ➤ Start Debugging

> ➤ Start Without Debugging

If you just want to deploy the application to the device to review how the application displays on the screen and its general function and do not intend to debug the application code, you can select the Start Without Debugging option. If you want to deploy the application onto the device to debug the code, select the Start Debugging option.

With both the development station and target device properly configured and connected, the application should deploy on the target device, as shown in Figure 17-11.

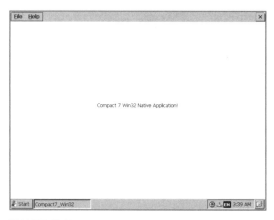

FIGURE 17-11

If the application fails to deploy to the target device, you need to go through the following checklist to figure out what the problem may be:

➤ Are CoreCon files included as part of the Compact 7 OS run-time image, or accessible from the Compact 7 target device's file system?

➤ Is the required CoreCon executable launched on the Compact 7 target device?

➤ Is the Compact 7 OS run-time image generated with the necessary registry to disable security to enable the development station to connect? Or is the CMAccept.exe executable launched to temporarily disable security to enable the development station to connect?

➤ If the CMAccept.exe executable is launched to temporarily disable security, did you attempt to connect before the time out?

➤ Are both the development station and target device attached to the same Local Area Network?

➤ Are the IP addresses assigned to the development station and target device within the same subnet?

To resolve CoreCon connection issues, read through Chapter 16, "CoreCon Connectivity," to better understand the requirements to establish CoreCon connectivity.

Debugging a Win32 Smart Device Application

The previous sections covered the steps to develop a Win32 smart device application, establish CoreCon connection to the target device, and deploy the application to the device.

As part of the development process, you are expected to encounter bugs in your code. You need to figure out an effective method to debug the code. This section provides information showing the debug message function you can inject in the application project to help with debugging.

Continue with the Win32 smart device application project already created, and work through the following steps to inject debugging function:

1. If the Win32 smart device application is still running on the target device, close the application from the device. With the Win32 smart device application project open, from the VS2008 Solution Explorer tab, double-click the Compact7_Win32.cpp file, in the Source Files folder, to open this file in the code editor window.

2. From the code editor window, locate the following block of code:

```
case IDM_HELP_ABOUT:
    DialogBox(g_hInst, (LPCTSTR)IDD_ABOUTBOX, hWnd, About);
    break;
```

3. Replace the preceding block of code with the following code to add a function to the output debug message before the DialogBox() function and another function to the output debug message after the DialogBox() function:

```
case IDM_HELP_ABOUT:
    //  Code added for Chapter-17

    //  Inject debug message Before the About message box is launched
```

```
OutputDebugString(L"Debug msg Before About msg box launch…..\n");

DialogBox(g_hInst, (LPCTSTR)IDD_ABOUTBOX, hWnd, About);

// Inject debug message After the About message box is closed
OutputDebugString(L"Debug msg After About msg box closed…..\n");
break;
```

Code snippet is from Chapter17_Snippet.txt

4. From the VS2008 Build menu, click Build Solution to build the project.

5. If you are continuing from the previous section, with CoreCon connection already established, you can skip to step 7.

6. Follow the earlier steps, in the "Connecting to a Target Device" section, to establish connection to the target device.

7. From the VS2008 Debug menu, click Start Debugging to deploy the application to the target device.

The application should deploy and launch on the target device just like the earlier step (refer to Figure 17-11).

Debug Messages from VS2008 IDE

As the application deploys and launches on the target device, the Output tab from the VS2008 IDE displays some messages showing the `Compact7_Win32.exe` executable is loading along with other DLLs, as shown in Figure 17-12.

FIGURE 17-12

In the earlier step, two instances of the `OutputDebugString()` function were added, one before and one after the `DialogBox()` function. The `DialogBox()` function in the project is designated to show the application's About message box. To trigger these two instances of the `OutputDebugString()` function, from the Compact7_Win32 application's Help menu, click About.

As the About message box is shown on the target device, the following debug message displays on the VS2008 Output tab:

```
Debug msg Before About msg box launch…
```

From the target device's About message box, click OK to close the About message box. After the About message box is closed on the target device, the following debug message appears on the VS2008 Output tab:

```
Debug msg After About msg box closed...
```

From the target device's File menu, click Exit to close the application. As the application is closed on the target device, an additional debug message displays on the VS2008 Output tab, as shown in Figure 17-13.

FIGURE 17-13

 If you are not able to see the debug messages display on the VS2008 Output tab, check to ensure the Debug option is selected for the "Show output from" combo box.

Set Breakpoint to Halt an Application

The VS2008 and Compact 7 development environment, when properly configured, can set a breakpoint to halt application execution as the application runs on the target device.

Continuing from the previous exercise, work through the following steps to set a breakpoint to halt the application execution:

1. From the VS2008 Debug menu, click Start Debugging to launch the application to the target device.

2. From the VS2008 Solution Explorer tab, double-click the `Compact7_Win32.cpp` file, in the Source Files folder, to open this file in the code editor window.

3. From the VS2008 code editor window, locate the following block of code:

```
case IDM_HELP_ABOUT:
    // Code added for Chapter-17

    // Inject debug message Before the About message box is launched
```

```
OutputDebugString(L"Debug msg Before About msg box launch…..\n");

DialogBox(g_hInst, (LPCTSTR)IDD_ABOUTBOX, hWnd, About);

//  Inject debug message After the About message box is closed
OutputDebugString(L"Debug msg After About msg box closed…..\n");
break;
```

4. From the VS2008 code editor window, place the mouse point over each of the
`OutputDebugString ()` functions, right-clicking your mouse; then select Breakpoint, and
click Insert Breakpoint, as shown in Figure 17-14.

FIGURE 17-14

5. After the breakpoints are set, the code editor window should look similar to Figure 17-15.

FIGURE 17-15

6. To trigger the breakpoint and halt the application execution, from the Compact7_Win32 application's Help menu, as it runs on the target device, click About.

7. At this point the Compact7_Win32 application on the target device halts. On the VS2008 code editor window, a yellow right-pointing arrow now displays on one of the breakpoints, as shown in Figure 17-16.

```
(Global Scope)                              ▼ ●WndProc(HWND hWnd, UINT message, WPARAM wF ▼
    switch (wmId)
    {
        case IDM_HELP_ABOUT:
            //  Codes added for Chapter-17

            //  Inject debug message Before the About message box is launched
            OutputDebugString(L"Debug msg Before About msg box launch.....\n");

            DialogBox(g_hInst, (LPCTSTR)IDD_ABOUTBOX, hWnd, About);

            //  Inject debug message After the About message box is closed
            OutputDebugString(L"Debug msg After About msg box closed.....\n");
            break;
        case IDM_FILE_EXIT:
            DestroyWindow(hWnd);
```

FIGURE 17-16

8. From the VS2008 IDE, you can press F10 to step to the next line of code, the `DialogBox` `()` function.

9. As you press F10 again to execute the `DialogBox` `()` function, the About message box displays on the target device.

10. From the target device's About message box, click OK to close. As the About message box closes, execution halts again on the next line of code.

11. You can right-click the mouse on the line of code with the breakpoint set to disable or delete the breakpoint and press F5 from the VS2008 IDE to resume program execution on the target device.

With a Win32 smart device application launched from the VS2008 IDE to a Compact 7 device with CoreCon connectivity, you can inject, delete, and disable breakpoints, as the application runs on the target device, without the need to redeploy the application.

SUMMARY

To develop an application for a Windows Embedded Compact 7 device that requires real-time behavior and needs to interact with low-level system resources efficiently, you need to develop the application in native code.

The Visual Studio 2008 IDE and the development resources available as part of the Platform Builder for Compact 7 software suite provide an effective environment to develop a native code application and deploy the application directly to the target device from the IDE, and the facility for you to debug the application as it executes on the target device.

18

Managed Code Application Example

WHAT'S IN THIS CHAPTER?

➤ Developing a managed code application for Compact 7 device

➤ Debugging a managed code application for Compact 7 device

Visual Studio 2008 provides a developer-friendly and efficient environment to develop a managed code application for a Windows Embedded Compact 7 device.

As part of the provided development resources, whether you work with C# or Visual Basic, the VS2008 IDE includes a large collection of controls to support managed code application development. You can use these managed code resources like Lego building blocks and simply drop multiple controls onto a Windows form to include the controls' functions as part of your Compact 7 application.

In addition to the managed code development resources provided as part of the VS2008 IDE, a large pool of managed code development resources is available from third-party companies and community projects.

This chapter works through the exercises, showing the steps to develop a managed code application using C# from the Visual Studio 2008 IDE and deploy the application to a Windows Embedded Compact 7 target device for testing and debugging.

PREREQUISITES AND PREPARATION

To complete the managed code application exercise in this chapter, you need to have the following:

➤ A Compact 7 OS run-time image, generated from the MyCompact7 OS design created as part of the exercise in Chapter 7, "OS Design," launched on a target device with the following components:

> ➤ CAB File Installer/Uninstaller

> ➤ .NET Compact Framework 3.5

> ➤ OS Dependencies for .NET Compact Framework 3.5

> ➤ CoreCon_v200_Compact7

> ➤ AutoLaunch_v200_Compact7

➤ The Compact 7 OS run-time image configured with the following registry to launch the CoreCon executable during startup:

```
[HKEY_LOCAL_MACHINE\Startup]
  "Process0"="ConmanClient2.exe"
  "Process0Delay"=dword:00002710
```

➤ Installed MyCompact7_SDK, generated from a MyCompact7 OS design in Chapter 7 to the development station.

➤ Both the development station and target device attached to the same Local Area Network, with DHCP service to provide an IP address dynamically. Or configure the development station and target device each with different IP addresses within the same subnet.

DEVELOPING A MANAGED CODE APPLICATION FOR COMPACT 7

The Visual Studio 2008 development environment is an efficient and effective environment to rapidly develop a managed code application for an embedded device with a graphical user interface (GUI) to help the end user interact with the device and other systems controlled by the device. This development environment abstracts the lower-level complicated code from the developer and provides a developer-friendly environment.

To develop a Compact 7 managed code application with a GUI from the VS2008 IDE is straightforward. Following is a list of the typical tasks to develop a managed code smart device application for a Compact 7 device:

1. Create a managed code smart device application project, in C# or Visual Basic, from the VS2008 IDE.

2. Adjust the Windows form's size and orientation for the application.

3. Write code to initialize the Windows form.

4. Select and place one or more controls, with functions to support the application, onto the Windows form.

5. Add code to initialize each control and set each control's properties.

6. Write code to each control's event handler.

7. Write more code…

8. Compile the project and deploy the compiled executable to the target device for testing and debugging.

The Compact 7 managed code application development environment provides a predictable and manageable development environment.

Creating a Managed Code Smart Device Application Project

The exercise in this section creates a managed code smart device application project using C#.

> *The process to develop, deploy, and debug a managed code smart device application for a Compact 7 device using Visual Basic is similar to C#.*
>
> *A simple Visual Basic serial port application project, VB2008_SerialPortApplication, is included as part of the code for this chapter.*

Work through the following steps to create a VS2008 managed code smart device application project:

1. From the VS2008 IDE File menu, select New, and click Project to bring up the New Project Wizard screen, as shown in Figure 18-1.

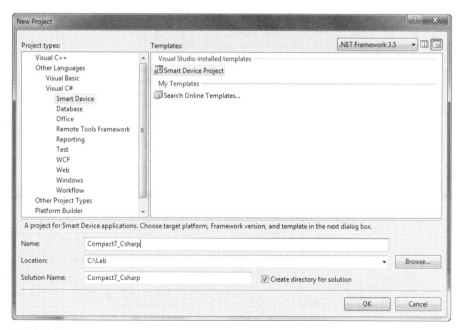

FIGURE 18-1

2. From the left pane, expand the Other Languages node followed by expanding the Visual C# node, and click Smart Device to bring up the Templates pane on the right.

3. From the Templates pane on the right, select Smart Device Project, and enter `Compact7_ Csharp` as the project name; click OK to bring up the Add New Smart Device Project screen, as shown in Figure 18-2.

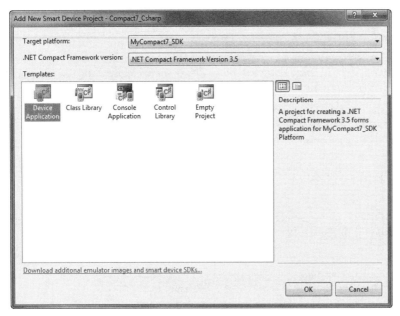

FIGURE 18-2

4. Select MyCompact7_SDK from the Target platform selection.

5. Select .NET Compact Framework Version 3.5 from the .NET Compact Framework version selection.

6. From the Templates pane, select Device Application, and click OK to complete the New Project Wizard steps.

At this point the VS2008 New Project Wizard creates the initial project workspace for the Compact7_Csharp application with an initial set of project files, which you can see in the VS2008 Solution Explorer tab, as shown in Figure 18-3.

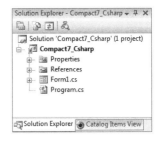

FIGURE 18-3

Add Code to a Managed Code Smart Device Application

With the application project created in the previous section, the exercise in this section adjusts the form and adds controls and codes for the project.

Continue from the exercise in the previous section and work through the following steps to add controls and codes to the project and other modifications:

7. From the Solution Explorer tab, double-click the `Form1.cs` file to bring up Form1 in the design window, with the Properties tab showing properties for Form1, as shown in Figure 18-4.

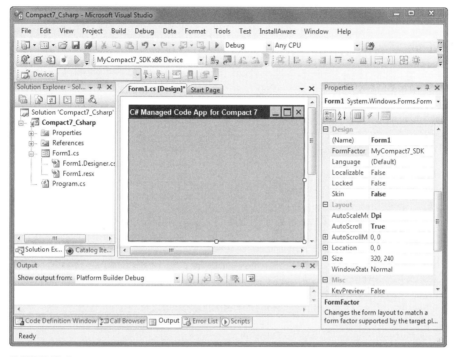

FIGURE 18-4

8. From the Design tab, right-click the mouse on the mainMenu1 control, and click Delete to remove this control from the project.

9. From the Properties tab, change the Text properties from Form1 to C# Managed Code App for Compact 7.

10. From the Properties tab, change the Size properties from the initial size to 320x240 to reduce the Windows form's size.

11. From the VS2008 View menu, click Toolbox to bring up the Toolbox tab, as shown in Figure 18-5. The different control categories are collapsed to show the available type of control, with the Device Components category expanded to show the controls available in this category. Take a tour to view different controls provided by VS2008 to support the managed code application.

FIGURE 18-5

To add a control onto Form1, you can simply double-click the selected control to place the control on the form. After the control is placed on Form1, you can drag and resize the control to the position that you want.

12. From the Toolbox tab, expand the Common Device Controls category, and double-click the Button and TextBox controls to place these two controls onto Form1, as textBox1 and button1.

13. Resize and move the textBox1 and button1 controls to the center of the form, and change the button1 control's caption to Hello World from the button1 control's text property, as shown in Figure 18-6.

FIGURE 18-6

14. To add code to the button1 control's click event, double-click the button1 control to bring up the code editor window, showing the button1 control's event handler codes, as shown in Figure 18-7.

15. Add the following code to the button1_Click () event.

FIGURE 18-7

```
private void button1_Click(object sender, EventArgs e)
{
    textBox1.Text = "1st Hello World message!";
    textBox1.Text = "2nd Hello World message!";
    textBox1.Text = "3rd Hello World message!";
    ;
    textBox1.Text = "Final Hello World message!";
}
```

Code snippet is from Chapter18_Snippet.txt

16. The preceding code will be used to demonstrate the debugging environment provided as part of the VS2008 IDE to support the managed code smart device application development for the Compact 7 device. From the VS2008 Build menu, click Build Solution to build the application.

Connecting to a Target Device

The process and requirements to establish connectivity from the development station to the target device to deploy a VS2008 managed code application is the same as the Visual C++ 2008 native code application. Refer to Chapter 16, "CoreCon Connectivity," and Chapter 17, "Visual Studio Native Code Application Example," to review the screen graphics for the required steps to establish CoreCon connectivity.

Work through the following steps to establish a connection between the development station and target device:

1. With the Compact7_Csharp managed code application project open, from the VS2008 Tools menu, click Options to bring up the Options screen.

2. From the Options screen's left pane, expand the Device Tools node, and click Devices to bring up the Device Configuration screen.

3. If MyCompact7_SDK x86 Device is not already selected, select this device, and click the Properties button to bring up the MyCompact7_SDK x86 Device Properties screen.

4. From the MyCompact7_SDK x86 Device Properties screen, click the Configure button to bring up the Configure TCP/IP Transport screen.

5. Select the Use Specific IP Address option, and enter the target device's IP address. Then, click OK to close the screen.

6. From the MyCompact7_SDK x86 Device Properties screen, click OK to close this screen.

7. From the Options screen, click OK to close this screen.

8. To initiate connection to the target device, from the VS2008 Tools menu, click Connect to Device to bring up the Connect to Device screen.

9. From the Connect to Device screen, if the MyCompact7_SDK x86 Device is not already selected, select this device, and click the Connect button to establish the connection and bring up the Connecting screen.

10. Upon a successful connection, the Connecting screen displays the Connection Succeeded message.

After connection the target device is established, you can click the Close button to close the Connecting screen.

Deploying a Managed Code Smart Device Application to the Target Device

With CoreCon connectivity established between the development station and the Compact 7 target device, you can deploy the Compact7_Csharp application directly from the VS2008 IDE to the target device.

From the VS2008 Debug menu, click one of the following options to deploy the application:

➤ Start Debugging

➤ Start Without Debugging

If you just want to deploy the application to the device to review how the application displays on the screen and its general function and do not intend to debug the application code, you can select the Start Without Debugging option.

If you want to deploy the application onto the device to debug the code, select the Start Debugging option.

Work through the following steps to deploy the Compact7_Csharp application to the target device:

1. From the VS2008 Debug menu, click Start Debugging to bring up the Deploy Compact7_ Csharp screen.

2. From the Deploy Compact7_Csharp screen, select the device associated with the application project, MyCompact7_SDK x86 Device, and click the Deploy button.

3. At this point, the Microsoft Visual Studio screen displays to indicate there are some deployment errors and provides the option for you to choose whether to continue, as shown in Figure 18-8.

4. When you click Yes to continue, the Compact7_Csharp application deploys and launches on the target device, as shown in Figure 18-9.

FIGURE 18-8

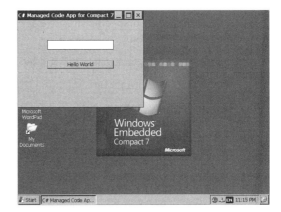

FIGURE 18-9

You can eliminate the error message in step 5 by changing one of the device properties within the Compact7_Csharp managed code smart device application project.

Work through the following steps to change this property:

1. With the Compact7_Csharp project active, from the VS2008 Solution Explorer tab, click to select the Compact7_Csharp managed code application project, under the Solution 'Compact7_Csharp' (1 project) node.

2. From the VS2008 Project menu, click Compact7_Csharp Properties to bring up the Compact7_Csharp properties window, as shown in Figure 18-10.

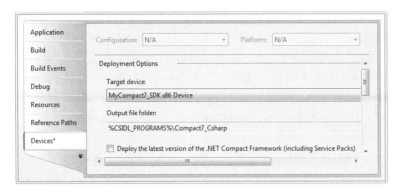

FIGURE 18-10

3. From the Compact7_Csharp properties window, click the Devices tab on the left to show Deployment Options. If the Devices tab does not display, click the small down-pointing arrow, just after the last tab item, to show additional options, and click Devices.

4. From the Deployment Options tab, uncheck the following option:

   ➤ Deploy the Latest Version of the .NET Compact Framework (Including Service Packs)

At this point, you should not encounter an error while deploying the Compact7_Csharp managed code application to the target device.

Debugging a Managed Code Smart Device Application

The previous sections covered the steps to develop a managed code smart device application in C#, establish a CoreCon connection to the target device, and deploy the application to the device.

As part of the development process, you are expected to encounter bugs in your code. You need to figure out an effective method to debug the code. This section provides information showing the debug message function you can inject into the application project to help with debugging.

Continue with the Compact7_Csharp smart device application project already created, and work through the following steps to inject the debugging function:

1. If the Compact7_Csharp smart device application is still running on the target device, close the application from the device.

2. With the Compact7_Csharp application project open, from the VS2008 Solution Explorer tab, double-click the `Form1.cs` file to bring up Form1 in the Design window.

3. From the Design window, double-click the Hello World button to bring up the code editor window, showing the `button1_Click` event handler codes.

4. To use the `Debug.WriteLine ()` function, you need to include the `System.Diagnostics` namespace. Scroll to the beginning of the `Form1.cs` code file, and add the following namespace after the existing namespace:

```
using System.Diagnostics;
```

Code snippet is from Chapter18_Snippet.txt

5. Scroll down to the `button1_Click ()` event handler code section. Add `Debug.WriteLine` function to the existing codes to send the debug message to the VS2008 IDE as follow:

```
private void button1_Click(object sender, EventArgs e)
{
    textBox1.Text = "1st Hello World message!";
    Debug.WriteLine ("1st Hello World message processed.");
    ;
    textBox1.Text = "2nd Hello World message!";
    Debug.WriteLine("2nd Hello World message processed.");
    ;
```

```
        textBox1.Text = "3rd Hello World message!";
        Debug.WriteLine("3rd Hello World message processed.");
        ;
        textBox1.Text = "Final Hello World message!";
        Debug.WriteLine("Final Hello World message processed.");
    }
```

Code snippet is from Chapter18_Snippet.txt

6. From the VS2008 Build menu, click Build Solution to build the application with the modified code.

7. If you continue from the earlier section in this chapter and establish connection from the development station to the target device, from the VS2008 Debug menu, click Start Debugging to deploy the application to the target device. Otherwise, work through the necessary steps to establish connection before deploying the application to the device.

8. From the C# Managed Code App for Compact 7 application screen on the target device, click the Hello World button.

After you click the Hello World button, the text box displays the following message:

```
Final Hello World message!
```

The VS2008 IDE's Output tab displays debug messages from the managed code application running on the target device, showing each of the `Debug.WriteLine ()` function's messages, as shown in Figure 18-11.

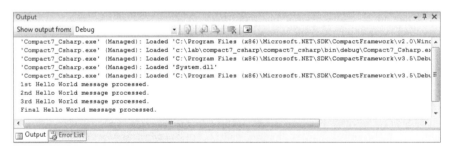

FIGURE 18-11

The debug messages on the VS2008 Output tab indicates all four instances of the `Debug.WriteLine ()` function have been executed.

Before continuing to the next step, it may be better to clear the existing debug messages on the VS2008 Output tab.

9. To set a breakpoint to halt program execution, from the VS2008 code editor window, navigate to the `button1_Click ()` event.

10. Set a breakpoint to halt the program at the following line of code, by right-clicking your mouse on the code; then select Breakpoint and click Insert Breakpoint. After the breakpoint is set, a big red dot appears to the left of the code, as shown in Figure 18-12.

FIGURE 18-12

11. To trigger the application to reach this breakpoint and halt execution, from the Compact7_Csharp application running on the target device, click the Hello World button.

12. After clicking the Hello World button, the text box on the Compact7_Csharp application shows the following:

➤ `1st Hello World message!`

At this point, the Compact7_Csharp application running on the target device halts. On the VS2008 code editor window, the line of code with the breakpoint is highlighted in yellow, as shown in Figure 18-13.

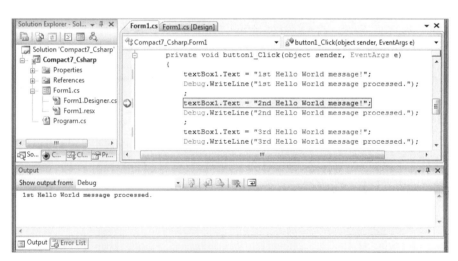

FIGURE 18-13

The Output tab on the VS2008 IDE shows the debug message from the first instance of the `Debug .WriteLine ()` function.

13. From the VS2008 IDE, you can click F11 to step through and execute each line of code, one by one. As you press F11 to step through the code, you can see the text box on the Compact7_Csharp application, running on the target device, displays a different instance of the Hello World message.

With a managed code smart device application launched from the VS2008 IDE to a Compact 7 device with CoreCon connectivity, you can set a breakpoint to halt execution, as the application runs on the target device, without the need to redeploy the application.

During the coding process, you can selectively inject functions to output debug messages and wrap these functions with conditional variables to have more granular control over when and where to trigger these debug messages.

SUMMARY

The Visual Studio 2008 IDE and the development resources available as part of the Platform Builder for Compact 7 software suite provide an effective environment to develop a managed code application, and deploy the application to the target device directly from the IDE and the facility, for you to debug the code as the application executes on the target device.

In addition to the controls and libraries provided as part of the VS2008 software to support a managed code application, there is a large collection of controls and libraries provided by third-party companies and community projects with resources to support just about anything you can think of.

To develop an application with a GUI that involves a database, needs access to the media player, communicates over the Internet, and interacts with other systems that do not require critical real-time performance, the VS2008 managed code environment provides the most efficient and effective environment to rapidly develop an application for a Compact 7 device.

19

Platform Builder Native Code Application Example

WHAT'S IN THIS CHAPTER?

➤ Developing a native code application with Platform Builder

➤ Debugging a Platform Builder subproject native code application

You can develop a Windows Embedded Compact 7 native code application as a VS2008 smart device application project or as a Platform Builder subproject to an OS design project.

As a subproject to the OS design, you can configure a Platform Builder native code application to compile as part of the OS run-time image. The development and debugging environment for a Platform Builder native code project is different from a VS2008 smart device native code project.

This chapter works through the exercises showing the steps to develop a native code application, as a subproject to the OS design, from the Platform Builder IDE, and deploy the application to a Windows Embedded Compact 7 target device for testing and debugging using a virtual machine as the target device.

PREREQUISITES AND PREPARATION

As part of the process to develop a native code application from the Platform Builder IDE, as a subproject to an OS design, the application is compiled as part of the OS run-time image. To support the Platform Builder native code application exercises in this chapter using a Virtual

PC machine (VM) as the target device, you need to create an OS run-time image for the VM. To complete the exercises in this chapter, you need to have the following:

➤ A VM configured with an appropriate bootloader to establish connectivity to the Platform Builder development station and download a Compact 7 OS run-time image.

➤ Both the development station and VM are attached to the same Local Area Network, with DHCP service to provide an IP address dynamically. Or configure the development station and VM each with different IP addresses within the same subnet.

DEVELOPING A VIRTUAL PC OS DESIGN

To support the exercises in this chapter, a VM is used as the target device. An OS design, MyVPC, based on the Virtual PC: x86 BSP, is created.

Work through the following steps to create the OS design project:

1. From the VS2008 File menu, select New, and click Project to launch the New Project screen.

2. From the New Project screen's left pane, select Platform Builder. Select OS Design from the right pane, enter **MyVPC** as the project name, and click OK to bring up the OS Design Wizard.

3. From the OS Design Wizard screen, click Next to bring up the Board Support Packages selection screen.

4. Select the Virtual PC: x86 BSP, and click Next to bring up the Design Templates selection screen.

5. From the Design Templates selection screen's left pane, expand the Enterprise Device folder, select the Industrial Controller template, and click Next to bring up the Application and Media selection screen.

6. From the Application and Media selection screen, click Finish to use the default for the remaining configurations, and complete the OS Design Wizard step.

7. After the OS Design Wizard step, the Catalog Item Notification screen displays to raise a security warning to indicate one or more of the components included in the OS design may pose a security risk. Click Acknowledge to acknowledge the warning, and close the warning screen.

8. At this point the OS Design Wizard creates the initial workspace for the MyVPC OS design project. From the VS2008 IDE, click the Catalog Items View tab, and expand the Virtual PC: x86 node under the BSP folder to select the required BSP components, as shown in Figure 19-1.

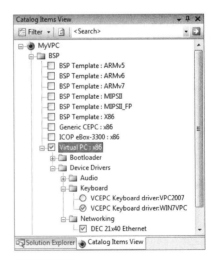

FIGURE 19-1

9. Select DEC 21x40 Ethernet and VCEPC keyboard drivers. If you use Virtual PC 2007, select VCEPC Keyboard driver: VPC2007. If you use Virtual PC on a Windows 7 development station, select VCEPC Keyboard driver: WIN7VPC.

10. At this point, the OS design project is configured to build in release mode with the KITL option enabled. From the VS2008 Build menu, click Build Solution to build the OS design and generate an OS run-time image.

The previous steps created the MyVPC OS design and built and generated a Compact 7 OS run-time image from the OS design, for a VM as the target device.

Using a Virtual PC as the Target Device

To use a VM as the target device, you need to create and configure a VM with the required bootloader to establish connectivity with the Platform Builder IDE to download an OS run-time image generated from the MyVPC OS design in the previous section.

A preconfigured VM and virtual hard drive (VHD) are provided as part of the Virtual PC BSP, which you can use as the target device, in the following directory:

```
$(_PLATFORMROOT)\VirtualPC\VM
```

To download a Compact 7 OS run-time image from the development station to the VM, you need to configure the development station and VM with appropriate network settings. For the exercise in this chapter, the Windows 7 development station and VM are both configured to use a Loopback Network adapter with the following static IP addresses:

➤ The static IP address configured for the Loopback Network adapter on the development station is 192.168.2.201.

➤ The static IP address configured for the Loopback Network adapter on the VM is 192.168.2.232.

The above static IP address configuration is just an example. You can use different IP addresses, as long as both of the addresses are within the same subnet. Instead of static IP, you can configure the development station and VM to use dynamic IPs from the same DHCP server.

You can find more information about using a Virtual PC as Compact 7 target device in Appendix A, "Virtual PC Connectivity."

Establish a Connection to a Virtual Machine

This section works through an exercise to create a target device connectivity profile, MyVM, and associate the MyVM profile with the VM.

Create a Target Device Profile for a VM

Work through the following steps to create a target device connectivity profile for the VM:

1. From the VS2008 Target menu, click Connectivity Options to bring up the Target Device Connectivity Options screen.

2. From the Target Device Connectivity Options screen's left pane, click Add Device to bring up the new device screen.

3. Enter MyVM as the New target device name, and click Add to add the new profile.

4. The default configuration for the newly created MyVM works well for the exercise in this chapter and does not need to be changed. Click Settings, to the right of the Kernel Download selection, to bring up the Ethernet Download Settings screen.

At this point, the Ethernet Download Settings screen is waiting for BOOTME messages from the bootloader launched on a Compact 7 device.

Configure the Virtual Machine

This section works through the steps to configure an IP address for the VM to establish connectivity with the Platform Builder IDE.

Continuing from the steps in the previous section:

5. Launch the virtual machine from the following directory:

```
$(_PLATFORMROOT)\VirtualPC\VM\CEVM.VMC
```

6. As the VM boots, click the spacebar to enter the setup, as shown in Figure 19-2.

7. From the Main Menu, press 2 to bring up the Select Boot Device configuration screen, and press 2 to select DEC21140 as the boot device.

8. Press 4 to bring up the Network Settings configuration screen.

9. Press 5 to bring up an IP address configuration.

10. Enter 192.168.2.232 and press the Enter key.

FIGURE 19-2

11. Press 0 to exit the Network Settings screen and move to the Main Menu.

12. From the Main Menu, press 7 to save settings.

13. Press 0 to exit and continue.

At this point the VM launches the bootloader and starts to broadcast a series of BOOTME messages, as shown in Figure 19-3.

As the Ethernet Download Settings screen detects the BOOTME messages, the VM's device ID is shown in the Active Target Devices list, as shown in Figure 19-4. From the Active Target Devices list, click the device ID. Then, click Apply to close the screen.

FIGURE 19-3

FIGURE 19-4

From the Target Device Connectivity Options screen, the VM device ID, detected on the Ethernet Download Settings screen, displays under the Kernel Download and Kernel Transport options. Click OK to close the screen.

The MyVM target device profile is now set up and associated with the $(_PLATFORMROOT)\ VirtualPC\VM\CEVM.VMC virtual machine.

Download an OS Run-time Image to a Virtual Machine

In the earlier sections, the MyVPC OS design is created and built to generate a Compact 7 OS run-time image. The MyVM target device connectivity profile is created and associated with the VM as the target device. To download an OS run-time image to the VM using the MyVM profile, you need to select MyVM from the VS2008 IDE's Device selection list, as shown in Figure 19-5, for the active OS design project.

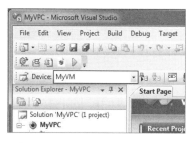

FIGURE 19-5

From the VS2008 Target menu, click Attach Device to bring up the Device Status screen and initiate the download process. At this point, the Platform Builder development station waits for BOOTME messages from the target device to connect and start the download.

From the exercise in the previous section, the bootloader running on the VM continues to broadcast BOOTME messages for about 2 minutes. If the VM is still sending BOOTME messages, the download will begin shortly. Otherwise, you need to restart the VM for it to launch the bootloader and broadcast the BOOTME messages again.

As the Platform Builder development station detects the BOOTME message from the VM target device and starts to download an OS run-time image to the device, the download progress is shown on the Device Status screen and on the VM window.

DEVELOPING A PLATFORM BUILDER NATIVE CODE APPLICATION FOR COMPACT 7

Continuing with the MyVPC OS design project created earlier in this chapter, you can create a native code application project, as a subproject to the MyVPC OS design, and compile the application as part of the OS run-time image.

Creating a Platform Builder Application Subproject

Work through the following steps to create a Platform Builder Win32 native code application as a subproject to the MyVPC OS design:

1. With MyVPC OS design open, from the VS2008 Project menu, click Add New Subproject to bring up the Subproject Wizard screen, as shown in Figure 19-6.

2. From the Available Templates pane, select WCE Application. Enter **PB7_Win32** as the subproject name, and click Next to bring up the Auto-Generated Subproject Files screen, as shown in Figure 19-7.

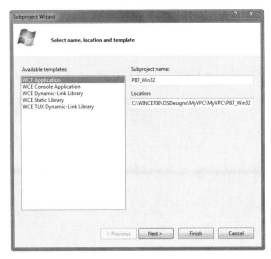

FIGURE 19-6

FIGURE 19-7

3. Select A Typical "Hello World" Application, and click Finish to create the subproject.

At this point, the PB7_Win32 native code application is created as a subproject to the MyVPC OS design. Continue with the following steps to add codes to the subproject.

4. From the VS2008 Solution Explorer tab, expand the Subprojects folder, followed by the PB7_Win32 node and then the Source files folder, as shown in Figure 19-8.

5. Double-click the PB7_Win32.cpp file to open the file in the code editor window. From the code editor window, locate the following block of code:

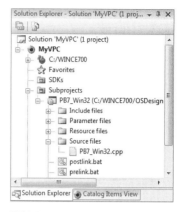

FIGURE 19-8

```
case WM_PAINT:
    hdc = BeginPaint(hWnd, &ps);
    // TODO: Add any drawing code here...
    RECT rt;
    GetClientRect(hWnd, &rt);
    DrawText(hdc, szHello, _tcslen(szHello), &rt, DT_CENTER);
    EndPaint(hWnd, &ps);
    break;
```

6. Replace the preceding block of code with the following code:

Available for download on Wrox.com

```
case WM_PAINT:
    RECT rect;
    GetClientRect (hWnd, &rect);
    hdc = BeginPaint(hWnd, &ps);
    RETAILMSG(1,(TEXT("Retail Msg before hello world….\n")));

    DrawText(hdc, TEXT("PB7_Win32 Hello World!"),-1,
                &rect, DT_CENTER|DT_VCENTER|DT_SINGLELINE);

    RETAILMSG(1,(TEXT("Retail Msg after hello world….\n")));

    EndPaint(hWnd, &ps);
    break;
```

Code snippet is from Chapter19_Snippet.txt

The two RETAILMSG() functions are added to demonstrate the debugging facility.

7. From the VS2008 Build menu, select Advanced Build Commands, and click Build Current BSP and Subprojects (blddemo -qbsp) to build the OS design, including the PB7_Win32 subproject.

Including an Application in the OS Run-time Image

By default, the PB7_Win32.exe executable from the subproject is configured to be compiled and included as part of the OS run-time image. You can view the files that are compiled and included as part of the OS run-time image as follows:

➤ From the VS2008 Solution Explorer tab, right-click your mouse on MyVPC, and click Show Build Image to bring up the nk.bin view window, as shown in Figure 19-9.

FIGURE 19-9

➤ From the nk.bin view window's left pane, expand the NK node, and select the (All files) folder to show the files included as part of the image, and locate the PB7_Win32.exe file on the right pane.

Downloading an OS Run-time Image to a Virtual PC

Following the steps from the earlier section, download the OS run-time image to the VM. When the OS run-time image launches on the VM, it does not do anything more than before.

Although the PB7_Win32.exe executable is compiled as part of the Compact 7 OS run-time image, it has not been configured to launch.

Refer to Chapter 23, "Auto Launching Applications," for more information about auto launching an application during startup.

DEBUGGING A PLATFORM BUILDER NATIVE CODE APPLICATION

As a subproject to the Compact 7 OS design, a Platform Builder native code application is compiled and included as part of the OS run-time image. As part of the application development and debugging process, you need to make changes to the application project, recompile the project to generate an updated executable for further testing and debugging, and repeat the process, over and over again, until you can generate an application executable that can deliver all the required functions with acceptable performance and user experience.

To recompile the OS design to generate an updated application executable for testing requires the newly generated OS run-time image to be downloaded to the target device to test the application, which is compiled as part of the OS run-time image. The repetitive tasks to recompile the OS design project and restart the target device to launch the bootloader to download the image are time-consuming and inefficient.

With the right setup and knowledge, you don't need to go through the process to recompile the OS run-time image, reset the target device, launch bootloader, and download the recompiled OS run-time image. Instead, you need to download only an OS run-time image to the target device once and use the same instance of the OS run-time image launched on the target device to support the testing and debug effort for multiple iterations of changes to the application project.

This section works through an exercise to show a simpler method to develop, test, and debug a Platform Builder native code application.

1. From the VS2008 Solution Explorer tab, click to highlight the MyVPC OS design project.

2. From the VS2008 Project menu, click Properties to bring up the MyVPC Property Pages screen.

3. From the left pane, expand the Configuration Properties node, and select Subproject Image Settings, as shown in Figure 19-10.

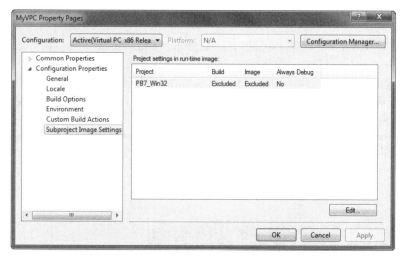

FIGURE 19-10

4. From the right pane, Project Settings in Run-Time Image pane, select PB7_Win32, and click Edit to bring up the Edit Run-Time Image Settings screen, as shown in Figure 19-11.

5. From the Edit Run-Time Image Settings screen, enable the following two options:

> ➤ Exclude from Build

> ➤ Exclude from Image

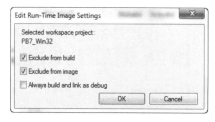

FIGURE 19-11

6. Click OK to close the Edit Run-Time Image Settings screen.

7. From the MyVPC Property Pages screen, click Apply followed by OK to save the settings and close.

8. From the VS2008 Build menu, select Advanced Build Commands, and click Build Current BSP and Subprojects (`blddemo -qbsp`) to build the OS design.

9. Follow the earlier steps to download the OS run-time image to the VM target device.

The preceding steps configure the OS design to exclude the PB7_Win32 subproject from the build and exclude the PB7_Win32.exe binary from the OS run-time image.

Building and Launching a Platform Builder Subproject Application

In the previous section, the OS design is configured to exclude the PB7_Win32 subproject from the build, generating an OS run-time image without the PB7_Win32.exe binary, and downloading the OS run-time image to the VM target device.

At this point, the OS run-time image downloaded and launched on the VM target device is built with the KITL option enabled, and established KITL connection between the Platform Builder IDE and the VM target device.

Work through the following steps to build the PB7_Win32 subproject and launch the compiled PB7_Win32.exe executable on the VM target device.

1. From the VS2008 Solution Explorer, right-click your mouse on PB7_Win32, and click Build, as shown in Figure 19-12, to build and generate the PB7_Win32.exe binary in the OS design's build release directory.

FIGURE 19-12

2. From the VS2008 Target menu, click Run Program to bring up the Run Program screen, as shown in Figure 19-13. All the programs in the OS design's build release directory can be launched on the target device from this screen.

3. From the Run Program screen, select `PB7_Win32.exe`, and click Run to launch the program on the VM target device.

As the `PB7_Win32.exe` executable launches on the target device, the PB7_Win32 Hello World! Message displays on the target device, and the following two retail debug messages display on the VS2008 Output window, as shown in Figure 19-14.

FIGURE 19-13

➤ `Retail Msg before hello world`

➤ `Retail Msg after hello world`

FIGURE 19-14

Rebuild and Relaunch a Platform Builder Subproject Application

The exercise in this section modifies the codes for the PB7_Win32 subproject, rebuilds the project, and launches the updated `PB7_Win32.exe` executable on the same instance of the VM target device with a Compact 7 OS run-time image launched from the previous exercise.

Continuing from the previous section, work through the following steps:

4. From the VM target device, close the `PB7_Win32.exe` application. Do not terminate the VM! Just right-click your mouse on the `PB7_Win32.exe` application, on the Compact 7 taskbar, and click Close to close the application.

5. From the VS2008 code editor window, with the `PB7_Win32.cpp` file open, locate the following block of code:

```
case WM_PAINT:
    RECT rect;
    GetClientRect (hWnd, &rect);
    hdc = BeginPaint(hWnd, &ps);
     RETAILMSG(1,(TEXT("Retail Msg before hello world...\n")));
     DrawText(hdc, TEXT("PB7_Win32 Hello World!"),-1,
```

```
                    &rect, DT_CENTER|DT_VCENTER|DT_SINGLELINE);

        RETAILMSG(1,(TEXT("Retail Msg after hello world….\n")));
         EndPaint(hWnd, &ps);
        break;
```

6. Change the preceding block of code to the following:

Available for download on Wrox.com

```
case WM_PAINT:
    RECT rect;
    GetClientRect (hWnd, &rect);
    hdc = BeginPaint(hWnd, &ps);

    RETAILMSG(1,(TEXT("Modified Debug Msg before hello world….\n")));

    DrawText(hdc, TEXT("Modified Hello World!"),-1,
                &rect, DT_CENTER|DT_VCENTER|DT_SINGLELINE);
     RETAILMSG(1,(TEXT("Modified Debug Msg after hello world….\n")));

    EndPaint(hWnd, &ps);
    break;
```

Code snippet is from Chapter19_Snippet.txt

7. From the VS2008 Solution Explorer window, right-click your mouse on PB7_Win32, and click Build to build the modified PB7_Win32 subproject.

8. From the VS2008 Target menu, click Run Program to bring up the Run Program screen.

9. From the Run Program screen, select PB7_Win32.exe and click Run to launch the modified PB7_Win32.exe executable on the VM target device.

As the PB7_Win32.exe executable launches again on the target device, the updated message, "Modified Hello World!" displays on the target device, and the following two debug messages are shown on the VS2008 Output window.

➤   Modified Debug Msg before hello world.

➤   Modified Debug Msg after hello world.

You can repeat the preceding process over and over again to make modifications to the code in the subproject, rebuild, and relaunch the application on the same instance of VM target device. The same process applies to a real target device.

Debug Messages

The Platform Builder native code exercises include the following function to send a debug message to the Output tab on the VS2008 IDE:

Available for download on Wrox.com

```
RETAILMSG(1,(TEXT("Retail build debug message….\n")));
```

Code snippet is from Chapter19_Snippet.txt

The preceding RETAILMSG() function sends the debug message to the VS2008 Output tab from an OS run-time image built in release mode with KITL. By injecting this function in the right places, with conditional variables to control the condition to send the debug message, you can put in place an effective debugging mechanism to trace your codes.

You can use the following DEBUGMSG() function to send a debug message to the VS2008 Output tab for the debug mode run-time image:

```
DEBUGMSG(1,(TEXT("Debug build debug message….\n")));
```

Code snippet is from Chapter19_Snippet.txt

SUMMARY

In addition to developing an application, the Platform Builder native code application development environment is the preferred environment to develop device drivers and library components.

As you can see from the simple exercises provided in this chapter, the Platform Builder IDE provides effective tools to help simplify development tasks and a useful debug facility to quickly help trace and identify potential problems.

20

Developing Embedded Database Applications

WHAT'S IN THIS CHAPTER?

➤ Introducing SQL Server Compact

➤ Exploring text file data storage and XML data serialization

➤ Understanding SQL Server Compact development and device requirements

➤ Using a remote SQL Server database in an application

➤ Using a SQL Server Compact database in an application

For Microsoft Windows Embedded Compact 7 devices, Microsoft SQL Server Compact 3.5 provides an efficient database capability with which applications can store and retrieve data. This chapter provides an introduction to SQL Server Compact for data manipulation on a Compact 7 device. As a lead-in, text file and XML data storage are covered. Access to a SQL Server from a Compact 7 device is also covered.

INTRODUCING MICROSOFT SQL SERVER COMPACT

Embedded devices typically capture input data from hardware and output processed data back to hardware. For example, a temperature sensor can digitize the temperature, an application or service can make decisions based upon that data as to heating and cooling required, and then output control signals to environment control devices to make temperature adjustments. Data can also be streamed to and from the device over serial and network services. Data will often need to be stored for later use, so a storage mechanism will be used. The data can simply be saved on storage media as a formatted text or binary file or as an XML file. Alternatively, it can be saved as a local file-based database or on a remote database server.

In this chapter Microsoft SQL Server Compact Edition is presented as a method to store, retrieve, and query such data locally. You see how to develop a simple SQL Server Compact database application that makes use of the Visual Studio 2008 Visual Designers. You work through some examples of application data storage using a number of methodologies, leading up to SQL Compact. You cover how to store and load data as a CSV file and as an XML data file. You also use a remote SQL Server for data storage and retrieval and finally do the same using SQL Compact.

Some Data to Store

Start by considering a simple table of data that you can store and load with an application. Consider an application on a device that programmatically plays music on Windows Media Player. A simple list of music files on a device and meta-information about those files could be stored so that it can be read into the custom media player application and turned into a drop-down list for track selection. A music playlist would consist of tracks, each with the field values for such things as the following:

➤ Track Number

➤ Title

➤ Artist

➤ Album

Table 20-1 shows some sample data.

TABLE 20-1: A Sample Music Playlist

TRACK NUMBER	TITLE	ARTIST	ALBUM
1	The Fool on the Hill	Beatles	Magical Mystery Tour
2	Chasing Pirates	Norah Jones	The Fall
3	Man of The Hour	Norah Jones	The Fall
4	Love of My Life	Queen	A Night At The Opera

You can generate such a list by querying the operating system shell for media content or the Internet for tracks and meta-information about them. This information is then written into a playlist file. Queries can be coded in the application to find certain tracks using the stored meta-information. You could also extend this list to include lists of Internet radio stations that the media player can play.

In this chapter after looking at SQL Server Compact, you develop a simple Playlist application to store and retrieve this data in a file or in a database.

MICROSOFT SQL SERVER COMPACT

Tabular or list data can be easily saved as text or an XML file. When data storage requirements are simple, those methods are quite efficient. When more complex data storage and manipulation is needed, a database is a more efficient option. Desktop applications tend to use a remote database server (such as Microsoft SQL Server) but that is not efficient for an embedded device, particularly because they are often disconnected. Microsoft Windows Embedded Compact 7 (Compact 7) has a file based database optional component, Microsoft SQL Server Compact 3.5 SP2 (SQL Compact). In this section you look at databases in general, have a quick look at two native databases engines in Compact 7, and then do a deep dive into SQL Compact in a Windows Embedded Compact 7 context.

What Is a Database?

Files are an excellent solution for storing data, particularly when it is mainly used in a serial manner such as a music file or a file that can load in its entirety when required. Databases are an alternative to file storage in which information is stored in a structured manner. Database tools and libraries that exploit that structure implement fast querying of the information in databases. For the music application, the meta-information could be stored in database tables, whereas the media files remain in the file system. Database software provides a range of functions to create, read, update, and delete (CRUD) database information.

A database can consist of tables, information about the relationships between the tables, queries to manipulate the data, and security information. Tables represent conceptual entities such as, in the music case, albums, artist, and track filenames. A music track would then be entered in the database as a filename, an album, and an artist. Some database queries for this music example could return all track filenames for an artist or for a specific album so that they can be turned into a media player playlist for playing.

Relational databases structure data into entities with relationships between them. With the playlist example, there could be three entities as tables:

➤ Tracks

➤ Artists

➤ Albums

The Artists table would list all the artists, whereas the Albums would list all the albums. Typically they would also contain meta-data specific to those entities. Both of these two tables would have a unique identifier for each record such as an integer. The Tracks table would then be constructed by recording the title of each track, an index for the artist, and an index for the album, as shown in Figure 20-1. For simplicity you can leave out the track filename, although in a real-world application, this and much other meta-data would be included (such as album art, publisher, date published, and so on).

FIGURE 20-1

Relational databases such as Microsoft SQL store data much more efficiently and lead to better integrity of the data. Language Integrated Queries (LINQ) and other .NET libraries simplify the coding of relational database functions. Also, .NET web and form controls can be seamlessly connected to a database source.

Where Is the Database?

The database can be stored on the local device or on a remote database server. For an always-connected device, a remote database server is a suitable database source. But if the device is only occasionally connected, such as a mobile handheld device, mobile phone, or a mobile data logger, a database on the device will be used. Device-based databases are usually file-based because this avoids the need to run an additional service on the device with which there is typically only one user, so a service is suboptimal. Microsoft Windows Embedded Compact 7 provides Microsoft SQL Server Compact Database V3.5 as a local database store. Compact 7 can also query a remote SQL Server.

Windows Embedded Compact Database Engines

Besides SQL Compact, Windows Embedded (Compact and CE) supports two native database engines, EDB and the older CEDB. Both can store databases as files on the devices with CEDB having access to the device object store. The object store is where nonvolatile data such as an address book is written. There is a native API for both database engines, which means they can be used directly from nonmanaged code. The native database engines for Windows Embedded Compact provide a compact, flat database structure optimized for compact and efficient storage and retrieval. These are managed by FileSystem.

CEDB is used by a lot of low-level things by the kernel. EDB is used by higher-level things such as the CAB installer, Media Player, and SQL Compact. CEDB will be included automatically in any Compact OS. EDB will be included in most systems that are GUI-based. They are located in the Platform Builder Catalog, as shown in Figure 20-2. Right-click them in the Catalog and you can have a look at the components that depend upon them.

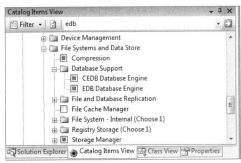

FIGURE 20-2

The focus in this chapter is on the database engine SQL Server Compact (SQL Compact), which is interacted with in a manner that mirrors the interaction with a SQL server in that the code and techniques are largely the same. The difference is that you connect to a local file rather than a remote service.

SQL Server Compact 3.5

The file-based access to a SQL database was available on earlier versions of the Windows Embedded Compact (CE) device, which was originally called SQL Server CE or similar. (The SQL Compact filenames and Managed Code classes still contain the CE moniker.) Although there was a capability to interact with them in a Structured Query Language (SQL) manner in native and Managed Code, the file and its interaction was tied to a CE device. The introduction of SQL Server

Compact facilitated the use of such files on a desktop, although this was initially permitted only for development purposes. This restriction has now been removed. SQL Compact on a desktop can now supplant some of the database interaction typically implemented using Microsoft Access where simple access to a few tables is required by a desktop application.

 Create a Managed Code (Compact Framework/Smart Device) SQL Compact Framework application, as in this chapter. Build the application but don't deploy it. Browse to the bin *directory and run the application on the desktop. You may have to modify the database file path. This proves two things:*

➤ *Compact Framework is in the main a true subset of the full Framework that the application will run.*

➤ *A desktop SQL Compact database file is the same on a desktop and a Compact device.*

You can use SQL Compact solely as a local data store or in unison with a remote SQL Server. In the first case an application reads and writes application data with the local file only. In the second case a query is sent to the server, which returns records stored locally in a SQL Compact database file. An application on the Compact device can modify the records and return them to the server in an asynchronous manner. A typical scenario is a traveling salesperson who at base will query the server for the clients in the area to which they are traveling, and for catalog data relevant to those clients. Orders will be generated as local database records on the device, which will then be uploaded to the server upon return to base.

The SQL Compact clients can be a Windows Embedded Compact (or CE) device or a Windows desktop such as a laptop. A client can interact directly with the SQL server or use SQL synchronization services via an IIS web server. As shown in Figure 20-3, a Compact 7 device can use the web to synchronize or use ActiveSync.

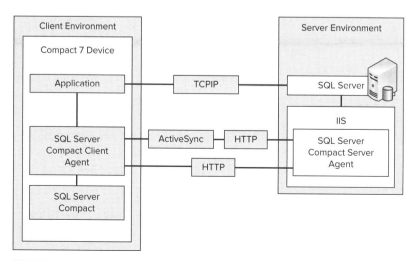

FIGURE 20-3

SQL Server Compact has three main components, with specific roles. There is a storage engine that stores the data in a binary manner as a local file. These files normally have an `.sdf` extension. The storage engine supports multi-use so that multiple applications can use it at the same time. There is a query processor that handles all the SQL queries to databases in the file. The third component is the synchronization engine for replication and synchronization with a backend SQL Server. The SQL Compact capabilities are for a device application to work directly with an `.sdf` file using SQL queries, to work with a remote SQL server, and finally integration with Visual Studio for development purposes.

The version of SQL Compact with Compact 7 is based upon Microsoft SQL Server Compact 3.5 SP2 and has some bug fixes not in SP2.

COMPACT DATABASE REQUIREMENTS

In this section you look at what is needed on the development machine, what is needed in the target operating system, and what is needed by a Managed Code application to build, run, and deploy a Compact SQL application on a Compact 7 device.

Compact 7 Device Requirements

Compact 7 has a native component and a Managed Code Provider for SQL Server Compact. Both are located in the Catalog, as shown in Figure 20-4. The Managed Code provider has a dependency on the native driver in that the Managed Code component calls the native component: With SQL Compact Managed Provider checked, SQL Compact (Native) is a required component.

Figure 20-5 shows a list of the SQL Compact DLLs on a deployed Compact 7 operating system that has the SQL Compact components included in Figure 20-4. The main DLL is `sqlcecompact35.dll`.

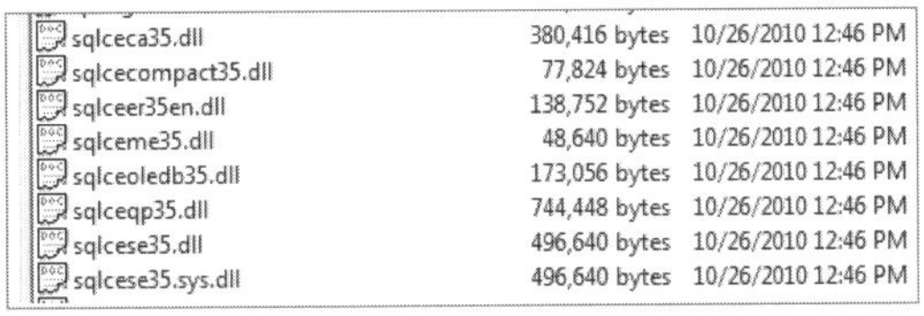

The Compact SQL file version with Compact 7 is a slightly later version (3.5.8154.0) than SQL Server Compact 3.5 SP 2 (3.5.8080.0) but is compatible with this for development

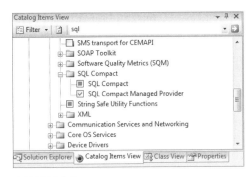

FIGURE 20-4

FIGURE 20-5

purposes. You should make sure that the required SQL Compact service packs are installed on your development machine for all the SQL Compact components. For SP2 the main DLL file is version 3.5.8080.0. You can see the installed versions in the Program and Features Control Panel applet on the right. For development purposes ensure that this is the 3.5.8080.0 version (or later) referenced from Managed Code; otherwise, the application will say it can't find this DLL when it runs, or the development system will try to download the development machine installed version to the

Compact device, which will fail. An alternative (and better) approach is to set the properties of the SQLServerCe reference to:

➤ Copy Local = False

➤ Specific Version= False

If you still have version problems with the SQL Compact, you may try referencing the version in Platform Builder as explained in the next section of this chapter. This will be the actual version on the system if the SQL Server Compact Catalog components are included in the image.

A typical development system will have the following installed:

➤ Visual Studio 2008 Professional (or higher)

➤ Visual Studio 2008 Service Pack 1

➤ Microsoft SQL Server Compact 3.5 SP2

➤ Microsoft SQL Server Compact 3.5 Design Tools SP1 (or later), which is installed with Visual Studio 2008 Service Pack 1

➤ Microsoft SQL Server Compact 3.5; for Devices SP2 also known as Microsoft SQL Server Compact 3.5 Service Pack 2 for Windows Mobile

➤ If using SQL Server then the following would also be installed: SQL Server 2008 Management Studio

Microsoft SQL Server Compact 3.5 is installed when Visual Studio 2008 is installed. The service packs need to be downloaded and installed. It is important that all these are installed, that they are updated, and that the DLL versions that you develop with are compatible with those on the device. Some other things to take care of follow:

➤ With Managed Code, set the `System.Data.SqlServer Ce` reference properties Copy Local and Specific Version both to False.

MANAGED CODE REQUIREMENTS

Note that SQL Compact 4 and the new Sync libraries as installed with Visual Studio 2010 do not run on Compact 7 systems. It is highly recommended that you have a development machine specifically for Compact 7 development with only the 2008 version of Visual Studio installed.

A typical Compact 7 SQL Compact application will be developed as Managed Code, although it can be done as a native application. The Managed Code namespace for SQL Compact classes follows:

```
System.Data.SqlServerCe
```

You can add a reference to this:

Right-click on References in Solution Explorer, choose Add Reference, and select `System.Data.SqlServerCe` from the .NET tab.

Alternatively you can add a reference to SQL Server Compact in Platform Builder located at:

```
$(_WINCEROOT)\Others\sqlcompact\managed\Retail
```

Right-click on References in the Solution Explorer and choose Add Reference. Select the Browse tab as in Figure 20-6, browse to that directory, and select file `system.data.sqlserverce.dll`.

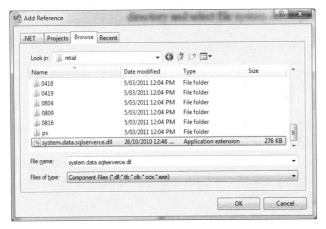

FIGURE 20-6

SqlCe Classes

A number of classes are in this namespace. They apply only to a SQL Compact database connection, not a SQL server database connection. Table 20-2 shows a list of the main ones.

TABLE 20-2: Some of the Main `SqlServerCe` Classes

CLASS	USE
SqlCeEngine	For creating new database files.
SqlCeConnection	To connect to the database file. It is only a reference to the `.sdf` file.
SqlCeCommand	A SQL query to be run against the connected database.
SqlCeResultSet	An updatable result from a query.
SqlCeDataReader	A forward-only reader of data rows from a data source.
SqlCeException	To return SQLCS specific errors, typically in a try catch.

When specifying a connection string, Compact 7 does not have a concept of a current directory. It is therefore best to specify an absolute path. On a development machine you can safely specify the root of the device, as follows:

```
conn = New SqlCeConnection("Data Source = \MyDatabase.sdf")
```

Code snippet is from a SQL Compact Connection String

A typical local-only database application can do the following:

➤ Create the database file if doesn't exist.

➤ Make a connection to the database.

➤ If new, create some data and insert it into the database.

➤ Query the database.

➤ Display the results.

➤ Modify the results and submit the records to the database.

➤ Close the connection.

The simplest way for an embedded developer is to write some code directly using the preceding classes. As an alternative, Visual Studio has data-oriented development controls that you can use to simplify this. Before walking through developing a Managed Code SQL Compact application using the direct approach, see how to build a simple "visual" application in Visual Studio using the visual data controls. This includes creating a SQL Compact database in Visual Studio. You then see how to connect this up to a DataGrid. When the application runs, it displays the data, and you can edit the database via this DataGrid. All this with only four lines of code!

BUILDING A SQL COMPACT DATABASE APPLICATION USING VISUAL DATA DESIGNERS

For this topic you create a Managed Code C# SmartDevice Windows Form application that can target your Compact device. Chapter 18, "Managed Code Application Example," covers building, deploying, and testing such an application.

Getting Started

Start by creating a C# Smart Device (Device Application) project targeting Compact Framework 3.5. Name it PlayList and set the Target Platform to Windows CE, or to your device's SDK if you have built and installed one.

In the Project Properties (Project Menu) on the Devices tab, make sure that that you uncheck Deploy the Latest Version of the .NET Framework (Including Service Packs). Otherwise Visual Studio will try to install the Framework (which is already in the OS) when you deploy the application, and the deployment will fail.

Add a reference to `System.Data.SqlServerCe` as in Figure 20-6 or via the .NET Add Reference tab.

Creating a New SQL Compact Server Database

To add a new database to the project, follow these steps:

1. On the Project menu, click Add New Item.

2. From the list of available Data templates, select Database File.

3. Enter **MyMusic.sdf** in the Name box.

4. Click Add.

   The Data Source Configuration Wizard opens with the new `MyMusic.sdf` file chosen as the data connection, and `MyMusicDataSet` is the dataset name.

5. On the Choose Your Database Objects page, click Finish. (No database objects are available because this is a new database.)

`MyMusic.sdf` and `MyMusicDataSet.xsd` are added to the project.

Creating a Table in the Database

To add a table to the database, follow these steps:

1. In the Solution Explorer, Open Server Explorer/Database Explorer by double-clicking `MyMusic.sdf`.

2. Under the Data Connections node, expand the `MyMusic.sdf` node.

3. Right-click Tables and then click Create Table. The New Table dialog box opens.

4. Name the table **Tracks**.

5. Create columns as specified in Table 20-3:

TABLE 20-3: The Tracks Database Table

COLUMN NAME	DATA TYPE	LENGTH	ALLOW NULLS	UNIQUE	PRIMARY KEY
TrackNumber	integer	Length4	No nulls	Yes	Yes
Title	nvchar	100	No nulls		
Artist	nvchar	100	No nulls		
Album	nvchar	100	No nulls		

6. If you haven't already, select the TrackNumber column, and set it as Primary Key (Yes) and Unique as Yes.

7. Then in the table below set Track Number Identity to True. This implements an auto-generation of Track Numbers when a track is added.

8. Click OK.

Populating the Table

To populate the table, follow these steps:

1. In Server Explorer, right-click the Tracks Table, and choose Show Table Data.

2. Enter some content for some tracks. Don't enter the Track Number because this is auto-generated.

3. To complete a track you need to enter data in the Title, Artist, and Album columns because you set then to non-null.

4. Click the row at the bottom when each track is entered.

5. Close the table, and reopen it to check that the data was written to the file.

Creating the Data Source

To create the data source, follow these steps:

1. Double-click `MyMusicDataSet.xsd` in the Solution Explorer. The blank dataset designer appears.

2. From the Server Explorer, drag the Tracks table and drop it on the dataset designer. The Tracks Table Adapter appears on the canvas.

3. Close the Dataset Designer.

Displaying a SQL Compact Table in a DataGrid

This part is quite easy! You need to add only a DataGrid control to the form and do some dragging and dropping. Follow these steps:

1. Show the form in Designer mode. At the bottom you see a mainMenu1 icon. Click this to see how far the menu comes down from the top. You use this later, so space needs to be left for it.

2. From the Toolbox, drag and drop a DataGrid onto the form.

3. Resize it to fill the form, and anchor it to all sides of the form, but leave space at the top for the menu.

4. From the Data menu, show the Data Sources window (not to be confused with Data Connections.)

5. From the Data Sources window, drag the Tracks node onto the form.

6. Build, deploy, and test the application.

The running application is shown in Figure 20-7.

FIGURE 20-7

Editing Data

For this application you would typically want some simple editing capabilities such as:

➤ Edit existing tracks

   ➤ Run an update query

➤ Add more tracks

   ➤ Run an insert query

➤ Delete a track

   ➤ Run a delete query

➤ Find a tracks

   ➤ Run a select query

Now to cover adding, editing, and deleting tracks using the DataGrid. It is quite easy to do!

Inserting, Updating, and Deleting Queries

If the TableAdapter in the Data Source has these SQL queries, it is simply a matter to action them via the DataGrid. Luckily when you added Tracks to the DataSet canvas, these were automatically created. Now have a look:

1. Load the DataSet visual designer: Double-click the .xsd file in the project (Solution Explorer).

2. Right-click on TracksTableAdapter (second line from bottom) and show its properties.

3. You see the Table Adapter SQL queries.

4. Expand them to see the parameterized queries, similar to Figure 20-8.

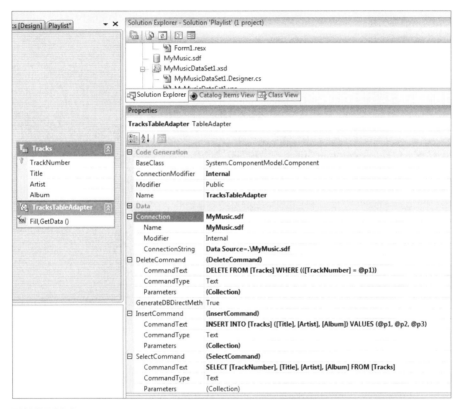

FIGURE 20-8

Adding an Edit and a View Form

The DataGrid in Compact Framework is a bit limited in that you can't edit cells directly in the grid. (There are some third-party grid controls that will do that though.) You have to copy the record into a form and edit there. A similar situation applies when you create a new record. Fortunately, the edit view form and a summary view form can be created for you.

1. Click the little right-pointing arrow at the top right of the DataGrid, as shown in Figure 20-9. (The left-pointing arrow in Figure 20-9 is right-pointing before the menu is displayed.) This shows only if the grid has a datasource.

2. From DataGridTasks, select Generate Data Forms.

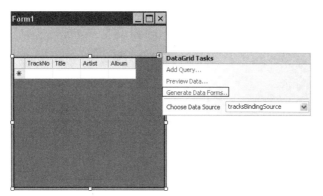

FIGURE 20-9

This generates the two forms, as shown in Figure 20-10.

FIGURE 20-10

The first form shows when you edit a track or create a new one. The second form displays whenever the grid is clicked. The track details for the row in the grid that was clicked are shown on the second form. You can either close it [X] and go back to the grid or choose to edit the record, in which case the edit form shows. You can then make changes to the track data. Click [X] to return to the grid from the edit form. At that point the changes are written directly back to the database; the grid is refreshed and displays.

When the forms generate, a menu appears at the top of the form to insert (add) a new track. If this is pressed when the application runs, a new record is created in the database, and the edit form shows.

3. Build, deploy, and test the application. Add some records and close the application.

Now you can observe that the changes were saved directly to the database file. If you just rerun the application from the application development machine, the database file will redeploy along with the application, overwriting the `.sdf` file. You need to rerun the application directly on the device after making the changes with the deployed run of the application.

4. On the device: Run File Explorer, and browse to `\Program Files`. Enter the Playlist folder, and run the application from there. Observe that the changes made were saved.

Enabling Record Deletes

You are almost done — without any coding so far!

You need to delete records, as follows:

1. To the menu at the top, add one more menu item beside New:

➤ Click on the menu item New.

➤ Click on Type Here and enter **Delete.**

2. Click away from that entry; then double-click on the menu item Delete to create a handler function for it.

3. When the edit and summary forms were created, there was some code-behind generated.

4. Insert the four lines of code, as shown here, into the Delete handler:

```
private void menuItem1_Click(object sender, EventArgs e)
{
    int current = dataGrid1.CurrentRowIndex;
    int currentTrackNo = (int)dataGrid1[current, 0];

    this.tracksTableAdapter.Delete(currentTrackNo);
    this.tracksTableAdapter.Fill(this.myMusicDataSet.Tracks);


}
```

Code snippet is from the inserted four lines of code to implement Delete in file delete.cs in the folder for the program PlaylistForm

This code gets the track number of the current row, deletes it in the database, and refreshes the DataGrid. This code perhaps should handle the case in which that track number isn't in the database.

5. Build, deploy, and test the application. Add some records, close the application, and rerun via File Explorer as previously done.

6. Observe that the changes were saved directly to the database.

There you are. You did it with only four lines of code!

A MEDIA PLAYLIST LIST APPLICATION

The next three sections will cover implementing the tracks functionality as a text file and as an XML file instead of using a database file to store and retrieve the data:

➤ This section outlines the tracks class that is used to programmatically implement much of the required functionality.

➤ The next section shows how to store and retrieve the data as a text file and as an XML file.

➤ The following section shows how to implement all of this as a Managed Code console application.

➤ The later sections of this chapter implement the same store and retrieve functions using a remote SQL Server and using a SQL Compact database file.

There are many high-level libraries to programmatically serialize program data into text, binary, and XML formats to store it and also to read it back in as meaningful information. In this section you look at the application requirements for the playlist that accept the save and load functions. The List functionality used here could be applied to any list structured data application and is independent of the method to store and retrieve the data.

To handle the playlist in a program, you start with a class called `track`, which encapsulates all the programming features of an individual track, such as the fields and methods to manipulate the track:

```
//The track class
[Serializable()]
public class track
{
    public track() { }

    public track(string Title, string Artist, string Album)
    {
        title = Title;
        album = Artist;
        artist = Album;
    }
    public string title;
    public string artist;
    public string album;
}
```

Code snippet is from the Track Class in the file program.cs in the project PlaylistConsole

This class has the three meta-data fields for a track (title, artist, and album) and two constructors. The track number is not included here because that is its index in the list to which it is added. Constructors are called to set up a class instance when a new instance of the class is created. The parameterless constructor is needed for XML serialization.

You can create an empty track or one with values. The Serializable attribute is needed for XML and is not needed for a CSV file.

A playlist is then a list of tracks:

```
public static List<track> Tracks;
```

Code snippet is from the Tracks playlist declaration: List of tracks as in the file program.cs in the project PlaylistConsole

A generic list class can implement a list of any data type and comes with methods to simply add, remove, filter, and reference list elements. The class also implements an iterator that facilitates simple looping through all items in a list. Generic Lists require a reference to `System.Collections` `.Generic` as a using statement at the top of the code file.

You need six functions to manipulate the playlist:

➤ Create the playlist.

➤ Display the playlist.

> ➤ Clear the playlist.
>
> ➤ Search the playlist.
>
> ➤ Save the playlist.
>
> ➤ Load the play list.

Playlist Functions

In this section the playlist functions are implemented.

Create the Playlist

It is useful to include some code to generate a new playlist of tracks that can then be saved and reloaded to test the storage functionality.

Available for
download on
Wrox.com

```
public static void CreateData()
{
        Tracks = new List<track>();
        Tracks.Add(new track("The Fool on the Hill","Beatles","Magical MysteryTour"));
        Tracks.Add(new track("Chasing Pirates","Norah Jones","The Fall"));
        Tracks.Add(new track("Man Of The Hour","Norah Jones","The Fall"));
        Tracks.Add(new track("Love Of My Life","Queen","A Night At The Opera"));
}
```

Code snippet is from the function to put some tracks into the playlist in the file program.cs in the project PlaylistConsole

new causes a new instance of the specified class to be generated. This code therefore generates a new list of tracks and adds four new tracks to the list.

Display the Playlist

Available for
download on
Wrox.com

```
private static void DisplayData(List<track> pTracks) {
    foreach (track track in pTracks) {
        // Write each track to the console
        Console.WriteLine(string.Format("{0},{1},{2}",track.title,
                            track.artist, track.album));
    }
}
```

Code snippet is from the function to display the playlist in the file program.cs in the project PlaylistConsole

This code iterates through the track data list to display the tracks.

Clear the Playlist

Available for
download on
Wrox.com

```
private static void ClearData() {
    Tracks.Clear();
}
```

Code snippet is from the function to clear the playlist in the file program.cs in the project PlaylistConsole

Search the Playlist

```
public static List<track> FindArtist(string Artist)
{   //The list query
    IEnumerable<track> query =
    Tracks.Where(track => track.artist.Contains(Artist));

    //Convert to a list.
    List<track>_tracks = query.ToList<track>();
    return _tracks;
}
```

Code snippet is from the function to search the playlist for an artist in the file program.cs in the project PlaylistConsole

This function will find all the tracks in the playlist for an artist and return them as a playlist. Although it could have been done by iterating through the original playlist and checking the artist for each track, LINQ, which reached maturity in.NET 3.5, simplified making SQL-like queries in the code of data structures. This requires the following directives at the top of any program using this capability:

```
using System.Data;
using System.Linq;
```

Code snippet is from the declarations needs for LINQ searching in the file program.cs in the project PlaylistConsole

Save and Load

The Save and Load functions are specific to the storage mechanism used. The other functions are independent of how the data is stored. The code for Save and Load will therefore be implemented in a number of ways to show CSV, XML data storage, and remote and local database storage. The program code is therefore the same for all methods used to load and save the data except for these two functions.

TEXT FILE DATA AND XML SERIALIZATION

In this section the functions to read and write the tracks data to a text file and with an XML file are implemented. The sample code as supplied has this implementation of the read and write functions.

Reading and Writing to a Text File

The playlist could be stored as a Comma Separated Values (CSV) text file. A CSV file is a text file consisting of lines as records. Each field value for a record is sequentially listed in the line separated by a comma. Text files are a universal way for passing data around because most computer applications can load, save, and transport them.

A music playlist would have tracks as records, with the following field values on every line: Track Number, Title, Artist, and Album.

If you were to save the music list data generated by the function CreateData(), as a CSV file, it would be written into a text file in the following format:

1, The Fool on the Hill, Beatles, Magical Mystery Tour

2, Chasing Pirates, Norah Jones, The Fall

3, Man of The Hour, Norah Jones, The Fall

4, Love of My Life, Queen, A Night At The Opera

Often the first line of such files would be a header which lists the field names in order. The Track Number possibly would not be stored because this would be generated from the order that it is read back in by.

CSV Text File Write Example

This code implements the process of writing the track information to a CSV text file. It also includes the name of the text file to which the data will be written and read.

```
static private string Filename="\\MyMusic.txt";

//CSV File writer.
public static void WriteData(List<track> pTracks)
{
    try
    {
        // Create an instance of StreamWriter to write text to a file.
        // The using statement also closes the StreamWriter.
        using (StreamWriter musicOut = new StreamWriter(Filename))
        {
            musicOut.WriteLine(string.Format("{0},{1},{2}", "title", "album",
"artist"));

            //Get each track from the list
            foreach (track track in pTracks)
            {
                // Write each track to the .csv file
                musicOut.WriteLine(string.Format("{0},{1},{2}",
                    track.title, track.artist, track.album));
            }
        }
    }
    catch (Exception e)
    {
        // Let the user know what went wrong.
        Console.WriteLine("The file could not be written:");
        Console.WriteLine(e.Message);
    }
}
```

Code snippet is the WriteData function from the project PlaylistConsole in the file csvTextReadWrite.cs.txt

CSV Text File Read Example

This code implements the process of reading the track information from a CSV text file.

```
//CSV File reader.
public static List<track> ReadData()
{
    List<track> tracks = new List<track>();
    char[] sep = new char[] { ',' };      //Used to split the string into its elements

    try
    {
        // Create an instance of StreamReader to read from a file.
        // The using statement also closes the StreamReader.
        using (StreamReader musicIn = new StreamReader(Filename))
        {
            string line;

            // Read and display lines from the file until the end of
            // the file is reached.
            while ((line = musicIn.ReadLine()) != null)
            {
                string[] musicdata = line.Split(sep);
                tracks.Add(new track(musicdata[0], musicdata[1], musicdata[2]));
            }
        }   //Note using opens AND closes the file
    }
    catch (Exception e)
    {
        // Let the user know what went wrong.
        Console.WriteLine("The file could not be read:");
        Console.WriteLine(e.Message);
    }
    return tracks;
}
```

Code snippet is the ReadData fucntion from the project PlaylistConsole in the file csvTextReadWrite.cs.txt

XML Serialization

Another approach would be to use XML serialization to store data. This is often implicitly used in applications as the `app.config` file (or `web.config` for web sites). XML serialization takes class instances and automatically writes the public properties and public fields as an XML file. It can also be used to transmit those records. To read the data back in, the class needs a parameterless constructor, as implemented in the track. Writing structured data as XML to a file is termed *serialization*, whereas reading it back in as XML and repopulating that data structure is termed *deserialization*. XML has the advantage over CSV and other text file formats in that it is far simpler to transfer, transform, query, and apply rules to XML data.

To implement serialization, you make use of the `System.Data.Xml.Serialization .XmlSerializer` class. This can serialize and deserialize whole data structures in one hit. This requires the following declaration at the top of the code:

```
using System.Xml.Serialization;
```

Code snippet is from the project PlaylistConsole in the file program.cs

XML Serialize Data Example

This code implements the process of writing the tracks information to an XML file. It includes the filename used. Note that you would normally use a .XML file extension. Using a .txt extension will enable the file to be opened on the device with a text file reader (Wordpad).

```
static private string Filename = "\\MyMusicXML.txt";

//Write tracks to XML file.
public static void WriteData(List<track> pTrack)
{
    try
    {
        //Create XML serialiser
        //We can serialise the whole list in one hit.
        //No need to iterate through the list
        XmlSerializer serializer =
        new XmlSerializer(typeof(List<track>));

        TextWriter writer = new StreamWriter(Filename);

        //Write XML to file
        serializer.Serialize(writer, pTrack);
        Console.WriteLine("XML data written");
        writer.Close();

    }
    catch (Exception e)
    {
        // Let the user know what went wrong.
        Console.WriteLine("The XML file could not be written:");
        Console.WriteLine(e.Message);
    }
}
```

Code snippet is the function WriteData from the project PlaylistConsole in the file XMLSerialize.cs.txt

XML Deserialize Data Example

This code implements the process of reading the track information to an XML file. Note that `Deserialize()` will return an object because it knows nothing of the data structure that was saved. The cast (`List<track>`) converts it to the required data type. If the data had been corrupted in any way, the cast would fail.

```
public static List<track> ReadData()
{
    List<track> tracks = new List<track>();
```

```
try
{
    //List that will be read into
    //List<track> xmlTracks;

    //Serializer
    XmlSerializer serializer =
    new XmlSerializer(typeof(List<track>));

    // A FileStream is needed to read the XML document.
    FileStream reader = new FileStream(Filename, FileMode.Open);

    //Use the Deserialize method to restore the data from the XML document.
    //Note. Need to cast restored data.
    tracks = (List<track>)serializer.Deserialize(reader);

    reader.Close();

    Console.WriteLine("XML data read back in.");
    DisplayData(Tracks);
}
catch (Exception e)
{
    // Let the user know what went wrong.
    Console.WriteLine("The XML file could not be read:");
    Console.WriteLine(e.Message);
}
return tracks;
}
```

Code snippet is ReadData from the project PlaylistConsole in the file program.cs

BUILDING THE MANAGED CODE DATA APPLICATION (TEXT AND XML)

To implement the PlaylistConsole Application, you need a Smart Device C# Application that uses .NET CF 3.5. You create a console application and add the previous Playlist functions. To the previous code implement the `main()` function and add a further function, as shown next.

You need a Retail mode Compact 7 device with the Compact Framework 3.5 component. Refer to Chapter 9, "Debug and Remote Tools," to see how to build, deploy, and test a Managed Code application on a Compact device. Your device also needs to have been built with the Managed SQL Compact component:

➤ Create a C# SmartDevice Console Compact Framework 3.5 application called PlayListConsole.

➤ The following is the shell of the program for the program. It is used for the CSV Text File and Serialization implementations of the data storage as well as for SQL Server and SQL Compact access. Replace the console program code with the following:

```csharp
using System;
using System.IO;
using System.Collections.Generic;
using System.Data;
using System.Linq;

//XML Serialization:
//Uncomment the next line
//using System.Xml.Serialization;

//Remote SQL:
//Add a reference to System.Data.SQLClient
//Uncomment the following:
//using System.Data.SqlClient;

//SQLCompact:
//Add a reference to System.Data.SQLServerCe
//Uncomment the next line
//using System.Data.SqlServerCe;


public static class PlaylistConsole
{

    public static List<track> Tracks;


    public static void Main()
    {
        CreateData();
        Console.WriteLine("Data as created.");
        DisplayData(Tracks);
        WriteData(Tracks);
        Console.WriteLine("Data written to file.");
        ClearData();
        Tracks = ReadData();
        Console.WriteLine("Data as read back in.");
        DisplayData(Tracks);
        Console.WriteLine("Doing query for tracks by Elton");
        DoAQuery();
    }

    public static void CreateData()
    {
    }

    private static void ClearData()
    {
    }

    public static void DoAQuery()
    {
    }
```

```csharp
        public static List<track> FindArtist(string Artist)
        {
        }

        public static void WriteData(List<track> pTrack)
        {
        }

        public static List<track> ReadData()
        {
        }

        [Serializable()]
        public class track
        {
        }

    }
```

Code snippet is the outline of the program from the project PlaylistConsole in the file program.cs

➤ Implement `DoQuery()` as follows:

```csharp
public static void DoAQuery()
{
    List<track> eltons = FindArtist("Elton");
    if (eltons.Count==0)
    {
        Console.WriteLine("No tracks found");
    }
    else
    {
        Console.WriteLine(string.Format("{0},{1},{2}",
                    "title", "album", "artist"));
        foreach (track Track in eltons)
        {
            Console.WriteLine(string.Format("{0},{1},{2}",
                    Track.title, Track.album, Track.artist));
        }
    }
}
```

Code snippet is the function to action the artist query as DoQuery in the project PlaylistConsole in the file program.cs

1. Add the Create, Display, Clear, and Search functions as previous.

2. Replace the `WriteData` and `ReadData` functions in the program with the contents of the file `csvTextReadWrite.cs.txt`. Include the filename when pasting the CSV implementation.

3. Build, deploy, and run the application on the device, noting the console output.

4. Check that the file `music.txt` is created in the root of the device's file system and examine its contents with Wordpad.

Now modify the program for the XML Serialization:

1. Replace the `LoadData()` and `SaveData()` functions with the contents of the file `XMLSerialize.cs.txt`. Also replace the filename when pasting with that for the XML file.

2. Uncomment the Serialization `using` reference at the top of the program file.

3. Build, deploy, and run.

4. Examine `MyMusicXML.txt` in the root of the device with Wordpad.

5. As a variation, you could create a Smart Device Windows Forms application and insert the Tracks list into a `ListBox` when loaded. When a track is selected from the `Listbox`, its meta-data is displayed in text boxes. The functions such as `Create`, `Clear`, `Load`, and `Save Search` could be called from command button events.

BUILDING A MANAGED CODE REMOTE DATABASE APPLICATION

With SQL Compact you again use the previous application. Change the filename used to have an .sdf extension, and change the `read` and `write` functions to use the database. The `write` function creates the database file if it doesn't already exist, so there is no need to create the file in preparation.

Preparation

1. Create a database on a SQL server called MyMusic.

2. Set it so that a specific user can access the database.

3. Make sure the SQL server permits remote access over TCPIP.

4. Determine the connection string for that user to the database on that server. An example follows:

```
private string connectionString =
    "Data Source=myserver;Initial Catalog=
MyMusic;Integrated Security=Integrated;User ID=myserver\\user1;Password=pwd";
```

Code snippet is from the project PlaylistConsole in the file sqlServerReadWrite.cs.txt

5. This would connect to the SQL server myserver, to the database MyMusic, using the credentials of `user1`.

6. In the project add a reference to `System.Data.SqlClient`.

7. Comment out the Serialization `using` reference and uncomment the SQL Remote `using` reference in the program.

Writing Fracks to a Remote SQL Server

In this function you do the following:

➤ Create a connection to the database.

➤ Open the connection.

➤ If the Tracks table exists, delete it (Drop Table).

➤ Create the Track table.

➤ Write each track in the Tracks list to the table.

➤ Close the connection.

Note the importance of capturing errors with the database actions.

1. Enter the connection string in place of the filename statement in the program.

2. Replace the `WriteData` function in the PlaylistConsole application with the following (or copy it from `sqlServerReadWrite.cs.txt`):

```
private static string connectionString =
"Data Source=myserver;Initial Catalog=MyMusic;Integrated Security=Integrated;
User ID=myserver\\user1;Password=pwd";

public static void WriteData(List<track> pTracks)
{
    SqlConnection conn = null;

    try
    {

        //Connect to the Compact SQL file
        conn = new SqlConnection(connectionString);
        conn.Open();

        //Drop the table
        SqlCommand cmd0 = conn.CreateCommand();
        cmd0.CommandText = "Drop TABLE Tracks";
        Console.WriteLine(cmd0.CommandText);
        cmd0.ExecuteNonQuery();

        //Create the table
        SqlCommand cmd1 = conn.CreateCommand();
        cmd1.CommandText = "Create Table Tracks";
        cmd1.CommandText += "(Title nvarchar(100),";
        cmd1.CommandText += "Artist nvarchar(100),";
        cmd1.CommandText += "Album nvarchar(100),";
        cmd1.CommandText += "Id int NOT NULL IDENTITY(1,1) PRIMARY KEY)";
        cmd1.ExecuteNonQuery();


        //Add a record to the table for each track.
        foreach (track track in pTracks)
        {
            SqlCommand cmd2 = conn.CreateCommand();
            cmd2.CommandText = "INSERT INTO Tracks ([Title], [Artist], [Album]) ";
            cmd2.CommandText += "Values('" + track.title + "', '";
            cmd2.CommandText += track.artist + "' , '" + track.album + "'  )";

            cmd2.ExecuteNonQuery();
        }
    }
```

```
        catch (SqlException e)
        {
            // Let the user know what went wrong.
            Console.WriteLine("The SQL data could not be written:");
            Console.WriteLine(e.Message);
        }
        finally
        {
            //Make sure that the connection is closed
            try
            {
                conn.Close();
            }
            catch { }
        }
    }
```

Code snippet is the function WriteData from the project PlaylistConsole in the file sqlServerReadWrite.cs.txt

Reading Tracks from a Remote SQL Server

In this function you do the following:

➤ Create a connection to the database.

➤ Query the database for all tracks.

➤ Read each track from the query.

➤ Add each track to the list.

➤ Write out the track details.

1. Replace the ReadData function in the PlaylistConsole application with the following (or copy it from sqlServerReadWrite.cs.txt):

Available for
download on
Wrox.com

```
public static List<track> ReadData()
{
    SqlConnection conn = null;
    List<track> tracks = new List<track>();

    try
    {
        //Connect to the Compact SQL file
        conn = new SqlConnection(connectionString);
        conn.Open();

        //Query for Tracks table
        SqlCommand cmd3 = conn.CreateCommand();
        cmd3.CommandText = "select * from  Tracks";
        Console.WriteLine(cmd3.CommandText);
        SqlDataReader sqlreader = cmd3.ExecuteReader();
```

```csharp
        //Copy records into Tracks list
        ClearData();
        while (sqlreader.Read())
        {
            int id = 137; //Dummy value
            string title = "";
            string artist = "";
            string album = "";

            for (int i = 0; i < sqlreader.FieldCount; i++)
            {
                string fieldname = sqlreader.GetName(i);
                switch (fieldname)
                {
                    case "Id":
                        id = (int)sqlreader[i];
                        break;
                    case "Title":
                        title = (string)sqlreader[i];
                        break;
                    case "Artist":
                        artist = (string)sqlreader[i];
                        break;
                    case "Album":
                        album = (string)sqlreader[i];
                        break;
                }
            }
            tracks.Add(new track(title, artist, album));
        }
        sqlreader.Close();

    }
    catch (SqlException e)
    {
        // Let the user know what went wrong.
        Console.WriteLine("The SQL data could not be read:");
        Console.WriteLine(e.Message);
    }
    finally
    {
        //Make sure that the connection is closed
        try
        {
            conn.Close();
        }
        catch { }
    }
    return tracks;
}
```

Code snippet is the function ReadData from the project PlaylistConsole in the file sqlServerReadWrite.cs.txt

2. Build and run the program.

3. Observe the output.

4. Examine the database table created on the SQL Server using SQL Server Management Studio.

BUILDING A MANAGED CODE COMPACT DATABASE APPLICATION

With SQL Compact you again use the same application as previously used. Here you change the filename used to have an `.sdf` extension and change the `read` and `write` functions to use the database. The `WriteData` function creates the database file if it doesn't already exist, so there is no need to create the file in preparation. The code is essentially the same except the classes are for SQL Compact and the connection is to the database file.

1. Remove the `System.Data.SqlServer` reference and add a reference to `System.Data.SqlServerCe` as in Figure 20-6 or via the Add Reference .NET tab.

2. Comment out the SQL Remote `using` reference at the top of the program and uncomment the SQL Compact `using` reference.

3. Remove the SQL connection string code.

Writing Tracks to a Compact Database File

In this function you do the following:

a. Create a connection to the database.

b. If the database file doesn't exist, create it and add the Tracks table.

c. Clear any tracks from the table.

d. Write each track in the Tracks list to the table.

Note again the importance of capturing errors with the database actions.

1. Replace the `WriteData` function in the PlaylistConsole application with the following (or copy it from `compactsqlReadWrite.cs.txt`) It includes the database filename:

```
public static string dbFilename = "\\MyMusic.sdf";

public static void WriteData(List<track> pTrack)
{
    SqlCeConnection conn = null;

    try
    {
        //Connect to the Compact SQL file
        conn = new SqlCeConnection(@"Data Source =" + dbFilename);

        //if (File.Exists(dbFilename)) File.Delete(dbFilename);

        //If the file doesn't exist create the database, add table and open it
        if (!File.Exists(dbFilename))
```

```
    {
        //Open SQL engine
        SqlCeEngine sqlEngine = new SqlCeEngine(conn.Connecti        g);
        sqlEngine.CreateDatabase();
        conn.Open();

        //Create the database and table
        SqlCeCommand cmd0 = conn.CreateCommand();
        cmd0.CommandText = "Create Table Tracks";
        cmd0.CommandText += "(Title nvarchar(100),";
        cmd0.CommandText += "Artist nvarchar(100),";
        cmd0.CommandText += "Album nvarchar(100),";
        cmd0.CommandText += "Id int NOT NULL IDENTITY(1,1) PRIMARY KEY)";
        cmd0.ExecuteNonQuery();
    }
    else
    {
        //Otherwise clear the table  (
        //Could drop table and recreate as above also
        //  ..That would be better as Ids would start from zero again.
        conn.Open();

        //Clear the records in the table
        SqlCeCommand cmd1 = conn.CreateCommand();
        cmd1.CommandText = "DELETE Tracks";
        Console.WriteLine(cmd1.CommandText);
        cmd1.ExecuteNonQuery();
    }

    //Add a record to the table for each track.
    foreach (track sqltrack in pTrack)
    {
        SqlCommand cmd2 = conn.CreateCommand();
        cmd2.CommandText = "INSERT INTO Tracks ([Title], [Artist], [Album]) ";
        cmd2.CommandText += "Values('" + track.title + "', '";
        cmd2.CommandText += track.artist + "' , '" + track.album + "'  )";
        cmd2.ExecuteNonQuery();
    }
}
catch (SqlCeException e)
{
    // Let the user know what went wrong.
    Console.WriteLine("The SQL data could not be written:");
    Console.WriteLine(e.Message);
}
finally
{
    //Make sure that the connection is closed
    try
    {
        conn.Close();
    }
    catch { }
}
}
```

Code snippet is the function WriteData from the project PlaylistConsole in the file compactsqlReadWrite.cs

Reading Tracks from a Compact Database File

In this function you do the following:

a. Create a connection to the database.

b. Query the database for all tracks.

c. Read each track from the query.

d. Add each track to the list.

e. Write out the track details.

1. Replace the ReadData function in the PlaylistConsole application with the following (or copy it from compactsqlReadWrite.cs.txt):

Available for download on Wrox.com

```csharp
//Read music list back from XML file.  Rename as ReadData to use
public  static  List<track> ReadData()
{
    SqlCeConnection conn = null;
    List<track> tracks = new List<track>();

    try
    {
        //Connect to the Compact SQL file
        conn = new SqlCeConnection(@"Data Source =" + dbFilename);
        conn.Open();

        //Query for Tracks table
        SqlCeCommand cmd3 = conn.CreateCommand();
        cmd3.CommandText = "select * from  Tracks";
        SqlCeDataReader sqlreader =   cmd3.ExecuteReader();

        //Copy records into Tracks list
        ClearData();
        while (sqlreader.Read())
        {
            int id = 137; //Dummy value
            string title ="";
            string artist ="";
            string album ="";

            for (int i = 0; i < sqlreader.FieldCount; i++)
            {
                string fieldname = sqlreader.GetName(i);
                switch (fieldname)
                {
                    case "Id":
                        id = (int)sqlreader[i];
                        break;
                    case "Title":
                        title = (string)sqlreader[i];
                        break;
```

```
                    case "Artist":
                        artist = (string)sqlreader[i];
                        break;
                    case "Album":
                        album = (string)sqlreader[i];
                        break;
                }
            }

            tracks.Add(new track(title, album, artist));
        }
        sqlreader.Close();

    }
    catch (SqlCeException e)
    {
        // Let the user know what went wrong.
        Console.WriteLine("The SQL data could not be read:");
        Console.WriteLine(e.Message);
    }
    finally
    {
        //Make sure that the connection is closed
        try
        {
            conn.Close();
        }
        catch { }
    }
    return tracks;
}
```

Code snippet is the function ReadData from the project PlaylistConsole in the file compactsqlReadWrite.cs

2. Build and run the program.

3. Observe the output.

4. You may wish to copy the database file back to the development machine using the Remote File tool and open it there.

SUMMARY

This chapter covered a large territory; enough for a book in its own right. You learned how to store and retrieve data in a number of ways including text files and database tables. You looked at the Microsoft SQL Compact 3.5 SP2 database technology in detail. This content is normally not covered in embedded operating systems books but left to the mobile devices books, to which you can refer for more detail. This content is important though for embedded devices because they are about data capture and manipulation and include the use of efficient and robust data storage and queries.

A further topic that could have been covered is the data synchronization between the SQL Compact database and a remote SQL server. This would cover topics such as merge replication, RDA, and the new Microsoft Sync Framework. They would take a few more chapters on their own, though, so you can go to MSDN and the mobile devices books for those topics. Although Merge Replication is simple to code, it can be difficult to configure for an embedded device. Also, note that Microsoft SQL Server Compact 4 is not available for Windows Embedded Compact 7 — at least not initially.

You can implement a form of merge replication with the existing code in this chapter. Just use the Remote SQL read and writes code to send and receive data to and from the SQL server. The result of a select (read) query from the server is written to the Compact database. An update query (write) to the SQL server will take changed records from the Compact database.

A desktop Managed Code application can connect to a Microsoft SQL Azure database in the cloud in exactly the same manner as outlined in the Remote SQL sections in this chapter except that the connection must use SSL encryption. SSL stands for Secure Socket Layer, the "s" in https. Unfortunately, the Compact Framework connection class does not support encryption and so a Managed Code application on a Compact 7 device cannot connect directly to a SQL Azure database. The recommended method is to use a web service to access a cloud database.

21

Silverlight for Windows Embedded

WHAT'S IN THIS CHAPTER?

➤ Introducing the Silverlight for Windows Embedded user interface development framework

➤ Using Silverlight for Windows Embedded development environment and tools

Silverlight is a user interface (UI) development framework that enables the designer and developer to work in parallel, leveraging the designer's graphic and artistic skill to create compelling UI for the application without the need to understand the application's complex programming logic and code. This enables the developers to do what they do best: write code, without being hindered by graphic design and related tasks.

Silverlight for Windows Embedded is an UI development framework for Windows Embedded Compact designed specifically to support embedded devices. Silverlight technology and development scenarios are broad subjects that can span across multiple books. It's not within this chapter's intention to cover Silverlight technology in detail.

This chapter provides a brief overview of Silverlight for Windows Embedded, talks about the differences between Silverlight for Windows desktop versus Silverlight for Windows Embedded, and offers a starting point to help you begin developing with Silverlight for Windows Embedded.

SILVERLIGHT: USER INTERFACE DEVELOPMENT FRAMEWORK

Initially, Silverlight was introduced to the market as a development framework for web applications, to deliver media rich content, designed to run inside a web browser with the required plug-in installed.

Although Silverlight technology is still generally known as a development framework for web applications that runs within a browser, Silverlight version 3 and later support out-of-browser applications. As Silverlight evolves, this technology is being adopted to support other platforms, including Linux, Mac OS, the latest Windows Phone 7 mobile platform, and Windows Embedded Compact.

Whether you use Silverlight to develop an out-of-browser application for the Windows desktop PC, a web application that runs in a browser, an application for Windows Phone 7, or a Windows Embedded Compact application, Silverlight is a UI development framework that enables the designer and application developer to work together seamlessly, doing what they do best, to jointly create an exciting and visually compelling UI for the application.

If you are new to Silverlight and want to learn more, there is plenty of information and tutorials about Silverlight available.

With hundreds of books written about Silverlight and thousands of technical articles and blog postings that talk about Silverlight, there is a large pool of information resources for you to draw from. A good place to start is the Silverlight web site at the following URL:

```
www.silverlight.net
```

SILVERLIGHT FOR WINDOWS EMBEDDED

Silverlight for Windows Embedded (SWE) is a UI development framework created specifically to support the Windows Embedded Compact development environment. Initially, SWE released as part of Windows Embedded CE 6.0 (CE 6.0) R3, based on Silverlight 2. It uses Expression Blend 2 to create the XAML code project for the UI. When working with SWE in the CE 6.0 environment, you need to manually port a XAML code project to a native code subproject for the CE 6.0 OS design.

For Compact 7, SWE is based on Silverlight 3 and uses Expression Blend 3 to develop a XAML code project for the UI. When working with SWE in the Compact 7 environment, the new Windows Embedded Silverlight tools, included as part of the Platform Builder for Compact 7 development tools, are provided to automate the process to port and update an Expression Blend XAML code project to a native code subproject for the Compact 7 OS design.

Although Silverlight applications for the Windows desktop and Windows Phone 7 environments are based on managed code, Silverlight for Windows Embedded is based on native code, written in C++, to generate an efficient executable to support Windows Embedded Compact devices typically built with limited hardware and processing resources. Other than the common XAML code shared by the Silverlight for Windows desktop, Silverlight for Windows Phone and Silverlight for Windows Embedded, the Silverlight for Windows Embedded application is not portable between platforms.

For more detailed information about the similarity and differences between Silverlight for Windows desktop and Silverlight for Windows Embedded UI development frameworks, visit the following URL:

```
http://msdn.microsoft.com/en-us/library/ee501848.aspx
```

DEVELOPMENT ENVIRONMENT AND TOOLS

Silverlight for Windows Embedded provides an environment that separates application development for a Compact 7 device into two separate environments: UI and programming logic.

As shown in the graphical presentation in Figure 21-1, the designer creates the Silverlight XAML code project for the application's UI based on design requirements specified in the contract, using Express Blend. Working in parallel, the developer, using Visual Studio 2008, develops code and implements programming logic for the application that functions behind the XAML UI code (code-behind).

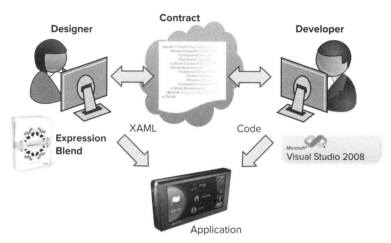

FIGURE 21-1

Combining the designer's artistic skill and the developer's technical skill, Silverlight for Windows Embedded provides an efficient and manageable environment to create an application, with a visually compelling user interface for an embedded device that helps to differentiate the device from the competition.

Required Software

To develop a Silverlight for Windows Embedded application, you need to have the following software installed to the development station.

Visual Studio 2008 with Service Pack 1

Visual Studio 2008 is the primary development environment to develop managed and native code applications for Windows Embedded Compact 7.

Platform Builder for Windows Embedded Compact 7

Platform Builder for Compact 7 is a plug-in to the VS2008 IDE and requires VS2008 to function. Platform Builder is the tool used to develop OS design and generate a custom Compact 7 OS run-time image for a designated device.

Expression Blend 3

Expression Blend 3 is the development tool used to create a XAML code UI project.

Windows Embedded Silverlight Tools

Windows Embedded Silverlight tools are provided as part of the Platform Builder for Compact 7. The tools automated the process to port SWE XAML code for the UI to native code. The following wizards are included as part of the Windows Embedded Silverlight tools:

➤ **Create Platform Builder Subproject Wizard** — This wizard converts an Expression Blend 3 XAML code project, created with the Silverlight for Windows Embedded application template, into a Compact 7 application subproject for the active OS design.

➤ **Update Silverlight for Windows Embedded Project Wizard** — This wizard is used to update the Compact 7 application subproject when the source project, the Expression Blend XAML code project that the subproject is derived from, is changed.

➤ **Windows Embedded Events Wizard** — This wizard is used to add C++ event handles to UI elements parsed from the Expression Blend XAML code.

Silverlight for Windows Embedded Template

The Silverlight for Windows Embedded Template is provided as part of the Platform Builder for Compact 7 software suite. Expression Blend 3 must be installed prior to installing this template.

Although Silverlight for Windows Embedded for Compact 7 is based on Silverlight 3, it does not support all the Silverlight 3 features. An Expression Blend 3 XAML code project created with this template is restricted to use features supported by Silverlight for Windows Embedded.

XAML: Extensible Application Markup Language

Extensible Application Markup Language (XAML) is an XML-based markup language created by Microsoft. Similar to HTML, XAML is an UI description language used to describe the structure and layout for the application's visual presentation.

The XAML language structure is similar to XML. Each element that describes the visual layout is enclosed in a bracket, as shown in the following sample:

```
<Element>
      Property1="value1"
      Property2="value2"
</Element>
```

The following XAML codes describe the visual presentation for the UI, as shown in Figure 21-2.

```
<UserControl
     xmlns="http://schemas.microsoft.com/winfx/2006/xaml/presentation"
     xmlns:x="http://schemas.microsoft.com/winfx/2006/xaml"
     xmlns:d="http://schemas.microsoft.com/expression/blend/2008"
     xmlns:mc="http://schemas.openxmlformats.org/markup-compatibility/2006"
```

```xaml
    x:Class="Chapter21.MainPage"
    Width="300" Height="300" mc:Ignorable="d">

<Grid x:Name="LayoutRoot" Background="GRAY">

    <!-- TextBox -->
    <TextBox
        Height="60"
        Margin="50,80,50,0"
        VerticalAlignment="Top"
        Text="This line of text extends beyond one line."
        TextWrapping="Wrap"
        FontSize="16"
        RenderTransformOrigin="0.5,0.5"
        >

        <TextBox.RenderTransform>
            <TransformGroup>
                <ScaleTransform/>
                <SkewTransform/>
                <RotateTransform Angle="-15"/>
                <TranslateTransform/>
            </TransformGroup>
        </TextBox.RenderTransform>

    </TextBox>

    <!-- Click Me button -->
    <Button
        Height="30"
        Margin="50,0,50,80"
        VerticalAlignment="Bottom"
        Content="Click Me"
        d:LayoutOverrides="VerticalAlignment"
        RenderTransformOrigin="0.5,0.5"
        >

        <Button.RenderTransform>
            <TransformGroup>
                <ScaleTransform/>
                <SkewTransform/>
                <RotateTransform Angle="-15"/>
                <TranslateTransform/>
            </TransformGroup>
        </Button.RenderTransform>

    </Button>

</Grid>

</UserControl>
```

Code snippet is from XAML_1.TXT

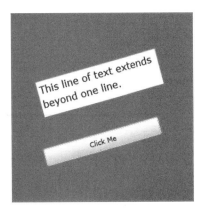

FIGURE 21-2

The preceding XAML code is created using Expression Blend 3.

Code-Behind

Code-behind is a term that refers to the code that joins the UI object defined by the XAML code with program and business logic code, which provides the function and features for the application. This is one of the key mechanisms that separates the application code from the visual presentation XAML code and enables the designer and application developer to work together, leveraging their unique expertise to deliver a compelling UI for the application without compromising the application's technical function and features.

For the Silverlight for Windows desktop and Windows Phone 7 environments, the code-behind is written in managed code. For the Silverlight for Windows Embedded environment, the code-behind is written in native code, using C++.

Following is a listing of the code snippet for the code-behind to the Click Me button's event handler.

```
// ========================================================================
// button_Click
// Description: Event handler implementation
// Parameters: pSender - The dependency object that raised the click event.
//             pArgs - Event specific arguments.
// ========================================================================
HRESULT MainPage::button_Click (IXRDependencyObject* pSender,
                                XRMouseButtonEventArgs* pArgs)
{
    HRESULT hr = E_NOTIMPL;

    if ((NULL == pSender) || (NULL == pArgs))
    {
        hr = E_INVALIDARG;
    }
    return hr;
}
```

Code snippet is from CODE_BEHIND.TXT

Contract Between Designer and Application Developer

For the designer and application developer to effectively work together, a contract (a design specification for the UI) between the designer and developer must be established to define the required features and event handlers for the UI, as shown in Figure 21-3.

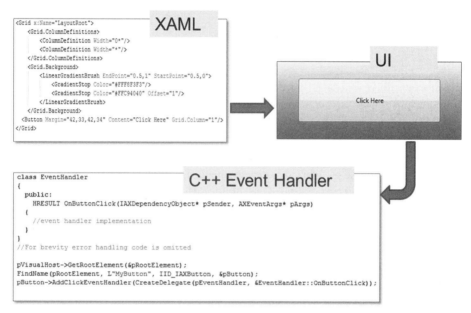

FIGURE 21-3

After the design specification and the contract between the designer and developer are established, the application developer and designer can start to work in parallel, doing what they do best.

During the development process, the designer can provide an Expression Blend XAML code project for the UI to the developer, who in turn uses the Windows Embedded Silverlight tools to convert and update the Expression Blend XAML code project to an application subproject for the Compact 7 OS design.

DEVELOPMENT PROCESS

To develop an application that leverages Silverlight for Windows Embedded for a Compact 7 device, the development process typically involves the following steps:

1. Create a Compact 7 OS design with support for Silverlight for Windows Embedded using Platform Builder.

2. Create XAML code to describe the UI using Expression Blend 3.

3. Create the necessary event handler for the XAML code.

4. Port the XAML code project to the native code subproject for Compact 7 OS design using the Windows Embedded Silverlight tool.

5. Develop programming logic codes for the native code subproject to provide the required functions and features.

6. Configure and compile the native code subproject as part of the Compact 7 OS design for testing, debugging, and deployment.

SUMMARY

In a traditional Windows form application, the application's code and user interface are tightly coupled. Throughout the development process, changes made to the UI often required the application developer to spend countless hours updating the application's code to adapt to the changes.

By separating the application's development into two separate environments, program logic and visual presentation, it enables these two separate development processes to work seamlessly in parallel. Silverlight for Windows Embedded provides an innovative and efficient environment to develop quality applications for Windows Embedded Compact devices with a visually compelling user interface.

In addition, by separating a complex development environment into two simplified environments that are easier to manage, it helps the development team to minimize code and reduce the overall development time.

22

Silverlight for Windows Embedded Application Examples

WHAT'S IN THIS CHAPTER?

➤ Developing XAML with Expression Blend 3

➤ Using Silverlight for Windows Embedded Tools

➤ Integrating a Silverlight for Windows Embedded application as part of the OS image

Developing a Silverlight for Windows Embedded (SWE) application for Windows Embedded Compact 7 device involves multiple steps, using Expression Blend 3 to develop the user interface and Visual Studio 2008 to develop the program and business logic.

This chapter works through the following exercises to show the steps to develop a Silverlight for Windows Embedded application for Compact 7:

➤ Create a Compact 7 OS design that supports SWE application.

➤ Create a SWE user interface project using Expression Blend 3.

➤ Port a SWE XAML code project to native code using the Windows Embedded Silverlight Tool.

PREREQUISITES AND PREPARATION

To work through the exercises in this chapter, you need to have the following installed to the development station:

➤ Visual Studio 2008 with service pack 1

➤ Platform Builder for Windows Embedded Compact 7

➤ Expression Blend 3

➤ Windows Embedded Silverlight Tools

➤ Windows Embedded Silverlight Tools - Blend Templates

DEVELOP A COMPACT 7 OS DESIGN WITH SILVERLIGHT SUPPORT

To support the SWE application, the Compact 7 OS run-time image needs to include the necessary Silverlight for Windows Embedded components.

Work through the following steps to create an OS design based on the Virtual PC BSP, using a Virtual PC machine (VM) as the target device, to support the SWE application exercises in this chapter:

1. From the VS2008 File menu, select New, and click Project to launch the New Project screen.

2. From the New Project screen's left pane, select Platform Builder. Select OS Design from the right pane, enter MySWE as the project name, and click OK to bring up the OS Design Wizard.

3. From the OS Design Wizard screen, click Next to bring up the Board Support Packages selection screen.

4. From the Board Support Packages selection screen, select the Virtual PC: X86 BSP, and click Next to bring up the Design Templates selection screen.

5. From the Design Templates selection screen's left pane, expand the Enterprise Device folder, select the Handheld template, and click Finish to use the default selection for the remaining configurations and complete the OS Design Wizard step.

6. At this point, the Catalog Item Notification screen displays to raise a security warning to indicate one or more of the components included to the OS design may pose a security risk. Click Acknowledge to acknowledge the warning and close the warning screen.

7. After completing the OS Design Wizard step, the initial workspace for the MySWE OS design project is created. From the VS2008 IDE, click the Catalog Items View tab, and expand the Virtual PC: x86 node under the BSP folder to select the following BSP components from the Virtual PC BSP:

➤ SoundBlaster 16 Audio.

➤ VCEPC Keyboard driver: WIN7VPC (If you use Virtual PC 2007, select VCEPC Keyboard driver: VPC2007.)

➤ DEC 21x40 Ethernet.

8. To support the SWE application, you need to include the following component from the `\Shell and User Interface` folder to the OS design:

➤ Silverlight for Windows Embedded

The preceding steps create the MySWE OS design, with XAML run-time support, configured to build a Compact 7 OS run-time image in release mode, with the KITL build option enabled, using a Virtual PC machine as the target device.

When an OS run-time image, generated with the KITL option enabled, is downloaded to the target device, a KITL connection is established between the development station and the target device.

With an active KITL connection to the target device, you can modify code for the subproject application, recompile the application, and launch the application on the target device for testing from the development station.

 To see more descriptive information about the steps to create a Compact 7 OS design project, refer to Chapter 7, "OS Design."

Continue with the following steps to build and generate the OS run-time image from the OS design, and download the image to a Virtual PC machine to support the SWE application development exercise:

9. From the VS2008 Build menu, select Build Solution to build the MySWE OS design to generate an OS run-time image.

10. After the build process in step 10 is completed, download the OS run-time image generated from the project to the Virtual PC machine.

 For information about establishing connectivity and downloading an OS run-time image to the target device, refer to Chapter 8, "Target Device Connectivity and Download."

DEVELOP THE SWE APPLICATION PROJECT USING EXPRESSION BLEND 3

In this section, you work through an exercise to create a SWE UI project using Expression Blend 3.

The main objective for this exercise is to show the steps to develop the SWE user interface in XAML code using Express Blend 3 and use the classic "Hello-World" approach to keep the project simple and easy to understand.

Work through the following steps to create the SWE UI project:

1. Create the following directory to store the SWE application project:

```
$(_WINCEROOT)\SWEAPP
```

2. Launch Microsoft Expression Blend 3.

3. From the File menu select New Project to bring up the New Project Wizard, as shown in Figure 22-1.

4. From the Project Types pane on left, select Windows Embedded.

5. On the right, select the Silverlight for Windows Embedded Application template and enter **XAML_Hello** as the name for the project.

6. Select the $(_WINCEROOT)\SWEAPP directory as the location to store the project, and click OK to create the initial project workspace with a blank canvas.

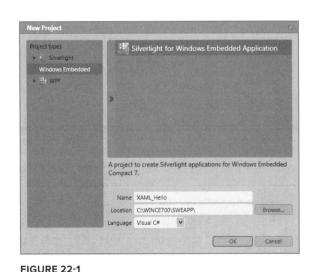

FIGURE 22-1

7. From the View menu, select Active Document View, and click Split View to show both the Design and XAML views, as shown in Figure 22-2.

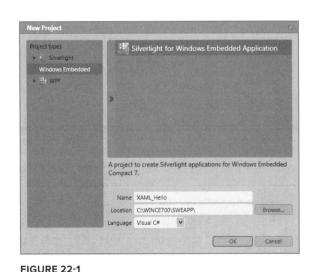

FIGURE 22-2

8. From the XAML code window, change the Width to 320 and Height to 240 to adjust the canvas to a smaller size.

9. From the Assets panel, select the TextBox control and draw a textbox on the canvas, change the text to **Hello World** and change the font to a larger size, 16pt, and bold.

10. From the Assets tab, select the Button control, and draw a button control on the canvas, as shown in Figure 22-3.

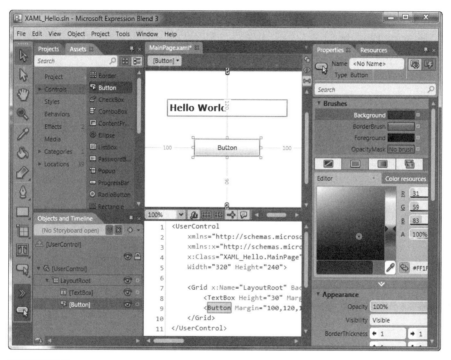

FIGURE 22-3

11. From the File menu select Save All to save the project.

PORT A XAML CODE PROJECT TO NATIVE CODE USING WINDOWS EMBEDDED SILVERLIGHT TOOLS

In the previous section, a simple SWE application project, XAML_Hello, is created. To use this project with Compact 7, you need to port the project from XAML code to native code as a subproject for the OS design.

In this section, you work through the following steps to port the XAML_Hello project to a Compact 7 OS design subproject, using the Windows Embedded Silverlight Tool (WEST):

1. With the MySWE OS design project active, from the VS2008 Tools menu, select Windows Embedded Silverlight Tools, and click Create Platform Builder Subproject to bring up the Create Platform Builder Subproject Wizard screen, as shown in Figure 22-4.

2. Click Next to bring up the project name and location screen.

3. Enter **SWE_Hello** as the project name.

4. Click Browse, and select the following folder for the Location entry, as shown in Figure 22-5, and click Next to show the Project Selection screen:

FIGURE 22-4

```
$(_OSDESIGNROOT)\MySWE\MySWE
```

5. From the Project Selection screen, click Browse, and navigate to the following folder to select the XAML_Hello.csproj project file, as shown in Figure 22-6:

```
$(_WINCEROOT)\SWEAPP\XAML_Hello\XAML_Hello
```

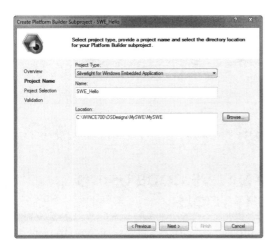

FIGURE 22-5

FIGURE 22-6

6. From the Project Selection screen, click Next to bring up the Validation screen, as shown in Figure 22-7.

7. From the Validation screen, click Finish to complete the process to port the XAML_Hello XAML code project to a native code subproject, SWE_Hello, for the MySWE Compact 7 OS design.

At this point, the WEST ported the XAML code project to native code and created the SWE_Hello native code application project in the following directory:

```
$(_WINCEROOT)\OSDESIGNS\MySWE\MySWE
```

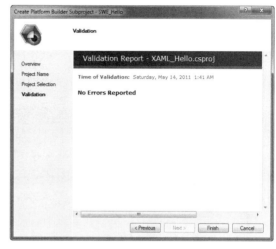

FIGURE 22-7

ADD THE SWE APPLICATION AS A SUBPROJECT, COMPILE, AND LAUNCH

In the previous section, the SWE_Hello application project is ported from an Expression Blend XAML code project to a native code application project, SWE_Hello. To include the application to the OS design, you need to add the SWE_Hello native code application as a subproject to the OS design.

Add Application as Subproject

Work through the following steps to add the SWE_Hello application as a subproject to the OS design:

1. With the MySWE OS design active, from the VS2008 Solution Explorer tab, right-mouse-click the Subprojects folder, and click Add Existing Subproject, as shown in Figure 22-8.

2. From the selection dialog, navigate and select the SWE_Hello.pbpxml project file from the following directory, and click Open to add the SWE_Hello application as a subproject to the MySWE OS design:

```
$(_OSDESIGNROOT)\MySWE\MySWE\SWE_Hello
```

FIGURE 22-8

Build and Compile a Subproject Application

Continuing from the exercise in the previous section, work through the following steps to configure the OS design to exclude the SWE_Hello subproject application from the OS run-time image to enable you to compile and build the SWE_Hello subproject without recompiling the OS design to save time:

1. From the VS2008 Solution Explorer tab, right-mouse-click the MySWE OS design project node, and click Properties to bring up the MySWE Property Pages screen, as shown in Figure 22-9.

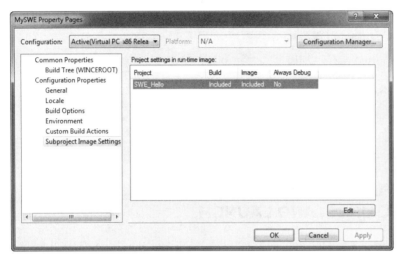

FIGURE 22-9

2. From the left pane, expand the Configuration Properties node to select Subproject Image Settings.

3. From the right pane, select SWE_Hello, and click Edit to bring up the Edit Run-Time Image Settings screen, as shown in Figure 22-10.

4. Enable the Exclude from Image check box, and click OK to close the screen.

5. From the MySWE Property Pages screen, click OK to close the screen.

FIGURE 22-10

6. From the VS2008 Build menu, select Targeted Build Settings, and uncheck the Make Run-Time Image After Building option.

7. From the VS2008 Solution Explorer tab, right-mouse-click the SWE_Hello node under the Subprojects folder, and click Build to compile and generate a binary executable for the application.

Launch the Subproject Application on the Target Device

During the first exercise in this chapter, an OS run-time image is generated from the MySWE OS design and downloaded to the target device using a Virtual PC machine as the target device. If the OS run-time image is not downloaded to the target device, download the image now.

The OS run-time image is generated with the KITL build option enabled. As the result, the VS2008 IDE establishes a KITL connection to the target device, after the OS run-time image is downloaded and launched on the target device. KITL connectivity between the VS2008 IDE and the target device is needed to launch the application from the build release directory to run on the target device.

Work through the following steps to launch the SWE_Hello application on the target device:

1. From the VS2008 Target menu, click Run Program to bring up the Run Program screen, as shown in Figure 22-11.

FIGURE 22-11

2. From the Run Program screen's Available Programs selection list, select the SWE_Hello.exe executable, and click Run to launch the program on the target device.

3. As the SWE_Hello.exe application executes on the target device, the application screen is shown on the target device's desktop, as shown in Figure 22-12.

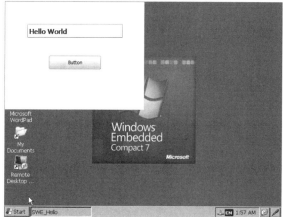

From this exercise, you can see the WEST simplified the process to port an Expression Blend XAML code project to a native code project.

FIGURE 22-12

ADD EVENT HANDLER TO SILVERLIGHT XAML CODE PROJECT

In the previous section, a simple SWE application UI is created in XAML code using Expression Blend 3 and ported to a native code application as a subproject to a Compact 7 OS design. The exercise in this section adds an event handler to this application for the button click event.

Continuing with the SWE application project created in the previous section, work through the following steps to modify the Silverlight XAML code application to add an event handler for the button control:

1. Launch Express Blend 3, and open the XAML_Hello SWE application project created earlier in this chapter.

2. From the Expression Blend View menu, select Active Document View, and click Split view to show both the Design and XAML views.

3. From the Design view window, click the Button control.

4. From the Properties panel's top-right corner, click the Events icon to list all available events associated with the Button control, as shown in Figure 22-13.

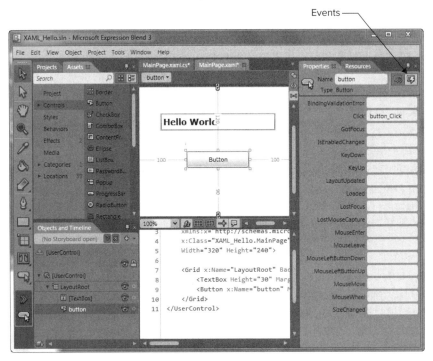

FIGURE 22-13

5. Enter **button** as the name for the control.

6. Double-click on the blank text box for the Click event to add a button_Click event. As you double-click on the Click event, the code editor window displays the MainPage .xaml.cs file, showing the code for the button_Click event, as shown in Figure 22-14.

7. From the File menu, click Save All to save the changes.

```
1   using System;
2   using System.Windows;
3   using System.Windows.Controls;
4   using System.Windows.Documents;
5   using System.Windows.Ink;
6   using System.Windows.Input;
7   using System.Windows.Media;
8   using System.Windows.Media.Animation;
9   using System.Windows.Shapes;
10
11  namespace XAML_Hello
12  {
13      public partial class MainPage : UserControl
14      {
15          public MainPage()
16          {
17              // Required to initialize variables
18              InitializeComponent();
19          }
20
21          private void button_Click(object sender, System.Windows
22          {
23              // TODO: Add event handler implementation here.
24          }
25      }
26  }
```

FIGURE 22-14

UPDATE THE SWE APPLICATION SUBPROJECT

In the previous section, the XAML_Hello Expression Blend project has been updated with an event handler added to the button control. The exercise in this section updates the SWE_Hello subproject with the change made to the XAML_Hello project using the Update Silverlight for Windows Embedded Project Wizard.

Work through the following steps to update the SWE_Hello subproject:

1. With the MySWE OS design active, from the VS2008 Solution Explorer, expand the SWE_Hello subproject under the \Subprojects folder.

2. Expand the \Resources files folder, and double-click the MainPage.xaml file.

3. From the VS2008 Tools menu, select Windows Embedded Silverlight Tools, and click Update Silverlight for Windows Embedded Project to launch this wizard and update the SWE_Hello subproject to reflect the change made to the XAML_Hello Expression Blend 3 project.

4. From the VS2008 Solution Explorer tab, expand the SWE_Hello subproject's \Source files folder, and double-click on the MainPage.cpp file to open this file in the code editor window.

5. Search for the button_Click event handler, and add the MessageBox function to display a message box when this event is triggered, as follows:

Available for download on Wrox.com

```
HRESULT MainPage::button_Click (IXRDependencyObject* pSender,
                                XRMouseButtonEventArgs* pArgs)
{
    HRESULT hr = E_NOTIMPL;

    if ((NULL == pSender) || (NULL == pArgs))
    {
        hr = E_INVALIDARG;
    }
        MessageBox (NULL, TEXT("Button clicked."), TEXT("SWE App"), MB_OK | MB_TOPMOST);
    return hr;
}
```

Code snippet is from Chapter22_Snippet.txt

6. Compile the SWE_Hello subproject, and launch the application on the target device.

7. After the SWE_Hello application is launched on the target device, click the button to show the message box.

CREATE A USER CONTROL

Continuing with the same XAML_Hello Expression Blend project and SWE_Hello Compact 7 subproject from the previous section, the exercise in this section adds a storyboard to the project to animate the Button control.

Work through the following steps to create a storyboard to animate the Button control:

1. Launch Express Blend 3, and open the XAML_Hello SWE application project created earlier in this chapter.

2. From the Objects and Timeline tab, click the + icon on the top-right corner, as shown in Figure 22-15, to bring up the Create Storyboard Resource screen, as shown in Figure 22-16.

FIGURE 22-15

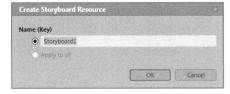

FIGURE 22-16

3. Use the default name, Storyboard1, and click OK and bring up the Objects and Timeline tab.

With an active storyboard, the Objects and Timeline tab displays the animation timeline for the storyboard, as shown in Figure 22-17.

The animation timeline is shown in the second increment, where you can associate a UI element's display to a different timeline. For example, you can make the button animate left to right by associating the button control's position moved by 50 pixels to the left at the 1-second timeline, moved right by 50 pixels at the 2-second timeline, moved by 50 pixels to the left at the 3-second timeline, and so on.

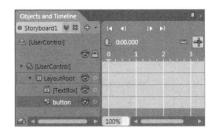

FIGURE 22-17

Work through the following steps to configure the storyboard to animate the Button control:

4. From the Objects and Timeline tab, select the Button control.

5. Click the 1-second timeline, and move the Button control to the left by about 50 pixels.

6. Click the 2-second timeline, and move the Button control to the right by about 50 pixels.

7. Click on the 3-second timeline, and move the Button control to the left by about 50 pixels.

8. From the Expression Blend File menu, click Save All to save the changes made to the XAML_Hello project.

UPDATE THE SWE APPLICATION SUBPROJECT TO INCLUDE ANIMATION

In the previous section, Storyboard1 is added to the XAML_Hello XAML code UI project to animate the Button control. The exercise in this section updates the SWE_Hello Compact 7 subproject to include the animation function and add codes to trigger the animation.

Work through the following steps to update the SWE_Hello project:

1. Launch the MySWE OS design from the VS2008 IDE.

2. From the Solution Explorer tab, expand the SWE_Hello subproject under the `\Subprojects` folder.

3. Expand the `\Resources files` folder, and double-click the `MainPage.xaml` file.

4. From the VS2008 Tools menu, select Windows Embedded Silverlight Tools, and click Update Silverlight for Windows Embedded Project to launch this wizard and update the SWE_Hello subproject to reflect the change made to the XAML_Hello Expression Blend 3 project.

5. From the VS2008 Solution Explorer tab, expand the SWE_Hello subproject's `\Source files` folder, and double-click the `MainPage.cpp` file to open this file in the code editor window.

6. Search for the `button_Click` event handler and replace the codes in the event handler with the following code to trigger the storyboard to animate the Button control.

Available for
download on
Wrox.com

```
HRESULT MainPage::button_Click (IXRDependencyObject* pSender,
 XRMouseButtonEventArgs* pArgs)
{
    HRESULT hr = E_NOTIMPL;

    if ((NULL == pSender) || (NULL == pArgs))
    {
        hr = E_INVALIDARG;
    }
       IXRStoryboard *pStoryboard;

    FindName(L"Storyboard1", &pStoryboard);
    if(pStoryboard)
    {
        pStoryboard->Stop();
        pStoryboard->Begin();
    }
       return hr;
}
```

Code snippet is from Chapter22_Snippet.txt

7. From the Solution Explorer tab, right-mouse-click the SWE_Hello subproject, and click Build to compile the project.

8. Download the OS run-time image to the target device.

9. After the OS image launches on the device, launch the SWE_Hello.exe application on the device.

10. Click the Button control to see the animation.

SUMMARY

Silverlight for Windows Embedded helps the device maker to create an exciting and visually compelling user interface for an embedded device. The Windows Embedded Silverlight Tool, included as part of the Compact 7 release, greatly simplifies the development process for Silverlight for Windows Embedded applications.

23

Auto Launching Applications

WHAT'S IN THIS CHAPTER?

➤ Launching an application during startup

➤ Configuring the registry to auto launch an application

➤ Auto launching an application using the Startup folder

➤ Using the AutoLaunch component

A Windows Embedded Compact 7 device is designed to perform designated functions. It's common for a Compact 7 device to be designed without the typical Windows desktop and launch a custom application as the device's primary user interface during startup.

For some Compact 7 devices, in addition to the need to automatically launch a custom application that functions as the primary user interface, the device needs to launch additional applications and services during startup to support the device's functions. Some of the applications may have dependencies and need certain system resources and other applications to be launched to function properly. Otherwise, launching these applications prematurely can cause system errors.

You can use different methods to automatically launch an application during startup. This chapter talks about the following options, which you can apply to your Compact 7 device:

➤ Configuring the system registry to auto launch an application during startup

➤ Placing an application in the `\Windows\Startup` folder for the OS to launch the application during startup

➤ Using the AutoLaunch component, from the AutoLaunch4CE project on the Codeplex site, to AutoLaunch multiple applications, with configurable time delays for each individual application, during startup

CONFIGURING THE REGISTRY TO AUTO LAUNCH AN APPLICATION

The Compact 7 system registry plays a key role in controlling the OS run-time image's startup process, launching device drivers and applications during startup.

As the Compact 7 OS run-time image launches, during the startup process, the system scans the HKLM\ Init registry key, looking for Launchxx entries and launches the associated application in numerical order, going from the lowest number to the highest number. For each Launchxx entry, a corresponding Dependxx entry contains information about the application's dependency, such as the following:

```
[HKEY_LOCAL_MACHINE\Init]
    "Launch90"="App1.exe"
    "Depend90"=hex:0a,00,14,00
```

Understanding the Compact 7 Startup Registry

To configure the Compact 7 registry to auto launch an application during startup, you need to understand how the Compact 7 OS uses the system registry to launch core OS components, which your application is dependent on.

During an OS design project's build process, all the registry entries from different components, configured to be part of the OS design, are merged into the REGINIT.INI file in the build release directory, to be compiled as part of the final OS run-time image. To review registry entries for a Compact 7 OS run-time image generated from an OS design project, the REGINIT.INI file is the best place to look.

Using the MyVPC OS design project from the exercise in Chapter19, "Platform Builder Native Code Application Example," as an example, searching through the REGINIT.INI file after the OS design project's build process, you can find a number of Launchxx entries under the HKLM\Init key, used by the Compact 7 OS to launch core system components, such as the following:

```
[HKEY_LOCAL_MACHINE\init]
    "Launch10"="shell.exe"
    "Launch20"="device.dll"

    "Launch30"="gwes.dll"
    "Depend30"=hex:14,00

    "Launch50"="explorer.exe"
    "Depend50"=hex:14,00, 1e,00
```

Based on the preceding registry entries, the shell.exe component, associated with the Launch10 entry, is the first to launch. The shell.exe component provides target control support.

The next in line to launch is the device.dll component, associated with the Launch20 entry. This is the device manager responsible for loading the audio, battery, keyboard, mouse, NDIS, notification LED, serial, and USB, and any other device drivers that expose the stream interface.

The next in line to launch, after the `device.dll`, is the `gwes.dll` component, associated with the `Launch30` entry. This is the Graphic Windowing and Event Subsystem (GWES) responsible for loading the display, printer, and touch screen drivers. The value for the associated `Depend30` entry, `hex:14,00`, indicates this component depends on the `Launch20` process (14 in hexadecimal = 20 in decimal) and needs to wait until the `device.dll` is fully loaded before launching the `gwes.dll`.

The next in line to launch after the `gwes.dll` component is the `explorer.exe` executable, associated with the `Launch50` entry. This component launches the Compact 7 desktop. The value for the associated `Depend50` entry, `hex:14, 00, 1E, 00`, indicates this component depends on the `Launch20` and `Launch30` processes (14 in hexadecimal = 20 in decimal; 1E in hexadecimal = 30 in decimal) and needs to wait until both the `device.dll` and `gwes.dll` are fully loaded before launching the `explorer.exe` executable.

Configure Registry to Launch Application During Startup

The MyVPC OS design project from Chapter 19 includes a Platform Builder native code application subproject, PB7_Win32. For Chapter 19, the MyVPC OS design is configured to generate an OS run-time image with KITL enabled, excluding the PB7_Win32 subproject from the build process and excluding the `PB7_Win32.exe` executable from the OS run-time image.

Using the same MyVPC OS design for the exercise in this section, you need to configure this OS design to generate an OS run-time image that includes the `PB7_Win32.exe` and launches this executable during startup.

Work through the following steps to configure the MyVPC OS design project to disable KITL; include the PB7_Win32 subproject as part of the build process, include the `PB7_Win32.exe` executable as part of the OS run-time image, and configure the OS run-time image to launch the `PB7_Win32.exe` executable during startup:

1. Launch the MyVPC OS design project from Chapter 19.

2. From the VS2008 Project menu, click MyVPC Properties to bring up the MyVPC Property Pages screen.

3. From the left pane, expand the Configuration Properties node, and click Subproject Image Settings.

4. From the right pane, select PB7_Win32, and click Edit to bring up the Edit Run-Time Image Settings screen.

5. From the Edit Run-Time Image Settings screen, uncheck the following items, and click OK to close the screen:

   ➤ Exclude from Build.

   ➤ Exclude from Image.

6. From the MyVPC Property Pages screen's left pane, click Build Options to bring up the build options configuration pane.

7. From the build options configuration pane on the right, disable KITL, and click OK to close the screen.

8. From the VS2008 Solution Explorer tab, double-click `OSDesign.reg` to open this registry file in the code editor window.

9. From the code editor window, append the following registry to the `OSDesign.reg` file:

```
[HKEY_LOCAL_MACHINE\init]
    "Launch90"="PB7_Win32.exe"
    "Depend90"=hex:14,00,1e,00,32,00
```

Code snippet is from Chapter23_Snippet.txt

10. From the VS2008 Build menu, click Build Solution to build the project and generate an OS run-time image.

11. Follow the steps from the exercise in Chapter 19 to download the OS run-time image to a Virtual PC machine to review the result.

With the preceding configuration, the OS run-time image generated from the project launches the `PB7_Win32.exe` executable during startup.

AUTO LAUNCH APPLICATION FROM STARTUP FOLDER

Another method to automatically launch an application when the Compact 7 OS starts is to place a copy of the application executable in the `\Windows\Startup` folder. When Compact 7 starts, it scans and launches any application found in this folder.

Work through the following steps to configure the MyVPC OS design to generate an OS run-time image and launch the `PB7_Win32.exe` application from the startup folder:

1. Continue with the MyVPC OS design from the previous exercise; from the VS2008 Solution Explorer tab, double-click `OSDesign.reg`, and open this file in the code editor window.

2. Remove the following entries from `OSDesign.reg` (These entries were added in the previous exercise to launch the `PB7_Win32.exe` during startup and need to be removed for the exercise in this section.):

```
[HKEY_LOCAL_MACHINE\init]
    "Launch90"="PB7_Win32.exe"
    "Depend90"=hex:14,00,1e,00,32,00
```

3. From the VS2008 Solution Explorer tab, locate and double-click `PB7_Win32.bib` to open this file in the code editor window.

4. Replace the `Modules` entry with `Files` as follows:

```
FILES
; @XIPREGION IF PLATFORM_FILES_MISC
PB7_Win32.exe  $(_FLATRELEASEDIR)\PB7_Win32.exe    NK
; @XIPREGION ENDIF PLATFORM_FILES_MISC
```

Code snippet is from Chapter23_Snippet.txt

> *When a BIB file entry is added under the Modules section, the file is included in the OS run-time image with the hidden attribute. The Compact 7 OS does not launch an executable with a hidden file attribute from the startup folder. Changing the file placement from the Modules section to the Files section removes the hidden attribute and makes the file visible.*

5. From the VS2008 Solution Explorer tab, locate and double-click on OSDesign.dat to open this file in the code editor window.

6. Append the following entry (this is a single entry within the same line) to the OSDesign.dat file, to copy the PB7_Win32.exe executable to the Compact 7 device's \WINDOWS\STARTUP folder:

Available for download on Wrox.com

```
Directory("\Windows\Startup"):-File("PB7_Win32.exe","\Windows\PB7_Win32.exe")
```

Code snippet is from Chapter23_Snippet.txt

7. From the VS2008 Build menu, click Build Solution to build the OS design project and generate an OS run-time image.

8. Follow the steps from the exercise in Chapter 19 to download the OS run-time image to a Virtual PC machine to review the result.

With the preceding configuration, the OS run-time image generated from the project launches the PB7_Win32.exe executable during startup.

USING THE AUTOLAUNCH COMPONENT

The AutoLaunch component is created to ease the tasks needed to launch one or more applications during Compact 7 startup. With this component, you can configure the Compact 7 device to launch multiple applications during startup and control these applications' launching sequence using configurable time delay to launch each application.

The AutoLaunch component is developed and packaged as a Compact 7 component and can be easily added to an OS design project, from the component catalog, and compiled as part of the OS run time image.

As of this book's writing, the AutoLaunch_v200_Compact7 component is the latest version, available from the Codeplex site at the following URL:

http://AutoLaunch4CE.Codeplex.com

Work through the following exercise to configure MyVPC OS design to launch the PB7_Win32.exe executable during startup with help from the AutoLaunch component:

1. Continue with the MyVPC OS design from the previous exercise; from the Catalog Item View tab, select and include the AutoLaunch_v200_Compact7 component in the OS design, from the \Third Party\Embedded101 folder.

2. From the VS2008 Solution Explorer tab, double-click `OSDesign.dat` to open this file in the code editor window.

3. Remove the following entry, entered as part of the previous exercise.

```
Directory("\Windows\Startup"):-File("PB7_Win32.exe","\Windows\PB7_Win32.exe")
```

4. Append the following registry entries in the `OSDesign.reg` file:

```
[HKEY_LOCAL_MACHINE\Startup]
    "Process0"="PB7_Win32.exe"
    "Process0Delay"=dword:00001388
```

Code snippet is from Chapter23_Snippet.txt

5. From the VS2008 Build menu, click Build Solution to build and generate a Compact 7 OS run-time image from the OS design.

6. Follow the steps from the exercise in Chapter 19 to download the OS run-time image to a Virtual PC machine to review the result.

With the preceding configuration, the OS run-time image generated from the project launches the `PB7_Win32.exe` executable during startup, with a 5-second delay (1388 in hexadecimal = 5000 in decimal).

AUTOLAUNCH MULTIPLE APPLICATIONS

With help from the AutoLaunch component, launching multiple Compact 7 applications during startup and controlling the applications' startup sequence is simple.

In the previous exercise, the AutoLaunch component is included in the OS design and configured to launch the `PB7_Win32.exe` executable during startup.

Continue with the MyVPC OS design from the previous exercise, and work through the following steps to configure the MyVPC OS design to generate an OS run-time image to launch multiple applications during startup:

1. From the Catalog Items View tab, select and add the following components to the OS design:

    ➤   WordPad

    ➤   Internet Explorer 7.0 Sample Browser

2. From the Explorer tab, double-click `OSDesign.reg` to open this file in the code editor window.

3. Add the following entry to `OSDesign.reg`, to configure the AutoLaunch component to launch these applications, with individual time delay:

```
[HKEY_LOCAL_MACHINE\Startup]
    ; Launch with 5 seconds delay
    "Process0"="PB7_Win32.exe"
```

```
"Process0Delay"=dword:00001388

; Launch with 10 seconds delay
"Process1"="IEsample.exe"
"Process1Delay"=dword:00002710

; Launch with 15 seconds delay
"Process2"="Pword.exe"
"Process2Delay"=dword:00003A98
```

Code snippet is from Chapter23_Snippet.txt

4. From the VS2008 Build menu, click Build Solution to build and generate a Compact 7 OS run-time image from the OS design.

5. Follow the steps from the exercise in Chapter 19 to download the OS run-time image to a Virtual PC machine to review the result.

With the previous configuration, the OS run-time image generated from the project launches the PB7_Win32.exe executable during startup, with a 5-second delay. Five seconds after launching the PB7_Win32.exe executable, the AutoLaunch component launches the IEsample.exe executable, a browser application. Ten seconds after launching the PB7_Win32.exe executable, the AutoLaunch component launches the Pword.exe executable, a WordPad word processor.

SUMMARY

Whether you use Windows Embedded Compact 7 to build a medical device, an engineering instrument, an industrial automation control system, an automation, or handheld portable devices, these devices are intended for the targeted market and designed to deliver specific functions. When powered on, these devices are designed to launch one or more customized applications developed to serve the device's purpose.

Automatically launching one or more applications during startup is a built-in feature provided by the Platform Builder for Compact 7 development environment to make your job easier. With help from resources provided as part of the AutoLaunch component, from the AutoLaunch4CE project on the Codeplex site, you have additional resources to help simplify the tasks needed to launch multiple applications, with configurable time delay for each individual application, to control the application startup sequence to ensure other application resources required by the application launch.

The AutoLaunch4CE component from the Codeplex site is provided with source code, which you can modify to add additional features to serve your purpose.

24

Application Deployment Options

WHAT'S IN THIS CHAPTER?

➤ Deploying a Compact 7 application

A Windows Embedded Compact 7 device is designed to serve designated functions and tasks, and requires a specialized application to serve the device's intended purpose.

Unlike the desktop PC environment, where it's common to distribute a software application as an installable package to the end-user, and allow the end-user to install the application on their PC, the specialized purpose of Compact 7 application needs to be deployed onto the Compact 7 device prior to distributing the device to the end-user.

To ensure the device can maintain an expected level of performance to serve the intended purpose, many Compact 7 devices are designed with restrictions to prevent the end-user from installing additional software to the device.

This chapter looks at different options to deploy an application on a Compact 7 device.

DEPLOYING COMPACT 7 APPLICATIONS

Throughout the Compact 7 development process, there may be different types of applications created to serve different purposes to support the development effort. Some of the applications are not intended to be distributed to the end user.

For an application that needs to be deployed as part of the Compact 7 device to the end-user, you need to consider the following factors as part of the application deployment plan:

➤ Throughout the device's life, will there be the need to update the application?

➤ Throughout the device's life, will there be the need to provide updated data to support the application?

➤ When the device needs to be serviced and requires the end-user to use a replacement unit, will there be the need for the end-user to export the device configuration and user data from the unit being replaced and import this data to the new replacement unit?

➤ When the device requires service due to system errors and failure, how will the device be serviced?

➤ Additional considerations unique to the device or industry you work in.

The type of device, application, and end-user scenario for the device can have a strong influence on your choice for deployment mechanism for applications on the Compact 7 devices.

OPTIONS

There are multiple options to deploy an application for Compact 7 devices.

➤ Deploy the application as an installable CAB file to install to a device, preconfigured with Compact 7 OS and required components to support an application installation packaged in CAB file format.

➤ Deploy the application to the Compact 7 device's local storage.

➤ Deploy the application as part of the Compact 7 OS run-time image created for the device.

➤ Deploy the application using a hybrid between the including portion of the application as part of the Compact 7 OS run-time image, and deploy part of the application to the device's local storage.

Deploying an Application: CAB Installable Package

For a Compact 7 device created to serve a targeted industry and designed to deliver specific functions, it's not likely to use the CAB installation package as an option to deploy the Compact 7 application.

To support a Compact 7 application installed from the CAB file installation package, the device must implement a Hive-based registry or some other method to persist configuration and application data when the device goes through a cold reboot or complete power reset, where the device loses power completely. Otherwise, the device reverts to the initial factory default state and cannot retain the application installed from a CAB file installation package.

Although the CAB file installation package is common and the preferred method to deliver a Windows Mobile and Windows Phone application, it's not recommended for Compact 7 devices designed to serve vertical markets.

The VS2008 IDE includes the Smart Device CAB Project Wizard, which you can use to create a CAB file installation package for you application. To access this wizard, work through the following steps:

1. From the VS2008 File menu, select New, and click Project to bring up the New Project screen.

2. From the New Project screen's left pane, expand the Other Project Types node, and click the Setup and Deployment node to show available setup templates, as shown in Figure 24-1.

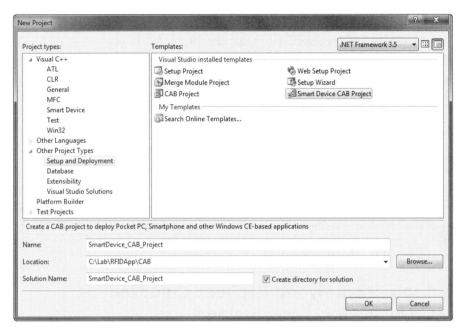

FIGURE 24-1

3. From the Templates pane on the right, select the Smart Device CAB Project, enter a project name, and click OK to create the project workspace to create a CAB file installation package.

From this point forward, the steps to create the CAB file installation package are the same as a standard setup project, where you specify the application binary and other project files, installation folder, and other project properties. When you build and compile the project, instead of producing the MSI and `setup.exe` files, the Smart Device CAB Project produces a CAB file.

Deploying an Application: Local Storage

For a Compact 7 device built with local storage that you can access from the Compact 7 file system, you can deploy an application to the local storage.

When deploying an application to the device's local storage, separate from the OS run-time image, the OS needs to be configured to launch the application from the local storage. For this option, the OS run-time image needs to implement a Hive-based registry to persist configuration and application data when the device resets or experiences a complete loss of power.

While this option provides flexibility, making it easier to update the application, it does have some drawbacks. When the device's configuration data on the local storage becomes corrupted, the application may not be able to launch as expected.

Deploying an Application: Compiled as Part of the OS Image

Deploying an application as part of the Compact 7 OS run-time image is one of the preferred methods. When the application is compiled as part of the image, the application and the default configuration always remain with the image. As long as the device's hardware can function, the Compact 7 OS run-time image compiled with the application always boots up with the application running, using the factory default configuration.

Configuring an OS design to include an application to be compiled as part of the OS run-time image involves the following steps:

➤ Add the BIB file entry to the OS design to include the application and all required support files.

➤ Add required registry entries, to support the application, as part of the OS design.

➤ Configure the OS design to launch the application during startup.

For a Compact 7 device deployed with the application compiled as part of the OS image, to update the application, the OS run-time image for the device needs to be updated. For a device that requires updates, this option is a potential drawback. While updating the device's OS run-time image in the field, a single failed attempt to update the OS run-time image can cause serious problems and can even render the device not able to boot.

Deploying an Application: Hybrid Between Compiled as Part of the OS Image and Local Storage

Although it may require additional effort and cost, using a hybrid method to deploy a Compact 7 application, with the mechanism to launch the application compiled as part of the OS image and from the device's local storage, you can overcome the drawbacks associated with the other methods.

Depending on the device's hardware resources and architecture, the hybrid method to deploy a Compact 7 application to a device may not work for some devices.

To deploy a Compact 7 application to a device, using the hybrid method, you need to include the following design considerations as part of your project's OS design and application development requirements:

➤ Include an application launcher as part of the design. The application launcher (AppLauncher) is to be compiled as part of the OS run-time image configured to launch as the device startup. When launched, the application launcher is responsible for launching the device's application, going through the following steps:

1. When launched, the AppLauncher attempts to retrieve configuration data from the device's local storage and launch the device's application based on the retrieved configuration data.

2. When the AppLauncher fails to retrieve configuration data from the device's local storage, it defaults back to launching the application compiled as part of the OS run-time image.

➤ Design the application in a way that enables it to execute when deployed as part of the OS run-time image or deployed to the device's local storage.

➤ Include the initial application as part of the OS run-time image.

➤ Future updates to the application are to be deployed to the device's local storage.

With the above design consideration, the device is deployed initially with the application compiled as part of the OS image. When an update to the application is needed, the updated application can be deployed to the device's local storage along with a configuration file to instruct the AppLauncher to launch the application from the local storage.

During a failed attempt to update the device's application, the device is still able to launch the initial application compiled as part of the OS image, and safeguard the device from being disabled as the result of a failed update attempt.

SUMMARY

There are multiple options to deploy an application to a Compact 7 device that lead to the same objective, to make the application accessible on the device. There are differences among these options for how each option handles a complete loss of power to the device and a failed attempt to update the application for the device.

Which ever option you choose to deploy an application to a target device, you need to understand the advantages and disadvantages of the different options.

PART IV
Deploy Windows Embedded Compact 7 Devices

25

Deploy OS Run-time Images

WHAT'S IN THIS CHAPTER?

➤ Deploying a Compact 7 OS run-time image

After the development process that created and configured a Windows Embedded Compact 7 OS design and generated an OS run-time image for distribution, you need to choose the best option to deploy the OS image to the target device.

This chapter talks about different options to deploy the OS image to the target device for distribution.

CONSIDERATIONS

You can configure Compact 7 devices designed with different processor architectures and hardware platforms to boot from different types of storage. Depending on the selected processor and the hardware's overall design, you need to consider the best option to deploy the OS image based on the target device's unique hardware architecture and application scenario.

ARM, MIPS, and x86 devices each have different implementations to boot and launch Compact 7 OS. This chapter talks about different options to deploy an OS run-time image to an x86 target device, using the eBox-3310A (eBox) as a target device.

The eBox is built with an x86 processor and designed to boot from the following sources:

➤ Network: Boot from the network using Preboot eXecution Environment (PXE).

➤ Removable storage: USB flash storage.

➤ Fixed storage: IDE hard disk.

➤ Fixed storage: IDE flash storage.

➤ Fixed storage: Compact Flash.

Network: PXE

PXE is one of the common methods in use to boot up and launch an OS run-time image from the network. When configured to boot from the network using PXE, a Compact 7 device acquires an IP address from a DHCP server and attaches to a TFTP server to download the OS run-time image to RAM and launch the image from RAM.

Booting from the network eliminates the need to have local storage, which can help lower the component cost for the device. For an application scenario such as an information kiosk, electronic billboard, and thin-client, booting from the network can help simplify ongoing administrative and maintenance tasks for the devices.

Following is an example application scenario:

➤ A department store needs to deploy information kiosks around the store to display active advertisements and product information based on each kiosk's location, where kiosks in the kitchen department display different content than the kiosks in the fashion department. As part of the ongoing administrative and maintenance tasks, the project requires these kiosks to change the display contents dynamically as needed.

➤ Windows Embedded Compact 7 devices are used to drive these information kiosks. Each of these Compact 7 devices has an integrated network interface with a unique MAC address. The MAC address is used to identify each individual kiosk and associate with the kiosk's location during installation.

➤ Each of these Compact 7–based kiosks is designed to boot from the network using PXE.

➤ Multiple Compact 7 OS run-time images are created with different display configurations to support kiosks built with different screen sizes, display resolutions, and orientations.

➤ A TFTP server is set up to serve the designated Compact 7 OS run-time image to each of the kiosks based on its MAC address.

➤ All the kiosks are configured to launch Internet Explorer during startup, pointing to a designated URL configured as part of the OS run-time image.

In the preceding application scenario, Compact 7 OS run-time images for all the kiosks are stored in one single TFTP server. To update a new Compact 7 OS run-time image for one particular group of devices or all the devices can be accomplished by updating the Compact 7 OS run-time images from one location, the TFTP server.

The advertisement and product information contents for the kiosks can easily be centralized on a local web server, which can be the same physical server as the TFTP server that stores the Compact 7 OS run-time images.

The preceding project provides a centralized location to update all the kiosks' display contents dynamically. If the kiosks require a major update, the Compact 7 OS run-time images for all kiosks can easily be updated from one central location, without the need to send technical personnel to service each individual kiosk.

This application scenario provides an effective method for the department store to communicate timely information to their customers with minimum effort. The system is designed to minimize the ongoing effort to manage and maintain the system, which translates to lower operating costs for the overall system and lowers the total cost for the project.

Removable Storage: USB Flash Storage

Although booting a Compact 7 OS image from removable USB flash storage may not be the best option for distribution, configuring the target device to launch the Compact 7 OS image from USB flash storage provides a convenient method to perform different testing and maintenance tasks on the device.

With USB flash storage, you can easily copy a Compact 7 OS image, an application, and a data file, needed for testing, from the development station without the need to set up a complex networking infrastructure just to download an OS image to the target device.

Fixed Storage: Hard Drive, IDE Flash, and Compact Flash

Deploying a Compact 7 OS run-time image to the device's fixed storage is the most common method.

For an x86-based device, a hard drive, an IDE flash, and Compact Flash storage, supported by the ATAPI block storage driver and FAT file system, are common storage options used to deploy a Compact 7 OS run-time image.

Hard Drive

The advantage for using a hard drive is the enormously large storage capacity. Currently, it's common to see a hard drive with storage capacity ranging from 250GB to more than 2TB.

However, because a hard drive uses spinning media with a mechanical reading mechanism, it does not function well in an environment that is subject to a high level of vibration. In addition, the operating temperature for most hard drives is limited to 0 to 55 degrees Celsius (32 to 131 degrees Fahrenheit).

IDE Flash Storage

IDE flash storage is built with nonvolatile flash memory designed with a controller and firmware to emulate an IDE hard drive. IDE flash storage is supported by the same device driver that supports a typical IDE hard drive, the ATAPI block storage driver, and a FAT file system.

Following are some of the IDE flash storage's characteristics:

➤ Available with a storage capacity ranging from 256MB to 16GB or more.

➤ No moving parts and can operate in an environment subject to a high level of vibration.

➤ Can operate in a broader range of operating temperatures than the hard drive. The industrial version can operate in −40 to +85 degrees Celsius (-40 to 185 degrees Fahrenheit).

Compact Flash

For an x86-based target device, Compact Flash has similar characteristics as the IDE flash storage. Although the Compact Flash is mechanically removable, the ATAPI driver and associated FAT file system treat the Compact Flash as fixed storage, similar to an IDE storage device that is not removable.

Compact Flash has similar characteristics to the IDE flash:

➤ Available with a storage capacity ranging from 256MB to 32GB or more.

➤ No moving parts and can operate in an environment subject to a high level of vibration.

➤ Can operate in a broader range of operating temperatures than the hard drive. The industrial version can operate in −40 to +85 degrees Celsius (-40 to 185 degrees Fahrenheit).

Bootloader

For an x86 device, it's common to configure the flash storage to boot to DOS and launch a Windows Embedded Compact OS run-time image or an Ethernet bootloader using LOADCEPC.EXE, a DOS-based bootloader, as part of the development environment setup.

Although DOS provides a convenient environment, with a file system compatible to the desktop PC, that enables you to easily copy and change contents on the storage device, it's an operating system. Whether you use Microsoft DOS or a derivative of DOS from another company, the DOS operating system has its own set of licensing requirements and costs and should not be used as part of a Compact 7 device configured for distribution to the end user.

For distribution, you need to configure the storage for the target device with an appropriate bootloader for Compact 7. For x86 devices, Platform Builder for Compact 7 provides two bootloaders that you can use:

➤ BIOSLoader

Provided as part of the CEPC BSP in the following directory:

```
$(_PLATFORMROOT)\CEPC\SRC\Bootloader\BIOSLoader
```

➤ Compact 7 Bootloader Framework

This is a new bootloader framework released as part of Compact 7, with source code. This bootloader framework provides common code and features to support ARM, MIPS, and x86 devices. The code for the x86 device is provided as part of the CEPC BSP in the following directory:

```
$(_PLATFORMROOT)\CEPC\SRC\Boot\
```

DEPLOYING AN OS RUN-TIME IMAGE

Although the Compact 7 OS provides a Windows shell similar to the Windows OS for the desktop PC, the Compact 7 OS is not intended for use as a general-purpose computer like the PC. A typical Compact 7 device is designed to deliver a specific function and configured to launch one or more applications during startup to perform the intended functions. Often, other than the required license sticker, Compact 7 devices distributed to their intended end user do not provide any indication that the devices are based on the Compact 7 OS.

When a target device is properly configured with a Compact 7 OS run-time image for distribution, it should behave as follows when powered on during normal operation:

1. The device's firmware, BIOS, or bootloader initializes the hardware.

2. The bootloader loads the OS run-time image into system memory. Optionally, the bootloader displays a splash screen as it loads the image to the system memory.

3. As the Compact 7 OS run-time boots up, it launches the application configured to run during startup.

The preceding steps need to be executed without any user interaction.

Image Deployment on RISC Platforms

The presence of some firmware responsible for the system boot is mandatory on any computer, but the size and the functionalities of this firmware vary widely from one system to another. The IBM-PC BIOS is a sophisticated piece of firmware that serves several purposes:

➤ Hardware initialization (IDE, PCI, USB, and so on)

➤ User configuration (CMOS setup)

➤ Real-mode IO interface based on software interrupts

➤ OS initialization (loading of a dedicated sector)

Several of these functionalities in the BIOS are nowadays obsolete, such as the real-mode IO interface (which explains the name: Basic Input Output System) or user configuration before the OS is initialized, which is confusing for the average user. Non-IBM-PC platforms such as ARM devices do not require complex bootloaders such as the PC BIOS; depending on the hardware configuration and system flexibility, the list may be reduced from zero to three items.

If the device is equipped with a NOR Flash that is large enough to contain the OS image, the Windows Embedded Compact 7 image may be installed at the CPU reset address and act as its own bootloader. This zero-bootloader solution, as shown in Figure 25-1, is not common because of several drawbacks including NOR flash speed, which is lower than DRAM speed, and the need to include all hardware initialization and maintenance code in the Compact 7 OAL.

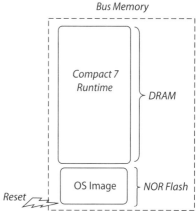

FIGURE 25-1

A more common solution in ARM designs is to include a built-in NAND Flash to store the Compact 7 image. This solution, as shown in Figure 25-2, requires a minimal bootloader responsible for hardware initialization (at least the DRAM components) and for the copy of the OS image from NAND Flash to DRAM. The list is in this case restricted to two items, and the bootloader code can be small:

➤ Hardware initialization (RAM, Clocks)

➤ OS initialization (NAND to DRAM copy)

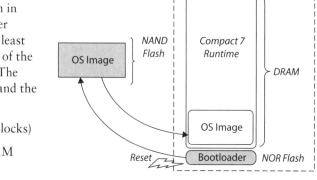

FIGURE 25-2

When the OS image is copied byte-to-byte from NAND Flash to DRAM by a minimal bootloader, you need an OS image file containing the exact memory mapping in DRAM. The NK.BIN file contains sections and does not correspond to the memory mapping of the image; you need to convert the NK.BIN file to an NK.NB0 file. Two command-line utilities can help you for that task:

➤ VIEWBIN.EXE to display the characteristics of your NK.BIN

➤ CVTBIN.EXE to convert the NK.BIN to NK.NB0

When the NK.BIN file is built, you can open a command shell window with the menu option Build ➪ Open Release Directory in Build Window. By launching VIEWBIN you can collect information about the NK.BIN for future CVRTBIN parameters.

```
viewbin nk.bin
ViewBin... nk.bin
Image Start = 0x00220000, length = 0x01CAC154
                Start address = 0x002258B0
Checking record #208 for potential TOC (ROMOFFSET = 0x80000000)
Found pTOC  = 0x81ec9688
ROMOFFSET = 0x80000000
Done.
```

Code snippet is Chapter25_Snippet.txt

CVRTBIN parameters may be listed with the -? argument:

```
cvrtbin -?
Unknown option... -?
Usage: cvrtbin [ options ] <filename>
Options:
    -s[re]      Generates SRE file from BIN
    -r[om]      Generates ROM file from BIN *

      * ROM conversion requires the following options to be set also...
```

```
-a[ddress]   Rom starting address
-w[idth]     Rom width 8, 16, or 32 bits
-l[ength]    Rom length as a hex value
```

Code snippet is from Chapter25_Snippet.txt

Use argument -r as you generate a raw ROM image; this option requires three parameters; *-address* and *-length* are listed in VIEWBIN output, and *-width* is your ROM width. Converting the NK.BIN file previously analyzed for a 32-bit ROM is done with the following line:

```
cvrtbin -r -a 0x00220000 -l 0x01CAC154 -w 32 nk.bin
ViewBin... nk.bin
Image Start = 0x00220000, length = 0x01CAC154
             Start address = 0x002258B0
Checking record #208 for potential TOC (ROMOFFSET = 0x80000000)
Found pTOC = 0x81ec9688
ROMOFFSET = 0x80000000
start 00220000 length 00000010
start 00220040 length 00000008
.................
.... Done.
```

Code snippet is from Chapter25_Snippet.txt

A minimal bootloader copying from NAND to DRAM is fast but shows its limitations as soon as you need multiple boot options, or an image update on the target. A more sophisticated boot mechanism is shown in Figure 25-3 where an intermediate bootloader offers user access before the OS image loads to DRAM.

With this technique, your NAND Flash can contain several images: one is the intermediate bootloader possibly obtained from the EBOOT.BIN file, and the other one is the final Compact 7 image. The NAND Flash may also be used as a persistent storage if a NAND file system is installed on a dedicated partition separated from ROM images.

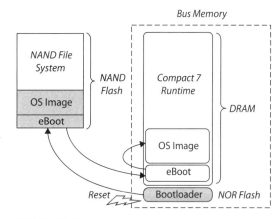

FIGURE 25-3

An intermediate bootloader is usually available as a source project in _WINCEROOT/PLATFORM/BSP_Name/SRC/BOOT/EBOOT. This standard EBOOT displays a menu on the debug link (serial, USB, and such) offering options to boot locally or download an OS image; it can also propose to write the downloaded OS image to NAND flash to finalize the installation of your device.

Windows Embedded Compact 7 does not impose any design choice for OS image deployment. You may use encryption to protect your devices during OS update or compression to reduce NAND flash footprint. The EBOOT project is a good starting point for these developments.

SUMMARY

Due to cost constraints, hardware architecture, and other design considerations, the option for deploying Compact 7 OS run-time image to an embedded device can be quite different for different projects. Although this is a norm for the seasoned developer in the embedded field, for the new developer coming from the desktop PC development environment, deploying an OS run-time image to a target device is often a confusing topic.

26

Bootloaders

WHAT'S IN THIS CHAPTER?

➤ Using Windows Embedded Compact 7 bootloaders

Bootloader is the code that initializes the hardware, places the Windows Embedded Compact 7 OS onto the hardware's memory, and launches the OS.

For new hardware, bootloader is the first piece of code to develop, as it is needed to download and launch the Compact 7 OS run-time image on the hardware.

Unless you develop a new target device from the ground up, using a processor or system-on-chip that does not support the current or previous version of Windows Embedded Compact, it's not likely that you need to develop new bootloader code from scratch. The chip vendor is likely to have reference development hardware that supports the Windows Embedded Compact 7 environment and can provide reference development hardware with a bootloader and BSP to support its product. Microsoft also provides sample bootloaders, with source code, as part of the Platform Builder for Compact 7 software suite, which you can use as the starting point to develop your bootloader.

Because the bootloader is the first piece of code to run on a device, there isn't other code running in the background to provide other services or help with debugging. To develop a bootloader for Compact 7, you must have a good understanding of the hardware platform, the processor, and the Compact 7 OS.

COMPACT 7 BOOTLOADER

There are different Compact 7 bootloader implementations for hardware built with different processor architectures, different types of storage, and different debugging connectivity, to support the development environment.

Bootloader plays a key role in the development process and provides the mechanism to deploy an OS run-time image, from the development station to the target device, for testing and debugging.

During the development process, it's expected to have situations in which the Compact 7 OS run-time image fails to complete the boot process on the target device. Because the OS fails to boot, it does not have sufficient resources in place to provide and send debug information back to the development station. In a situation like this, a quality bootloader with a debugging facility can be helpful to provide status information to help with the debugging process.

Although there are bootloaders created to launch the OS image from local storage, there are bootloaders for some devices created specifically to support the development environment, to download the OS image from the development station to the device's memory, and not intended for distribution with the device to the end user.

Some devices are shipped with multipurpose bootloaders, to launch an OS run-time image from local storage during normal usage, to update the OS run-time image in the ROM by downloading the new image through a network connection.

In some cases, the hardware vendor for the target device may provide multiple bootloaders for the device, each serving a different purpose.

Following are bootloaders provided as part of the Platform Builder for Compact 7 to support an x86 processor-based device:

➤ Ethernet booloader (Eboot)

➤ Serial bootloader (Sboot)

➤ DOS bootloader (Loadcepc)

➤ BIOS bootloader (BIOSLoader)

➤ Compact 7 bootloader framework (WCELDR)

ETHERNET BOOTLOADER (EBOOT)

The Ethernet bootloader, Eboot, is a network bootloader designed to download Compact 7 OS run-time images from the development station to the target device over a network connection. The Eboot bootloader cannot function on its own. You need to use another bootloader to launch Eboot.

When launched by another bootloader (Loadcepc or BIOSLoader), the Eboot bootloader performs the following tasks:

➤ Acquires an IP address from a DHCP server

➤ Broadcasts a BOOTME packet to initiate connection with a Platform Builder development station

➤ After establishing connection with the development station, initiates a Trivial File Transfer Protocol (TFTP) session to download Compact 7 OS run-time image from the development station to the device

SERIAL BOOTLOADER (SBOOT)

The Serial bootloader, Sboot, is designed to download a Compact 7 OS run-time image from the development station to the target device over a Serial port connection. The Sboot bootloader cannot function on its own. You need to use another bootloader to launch Sboot.

Because the data transfer speed over a serial connection is extremely slow compared to an Ethernet connection, the Sboot bootloader is not commonly used.

LOADCEPC

The Loadcepc bootloader is designed to support an x86 processor-based device and is provided as part of the CEPC BSP for use in the development process. The Loadcepc requires the target device to boot to DOS to function.

The Loadcepc bootloader can launch a Compact 7 OS run-time image, an NK.BIN file, from the target device's local storage. It can be used to launch the Eboot.bin and Sboot.bin bootloader, from the target device, to establish connection to the development station to download an OS run-time image.

The Loadcepc bootloader is provided as part of the CEPC BSP for Compact 7, in the following directory:

```
$(_PLATFORMROOT)\CEPC\SRC\BOOTLOADER\DOS
```

Following are some of the Loadcepc bootloader usage examples:

```
; Launch the NK.BIN file, CE OS run-time image, with 2 parameters.
; The /C switch specify the COM port for sending serial debug messages.
; The /L switch specify the display resolution
Loadcepc /C:1 /L:1024x768x16 NK.BIN

; Launch the EBOOT.BIN file, Eboot loader with the following parameters.
; The /C switch specify the COM port for sending serial debug messages.
; The /L switch specify the display resolution
; This is used in the environment with DHCP service, and both the target
; device & development station are on the same subnet.
Loadcepc /C:1 /L:1024x768x16 EBOOT.BIN

; Launch the EBOOT.BIN file, Eboot loader with the following parameters
; The /e switch specify 0x320 I/O port, IRQ-5, 192.168.1.232 static IP
; for target device with a NE2000 interface.
; The /L switch specify the display resolution
Loadcepc /e:320:5:192.168.1.232 /L:800x600x16 EBOOT.BIN
```

For an x86 processor-based device, the Loadcepc and Eboot combination have been the most common setup for development purposes for all the previous versions of Windows Embedded Compact and is still one of the preferred setups for Compact 7. The DOS environment provides the FAT file system service to easily copy and move files as needed during development. The FAT file format is accessible by the Compact 7 file system, which provides a common file system between the DOS and Compact 7 environment to support development activities.

When using the Loadcepc bootloader to support the x86 device's development environment, it's common to configure the x86 device to boot to DOS with the following menu options, as shown in Figure 26-1:

1. Load OS image from local storage.

2. Load OS image from development station with DHCP service.

3. Load OS image from development station with static IP 192.168.2.232.

4. Clean Boot (no commands)

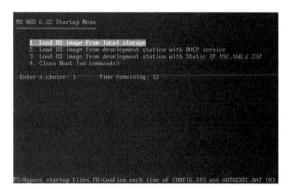

FIGURE 26-1

BIOSLOADER

The BIOSLoader is designed to support an x86 processor-based device and is dependent on the BIOS firmware that all x86 processor-based devices are built with. The BIOSLoader does not contain the code to initialize system hardware for the target device. It's dependent on the x86 BIOS to initialize system hardware.

You can configure the BIOSLoader to launch a Compact 7 OS run-time image from the local storage. You can also configure it to launch the Eboot bootloader to establish connectivity with the development station to download an OS run-time image.

Following are the startup sequences for a typical x86 processor-based device:

1. After power is applied to the device, the x86 processor jumps to the reset vector address and executes the BIOS code.

2. The BIOS code initializes the hardware and searches for a bootable storage device.

3. After detecting a bootable storage device, the BIOS locates and loads the master boot sector (MBR) to the system memory.

4. As the MBR code runs, it searches for the boot sector image on a valid partition, loads the boot sector image into the system memory, and kick starts the boot sector code.

5. As the boot sector code runs, it finds and loads the BIOSLoader.

6. As the BIOSLoader runs, it finds and loads the OS run-time image into system memory and jumps to the starting address to launch the image.

The BIOSLoader is provided as part of the CEPC BSP for Compact 7, in the following directory:

```
$(_PLATFORMROOT)\SRC\BOOTLOADER\BIOSLOADER
```

Chapter 27, "BIOSLoader," provides more information about BIOSLoader and works through an exercise showing the steps to configure and use BIOSLoader for a Compact 7 device.

COMPACT 7 BOOTLOADER FRAMEWORK

A new bootloader is released as part of the new Platform Builder for Compact 7 resources. This new bootloader framework provides the foundation, with common code shared by all processors supported by Platform Builder for Compact 7, including ARM, MIPS, and x86. Using this new bootloader framework as the foundation, you can develop a full-featured bootloader to support your hardware.

This new bootloader includes all features needed to support the development environment and device for distribution. You can configure it dynamically to accomplish the following:

➤ Configure to launch a Compact 7 OS run-time image from local storage.

➤ Configure to launch the built-in Ethernet loader, to send BOOTME messages to establish connectivity with a Platform Builder development station and initiate TFTP to download an OS run-time image from the development station.

➤ Configure network settings.

➤ Configure a static IP address and save configured IP address settings.

➤ Configure KITL settings.

➤ Configure VMINI settings.

➤ Configure display settings.

➤ Configure serial debug port settings.

The source code for this new bootloader framework is provided as part of the Platform Builder for Compact 7 software. The common code shared by different processors are provided in the following directory:

```
$(_PLATFORMROOT)\COMMON\SRC\COMMON\BLDR
```

The new bootloader codes specific to the CEPC BSP are provided in the following directory:

```
$(_PLATFORMROOT)\CEPC\SRC\BOOT
```

There are two versions of this new bootloader framework: console mode and serial port mode. For a bootloader generated in console mode, the bootloader configuration menu is accessible from the console window. For a bootloader generated in serial port mode, the bootloader configuration menu is redirected to the serial port and is accessible through a serial terminal connection, which you can use a program like Hyper Terminal to access.

Figures 26-2 through 26-6 show the configurable settings available for this new bootloader:

> ➤ Main configuration settings menu
> ➤ Boot device selection menu

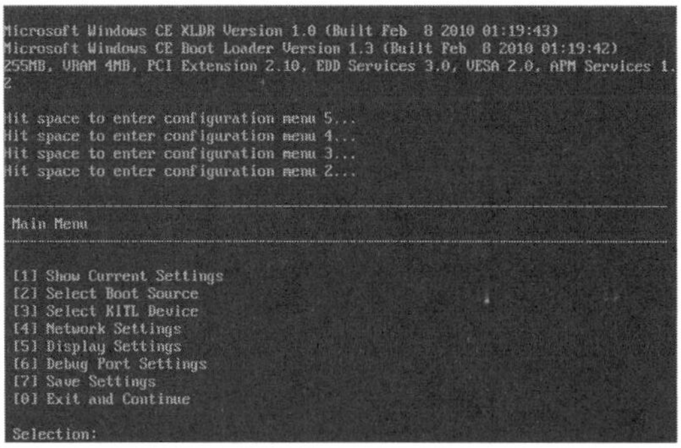

FIGURE 26-2

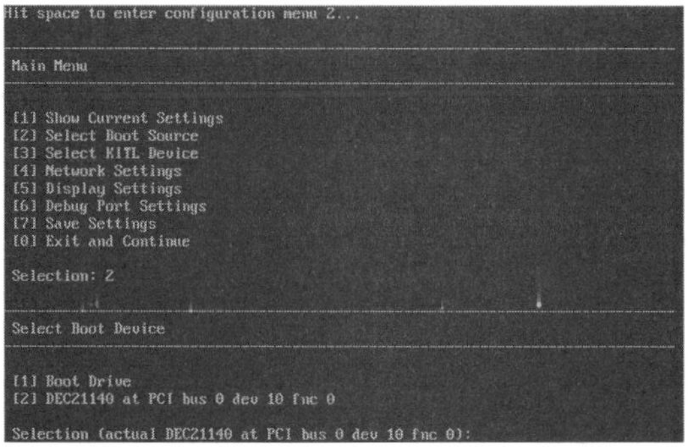

FIGURE 26-3

> ➤ Network settings configuration menu
> ➤ Display settings configuration menu

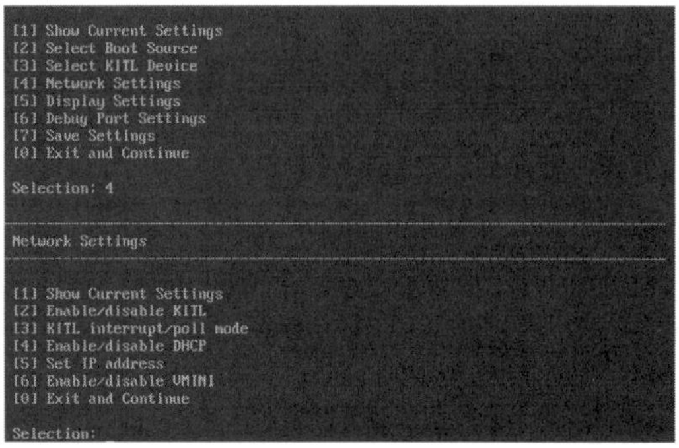

FIGURE 26-4

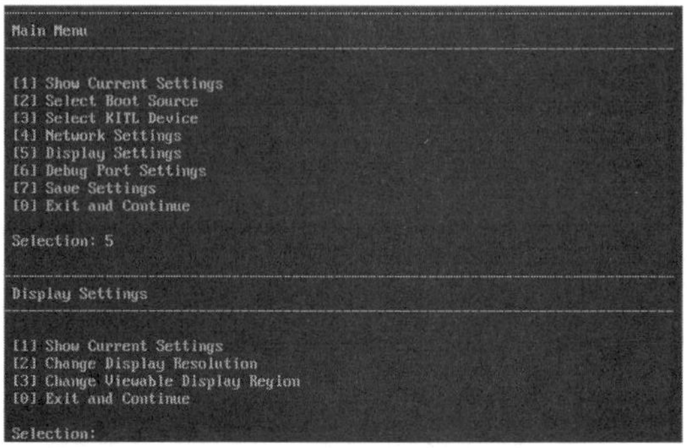

FIGURE 26-5

> ➤ Serial debug port configuration menu

The new bootloader framework provided as part of the Compact 7 release includes comprehensive functions and features to support just about any device. You can use all or part of the codes provided as part of this bootloader framework to develop a bootloader tailored to meet your device's specific requirements.

The sample Virtual PC machine, provided as part of the Virtual PC BSP, is preconfigured with

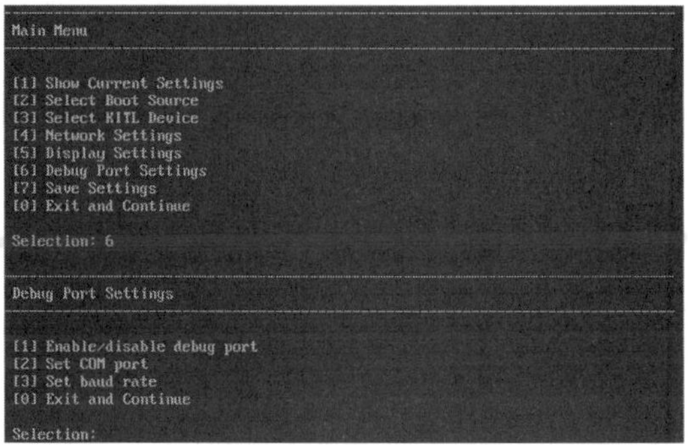

FIGURE 26-6

this new bootloader in console mode, which you can use to review the features available for this bootloader.

SUMMARY

For any embedded device that requires the use of an operating system, bootloader code is one of the lowest levels and most challenging to develop.

Because the bootloader is the first piece of code to run on the device during power-on, there aren't other codes already launched or running in the background to help access the system hardware and file system. As a developer, you need to have a thorough understanding about the hardware and operating system to develop efficient and quality bootloader codes.

As a development tool, with the primary objective to deliver efficient and effective development tools to help simplify your tasks to develop solutions for the Windows Embedded Compact platform, the Platform Builder for Compact 7 provides the necessary tools and resources to simplify your developer efforts, including a full range of quality bootloaders to support different development scenarios.

27

BIOSLoader

WHAT'S IN THIS CHAPTER?

➤ Using BIOSLoader

The x86 BIOS bootloader (BIOSLoader) is a bootloader provided as part of the Platform Builder for the Compact 7 development tool to support x86-based devices.

The BIOSLoader does not have the function to initialize system hardware: it is dependent on the x86 device's system BIOS to initialize the hardware, and is launched by the system BIOS.

You can configure the BIOSLoader to launch a Compact 7 OS run-time image and Ethernet bootloader from the device's local storage.

BIOSLOADER STARTUP PARAMETERS

When an optional BOOT.INI configuration file is available, BIOSLoader reads and parses the following startup parameters from the file:

➤ Boot setting

➤ Debug setting

➤ Display setting

➤ Network setting

The BIOSLoader uses the boot and network settings during the startup process. The display and debug settings can be passed to the Compact 7 OS run-time image when the OS image and associated device drivers are configured to use these parameters and generated with the following build option:

➤ Enable eboot space in memory.

To find out the BIOSLoader's configurable parameters, you can review the sample `BOOT.INI` configuration file, provided as part of BIOSLoader, in the following directory: `$(_PLATFORMROOT)` `CEPC\SRC\BOOTLOADER\BIOSLOADER\BOOTDISK`.

Through the `BOOT.INI` configuration file, you can configure the BIOSLoader to delay the process to launch an OS run-time image. During the delay period, you can configure the BIOSLoader to launch an Ethernet bootloader, `EBOOT.BIN`, or an alternative OS image, when a numeric key is pressed.

The following sample entries configure the BIOSLoader with alternative options to launch `EBOOT` `.BIN`, an Ethernet bootloader, and a secondary OS image, `NK2.BIN`:

Available for download on Wrox.com

```
Delay=10
BinFile=NK.BIN
BinFile1=EBOOT.BIN
BinFile2=NK2.BIN
```

Code snippet is from Chapter27_Snippet.txt

The preceding entries configured the BIOSLoader to function as follow:

➤ During startup, delay 10 seconds before attempting to launch `NK.BIN`, the primary Compact 7 OS run-time image.

➤ If the "1" key is pressed before the delay time expires, the BIOSLoader stops the delay and launches `EBOOT.BIN` instead, an Ethernet bootloader.

➤ If the "2" key is pressed before the delay time expires, the BIOSLoader stops the delay and launches `NK2.BIN` instead, an alternative Compact 7 OS run-time image.

BIOSLOADER FILES AND UTILITY

The BIOSLoader is provided as part of the CEPC BSP, installed to the development station as part of the BSP, under the CEPC BSP's `\SRC\BOOTLOADER\BIOSLOADER` directory. There are five subdirectories under the preceding BIOSLoader directory:

1. This directory contains the boot sector code. This code is separated into four folders, each containing the code for the EXFAT, FAT12, FAT16, and FAT32 file systems. The boot sector code is responsible for loading the BIOSLoader into system memory for the jump to the startup routine. Precompiled boot sector images for the four different file systems are provided in the `\IMAGES` folder.

2. `\DISKIMAGES`: This directory contains two floppy disk images and two folders containing the files for each of the floppy images.

   ➤ `\BOOTDISK`: This subfolder contains the files for the `BOOTDISK.144` bootable floppy image, which boot to BIOSLoader and launch the included Ethernet bootloader.

   ➤ `\SETUPDISK`: This subfolder contains the files for the `SETUPDISK.144` bootable floppy image, which boot to MS DOS 6.22. This floppy contains the BIOSLoader binary and the necessary utility to prep the storage device to boot using BIOSLoader.

3. \INIPARSER: This directory contains the codes to parse configuration parameters from the BOOT.INI file for the BIOSLoader.

4. \LOADER: This folder contains the codes for the loader, with the following three subfolders:

➤ \FIXED: This folder contains the loader codes to support fixed storage (nonremovable).

➤ \FLOPPY: This folder contains the loader codes to support the floppy disk.

➤ \Images: This folder contains the precompiled loader for different file systems.

5. \UTILITIES: This folder contains the codes for three different utilities:

➤ \BINCOMPRESS: This folder contains the codes for BINCOMPRESS.EXE, the utility used to compress or decompress .BIN run-time images for use with the BIOSLoader.

➤ \CESYS: This folder contains the codes for CESYS.EXE, the utility used to copy the boot sector image to the storage device.

➤ \DISKPART: This folder contains the codes for DISKPARK.EXE, the utility used to prepare storage partitions for EXFAT, FAT16, and FAT32 file systems.

USING BIOSLOADER

For an x86-based device that supports booting from IDE, Compact Flash, and USB flash storage, you can configure the BIOSLoader to launch a Compact 7 OS run-time image from these storages.

You need the following components to prepare a storage device to launch a Compact 7 OS image using BIOSLoader:

➤ Boot sector image: BSECT.IMG

➤ CESYS.EXE utility

➤ BIOSLoader image: BLDR

Boot Sector Image: BSECT.IMG

You need to use a boot sector image that supports the storage device's configured file system. Precompiled boot sector images for EXFAT, FAT12, FAT16, and FAT32 file systems are in the \IMAGES subfolder under the \BIOSLOADER\BOOTSECTOR folder. When using one of the precompiled boot sector image files, such as FAT32_BSECT.IMG, you need to rename the file as BSECT.IMG. Source codes for the boot sector are in the subfolders with the folder name corresponding to the supported file system name.

CESYS.EXE Utility

The CESYS.EXE utility is needed to copy the boot sector image to the file system boot partition's first sector.

BIOSLoader Image: BLDR

You need to use a BIOSLoader image, BLDR, that supports the storage device's file system. Precompiled BIOSLoader images for EXFAT, FAT12, FAT16, and FAT32 file systems are in the \IMAGES subfolder under the \BIOSLOADER\LOADER folder. When using one of the precompiled BIOSLoader image files, such as BLDR_FAT32, you need to rename the file as BLDR. Source codes for the BIOSLoader, BLDR, are in the subfolders with folder name corresponding to the supported file system name.

Preparing a Storage Device with BIOSLoader

Following are the steps to prepare a storage device to launch a Compact 7 OS image with BIOSLoader:

1. Format the storage device with the FAT file system.

2. Use the CESYS.EXE utility to copy the BSECT.IMG, the boot sector image, to the file system boot partition's first sector.

3. Copy the BIOSLoader image, BLDR, to the storage device.

4. Copy the Compact 7 OS run-time image, NK.BIN, to the storage device.

5. Copy BOOT.INI, the startup configuration file, to the storage device. The BOOT.INI file is optional. Without this file, the BIOSLoader simply launches the NK.BIN OS image.

You can review the MKDISK.BAT batch file from the BIOSLoader setup disk in the following directory to see the process to prepare a storage device with BIOSLoader:

```
$(_PLATFORMROOT)\CEPC\SRC\BOOTLOADER\BIOSLOADER\DISKIMAGES\SETUPDISK
```

Chapter 28, "The DiskPrep Power Toy," talks about the DiskPrep utility. This utility is created to help simplify the tasks to configure a storage device with BIOSLoader to launch a Compact 7 OS image.

Startup Splash Screen

By default, the BIOSLoader launches a splash screen, using the SPLASH.BMX graphic file, during startup. You can configure the BIOSLoader to show a graphic of your choice by replacing the SPLASH.BMX graphic file with one of your own.

Following are the steps to create the SPLASH.BMX graphic file:

1. Create a 256-color bitmap graphic file that fits the screen size for your device, and name the file SPLASH.BMP.

2. Create a temporary folder as the workspace, such as C:\BMX.

3. Copy the BINCOMPRESS.EXE executable from the following directory to C:\BMX.

```
$(_PUBLICROOT)\COMMON\OAK\BIN\i386
```

4. From the Startup menu, run the CMD command to launch a DOS command window.

5. From the DOS command window, navigate to the `C:\BMX` directory.

6. From the `C:\BMX` directory, enter the following command to compress the `SPLASH.BMP` file to `SPLASH.BMX`:

```
BinCompress /C SPLASH.BMP SPLASH.BMX
```

You can replace the `SPLASH.BMX` file from the flash storage with your own startup splash screen.

Windows CE Splash Generator

Window's CE Splash Generator (CE Splash) is a utility created by Chris Tacke to simplify the tasks needed to convert different type of graphic files into the compressed BMX file format to use as a splash screen for Windows Embedded Compact.

The CE Splash utility is released to the community on the Codeplex site. As of this book's writing, the CE Splash utility is able to support the following image file formats:

➤ BMP

➤ GIF

➤ JPG

➤ PNG

You can find the CE Splash utility at the following URL: `http://splashce.codeplex.com`.

SUMMARY

Bootloader is one of the low-level components within an embedded system. When properly configured, you don't notice its existence. When developing a new device without a working bootloader, developing a bootloader can be challenging.

The BIOSLoader is a stable bootloader for x86 devices with flexible configuration to launch a Compact 7 OS image from the local storage, with optional configuration to launch an Ethernet bootloader to download an image from a Platform Builder development station, or another alternative OS image from the local storage for testing and administrative purposes.

28

The DiskPrep Power Toy

WHAT'S IN THIS CHAPTER?

➤ Introducing the DiskPrep power toy features

➤ Using the DiskPrep power toy

DiskPrep is a Windows CE power toy created to help simplify the process to configure different types of bootable storage with BIOSLoader to launch the Windows Embedded Compact OS run-time image. It can also configure the bootable storage to launch an Ethernet bootloader to download an OS run-time image from the Platform Builder development station.

The DiskPrep utility is designed to run on a Windows 7, Vista, or XP desktop or notebook PC. Microsoft released this utility under the Microsoft Public License. The DiskPrep utility is available for download from the following URL:

```
http://code.msdn.microsoft.com/DiskPrep
```

The DiskPrep power toy is designed to support x86 devices and can work with the following types of storage devices, providing the x86 target device can boot from these storage devices:

➤ IDE hard drive

➤ IDE flash storage

➤ Compact Flash

➤ SD memory card

➤ Micro-SD memory card

➤ USB flash storage

➤ SATA hard drive

➤ SATA flash storage

You can use the DiskPrep power toy to configure bootable flash storage to launch the Ethernet bootloader and OS run-time image for previous versions of a Windows Embedded Compact device, built with x86 processor.

This chapter provides information about the DiskPrep power toy and works through the exercise showing the steps to use this power toy.

PREREQUISITES AND PREPARATION

To use DiskPrep, you need a Compact 7 OS run-time image or an Ethernet bootloader configured to support the target device. In addition, you also need a bootable flash storage for the target device.

Following are two different DiskPrep usage scenarios:

1. To configure bootable flash storage for the target device to launch an Ethernet bootloader, EBOOT.BIN, to download a Windows Embedded Compact OS run-time image from the Platform Builder development station

2. To configure bootable flash storage for the target device to launch a Windows Embedded Compact OS run-time image, NK.BIN

DiskPrep to Launch EBOOT.BIN

To configure bootable flash storage for a target device, with a BIOSLoader, to launch EBOOT.BIN using DiskPrep, you need to have the following:

➤ Target device built with an x86 processor, with an Ethernet interface

➤ Windows Embedded Compact Ethernet bootloader, EBOOT.BIN, for the target device

➤ Flash storage device that can be configured as the boot device for the target device

➤ Mechanism to attach the flash storage device to the development station

DiskPrep to Launch NK.BIN

To configure bootable flash storage for a target device, with BIOSLoader, to launch NK.BIN using DiskPrep, you need the following:

➤ Target device built with an x86 processor

➤ Windows Embedded Compact OS run-time image, NK.BIN, generated in release mode with KITL disabled

➤ Flash storage device that can be configured as the boot device for the target device

➤ Mechanism to attach the flash storage device to the development station

USING DISKPREP POWER TOY

The DiskPrep utility can be used to configure different types of storage, for x86 based devices, with BIOSLoader to launch a Windows Embedded Compact OS run-time image or an Ethernet bootloader. In addition, this utility can also be used to configure a virtual hard disk (VHD) for the Virtual PC to launch Windows Embedded Compact OS run-time.

The exercises in this section show the steps to accomplish the following:

➤ Configure the Compact Flash (CF) storage for an eBox-3310A to boot to a Compact 7 OS run-time image

➤ Configure the VHD for a Virtual PC to boot to a Compact 7 OS run-time image

Configuring Compact Flash with BIOSLoader for eBox-3310A

To use the DiskPrep utility to configure the flash storage device to become bootable, with BIOSLoader, to launch a Windows Embedded Compact OS run-time image or Ethernet bootloader, you need to have a mechanism to attach the flash storage device to the development station, as removable storage. The DiskPrep utility cannot configure fixed storage.

You can use one of the following methods to attach a flash storage device to the development station:

➤ Use an USB to IDE adapter for IDE flash storage

➤ Use an USB to Compact Flash adapter for Compact Flash storage

➤ Use an USB to SD adapter for SD flash storage

➤ USB flash storage can be attached directly to the development station's USB host interface

Whether you use USB to IDE, USB to Compact Flash, and USB to SD flash adapters or USB flash storage, the steps and process to configure the flash storage using DiskPrep is the same.

The steps to configure the flash storage to launch `EBOOT.BIN` or `NK.BIN` are the similar.

Using an eBox-3310A as the target device with Compact Flash as the boot device, the exercise in this section configures the Compact Flash with BIOSLoader, using DiskPrep, with the following features:

➤ During startup, delay 10 seconds before launching the Windows Embedded Compact OS run-time image. Before the 10 second delay expires, you can press 1 to trigger the BIOSLoader to launch `EBOOT.BIN` instead.

For this exercise, the Compact Flash is attached to the development station using a USB to Compact Flash adapter. Work through the following steps to configure the Compact Flash:

1. Create the following folder to use as the workspace for the exercise:

`C:\TEST`

2. Copy the following files to the `C:\TEST` folder:

➤ The DiskPrep utility's executable, `DISKPREP.EXE`

➤ Compact 7 OS run-time image, `NK.BIN`, for the target device, eBox-3310A

➤ Compact 7 Ethernet bootloader, `EBOOT.BIN`, for the target device, eBox-3310A

3. Use Notepad to create a text file with the following contents and save the file as BOOT.INI to the C:\TEST folder:

```
# BIOSLoader configuration file

# Primary File to Load on startup:
BinFile=NK.BIN

#
# Device name root string:
DeviceNameRoot=eBox

# Boot delay (in seconds) in which to select the alternative image
Delay=10

# Alternative image
# While booting hit the key corresponding to the suffix char
# (e.g. "1" for BinFile1) to boot the alternative image
BinFile1=EBOOT.BIN

# Video Setting:
Video=on

# Physical screen width
# Must be >= DisplayWidth
PhysicalWidth=640

# Physical screen height
# Must be >= DisplayHeight
PhysicalHeight=480

# Display Depth
# Possible values are 8, 15, 16, 24, 32
DisplayDepth=16

# Display width
DisplayWidth=640

# Display height
DisplayHeight=480

# Debug zone (Use with eboot):
#    1 - error
#    2 - warning
#    4 - info
DebugZone=0x00000007
```

Code snippet is from Chapter28_Snippet.txt

4. Attach the USB to Compact Flash adapter to one of the development station's USB interfaces.

5. After the system recognizes the Compact Flash, launch the DiskPrep utility, DISKPREP.EXE, and bring up the DiskPrep screen, as shown in Figure 28-1.

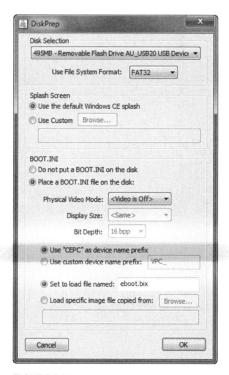

FIGURE 28-1

6. From the Disk Selection drop-down list, select the Compact Flash as the device to configure.

7. From the Use File System Format selection, select FAT or FAT32.

 The FAT file system is limited to support file partitions up to 2 GB in size. If you are using flash storage that is larger than 2 GB, select FAT32.

8. Toward the bottom of the DiskPrep program screen, select the Load Specific Image File Copied From option, and click Browse to bring up the Select File to Execute on Boot screen, as shown in Figure 28-2.

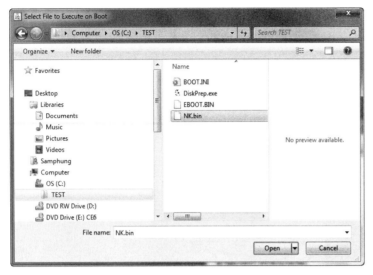

FIGURE 28-2

9. From the Select File to Execute on Boot screen, navigate to locate the C:\TEST\NK.BIN file, select the file, and click Open. At this point, the DiskPrep screen should look similar to Figure 28-3.

10. From the DiskPrep screen, click OK to configure the Compact Flash. At this point, the Confirm Dangerous Action screen displays to warn the action will destroy all data on the Compact Flash, as shown in Figure 28-4.

FIGURE 28-3

FIGURE 28-4

11. From the Confirm Dangerous Action screen, Click OK to acknowledge and bring up the DiskPrep Progress screen, as shown in Figure 28-5.

FIGURE 28-5

12. As the DiskPrep utility configures the Compact Flash, a series of messages display on the screen to indicate progress, such as:

> ➤ Purge Any Existing Volumes

> ➤ Creating Target File System

> ➤ Copy Target Files

> ➤ Making Disk Bootable

13. After the DiskPrep utility finishes configuring the Compact Flash, the Success screen displays to indicate disk preparation is completed.

14. Click OK to complete and close the DiskPrep utility.

The Compact Flash is now configured as a bootable device that boots to BIOSLoader. Using Windows Explorer to view the Compact Flash's contents, you can see the following files are copied to the Compact Flash by the DiskPrep utility:

➤ BLDR — BIOSLoader

➤ BOOT.INI — Startup configuration file

➤ NK.BIN — Compact 7 OS run-time image

➤ SPLASH.BMX — Splash screen graphic file

Using the Compact Flash configured with the preceding configuration as the boot device, the eBox-3310A boots to BIOSLoader, showing the SPLASH.BMX graphic as the splash screen during startup, and launches the NK.BIN OS run-time image, without other options.

Next, copy the C:\TEST\BOOT.INI configuration file prepared in step 3 to the Compact Flash, overwriting the existing BOOT.INI file, and copy C:\TEST\EBOOT.BIN to the flash storage.

Using the updated Compact Flash as the boot device, the eBox-3310A boots to the BIOSLoader, showing the SPLASH.BMX graphic as the splash screen during startup, and launches the NK.BIN OS run-time image with a 10-second delay. When you press 1 before the 10-second delay expires, it stops the delay and launches the EBOOT.BIN Ethernet bootloader. Otherwise, it launches NK.BIN after a 10-second delay.

Configuring Virtual Hard Disk with BIOSLoader for Virtual PC

Using DiskPrep, you can create a Virtual Hard Disk (VHD), for Windows 7 Virtual PC and Virtual PC 2007 virtual machines, configured to launch a Compact 7 OS run-time image with BIOSLoader.

The DiskPrep utility is created to operate in the 32-bit environment. Although it can sometimes function in the 64-bit environment, it has known issues when run in a 64-bit environment. It's advised for you to perform the following exercise on a 32-bit machine.

A virtual hard disk created on a 32-bit machine is able to function as expected on a 64-bit machine.

Work through the following steps to create a Compact 7 Virtual Hard Disk:

1. Develop an OS design using the Virtual PC BSP.

2. Configure the OS design to generate an OS run-time image in release mode, with KITL disabled.

3. Copy the NK.BIN OS run-time image file to the C:\TEST folder.

4. Launch the DiskPrep utility.

5. From the DiskPrep screen's Disk Selection, select the following:

   ➤ VHD I Create or Specify When I Click OK

6. From the DiskPrep screen, select the following option:

   ➤ Load Specific Image File Copied From

7. Click Browse to bring up the Select File to Execute on the Boot screen.

8. From the Select File to Execute on the Boot screen, navigate to locate the C:\TEST\NK.BIN file, select the file, and click Open. At this point, the DiskPrep screen should look similar to Figure 28-6.

9. From the DiskPrep screen, click the OK to bring up the Create or Select Virtual Hard Disk screen.

10. From the Create or Select Virtual Disk screen, select the following options:

    ➤ Select the Create a New Virtual Hard Disk (VHD) Option.

    ➤ Change the Size to 64MB.

    ➤ Select the Dynamically Expanding Option.

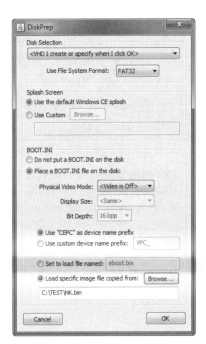

FIGURE 28-6

11. Enter C:\TEST\MyVirtualPC as the name and location to create the new VHD, as shown in Figure 28-7, and click OK.

12. As you click OK, the Confirm Dangerous Action screen is raised. Click the OK to acknowledge and bring up the DiskPrep Progress screen.

FIGURE 28-7

13. After the DiskPrep completes the process to create the new VHD, the success screen is shown to indicate the process completed. At this point, MyVirtualPC.VHD, a virtual hard disk, is created in the C:\TEST folder.

To use the MyVirtualPC.VHD virtual hard disk, you need to create a virtual machine and configure the virtual machine to use MyVirtualPC.VHD.

SUMMARY

The DiskPrep power toy can simplify the tasks needed to configure bootable storage for x86 devices, with BIOSLoader, to launch a Windows Embedded Compact OS run-time image and Ethernet bootloader.

Using the DiskPrep power toy, configuring a bootable storage with BIOSLoader to launch a Windows Embedded Compact OS image with the options to launch an Ethernet bootloader or alternative Compact 7 OS image for development, testing, and other administrative purposes is a straightforward process.

PART V
Device Drivers, Boot Loader, BSP, and OAL Development

29

An Overview of Device Drivers

WHAT'S IN THIS CHAPTER?

➤ Defining device drivers and componentized operating systems

➤ Using out-of-the-box Compact 7 device drivers

➤ Understanding custom and third-party device drivers

This chapter provides an introduction to device driver concepts as part of an embedded operating system, an overview of Compact 7 device drivers, and an introduction to drivers in the Public folder.

WHAT IS A DEVICE DRIVER?

A componentized operating system such as Windows Embedded Compact enables you to customize an embedded operating system by selecting only those drivers and applications that are needed and relevant. This enables you to make a smaller footprint.

When you add new hardware to a computer system, the operating system can't use it until a suitable device driver is loaded for it. The system searches for a driver from a list of available drivers, and if found the system loads the driver; otherwise, you need to download or install the driver from media supplied with the hardware.

A device driver provides an interface between the operating system and the device and handles the transfer of data between the two. It also manages the configuration of the device and reads its status. For example, a serial port driver moves data from the port's receive data register upon reception to a software buffer that applications can use. It places data in the transmit register when an application sends data, enabling the hardware to handle the transmission from there. Operating system calls to the driver configure such things as the baud rate and number of stops bits for the port. An application can check the status of the port through operating system calls to the driver.

A device driver provides input/output (I/O) through ports written to and read from by the device driver. The device driver manages the functional configuration of the device and checks its status. Finally, the hardware can generate interrupts that are also handled by the device driver.

Windows Embedded Compact 7 (Compact 7) provides a wide range of out-of-the-box device drivers that you can select from the Platform Builder Catalog, which covers a broad range of devices. You can add device drivers for unlisted devices and develop custom drivers as well.

System Concepts

The hardware for a device is typically one or more integrated circuits that connect into the computer system's memory, buses, ports, and interrupts. The system's processor communicates with the device through certain memory addresses and ports that must be unique for that device in that system. Certain system level interrupts may also be assigned to that device, whereas the actual hardware interrupts are chained together with other devices.

Communication with a hardware device IC will be via its hardware registers. The three classes of registers are configuration, status, and data.

Configuration

The device control registers will determine how the device will function. The driver will write values into these to specify things such as device enable/disable, data rates, message formats, and interrupts.

Status

You can poll the status of the device at any time by reading the status registers. The status would indicate if the data has been sent or received, the state of output control pins, if an ADC (Analog to Digital Converter) conversion has been completed, and what error (if any) has occurred. You can also use polling when a number of devices share the same interrupt. The devices are queried to determine which caused the interrupt.

I/O

A computer system performs I/O through hardware ports. These ports can be for GPIO (General Purpose I/O), serial ports, and network access or provide access to dedicated hardware such as timers, counters, ADC, and DAC (Digital to Analog Conversion). These ports typically have registers for configuring the I/O, for reading its status, and for the data reads and writes.

Interrupts and Events

You can implement a device driver so that it periodically polls the status registers to determine if an event has occurred. Alternatively, it may make use of interrupts that generate events that can be trapped and responded to by software handlers. An *interrupt* is a signal that can occur at any time (asynchronous) and causes the processor to temporarily change for that handling in a manner so that when the handler completes, it resumes exactly where it previously left off. That way interrupts can occur randomly without impacting directly upon the main processing. The main processing though will make use of the data stored by an interrupt input and output indirectly via an interrupt.

Interrupts can be generated by the hardware though single bits in an individual or nested manner. The ports are often configurable for interrupts for a range of events, such as upon data reception and when data transmission is complete. Also, interrupts can be generated by software interrupts.

A polling driver normally sleeps between status checks to minimize the load on the CPU. It is a useful methodology when certain I/O events that need to be trapped do not generate interrupts. This sort of driver may in turn generate a software interrupt so that it can be handled at a higher level.

An Example

Consider the 16550 Universal Asynchronous Receiver/Transmitter (UART), as shown in Figure 29-1. This, a predecessor or a variant of it, is used in most PC RS232 serial systems. Even high-speed serial devices are modeled on it. There are control registers, status registers, and data registers. Pins on the right are the port's input and output signal and data pins. Pins on the left provide the hardware interface to the computer system buses enabling register selection through the address bus ($A_2 \ldots A_0$), data movement with the selected register through the data bus ($D_7 \ldots D_0$), and various control signals to manage that movement, such as the chip select and read and write signals. Interrupts from the device are provided by the /TXRDY, /RXRDY, and /XOUT signals.

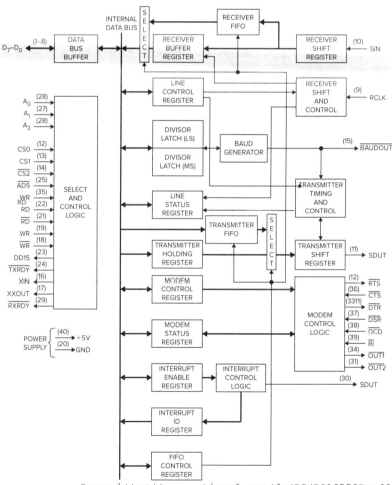

SOURCE: http://www.national.com/ds/PC/PC16550D.pdf

FIGURE 29-1

For an x86 system, this device would map into the CPU's port address space at 3F8H for COM1 and 2F8H for COM2. The interrupts would connect to the CPU's interrupts via a PIC controller using system interrupts IRQ4 and IRQ3 respectively.

16550 Configuration

The 16550 device driver would handle the configuration of the device by writing to its control registers. These would affect its mode of transmission and reception such as the baud rate and the number of start and stop bits. The device can also be turned on or off through the control registers.

16550 Status

The status of the device can be polled at any time by reading the status registers. The status would indicate if the data has been sent or received, the state of output control pins such as /CTS and /DSR, and what error (if any) has occurred.

16550 I/O

When the device is enabled, transmission occurs when data is written to the transmitter FIFO or the transmit holding buffer. The device moves the data to the shift register and serial shifts it out bit by bit. When data is received serially, it enters via the receiver shift register and shifts into the receiver FIFO or the receive buffer register. The input pins /CTS, /DSR, and /DSR can be configured to enable some external control of the transmission, whereas /RTS and /DTR can indicate to an external device the system state of the reception.

16550 Interrupts and Events

The 16550 can generate interrupts on such events as when the transmit buffer is empty, the receive buffer has data, the input control pins change state (/CTS, and so on), and on an error such as buffer input overrun.

A 16550 Device Driver

A 16550 device driver would handle the configuration of the device control registers through a standard serial DCB structure that has fields that set such things as its baud rate, handshaking modes, and interrupt configuration. The device driver would have a transmit thread and a receive thread that would wake and move data upon transmit and receive interrupts respectively. Their tasks are to seamlessly move the data between the hardware registers and the software buffers. A serial application would interact with those software buffers through a driver API. The API would also handle the reading and writing of the DCB for reconfiguration of the device and would enable the determination of the status of the device, such as that of the input control pins. Interrupts would also be delegated through the API.

OPERATING SYSTEM STRUCTURE

An operating system facilitates application access to system hardware and software resources though device drivers. This can be via a defined set of interrupts. A more extensible approach is to use drivers with defined interfaces to the OS, many of which make use of the underlying interrupt architecture.

An Operating System as Interrupts

It is a simple matter to build a basic operating system for a microcontroller if it supports indexed (vectored) software interrupts. That is, when a software interrupt is asserted by software, or by hardware, an index is supplied that is automatically used to look up the address to vector to for the interrupt from within a lookup table of interrupt addresses. DOS is essentially such an operating system. For example MSDOS interrupt 23H is the Control-C handler.

An x86 operating system typically has two levels of interrupts. At one level are the hardware generated interrupts; at a higher level are the system level interrupts. The hardware generates a hardware interrupt to the system that must then map this to a system level interrupt. The processor orchestrates deciphering between interrupts that are daisy-chained together on the same interrupt, such as COM1 and COM3. The x86 systems typically have a Programmable Interrupt Controller (PIC)[1] that takes a number of interrupts as input and outputs as one interrupt to the microprocessor. The processor can then send messages to the interrupts to see which one responds to being the source of the interrupt.

An Operating System as Drivers

Although the underlying architecture is actually a system of interrupts, memory, and port accesses, it is simpler to think of an operating system as an architecture based upon drivers that interface to the hardware and the operating system. There is typically a hardware abstraction layer (HAL) implemented for any system that drivers communicate with and with the higher level operating system. In that way, an operating system can run on a variety of systems with the same binary upper-level software.

WINDOWS EMBEDDED COMPACT DRIVERS

Compact 7 is a componentized operating system in that apart from a core set of drivers, components can be optionally added depending upon the system functional requirements and system capabilities. These components are individually selectable via the Catalog. They are also selected at a macro level when you choose a Board Support Package (BSP) or a template for an OS. When you add a component, its dependencies are generally automatically added. When the OS is built, the driver's DLL is included in the image as well as its resources and Registry settings.

Components in the Catalog consist of Device Drivers, Board Support Packages, Services, Applications, Libraries, and Resources. Out-of-the-box drivers installed with the Compact 7 development system are Product Quality Developed (PQD) or Microsoft Validated. PQD means they have been developed and tested in-house by Microsoft for Compact 7. Microsoft Validated means that they have been developed by a third party but have been validated by Microsoft for Compact 7.

Compact 7 drivers interface to a Graphical Windows and Events Sub System (GWES), the file system, and Device Manager. A BSP is essentially a collection of device drivers plus configuration information.

GWES and File System

GWES implements the graphical user interface (GUI) aspects of the operating system. This includes the Windows messaging system for Windows events. The file system drivers implement the storage aspects of the OS. ATAPI, FAT, SDIO Memory, and Compact Flash drivers interface to the file system.

The GWES provides the nuts and bolts of the GUI operating system. Drivers that interact with it, interface with it in a nongeneral (native) manner. Video drivers, the keyboard, mouse, touch and printer drivers interface directly to GWES because this implements the GUI operating system *window icon menu pointing device (WIMP)* metaphor first championed by Xerox PARC. The events aspect of GWES is the passing of Windows events as messages to the OS GUI. For example, a mouse click on a window may generate a MOUSE_DOWN event that can be consumed by the window's application.

Device and Services

Drivers other than GWES and file system drivers are loaded and managed by the Device Manager. These all implement the stream interface. For example, power management and notification LEDs are implemented as stream drivers. Services load components such as the Web Service, FTP Service, and so on. These components are not drivers though. Services are essentially a software construct with no direct hardware aspects.

Board Support Packages

A Board Support Package (BSP) is a collection of drivers for the board's hardware, a specification of its configuration for its memory map and ports, and a boot mechanism. For development purposes, it also needs a mechanism for downloading and booting a developmental OS image. Because of its dependence upon drivers, a BSP will be operating system dependent, and operating system version dependent. Without it, it is difficult to do any OS development; although, the system SDK is all you need for application development.

If you purchase a development board for embedded operating system development, you must have the built (binary) BSP. Often the BSP is available in a source form with the source format requiring a significant investment. For a large commercial development though, this expense may be necessary because it may enable you to solve an issue by debugging the BSP drivers. Also if a new version of the OS is available and the OEM doesn't supply a new BSP, it may enable you to migrate the BSP to the new version.

Drivers in the Compact 7 Catalog

The Compact 7 hardware device drivers are listed in the Visual Studio 2008 Catalog under \Device Drivers. These are CPU-independent but are specific to the hardware they support. For example, as shown in Figure 29-2, the Serial Driver COM16550 is used by a variety of compatible serial devices on most Compact 7 systems, regardless of the BSP CPU. If the source code is available for these drivers, it is found under the $(_PUBLIC) folder. Multiple instances of this driver all use the same driver DLL.

The Catalog lists higher level device drivers under \CoreOS\CEBase. For example, Battery and Notification LEDs drivers are under \CoreOS\CEBase\Core OS Services. If you install third-party drivers, they will be typically found under the Vendor's branch below the Third Party Catalog branch.

FIGURE 29-2

When selecting items in the Catalog, if they have a square box, you can select them. When selected the item is checked with a green tick. If the box is filled with green, it is required by another component and can't be unselected. You can right-click on it and find out what requires it (the Reasons for Inclusion of Item) If a component is preceded by a circle in the Catalog, there will be one or more others under the same branch. This means that you can only select one of them. If an item when selected shows a red cross, it can't be used by the OS as configured. You can right-click on it to see why it is excluded (Reasons for Exclusion of Item).

Drivers in the PUBLIC Folder

The $(_PUBLIC folder) contains the hardware-independent components of the operating system. The PUBLIC\Common\OAK\Drivers directory contains the hardware-independent drivers in source form.

The orange icons indicate that there are subprojects are under the folder, whereas the blue icons indicate that the folder is a single driver project. For example, the serial folder has a number of serial library projects that are linked together to form the serial 16550 DLL driver.

When the OS is built, this source is used to build the driver .lib files and then to bind them into driver DLLs. This code can be debugged if there is an issue with a driver or modified if a custom driver is to be developed for hardware similar to the hardware for an existing driver. Although this source code can be modified and the driver rebuilt, this is not a good idea because it's best to maintain an original copy of the source and because these files can get overwritten with an update to the OS development platform. It is better to make a copy of the folder and modify that. Compact 7 has a simple (yet problematic) method for cloning these driver projects into the current OS subproject folder. That way the driver can be debugged and modified without an impact upon the original source.

Drivers in the PRIVATE Folder

When you select the Shared Source installation option, you see the $(_PRIVATE) folder that contains the source code for the operating system,. When an OS is built, the installed binaries for these folders are used.

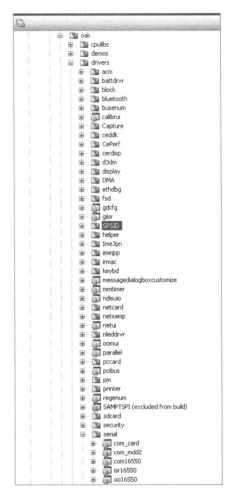

FIGURE 29-3

The source within is not built. The Microsoft CE Shared Source Licensing Program enables this source to be modified and built and the components distributed. This may be needed with new hardware. Some examples of drivers under this folder are the storage drivers in \PRIVATE\winceos\COREOS\storage.

 Unlike with some of the previous Windows Embedded CE Platform Builder installations, the $(_PRIVATE) folder is not available in the trial version of Windows Embedded Compact 7 Platform Builder.

CUSTOM DRIVERS

The first maxim for a device is that to use a device in Compact 7 you need a driver. Either it will be a driver specific to that device, or the device will belong to a class of devices that uses the same driver. For example, a specific video driver is needed in a Compact 7 system, whereas a USB memory stick does not need a specific driver — just the USB storage class. Before using a device in Compact 7, you need to make sure that a suitable driver is available, which can be quite frustrating! One reason to use Windows Embedded Standard for an embedded device is the broad spectrum of devices available for it. Anything that runs on a Windows desktop can run on Windows Embedded Standard[2] using the same drivers. Only a subset of these also have a Compact 7 driver. Desktop Windows drivers do not work in Compact 7. For example, there is no support for TWAIN in Compact 7, so you can't attach a scanner to a Compact 7 device.

When a hardware component is added to a Compact 7 system, whether it plugs into USB or a BUS, or whether it is hard-wired into the system's circuitry, as a first preference you should use drivers in the Compact 7 Drivers branch of the Catalog. They have been developed in-house by Microsoft, tried, tested, and approved and carry the tag PQD (Production Quality Developed). Third Party drivers in the Catalog may also be used but these may or may not be Microsoft Validated. If the component does not have a suitable driver in the Catalog, you need to add a custom driver to the Compact 7 image. The lack of an existing driver for a component could be because of a variety of reasons. It could be because it's a totally different hardware; it's similar to an existing device but a variant of the chip set; it's the same hardware as an existing device but with a different configuration; or it could be a device class not implemented on the system. Another (frustrating) scenario is when there is a driver for a previous version of Windows Embedded CE but not for Compact 7.

One possibility is that the driver is supplied in source code, in which case it can be added to the OS BSP and built from there. Alternatively, the hardware device comes with an existing Compact 7 installation package for Compact 7. The simplest solution in that case is to build the OS including the installation package, run the OS, run the installation, and capture the Registry changes and files added. Then add these to the OS image. Another possibility is that the driver is supplied as a binary DLL plus Registry settings. These can be added directly to the OS image. Finally if a device does not meet any of the these instances, a custom driver needs to be developed.

Custom Driver Development

As a minimum, a Compact 7 driver consists of the driver DLL plus Registry settings. In a worst-case scenario, the custom driver needs to be built from the ground up. A simpler case is where an existing driver can be cloned and modified.

The simplest scenario is where the only changes required are in the Registry settings. For example, the device might be a USB device that is exactly the same as an existing device, except its VendorID/ProductID (which identifies the device and its required DLL) is different. In this case, the same binary DLL can be used, with modified Registry settings.

The typical scenario is that an existing driver's source code can be cloned and the source modified to fit the required device. For example, if a high-speed serial device such as an OX16C954 were integrated into a Compact 7 system, the starting point would be the Compact 7 16550 driver because the OX16C954 can operate in a 550 mode. Then you would clone the 16550 driver from the Public folder and suitably modify it. For drivers in the Public folder (`Public\Common\OAK\Drivers`) you can clone a copy into the OS subprojects folder. See `http://embedded101.com/Articles.aspx` for further information on cloning device drivers.

For a driver that needs to be developed from scratch, you need to add a DLL project to the OS and add a suitable interface definition (DEF file) and add the required header references for a driver and linkage references. This would normally be done as a Stream Driver, which has a standardized OS interface. Development of a Stream Driver will be covered in Chapter 32, "Stream Interface Drivers," and Chapter 33, "Developing a Stream Interface Driver."

The developed driver needs to be developed and tested with a Debug version of the OS. Tools such a TUX Test Harness should also be used in its testing.

Use a Third-Party Driver Binary

Where the required DLL and Registry settings are available for a device, a targetless subproject is developed to include these in the OS. In the sources file for the project, `TARGETTYPE` is set equal to `NOTARGET`, and `postlink.bat` is set to copy the DLL to the `FlatRelease` directory for the OS. Its BIB file specifies that the DLL is included in the image, in the kernel space if required. The subproject's Registry file contains the required Registry settings. The project is set to be included in the image, so when the BuildRel runs, the project is run. As there is no C++ building required, the project is not touched until the late phase of an OS build. There is no debugging of this kind of driver.

Chapter 44, "FTDI Devices," shows how to create a driver project for this scenario.

SUMMARY

An understanding of device drivers is a key to comprehending the requirements for development of a customized embedded operating system such as Windows Embedded Compact 7. A device driver interfaces between the hardware and the operating system and provides an application programming interface for its configuration, status reads, I/O reads and writes, and an interrupt mechanism if required. You can select out-of-the-box Compact 7 drivers from the Catalog or use third-party device drivers and custom device drivers.

NOTE

1. Or in later x86 systems, the Advanced Programmable Interrupt Controller (APIC).

2. More specifically, you can configure any Windows 7 compatible device to run on a Windows Embedded Standard 7 system.

30

Device Driver Architectures

WHAT'S IN THIS CHAPTER?

➤ Introducing device driver software architectures

➤ Exploring the Windows Embedded Compact 7 kernel

➤ Defining kernel and user mode drivers

➤ Using monolithic and layered drivers

➤ Understanding stream, block, bus, and USB drivers

This chapter considers some key perspectives from which device drivers can be compared. It provides an overview of Compact 7 device drivers and how they are structured and relate to the operating system kernel. There are also some activities in this chapter dealing with the Bluetooth driver stack.

INTRODUCING DEVICE DRIVER ARCHITECTURES

Device drivers provide the interface between device hardware and the operating system. They can be structured in a number of ways. This section provides an introductory look at the different architectures you can use with device drivers.

What Is a Hardware Device Driver?

A hardware device driver is a software component that abstracts the underlying functionality of a physical device into the OS, as shown in Figure 30-1. That is, it makes the device functionality available to the OS and software entities that run on that system via a top-level interface. The device just plugs into the OS via the device driver. Applications therefore do not need to recode all the

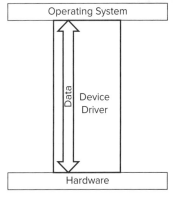

FIGURE 30-1

low-level hardware access code because that is all encapsulated in the device driver.

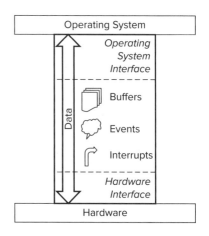

FIGURE 30-2

As shown in Figure 30-2, at the top level of the driver architecture is an interface that plugs the driver into the OS. At the bottom is an interface to the underlying hardware in terms of ports, registers, memory, and interrupts. In between these two interfaces, the device driver implements buffers for moving data between the interfaces, interrupts handlers to handle hardware generated events, and threads to respond to these events in a coherent manner. The device driver can also handle software and hardware configuration parameters submitted to it by the OS as well as status and data requests.

Between the top-level interface to the OS and the low-level interface to the hardware, you can use a variety of architectural structures to implement the driver functionality in between them, as shown in Figure 30-3. Some drivers (monolithic) are implemented amorphously bottom to top specifically for the driver in question. Other drivers (layered) are implemented in standardized layers in a much more structured manner.

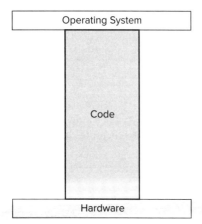 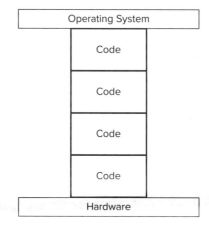

FIGURE 30-3

What Then Is a Virtual Device Driver?

A virtual device driver has the top interface of the driver architecture without the hardware interface. That is, it plugs into the OS as a serial device, a keyboard, or other device without implementing the lower interface to hardware. It builds upon other device drivers. For example, a USB serial device driver at its top level interfaces to the OS as a serial device and encapsulates a USB hardware driver as its lower level transport. Another virtual serial device could use a network as its transport. As shown in Figure 30-4, a virtual device driver

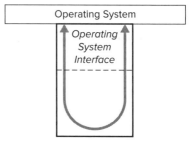

FIGURE 30-4

can implement the lower part of its functionality by calling back to the OS to invoke other drivers hosted by the OS.

Driver Stack

You can also consider a virtual device driver as part of a software stack where at the top is the operating system, at bottom is the hardware, and in between is a stack of device drivers. Each of these drivers loads as a separate device driver by the operating system. This is different to the layered device driver approach because that results in only one driver, one driver DLL, and one driver to be loaded. The layers generally build as library files linked together to form the one DLL file. With a software stack, a DLL loads for every driver in the stack. As the OS loads each driver, it must have a direct interface with the OS, as shown in Figure 30-5 (on left). Usually this connection is just assumed when drivers are stacked on top of each other (refer to Figure 30-5, on the right).

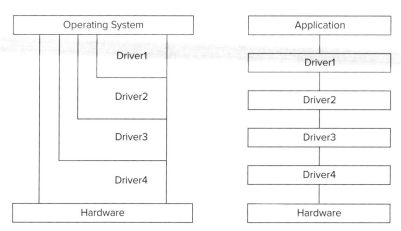

FIGURE 30-5

The driver stack may not be a single stack because there may be several paths from an application to the hardware through the interconnected driver stack, as shown in Figure 30-6. This is the Compact 7 Bluetooth Driver stack. An application may use Bluetooth via interfaces such as follows:

➤   SDP (Service Discovery Protocol)

➤   OBEX (Object Exchange)

➤   RfComm (Bluetooth Serial)

➤   Winsock (networking sockets)

➤   PAN Profile (personal area network: Bluetooth sharing)

➤   HID Profile (Human Interface Devices: keyboard and mouse)

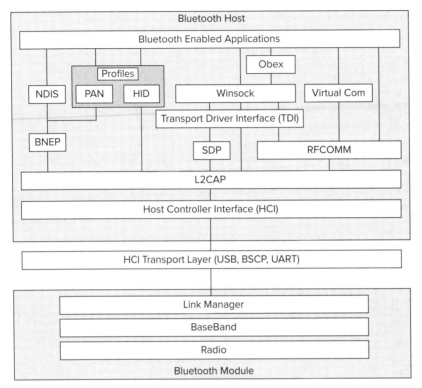

FIGURE 30-6

Driver Loading and Use

Another important aspect of a device driver is its configuration at loading and cleanup at unloading. This software as part of the device driver handles the instantiation of the buffers; the hooking up of the device interrupts into the operating system interrupt system, and the creation of the needed threads. It must put the device driver into a deterministic state including initializing the underlying hardware into a suitable initial state. The unloading of the driver unhooks the interrupts, releases the buffer resources, and causes the threads to exit or terminate. A driver management component of the operating system launches the device loading software, as shown in Figure 30-7. This assumes nothing about the initial state of the hardware and uses initialization parameters from the Registry. The same driver manager loads the drivers of the same class.

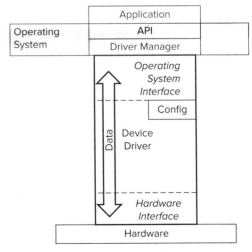

FIGURE 30-7

Two key aspects of a driver's configuration are when it is loaded and in which memory space it is loaded. Drivers can load at boot time because they are configured in registry to do so or because the operating system finds them through bus interrogation. Other drivers load only when they are plugged into the system or on demand when applications invoke their loading. Some drivers are uninstallable when loaded; others are not. Also, drivers can load into the kernel or user memory space, or both.

In Windows Embedded Compact 7, a device driver is implemented as a DLL with some exported entry ports so that the OS can perform such functions as to initialize it when it is loaded. The DLL can also implement functions that the driver manager interprets for the drivers' application interface such as to open and close an I/O stream and to read and write data with that stream. Applications do not call these functions directly to interact with the driver because this is done through the operating system driver manager that loaded it, as shown in Figure 30-7. Therefore all drivers of the same class have the same application programming interface (API) provided by the manager that loads them. Most drivers also provide a low-level interface to enable driver-specific custom calls.

In summary, following are the key aspects of a device driver's architecture:

➤ In what mode is a driver loaded?

➤ Is it a native or stream driver?

➤ Is it a monolithic or layered driver?

➤ Is it a hardware or virtual driver?

➤ When a driver is loaded, is it installable after start-up and can it be uninstalled?

➤ The driver API.

➤ The class of the driver.

In the rest of this chapter you examine the first three questions in detail. The fourth question has already been sufficiently covered in this section. The other questions are covered as part of subsequent chapters.

KERNEL AND USER DRIVER MODES

The kernel implements the core functions of the operating system. System reliability requires that user application drivers cannot halt the OS by corrupting, blocking, or overloading the kernel. To implement that requirement, Compact 7 like a lot of operating systems has two modes under which processes and threads can operate. The kernel runs in kernel mode, which is a protected mode. User applications run in user mode, which prohibits direct access to the kernel and its resources. Drivers can be loaded in kernel and user modes. Kernel mode drivers get full protection from both user applications and user mode drivers. A crashed user mode driver can't bring the system down and can typically be restarted.

As shown in Figure 30-8, every driver that runs in a Windows Embedded Compact system runs in either kernel mode or user mode. Applications whether they are native or managed run in user mode. Services, such as http, ftp, and so on run in user mode. Drivers are configured to run in user mode or kernel mode (or both) via the Registry.

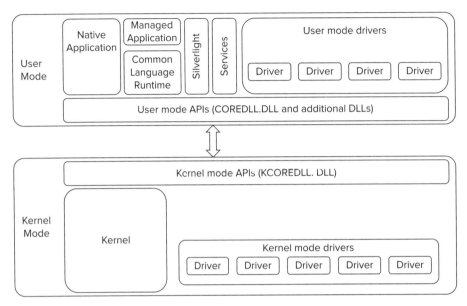

FIGURE 30-8

Kernel mode drivers have full access to the system operating system and hardware. A driver that needs to hook into the OS interrupts needs to run in kernel mode. If it needs to manipulate hardware registers directly, it needs to run in kernel mode. A virtual driver would be configured in user mode because it doesn't need direct access to hardware. A user mode driver can access the kernel resources but only indirectly via a reflector service that buffers user mode access to the operating system resources and kernel mode drivers. User mode drivers access operating system features (including kernel mode drivers) via coredll.dll, whereas kernel mode drivers access the operating system via a similar entity, k.coredll.dll. These two APIs essentially mirror each other, but there are some differences. User mode drivers can access the user shell functionality but have access to only a subset of the OS functionality, whereas kernel mode drivers don't have direct access to the user shell.

This separation of driver modes leads to improved system stability and recoverability. In some earlier versions of Windows CE, drivers all ran in user mode but could make a call to be elevated to kernel mode. There were no restrictions on this. An errant driver could easily crash or lock up the system. In later versions of Windows CE/Compact, drivers must be designated as being in kernel or user mode when loaded. User mode drivers are isolated from other drivers and the kernel is isolated from them. A compromised user mode driver can't crash the system, whereas a malfunctioning kernel mode driver can corrupt kernel data structures and crash the system. A user mode driver can be restarted without rebooting the operating system whereas kernel mode drivers cannot be restarted. Kernel mode drivers have a more efficient access to system resources than user mode drivers.

An OEM can choose whether its driver is loaded in kernel or user mode. Kernel mode driver loading though can occur only at startup. Registry flags determine the mode in which it is loaded. A driver loaded in kernel mode must have a K or Q flag in its BIB file entry. The Q flag means it may be loaded in either mode, whereas K means kernel mode only.

As shown in Figure 30-9, running in kernel mode are the kernel, its API, kernel mode drivers, the network stack, and driver managers, which load and manage those drivers.

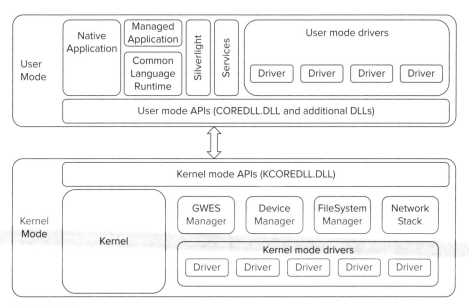

FIGURE 30-9

When a driver is loaded in kernel mode by Device Manager, device.exe is used whereas when a driver is loaded in user mode, udevice.exe is used. When a user mode application or driver references a kernel mode driver, a reflector service is created by Device Manager in the kernel to provide this indirect access, as shown in Figure 30-10 (on right).

Also, when an application accesses a user mode driver, a reflector is created for the driver as shown in Figure 30-10 (on left)

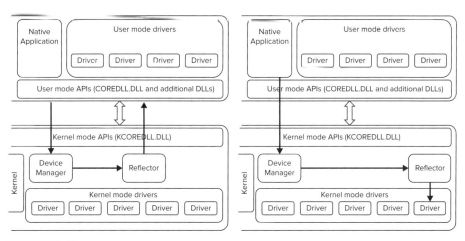

FIGURE 30-10

NATIVE AND STREAM DRIVERS

What loads a driver determines the operating system interface that must be implemented by the driver. Some core operating system drivers are loaded by GWES Manager (Graphical Windows and Event System), whereas most are loaded by Device Manager. Drivers loaded by GWES are native drivers because they are specific to the function they provide, whereas those loaded by Device Manager are stream drivers.

Native drivers expose an API other than the stream interface. Each native driver implements functions specific to its purpose. Compact 7 native drivers loaded by GWES encompass display and I/O devices such as the following:

➤ Display

➤ Keyboard

➤ Mouse and touch

➤ Printer interface

GWES supports all the windows, dialog boxes, controls, menus, and resources that make up the Windows Embedded Compact user interface (UI), which enables users to control applications. In Compact 7 there is a change from CE 6 in that GWES drivers are loaded by gwesuser.exe rather than gwes.dll. Also the GWES interface required for each of these is specific to the functionality of the driver. For example, a display driver implements functions such as shown in Table 30-1.

TABLE 30-1: Some Display Driver Functions

DisplayInit	DrvSetPalette	ContrastControl
DrvGetModes	DrvMovePointer	DrvGradientFill

These functions would not make any sense in a mouse, keyboard touch, or printer driver. A printer driver can implement eight functions relevant to printing documents, as shown in Table 30-2.

TABLE 30-2: Printer Driver Functions

DrvEndDoc	DrvStartDoc	DrvStartPage
GetPrinterInfo	PrinterClose	PrinterOpen
PrinterSend	ReportPrinterStatus	

This demonstrates that the interfaces for native drivers are specific to the class of driver.

The drivers loaded by the Device Manager are called stream drivers because their software functionality mimics the streaming of data to and from a file. Stream drivers suit devices that can be considered a data source, a data sink, or both. In the earlier versions of Windows CE, many more core OS drivers were of native structure, whereas only a few specific Compact 7 drivers are native. For example, the power driver was a native driver prior to CE 5 and was recast as a stream driver from CE 5 onwards.

All stream drivers have a common software interface consisting of up to 13 functions, as shown in Table 30-3. The XXX in the function names is replaced with the stream prefix, such as COM with a serial driver. This makes their development and testing a lot simpler because a driver needs to implement only this interface and link to coredll. With appropriate Registry settings, Device Manager, through `device.exe`, loads the driver and manages it.

TABLE 30-3: The Stream Driver Interface Functions

XXX_Init	XXX_DeInit	
XXX_Open	XXX_Close	XXX_PreClose
XXX_Read	XXX_Write	XXX_Seek
XXX_PowerUp	XXX_PowerDown	XXX_IOControl
XXX_PreDeinit	XXX_Cancel	

Applications get indirect access to the driver via the Device Manager using the stream driver API, which is a file I/O API (CreateFile, ReadFile, WriteFile, Close, and so on), not the stream driver interface functions.

Native and stream drivers are summarized and compared in Table 30-4.

TABLE 30-4: Native Versus Stream Drivers

	NATIVE DRIVER	STREAM DRIVER
Device characteristics	Any device that can't be supported by a stream driver	Any device that supports I/O operations similar to file I/O
Device type	Input and output such as display, keyboard, mouse, and touch	Many
API	Custom API specific to type of driver	Stream Interface
Loaded by	GWES	Device Manager
When loaded	Usually at boot time	Boot time, on device detection, by application
Mode	Kernel mode	Kernel and user modes
Application Access	Via the operating system	Through the file system

MONOLITHIC AND LAYERED DRIVER MODELS

As previously discussed, a driver can be constructed from a software perspective as a single entity or as a number of software layers. The driver interface to the OS is called the Device Driver Interface (DDI), as shown in Figure 30-11. With layered drivers, the interface between layers is called a Device Driver Service Interface (DDSI).

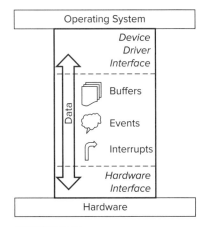

FIGURE 30-11

Monolithic Drivers

A monolithic driver implements both the DDI and the hardware interface. There are no DDSIs because the driver implements everything from the DDI down to the hardware. At the top, the device driver implements all the required and optional DDI functions so that it can be loaded into the OS and function correctly. The hardware interface at the bottom can directly interface to device hardware ports and memory. The device hardware interrupts are handled indirectly. These interrupts would normally connect to the target system's interrupt system so the device driver interrupt handler must be configured to trap interrupts from its device and maps them into the operating system's interrupts. In between the DDI and hardware are everything including initialization, de-initialization, configuration, state management, power management, and management of buffers and implementation interrupt handlers.

A monolithic driver is used when there is not a shared source for the required DDI functions. Because there are not DDSI interfaces to slow things down, it is written to implement its functionality as efficiently as possible. In general, this makes its development more difficult as all aspects of the driver, top to bottom, come to play when trying to debug the driver. Though if the interface to the OS is functionally similar to the hardware interface, then the implementation can be easier than the general case.

You would create a new monolithic driver from scratch if there is no alternative. Alternatively, you could clone an existing monolithic driver with the required DDI that is based upon similar hardware and modify to suit. Some examples of drivers that would typically be monolithic are display, block, network, Notification LEDS, and printer drivers. A display driver would be monolithic because its DDI would be tightly bound to the hardware, and it needs to be efficient. You can find examples of these in the $(_WINCEROOT)\public\COMMON\oak\drivers directory.

The DDI of a monolithic driver can be a stream or native interface. Many native drivers are implemented as monolithic drivers because of their nonstandard interfaces.

Layered Drivers

With Compact 7, layered drivers are typically architected as two layers, MDD (Model Device Driver Layer) and PDD (Platform Device Driver Layer) with a DDSI in between. The MDD is the layer at the top that interfaces to the operating system and implements the DDI, as shown in

Figure 30-12. The DDI can be a stream or native interface. The PDD is the bottom layer that implements the interface to the hardware and the DDSI that the MDD uses to call it. The same MDD can be used with a variety of platforms, each with a different PDD. This reuse is further facilitated because Microsoft provides a vast range of well-developed MDDs with sample PDDs that can be cloned and modified for different targets.

An MDD implements the operating functionality common to all devices of the same driver class. This would include operating system-specific things such as the interrupt handler. MDDs typically can be reused without modification. Normally it's just the lower and the middle parts of the PDD that need to be implemented for a specific device. The code reuse that layered drivers afford can mean simpler code development and

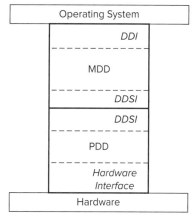

FIGURE 30-12

driver debugging than with a monolithic driver. But because of the DDSI interface, layered drivers might not be as efficient from performance and memory perspectives as monolithic drivers. But given that I/O is often much slower than CPU throughput and the memory capability of embedded devices is on the rise, this is probably being overcautious.

Note that layered drivers can consist of more than two layers. There would be a unique DDSI at the top of each layer below the MDD. Each layer would call the lower layer through that layer's DDSI and be called through its DDSI layer by the layer above it. Layers typically compile in Compact 7 into a library file. All the layer libraries, and others libs, are then linked into the driver's DLL file.

There are MDD/PDD drivers for many driver classes such as serial and audio. Apart from the DDI implementation, each provides an API specific to the driver class via the stream IOCTL interface (see Chapter 32). These APIs are additional to the API provided by the driver manager. For example, a serial driver is a stream driver and supports the stream API, and will be loaded by Device Manager (see $(_WINCEROOT\public\COMMON\oak\drivers\serial). All serial drivers in addition support calls such to configure the serial port (baud rates, bits, and so on) and to get its status. This enables a serial device, when loaded, to be used by any application that supports the specific serial interface. The serial device transport could be RS232, Bluetooth, or Infrared; for any serial application that makes no difference. Alternatively, the serial device could be interacted with using the lower level stream interface.

The wavedev driver is implemented as a MDD/PDD driver with the MDD implementing a stream interface, so it will be loaded by Device Manager (see $(_WINCEROOT) \public\COMMON\oak\ drivers\wavedev). The wavedev API supports such audio specific functions to start, stop, and pause the audio stream and to set the volume. With Compact 7, you would usually add and use the WaveForm Audio component and use its audio API because this provides a more application-focused functionality. For example, it has a PlaySound function to directly play a sound file. This is a virtual driver providing a layer over the wavedev driver. (The WaveForm component is actually a requirement of the audio drivers.)

Monolithic Versus Layered Drivers

Monolithic and layered drivers are summarized and compared in Table 30-5.

TABLE 30-5: Monolithic Versus Layered Drivers

	MONOLITHIC DRIVER	LAYERED DRIVER
Architecture	One entity.	A number of interfacing layers.
Number of layers	One.	Typically two (MDD,PDD) but can be more.
Reuse	Only for similar drivers, with similar hardware.	MDD is typically used for a range of PDDs.
Development ease	Harder.	Simpler.
Run-time efficiency	Can be more efficient.	Can be less efficient.
Operating system interface	Can be used for unique OS interface.	Normally requires an existing MDD.
DDI Interface type	Stream or native.	Stream or native.

STREAM, BLOCK, BUS, AND USB DRIVERS

As introduced in this chapter, stream device drivers are used when the device acts as a data source, a data sink, or both. This is the most common device driver architecture used in Windows Embedded Compact. Data is streamed to or from the device in a serial manner, on a per byte basis. Stream drivers are covered in detail in Chapters 32 and 33.

Two other driver formats are block and bus drivers. They may actually be implemented as stream drivers though. A block driver reads and writes data as fixed sized blocks. Individual bytes within a block cannot be addressed on the device for reading and writing. A bus device driver controls a bus such as a PCI, a USB, an SD, an I2C, and an ISA (PC104). Note that PCMCIA/Card Bus is not supported in Compact 7, whereas the I2C bus has been added. Bus drivers determine the correct driver for devices connected to them and therefore load them with their correct drivers.

Mass storage devices such as hard disk drives, flash memory cards, CDs and DVDs, various USB storage devices, and RAM disks would be loaded with a block driver. Common block sizes, the quantum of data accessed at any one time, are 512, 1K, 2K, and 4K bytes. The operating system file system is implemented to store a file as a number of blocks. Block drivers are generally implemented as stream drivers with the block movements implemented in the driver IOCTL interface (see Chapter 32, "Steam Interface Driver"). Most block drivers are based upon the ATAPI interface (Advanced Technology Attachment with Packet Interface). A block driver can typically connect to the system via a bus driver.

A bus driver is loaded at start up, and when loaded it interrogates the bus for devices (Bus Enumeration), with each device on the bus in turn responding with information about itself such as its Vendor ID and Product or Device ID. The bus driver uses these IDs to look up in the Registry to determine the device driver to use and its parameters for loading using Device Manager. The Vendor ID is the vendor identification code and Product or Device ID identifies the device on the bus.

On a USB bus, devices return a VID (Vendor ID) and a PID (Product ID). On a PCI, bus devices return a VEN (Vendor ID) and DEV (Device ID). For a Windows desktop system, you can see these identification codes in the properties of a driver in Device Manager. (Look at the Details tab and select Hardware IDs). OEMs and third parties maintain lists on the web of these IDs to search and identify devices and to help find drivers for devices.

On a hot pluggable bus (such as USB), devices can be added and removed any time after start up because the bus electrically supports this and because insertion and removal signals are generated on the bus by the device for the bus controller. These signals cause the bus controller to load and unload the device's driver.

There are USB Hosts and USB Devices. Most PCs act as USB Hosts, whereas devices such as memory sticks act as USB Devices. When a system has the USB host controller it gets information about the inserted device so that it can find the device in the Registry and load the device driver. This information may point to a specific driver (VID&PID) for the device or to a device class for which the class driver is used, as per the USB class IDs in Table 30-6. That is why most USB memory sticks can be inserted into a system without preloading the driver or searching updates for the driver. When a USB device is inserted for the first time, there will typically be two or more drivers to be loaded. The first will be the hardware driver (EHCI, OHCI, or UHCI controller), which will be followed by one or more drivers for functions such as Mass Storage.

TABLE 30-6: Some USB Class IDs

ID	CLASS
01	Audio
03	Human Interface Device (HID)
08	Mass Storage
07	Printer
09	Hub
58	Xbox
E0	Wireless

It is important to be clear about the difference between a bus driver and device driver that runs on a bus. The bus driver is typically part of the Board Support Package (BSP) because the buses are part of the board design and therefore determined by the board OEM. Developers are normally not concerned with developing bus drivers unless they are porting or developing a new BSP. Even then they would probably use the bus driver source code or binary available in Compact 7 for that board's CPU. A driver for a device on a bus is called a client driver.

For example, a serial device on a PCI bus can have a client driver, whereas the PCI bus can have a bus driver. The PCI bus driver is responsible for hardware configuration, hardware power control, bus address translation, and loading and unloading the client drivers. The client driver is identified for the bus that it is on and normally links with the bus driver for certain functions such as power management.

Many bus client device drivers are bus-agnostic in that they can execute on a number of buses. That means that the same driver can be used to load the device regardless of whether it connects to the system via a PCI bus, a USB bus, or whatever. This is a desirable feature because it results in code reuse and can ease migration between platforms. A bus-agnostic driver can get its resources via the Registry and hook into the bus on which it is present for things such as power state. It can avoid calling the OS for hardware-specific functions. Some examples of bus-agnostic drivers are the NE2000 network and COM16550 serial drivers.

HOW TO CHECK IF THE BLUETOOTH STACK IS LOADED

This project is contained in the source code zip file for this project in the directory `BTStackCheck`. The code snippets used here are also in source code zip file as `chapter30Code.txt`.

In this activity you create a native code application that attempts to see if the Bluetooth stack is loaded. This checks only to see if the operating system Bluetooth stack drivers have been loaded, regardless of whether the Bluetooth hardware device is present. For this activity a suitable Bluetooth USB dongle is required that has the Cambridge Silicon Research (CSR) hardware (as many do) because this is the default Bluetooth hardware driver that is included in the catalog. The help documentation says that no hardware driver is provided, just everything in the stack above; but the CSR one is there, as `bthcsr.dll`.

First, you need to check that your Bluetooth dongle works:

1. Insert it into your desktop system and let it load the drivers.

2. Examine it under Device Manager/Bluetooth Radios. You should see two entries:

   ➤ CSR Bluetooth Radio

   ➤ Microsoft Bluetooth Enumerator

Now create the test application and try it out on the OS before the Bluetooth stack has been added:

1. Start with a Compact 7 Retail image that runs on hardware.

2. Add a new a new native code application:

   ➤ Console Application

   ➤ BTStackCheck

   ➤ Simple Console Application

➤ In Solution Explorer/Properties (OS, not the Subproject), set it to be built in debug mode and excluded from the image (as in Figure 31-6).

3. Double-click the project in Solution Explorer to open its `BTStackCheck\sources` file. Add the following at the bottom of the file:

```
INCLUDES= \
    $(_PUBLICROOT)\COMMON\SDK\INC;   \
    $(_PUBLICROOT)\COMMON\DDK\INC;   \
    $(_WINCEROOT)\Public\Common\Sdk\Inc
```

Code snippet is from include directory references in the file sources

4. Add the following at the top of sources:

```
WINCEREL=1
```

Code snippet is from the project type reference in the file sources

5. Build BTStackCheck by right clicking on the BTStackCheck project and selecting Build to check that all is OK. Resolve any issues.

6. Open the source file, `BTStackCheck.cpp`, in the BTStackCheck project and add the following header references at or near the top:

```
#include <windows.h>
#include "Bt_api.h"
```

Code snippet is from header file references in the file BTStackCheck.cpp

7. Do another build or attempt to open these header files; just to make sure that they are correctly referenced.

8. Add the following code inside the main function before the return statement:

```
// Make sure BT stack is up
  BOOL fStackUp = FALSE;
  RETAILMSG(1,(_T("BT Stack STARTING")));
  for (int i = 0 ; i < 30 ; ++i)
  {
    HANDLE hBthStackInited = OpenEvent (EVENT_ALL_ACCESS, FALSE,
      BTH_NAMEDEVENT_STACK_INITED);
    RETAILMSG(1,(_T("BT Stack Got handle.")));
    if (hBthStackInited)
    {
      DWORD dwRes = WaitForSingleObject (hBthStackInited, 3333);
      CloseHandle (hBthStackInited);
      if (WAIT_OBJECT_0 == dwRes)
      {
        RETAILMSG(1,(_T("BT Stack FOUND .. in loop")));
        fStackUp = TRUE;
```

```
      break;
    }
    else if (WAIT_TIMEOUT == dwRes)
    {
     RETAILMSG(1,(_T("BT wait  timed out")));
    }
    else if (WAIT_ABANDONED == dwRes)
    {
     RETAILMSG(1,(_T("BT wait  abanded")));
    }
    else
    {
     RETAILMSG(1,(_T("BT unknown wait exit")));
    }
    RETAILMSG(1,(_T("BT Stack Waiting")));
    Sleep (1000);
  }
}
if (! fStackUp)
{
  RETAILMSG(1,(_T("BT Stack NOT found")));
}
else
{
  RETAILMSG(1,(_T("BT Stack FOUND")));
}
RETAILMSG(1,(_T("BT Stack DONE")));
```

Code snippet is from code to implement the stack check in main in the file BTStackCheck.cpp

9. Build the application and resolve any issues.

10. Run your OS.

11. Run the application:

   ➤ Select Target-Run Programs, and choose BTStackCheck

12. It continuously loops and eventually reports that the stack is not present. Look in the Output windows in the IDE.

13. Insert the Bluetooth USB dongle into the system. It asks for the driver. Enter **bthcsr.dll**. It won't find it because you haven't added it to the OS yet.

Now shutdown the OS and modify it to include the Bluetooth stack:

1. Add USB Host components under Device Drivers/USB in the Catalog, if they are not there already:

   ➤ USB Host Support.

   ➤ That will automatically add all three USB Host Controllers.

   ➤ Add some USB Class drivers while you are about it.

2. Add the required Bluetooth Components:

   ➤ Go to the top of the Catalog and search for Bluetooth.

➤ Bluetooth Stack and Universal Loadable Driver.

➤ Add other Bluetooth components depending upon what you have; or add them all.

3. Rebuild the OS in Retail mode.

4. Run the OS.

5. Insert your Bluetooth dongle into the Compact 7 system. It doesn't ask for the driver because it is included and configured in the OS.

6. Rerun the application as you did previously.

7. It now reports that it found the Bluetooth stack, if all is well!

Actually it may report that the stack is in place if the dongle is inserted. It does not check the hardware. You need to add some control panel components to check that.

USING THE COMPACT 7 BLUETOOTH COMPONENTS

In this activity you learn how to configure and use Bluetooth with Compact 7. This includes adding some Silverlight Control Panel items and pairing a Bluetooth HID device such as a mouse or keyboard.

Start with configuring the OS Bluetooth components and building the modified OS:

1. Revisit step 2 in the previous section and make sure that the following components are also added:

➤ Both Bluetooth HID components.

➤ The Bluetooth Settings UI. Note that Silverlight is automatically added. Check Shell and User Interface/Silverlight for Windows Embedded.

2. Under Shell and User Interface/User Interface add the following:

➤ Control Panel, Silverlight for Windows Embedded

➤ Some of the under unchecked settings components such as Date Time, Display, Network. These all require the Silverlight Control Panel.

3. Under Shell and User Interface/Graphical Shell add the following:

➤ Sample Home Screen

➤ The Silverlight-based Message Box, if you want

4. You might also want to add Internet Explorer 7.0 Silverlight for Windows Embedded and the Internet Options Control Panel for Windows Embedded. Another is CAB Installer based on ConfigManager v1 and CSPs. (That's for Silverlight.) You can find them by searching the catalog.

5. Build and run the OS.

The OS should start and the Home Screen should appear. Now check that Bluetooth started and pair a mouse or keyboard.

1. Select Settings.

2. Scroll down to where Bluetooth appears and select it.

3. Turn on Bluetooth if it's not already on. The silver button on the left toward the top should have a blue icon. Press it if it's not blue.

4. After a while some of the buttons should be enabled.

5. Press Add New and set the mouse (or keyboard) to be discoverable.

6. When the mouse (or keyboard) displays, click the device and then press Pair Device.

7. Complete any pairing instructions. A paired mouse is shown in Figure 30-13.

8. You now can use the paired device.

9. Experiment with the other Bluetooth settings.

10. Try pairing with other Bluetooth devices such as a phone or laptop.

11. Return to the Home Screen and explore the other settings.

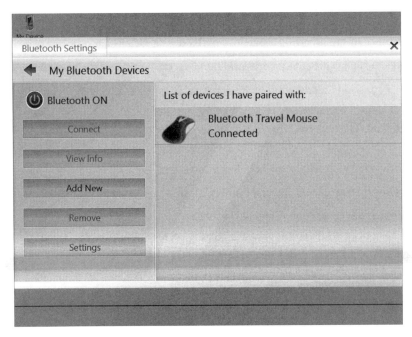

FIGURE 30-13

SUMMARY

This chapter introduced the concept of a device driver as the interface between the operating system and hardware. The different architectures for device drivers and how they can load in kernel and user modes was also explored. Bluetooth was added into a Compact 7 image explaining how to use it. The next chapter provides an in-depth look at interrupts with respect to drivers, which is key to how they function. The following chapter covers stream drivers in detail.

31

Interrupts

WHAT'S IN THIS CHAPTER?

➤ Understanding interrupts

➤ Exploring Compact 7 Interrupt Architecture

➤ What are installable Interrupts?

➤ Using Compact 7 Message Queues

➤ Understanding watchdog timers

➤ Using the eBox 3300 watchdogs to generate interrupts

➤ Creating a native DLL project and application that calls it

This chapter covers everything you need to know to get started with implementing and using interrupts with a Compact 7 system. It introduces interrupts and then discusses the Compact 7 interrupt architecture for IRQs, ISTs, and system interrupts. Watchdog timers are then introduced and a detailed example explains how to use them to generate system interrupts and how to trap these in user code. Also, you learn how to create a native DLL subproject as well as a native application subproject that calls the DLL.

POLLING AND INTERRUPTS

When the state of the hardware changes, such as when a serial port receives data or transmission is completed, the device driver needs to know about this change so that it can handle the changed state. Consider a UART serial transmission device. For reception, the device driver needs to move the data from the hardware buffer into its software buffer before more data arrives and overwrites it. Also, the system will need to copy data for transmission from software buffers to the hardware buffers as transmissions are completed. The issue then is, how does the system know to respond to changes of state by the hardware? Software can use two different methods to handle hardware changes of state: polling and interrupts.

With polling, a separate thread runs that continuously checks the state of a hardware register or hardware flag. If it has changed, then the change is acted upon. Such a thread would typically sleep for a period in its loop to not overburden the CPU, as shown in Figure 31-1. Polling in this manner is effectively a periodic activity. If the period is too long, some events may be missed. If the period is too short, the thread may consume too much of the CPU time. Polling is suitable where the hardware in question doesn't raise interrupts or where only the occasional poll is required. Polling can be simpler to implement than interrupts.

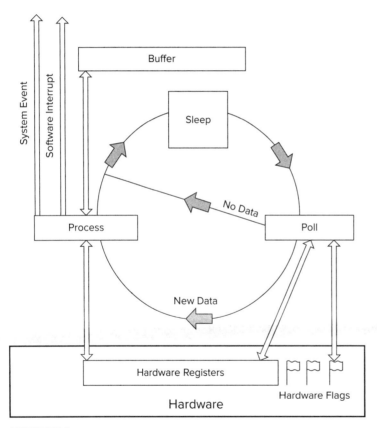

FIGURE 31-1

If polling is used in a driver, then it does nothing more than move the data between its buffers and hardware as it becomes available. Higher level threads use the data. To do this, after processing the polled data, the driver can generate a software interrupt for use by the operating system or action, an operating system event that would be trapped by another thread waiting on that event, as shown in Figure 31-2.

Rather than polling the hardware flags, you can configure them to generate interrupts. With interrupts, the change of state in the hardware generates an interrupt that is handled by the CPU's interrupt mechanism. When the processor receives an interrupt, it saves the current processor context and then quickly changes context to process the event. It then returns to the original context.

As shown in Figure 31-3, the steps for handling an interrupt are as follows:

1. The CPU is interrupted by hardware and saves its state on the stack.

2. The CPU then jumps to the interrupt handler to handle the interrupt.

3. The data is moved between the hardware registers and the buffers.

4. The source of the interrupt in the hardware is cleared.

5. A system event is generated for higher level processing. This is not handled immediately because the thread that handles it is a lower priority.

6. The CPU is signaled that the interrupt is handled, and the handler exits. The CPU returns to the state that it was in prior to the interrupt.

7. The higher level thread waiting on the system event further processes the data transfer.

A variation of this sequence is that the handler only signals the event. In this scenario, the interrupt is cleared by the higher level blocked thread when it completes the data transfer between the hardware registers and its buffers directly. This is essentially what Compact 7 does via the kernel.

With I/O-oriented microprocessors that have counters, timers, Analog to Digital Converters (ADC), and Digital to Analog Converters (DAC) as part of the core, those peripherals generate an interrupt specific to the source. In general though, interrupts from peripheral

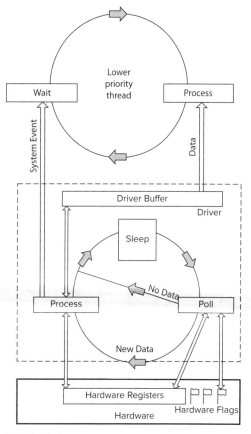

FIGURE 31-2

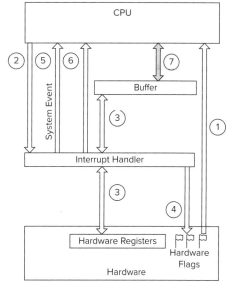

FIGURE 31-3

hardware external to the processor connect to the CPU via a common pin. When an interrupt occurs in this manner, the CPU has to determine the source of the interrupt so that it can determine which interrupt handler to call. In some cases hardware interrupts are chained together and an initial handler must poll the hardware to determine the interrupt source.

Usually after an interrupt has been raised with the CPU, it can't process any more interrupts, or any more interrupts at the same or lower priority. Therefore it is important to quickly handle interrupts. To that end, the interrupt handler normally does nothing more than determine the interrupt source and pass that to the operating system.

COMPACT 7 INTERRUPT ARCHITECTURE

The interrupt mechanism is initiated by a hardware interrupt which manifests at the CPU as an IRQ (Interrupt Request). A Windows Embedded Compact 7 driver will handle an interrupt as two routines: The ISR and the IST. The ISR is the Interrupt Service Routine, which is the first routine called when an interrupt occurs. The IST is the Interrupt Service Thread, which gets called later.

The Compact 7 Interrupt mechanism is shown in Figure 31-4 and is discussed in detail in the following sections.

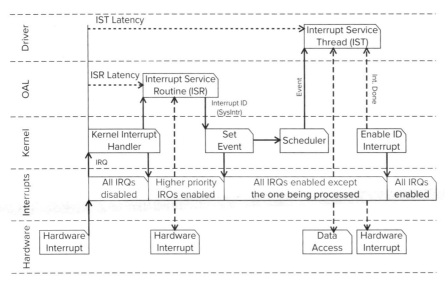

FIGURE 31-4

Setup

The ISR and IST have to be enabled through the operating system before they can handle the interrupt.

➤ When the driver is loaded, or when it is enabled, the ISR is registered to handle an IRQ.

➤ When the driver is loaded, a high priority thread is started that loops. The thread blocks waiting for an event. When unblocked, it processes the interrupt data and then blocks on that event until it is signaled again.

Interrupt Sequence

The following outlines the interrupt sequence as in Figure 31-4:

1. Hardware generates an interrupt on the CPU's IRQ pin.

2. CPU disables all other IRQs on that pin.

3. Kernel gets the interrupt and calls the associated ISR, in a high-priority thread.

4. Kernel reenables higher priority IRQs.

5. ISR determines the interrupt source from hardware and returns the system interrupt ID to the kernel via `SetEvent`.

6. ISR exits.

7. Kernel enables all IRQs except the current one.

8. The event is scheduled.

9. The IST is unblocked and runs until data access is complete.

10. IST signals hardware that the interrupt has been handled and then blocks on the same event.

Interrupt Service Routine (ISR)

The Interrupt Service Routine (ISR) is what runs initially in response to a hardware interrupt. Its job is to determine the source of the interrupt for the system configuration; that is, to determine the Operating System Interrupt (SYSINTR) when a hardware interrupt occurs. For installable interrupts, the ISR calls down the chain to all installed interrupt handlers for that hardware interrupt. Each consults its hardware to determine if it was the source or passes it further down the chain. The ISR cannot have any operating system dependencies, such as Win32.

Interrupt Service Thread (IST)

An interrupt service thread (IST) is a thread that runs as an infinite loop that blocks on events fired by the kernel when the ISR informs it that a certain system interrupt needs to be signaled. This thread is normally a high-priority thread (often priority zero) and is started by the device driver that depends upon it. Its blocking call to `WaitForSingleObject` unblocks when the SYSINTR that it is waiting for is signaled. While the ISR could move the data to and from the hardware for this interrupt, it is better to do this in the IST.

Latency

Latency is the time that a device takes to respond to an event. For Windows Embedded Compact interrupts, there is the ISR latency and the IST latency. Obviously, the ISR latency is shorter than the IST latency because it has to occur first. Both are subject to jitter because there is some indeterminacy for when the hardware event occurs for CPU instructions and the time it takes to change context. The CPU clock speed and thread quantum size can also impact upon latency, particularly for the IST. Finally, the priority that the IST runs in can have a major impact on its latency; therefore it is desirable that the IST run at priority zero.

Latency impacts directly upon the maximum frequency at which the event can reoccur. During ISR latency no new IRQs can be received. During IST latency, the same interrupt can't be received. (Remember that the IRQ is the hardware interrupt that the CPU receives. Multiple interrupts will normally cause the same IRQ. Therefore one IRQ will cause one of a number ISTs to be actioned. The ISR works out which system interrupt event needs to be sent.)

Another aspect of latency is determinism. The ISR latency is reasonably deterministic, whereas IST latency is less deterministic, depending upon what priority it runs at. The indeterminacy results in latency *jitter*, which means that if the latency period is measured over a number of interrupts, there will be some variance in the measured latency. In a situation of high CPU load, there is much more jitter with the IST than with the ISR. Jitter is how much the latency can vary.

There is a test application in Compact 7, ILTiming, that can be used to measure both latencies for a system interrupt. This tool uses the system tick interrupt as the test interrupt vector. It injects an interrupt into the system periodically; the period is an integral number of timer ticks. You can set the priorities of IST and a number of other threading options. The application runs for a specified number of interrupts, measuring the latencies for each interrupt, and returns some statistics on the latencies. The built application can be copied to the Release directory and run from there. Run it with the command line parameter -h to get its help messages. ILTimining.exe is located in:

```
$(_PUBLICROOT)\COMMON\oak\target\<CPU>\<Retail|Debug|Checked>
```

with the source code in:

```
$(_PUBLICROOT)\platform\common\src\<CPU>\common\timer
```

The application requires some modifications in the BSP in the OAL but not in the kernel. In addition to injecting timer actioned interrupts, there needs to be some hooks in the system interrupt chain to log the interrupts. Fortunately the Compact 7 VM BSP does support the ILTiming application, so the application can be copied to a VM and the latency jitter can be measured. A variant of this uses an external interrupt to inject real interrupts into the system from an oscillator. With this the latencies can be observed when the system receives a varied rate of interrupts.

The eBox 3300, discussed later in this chapter, also supports ILTiming. Running the tool on this system is perhaps more meaningful than on the VM because it uses a real hardware timer, whereas the VM has a simulated software timer and is subject to the timing indeterminism of any application running on Windows because it is nonpreemptive.

Chapter 36, "Introduction to Real-Time Applications," covers jitter in more detail.

System Interrupts and Hardware Interrupts

You need to clearly distinguish between hardware interrupts and system interrupts. Hardware interrupts are the Physical Interrupts (IRQs) that occur, whereas the system interrupts are the Logical Interrupts (SYSINTR). The logical interrupts are fed up the software stack to user mode applications and drivers, not the hardware interrupts. The IRQs for a typical x86 system are shown in Table 31-1. Physical interrupts can have more than one source, which also means that logical interrupts can share the same physical interrupt. For example, COM1 and COM3 share the same physical interrupt IRQ4. If an OS is configured to use both, a separate SYSINTR value is created via a kernel call for each when the driver is installed. The ISR or IST is tasked with distinguishing between both using the hardware and then forwarding the correct SYSINTR.

TABLE 31-1: Physical (Hardware) IRQs for a Typical x86 PC

IRQ	USUAL FUNCTION/DEVICE
0	System Timer
1	Keyboard
2	2nd IRQ controller
3	COM2: and COM4:
4	COM1: and COM3:
5	Free (used by LPT2: or sound card)
6	Floppy disk
7	LPT1:
8	Real-Time Clock (RTC)
9	Free (may be labeled/appear as IRQ 2)
10	Free (often used by sound cards)
11	Free
12	PS/2 mouse
13	Math coprocessor on CPU (used)
14	Primary IDE
15	Secondary IDE

A CPU often has only one or two interrupt inputs. So that they can support a much larger number of interrupts, an external device such as a Programmable Interrupt Controller (PIC) can be used that has a number of interrupt inputs funneled into a single interrupt for the CPU. The ISR then queries the PIC to determine the source of the interrupt.

Installable Interrupts

Installable interrupts can be installed any time after the operating system has been started, particularly after the OAL boot phase, whereas the physical OS interrupts are part of the BSP and are therefore installed as part of the OAL phase. Only interrupts that are bound to the hardware and therefore to the target hardware should be installed then. Interrupts for most drivers should be implemented as installable interrupts because they are then not tied to specific platforms.

An installable interrupt links in via the kernel to an existing IRQ so that it can be queried as to whether it is the source of the interrupt. When the driver installs it, a SYSINTR is designated for it so that the ISR can return it to the kernel if it indicates that it is the source of the interrupt. The kernel then signals this system interrupt so that the driver's IST can respond.

ILTiming is implemented using an installable interrupt that hooks into the system timing. There is a Generic Installable Interrupt Service Routine (GIISR) code in the following:

```
$(_PUBLICROOT)\COMMON\oak\drivers\giisr
```

In the next few sections of this chapter you use an installable interrupt to capture interrupts from a watchdog timer.

WATCHDOG TIMER

A Watchdog Timer (WDT) is a timer that triggers a system reset or some other system resolution event when it times out. Software on the device needs to signal the timer to restart its count regularly to avoid the timeout action. This is often called "petting the dog." The purpose of a watchdog timer, also called computer operating properly (COP), is to restart the system when it has become errant. If the device hangs for whatever reason, the timer automatically resets the system or signals a handler to take a corrective action. That way, after a maximum period, the system always restores to a normal state if errant. Many microprocessors, many Systems on a Chip (SoC), and some System I/O chips have an inbuilt watchdog timer, although this function can also be implemented in software. A hardware watchdog timer is a better option because no matter what state the system software is in, the hardware can always force a reset if required. Windows Embedded Compact 7 has support for a software watchdog, although it can be configured to use a hardware watchdog if available.

When you configure a watchdog timer, you need to configure two properties besides enabling or disabling it. You configure the watchdog timer timeout and what to do when it does time out.

Some possible timeout actions are:

➤ System reset

➤ An interrupt

➤ Operating system event

➤ Kill the process that started the WDT

➤ No action

The purpose of the WDT determines what action should be taken. A system reset should be considered a drastic reaction, but if the system is a standalone, remote embedded system, then this may suit the WDT's purpose. The purpose of the WDT depends on what initiated the WDT. If it were part of the system initialization, then reset would probably be appropriate. If a process started it, then the action may be to kill the process and to recover its resources.

For software watchdog timers, the timeout period needs careful consideration for thread quantum and thread priorities. A process starts the WDT. The WDT periodically runs as a thread to update its counter and in doing so runs at a certain priority. Compact 7 is a preemptive multitasking operating system, and if this thread is not of sufficient priority, it will be preempted by other threads or has to take its turn with other threads of the same priority. The timeout period therefore should be many operating system thread quantums (which for Compact 7 is typically 100mS). Even if the WDT thread is of high priority, the thread that is to "pet" it may only be of low priority, and may be continually preempted before it gets a chance to interact with the WDT. Hardware WDTs don't suffer from these issues.

Another issue with a watchdog timer reset is the corruption of the file system (or even the registry), which could happen if a write is not completed because of a reset. Earlier versions of Windows could suffer file system corruption if turned off rather than shutdown. A transaction-safe file system must be used if you use a WDT reset. See "Transaction-Safe FAT System (TFAT)" in the catalog. Also a Compact 7 system often takes minutes to reboot and restart apps that would result in a long system outage. And related to this, the WDT should be one of the last things to start; otherwise, the system may keep rebooting, never completing startup because the "petting" application never gets a chance to do a pet before the WDT times out.

In summary, watchdog timers are OK for small microprocessors but are possibly not a solution for operating systems. The system and application code should be constructed in a manner so that they are verifiably correct and can directly handle all possible errant conditions. Would you want a life support system suddenly doing a WDT reset?

Compact 7 Watchdog API

The Compact 7 kernel provides an API for software watchdog timers:

➤   `CreateWatchDogTimer` (Called by the process initiating the WDT)

Table 31-2 lists the default actions to take at timeout.

TABLE 31-2: WDT Timeout Actions

VALUE	DESCRIPTION
WDOG_KILL_PROCESS	Terminate the process to be watched.
WDOG_NO_DFLT_ACTION	Take no default action.
WDOG_RESET_DEVICE	Reset the device.

This returns a handle for the following functions:

➤   `StartWatchDogTimer` — Starts the timer

➤   `StopWatchDogTimer` — Stops the timer

The handle is forwarded to the threads that refresh (pet) the WDT using the following:

➤   `RefreshWatchDogTimer` — Refresh the timer

The sample code for this chapter contains a console application for exercising the Compact 7 software WDT. See the folder SWWDT on the book's website.

The Private Compact 7 code (if you have access to it) for the watchdog timer is in:

```
$(_PRIVATEROOT)\WINCEOS\COREOS\NK\KERNEL\watchdog.c
```

Using WatchDog Timers in System Development

Causing a development system to automatically reset via a WDT, while useful to do once, doesn't help with the OS development. WDTs configured to generate interrupts are a good example of installable interrupts and are a good demonstration of how to implement them. Now look at an x86 SoC that has an built-in hardware WDT.

The Vortex86 SoC Watchdog Timer

The Vortex86 is an example of a SoC that has a watchdog timer. As shown in Figure 31-5, the South Bridge has two independent hardware watchdog timers: WDT0 and WDT1. This is used in the eBox 3300 Embedded PC.

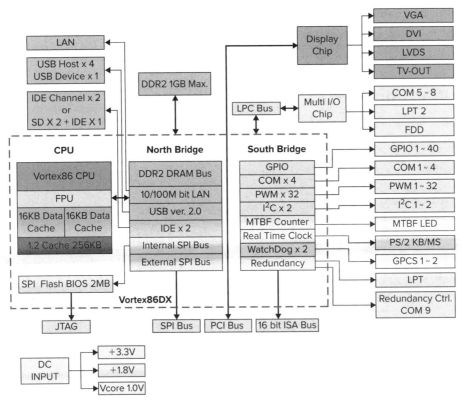

FIGURE 31-5

There is a programming guide to the Vortex86DX WDT on page 29 of the following PDF:

```
www.embeddedpc.net/Compact7Book/DMP_Vortex86_Series_Software_Programming_
Reference_v1.pdf
```

The main Vortex86 WDT features are in Table 31-3, and the WDT1 function configuration data for bits 7 to 4 of port 0x69 are in Table 31-4.

TABLE 31-3: The Vortex86 WDT Features

	WDT0	WDT1
Index Port	0x22	—
Data Port	0x23	—
I/O Ports	—	0x68 to 0x6D
Counter	24 bit	24 bit
Timeout Range	30.5uS to 512 sec	30.5uS to 512 sec
Resolution	30.5uS	30.5uS
Interrupts	System reset, NMI. IRQ	System reset, NMI. IRQ

TABLE 31-4: WDT Function (Port 0x69, Bits 7 to 4)

CODE	WDT FUNCTION
0000	Reserved
0001	IRQ3
0010	IRQ4
0011	IRQ5
0100	IRQ6
0101	IRQ7
0110	IRQ9
0111	IRQ10
1001	IRQ12
1010	IRQ14
1011	IRQ15
1100	NMI
1101	System reset
1110	Reserved
1111	Reserved

Following are the steps to set up WDT0:

1. Set Bit 6 = 0 to disable the timer.

2. Write the desired counter value to 0x3B, 0x3A, 0x39 (24 bits, 3B is MSB).

3. Set Bit 6 = 1 to enable the timer; the counter begins to count up.

4. When the counter reaches the setting value, the timeout will generate a signal setting by index 38h bit[7:4] (e.g., 1011 = IRQ15).

5. BIOS can read index 3Ch Bit 7 to decide whether the watchdog timeout event will happen.

6. Write 1 to bit 6 of 0x3C to clear ("pet") the WDT.

7. Set Bit 6 = 0 to disable the timer. This also clears the counter at the same time.

Following are the steps to set up WDT1:

1. Write time into register 0x6A-0x6C (24 bit, 6A is MSB).

2. Set the timeout signal in register 0x69, bits 7 to 4. (e.g., 1011 = IRQ15).

3. Set register 0x68 bit 8 to enable WDT1.

4. Write any value to register 67H to clear ("pet") the WDT.

5. Clear register 0x68 bit 8 to disable WDT1.

The Compact 7 Message Queue API

When an IST receives an interrupt from the ISR, it needs to signal the user application, or any other entity that is dependent upon it, that a message is available and pass data to it — and potentially get data from it. Compact 7 has an interprocess message queue API for setting up a message queue at both ends as well as for sending and receiving data over the queue. The receiving end can synchronize with the sender by waiting on messages to be available. A queue has a single direction; one is designated the writer, and the other is designated the reader. The main API functions follow:

➤ CreateMsgQueue()

➤ CloseMsgQueue()

➤ WriteMsgQueue()

➤ ReadMsgQueue()

The first function takes as parameters a name as a string and an options structure and returns a handle that the other three functions use as a parameter. The two processes create their ends of the queue separately; they need to use the same name. The options include whether the process that is instantiating the queue is a writer or reader. (There must be one of each.) The WriteMsgQueue parameters include a pointer to the source buffer and how many bytes to send. It also has a timeout period, which is normally set to 0 so that the writer doesn't block on the transmission. ReadMsgQueue has the same parameters plus a parameter for the number of bytes received. Its timeout though is typically set to INIFNITE or a period in milliseconds so that it can block on the IST events.

To pass an event indicating that an interrupt has been received by the IST, the IST will be configured as the message queue writer and write a dummy value into the message queue upon each interrupt. The receiving entity that is to be blocked waiting for that event signal from the IST is configured as the message queue reader and blocks on a `ReadMsgQueue` with a nonzero timeout. You can also use `WaitForSingleObject` for the reader synchronization, using the same handle and a timeout as parameters.

A WATCHDOG TIMER DRIVER AND APPLICATION

In the code for this chapter is a complete Compact 7 WDT test application and drivers for the eBox 3300-Vortex86DX (and MX) watchdog timer. This section will discuss the structure and function of this code. The next section will cover using the code. It can be configured to reset the device or generate IRQs 3 to 7, 9, 10, 12, and 14. There are four Compact 7 projects in this bundle:

➤   `WDT_ISR` — WDT IRQ handler

➤   `WDT_DRV` — WDT driver

➤   `WatchdogWrapperDLL` — Native code wrapper for the driver

➤   `WatchdogWrapperDLL` — Native code application to test the WDT via the wrapper

As the code for WDT1 is simpler, you track its coding in the next section.

WDT_ISR

`WDT_ISR` implements an installable interrupt for the Vortex86.

The configuration information and values for WDT1 follows:

➤   DWORD SysIntr

    ➤   The system interrupt for WDT1 if enabled.

        ➤   Upon an interrupt this gets passed to the kernel, which fires an event that unblocks the IST.

    ➤   SYSINTR_CHAIN if not enabled

        ➤   The interrupt gets passed on to any other ISR in the chain to see if it can handle it. For this interrupt there will be no other interrupts in the chain.

➤   UCHAR IIRaddr

    ➤   Port Ox6d if enabled; zero otherwise.

    ➤   The configuration port for what to do upon an interrupt.

➤   UCHAR Mask

    ➤   0x80 if enabled.

    ➤   Zero otherwise.

➤ BOOL M6117

   ➤ False for WDT1.

The key functions in this driver follow:

➤ CreateInstance()

   ➤ This does nothing other than store configuration information such that the ISR does not pass the WDT1 system interrupt to the kernel.

➤ DestroyInstance()

   ➤ Removes the instance configuration information.

➤ IOControl()

   ➤ The IOCTL handler.

   ➤ There is one IOCTL implemented: IOCTL_ISR_INFO.

   ➤ It writes configuration information.

   ➤ The WDT_DRV would send information such that the ISR does pass on WDT1's system interrupt.

➤ ISRHandler()

   ➤ Returns with the value SYSINTR_CHAIN if interrupts are not enabled for WDT1.

      ➤ This means that the signal will be passed farther up the chain.

   ➤ If WDT1 is enabled, then it gets WDT1's system interrupt (SYSINTR) and returns that to the kernel.

```
DWORD ISRHandler(DWORD InstanceIndex)   //For WDT1 InstanceIndex=1
{
    UCHAR Mask;
    DWORD RetVal;
    volatile UCHAR RdPort = 0;

    //Used in latency timing:
    WRITE_PORT_UCHAR((PUCHAR)0x79,0);    /////////11111 .. GPIO Port 1
    WRITE_PORT_UCHAR((PUCHAR)0x78,0);    /////////00000 .. GPIO Port 0

    Mask = g_Info[InstanceIndex].Mask;
```

Code snippet is from ISR Handler in WDT_ISR.cpp (Project WDT_ISR)

➤ Check if the WDT is enabled and return if not.

This section will discuss the structure and function of this code. The next section will cover using the code.

```
    if (g_Info[InstanceIndex].IIRaddr == 0)
        return SYSINTR_CHAIN;
```

Code snippet is from ISR Handler in WDT_ISR.cpp (Project WDT_ISR)

➤ Check if an interrupt has occurred:

```
//The following will read the contents of port 0x6d for WDT1
RdPort = READ_PORT_UCHAR((PUCHAR)g_Info[InstanceIndex].IIRaddr);

/If bit 5 of the result (0x80) is  then it's an interrupt, so get the SysIntr
RetVal = (RdPort & Mask)? g_Info[InstanceIndex].SysIntr : SYSINTR_CHAIN;

//If not an interrupt then return
If (RetVal== SYSINTR_CHAIN)  return SYSINTR_CHAIN;
```

Code snippet is from ISR Handler in WDT_ISR.cpp (Project WDT_ISR)

➤ Clear the hardware interrupt:

```
WRITE_PORT_UCHAR((PUCHAR)g_Info[InstanceIndex].IIRaddr,0x80);
```

Code snippet is from ISR Handler in WDT_ISR.cpp (Project WDT_ISR)

➤ Return the SYSINTR for WDT1:

```
    return RetVal;
}
```

Code snippet is from ISR Handler in WDT_ISR.cpp (Project WDT_ISR)

WDT_DRV

This handles the configuration of the ISR as well as starting and stopping the IST. A user mode application calls functions in this driver to configure the WDT using IOCTLs. This code is rather complex and long, so examine some of the key functions in WDT_DRV.cpp in this project. Many of the functions write directly to the ports as discussed in the ISR.

➤ IO_Control

    ➤ The application gateway (API) to the driver for these and other functions

➤ Enable/disable WDT1

    ➤ See WDT1Enable()/WDT1Disable()

➤ WDT1 timeout count

    ➤ See WDT1SetEvent()

➤ Start/stop the IST

    ➤ See StartIst() (and below)/StopIst()

➤ Set Mode: Interrupt/Reset/None

    ➤ See WDT1SetEvent()

    ➤ Called when the IST has handled the interrupt

StartIST()

`StartIST()` configures the message queue, loads the ISR into the interrupt chain, starts the event that the IST waits on, starts the IST thread, and so on.

➤ Start the message queue:

```
pOpenContext->hMsgQ = CreateMsgQueue(MSGQ_NAME, lpopt)
```

Code snippet is from StartIST in WDT_DRV.cpp (Project WDT_DRV)

➤ Install the ISR handler (`WDT_ISR`):

```
pOpenContext->hIsr = LoadIntChainHandler(_T("WDT_ISR.dll"),_T("ISRHandler"),
        pOpenContext->Irq);
```

Code snippet is from StartIST in WDT_DRV.cpp (Project WDT_DRV)

➤ Get System logic interrupt:

```
KernelIoControl(
    IOCTL_HAL_REQUEST_SYSINTR,
    &pOpenContext->Irq,sizeof(pOpenContext->Irq),
    &pOpenContext->SysIntr,sizeof(pOpenContext->SysIntr),
    NULL
);
```

Code snippet is from StartIST in WDT_DRV.cpp (Project WDT_DRV)

➤ Pass the ISR details to the kernel (note the IOCTL: `IOCTL_ISR_INFO`):

```
KernelLibIoControl(pOpenContext->hIsr,IOCTL_ISR_INFO,
        &info,sizeof(ISR_INFO),NULL,0,NULL);
```

Code snippet is from StartIST in WDT_DRV.cpp (Project WDT_DRV)

➤ Create the event that the IST blocks on:

```
pOpenContext->hEvent = CreateEvent(NULL,FALSE,FALSE,NULL);
```

Code snippet is from StartIST in WDT_DRV.cpp (Project WDT_DRV)

➤ Initialize the system interrupt, including linking it to the event:

```
InterruptInitialize(pOpenContext->SysIntr,pOpenContext->hEvent,NULL,0)
```

Code snippet is from StartIST in WDT_DRV.cpp (Project WDT_DRV)

➤ Create thread:

```
pOpenContext->hThread = CreateThread( .. )
```

Code snippet is from StartIST in WDT_DRV.cpp (Project WDT_DRV)

➤ Set thread priority; note it is top priority:

```
CeSetThreadPriority(pOpenContext->hThread,0)
```

Code snippet is from StartIST in WDT_DRV.cpp (Project WDT_DRV)

➤ Start the thread:

```
ResumeThread(pOpenContext->hThread);
```

Code snippet is from StartIST in WDT_DRV.cpp (Project WDT_DRV)

IST Thread

The IST thread code is within this driver's code. This is simply a separate thread that is launched when WDT1 is enabled that blocks waiting for the WDT1's system interrupt event to occur, which is fired by the kernel when the ISR sends SYSINTR to the kernel. When it receives the event, it does some processing and then loops back waiting for another interrupt event. The IST is can be configured to generate a Windows event or insert a message into a Windows CE message queue. Windows events are trapped by Windows forms but are not guaranteed to be delivered. If another message arrives before the first is handled, one of the messages will be lost. The message queue is a better option because it is an interprocess FIFO. One process can put messages into the queue; another receives them in that order. Also, for console applications, message queues are simpler to implement. A simplified version of the IST in WDT_DRV.cpp is in the code for this chapter in the folder WatchdogTimer.

```
DWORD WINAPI WdtIst(LPVOID lpv)
{
    PDEVCONTEXT pDevContext = (PDEVCONTEXT)lpv;
    DWORD result = 0;

    //Clear any pending interrupts
    InterruptDone(pDevContext->SysIntr);

    while(!pDevContext->bKillFlag) {

        //Block on the system interrupt
        result = WaitForSingleObject(pDevContext->hEvent,INFINITE);

        //Used in latency timing:
        WRITE_PORT_UCHAR((PUCHAR)0x79,0xff);   ////////11111     GPIO Port 1

        if (result == WAIT_OBJECT_0) {
```

```
            DisableWdt(pDevContext->WdtID);
            if (pDevContext->hMsgQ != (HANDLE)NULL)
            {
                //Write 137 to the message queue
                DWORD buff=137;
                DWORD flags = 0;
                BOOL res = WriteMsgQueue(
                pDevContext->hMsgQ,&buff,sizeof(buff),0,MSGQUEUE_MSGALERT);
            }

            WRITE_PORT_UCHAR((PUCHAR)0x79,0);    /////////11111

            InterruptDone(pDevContext->SysIntr);
            EnableWdt(pDevContext->WdtID);


        }
    }

    CloseMsgQueue(pDevContext->hMsgQ);
    return 0;
}
```

Code snippet is from WdtIst in WDT_DRV.cpp (Project WDT_DRV)

The Test Application

The test application is implemented as two native code platform builder projects. The application itself is a console application that calls a DLL. The DLL project is a wrapper in that it abstracts (or wraps) the WDT_DRV driver functionality into a small number of meaningful functions that the application can use to invoke the watchdog timer.

See "Creating a Console Application with a Dynamic Link Library" later in this chapter to learn how to create a console application subproject as well as a native DLL subproject that the application uses. All code is available.

The Wrapper DLL

This implements four key functions:

➤ ConfigureWDT (parameters)

➤ General purpose function to configure the WDT.

➤ WaitWDT (DWORD timeout);

➤ Wait for a message to be received on the message queue and read it.

➤ OpenWDT ()

➤ Open the message queue and start the IST/ISR.

➤ CloseWDT ()

➤ Shut down the IST/ISR and close the message queue.

```
//Configure the WDT via IOCTLs
WatchDogNativeWrapper_API    void ConfigureWDT(DWORD wdt_no, DWORD action,
        DWORD param, HWND hndl);

//Wait on the driver to send a DWORD via the message queue
WatchDogNativeWrapper_API    DWORD WaitWDT (DWORD timeout);

//Open the message queue
WatchDogNativeWrapper_API    bool OpenWDT();

//Close the message queue
WatchDogNativeWrapper_API    void CloseWDT();
```

Code snippet is from WatchDogNativeWrapper.h (Project WatchDogNativeWrapperDLL)

Both the driver and this wrapper use the same name for the message queue, `"WDTMMessageQ"`. The driver in creating the message queue configures it as a writer, whereas the wrapper creates it as a reader. The wrapper therefore can block waiting for messages to be written to the queue.

The four parameters for `ConfigureWDT()` follow:

➤ WDT Index: 0 or 1.

➤ Action: As in the following table.

  ➤ These map onto the IOCTLs in `WDT_DRV`.

➤ Further parameters, see the following table.

➤ Null.

The Actions and Further parameters are specified in the file `wdt.h`. Table 31-5 lists the Action parameters.

TABLE 31-5: The ConfigureWDT Action Parameter Values

MACRO	VALUE	ACTION
IOCTL_WDT_RESET	0x00	Triggers watchdog timer
IOCTL_WDT_DISABLE	0x01	Disables watchdog timer
IOCTL_WDT_ENABLE	0x02	Enables watchdog timer
IOCTL_SET_IRQ	0x03	Sets watchdog timer to generate IRQ
IOCTL_GET_IRQ	0x04	Sets watchdog timer to generate IRQ
IOCTL_SET_REBOOT	0x05	Sets watchdog timer to reboot system
IOCTL_SET_TIMER_REGISTER	0x06	Sets time of watchdog timer
IOCTL_GET_TIMER_REGISTER	0x07	Gets time of watchdog timer
IOCTL_SET_CALLBACK_MSGQ	0x0A	Starts the IST

Further parameters:

➤ For `IOCTL_SET_IRQ` this specifies the action to take on an interrupt. Zero means reset; 1 to 10 maps on interrupts 3 to 15.

➤ For `IOCTL_SET_TIMER_REGISTER`, this is the timer count in milliseconds (24 bits).

The Console Application

Following is the test application source code, `WatchDogTimerApp.cpp`. The application configures WDT1 for system interrupt 15, with a period of 2 seconds between interrupts. It then starts the watchdog timer. It loops 10 times. In each loop it blocks waiting to receive a message from the queue with a timeout of 3 seconds. It then checks the reception to see if the correct value (137) was received, if there were a timeout, or if an error occurred. During all this many messages display in the Output window, including messages from the IST. Debug Message Zones can be enabled for the driver as well.

```cpp
#include "stdafx.h"
#include "wdt.h"
#include <msgqueue.h>
#include "WatchDogNativeWrapper.h"

DWORD count = 0;  //Counter for interrupts

int WINAPI WinMain(HINSTANCE hInstance,
                   HINSTANCE hPrevInstance,
                   LPTSTR    lpCmdLine,
                   int       nCmdShow)
{

    //Configure the WDT
    ConfigureWDT(1,IOCTL_WDT_DISABLE,0,NULL);             //Disable
    ConfigureWDT(1,IOCTL_SET_IRQ,10,NULL);               //IRQ_15
    ConfigureWDT(1,IOCTL_GET_IRQ,0,NULL);                //Get IRQ
    ConfigureWDT(1,IOCTL_SET_TIMER_REGISTER,2000,NULL);  //Timer period in mS
    ConfigureWDT(1,IOCTL_GET_TIMER_REGISTER,0,NULL);     //Get Timer period

    //Start the IST
    bool res = OpenWDT();
    if (!res) {
        return 0;
    }

    DWORD count =0;

    //Loop 10 times (each loop is either a timeout or interrupt:
    //App and driver will close in max 30 sec.
    while (count++ < 10) {

        //Wait for message from driver, 3 second timeout
        DWORD result = WaitWDT(3000);
        bool OK= true;
```

```
//Check to see what happened
switch (result)
{
    case 137:
        //Success
        RETAILMSG(1,
        (_T("App. Interrupt: 137 correctly received Counter: %d"),count));
        break;
    case 0:
        //Probably a timeout
        RETAILMSG(1,(_T("App. Timeout. Counter: %d"),count));
    case DWORD_MAX:
        //An error so abort
        RETAILMSG(1,(_T("App. Error in message q so quitting")));
        OK = false;
        break;
    default:
        RETAILMSG(1,
        (_T("App. Incorrect value received. Expected 137. Got %d"),result));
        break;
}

//If error then exit loop
if (!OK)
{
    break;
}
}

//Done so stop the IST
CloseWDT();
RETAILMSG(1, (_T("App. Done")));
return 0;
}
```

Code snippet is from WatchDogTimerApp.cpp (Project WatchDogTimerApp)

USING THE WDT TEST APPLICATION

In this section, the supplied projects for the Compact 7 WDT test application and drivers for the eBox 3300-Vortex86DX (and MX) watchdog timer are built and tested. There are four projects in the WatchDogTimer folder in the source code for this chapter.

1. You need the following:

    ➤   eBox 3300

    ➤   Compact 7 eBox 3300 OS project that has been built and run with KITL and Kernel Debug enabled

    ➤   Source code for this chapter

2. Copy the WatchDogTimer folder to the OS project SubProjects folder.

3. Add each of the projects separately, or just select the `dirs` file in the root of the Watchdog folder.

> ➤ This adds all four projects.

4. Set all subprojects to be built in debug mode.

5. Set the driver and ISR to be included in the image, and set the application and wrapper DLL to not be included in the image.

6. Build all subprojects.

7. You won't need to do a complete Sysgen. Do the following:

> ➤ Menu ➪ Build ➪ Copy files to the Release Directory

> ➤ Menu ➪ Build ➪ Make Run-Time Image

8. Download and run the image.

9. When started, run WatchDogTimerApp from Target\Run Programs.

10. Observer the Output window.

11. Change the settings in the application, only rebuild the application, and then rerun it.

> ➤ Change the interrupt and timeout.

> ➤ You don't need to rebuild/download the image again.

13. Try it in reset mode — once!

14. Try enabling the Debug Message Zones for the IST.

The typical output from the application is shown below. The messages from the IST (PID:400002) and those from the application/wrapper (PID:100000a) IOCTL 1 mean the driver is stopping the IRQ/IST:

```
4294955820 PID:400002 TID:4ed0016 IST WaitForSingleObject() OK
4294955820 PID:400002 TID:4ed0016 WDT event caught in IST
4294955820 PID:400002 TID:4ed0016 IST Writing 137 to message queue in IST
4294955820 PID:100000a TID:102000a Upper Event Occurred
4294955820 PID:100000a TID:102000a Driver sent: 137 Bytes Received: 4
4294955820 PID:100000a TID:102000a App. Interrupt: 137 correctly received Counter: 10
4294955820 PID:100000a TID:102000a IOCTL:  1
4294955821 PID:100000a TID:102000a IOCTL TestIOCTLsApp: Stream is open: WDT1:
4294955821 PID:100000a TID:102000a TestIOCTLsApp: IOCTL success IOCTLNo: 1
4294955822 PID:100000a TID:102000a App. Done
```

CREATING A CONSOLE APPLICATION WITH A DYNAMIC LINK LIBRARY

For this activity you need an existing OS image project that has been built and runs with Kernel and KITL debugging enabled.

In Platform Builder, you can add a native code console application by right-clicking the SubProjects icon in the `Solution` folder and selecting Add New SubProject. Then select WCE Console Application, give it a name (e.g., MyApp), and select Next. Typically, you would select the second option ("Simple console application") and finish. This generates a project in a folder below the OS `SubProjects` folder with the name that you gave the subproject. To create a native DLL project, you do the same except you would select WCE Dynamic-Link Library instead of WCE Console Application. (Call it MyDLL.) For this project select a DLL that exports some symbols.

Configure both projects to be excluded from the image and to be built as follows:

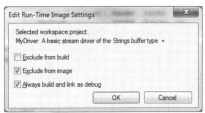

➤ Right-click on the OS project in the Solution Explorer.

➤ Select Properties, then Configuration Properties, then SubProject Image Settings.

➤ Select the project and configure the dialog as in Figure 31-6.

FIGURE 31-6

By doing this you can modify the subprojects and rebuild them while the OS is running without rebuilding the OS.

Following are a couple of hints to avoid some confusion with terminology with respect to native projects:

➤ When a SubProject is created, the sources file (called sources) sets out how the project is to be built and linked. This is a text file.

➤ The sources file is not to be confused with the project source file, which is named with the .cpp extension (e.g., `MyApp.cpp`). This implements the module's functionality.

The DLL Project

Open the header file for the project (not `stdafx.h`). Remove the class declaration and the line starting with an extern declaration. It's simpler to access everything only via a function for an embedded application. Similarly, in the source file (.cpp) remove the class implementation at the implementation of the exported variable. See that the function returns 42.

Build the DLL project.

The Console Application

The project needs to reference the DLL project for compilation and for linkage.

➤ At the top of the console application's source (.cpp) file, put a reference to the DLL such as the following:

```
#include   "MyDLL.h"
```

Code snippet is from the Application DLL Reference. Code is from MyApp\MyApp.cpp. (Also in Chapter31AppDLLSnippets.txt.)

➤   Open the sources file for this project. (Double-click the subproject in the Solution Explorer.) Insert the following code at the bottom (or edit if it already exists) where MyDLL is your DLL project name:

Available for
download on
Wrox.com

```
INCLUDES= \
$(_PUBLICROOT)\COMMON\SDK\INC;$(_PUBLICROOT)\COMMON\DDK\INC; \
    $(SG_OUTPUT_ROOT)\oak\inc;..\MyDLL;
```

Code snippet is from the Application Header Folder References. Code is from MyApp\sources. (Also in Chapter31AppDLLSnippets.txt.)

➤   Make sure each of the first two lines of that code end with \.

➤   This is the line continuation character in the sources file.

➤   Also make sure that there is a blank line above the inserted code.

➤   Check that the header reference is correct by right-clicking the application source file, and choose to open the header file (first option).

➤   Add some code to use the DLL function in the application main function before its return statement as follows:

Available for
download on
Wrox.com

```
int num = fnMyDLL();
```

Code snippet is from the Application Calling DLL. Code is from MyApp\MyApp.cpp. (Also in Chapter31AppDLLSnippets.txt.)

➤   Try building the application. If all is well it should fail only at the linkage stage.

➤   Find the following code in the sources file:

```
TARGETLIBS= \
    $(SG_OUTPUT_ROOT)\sdk\lib\$(_CPUINDPATH)\coredll.lib  \
```

➤   Add a `MyDLL.lib` reference immediately after the second line so that sources code sequence is:

Available for
download on
Wrox.com

```
TARGETLIBS= \
    $(SG_OUTPUT_ROOT)\sdk\lib\$(_CPUINDPATH)\coredll.lib  \
    ..\MyDLL\obj\$(_TGTCPU)\$(WINCEDEBUG)\MyDLL.lib
```

Code snippet is from the Application DLL Linkage. Code is from MyApp\sources. (Also in Chapter31AppDLLSnippets.txt.)

This last action links the lib file for the DLL into the application, so the application build can complete. When the application runs it expects to load `MyDLL.dll` and the interface to it for the function.

Testing the Projects

The application should now be able to run in your Compact 7 system.

➤ Build the application.

➤ Run the application in your OS via the Target Control menu or the Run Programs dialog.

➤ Put a breakpoint at the function call to the DLL in the application, run the application again, and step into the DLL (F11) to see that it is all works correctly.

SUMMARY

This chapter starts by explaining the differences between polling and interrupts for scheduling responses to hardware events. It examines the Windows Embedded Compact 7 Interrupt architecture and its uses in device drivers. Watchdog timers as a source of interrupts were considered along with a sample driver and application that implements a watchdog timer for the eBox hardware. Finally, how to create a native Platform Builder DLL project and an application project that uses it were explained.

32

Stream Interface Drivers

Stream interface drivers are the most common type of drivers implemented in Windows Embedded Compact 7. This chapter is a deep dive into the detail that you may need for implementing fully functional Stream Drivers. At the end is simple console application that tests for the presence of a Stream Driver.

LOADING A DRIVER

How and when a Stream Interface Driver (Stream Driver) loads depends much on the purpose of the driver and its registry settings. As a lead into Stream Drivers, this section examines what happens when you load any driver.

When Is a Driver Loaded?

A Windows Embedded Compact 7 device driver is either loaded at startup, when the device is physically connected to the system if it is "plug and play" or when an application initiates the loading. Some devices automatically load at startup because the system requires them for a dedicated function such as a display. Some devices load at startup because the system is configured to attempt to load them at startup if physically present in the system. Other devices load at startup because a bus driver finds them. Devices can also be loaded by a bus driver at later stage when they are inserted into the device. Alternatively, applications may initiate their loading.

Registry

As previously discussed, each driver is loaded by one of the managers GWES, FileSys, or Device Manager. These make use of the system registry to identify the device, its DLL, and its required parameters. If the device isn't listed in the registry, it can't be loaded, although drivers loaded programmatically can use registry settings written in advance by the application. The registry is a special storage location on a Windows device that acts as a database of the hardware, software, and users of the device. Device driver registry details are stored under HKLM\Drivers. (HKLM means Home Key Local Machine.) Drivers automatically loaded need to be in specific registry locations, whereas other drivers can be anywhere because the calling code can specify the registry location. The drivers that have been loaded are listed under the HKLM\Drivers\Active key.

GWES driver registry keys are located in different locations. The display driver information as used by GWES is possibly in a key under HKLM\System\GDI but defaults to ddi.dll if not found there. The keyboard and touch drivers are separate keys under HKLM\Hardware\DeviceMap, and the mouse is handled by the keyboard entry.

Stream Drivers loaded at startup are found by the bus enumerator. The HKLM\Drivers\BuiltIn key specifies the bus enumeration DLL and typically the location to start the enumeration from (which is typically the same location [Root]). At startup the bus enumerator searches for registry entries from there for buses and built-in devices and attempts to load them with the registry information found. Built-in devices typically connect directly to the CPU and not on a bus; although built-in registry entries can specify other more loosely coupled devices to be loaded at startup.

Table 32-1 summarizes the locations of driver registry keys.

TABLE 32-1: Some Compact 7 Driver Registry Keys

DRIVER	UNDER KEY
Root	HKLM\Drivers
Active	HKLM\Drivers\Active
Stream: Load at start up	HKLM\Drivers\BuiltIn
Bus (not drivers for devices on a bus)	HKLM\Drivers
Keyboard (and mouse) and touch	HKLM\Hardware\DeviceMap
Display	HKLM\System\GDI
File system and storage devices	HKLM\System\StorageManager

The system registry contains information about the driver and covers such details as the following:

- Driver name
- Driver DLL name
- Vendor ID/Device ID or PID
- Driver class GUID (Globally Unique Identifier)
- Mode to load in (kernel/user)
- Memory location
- Interrupt
- Boot order
- Initialization data

When the driver loads, the system loads the named DLL from \Windows in the kernel or user mode (default is kernel) using the specified resources and initialization. If the driver resources are available (for example, the target hardware) then the driver loads. Other drivers are identified at boot through bus interrogation.

Built-In Drivers

GWES drivers load at startup in kernel mode using driver-specific registry keys. Stream Drivers load at startup in kernel mode or user mode depending upon the registry setting. The buses load at startup in kernel mode. The order in which Stream Drivers load is determined by their order of registry setting. Devices of a lower order value load before others of a higher value. Devices of the same order value load at about the same stage of the OS startup.

Installable Drivers

An installable driver is one that loads after the operating system starts. These are installed when a device requiring the driver is inserted into a bus on the device or when an application calls for the driver to load. Installable drivers are generally uninstallable. All installable drivers will be Stream Drivers.

Bus Drivers

Examples of buses are PCI, USB, and PC104 (ISA). A bus driver queries buses under its control for devices present there. This is called bus enumeration. Devices on a bus respond with information that can identify them via the registry. If the device is found, it loads. An installable driver is searched for using its Vendor ID/Device ID on a PCI bus (or Vendor ID/Product ID on a USB bus) and if this is not found, the driver class GUID is searched for. In this manner, an OEM's driver is used in preference to the generic class driver. On the other hand, an OEM doesn't need to supply a driver if the device conforms in structure and function to a specific class driver. That is why USB memory sticks normally do not need a driver when inserted into a system. The USB storage class driver is used. There is also a third identifier that can be used, the device serial number. When an installable device's driver is installed, if the device has an ID, information is stored in the registry for the specific device about the driver and installation against the port used. When the device is reinserted, this is used in preference to reinstallation to implement a fast setup of the device. USB devices that have to be reinstalled every time they are inserted are not making an ID available.

FileSys

FileSys loads the file system drivers such FATFS, UFDS, and so on. They can load automatically at startup or when media is mounted via a block driver. In the first case the registry entries are located in `HKLM\Systems\StorageManager\Autoload`. When a block driver loads, it sends a request to mount a media device to the Storage Manager, which then requests information about the device profile. The driver for the partition loads and then file system drivers load as per the partition type. Profile information is in `HKLM\System\StorageManager\Profiles`.

STREAM DRIVERS

A majority of Windows Embedded Compact 7 drivers are implemented as Stream Drivers. Any device that can be modeled as producing and consuming data in a stream can have a device driver implemented as a Stream Driver. Drivers as diverse as serial, battery, backlight, NLED, accelerometer, and I2C are all implemented as Stream Drivers. For layered Stream Drivers, the MDD, the part that interfaces to the OS, implements the stream interface. Even the RELFSD driver, which enables the mounting of the Release Directory File System on a development system, has a pseudo Stream Driver interface so that Device Manager can load it.

Why Stream Drivers?

Stream Drivers, unlike native drivers, all interlock with the operating system in a standard manner but have the flexibility via IOCTLs to implement specific functionality. This standardization results in a generic functional interface between the drivers and their operating system manager, Device Manager. Driver source code consists of a set of functions that all Stream Drivers implement in part or in full. The same API is used to load, unload, and perform data streaming with the driver. Yet IOCLs provide a "backdoor" interface for implementing driver-specific functionality and for low-level operating system functions such as power management.

Stream Driver Architecture

Figure 32-1 shows the Stream Driver architecture. An application makes calls to the Device Manager to load a Stream Driver. The system or an application can similarly initiate the loading of a driver.

An application can make calls through the FileSystem to the Device Manager to open a stream to a device driver that has been loaded, whether loaded by the system or by an application. The Device Manager passes the open call through to the Stream Driver, which returns a file handle. This handle can then be passed back to the application that can use it to make calls back down to the driver to stream data to and from the driver. Typically, references to buffers pass between the application and the driver, which pass data between the two. The Stream Driver accesses the hardware to get data directly, or it is passed to it via the ISR/IST interrupt mechanism. A Stream Driver can implement power management for its device through the two power interface functions or through the IOCTL interface.

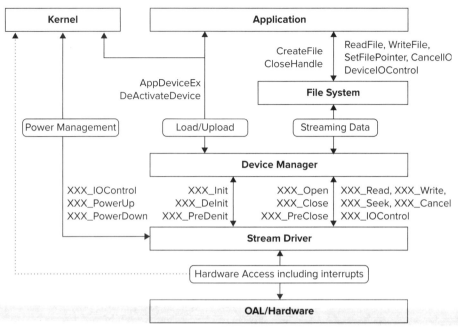

FIGURE 32-1

When the application has no further use for the stream, it closes the stream. This causes the Device Manager to call on the driver to wake up the driver stream context threads if needed and calls on the driver to remove the resources assigned to its open context when it opened. Similarly, if the driver is installable, the application can request that it be unloaded. (It needs to have a handle to the stream though to make this call). The Device Manager wakes up the driver if necessary and calls on the driver to invalidate any handles to it and then unloads the driver by removing any device context resources allocated to the device driver when the driver loaded.

The operating system uses the same API (`AppDeviceEx`) for loading drivers built-in or bus drivers. A bus driver also uses the same API for loading and unloading drivers for devices on its bus.

As discussed in Chapter 30, "Device Driver Architectures," a Stream Driver loaded in kernel mode is loaded by `device.exe`, whereas one loaded in user mode is loaded with `udevice.exe`. An application assesses whether a driver is in kernel mode or user mode via a reflector. This protects the OS while allowing some kernel access to the application (which runs in user mode) and to user mode drivers it may call.

STREAM DRIVER FUNCTIONS

When the Device Manager loads a Stream Driver, it requires that the driver DLL implement all or part of its Device Driver Interface (DDI). This is implemented in the driver's source file as up to 13 entry points (functions) with the `XXX_` prefix in their names where `XXX` is the prefix for the driver as specified in its registry entries. For example a serial port can use the prefix `COM`, so `COM_Open` will be the interface function called when an application opens that serial stream. You can also implement the driver without using a prefix by specifying DEVFLAGS_NAKEDENTRIES in the driver's flags in its registry entries. A serial driver with that flag would then implement Open instead of COM_Open.

Table 32-2 lists the complete set of Stream Driver interface functions, the corresponding API call, what calls them, whether you have to implement them in a Stream Driver, and the value to return from the stream interface function to indicate to the caller that the function call was successful. Functions indicated as being actioned by a user application can also be called by another driver that is a "wrapper" around the driver.

TABLE 32-2: The Stream Driver Function and API Calls to Action

FUNCTION	CALLING FUNCTION	ACTIONED BY	REQUIREMENT	RETURN VALUE
Loading/Unloading				
DllEntryPoint	ActivateDeviceEx or ActivateDevice	OS or user application	Mandatory	TRUE
XXX_Init			Mandatory	Nonzero
XXX_PreDeinit	DeactivateDevice	User application	Optional	TRUE
XXX_Deinit			Mandatory	TRUE
Application				
XXX_Open	CreateFile	User application	Required	Nonzero
XXX_Read	ReadFile	User application	Required	Nonzero
XXX_Write	WriteFile	User application	Required	Nonzero
XXX_Seek	SetFilePointer	User application	Optional	Nonzero
XXX_IOControl	DeviceIOControl	User application	Required	TRUE
XXX_PreClose	CloseHandle	User application	Optional	TRUE
XXX_Close			Required	TRUE
XXX_Cancel	CancelIO	User Application	Optional	TRUE
Power Management				
XXX_PowerDown	NA	OS	Optional	void
XXX_PowerUp	NA	OS	Optional	void

Not all functions are required to load a driver. A minimal set is XXX_Init and XXX_Deinit. Functions tagged as mandatory are required for the driver to load and unload by the Device Manager. You can leave out the optional functions if their specific functionality is not required. The other functions to do with data I/O tend to be collectively required if any IO is to be implemented with the driver, which is what you would normally do with most drivers. There are various combinations of functions so that if one is present, the other must be there or else the driver won't load. You can experiment with combinations of functions added or removed from the driver's interface. For example, if XXX_Open is implemented, then XXX_Close must also be. The simplest way to resolve this is to implement all the nonoptional functions initially as dummy functions so that they return the true or 1 value so that the Device Manager reports that the call was successful. An alternative option for dummy functions might be to return false or 0 after setting a custom error, which in the system would mean not implemented.

For XXX_Read and XXX_Write, the number of bytes read or written as the nonzero value can be returned; although, this is not mandatory because this value is a returned parameter and the calling code needs to only check for a nonzero returned value. For XXX_Seek, the file pointer may be returned. For some of the other functions where a pointer to a structure is generated, the pointer can be cast into the return variable because a null pointer will cast to zero.

Stream Driver Function Details

The Stream Driver interface functions are typically implemented in the one source file along with any ancillary functions required by them that are tightly coupled to these functions. XXX_Init and XXX_Deinit are the only ones that must be implemented for a Stream Driver, but typically all except the power functions would be implemented, even if some are just dummy functions. The hAsyncRef parameter for stream I/O functions is for asynchronous I/O and is passed as NULL for synchronous I/O.

XXX_Init

```
DWORD XXX_Init(LPCTSTR pContext, LPCVOID lpvBusContext)
```

This is the function that the operating systems calls when loading the device driver, after loading the DLL (through dllMain). Its main task is to set up the driver context and read in the registry values and configure a device context structure. It may also limit the number of instances of a driver. It is called once for every instance of the driver.

XXX_Init also sets up any data buffers required by the driver and links them into the device context.

It can return a pointer to a device context structure cast as a DWORD, which then inputs to Open, DeInit, PreDeinit as hDeviceContext.

XXX_PreDeinit

```
BOOL XXX_PreDeinit(DWORD hDeviceContext)
```

This invalidates the driver and wakes any sleeping threads and wakes it from a lower power mode. This occurs before XXX_Deinit so that it can properly perform the shutdown of the driver.

XXX_Deinit

```
BOOL XXX_Deinit(DWORD hDeviceContext)
```

This is called when the driver is unloaded. It releases any resources assigned to the driver during XXX_Init.

XXX_Open

```
DWORD XXX_Open(DWORD hDeviceContext, DWORD AccessCode, DWORD ShareMode)
```

This is called when an application opens the stream for data I/O. Its primary task is to generate an open context for the driver to use in its read, write, seek, and IOCTL functions. This open context is different from the device context in that there is only one device context for each driver instance, whereas there is one open context generated for each XXX_Open call to the driver instance. There can be more than one opened handle to a driver instance at a time, so these multiplied opened contexts must resolve this multiple simultaneous use. One way to do this is to limit the number of open contexts to 1. Another method used is to have an array of contexts limiting the number of contexts to the size of the array. A third method uses a linked list of contexts created on the heap as required.

It can return a pointer to a open context structure cast as a DWORD, which then inputs to Read, Write, IOControl, etc. as hOpenContext.

XXX_Read

```
DWORD XXX_Read(DWORD hOpenContext, LPVOID pBuffer, DWORD Count ,HANDLE hAsyncRef)
```

This reads data from the device's data buffer or hardware into a buffer supplied by the calling application.

XXX_Write

```
DWORD XXX_Write(DWORD hOpenContext, LPCVOID pBuffer, DWORD Count, HANDLE hAsyncRef)
```

This copies data from the supplied buffer into the driver's data buffer or hardware.

XXX_Seek

```
DWORD XXX_Seek(DWORD hOpenContext, long Amount, DWORD Type)
```

This function moves the driver's data pointer. This function would not normally be used because it is a legacy function from tape drive mechanisms. It could be implemented within the driver to implement a custom function.

XXX_IOControl

```
BOOL XXXIOControl(DWORD hOpenContext,
                  DWORD dwCode,
                  PBYTE pBufIn,
                  DWORD dwLenIn,
                  PBYTE pBufOut,
                  DWORD dwLenOut,
                  PDWORD pdwActualOut,
                  HANDLE hAsyncRef)
```

This implements a range of driver-specific functions. The calling application provides an IOCTL number that the Device Manager supplies to this function. It then typically uses a switch statement to determine what driver-specific function to action. Subclasses of Stream Drivers implement the same set of IOCTLs so that they can provide the same set of functionality. There are also system-specific IOCTLs such as for power management that drivers can register to receive notifications for.

Although this function is not mandatory, it is safest to implement at least a dummy function. Some of the kernel functions may make a call to this to determine if it supports certain functionality.

XXX_PreClose

```
BOOL XXXPreClose(DWORD hOpenContext)
```

This is called prior to XXX_Close when the stream is closed by an application. It wakes any sleeping threads relevant to the open context and marks the open handle as invalid.

XXX_Close

```
BOOL XXXClose(DWORD hOpenContext)
```

This releases the resources assigned to the open context by XXX_Open and releases the context.

XXX_Cancel

```
BOOL XXX_Cancel(DWORD hOpenContext, HANDLE hAsyncHandle)
```

This cancels any pending asynchronous I/O initiated by the open context.

XXX_PowerDown

```
void XXXPowerDown(DWORD hDeviceContext)
```

This is called when the system or an application calls for the device to power down.

XXX_PowerUp

```
void XXXPowerUp(DWORD hDeviceContext)
```

This is called when the system or an application powers up the device.

STREAM DRIVER CONFIGURATION

A Stream Driver is configured in terms of its registry entries and BIB file entry. The registry entry can include, amongst other things, a specification of the name to use for the driver in terms of its prefix.

Driver Naming Conventions

Stream Drivers are typically named by their *legacy name*, which is the prefix with the instance name post-pended:

XXXN: where XXX is the driver prefix as in its registry key and N is the device instance index. Note the colon on the end.

For example, serial ports would be named COM1:, COM2: and so on. The instance index can range from 0 to 9 with Compact 7, which limits the number of instances of a driver to 10. When a driver is opened by an application it calls CreateFile with this name as a parameter. For example CreateFile(_T("COM1:", ...).

Alternatively, because Stream Drivers are loaded by the Device Manager, they can be referenced with respect to \$device. The format follows:

\$device\XXXN where XXX is the prefix and N is the index.

N can be greater than 9. For example CreateFile(_T("\$device\COM11...) would open COM11. There is no colon in this syntax.

Remember that in C/C++ code, which is what is used for device driver code, the backslashes are implemented as the escape sequence \\.

Stream Drivers loaded on a bus have the following format for their names on the system:

\$bus\BUSNAME_BN_DN_FN where:

➤   BUSNAME is the name of the bus, e.g., PCI.

➤   BN is the bus number in the bus channel, typically 0 or 1.

➤   DN is the device number, which is an index based upon the order in which the device was loaded on the bus, e.g., 0,1,2,3,4, and so on.

➤   FN is the function number.

For example, \$bus\PCI_1_2_0 would be the third device (indexed from 0) on the second PCI bus with function 0. This may be a serial port but would not be used as an application to open a stream with it. The bus naming would be used for unloading, reloading, and power management of such drivers. The legacy or $device format name would be used for data access to such a device by an application.

Registry Entries

When a Stream Driver is loaded, whether automatically as a built-in driver or on a bus, or manually by an application, the driver cannot be loaded if it is not in the registry. An application may resolve this by first loading the required entries into the registry before actioning the loading. The registry entries for a Stream Driver that the device manager uses are a subset of the following:

➤   Prefix

  ➤   Which is whatever XXX is for the driver, e.g., COM.

➤   DLL

  ➤   The driver DLL name, e.g., serial16550.dll.

➤   Index

  ➤   The driver instance number.

➤ Order

    ➤ The relative order that the driver is loaded if `BuiltIn`.

➤ IClass

    ➤ A device interface GUID for an interface it implements.

➤ Flags

    ➤ An OR listing of applicable flags for the driver.

➤ UserProcGroup

    ➤ User mode drivers can be loaded in the same host process.

➤ Driver parameters

    ➤ Data used by the driver.

The DLL entry is the only one that is mandatory, while typical streams also have a prefix and a flag to indicate the mode to load the driver in. The DLL entry is only the filename and doesn't include the path because all drivers are located in `\Windows`, and the Device Manager expects to find them there. If no indexes are specified in the registry entry for the driver, they are automatically generated as loaded incrementing from 1, using the same registry entries. If a specific index is used, there needs to be a separate registry entry for each instance. The order is relative in that drivers of the same order load at about the same time in the boot process. All drivers that don't have an order load last. Order should be used to enforce dependency requirements. For example a device driver that uses a serial port for its interaction with the system should have a higher order (later) than the serial upon which it depends.

The Flags entry can be a logical or combination of the flags as in Table 32-3.

TABLE 32-3: Stream Driver Flags

FLAG	VALUE	PURPOSE
DEVFLAGS_NONE	0x00000000	No flags set.
DEVFLAGS_UNLOAD	0x00000001	Loads driver and unloads after calling XXX_Init.
DEVFLAGS_LOADLIBRARY	0x00000002	Loads via LoadLibrary rather than LoadDriver.
DEVFLAGS_NOLOAD	0x00000004	Stops it being loaded although may be in BuiltIn. Need to clear this for subsequent loading.
DEVFLAGS_NAKEDENTRIES	0x00000008	No prefix used in driver name.
DEVFLAGS_USERMODE	0x00000010	Load in user mode. If not set then load in kernel mode.
DEVFLAGS_IRQ_EXCLUSIVE	0x00000100	Bus loads this driver only if it has exclusive use of its IRQ.
DEVFLAGS_BOOTPHASE_1	0x00001000	Required for loading hive registry.

There can also be other registry entries under the driver's key that the driver decodes and uses.

The registry for a simple Stream Driver `MyDriver` is shown next. This loads at startup using the named `MyDriver.dll`, in relative order 4 (not 4th), using the prefix `MYD` and is named `MYD1`: It loads in user mode. If the Flag entry were removed or made 0, then the driver can load in kernel mode subject to its BIB entry.

Available for
download on
Wrox.com

```
[HKEY_LOCAL_MACHINE\Drivers\BuiltIn\MyDriver]
       "Dll"="MyDriver.dll"
       "Order"=dword:4
       "Prefix"="MYD"
       "Flags"=dword:10
```

Code snippet is from a simple Stream Driver registry entry

BIB Entries

As covered previously, the BIB file specifies which files are included in the image and what type of file it is. Drivers need to be in the Modules section of the BIB file, not the Files section. The BIB entries' flags can also indicate whether it is to be available in kernel space or user space. A kernel driver typically has the flags SHK, which means system, hidden, and kernel. Instead of K, Q can be used, which means that the driver can load in kernel mode and user mode. In that case two versions of the driver DLL load with the kernel mode version named with k. prepended. For example `MyDll.dll` would be located in user space as `MyDll.dll` and in kernel space as `k.MyDll.dll` if its Q flag is set. In the following examples, `MyDriver` can be loaded only in user mode and `MyKDriver` can be loaded only in kernel mode, whereas `MyQDriver` can be loaded in either mode.

Available for
download on
Wrox.com

```
MODULES
MyDriver.dll    $(_FLATRELEASEDIR)\MyDriver.dll    NK
MyKDriver.dll   $(_FLATRELEASEDIR)\MyKDriver.dll   NK    SHK
MyQDriver.dll   $(_FLATRELEASEDIR)\MyQDriver.dll   NK    SHQ
```

Code snippet is from some BIB file entries for Stream Drivers

Kernel Mode Load

To load a driver in kernel mode, there are three requirements:

➤ Registry flag bit 4 must be clear, that is, no `DEVFLAGS_USERMODE` flag.

➤ K flag must be set in the BIB file (or Q).

➤ It is `BuiltIn` (loaded as startup) or loaded by a bus.

That is, a user application can load drivers only in user mode.

User Mode Load

The following are the requirements to load a driver in user mode:

➤ Registry flag bit 4 must be set, that is, DEVFLAGS_USERMODE flag must be included.

➤ K flag must not be set in the BIB file.

   ➤ Q flag can be set.

➤ The driver registry settings can be in BuiltIn or placed elsewhere, typically under HKLM\Drivers.

➤ If placed elsewhere, then a user application can action its loading with a call to ActivateDeviceEx passing the driver key name and location in the registry as a string.

The following code loads a driver whose registry information is in HKLM\Drivers\MyDriver.

```
TCHAR szDevKey[]   = _T("Drivers\\MyDriver");
TCHAR szDefaultString[] = _T("RegIninData: Placed in the driver's Active reg. entry.");
REGINI RegIniData[] = { _T("DefaultString"),
       (LPBYTE)szDefaultString,
       sizeof(szDefaultString),REG_SZ };
HANDLE hStr = ActivateDeviceEx( szDevKey, RegIniData, 1, NULL );
```

Code snippet is from typical code to load a Stream Driver

Imaging a Developmental Driver

In development mode with Compact 7, with the driver as a subproject, for the driver to be included in the image along with its BIB, DB, DAT, and registry entries with the OS built, you just need to configure it in the Solution Explorer/Project Properties/SubProjects with Include in the Image checked for the driver subproject. When the build runs, it merges the parameter files into the system files.

DRIVER CONTEXT

A Stream Driver has two types of contexts. One is for the driver, and the other is for any streams opened with It.

Device Context

As mentioned previously, the driver context is established in XXX_Init, and there is only one driver context for each loaded driver. This context is represented by a structure that stores information about the driver that it gets from its registry entries. The structure is specific to the driver. The number of instances of the driver are stored in the device context, so XXX_Init can limit the number of such instances. The number of opened streams to the driver can also be a device context and can be used to limit the number of such streams that are open. If multiple streams are permitted, the device driver needs to employ multitasking mechanisms to function currently. A typical code for XXX_Init is shown here.

```
PDEVCONTEXT pDevContext;
HKEY hKey;

//Get registry information
hKey = RegDeviceOpen((LPCWSTR)pContext);
. . . .
. . . .
RegCloseKey(hKey);


//Check whether driver has been loaded, and check its index
. . . .
. . . .

//Create an instance of the device context on the heap
pDevContext = (PDEVCONTEXT)LocalAlloc(LPTR,sizeof(DEVCONTEXT));
if (pDevContext == NULL){
    return NULL;
}

// Initialize the device context
pDevContext->hMsgQ=NULL;
pDevContext->dwSize = sizeof(DEVCONTEXT);
. . . .
. . . .
pDevContext->OpenCount = 0;

InitializeCriticalSection(&pDevContext->CS);

return (DWORD)pDevContext;
```

Code snippet is from the outline of a typical XXX_Init stream function (From the WDT_DRV project in Chapter 31)

The device context structure is pointed to by pDevContext where PDEVCONTEXT is a structure specific to the driver and contains all the driver details that it needs in its stream functions. The structure for this driver is shown in the following code.

```
typedef struct tagDEVCONTEXT {
    CRITICAL_SECTION CS;      // Sync Object
    DWORD dwSize;             // size of struct
    int   OpenCount;          // Opened count
    int   WdtID;              // WDT ID
    int   Irq;                // IRQ
    DWORD SysIntr;            // System logic interrupt
    HANDLE hThread;           // Thread's handle
    HANDLE hEvent;            // Event's handle btw IST and IRQ
    HANDLE hMsgQ;             // Message Q handle
    LPWSTR lpszName;          // Message Q name
    DWORD  interruptCounter;  // Counts the number of interrupts
    HANDLE hIsr;              // Isr's handle
    volatile BOOL bKillFlag;  // Ist quit flag
    HWND   hWnd;              // Window handle
    }DEVCONTEXT,*PDEVCONTEXT;
```

Code snippet is from a device context structure (From the WDT_DRV project in Chapter 31)

Stream Context

A stream open context may be created when a stream to the driver is opened and is disposed of when the stream is closed. That is, if more than one open stream to a driver is permitted, for every opened handle to the stream, there is a separate open context. This is also a structure specific to the driver and is created and initialized in XXX_Open. A pointer to the driver device context is passed to this function, so it can determine if this additional context is supported by the driver and hardware among other things. Some of the code for COM_Init for the 16550 serial driver is shown next. In this, the open context structure is created and partially initialized.

```
// Allocate an Open Context structure
pOpenHead    = (PHW_OPEN_INFO)LocalAlloc(LPTR, sizeof(HW_OPEN_INFO));
if ( !pOpenHead ) {
    DEBUGMSG(ZONE_INIT | ZONE_ERROR,
                (TEXT("Error allocating memory for pOpenHead, COM_Open failed\n\r")));
    return(NULL);
}

// Init the structure
pOpenHead->pSerialHead = pSerialHead;  // pointer back to our parent
pOpenHead->StructUsers = 0;
pOpenHead->AccessCode = AccessCode;
pOpenHead->ShareMode = ShareMode;
pOpenHead->CommEvents.hCommEvent = CreateEvent(NULL, FALSE, FALSE, NULL);
pOpenHead->CommEvents.fEventMask = 0;
```

Code snippet is from partial code for initializing the open context of a Stream Driver (From the Compact 7 Catalog Com16550 driver)

DRIVER CLASSES

Besides implementing the stream interface, a driver may implement a specific set of IOCTLs. In reality, most functionality is implemented by this "backdoor" because it enables far greater flexibility than the read-and-write driver functions. For example, drivers that implement power management implement a standard set of IOCTLs. Drivers that implement serial devices also implement a standard set of IOCTLs.

Many drivers implement an alternative interface by implementing a specific set of IOCTLs. Compact 7 formalizes this by specifying a number of predefined interfaces, as shown in Table 32-4. Devices that implement the IOCTLs for an interface belong to the associated class. This can be indicated by adding a class GUID entry into a driver's registry settings as a subkey IClass, or the Device Manager function AdvertiseInterface can be used. Custom interfaces classes can also be defined. If a driver implements the interface for a driver class though, then it must fully implement the functionality because system components that use it assume that the functions are fully executed.

TABLE 32-4: Compact 7 Interface Classes

INTERFACE
BATTERY_DRIVER_CLASS
BLOCK_DRIVER_GUID
CDDA_MOUNT_GUID
CDFS_MOUNT_GUID
DEVCLASS_CARDSERV_GUID
DEVCLASS_DISPLAY_GUID
DEVCLASS_KEYBOARD_GUID
DEVCLASS_STREAM_GUID
FATFS_MOUNT_GUID
FSD_MOUNT_GUID
NLED_DRIVER_CLASS
PMCLASS_BLOCK_DEVICE
PMCLASS_DISPLAY
PMCLASS_GENERIC_DEVICE
PMCLASS_NDIS_MINIPORT
STORE_MOUNT_GUID
STOREMGR_DRIVER_GUID
UDFS_MOUNT

For example, the registry entry for the Catalog NLED driver is shown below including its IClass definition. The IClass GUID is the same value as NLED_DRIVER_CLASS as defined in $(_PUBLICROOT)\ COMMON\sdk\inc\nled.h. This means that it can implement the NLED interface IOCTLS, IOCTL_NLED_ GETDEVICEINFO, IOCTL_NLED_SETDEVICE, IOCTL_NLED_POSTINIT as specified in nled.h.

```
[HKEY_LOCAL_MACHINE\Drivers\BuiltIn\NLed]
  "Prefix"="NLD"
  "Dll"="nleddrvr.dll"
  "Flags"=dword:8                        ; DEVFLAGS_NAKEDENTRIES
  "Order"=dword:0
  "Ioctl"=dword:1050408                  ; IOCTL to use for PostInit callback
  ; nled.h: CTL_CODE(FILE_DEVICE_NLED, 0x102, METHOD_BUFFERED, FILE_ANY_ACCESS)
  "IClass"="{CBB4F234-F35F-485b-A490-ADC7804A4EF3}"
```

APPLICATION STREAMING APIS

A stream's IO is performed by a combination of functions, as shown in Table 32-5. You can use the API functions in an application performing IO on the stream. The calls require the stream's handle, as returned from `CreateFile`, a data buffer pointer, and some indication of how much data is moved. The device manager takes those parameters and passes them to the corresponding driver function along with the open context for the stream pointed to by the handle. The driver functions are not what are called by the user application. The driver functions are an interface to the Driver Manager, not an application.

TABLE 32-5: Stream IO API

API	Driver	Example API call
CreateFile	XXX_Open	HANDLE **hStr** = CreateFile(_T("MDY1:"), GENERIC_READ | GENERIC_WRITE,0, NULL,OPEN_EXISTING, NULL,0);
ReadFile	XXX_Read	BOOL rs = ReadFile(**hStr**,bufferIn , 12, &dw, NULL);
WriteFile	XXX_Write	BOOL rs = WriteFile(**hStr**, bufferOut , 12 &dw,NULL);
DeviceIOControl	XXX_IOControl	BOOL rs = DeviceIoControl(**hStr**,IOCTL_NO,NULL,0, NULL, 0,&dw,NULL);
CloseHandle	XXX_Close	BOOL res = CloseHandle(**hStr**);

In the preceding examples the buffers are pointers to storage in the application. The `12` parameter is the number of bytes to pass from or to the buffer. The actual number of bytes, especially for the read, may be different as indicated by the returned value of `dw`. With the `DeviceIOControl` call, `IOCTL_NO` is the number of the `IOCTL` to be actioned by the driver. All API functions return a `true` or `false` to indicate success or otherwise, except for `CreateFile`, which returns a `NULL` or `INVALID_HANDLE_VALUE` (which equates to the casting of –1 to a file handle) if there was an error. If the call fails, `GetLastError` can be used to determine the reason for the failure.

Asynchronous I/O

Data can be passed between an application and a driver directly, where the driver uses the buffer pointer to immediately access the user space, or by the driver making a copy of the input user buffer and then continuing to process the I/O while the application returns to its processing. Or the driver can create an alternative reference to the buffer within its own context that refers to the same physical location.

The I/O covered thus far is assumed to be synchronous, which uses the user buffer directly. When an application makes a call to write data to the stream, the call doesn't return until the data has been copied from its buffer by the driver. A synchronous read means that the application's call doesn't return until the required data has been copied to the application's buffer by the driver. With asynchronous IO, these calls return allowing the application to continue doing other things while the driver completes the data transfer.

Asynchronous I/O can be of use where the data stream, at the hardware or external level, is slow. This might occur, for example, where data is transferred over a slow wireless network connection. Another use for asynchronous I/O is where the data to be moved is large, such as with a system backup or for the transfer of a video file.

Compact 7 adds some asynchronous I/O functionality to the Stream Driver interface. There is a 13th interface function XXX_Cancel. Also, the handle parameter hAsyncRef, which is passed to the driver functions as NULL for synchronous I/O, is used for asynchronous I/O. XXX_Cancel is called when the application calls CancelIo on the stream (using its open handle) to cancel any asynchronous I/O in progress. This should terminate any threads transacting the transfer, release any memory structures created by the driver for the transfer, and void any associated handles (apart from the open handle). For drivers that don't use asynchronous IO, the hAsynchRef parameter can be left out of all interface function parameters, as well as the XXX_Cancel function.

Asynchronous buffers need to be used for asynchronous I/O because the application's buffer will be out of context after the read or write returns to the application. The driver can't access the buffer pointed to by the application at this point, even though the transfer is incomplete. The CreateAsynchIoHandle generates a reference to the buffer for the absolute system address, which is what the hAsyncRef parameter is.

The driver must call CompleteAsyncIo when the transfer is complete and can call SetIoProgress during the transfer to indicate how the transfer is progressing in terms of bytes transferred. GetOverlappedResult can get that progress for the application and can be called synchronously and can therefore block until the transfer is complete. The application needs to eventually block on the transfer waiting for the completion, or have a separate thread doing so, before the target buffer is used again by the application. There are some limitations with using asynchronous I/O with user mode drivers.

POWER MANAGEMENT

A Compact 7 device may or may not implement power management depending upon its purpose and upon the target hardware. For example, a handheld device or mobile phone would need to implement power management, whereas an always-on mains powered home climate control system need not. Power management can reduce the power consumption of a device by shutting down hardware or by putting it in a low power state. The CPU clock speed can be scaled down or even stopped if the CPU and memory can maintain state when the CPU is in this state. Also, with multicore CPUs, Compact 7 permits the shutting down of cores to save power.

Devices can also support power management by supporting all or some of the device power states. If they do, as the system changes state, they can do so as well. To do so they may implement the Stream Driver power functions (XXX_PowerUp or XXX_PowerDown) or implement the system power management IOCTLs. The recommended method is the IOCTLs.

Power Management Interface

This interface is a standard set of IOCTLs that a driver can implement, as shown in Table 32-6.

TABLE 32-6: Power Management Interface IOCTLs

POWER MANAGEMENT IOCTL	FUNCTION DESCRIPTION
IOCTL_POWER_CAPABILITIES	Checks device-specific capabilities.
IOCTL_POWER_GET	Gets the current device power state.
IOCTL_POWER_SET	Requests a change from one device power state to another.
IOCTL_REGISTER_POWER_RELATIONSHIP	Notifies the parent device so that the parent device can register all the devices that it controls.

➤ IOCTL_POWER_CAPABILITIES — If a driver does not implement this, the Power Manager assumes that the driver does implement the other power IOCTLs and does not send them. During initialization, through IOCTL_POWER_CAPABILITIES, the device driver should put the device into D0 and report its device capabilities as accurately as possible when queried by the Power Manager.

➤ IOCTL_REGISTER_POWER_RELATIONSHIP — This call notifies the parent device so that it can register all devices that it controls. It is actually up to the device driver to do the power management registration within this call. The OS ignores anything sent back.

➤ IOCTL_POWER_GET — The Power Manager knows the device power state of all power-manageable devices. It does not generally issue an IOCTL_POWER_GET call to the device unless an application calls GetDevicePower with the POWER_FORCE flag set.

➤ IOCTL_POWER_SET — All drivers that account for power must handle this call. The driver should set the device's state to the requested value. An application should not call this control directly to set the device power. Instead, it should use the SetDevicePower function, which goes through the Power Manager.

Compact 7 Power States

Compact 7 has system power states and device power states, and the two are coupled.

System Power States

Compact 7 defines four different power states for the operating system, as shown in Table 32-7.

TABLE 32-7: Compact 7 System Power States

OS POWER STATE	DESCRIPTION
On	The device is full active, and a user can use all the peripherals. The power consumption is at maximum.
User Idle	The user is not using the device after a time out; the power consumption can be reduced by, for example, decreasing the display backlight intensity and disabling peripherals.
System Idle	After application inactivity, the Power Manager switches to this state.
Suspend	In this state the device consumes the least amount of power possible, but the device cannot be used. The processor clock is decreased (or in a suspend state if supported); the peripherals are usually turned off, but the dynamic RAM is still refreshed. (Static RAM doesn't require refreshing.)

Device Power States

Compact 7 defines five device power states, as shown in Table 32-8. A device can implement all or a subset of these states. The only mandatory state is D0, Full on.

TABLE 32-8: Compact 7 Device Power States

DEVICE POWER STATE	REGISTRY KEY	DESCRIPTION
Full on	D0	The device is on and running. It is receiving full power from the system and is delivering full functionality to the user.
Low on	D1	The device is fully functional at a lower power or performance state than D0. The D1 state is applicable when the device is used; however, peak performance is unnecessary, and power is at a premium.
Standby	D2	The device is partially powered and has automatic wake-up on request.
Sleep	D3	The device is partially powered and has device-initiated wake-up, if available. A device in state D3 is sleeping but capable of raising the system power state on its own. It consumes only enough power to do this, which must be less than or equal to the amount of power used in state D2.

DEVICE POWER STATE	REGISTRY KEY	DESCRIPTION
Off	D4	The device has no power. A device in state D4 should not be consuming any significant power. Some peripheral buses require static terminations that intrinsically use nonzero power when a device is physically connected to the bus. A device on such a bus can still support D4.

The operating system and device power states map as follows:

➤ On -> D0

➤ User Idle -> D1

➤ System Idle -> D2

➤ Suspend -> D3

Class Power Management Interfaces

Besides the main Power Management interface, there are also defined power management interfaces for the driver classes, as shown in Table 32-9. A device driver registers that it implements one of these by calling `AdvertiseInterface`. `RequestPowerNotifications` may also need to be used in setting up the driver for power management.

TABLE 32-9: Driver Class Power Management Interfaces

INTERFACE	DEVICE TYPE
PMCLASS_BLOCK_DEVICE	Storage device
PMCLASS_DISPLAY	Display device
PMCLASS_NDIS_MINIPORT	Network device
PMCLASS_GENERIC_DEVICE	All other devices

Compact 7 Power Management Architecture

To support power management, a driver must be a Stream Driver and implement the power IOCTLs and a set of power states as in the previous two sections. Power management of a device driver requires close and accurate coupling of it with the OS Power Manager. The driver needs to be registered with Power Manager and must respond correctly when called by it. A device driver cannot unilaterally change its power state. It can make the request to the OS, which decides in the context of its state and the state of other drivers. If the OS approves this, the driver is signaled to change state. A similar caveat applies to applications. They also have to request power state changes of devices (and the system) through the Power Manager. Figure 32-2 shows the Power Management Architecture for a Compact 7 system.

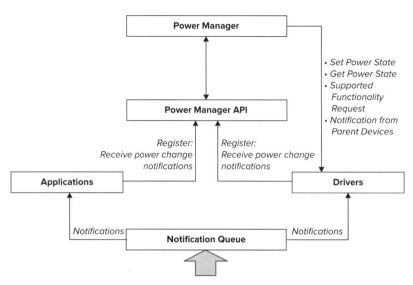

FIGURE 32-2

Power Management API

Table 32-10 shows the main functions used for power management.

TABLE 32-10: Power Management Functions

FUNCTION	ACTION
DevicePowerNotify	Requests that the Power Manager changes the power state of a device
GetDevicePower	Returns the current power state for a device
GetSystemPowerState	Returns the current system power state currently in effect
PowerPolicyNotify	Notifies the Power Manager of the events necessary to implement an OEM power policy
ReleasePowerRequirement	Requests that the Power Manager releases a power requirement previously set with SetPowerRequirement
RequestPowerNotifications	Enables applications and drivers to register for power notification events
SetDevicePower	Sets the device power state for a device
SetPowerRequirement	Notifies the Power Manager of an application device power requirement
SetSystemPowerState	Sets the system power state
StopPowerNotifications	Disables power notification events

Power Management in a Stream Driver is implemented along with a test application as part of the next chapter.

AN APPLICATION TO TEST IF A STREAM IS LOADED

The following code when implemented as the main( ) of a Compact 7 Console application tests if the stream MYD1: has been loaded. You can use it to test any stream loaded by changing the prefix used.

```
LPCTSTR   wstream =  _T("MYD1:");
HANDLE hStr =  CreateFile(wstream, GENERIC_READ | GENERIC_WRITE, 0, NULL, NULL, 0);
if (hStr == (HANDLE)-1) {
    RETAILMSG(1, (_T("BasicTestApp: Cannot open stream:  %s"),wstream));
}
else
{
    RETAILMSG(1, (_T("BasicTestApp: Opened stream: %s"),wstream));
}
```

Code snippet is from a console application to test if a Stream Driver has been loaded

SUMMARY

This chapter covered Stream Drivers in great depth. It covered loading drivers, the Stream Driver structure and function, configuring Stream Drivers, stream IO, and power management. In the next chapter you see how to implement a Stream Driver using a wizard that can do a lot of the leg work for you.

33

Developing a Stream Interface Driver

WHAT'S IN THIS CHAPTER?

➤ Understanding stream driver development

➤ Implementing a string buffer stream driver

➤ Using the CEDriverWiz Stream Driver Wizard

➤ Exploring device and open driver context

➤ Accessing the registry from a driver

➤ Using stream driver test applications

➤ Using a stream driver with Power Management

This chapter considers aspects of the development of a stream driver in detail. After a quick review of the stream architecture, the sample stream driver project as installed with Compact 7 is covered. This chapter then presents a stream driver that implements a string buffer that can be written to and read from synchronously. It also implements some custom IOCTLs. The full source for this project is available and can be built and loaded without any further development. A wizard for creating stream drivers, CEDriverWiz, as available on Codeplex, is introduced and used to implement the same string buffer project along with a number of test applications. Finally, a stream driver with Power Management is implemented.

STREAM INTERFACE DRIVER DEVELOPMENT OVERVIEW

All Compact 7 drivers are coded as DLLs and therefore implement the DLL entry point (DllEntrypoint/DLLMain), the normal entry point for any Windows DLL whether a driver or just an application library (API DLL). Normally, the operating system uses the LoadDriver to load a driver's DLL when its manager loads the driver, whereas LoadLibrary is always used to load an API DLL. LoadDriver makes sure that the driver is never paged out. A driver can be loaded using LoadLibrary and be paged out though using a registry setting. The source code for a driver DLL implements the functions required for the interface to the OS through which the driver interacts with the OS. For native drivers, these functions are specific to the type of driver. For a stream driver there is the standard set of functions, a specific API to load and interact with the driver, and some standard registry locations for stream driver configuration entries. Within the set of 13 functions for a Compact 7 stream driver, some must be implemented; some if implemented require others to be implemented, whereas others need to be implemented only if specific functionality is required. Besides the standardized interface provided by these functions, the IOControl (IOCTLs) interface provides a customizable interface for stream drivers. But even with this, there are standard sets of IOCTLs that a driver will implement depending upon the class of the driver and depending upon whether it implements Power Management.

Having considered the device driver architecture concepts and issues as covered in Chapters 29 to 32, and chosen to implement a driver as a stream driver because of its formal architecture, the driver development requires planning to address the issues previously raised and other driver-specific issues. The following is a list of items to consider:

- ➤ Stream functions to implement
- ➤ I/O functionality when loaded
- ➤ When loaded/how loaded
- ➤ Configuration
- ➤ Hardware
- ➤ Device context
- ➤ Open context
- ➤ IOCTLs
- ➤ Power
- ➤ Testing

Table 33-1 expands upon that list. (See the previous few chapters for item details.)

TABLE 33-1: Stream Driver Planning Items

ITEM	ITEM ASPECTS	DESCRIPTION/ISSUES/EXAMPLES	FILE (EXTENSION)
Functions to implement	Which of the 13 stream functions?	All 13 or a suitable subset.	CPP H DEF
I/O functionality when loaded	What does the driver do?	For example, implements a string buffer that can be written to and read from.	
Architecture	Monolithic	Implement DLL as one.	Various
	Layered	Implement as multiple libs with DDSI interfaces. Use existing MDD. Implement PDD. (See Chapter 30)	
Loading	When By what Mode	See Configuration.	
Interface Classes	What stream classes does it implement?	See Table 32-4, "Compact 7 Interface Classes."	
Configuration	Mode	Kernel User	REG BIB
	When loaded	At startup, by OS. Also load order. On demand by application. On demand by a bus driver.	
	Stream and DLL name	For example, MyDriver DLL = `mydriver.dll`	
	Suffix	For example, MYD, COM, SDT, and so on.	
	Index	For example, 1 or not specified.	
	IClass	For example, `PMCLASS_GENERIC_DEVICE`	

continues

TABLE 33-1 *(continued)*

ITEM	ITEM ASPECTS	DESCRIPTION/ISSUES/EXAMPLES	FILE (EXTENSION)
Hardware	Virtual	Underlying drivers for which this driver is a "wrapper" or is part of a software stack with. (See Chapter 30)	
	Memory	The MemBase and MemLen registry entries specifying the relative starting address that the driver will use and length of this memory window.	
	Ports	Microprocessor or chipset ports or hardware registers used by the driver.	
	Interrupts	Are they System on a Chip (SOC)? Are they installable?	
Device Context	Single instance or multiple instances	Should the driver be loaded only once?	CPP H
	Buffers	Buffers and other driver data structures are typically created for each driver instance.	
	Synchronization & Messaging	System Events Message Queues	
Open Context	Single instance or multiple instances	Should the driver permit only one stream to be opened with it at a time?	CPP H
	Buffers	If multiple streams, what structures are needed for each open context?	
I/O	Synchronous	Will I/O calls to the driver need to return before completion?	CPP H
	Asynchronous	Will multiple simultaneous I/O calls to a driver be permitted, which can have random access to the same buffer?	

ITEM	ITEM ASPECTS	DESCRIPTION/ISSUES/EXAMPLES	FILE (EXTENSION)
IOCTLs	Class	Any class-specific IOCTls that need to be implemented depending upon what stream class the driver ascribes to.	CPP H
	Power	See Power.	
	Other	Any device-specific IOCTLs that implement functionality that applications may use.	
Power	Is the device to be power managed?	What device power states will it implement? What will be its responses?	CPP H
	Stream Functions	Are the stream power functions to be used?	
	IOCTLs	Or will the standard power IOCTLs be used?	
Testing	Coded	Debug print statements PB Debugging Test Applications	CPP H
	Test Tools	Remote Tools CETK JTAG	

 For simplicity, the xxx_ prefix *is dropped from the stream function names in some of the discussions in this chapter.*

THE STREAM INTERFACE FUNCTIONS

Previous versions of Windows Embedded CE had 12 stream interface functions. Compact 7 has 13 (see Table 33-2) with the addition of Cancel for canceling asynchronous I/O. These functions implement functionality related to:

➤ Loading/unloading the driver

➤ Application I/O

➤ Power management

TABLE 33-2: The Stream Driver Functions

LOADING/UNLOADING	APPLICATION I/O	POWER MANAGEMENT
DllEntryPoint or DllMain	XXX_Open	XXX_PowerDown
XXX_Init	XXX_Read	XXX_PowerUp
XXX_PreDeinit	XXX_Write	
XXX_Deinit	XXX_Seek	
	XXX_IOControl	
	XXX_PreClose	
	XXX_Close	
	XXX_Cancel	

In Chapter 32, "Stream Interface Drivers," these functions are discussed in detail. A summary of their functionality follows:

They are called by Device Manager, not directly by an application. There is an application programming interface (API) for calling the functions via Device Manager. When implemented, the XXX in the function names is replaced by the stream prefix. The functions each have a specific parameter list and generally return a value to the operating system that indicates success or otherwise of the operation. Not all functions have to be implemented. The functions when coded are compiled into a driver DLL that is loaded according to its registry settings.

A Minimal Stream Driver

Two stream functions, apart from the DLL entry point, are required to build and load a stream driver. They are Init and Deinit. A driver that has only those parts of the stream can load but cannot be functionally useful because it cannot be actioned to perform any I/O because it provides no open context to obtain a stream handle. It may be of use to perform some system functionality, say at startup, and then no longer be required. It can't be programmatically unloaded because the API function to unload a stream driver requires a handle to the stream that is generated via Open. It may be configured with the DEVFLAGS_UNLOAD flag to unload after Init has run.

PreDeinit optionally can be implemented to wake up any hardware prior to Deinit. If it is implemented, then PreClose must be implemented.

A Stream Driver with Open Context

A stream driver with open context is required to perform I/O. The minimum list of functions for open context apart from loading and unloading the driver is:

➤ XXX_Open

➤ XXX_Close

➤ XXX_Read

➤ XXX_Write

To perform I/O with the device driver, the application can open the stream, perform reads and writes, and then close the stream.

IOControl is optional, although most stream drivers make heavy use of this function. Seek is also optional and not normally used. It's a legacy function from when stream drivers were for serial media devices such as tape drivers. A developer is at liberty to implement the Seek function as they want. The optional PreClose function can be implemented to wake up any open context threads that may be in a sleep state so that they can be shut down. The Cancel function is included only if asynchronous I/O is to be performed.

Stream Power Functions

Stream power functions are normally not implemented. The recommended method for implementing power functionality in a device driver is to use the system power IOCTLs. These functions operate in kernel mode, so the driver must be loaded in kernel mode for these functions to operate as required. Also there are significant coding restrictions on these stream power functions. For example, they cannot make system calls, and unhandled exceptions can cause the system to halt. PowerDown should only power the device hardware down and do it quickly without blocking. PowerUp should only do a hardware level recovery of the device, quickly and without blocking.

A SIMPLE STREAM DRIVER PROJECT

To create a new stream driver project, you could create a new DLL subproject in Platform Builder and work though adding all of the required code. You could also copy an existing sample project to your SubProjects folder and include it, as explained in this section. Or you could use a Project Wizard to generate the driver files. In the next section, the structure and content of a Stream Driver project is covered in detail. A subsequent section in this chapter focuses on using a wizard. In this section you look at the sample driver provided in Compact 7. This is in $(_WINCEROOT)\platform\BSPTemplate\src\drivers\streamdriver.

1. Copy that folder into your operating system SubProjects folder.

2. Add it to your subprojects as follows:

    i. Right-click on SubProjects in Solution Explorer.

    ii. Choose Add Existing SubProject.

    iii. Browse to the added folder, typically in (for example):

        $(_WINCEROOT)\OSDesigns\MyOS\MyOS\StreamDriver

    iv. Select the sources file in that folder.

3. Look at the .cpp and registry files. This driver is a shell for a stream driver with significant details about each function. Its registry is configured so that the driver is loaded at startup.

4. Try building the driver; it should fail. If so, add the following includes directive at the bottom of this project's sources file and rebuild. To edit the project sources file double-click on the subproject in Solution Explorer.

```
INCLUDES= \
$(_PUBLICROOT)\COMMON\SDK\INC; \
$(_PUBLICROOT)\COMMON\DDK\INC; \
$(SG_OUTPUT_ROOT)\oak\inc;
```

Code snippet is from code to be added at the bottom of the sample StreamDriver
sources project file in ch33codesnippets.txt

5. Set the subproject properties (from the Solution Explorer) to Build with the Image, Include in the Image, and Build as Debug mode. (See Figure 33-3 later in this chapter)

6. Build the operating system.

7. Run the operating system. Search through the Debug Output for StreamDriver, and you find that that there was error in loading the driver. There was an access problem because it's not in the Modules section of the BIB file. There is also another issue to resolve:

   ➤ BIB File — Add Modules above the entry for the driver DLL.

   ➤ `Streamdriver.dll` — Browse to the `Init( )` function. Note that it returns zero. This is a failure so it will load and then unload immediately. It needs to be changed to return 1.

8. Shut down the operating system, and make those two corrections.

9. Rebuild the driver with those corrections as follows:

   Run Copy Files to The Release Directory (Build menu).

   Run MakeImage (Build menu).

10. Rerun the operating system and search the Debug Output for Streamdriver again. You can see that it loaded this time.

11. Use Remote Tools such as Registry Editor and Process Viewer to check if the driver is loaded: Start the Remote Registry editor and browse to `HKLM\Drivers\Active`; search through it for the driver, which has the prefix `SDT1`.

12. Look for the Streamdriver module loaded in Process Viewer running against the kernel (`nk.exe`).

13. Also look for it under Drivers in the System Information Remote Tool. What is needed is some test applications to test the stream.

A COMPACT 7 STREAM DRIVER PROJECT

This section covers a string buffer stream driver in detail as an example of a simple stream driver. This driver project is in the zip file for this chapter as MyDriver.

The primary outcome of a Stream Driver project is the driver DLL with its operating system configuration and registry settings. You can develop a Compact 7 Stream Driver project as a typical Platform Builder subproject in Visual Studio 2008 with the following files:

- ➤ Project files
    - ➤ Project (.pbpxml)
    - ➤ sources (just called sources without an extension)
- ➤ Code files
    - ➤ Stream interface header file (.h)
    - ➤ Stream interface source file (.cpp)
    - ➤ Stream interface module definition file (.def)
- ➤ Parameter files
    - ➤ Binary Image Builder (BIB) file (.bib)
    - ➤ Shortcuts file (.dat)
    - ➤ Database file (.db)
    - ➤ Registry file (.reg)
- ➤ Batch files
    - ➤ ProSysgen.bat
    - ➤ Prelink.bat
    - ➤ Postlink.bat

ProjSysgen typically has the same unchanged content for all projects.

The Platform Builder Project (XML) file (.pbxml) lists the operating system configuration files in the project and the project title. The sources file lists all the meta-information that Platform Builder needs to know to load and build the project. There may also be a DIRS file that points to project dependencies, as with a layered driver.

A typical driver project as displayed in Solution Explorer is shown in Figure 33-1. The Module Definition file is not typically shown, although it needs editing.

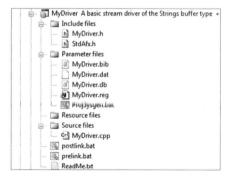

FIGURE 33-1

The stream driver functionality and configuration are implemented in the code files and the registry file. The BIB file can specify that the driver DLL is included in the image and whether it is to be placed in the kernel or user memory when loaded. (This is related to but separate from registry flags that determine how the driver is loaded.) There may also be a Catalog file (.pbcxml = Platform Builder Catalog XML) with a SYSGEN variable definition for the driver. If precompiled headers are used, there also are StdAfx.h and StdAfx.cpp files in the project.

The source code file implements the 13 interface functions, or a subset of them. These functions must conform to the interface that the Device Manager requires because that is what uses them. The source code may also implement other functions that the interface functions use. The header file contains any IOCTL definitions that the driver uses. Applications that use this interface to the driver need to include the header file. They do not need the function prototypes for the driver stream interface functions because no application connects directly to them. The module definition file is just a listing of the functions that the DLL implements without statements of their parameters and return types. This is used in the generation of the DLL to implement the interface.

The sources File

The sources file species the resources and configurations information for building the driver. A typical driver sources file is shown next:

```
WINCEREL=1
RELEASETYPE=LOCAL
_ISVINCPATH=$(_WINCEROOT)\public\common\sdk\inc;
_OEMINCPATH=$(_WINCEROOT)\public\common\oak\inc; \
     $(_WINCEROOT)\public\common\sdk\inc;

TARGETNAME=MyDriver
FILE_VIEW_ROOT_FOLDER= \
    ReadMe.txt \
    prelink.bat \
    postlink.bat \

FILE_VIEW_RESOURCE_FOLDER= \

FILE_VIEW_INCLUDES_FOLDER= \
  StdAfx.h \
  MyDriver.h \

SOURCES= \
  MyDriver.cpp \

TARGETLIBS= \
     $(SG_OUTPUT_ROOT)\sdk\lib\$(_CPUINDPATH)\coredll.lib

PRECOMPILED_CXX=1
PRECOMPILED_PCH=StdAfx.pch
PRECOMPILED_INCLUDE=StdAfx.h

TARGETTYPE=DYNLINK
POSTLINK_PASS_CMD=postlink.bat
PRELINK_PASS_CMD=prelink.bat

FILE_VIEW_PARAMETER_FOLDER= \
  MyDriver.bib \
  MyDriver.reg \
  MyDriver.dat \
  MyDriver.db \
```

```
ProjSysgen.bat \

INCLUDES= \    $(_PUBLICROOT)\COMMON\SDK\INC; \
    $(_PUBLICROOT)\COMMON\DDK\INC; \
    $(SG_OUTPUT_ROOT)\oak\inc;. \
```

Code snippet is from a typical stream driver Compact 7 sources project file

In Compact 7 some of the build macros as used in the sources file have changed. For example, $(SG_OUTPUT_ROOT) *replaces* $(_PROJECTROOT)\cesysgen. *These need to be changed if porting a CE 6 driver project to Compact 7. Refer to "Build Porting Guide for Windows Embedded Compact 7" in the Compact 7 documentation.*

The directives in this sources file have the following meanings:

➤   WINCEREL=1

  ➤   Causes the subproject build to copy the target to the flat release directory after the build has been completed.

➤   RELEASETYPE=LOCAL

  ➤   Build as a subproject.

➤   TARGETNAME=MyDriver

  ➤   Driver filename will be MyDriver.DLL.

➤   TARGETTYPE=DYNLINK

  ➤   Build a DLL.

➤   INCLUDES

  ➤   Directories to search for header files apart from the project directory.

➤   FILE_VIEW_PARAMETER FOLDER

  ➤   Headings under which files are placed in Solution Explorer.

The Project Parameter Files

The parameter files provide configuration information related to the driver. As with all subprojects, they are the registry file, the BIB file, the DAT file, and the DB file. The DAT and DB files are typically not used with a driver. If the driver is configured to be included in the image, then its parameter files (Registry, BIB, DAT, and DB) are all merged into the corresponding system files during MakeImage. If the driver is not included, then its parameter files (except the BIB one) can be copied or conditionally included in the OS project parameter files. Alternatively, the registry files can be programmatically added to the registry before the driver is loaded.

The Registry File

The only required entry is the name of the DLL file as the *DLL* subkey. Normally though, the three-letter *Prefix* will be included; otherwise, the stream will be implemented with "naked" function names.

If the driver is to load in user mode, then the registry must include the DEVFLAGS_USERMODE flag (value = 16= 10_2)

```
Flag= DEVFLAGS_USERMODE
```

Or

```
Flag= dword:10
```

Otherwise, it can be loaded only in kernel mode. Note that Flag=0 will cause the driver to be loaded in kernel mode.

If the driver is to have a specific index (and only one instance is to load) then this can be included; otherwise, the OS can "find" an index starting at 1 for every instance of the driver loaded. Example:

```
Index=0
```

If the driver has any dependencies, then these can be specified in the DependsOn driver subkey requiring them to be loaded before this driver.

The IClass subkey can specify any driver class interfaces its implements. Other driver-specific subkeys can be added such as *IRQ* number. Example:

IRQ=10

If the driver loads at startup, then a relative Order value appears in the registry entry, and the driver entries are under HKLM\Drivers\Builtin. If the driver programmatically loads, then it can be placed anywhere because the application specifies its location. Typically though, it is placed under HKLM\Drivers.

A registry file for a driver loaded at startup in kernel mode is shown here:

Available for download on Wrox.com

```
[HKEY_LOCAL_MACHINE\Drivers\BuiltIn\MyDriver]
    "Dll"="MyDriver.dll"
    "Order"=dword:4
    "Prefix"="MYD"
    "Flags"=dword:0
```

Code snippet is from a simple stream driver registry entry that will loaded at startup in kernel mode

The following is the registry to load the same driver programmatically in user mode:

Available for download on Wrox.com

```
[HKEY_LOCAL_MACHINE\Drivers\MyDriver]
    "Dll"="MyDriver.dll"
    "Prefix"="MYD"
    "Flags"=dword:10
```

Code snippet is from a simple stream driver registry entry that can be loaded programmatically in user mode

The BIB File

The BIB file specifies that the driver is a module. Its DLL file needs to be included in the image and located in the FlatRelease directory after building and can be loaded in kernel mode, user mode, or both. A BIB entry for a driver to be loaded in kernel mode follows:

```
MODULES
MyDriver.dll   $(_FLATRELEASEDIR)\MyDriver.dll                NK   SHK
```

Code snippet is from a BIB entry for a driver that can be loaded at startup in kernel mode

The following is a BIB entry required to load the same driver programmatically in user mode:

```
MODULES
MyDriver.dll   $(_FLATRELEASEDIR)\MyDriver.dll                NK
```

Code snippet is from a BIB entry for a driver that can be loaded programmatically in user mode

Stream Functionality

Stream functionality is implemented mainly in the source code file (.cpp) that implements all of the stream functions for the driver. The header will contain only driver definitions that applications that interact with it may need. Driver-specific custom IOCTLs can be declared in the header file. The stream interface driver functions are not prototyped in the header file because they are not used directly by the application. The module definition file lists all the stream function to be used in the interface, by name only. There may also be DLL-specific specifications in the module definition file. It is possible though to not use a module definition file and make suitable declarations in the source code file and in the sources file.

A stream driver module definition file follows that does not implement Seek, PowerUp, PowerDown, and Cancel. The Seek entry is not included because it is commented out with the semicolon.

```
LIBRARY MyDriver
EXPORTS

    MYD_Init
    MYD_Deinit
    MYD_PreDeinit
    MYD_Open
    MYD_PreClose
    MYD_Close
    MYD_Read
;   MYD_Seek
    MYD_Write
```

Code snippet is from a module definition file for a stream driver

A simple header file follows that defines a buffer of 1024 characters and five simple IOCTL:

```
#define BUFFER_SIZE  1024
typedef struct tagMYD_DEVCONTEXT {
    LPTSTR  Buffer;    // Buffer used for read and write
}MYD_DEVCONTEXT,*PMYD_DEVCONTEXT;

#define IOCTL_MyDriver_0        1000
#define IOCTL_MyDriver_1        1001
#define IOCTL_MyDriver_2        1002
#define IOCTL_MyDriver_3        1003
#define IOCTL_MyDriver_4        1004
```

Code snippet is from a simple header file with some custom IOCTLS and a buffer definition

The Source Code File

This stream driver source code file implements a simple string buffer, as specified in the previous header file that is written to and read from by stream functions. It also implements the IOCTLs in the header file. Each driver instantiated has its own buffer because the buffer is part of the device context.

Includes and Declarations

The following is needed at the top of the source code file:

```
#include <windows.h>
#include <tchar.h>
#include "stdafx.h"
#include "MyDriver.h"

//The device context
PMYD_DEVCONTEXT    pDevContext;
```

Code snippet is from Declarations in mydriver.cpp

XXX_Init and XXX_Deinit

Init creates the device context and then creates the buffer that it points to. The header file defines the device context structure. Deinit frees the memory allocated to the buffer and then disposes of the device context:

```
/////////////////////////////
// pContext is the driver's active key as copied under HKLM\Drivers\Active
// That is it the string name of the key
///-------------------------------------------------------------------------
DWORD MYD_Init( LPCTSTR pContext, LPCVOID lpvBusContext )
{
    DWORD dwRet = 0;

    // Initialize device context.
    pDevContext =
        (PMYD_DEVCONTEXT )LocalAlloc( LPTR, sizeof (MYD_DEVCONTEXT));
    if (pDevContext == NULL)
```

```
    {
        return 0;
    }

    //Allocate space for the string buffer
    pDevContext->Buffer =
            (LPWSTR)LocalAlloc( LPTR, BUFFER_SIZE * sizeof(WCHAR));

    if ( pDevContext->Buffer == NULL)
    {
        return 0;
    }

    //Return non zero value
    dwRet = (DWORD) pDevContext;
    return dwRet;
}
```

Code snippet is from Init stream function in mydriver.cpp

```
BOOL MYD_Deinit(DWORD hDeviceContext)
{
    BOOL bRet = TRUE;

    //Get the device context.  Could also use the global pDevContext
    PMYD_DEVCONTEXT pDevContext = (PMYD_DEVCONTEXT)hDeviceContext;

    //Release the context
    LocalFree(pDevContext->Buffer);
    LocalFree(pDevContext);

    return bRet;
}
```

Code snippet is from Deinit stream function in mydriver.cpp

XXX_Open and XXX_Close

No Open Context-specific functionality is required in this case:

```
DWORD MYD_Open(DWORD hDeviceContext, DWORD AccessCode, DWORD ShareMode)
{
    DWORD dwRet = 1;
    return dwRet;
}

BOOL MYD_Close(DWORD hOpenContext)
{
    BOOL bRet = TRUE;
    return bRet;
}
```

Code snippet is from the Open and Close functions in mydriver.cpp

FunctionXXX_Read and XXX_Write

The `Write` function writes the supplied string to the buffer, whereas `Read` reads it back:

```
DWORD MYD_Write(DWORD hOpenContext, LPCVOID pSourceBytes, DWORD NumberOfBytes)
{
    DWORD dwRet = 0;

    // Copy the smaller of buffer size and number of bytes sent..
    dwRet = min(BUFFER_SIZE, NumberOfBytes);
    wcsncpy(  (LPWSTR)pDevContext->Buffer,(LPWSTR)pSourceBytes, dwRet);

    // Return number of bytes written.
    return dwRet;
}
```

Code snippet is from the Write stream function in mydriver.cpp

```
DWORD MYD_Read(DWORD hOpenContext, LPVOID pBuffer, DWORD Count)
{
    DWORD dwRet = 0;

    // Copy the smaller of buffer size or string size.
    dwRet = min(BUFFER_SIZE, Count);
    wcsncpy( (LPWSTR)pBuffer,(LPWSTR)pDevContext->Buffer, dwRet);

    // Return number of bytes read.
    return dwRet;
}
```

Code snippet is from the Read stream function in mydriver.cpp

XXX_IOControl

`XXX_IOControl` implements the IOCTL interface. It returns true for the five IOCTLs as specified in the header file and false for any other values:

```
BOOL MYD_IOControl(DWORD hOpenContext,
                   DWORD dwCode,
                   PBYTE pBufIn,
                   DWORD dwLenIn,
                   PBYTE pBufOut,
                   DWORD dwLenOut,
                   PDWORD pdwActualOut)
{
    BOOL bRet = true;
    switch (dwCode) {
        case IOCTL_MyDriver_0:
            bRet = true;
            break;
        case IOCTL_MyDriver_1:
```

```
            bRet = true;
            break;
        case IOCTL_MyDriver_2:
            bRet = true;
            break;
        case IOCTL_MyDriver_3:
            bRet = true;
            break;
        case IOCTL_MyDriver_4:
            bRet = true;
            break;
        default:
            bRet=false;
            break;
    }
    return bRet;
}
```

Code snippet is from the IOControl stream function in mydriver.cpp

BUILDING A STREAM DRIVER FOR TESTING

For driver development you can typically use a Retail OS, with Kernel Debug and KITL enabled. Use a Debug build of the OS if some driver-OS interaction needs resolution. You can configure the stream driver to load in user mode upon demand if you implement a driver loading application or configure it as Builtin and include it in the image (deselect Exclude from Image). For development purposes it is simplest to set the driver project to be built when the image is built (deselect Exclude from Build), to not include in the image (select Exclude from Image), and build as Debug (select Always Build and Link as Debug) in the project properties (via Solution Explorer), as shown in Figure 33-2. That way you can run the OS image and make changes to the driver source, and rebuild and reload without restarting or rebuilding the OS. You need to unload the driver from the OS before rebuilding it. Figure 33-3 shows how to configure the driver to include in the image.

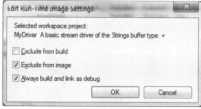

FIGURE 33-2

FIGURE 33-3

Typically you would disable MakeImage After Building (Build Menu ⇨ Targeted Build Settings). To build you can then right-click the project in Solution Explorer and choose Build or Rebuild. If some subproject drivers are configured to be included in the image, the Build All Subprojects can result in MakeImage running every time regardless of that setting.

If you need to include the driver in the OS because it needs to run at startup (and/or it needs to run in kernel mode) then build the OS once with the driver so configured. Have it configured as Build/Include/Debug. Then to change the driver, disconnect the OS, make changes to the driver, and then just do MakeImage. Then restart the OS.

Test the String Buffer Stream Driver

This activity encompasses building the string buffer driver, as discussed in this section, and launching it at startup as a Builtin driver. The driver project is included in the source code for this chapter. It is configured to load at startup in user mode. You need a Retail build Compact 7 OS project that has KITL and Debug Kernel both enabled.

1. Extract the MyDriver project from the zip file for this chapter to your OS SubProject folder, and add the project to the OS project. (Choose the sources file.)

2. Set the project to be built in Debug mode and to be included in the image (refer to Figure 33-3).

3. Build the OS and launch it.

4. In the project source code are some debug messages that should display in the Output window while the OS loads.

5. Search the Output window for MyDriver.

6. You can again use the Remote Tools, as in "A Simple Stream Driver Project" in this chapter to see that the driver loaded. The next section of this chapter remakes this stream driver project, along with some test applications using a Stream Driver Project Wizard.

CEDRIVER WIZARD

In Platform Builder, there are five types of subprojects that you can create and add to an OS project, as shown in Figure 33-4.

When you select one and give it a name, you run through a wizard to cover options relevant to that project. It would be useful if there was also a stream driver sub project type as a sixth option. It would cover options such as:

➤ Driver name

➤ Driver prefix

➤ Kernel mode, user mode, or both

➤ Inbuilt, dynamic, or both

➤ IOCTLs

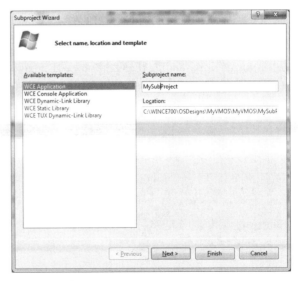

FIGURE 33-4

➤ Use Retail and/or Debug Messages

➤ Driver metadata such as Vendor

➤ Create a Catalog file

➤ SYSGEN variable name

It is also be useful if there are some test applications automatically generated specifically for the stream to test:

➤ That the driver loaded

➤ Adding registry setting for dynamic loading of driver

➤ Dynamically loading the driver

➤ Read/Write I/O

➤ IOCTL I/O

➤ Unload the driver

CEDriverWiz was created to do all this and is on Codeplex as a zipped-up installer:

```
http://CEDriverWiz.codeplex.com
```

It plugs into Visual Studio via the Tools menu. Setup instructions are on the web site and contained in the zip file. When installing for Visual Studio 2008 and Compact 7, you have the option to set up the wizard to be listed on the External Tools menu or as a Platform Builder script. The latter is the preferred option.

Although the functionality is the same for a Compact 7 developer, the Platform Builder script was an easier option for the development of the wizard code because when these scripts run, Build environment variables are available to the wizard, making it easier to determine where Compact 7 is installed and where the current OS project is. External Tools have only Visual Studio environment variables available to them, so when the wizard runs from here, it has to make some intelligent guesses about these locations.

Platform Builder Scripts

Platform Builder Scripts are a new feature with Compact 7. When you create a script, they are saved in your Documents folder under PBScripts. A typical script for CEDriverWiz that is installed if you choose the script option is shown here:

```
VSVersion = 9.0
Name=CEDriverWiz
RunPBCmd("C:\Program Files\Embedded101\CEDriverWiz\CEDriverWiz.exe")
```

You can configure the scripts to run anything that can start from a command line, including batch files and GUI applications. They have the advantage over External Tools because they have the same environment as the Build prompt (Build-Release Directory). Their primary purpose is so that developers can script custom builds for their projects, but they have a wider possible use for any in context application such as custom a subproject wizard.

To run an existing script:

1. From the Tools menu select Platform Builder then select Configure Scripts.

2. Select an existing script from the drop-down list Script.

3. Press Run.

The last run script is directly available as follows:

➤ From the Tools menu select Platform Builder then select Run Active Script (the current script will show on that menu).

To create a new script:

1. From the Tools menu select Platform Builder then select Configure Scripts.

2. Press New and give it a Display Name.

3. Press Add to add commands to the script from a menu of PB relevant commands.

4. Press Source to directly edit the script.

5. Press Save to save the script in the PBScripts folder.

It can now be run.

You can also add Shortcut keys to a script.

Using CEDriverWiz

CEDriverWiz generates a stream driver project that can implement a simple string buffer with synchronous I/O, as per the MyDriver project previously covered in this chapter.

➤ XXX_Init creates the buffer on the heap.

➤ XXX_Write takes a string as input and puts it into the buffer.

➤ XXX_Read returns the number of characters requested from the buffer up.

➤ XXX_DeInit disposes of the buffer from the heap.

The wizard also optionally generates a number of test applications for the driver. The wizard for this is shown in Figure 33-5.

When the wizard starts, it determines the location of the OS project. It generates projects under that location in a folder with the same name as the stream. To create a stream project, you give it a stream name and stream prefix (three characters). You can choose to have Retail and Debug messages inserted into the stream's functions to output messages to the Debug window when they are called. Precompiled headers and IOCTLs are also options.

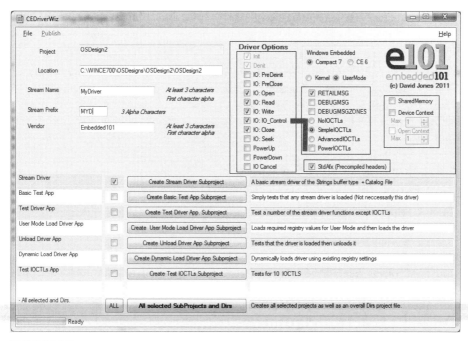

FIGURE 33-5

SubProjects

You can choose to generate just the Stream Driver Project or any of the test applications. You can also choose to generate all the projects. All projects are generated as subprojects of the current OS project with the stream name substituted in all filenames and other configuration names. The stream prefix is also substituted for XXX in the driver source file and in all `CreateFile` statements in the other projects that open the stream in those projects. All subprojects include a reference to the driver header file. When the driver is generated, a `Catalog` file can be generated just for the driver via the Publish menu. Alternatively, a `Catalog` file can be generated that enables individual selection of the subprojects generated. When the `Catalog` file is generated, a refresh of the Catalog is required.

The subprojects are:

➤ The stream driver — This is the actual stream driver project.

➤ BasicTest application — Tests for the presence of any stream driver

➤ Driver application — Tests the driver read/write I/O

➤ Load Dynamic application — Loads the driver in user mode assuming registry values are in place

➤ Load User Mode application — As per dynamic load application but writes the registry values first

➤ Unload driver — Unloads the driver

➤ TestIOCTLs application — Tests the IOCTLs interface

A BasicTest application requires the stream name such as COM1: as a command-line parameter. Unlike the other applications, it isn't stream driver-specific. All the other test applications assume that the driver index is 1.

The code in these subprojects demonstrates the opening and closing of a stream and performs I/O with a stream. Table 32-2 lists the Device Manager API functions used in these applications against the stream functions they indirectly activate. Table 32-5 also lists the stream and API functions and gives sample API function calls for stream drivers. The next chapter looks at a stream driver application in more detail.

Adding Wizard SubProjects to the OS Project

The root of the stream driver project is one directory deep from the SubProjects folder, for example in

```
$(_WINCEROOT) \OSDesigns\MyOS\MyOS\MyDriver
```

That folder has a dirs file if you chose the option to add all subprojects. If you choose that when adding an existing SubProject, then all the subprojects are added in one step. Alternatively, you can browse one folder deeper into each subproject and add them individually. Finally, if the Catalog file was generated, then the subprojects can be added under ThirdParty/VendorName/StreamName where VendorName is the name entered when the projects were generated, and StreamName is the name of the driver.

Creating a Stream Driver

You need a Retail build OS project with KITL and Kernel Debug enabled. Remove the previous MyDriver project.

1.   Download and install the wizard.

2.   Run the wizard and create all the subprojects. Configure the stream driver as follows:

  ➤   Name MyDriver

  ➤   Prefix MYD

  ➤   No Seek, Power, and Cancel functions

  ➤   Compact 7

  ➤   Include Retail messages

  ➤   User Mode

  ➤   No IOCTLs

  ➤   Device Context of 1

  ➤   No Shared memory

  ➤   No Open Context

3.   Configure all the projects as Build/Not in Image/Debug as in Figure 33-2.

4.   Build all the subprojects.

Testing the Stream Driver

Besides using the Platform Builder tools to test for the presence of a loaded driver, the CEDriverWiz created a number of applications to test its functionality. In the following exercise you use some of them to do so. The next chapter covers their implementation.

1. Start your OS. (You don't need to remake it.)

2. Run the LoadDynamic application using the Target-Run Programs menu. Note the Debug messages. It fails because the registry values required are not there.

3. Run the LoadUserMode application; this should succeed. See Debug output.

4. Run the BasicTest application. This requires a parameter in the box at the bottom of the Run Program dialog. This will be the stream prefix and its index, for example MYD1: There is only one instance of the driver so 1 is correct. Again note the Debug output. You should see that the driver was able to be opened and closed.

You can use this application to test for the presence of any stream driver, not just the one created by the wizard. Try it with COM1: if your system has a COM port. All other test applications are bound to the generated stream and its first instance.

5. Similarly run the driver App. (No parameters are required.) This opens the driver, writes to it, reads back from it, and verifies that the in and out values are the same. It then closes.

6. Run the application to unload the driver; then run the driver app again. It should fail because the driver is not loaded.

7. Run the LoadDynamic application again. It should now succeed because the registry values are still there. Test this with the applications.

8. Try setting Breakpoints in the driver and in the application, and run them again to see that you can debug both.

9. Try loading a second instance and test for its presence with the BasicTest application and, say, MYD2. (Replace MYD with your prefix.) Modify the applications to use this prefix in CreateFile; rebuild and test.

10. Use the Remote Tools, as in "A Simple Stream Driver Project" in this chapter, to check the loading of the driver and the entry of the driver registry settings.

Load the Driver at Startup

The registry settings are appropriate for loading the stream driver at startup in user mode. To do so you need to add the project needs to the operating system:

1. Detach the OS.

2. Configure just the driver to be included in the OS: Build/Include/Debug.

3. Rebuild the driver project.

4. From the Build menu, run Copy Files to the Release Directory.

5. From the Build menu run Make Run-time Image (MakeImage).

6. Start the OS and run the test applications. You do not need to load the driver. Try unloading it.

You can't dynamically load the driver in kernel mode using a user application. You need to configure the BIB file for kernel mode and change the registry flag entry.

7. Open the BIB file and add SHK flags on the end of the driver line with a space after NK. SHK means System, Hidden, and placed in Kernel space. For example:

```
MyDll.dll   $(_FLATRELEASEDIR)\MyDll.dll          NK SHK
```

8. In the registry file change the `Flags` value from `dword:10` to `dword:0`. The flag `0x10` means load in user mode; 0 means kernel mode.

9. Repeat the previous steps 1 to 6.

10. Try SHQ in 7 and try running the user mode loading application. Q means that you can load the driver in both user mode and kernel mode.

IMPLEMENTING IOCTLS

You can add IOCTLs to the stream project when generated by the CEDriverWiz Wizard. The Simple IOCTLs option just adds five successive IOCTLs from a base value. Advanced IOCTLs add five IOCTL values that are unique for the OS using the CTL_CODE macro. The IOCTLs are defined in the driver's header file and deduced in the XXX_IOControl function in the driver when a call is made to it. That function takes as a parameter an IOCTL value, and if the value is found in the switch statement, it returns true. Otherwise it returns false. To use the stream IOCTL interface, an application needs to include the stream header file. The IOCTL test application sends ten IOCTL values starting from the first so that five succeed and the next five fail.

1. Create a driver with Simple IOCTLs.

2. Build the driver and run the OS.

3. Run the TestIOCTls application.

4. Note that five pass and five fail.

5. Repeat 1 to 4 for Advanced IOCTls.

6. Note the values generated.

DRIVER CONTEXT AND SHARED MEMORY

The stream `Init` function is called each time the driver is loaded. The global data in the DLL is specific to each instance of the driver. For example if

```
int count=0;
```

is included below the header file included in the driver source file, then when `Init` runs, the count is always zero. How can driver instances know how many instances have loaded? This may be of importance for determining what hardware to access in the driver, or for limiting the number of instances to one if there is only one set of relevant hardware available.

DLLs can implement shared memory in two ways. The simplest uses named data segments. The second more complex method uses memory mapped files. The data segments approach is suitable for simple data such as a counter but not for structured data and pointers.

The following code implements the device counter (devCount) that can be incremented in each Init function and decremented in each Deinit function.

1. Place the first three lines of code in the global part of the driver DLL code.

2. Place the two lines from SECTIONS at the bottom of the driver's .def file. (Remember it may not show in the driver project although it is used in the build. Explore the driver's project directory to access it.)

3. Also add the Init and Deinit code to those functions.

Available for download on Wrox.com

```
#pragma data_seg(".MYSEG")
static DWORD devCount=0;
#pragma data_seg()


SECTIONS
      .MYSEG    READ WRITE SHARED

//In MYD_Init
devCount++;
RETAILMSG(1,(TEXT("MyDriver: Instance No.: %d\n"), devCount ));

//In MYD_Deinit
devCount--;
RETAILMSG(1,(TEXT("MyDriver: No instances now.: %d\n"), devCount ));
```

Code snippet is from implementing a device instance counter in Ch33Codesnippets.txt

4. Configure and build the driver as an installable user mode driver (not in kernel mode).

5. Select Copy Files to Release directory, rebuild the driver, and then run MakeImage.

Run the operating system, and run the application to load the driver in user mode. Run the application to unload it. Load several instances of the driver and then unload them (You need to provide an instance number on the command line for all but MYD1:). With each action the instance count is tracked.

Perhaps this information could have been inferred from the driver's index, but that would be invalid if an instance were unloaded that was not the last one loaded.

Try implementing some code in Init to limit the number of driver instances to one or two instances.

REGISTRY ACCESS FROM A DRIVER

When XXX_Init runs, the pContext parameter that is passed to it is a LPCTSTR string data type which names the HKLM\Drivers\Active string, and the driver instance that it is loaded under, relative to HKLM. It can be used to access registry information about the driver, from within the driver. Here is a function that gets the instance name as the original key entry for the driver (lpKeyName) and the driver's active name (lpActiveKeyName). The active name is the string that an application would use to open the stream, such as MYD1:. The function also extracts the index from this.

```
DWORD index=0;
WCHAR ActiveKeyName[8] ;
LPWSTR lpActiveKeyName;
TCHAR KeyName[256] = {0};
LPWSTR lpKeyName;

Void  RegDeviceOpen(LPCWSTR lpActiveKey )
{
    HKEY hKey;
    DWORD ValueType,ValueSize;
    DWORD Disposition;

    //Open the driver instance active registry entry
    RegCreateKeyEx(HKEY_LOCAL_MACHINE,
        lpActiveKey,
        0,
        NULL,
        0,
        0,
        NULL,
        &hKey,
        &Disposition);

    ValueSize = sizeof(szKeyName) * sizeof(TCHAR);
    RegQueryValueEx(hKey,
        _T("Key"),
        0,
        &ValueType,
        (LPBYTE)KeyName,
        &ValueSize);

    //Store the driver key
    lpKeyName  = (LPWSTR) lpKeyName;

    ValueSize = 8*sizeof(WCHAR);
    RegQueryValueEx(hKey,
        _T("NAME"),
        NULL,
        &ValueType,  //REG_SZ
        (LPBYTE) &ActiveKeyName,
        &ValueSize);
    RegCloseKey(hKey);

    //Get index
    index = (BYTE)ActiveKeyName[3] - (BYTE) '0';

    //Store the active name string, eg MYD1:
    lpActiveKeyName  = (LPWSTR) ActiveKeyName;

    return;
}
```

*Code snippet is from stream driver function to extract registry information from
the initial device context in Ch33Codesnippets.txt*

This function would be called from `Init` as:

```
RegDeviceOpen((LPCWSTR)pContext);
```

Code snippet call from XXX_Init to get registry information in Ch33Codesnippets.txt

You can use the `lpKeyName` string to open the driver's registry key to extract specific information about the driver as configured in its subproject registry entries.

IMPLEMENTING POWER MANAGEMENT

This section implements a rudimentary Power Management (PM) system for a device driver. The system is implemented as the four Power Management IOCTLs and registers the device for system requests to change its power state, and responds to queries about its power state. This PM system does not implement a message queue to handle power requests and does not attempt to send any requests to change its power state because of any inactivity, and so on by itself. The code in this section is in the code snippets file. The driver subproject is also included in the folder MorePower.

1. Create a new stream driver with the CEDriverWiz Wizard with the following configuration:

➤ Stream Name: MorePower

➤ Suffix: MPW

➤ Driver in kernel mode

➤ Enable Driver I/O

➤ Disable the PowerUp/PowerDown functions

➤ Seek is not needed

➤ Disable Driver Context

➤ Enable Advanced IOCTls

➤ Enable Retail Mode macros

➤ Enable Power IOCTLs

The last option adds the four power IOCTLs:

➤ `IOCTL_POWER_CAPABILITIES`

➤ Checks device-specific capabilities

➤ `IOCTL_POWER_GET`

➤ Gets the current device power state

➤ `IOCTL_POWER_SET`

➤ Requests a change from one device power state to another

➤   `IOCTL_REGISTER_POWER_RELATIONSHIP`

         ➤   Notifies the parent device so that the parent device can register all the devices that it controls

These IOCTLs as added by the wizard need implementation and return false to indicate to the operating system that PM has not been implemented.

2. Add the following declarations, the `#include` entries at the top of the driver source code file:

```
#include <pm.h>
//#include <windev.h>   //CTL_CODE
#include <memory.h>
void InitPower();
```

> *Code snippet is from Driver PM includes function prototype in Ch33Codesnippets.txt*

➤   `pm.h` is the PM header file.

➤   `windev.h` is needed for the `CTL_CODE` macro that is used to define the four PM IOCTLs. It's commented out because it would have already been included because the Advanced IOCTLs were enabled.

➤   `memory.h` is needed for copying memory buffers.

➤   The `InitPower` declaration is a function prototype. It initializes the device PM structures and needs to be called from `Init`.

The device needs a variable to represent its state, D0 to D4. This is implemented as an `enum`. Also, the first IOCTL needs a structure to return information about its capabilities, such as which device power states it implements in the `DeviceDx` field, as a bit mask. Because this is a simple PM implementation, you implement all states, so the mask will be `0x1f`. `InitPower`, as called by `Init`, initializes both of these.

3. Add the following code above the driver `IOControl` function:

```
//The device current power state
enum _CEDEVICE_POWER_STATE  PowerState;

//The device capabilities
POWER_CAPABILITIES *  pPower;

//Initialise device power state and set up capabilities structure
void InitPower()
{
    PowerState= D0;

    pPower =
          (PPOWER_CAPABILITIES )LocalAlloc( LPTR, sizeof (POWER_CAPABILITIES));

    pPower->DeviceDx = 0x1f;  //= Implements all states
    pPower->WakeFromDx = 1;  //Can awaken
    pPower->InrushDx = 0;
```

```
        pPower->Power[0]=8;
        pPower->Power[1]=4;
        pPower->Power[2]=2;
        pPower->Power[3]=1;
        pPower->Power[4]=0;
        pPower->Latency[0]=0;
        pPower->Latency[1]=0;
        pPower->Latency[2]=0;
        pPower->Latency[3]=0;
        pPower->Latency[4]=0;
        pPower->Flags=POWER_CAP_PARENT ;
    }
```

Code snippet is from InitPower and device PM structures in Ch33Codesnippets.txt

Most of the values in the power capabilities structure are only dummy values for the device driver. DeviceDx is what is important because the OS uses this to determine which states it should tell the driver to change to when the OS changes state. The actual state changes get mapped by the driver to its subset of its implemented states.

So that the operating system knows that this device driver implements the generic stream interface Power Management (the four IOCTLs) it needs a further registry entry.

4. Add the following to the driver's registry file:

```
"IClass"="{A32942B7-920C-486b-B0E6-92A702A99B35}"
```

This is defined in pm.h as PMCLASS_GENERIC_DEVICE.

After the driver's Init function runs, with the driver registered as implementing this power interface, the OS can action the first PM IOCTL, IOCTL_POWER_CAPABILITIES, to determine the driver's capabilities. It needs to copy the power capabilities structure into the supplied buffer and return true.

5. Implement the first PM IOCTL as follows:

Available for download on Wrox.com

```
case IOCTL_POWER_CAPABILITIES:
// Checks device-specific capabilities
    dw = sizeof(POWER_CAPABILITIES);
    if (dwLenOut != dw) return false;

    memcpy((void *) pBufOut, (void *) pPower, dw);

    *pdwActualOut = dw;
    bRet = true;
    break;
```

Code snippet is from IOCTL_POWER_CAPABILITIES in Ch33Codesnippets.txt

The second IOCTL gets the current power state of the device and returns it to a supplied buffer. This IOCTL is not normally used by the OS, but applications can query it either directly, by actioning the IOCTL, or by calling GetDevicePower( ).

6. Implement the second IOCTL as follows:

```
case IOCTL_POWER_GET:
// Gets the current device power state.
    dw  = sizeof(CEDEVICE_POWER_STATE);
    if (dwLenOut != dw) return false;

    pBufOut = (PBYTE) &PowerState;

    memcpy((void *) pBufOut, (void *) &PowerState, dw);

    *pdwActualOut = dw;

    bRet = true;
    break;
```

Code snippet is from IOCTL_POWER_GET in Ch33Codesnippets.txt

The third IOCTL requests the device driver to change state and should be actioned only by the OS PM. Applications and other devices should not attempt to call this but should send a request to the OS to do so. A PM message queue would then send the request if approved, but because you haven't implemented a PM message queue for the driver, this is not a functional option with the driver.

7. Implement the third IOCTL as follows:

```
case IOCTL_POWER_SET:
// Requests a change from one device power state to another.
    dw  = sizeof(CEDEVICE_POWER_STATE);
    if (dwLenOut != dw) return false;

//Copy the power state as requested into the device power
    memcpy((void *) &PowerState , (void *) pBufOut , dw);

//Copy it back to the OS
    memcpy((void *) pBufOut, (void *) &PowerState, dw);

    *pdwActualOut = dw;
    bRet = true;
    break
```

Code snippet is from IOCTL_POWER_SET in Ch33Codesnippets.txt

The fourth IOCTL is a simple one because it is only a dummy. It gets actioned by the driver's "parent" but needs to return only true. It is of more importance for a device on a bus.

8. Implement the fourth IOCTL as follows:

```
case IOCTL_REGISTER_POWER_RELATIONSHIP:
// Notifies the parent device so that the parent device
// can register all the devices that it controls.
    dw = 0;
    pBufOut=NULL;
```

```
    *pdwActualOut = dw;
    bRet = true;
    break;
```

Code snippet is from IOCTL_REGISTER_POWER_RELATIONSHIP in Ch33Codesnippets.txt

9. Configure the project to be included in the OS and built as Debug.

10. Build the device driver and resolve any issues.

11. Build the OS. Place some breakpoints in the IOCTL branches and in `InitPower` and start the OS.

`InitPower` runs during `Init` and the first and fourth IOCTLs run afterward. After a while the OS goes into Idle mode and requests that change of the driver.

12. Perform any task with the OS and see the power state change back to D0. Click Suspend in the Start Menu, leaving the mouse unmoved after clicking. The power state changes when the system is put in Suspend mode; note the changes when the mouse moves again.

13. Create a simple Console subproject with the following code:

Available for download on Wrox.com

```
#include <pm.h>

int _tmain(int argc, TCHAR *argv[], TCHAR *envp[])
{
    CEDEVICE_POWER_STATE State;

    DWORD res = GetDevicePower((LPWSTR)_T("MYD1:"),POWER_NAME,&State);
    RETAILMSG(1,(TEXT("GetDevicePower: MYD_IOControl Power = D%d \n"),(DWORD)State));

    return 0;
}
```

Code snippet is from an application to get the power state from a device in Ch33Codesnippets.txt

This application indirectly actions the `IOCTL_POWER_GET` via the operating system Power Management API.

14. Build the console application and run it to test Power Management functionality.

SUMMARY

This chapter covered how to build a custom stream driver with device context, shared memory, IOCTLs, and Power Management. You were introduced to the CEDriverWiz Project Wizard for creating customized stream drivers and related test applications. The next chapter covers application development and driver testing.

34

Stream Driver API and Device Driver Testing

In the previous few chapters, the focus was on developing the stream driver. This chapter focuses on testing a stream driver using applications that implement the stream API and Platform Builder driver test features.

DEBUGGING OVERVIEW

Having implemented a stream driver and resolved any compile and build issues, the next task is to fully test the driver. This determines that the driver functions correctly, that it can perform under load, and that it is "a good citizen" in the system. If the driver functions correctly, it can load and unload as required and perform all IO functions that it is designed to do. (For the strings buffer example for the driver to perform correctly, it should properly store a string written to it and return the same string when the stream is read from.) A driver should continue to perform correctly when under load. This would be of more significance when the driver implements threads and interrupts or is designed for multiple simultaneous accesses to a stream. The driver must handle all calls to it, and all its interrupts must be captured by the driver and passed up the software stack to applications using the driver. Being a good citizen in the system means that it must not corrupt or degrade the operating system in any way. It must not hog any shared system resources. It must not generate memory leaks.

To test a software entity, you can simply put print statements in the code to report that it gets to certain points in the code and to report values of variables at those points. Although that is simple enough to implement with an application, a driver normally won't have a visible output context to display such messages. They may be captured by a debug window but in general drivers won't have the capability to use stdin, stdout, and stderr that a typical console application can use. Test applications can be used to test the functionality of a device driver as introduced with CEDriverWiz in the previous chapter. This chapter looks at these in more detail. Platform Builder provides a number of macros that can output print messages from a driver (or application) to its Debug window. This chapter examines these macros and other Platform Builder debug tools such as the Remote Tools and Windows Embedded Test Kit (CTK). A number of the test methods covered in this chapter have been touched on in previous chapters. They are covered in more detail in this chapter.

BUILD CONFIGURATIONS

A Compact 7 image can be configured in one of three modes:

➤ Debug

➤ Retail

➤ Checked

Whereas a subproject, whether a driver or a native application, is configured separately and can have Debug mode enabled or disabled. That is, it is possible to have a Retail OS with a debug driver. When the operating system, driver, or application is built in debug mode, software symbols are inserted into the runtime as well as mechanisms to implement breakpoints and evaluate the state of those symbols when breakpoints occur.

There is also the Ship build option for Release mode to remove all debugging from the build. This would be used to implement a build for systems that are to be shipped. To implement this, set the environment variable WINCESHIP *to 1 in the OS properties (where KITL and Kernel Debug are set). This defines the compile time flag* SHIP_BUILD. *This flag can be used to conditionally compile code. If set, the OS does not output debug messages. If not set, the OS implements the debug messaging.*

A Debug build of the operating system has not been optimized, whereas a Retail build has been optimized for speed. A Checked build is a Debug build that has been optimized. Compared to a Retail build, a Debug OS build can take a long time to start up, whereas a checked build can start quicker than a Debug build. The level of support for debugging differs between OS builds, as shown in Table 34-1.

TABLE 34-1: Compact7 OS Build Features

CONFIGURATION	DESCRIPTION
Debug	• Uses `.lib` files from `$(_WINCEROOT)\Public\Common\Oak\Lib\<CPU>\Debug` • Places object files in directories that are named Debug • Uses Microsoft format to provide full symbolic debugging information • Provides the ability to turn debug zones on and off • Does not provide optimization. (Optimization generally makes debugging more difficult.) • Sets the environment variable `WINCEDEBUG=debug`
Release	• Uses `.lib` files from `$(_WINCEROOT%)\Public\Common\Oak\Lib\<CPU>\Retail` • Places object files in directories named Retail • Provides no symbolic debugging information • Optimizes for speed • Has a smaller run-time image than the run-time image that is built from the Debug configuration of the same OS design • Sets the environment variable `WINCEDEBUG=retail`
Checked	• Uses `.lib` files from `$(_WINCEROOT)\Public\Common\Oak\Lib\<CPU>\Checked` • Places object files in directories that are named Checked • Uses Microsoft format to provide full symbolic debugging information • Provides the ability to turn debug zones on and off • Optimizes for speed • Sets the environment variable `WINCEDEBUG=checked`

To debug a driver or native code application with Compact 7, you need to enable KITL and Kernel Debugger. (That is separate to setting Debug OS build.) For driver and application development, it is more efficient to use a Retail Build of the OS and Debug builds of native applications and drivers. If the driver or application doesn't need to be run at startup, then exclude it from the image because the source code can be modified, and it can be rebuilt without stopping the operating system when loaded. If, however, what happens in the operating system just before and/or immediately after a driver is called needs examination, then a Debug (or Checked) build of the OS is needed. Similarly, if it is an operating system driver or the kernel that needs debugging, then a Debug build of the OS is needed.

FIRST SOME SIMPLE CHECKS

After an image has been built that includes a custom driver, you can examine the image file to check that the driver file is in the image and that its registry setting are included. You can check these by opening the image file:

1. Go to Solution Explorer.

2. Right-click on the Operating System Project.

3. Choose Show Built Image.

Three branches show: Boot Registry, Registry, and (All Files).

4. Expand the (All Files) branch, and search for the driver DLL file.

5. When the OS is loading, it runs Boot Manager to load the system OAL. During this phase it has a separate set of registry entries: Boot Registry. You can ignore this for now.

6. Expand the Registry branch and find the driver's registry under `HKLM\Drivers\Builtin` if it is to be loaded at startup, or under `HKLM\Drivers` if not. Check that the correct subkey values are in place for the driver.

If the driver file isn't in the image, check that the driver subproject BIB file is correct, including that it is syntactically correct. If the entries are there, check that the driver should be included in the image. If the registry entries are not included, then check the syntax of the registry file and again check that the driver should be included in the image.

Some of the interim build files in the FlatRelease directory can be useful for determining configuration issues. The Fmerge tool runs once for each parameter file type (BIB, REG, and so on) to create one such file to be built into the image. `Reginit.ini` contains all the merged registry settings. `PBUserProjects.bib` contains all the merged data from BIB files from subprojects. Similarly `PBUserProjects.reg` contains the merged subproject registry entries from subprojects prior to merging with `reginit.ini`.

Hint: Always close the image file when done. Otherwise, the next MakeImage will fail at the end.

BREAKPOINTS

A simple mechanism for examining the functionality of a device driver is to put breakpoints at the start of each function. This can be used to simply check that the stream functions are being called. Also you can step through each function and examine how it performs, after a breakpoint has been reached. To do this though you need Kernel Debug and KITL enabled in the OS and the driver built with Debug enabled. If the OS is built in Debug mode, then you can step out of the driver and examine OS functionality. Also breakpoints can be put in the OS code where that source is available.

You can globally disable and re-enable existing breakpoints at a later stage when required. With Compact 7, Platform Builder breakpoints can have conditions. You can enable these as follows:

1. Create a breakpoint by clicking in the margin next to line for which the breakpoint is required.

2. Right-click the same line, Breakpoint/Breakpoint Properties, and then choose the Condition tab.

3. Enter the required condition.

The condition can be any expression that evaluates to true or false. There are a couple of variables that can be used in the expression:

➤ `$BPHITCOUNT` — Can be used in the expression to make it conditional upon the number of breakpoint hits

➤ $CALLSTACK — Contains ("functionname") which returns true or false if the callstack (functions that have been called to get to this point) contains a certain function

When at a breakpoint you can check the values of variables and structures using Quickwatch or Watch. For entities that are type pointers or structures, you can drill into the values they reference.

DEBUG MACROS

Compact 7 running under Platform Builder supports a raft of debug macros that formalize the insertion of print statements in code for debug purposes, as shown in Table 34-2. They are generally conditional, in that there is a Boolean expression that is evaluated to determine if the output is to occur. Some macros can be globally turned off and on. They are generally also dependent upon the type of operating system build. There are simple "Writeline" style macros such as RETAILMSG and DEBUGMSG. There are also the DEBUGZONE (and RETAILZONE) macros for code location specific messages. There are also assert macros.

TABLE 34-2: Compact 7 Debug Macros

MACRO	OS BUILD MODE	DETAILS
RETAILMSG	Any except Ship	Conditionally outputs to the Debug window in printf format
DEBUGMSG	Debug, Checked	As per RETAILMSG
ERRORMSG	Any except Ship	As per RETAILMSG but message with "ERROR"
DEBUGZONE	Debug	Combined with DEBUGMSG and other macros, can turn debug messages on and off within a certain region (zone) of code (within a function)
ASSERT	Debug and Checked	Evaluates the supplied parameter expression and performs a DebugBreak if false; doesn't require dpCurSettings as used in DEBUGMESSAGEZONES
DEBUGCHK	Debug and Checked	As per ASSERT but requires dpCurSettings
ASSERTMSG	Debug and Checked	As per ASSERT but outputs supplied message as well
RETAILLED	Any except Ship	Conditionally outputs pattern using WriteDebugLED, which is implemented by OEM in NLED driver
DEBUGLED	Debug and Checked	As per RETAILLED

 It is often safest to encapsulate macro parameter expressions in brackets to avoid any unintended consequences in the macro expansion.

Message Macros

The message macros conditionally output a message string using the `printf` C-code format for including the values of variables. Some examples follow:

```
RETAILMSG(1,(_T("MyDriver: Init No. devices: %d\n"),devCount));
DEBUGMSG(1,(_T("MyDriver: Close\n")));
ERRORMSG((devCount== 0),(_T("MyDriver: Init No. devices: %d\n"),devCount));
```

Code snippet is from some Compact 7 debug macro examples

The first always prints, displaying the value of devCount, with all OS builds except Ship. The second prints the string in Debug and Checked builds. The third displays the debug message in all except the Ship build if devCount is zero.

Assert Macros

Whereas the previous message macros conditionally print a message without possibly breaking execution, the assert macros, ASSERT, DEBUGCHK, and ASSERTMSG, output a message and break execution if the condition is true. These are useful for stopping on a major execution error or unexpected condition. Some macro examples follow with the output if devCount is zero:

```
ASSERT(devCount ==0);
Output:
Unknown: DEBUGCHK failed in file C:\WINCE700\MyOS\MyOS\MyDriver\mydriver.cpp at line 32

DEBUGCHK(devCount ==0);
Output:
Unknown: DEBUGCHK failed in file C:\WINCE700\MyOS\MyOS\MyDriver\mydriver.cpp at line 32

ASSERTMSG((_T("Device Count is zero")), (devCount ==0));
Output:
Device Count is zero.
Unknown: DEBUGCHK failed in file C:\WINCE700\MyOS\MyOS\MyDriver\mydriver.cpp at line 32
```

DEBUGCHK is used in driver code where Debug Zones are implemented because they make use of code inclusions with Debug Zones.

Debug Zones

Debug Zones enable debug zones to be turned on and off within a driver function while the operating system runs and the driver loads. When zones are enabled, macros for that zone are inserted as the conditional parameter in DEBUGMSG macro so that the macro is only actioned if the zone is turned on. The DGAPI.h header needs to be included, which implements Debug Zone macros (except DEBUGMSG). Debug Zones are only built for Debug and Checked builds. There is a similar set of macros for Retail builds that work in all except Ship builds.

The following is an example of the code required to implement Debug Zones within a driver's code. CEDriverWiz can generate this when you select the DebugMessageZones option when a stream driver generates.

The required header reference:

```
#include <Dbgapi.h>
```

Code snippet is from header reference code snippet in DebugZonesSnippetst.txt

Mask and Zone defines (can be in the driver header file):

```
#ifdef DEBUG
#define DTAG      _T("MyStream STR: ")
#define DEBUGMASK(bit) (1<<(bit))
#define MASK_ERROR      DEBUGMASK(0)
#define MASK_WARNING    DEBUGMASK(1)
#define MASK_INIT       DEBUGMASK(2)
#define MASK_DEINIT     DEBUGMASK(2)
#define MASK_IO_CALLS   DEBUGMASK(3)
#define MASK_POWER      DEBUGMASK(4)
#define MASK_IOCTLS     DEBUGMASK(5)
#define MASK_INFO       DEBUGMASK(6)
#define MASK_POWER      DEBUGMASK(7)

#define ZONE_ERROR      DEBUGZONE(0)
#define ZONE_WARNING    DEBUGZONE(1)
#define ZONE_INIT       DEBUGZONE(2)
#define ZONE_DEINIT     DEBUGZONE(2)
#define ZONE_IO_CALLS   DEBUGZONE(3)
#define ZONE_POWER      DEBUGZONE(4)
#define ZONE_IOCTLS     DEBUGZONE(5)
#define ZONE_INFO       DEBUGZONE(6)
#define ZONE_POWER      DEBUGZONE(7)
#endif
```

Code snippet is from Mask and zoned defines code snippet in DebugZonesSnippetst.txt

The Debug Zone structure:

```
#ifdef DEBUG
DBGPARAM dpCurSettings = {
    _T("AAAA Driver"),{
            _T("Errors"),_T("Warnings"),_T("Init"),
            _T("Deint"),_T("IO Calls"),_T("Power"),
            _T("IOCTLs"),_T("Info"),_T("Undefined"),
            _T("Undefined"),_T("Undefined"),_T("Undefined"),
            _T("Undefined"),_T("Undefined"),_T("Undefined"),
            _T("Undefined")},
            MASK_INIT | MASK_ERROR  | MASK_WARNING
};
#endif
```

Code snippet is from Debug Zone Structure code snippet in DebugZonesSnippetst.txt

Registering the structure in `DLL_PROCESS_ATTACH` (in bold):

Available for download on Wrox.com

```
BOOL WINAPI
DllEntryPoint(HANDLE hinstDLL,
              DWORD dwReason,
              LPVOID /* lpvReserved */)
{
    switch(dwReason)
    {
    case DLL_PROCESS_ATTACH:
#ifdef DEBUG
        DEBUGREGISTER((HINSTANCE) hinstDLL);
#endif
            break;
```

Code snippet is from registering the structure code snippet in DebugZonesSnippetst.txt

Making use of a Debug Zone in `XXX_Init( )`:

Available for download on Wrox.com

```
DEBUGMSG(ZONE_INIT,(TEXT("MyDriver: MYD_Init %s\n"),pContext));
```

Code snippet is from making use of a Debug Zone code snippet in DebugZonesSnippetst.txt

Turning Debug Zones On and Off

A zone needs to be turned on for its messages to be displayed by default Zones. This can be enabled by configuration, through the IDE, or programmatically.

Enabling Debug Zones Through Configuration

In the example, three zones are configured to be on when the driver is loaded: ZONE_INIT, zone_error, and zone_warning. This is because at the bottom of dpCurSettings is the list of zones to enable:

```
MASK_INIT | MASK_ERROR  | MASK_WARNING
```

Enabling Debug Zones Using Platform Builder

You can also use Platform Builder to turn zones on and off as follows:

1. Create a stream driver subproject with CEDriverWiz with the Debug Zones option checked and in Kernel Mode.

2. Add the driver to your OS and configure it to be included in the image and built in debug mode.

3. Set the OS to be built in debug mode.

4. Build the OS and launch it.

5. In Platform Builder, click the Target menu, and then click CE Debug Zones.

6. When the Debug Zones dialog box finishes initializing the list of loaded libraries, select driver DLL from the list.

7. Enable or disable the active debug zones by selecting them in the Debug Zones list.

8. Click Apply to accept the changes; or click OK to accept the changes and close the dialog box.

Enabling Debug Zones Programmatically

You can also programmatically change the active debug zones in code at any stage by setting `dpCurSettings.ulZoneMask`. For example, if you want to output only power messages, you set the debug mask as follows.

```
dpCurSettings.ulZoneMask = MASK_POWER;
```

Code snippet is from Enabling Debug Zones programmatically code snippet in DebugZonesSnippetst.txt

Target Control

Debug Zones can be examined with the `zo` Target Control command.

USING REMOTE TOOLS

You can use the various Compact 7 Remote tools (refer to Chapter 9, "Debug and Remote Tools") to check on the functionality of a device driver. There is also an API that can facilitate the development of custom tools. Table 34-3 is a summary of the uses of the Remote Tools in driver debugging.

TABLE 34-3: Remote Tool Driver Debugging

REMOTE TOOL	CHECKS
File Viewer	That the loaded image has the driver `DLL in\Windows`.
Registry Editor	That driver registry settings are in the registry as configured. That the driver is loaded by searching for it under `HKLM\Drivers\Active`.
System Information	That the driver is loaded.
Process Viewer	Can examine the processes running on a system. You can drill into the threads and modules loaded by a process with a view to determining under what process a driver (module) is loaded.
Kernel Tracker	Useful to examine threads, events, and other synchronization entities, deadlock, interrupts, and so on.
Performance Monitor	This facilitates looking at performance indicators. You can track such things as kernel time, user time, and memory usage as graphs and tables. Custom metrics can be implemented in code.
Profiler	This facilitates tracking the time function calls take and determines where most of the system time is consumed and can therefore locate bottlenecks.
Resource Leak Detector	Memory leaks.

STREAM DRIVER API AND TEST APPLICATIONS

Test applications to load, unload, and perform IO with a stream driver are useful for debugging a driver, particularly when combined with breakpoints and debug messages. Stream drivers are loaded via the Device Manager, which results in a standard API for implementing loading, unloading, and IO with a stream. As introduced in the previous chapter, CEDriverWiz can generate custom test applications to test a stream driver. This following section looks at the source code for those samples as an example of using the Stream API.

The Stream Driver API

In Chapter 32, "Stream Interface Drivers," and reprised again in Chapter 33, "Developing a Stream Interface Driver," the stream application programming interface (API) functions were mapped to their corresponding stream driver functions (refer to Tables 32-2 and 32-5).

Loading the Stream Driver

If the driver has not been configured to be loaded at startup, then it can be dynamically loaded by an application. The following code snippet assumes that the registry settings required for the driver, `HKLM\Drivers\MyDriver`, are in the registry. The MyDriverLoadUserMode sample application implements the following code snippet after writing the required registry values. `MyDriverLoadDynamic` implements this code without first writing to the registry.

Available for download on Wrox.com

```
//Assumes registry keys exist
TCHAR szDevKey[]  = _T("Drivers\\MyDriver");

TCHAR szDefaultString[] = _T("A message");
REGINI RegIniData[] = { _T("DefaultString"),
    (LPBYTE)szDefaultString,
    sizeof(szDefaultString),
    REG_SZ };

//Load the driver
HANDLE hStr = ActivateDeviceEx( szDevKey, RegIniData, 1, NULL );

//Check the result
if (hStr == ((HANDLE)0))  //-1 0rev
{
    RETAILMSG(1,(_T("MyDriver MYDx: Load failed")));
    return (int) hStr;
}
else
{
    RETAILMSG(1,(_T("MyDriver MYDx: Loaded OK")));
}

return 0;
```

Code snippet is from loading a stream driver as in the MyDriver test application
MyDriverLoadApp (mydriverloadapp.cpp)

Unloading the Stream Driver

The following code opens the stream, gets the required device information, and then closes the stream using it.

```
//Need a handle to the driver to get its device information
HANDLE hStr = CreateFile( _T("MYD1:"),
                               GENERIC_READ | GENERIC_WRITE,
                               0,
                               NULL,
                               OPEN_EXISTING,
                               0,
                               0);

//Get the device information
DEVMGR_DEVICE_INFORMATION DeviceInfo =
                          { sizeof(DEVMGR_DEVICE_INFORMATION) };
GetDeviceInformationByFileHandle( hStr, &DeviceInfo );

// Be sure to close the file handle before we unload the driver!
CloseHandle( hStr );

//Unload the driver
DeactivateDevice( DeviceInfo.hDevice );
```

Code snippet is from unloading a stream driver as in the MyDriver test application MyDriverUnloadApp (mydriverunloadapp.cpp)

Opening and Closing a Stream

The driver needs to be loaded before opening the stream.

```
//Open the stream
HANDLE hStr = CreateFile(_T("MYD1:"), GENERIC_READ | GENERIC_WRITE,
     0, NULL, OPEN_EXISTING, 0, 0);

if (hStr == (HANDLE)-1)
    RETAILMSG(1, (_T("MyDriverApp: Cannot open MYD1:")));
    return (int)hStr;
}
//Stream opened
RETAILMSG(1, (_T("MyDriverApp: Openned MYD1:")));

// Close the driver stream.
CloseHandle(hStr);
```

Code snippet is from opening and closing a stream driver as in the MyDriver test application MyDriverApp (mydriverapp.cpp)

Writing and Reading with a Stream

You need to open the stream before writing and reading, and close the stream afterward.

Available for
download on
Wrox.com

```
//Write a string to the driver.
DWORD dwWritten;
TCHAR * pString =
_T("This is a test of the MyDriver Driver. This is only a test.");
WriteFile(hStr, pString, (_tcslen(pString)) * sizeof(TCHAR), &dwWritten, NULL);

// Read string from driver.
WCHAR wch[256];
DWORD dwBytesRead;
BOOL rs = ReadFile(hStr, wch, dwWritten, &dwBytesRead, NULL);

if (rs)
{
    RETAILMSG(1, (_T("MyDriverApp: Read OK")));
    if (dwWritten==dwBytesRead)
        {
RETAILMSG(1, (
_T("MyDriverApp: (OK) Num bytes read = num written. %d"),dwBytesRead ));
    }
        else
        {
RETAILMSG(1,
(_T("MyDriverApp: (Problem) Num bytes read %d != num written %d." )
                    ,dwBytesRead, dwWritten));
    }
}
else
{
    RETAILMSG(1, (_T("MyDriverApp: Read Failed")));
}
```

*Code snippet is from opening and closing a stream driver as in the
MyDriver test application MyDriverApp (mydriverapp.cpp) driver.*

Stream IOCTls

The same stream handle that was returned when the stream was opened and used for stream reads
and writes is used in a stream IOCTL call. The code that follows calls IOCTL number 1024. It is only
a simple call to the IOCTL. A more complex call would implement a call that requires a return value.

Available for
download on
Wrox.com

```
DWORD dw;
IOCTLNO = 1024;
BOOL successIOCTL = DeviceIoControl(hStr,IOCTLNO ,NULL,0,NULL, 0,&dw,NULL);
if (!successIOCTL)
{
    RETAILMSG(1,(_T("TestIOCTLsApp: IOCTL error IOCTL No: %d"), IOCTLNO));
}
else
{
    RETAILMSG(1,(_T("TestIOCTLsApp: IOCTL success IOCTLNo: %d"), IOCTLNO));
}
```

*Code snippet is from calling a stream driver IOCTL as in the MyDriver test
application MyDriverTestIOCTLSApp (mydrivertestIOCTLSapp.cpp) code*

WINDOWS EMBEDDED TEST KIT (CTK)

Windows Embedded Compact Test Kit (CTK) (formerly called CETK) is a tool for testing the functionality and performance of drivers in a formal manner. It facilitates much deeper testing of a driver and is a must for any driver that is to be shipped. CTK can help you build and manage large test suites for regression and stress testing. Instead of adding a console application to your OS design and running that application on the target device, you add a test DLL to your OS design that is called by the CTK.

Creating Your Test DLL for the CTK

Creating a test DLL for the CTK is similar to creating a console application; both are subprojects of your OS design.

To create a CTK test DLL, follow these steps:

1. Open your previously created OS design in Visual Studio.

2. In the Solution Explorer window, right-click the Subprojects folder, and then click Add New Subproject from the shortcut menu.

3. In the Subproject Wizard window, select WCE TUX Dynamic-Link Library from the available templates list.

4. In the Subproject name field, type `MyDriverTUXTest` for your test application, and then click Next.

5. Click Finish.

Your new subproject MyDriverTUXTest appears under the Subprojects folder in Solution Explorer.

If you expand the subproject node, you find the Source files folder. The folder contains three files: `MyDriverTUXTest.cpp`, `Globals.cpp`, and `Test.cpp`. Your test must be added to `Test.cpp`, which contains the following code.

```
#include "main.h"
#include "globals.h"
TESTPROCAPI TestProc(UINT uMsg, TPPARAM tpParam, LPFUNCTION_TABLE_ENTRY lpFTE)
{
    // The shell doesn't necessarily want us to execute the test.
    // Make sure first.
    if(uMsg != TPM_EXECUTE)
    {
        return TPR_NOT_HANDLED;
    }
    // TODO: Replace the following line with your own test code here.
    // Also, change the return value from TPR_SKIP to the appropriate
    // code.
    g_pKato->Log(LOG_COMMENT, TEXT("This test is not yet implemented."));
    return TPR_SKIP;
}
```

Modify the `Test.cpp` file to include calls to `ActivateDeviceEx`, `CreateFile`, `CloseHandle`, and `DeactivateDevice`, just as you did in the driver test applications. You can then add any additional calls specifically required for testing the driver, such as `WriteFile`, `ReadFile`, and `DeviceIoControl`. For example, in the `Test.cpp` file, replace the code lines after the TODO comment with the following code.

```cpp
g_pKato->Log(LOG_COMMENT, TEXT("Stream driver TUX test starting"));
HANDLE hActiveDriver = NULL;
HANDLE hDriver = NULL;
bool bReturn = false;

//Load the driver
hActiveDriver = ActivateDeviceEx(_T("\\Drivers\\MyDriver"), NULL, 0, NULL);
if (hActiveDriver == INVALID_HANDLE_VALUE)
{
    g_pKato->Log(LOG_COMMENT, TEXT("Unable to load stream driver."));
    return TPR_FAIL;
}

// Open the driver
hDriver = CreateFile (_T("MYD1:"),
    GENERIC_READ| GENERIC_WRITE,FILE_SHARE_READ | FILE_SHARE_WRITE,NULL,OPEN_EXISTING,
    FILE_ATTRIBUTE_NORMAL,NULL);
if (hDriver == INVALID_HANDLE_VALUE)
{
    g_pKato->Log(LOG_COMMENT, TEXT("Unable to open stream driver."));
    return TPR_FAIL;
}

// Add test code here
// . . . .
// . . . .
// Close the driver
if (hDriver != INVALID_HANDLE_VALUE)
{
    bReturn = CloseHandle(hDriver);
    if (bReturn == FALSE)
    {
        g_pKato->Log(LOG_COMMENT, TEXT("Unable to close stream driver."));
    }
}
// Ask the Device Manager to unload the driver
if (hActiveDriver != INVALID_HANDLE_VALUE)
{
    bReturn = DeactivateDevice(hActiveDriver);
    if (bReturn == FALSE)
    {
        g_pKato->Log(LOG_COMMENT, TEXT("Unable to unload stream driver."));
    }
}
return TPR_PASS;
```

Code snippet is from CETK TUX driver test with MyDriver stream driver in CTK.txt

To build the new project `MyDriverTUXTest`, right-click the subproject in Solution Explorer, and then click Build.

Adding Your Test DLL to the CTK

After you successfully build your test DLL, you can then add it to the CTK.

To Add a Test DLL to the CTK

1. Open the Start menu, and run the Windows Embedded Compact Test Kit.

2. In the Getting Started pane, select Create a Custom Test Pass Template.

3. On the Test Pass Templates tab, select the My Templates node, and then click New.

4. Rename the new template `MyDriverTestTemplate`, and then click Done.

5. In the Getting Started pane, select Create a Custom Test Case.

6. Click the New Category button, and then rename the new category **My Category**.

7. Click the New Test button, and then rename the new test **MyDeviceDriverTest**.

8. Verify that the value for Category is My Category.

9. In the Run type list, select Fully Automated.

10. In the Test harness list, select Tux.

11. In the Supported architectures list box, select x86 (Device), which opens the Add/Remove Test Files dialog box.

12. Click Browse, navigate to the `MyDriverTUXTest.dll` file, select it, and then click OK.

13. On the Test Case Information tab, click Save, and then click Done.

Running Your Test from Within the CTK

To execute your DLL test from within the CTK, you must have an active device connection available. Before getting started with the next steps, ensure that you have:

➤ A complete build of your OS image

➤ Loaded your runtime image on your target device

After your debugging session is established, you are ready to run your test from the CTK.

To run your test from within the CTK:

1. Open the Start menu, and then run the Windows Embedded Compact Test Kit (CTK).

2. In the Getting Started pane, select Connect to Device.

3. When the Select a Device dialog box appears, under the Platform Builder node, select the name of your device, and then click OK.

    ➤ The Connecting to Device dialog box appears briefly while the CTK attempts to establish a connection.

4. On the CTK toolbar, click Remove Test Pass from Selected Connection.

> ➤ For development purposes, it is only necessary to include a single test as part of the test pass.

5. In the Test Case Explorer pane, select the Test Case Explorer tab.

6. Expand the My Category node that you created in step 6 of "Adding Your Test DLL to the CTK."

7. Right-click `MyDeviceDriverTest`, and then click Add to Current Test Pass from the shortcut menu.

> ➤ You must now have a single test selected for your test run.

8. To save your test pass, click the File menu, and then click Save.

9. On the CTK toolbar, click Run Test Pass.

OTHER COMPACT 7 DEBUGGING FEATURES

Some of the other debug features that can assist with driver (and operating system) development are:

➤ Target Control

➤ CeDebugX

➤ eXDI

Target Control

Target Control is a service that is interacted with via a command shell. In Platform Builder, this is via Target Menu/Target Control. On the device at a command shell, you can also enter Target Control commands, which are summarized in Table 34-4.

TABLE 34-4: Target Control Commands

COMMAND	DESCRIPTION
dd	Displays memory values
df	Displays memory values but to a file
gi	Gets information on processes or processes with threads; modules; critical sections that have threads waiting; and events
kp	Kills a process
log	Interacts with CeLog Event Tracking subsystem
mi	Gets kernel information
prof	Controls the kernel profiler if included
zo	Performs debugging zone operations

CEDEBUGX

CeDebugX is a newer feature in Compact 7 and is an extension to the PB debugger. When the operating system is at a breakpoint, it can be used to examine things such as threads, processes, modules, synchronization objects, heaps, GDI objects, windows, message queues, and other objects through the Target Control Window. It is particularly useful for examining a crash, hang, or deadlock. Table 34-5 shows the main commands.

TABLE 34-5: CeDebugX Commands

COMMAND	DESCRIPTION
!help	Lists all available commands.
!refresh	Synchronizes the extension with the current state of the system. This command must be invoked after every run/break cycle or any time the state of the system changes.
!diagnose	Performs an automatic diagnosis of all crashes or hangs present in the current state at break time.
!xml	Logs positive diagnoses and detailed system information in an XML file and displays the formatted data in a browser window.

An example of a command is

```
!diagnose all
```

that runs through all available diagnostic procedures to diagnose a failure of unknown type.

eXDI

eXDI enables hardware-assisted debugging, which relies on a technology called JTAG (from Joined Test Action Group, the specification committee). JTAG is an electronic circuitry integrated in modern CPUs that enables an external device to read or write CPU inputs and outputs through a serial line. Using the serial JTAG port, you can interact directly with the CPU by sending instructions and reading the results without the help of BUS and RAM. JTAG gives you full control on the computer, it is less invasive than software debuggers, and it requires no special software on the device. In return, JTAG input and output is fully dedicated to a specific CPU, and chip makers or tool editors often choose to develop dedicated real-time controllers called JTAG Probes to perform the low-level serial communication task. The communication protocol between the development workstation and the JTAG Probe is proprietary and is implemented in a special Platform Builder plug-in called eXDI. When you use hardware debugging with Windows Compact, you need to acquire a JTAG Probe and install the corresponding eXDI plug-in on Platform Builder. Hardware-assisted debugging offers the same services as the standard Kdstub kernel debugger. Platform Builder requires access to the image file, nk.bin, and can make use of files in the FlatRelease directory.

SUMMARY

Driver testing is a necessary phase of driver development. It is important for establishing that the driver is correctly configured, that it functions correctly, that it is robust, and that it doesn't corrupt the operating system. You can use a wide range of tools to test a stream driver, starting with simple checks, through debug messaging and test applications to the CTK. All have a place in any driver developer's toolbox.

35

The Target System

WHAT'S IN THIS CHAPTER?

➤   Understanding the Board Support Package (BSP)

➤   Examining bootloaders

➤   Understanding the OEM Adaptation Layer (OAL)

➤   Using the Kernel Independent Transport Layer (KITL)

In Chapter 6 the BSP was introduced, Chapter 26 introduced the bootloader, and Chapter 27 covered the BIOS bootloader. This chapter takes a deeper look at the BSP and its components, the bootloader, OAL, and KITL. A custom OAL IOCTL is implemented.

BSP OVERVIEW

A Windows Embedded Compact 7 target system requires a Board Support Package (BSP) to develop and run the operating system. For a shipped system, it enables the system to boot and run in terms of the specific hardware that the target has. For development it supports additional features such as the download and debugging of an operating system image. Although the Platform Builder installed base of Compact 7 supports a range of CPUs and devices, a BSP can support target board-specific components and configurations.

A Compact 7 target system will have as its core a CPU that is either a MIPS (MIPS II and MIPS II Floating Point), an ARM (v5, v6, v6 MP, or v7), or an x86 (32 bit and 64 bit). Compact 7 is the first OS in the Embedded Compact/CE series to also support multicore CPUs, and if this to be used, then the BSP has to implement it. A CPU requires a chipset to handle interrupts and other things such as Input/Output (IO). Compact 7 also has a requirement that the target system have a Memory Management Unit (MMU). This enables the operating system to map memory mapped components (such as RAM and non-serial ROM) into its virtual address space (which is what it uses once booted) in a disjointed manner with respect to their actual physical memory address space. Although Windows Embedded CE 6 supported 4G virtual address, it supported only 512M of actual RAM. Compact 7 supports up to slightly less than 4G of RAM. A Compact 7 may have a display component or it can exist without one (headless). For development purposes, the system also needs a peripheral such as a network adapter, serial port, or USB for downloading and debugging an operating system.

A Compact 7 Operating System image is a single file that has been built for the target hardware making use of the BSP (typically called `nk.bin`). This image file may be in ROM or storage on the device or need to be downloaded. It is the job of the board's bootloader to load that image into RAM. It is then the job of the BSP components in the image to interface between the hardware and the operating system.

In this chapter you examine the key components of a BSP.

SOME COMPACT 7 TARGET BOARDS

Many embedded systems are implemented as a SOC or SOM. A SOC is a System on a Chip where the CPU and most of the chipset for the CPU are all on the same substrate. (See Figure 31-5 for an example of a SOC.) A board that uses a SOC can be a lot smaller than one that is not. A SOM is a System on a Module. It implements the main parts of a Single Board Computer (SBC) on a smaller board, which then plugs into a board that implements the I/O connectivity. SOMs simplify system development further because only the I/O has to be implemented.

Some representative examples of some Compact 7 target systems are shown in Figure 35-1 through Figure 35-3. They are in order:

➤ The ICOP VDX-6328D (Vortex SOC: x86) Board

➤ The Phytec phyCore-LPC3250 (ARM9) SOM Board

➤ The BeagleBoard (Texas Instruments OMAP3530 SOC (ARM-7))

FIGURE 35-1

FIGURE 35-2

FIGURE 35-3

BSP COMPONENTS

A BSP can consist of a bootloader, the OEM Adaptation Layer (OAL), board-specific device drivers, configuration files, and the kernel-independent transport layer (KITL), as shown in Figure 35-4. The bootloader is responsible for getting the OS image loaded into RAM and calling the OAL to start. The OAL is the general interface between the OS and the hardware after the OS is loaded into RAM. The device drivers are for the board components, and the KITL enables the debugging of the OS when it is being developed. The configuration files are board specifications (for example, RAM size and location) and batch files, which are used in building the OS image.

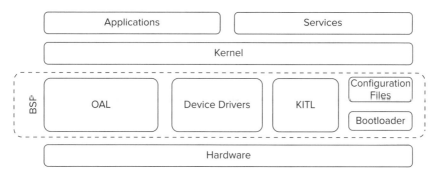

FIGURE 35-4

A BSP is board-specific. Although it can have many aspects that are common to other systems using the same CPU, a BSP has to be configured and built specifically for the target system. It is also OS version–specific in that a CE 5 BSP required a lot of upgrading to work in CE 6. Modifications may also be needed to make a CE 6 BSP work with Compact 7. (Although far less is required than for CE 5 to 6.) Also, if you have only the binary (built) version of the BSP and therefore lack access to the BSP source code, you can't port a Windows Embedded CE BSP to Compact 7.

Porting a BSP to Compact 7 and developing a new BSP is beyond the scope of this book. For further information on these processes see the "Windows Embedded Compact 7 White Papers" at www.microsoft.com/windowsembedded/en-us/develop/windows-embedded-compact-7-white-papers.aspx.

SDKs and BSPs

A board Software Development Kit (SDK) is not a BSP. A Windows Embedded CE/Compact development board or consumer product comes with a built-in Windows Embedded CE/Compact image. An SDK is supplied, which enables application development for the device but that won't facilitate the building of a new OS image. For example, with Windows Mobile/Windows Phone, you can get only an SDK, not a BSP. If the image has an installer and if its security settings permit, then you might install third-party devices or even develop them as native code. But you can't use any Windows Embedded CE/Compact Operating features from the Platform Builder Catalog. You can't build a new OS image for a Windows Mobile/Phone device in Platform Builder. Only the Mobile/Phone OEMS have access to those BSPs.

BSP Folders

Each BSP is located as a separate folder under $(_WINCEROOT)\platform. If you clone a BSP, this can create a duplicated folder there. If a new BSP is installed, it will be placed there, even though it appears under Third Party in the Catalog. It is desirable that code used by all BSPs be as common as possible. This common code is located under $(_WINCEROOT)\platform\common. There is code under this folder that is common to BSPs for the same CPU or SOC and code that is common to all BSPs. Compact 7 also has the $(_WINCEROOT)\platform\BSP Template folder, which has some source code and guidance for developing a new BSP. BSP folder structure is discussed in detail in a later section.

BOOTLOADER

When a microprocessor does a cold start (when it is first powered up) it is in an unknown state. It therefore starts executing from a specific memory address or loads a memory address to start from, from a specific address in memory. With both cases there is a ROM in those start locations that has a basic input/output program (BIOS) that initializes the system and starts it running. If the required code for the system is small and can fit into the same ROM, then the system continues to run that code until shutdown. If an OS is to be loaded, then this startup program can run until it has initialized the system as required by the OS, it has loaded the OS into RAM, and it has called the OS to start. The loading into RAM of the OS is required because a typical OS won't fit into a memory addressable ROM but can be stored in media such as serial ROM, storage such as a hard disk, or accessed as a network download.

With Windows Embedded Compact and other embedded OSs, there is a bootloader responsible for starting the OS as previously described. Some may do it in a two or more step manner because the initial startup program is too small or because the startup program on the target system is general purpose. For example, the CEPC-loadcepc startup process first boots to DOS via BIOS and runs loadcepc, which loads and starts the boot manager Eboot. Eboot downloads and starts up a Compact 7 CEPC image. Many OEM Compact 7 development systems have a startup program specific to the development system that can directly load and start an image from ROM or from a download. The new Virtual PC BSP implements this functionality and therefore runs the BIOS bootloader at startup after prompting for boot options.

The job of the bootloader therefore is at startup to initialize the system hardware enough so it can copy the OS image into memory and call the operating system to start. The operating system then calls back through the OAL to continue the OS configuration and startup. Bootloaders are BSP- or board-specific. As discussed in Chapter 26, "Bootloader," Platform Builder provides a number of out-of-the-box bootloaders that you can use to start a Compact 7 OS.

The main steps of the boot sequence with the bootloader follow:

1. When the system is powered on or reset, execution begins at the bootloader's entry point. This code performs minimal hardware initialization.

2. The bootloader initializes the serial debug output and also initializes the download transport (such as Ethernet) that downloads the runtime OS image onto the device. The runtime image is typically called `nk.bin` or `nk.nb0` (if in ROM).

3. The bootloader downloads the runtime OS image onto the device. It might store the runtime image in RAM or in nonvolatile storage, such as flash memory.

4. The bootloader locates the entry point of the runtime OS image, as specified by the last record of `nk.bin` or `nk.nb0`, and jumps to that address.

5. OAL takes over.

6. Eventually the kernel is started, which then calls back into the OAL to finish the OS boot.

The older bootloader is BLCommon, whereas the newer one is CE Boot in Compact 7. The DOS-loadcepc mechanism uses the older style bootloader, whereas the BIOS bootloader (Chapter 27) as used in the Compact 7 VPC uses CE Boot. CE Boot is preferred for newer systems because code reuse is far greater, making implementation far easier. It provides a set of libraries that implement most of the bootloader features, requiring development of only the platform-specific code. The CE Boot Framework is shown in Figure 35-5.

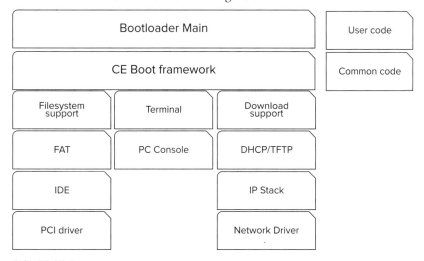

FIGURE 35-5

The bootloader typically emits some debug messages during its phase. These are typically sent over a serial port and allow some user input for such things as:

➤ Image source (Ethernet, Local, Serial, USB, and so on) .

➤ Network configuration (DHCP or Static IP, and so on)

➤ Display settings

➤ KITL and Debug settings

Figure 35-6 shows the bootloader options for the Compact 7 VPC.

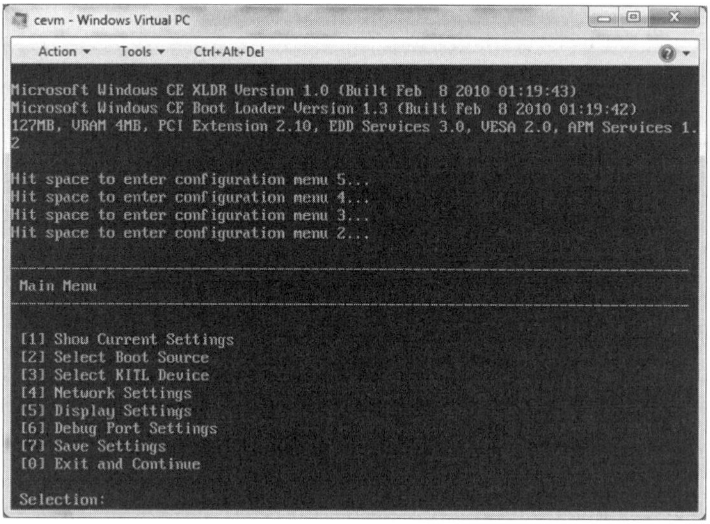

FIGURE 35-6

The bootloader sample code for each supported BSP is located in $(_WINCEROOT)\Platform\ <BSP>\Src\Bootloader. Note that in the VPC BSP there are two bootloaders.

XLDR

As mentioned previously, sometimes system constraints prevent the loading of the complete bootloader in one step. A further example of such a constraint is where the CPU has a small amount of internal RAM that can be used immediately but has a larger amount of external RAM for which the CPU buses must be initialized before it can be used. XLDR is a lighter weight loader that can load eboot in two stages. The Compact 7 VPC BIOS bootloader actually uses this mechanism. XLDR initializes the external RAM interface and loads the main bootloader into it.

OAL

The kernel provides the base OS functionality for any Windows Embedded Compact based device. This functionality includes process, thread, and memory management. The kernel also provides some file management functionality. Kernel services enable applications to use this core functionality. The kernel binaries, as installed with Platform Builder, are CPU-specific. The BSP, through the OAL, enables the CPU kernel binary to be used by the specific target board. The kernel, through the OAL, can access hardware components that it needs, such as interrupts, timers, IOCTLs, and so on, as shown in Figure 35-7.

In CE 5, the kernel was a single binary with a different version that existed depending upon whether KITL and profiling were required. The kernel library (`kernel.lib`) was statically linked to the BSP's OAL when the OS was built. Starting with CE 6, the kernel is dynamically linked at startup to the OAL, so only its DLL needs to be included in the image. There are three binaries: `oal.exe`, `kernel.dll`, and `kitl.dll` (refer to Figure 35-7). KITL is an optional component of the OS for development purposes.

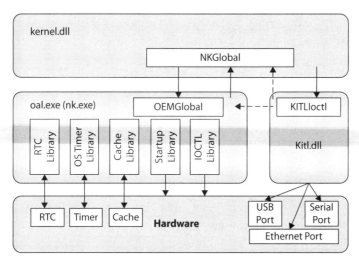

Not all OAL libraries are shown

FIGURE 35-7

Continuing the boot sequence at step 5 (as in the "Bootloader" section):

5. The OAL puts the CPU in a known state, initializes hardware, and initializes the kernel's global variables.

6. The OAL locates the entry point of the kernel by using a table of contents and jumps to that address.

7. The kernel calls various OAL functions to perform initializations, including those described here:

> ➤ The kernel exchanges global pointers with the OAL. From this point on, the kernel has access to all functions and variables defined by the OAL in the OEMGLOBAL structure, and the OAL has access to all functions and variables defined by the kernel in the NKGLOBAL structure.

> ➤ The OAL initializes the debug serial port on the device by using a process similar to the bootloader's debug serial port initialization process.

> ➤ The OAL initializes the rest of the hardware interfaces on the device.

> ➤ The OAL initializes and starts the KITL subsystem if KITL is used.

8. The kernel completes its initialization tasks.

9. The kernel starts executing its first thread.

There are many required functions in the OAL that the kernel needs to invoke. Some of them are listed in Table 35-1.

TABLE 35-1: Some of the Required x86 OAL Functions

PROGRAMMING FUNCTION	DESCRIPTION
OEMGetRealTime	Retrieves the time from the real-time clock (RTC)
OEMGetTickCount	Retrieves the number of milliseconds that have elapsed since Windows Embedded Compact started
OEMIdle	Places the CPU in the idle state when there are no threads ready to run
OEMInit	Initializes all hardware interfaces for the device
OEMInterruptDisable	Disables the specified hardware interrupt
OEMInterruptDone	Signals completion of interrupt processing
OEMInterruptEnable	Performs hardware operations necessary to enable the specified hardware interrupt
OEMInterruptMask	Masks or unmasks the interrupt according to its system interrupt (SYSINTR) value
OEMInitDebugSerial	Initializes the debug serial port on the device
OEMIoControl	Provides a generic I/O control code (IOCTL) for OEM-supplied information
OEMPowerOff	Is invoked when the user presses the OFF button or the Graphics, Windowing, and Events Subsystem (GWES) times out on its power-down timer
OEMSetAlarmTime	Sets the real-time clock alarm
OEMSetRealTime	Sets the real-time clock
OEMWriteDebugByte	Writes a byte to the debug monitor port
OEMWriteDebugString	Writes a string to the debug monitor port

Through OEMIoControl, the kernel needs to action OAL IOCTLs. As a sample, the power management IOCTLs follow:

➤   IOCTL_HAL_DISABLE_WAKE

➤   IOCTL_HAL_ENABLE_WAKE

➤ `IOCTL_HAL_GET_POWER_DISPOSITION`

➤ `IOCTL_HAL_GET_WAKE_SOURCE`

➤ `IOCTL_HAL_PRESUSPEND`

➤ `IOCTL_HAL_REBOOT`

Custom IOCTLs can also be added to the OAL, as demonstrated in a later section.

KITL

The kernel independent transport layer (KITL) provides a transport layer for the board under development to communicate with the Platform Builder on the development system. It is used by many Platform Builder tools such as kernel debugger, remote tools, debug message service, Target Control, remote file system (RELFSD), and so on. The Platform Builder debugger requires KITL to communicate with a target system. The target system needs to be configured and built for KITL. KITL can use a number of transports:

➤ Ethernet (most common)

➤ USB RNDIS

➤ Serial

➤ Custom

The two main functions for KITL are shown in Table 35-2.

TABLE 35-2: The Main KITL Functions

FUNCTION	DESCRIPTION
OEMKitlInit	Fills the `KITLTRANSPORT` structure with appropriate function pointers.
OEMKitlIoctl	Handles platform-specific KITL I/O control calls.

KITL is a separate component in the BSP from OAL. It can be removed from an image, especially one to be shipped. Common KITL code is located in:

`$(_WINCEROOT)\platform\common\src\common\Kitl`

When KITL and Kernel Debug are enabled, you can step through native code applications and drivers if they are built in Debug mode (but not through managed code). If the Release Directory File System (RELFSD) Catalog component (located under Storage Manager) is included in the operating system, applications and drivers not included in the image can be modified and rebuilt without stopping the operating system. RELFSD refers to the Release Directory, so any application and drivers in there that are refreshed or added are available to be run from the Target Control or Target/Run Programs. Make sure applications are exited and drivers are unloaded before refreshing (rebuilding them). There is also the KITL setting Enable Access to Desktop Files, on the Core Service Setting tabs of Target Device Connectivity Options, which must be set to enable the RELFSD functionality.

VMINI

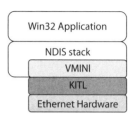

If a board has only one network connection and its Compact 7 OS is being developed using KITL over that network, then if KITL is the only function of the network card, the target system cannot test the system's network functionality. For example, Internet Explorer can't access the Internet. VMINI is a virtual NDIS miniport that uses KITL over Ethernet to enable Win32 applications to access the network when KITL over Ethernet is enabled, as shown in Figure 35-8.

FIGURE 35-8

VMINI requires a wired network adapter and can be configured to use a static IP or to use DHCP as follows:

```
; Enable static IP address for VMINI1
[HKEY_LOCAL_MACHINE\Comm\VMINI1\Parms\Tcpip]
    "EnableDHCP"=dword:0 ; Enable/Disable the DHCP
    "IPAddress"="192.168.1.3"
    "SubnetMask"="255.255.255.0"
```

VMINI, being a part of KITL, can therefore be a part of the BSP. You can remove the VMINI shared Ethernet library by setting IMGNOSHAREETH and BSP_NOSHAREETH to 1 (OS Property Pages/Environment Tab). Also, if network KITL is not enabled for an OS, then VMINI isn't available. In this case the network adapter can be used by the OS as part of the product, but it can still be used for an OS download. A development system that has two network adapters can be configured to use one for download and debugging and the other as the product Ethernet.

BSP CONFIGURATION FILES AND FOLDERS

In building a BSP a number of configuration and batch files are used. In Solution Explorer you see two folders, Parameter Files and src, in the BSP's folder under the platform tree. The Parameter Files configure the BSP build, as shown in Table 35-3.

TABLE 35-3: BSP Parameter Files

FILE	PURPOSE
config.bib	The memory configuration of the board.
platform.bib	BIB settings for all components of the BSP. Typically some components of the BSP are optional, so their BIB settings are conditional so that only the selected options are included in the image.
platform.dat	Not used.
platform.db	Not used.
platform.reg	Registry settings for all components of the BSP. Typically some components of the BSP are optional, so their registry settings are conditional.

FILE	PURPOSE
`sources.cmn`	Starting point of the BSP build process. All source files in directories below it in the BSP are dependent upon it. Provides include directories and libraries to link.
`<bsp>.bat`	BSP environment variables to use in the build process. In particular it specifies devices in the BSP that can be included in the build. (`<bsp>` is the name of the BSP.)

Expanding the src folder of a BSP in Solution Folder, you see the following folders, as shown in Table 35-4. (There may be some BSP-specific folders as well.)

TABLE 35-4: BSP Folders in Solution Explorer

BSP FOLDER (IN SOLUTION EXPLORER)	PURPOSE
`inc`	Contains header files.
`boot`	Bootloader build directory.
`bootloader`	Networked Bootloader build directory.
`common`	Contains code common to different components of the BSP. Typically contains code common to the Bootloader and OAL.
`drivers`	Contains BSP specific drivers.
`KITL`	KITL build directory.
`oal`	OAL build directory.

From the File Explorer view of a BSP, you see the following folders, as shown in Table 35-5.

TABLE 35-5: BSP Folder in File Explorer

BSP FOLDER (IN FILE EXPLORER)	PURPOSE
`CATALOG`	Contains the BSP's catalog file
`CESYSGEN`	Contains the BSP makefile
`FILES`	Contains most of the platform and driver's parameters files, plus some locality strings relevant to the BSP
`src`	Contains the files needed for building the BSP

When the Platform Builder is loaded or when the Catalog is refreshed, all BSP Catalog directories are accessed to refresh the BSPs listed in the catalog. A BSP Catalog file may include optional subitems. For example, eBox3300MX has a broad range of optional components, as shown in Figure 35-9. The network adapter is not an option. The Virtual PC requires a choice between two keyboards, which are determined by the version of VPC being used. To get application network access with the VPC, the network adapter has to be selected, and the VPC networking has to be configured.

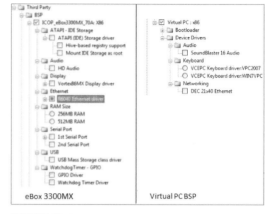

FIGURE 35-9

Drilling into the `src` directory via File Explorer, you see `dirs` and `sources` files. These are used to recursively build the BSP as per the normal Platform Builder build process. During the build, use is also made of the `$(_WINCEROOT)\platform\common\src\inc` directory for common OAL and some USB header files. These are the interfaces that the kernel uses to call the OAL and are implemented as board- or CPU-specific code. BSP source code that is generic to the BSP's CPU is located in the CPU directory below the platform common `src` directory.

For development, only the Catalog and Files directory folders are required. When a binary-only version of a BSP is obtained, this is what is supplied. The other two folders (CESYGEN and src) are needed only if the BSP is to be modified, as when porting to a later version of the OS, or if there is a bug in the BSP functionality that requires stepping through BSP source code.

DEVICE DRIVERS

The device drivers that would be a part of the BSP are those that are integral to the board, plus those for devices normally supplied with the board. The device drivers integral to the board would be the required drivers for SOC peripherals and any other devices implemented on the board. Some of these would be optional, which would be reflected in the BSP's catalog file. The BSP components have their SYSGEN listed in the `<bsp>.bat` file. Any other devices that may be supplied with the system could have their driver shipped with the BSP. For example, if the board OEM ships a certain touch screen with the board, then its display and touch drivers would be an option in the BSP catalog file.

Browsing through the BSP driver folders, you can find drivers such as network, ehci (USB), keyboard, mouse, and audio drivers.

Any BSP-specific driver build folders are located in the drivers subfolder of the BSP's `src` folder. For example, the VPC BSP drivers folder has mouse, keyboard, network, and sound driver folders. Other platform independent drivers are located in `$(_WINCEROOT)public\common\oak\drivers` folders.

DEVELOPING A BSP

This section outlines some of the issues with developing a new BSP from an existing one. The "White Papers" referred to at the start of this chapter provide details for BSP development and porting.

Developing a new BSP is generally not a simple task. To do so requires a lot of background knowledge and experience with Windows Embedded Compact. A simpler task is to adapt an existing BSP for a similar target by cloning it, implementing the bootloader and OAL, customizing the configuration, and adding any new drivers or replacing any that are different.

Cloning a BSP

As covered previously, a BSP for a board that has the same CPU and similar components can be cloned. This creates a new folder under the platform folder for the new BSP. Only modify code under this copied folder. Do not modify any other code because this can break other aspects of Platform Builder. Cloning a BSP was covered in Chapter 6.

Implement Bootloader and OAL

If the new target hardware is similar to the existing BSP's hardware, then the same bootloader might work. If this is not sufficient, the bootloader code might (hopefully) need only some small reconfiguration and rebuilding. You do, however, need to get this working first. If the task requires a major effort, then the bootloader architecture CE Boot might be a better option.

Customize Configuration

Customize the memory configuration, interrupts, any GPIO, peripherals, and system initialization requirements.

Add Drivers

Add the drivers that are new, and remove ones that are not relevant. For example, the PCMCIA driver is no longer supported. Initially, add only those that are absolutely necessary. You may have to port the existing driver projects to Compact 7.

Testing

Once the bootloader is working with the new target system, an operating system project for it can be attempted. It is probably best to start with the simplest OS template, such as the Small Footprint Device Design Template and build up from there.

ADDING AN IOCTL TO THE OAL

In this activity, you add a new IOCTL and its handler inside the OAL of a cloned Virtual PC BSP. It's best to use a cloned BSP because this activity can modify the BSP's source code.

The OAL IOCTLs that an application can call is limited because it runs in user mode. User mode threads have limited access to kernel functionality. To test the new IOCTL, add a simple stream driver that loads at startup in kernel mode. This driver can call the kernel in its XXX_Init function.

To add a new IOCTL to the BSP's OAL you need to:

1. Define the IOCTL index in the list of the BSPs' OALs.

2. Specify the function that handles the IOCTL.

3. Associate the IOCTL and its handler function.

4. Implement the IOCTL handler.

5. Rebuild the OAL.

6. Remake the OS image.

Getting Started

Clone the Compact 7 Virtual PC BSP as in Chapter 6 but for the VPC BSP. Only complete the section "Clone an Existing BSP." None of the other sections in that chapter are relevant here. Create, build, and test a Debug build of the OS with the cloned BSP.

Defining a New IOCTL

A new IOCTL

```
x86_IOCTL_VPC_MY_FUNC _NUM
```

is to be defined. Defining a new IOCTL for an OAL requires three new entries the BSP source code.

1. In Solution Explorer navigate to the `$(_WINCEROOT)\PLATFORM\<Your cloned BSP>\src\ inc` folder.

2. Open `vpc_ioctl.h`.

Define the IOCTL enum

The first entry is its `enum` definition in the header file:

3. Find the IOCTL `enums`:

   ➤ From the top do a Quick Search for `enum`. (There is only one in the file.)

4. Add the additional name-value pair to the IOCTL `enum` definition after the last `enum` entry (the `x86_IOCTL_VPC_MY_FUNC _NUM` line as below):

Available for
download on
Wrox.com

```
typedef enum {
    x86_IOCTL_VPC_GETVERSION_NUM                    = OEM_IOCTL_BASE + 0,
        ... ...
        ... ...
    x86_IOCTL_VPC_FUNC_MOUSEGETLOCATION_NUM         = OEM_IOCTL_BASE + 6,
    x86_IOCTL_VPC_MY_FUNC_NUM                        = OEM_IOCTL_BASE + 7
};
```

Code snippet is for the IOCTL x86_IOCTL_VPC_MY_FUNC enum definition (As in chapter sample code vpc_ioctl.h.txt)

Define the New IOCTL

The second entry the IOCTL's `#define` also in the header file:

5. Find the IOCTL `#defines`:

➤ Scroll down to the `#define` entries for the IOCTLs in the same file (or do a Menu-Edit-Quick Search).

7. Add a `#define` for the new IOCTL after the last IOCTL entry (the `x86_IOCTL_VPC_MY_FUNC _NUM` line as below):

```
#define x86_IOCTL_VPC_GETVERSION            x86_DEFINE_IOCTL(x86_IOCTL_VPC_GETVERSION)
        ... ...
        ... ...
#define x86_IOCTL_VPC_FUNC_MOUSEGETLOCATION
                x86_DEFINE_IOCTL(x86_IOCTL_VPC_FUNC_MOUSEGETLOCATION)
#define x86_IOCTL_VPC_MY_FUNC  x86_DEFINE_IOCTL(x86_IOCTL_VPC_MY_FUNC)
};
```

Code snippet for the IOCTL #define x86_IOCTL_VPC_MY_FUNC (as in chapter sample code vpc_ioctl.h.txt)

8. A corresponding BOOL function needs to be declared in the same header file for the new IOCTL. If you scroll below the `#defines` in the file, you will find some function such as (parameters have been left out):

```
BOOL BSPIoCtlVpc(..);
BOOL BSPIoCtlPostInit(..);
```

Add the following function definition below the last existing function definition in the file:

```
BOOL BSPIoCtlMyFunc(UINT32 code, void *lpInBuf, UINT32 nInBufSize,
                void *lpOutBuf, UINT32 nOutBufSize, UINT32 *lpBytesReturned);
```

Code snippet is the IOCTL function definition (as in chapter sample code vpc_ioctl.h.txt)

10. Save `vpc_ioctl.h`.

Associate the IOCTL with Its Function Handler

1. Navigate to the `PLATFORM\<Your cloned BSP>\src\oal\oallib\Source files` folder.

2. Open `globals.c`.

3. Do a Quick Search for `g_oalIoCtlTable`.

This structure is used by `OEMIoControl` to associate an IOCTL and its handler function. In this case you want to associate `x86_IOCTL_VPC_MY_IOCTL` with `BSPIoCtlMy_IOCTL`:

4. Add an entry to associate the new IOCTL and its handler as in the last line in here. (Add it before the line `#include <ioctl_tab.h>`).

```
{ x86_IOCTL_VPC_GETVERSION,                    0,        BSPIoCtlVpc              },
    . .  .   . . .
    . .  .   . . .
{ x86_IOCTL_VPC_FUNC_MOUSEGETLOCATION,         0,        BSPIoCtlVpc              },
{ x86_IOCTL_VPC_MY_FUNC,          0,        BSPIoCtlMyFunc               },
```

Code snippet is the IOCTL entry in globals.c (as in chapter sample globals.c.txt)

5. Save `globals.c`.

Implement the IOCTL Function Handler

1. Right-click the `oallib` folder, and add a new file to the OAL library.

2. Select `C++ file (.cpp)` and name the file `myioctl.cpp`.

3. Open `myioctl.cpp` for editing.

4. Implement the source file as follows:

```cpp
#include <windows.h>
#include <vpc_ioctl.h>
extern "C"
{
    BOOL BSPIoCtlMyFunc(UINT32 code, void *lpInBuf, UINT32 nInBufSize,
            void *lpOutBuf, UINT32 nOutBufSize, UINT32 *lpBytesReturned)
    {
        RETAILMSG(1,(TEXT("MyIOCTL IOCTL has been invoked!\r\n")));
        return TRUE;
    }
}
```

Code snippet is from the IOCTL Handler Function (as in chapter sample code myioctl.cpp.txt)

5. This IOCTL handler prints a message on the debug output when invoked.

6. Save as `myioctl.cpp`.

Build the New OAL IOTL

1. Right-click the `oal` folder and select `build` to compile `oallib` and relink `oalexe` with the new version.

2. Run the Make Run-Time Image step to include the new version of `oal.exe` in the OS Image.

3. The new IOCTL is now ready to be called from drivers or other kernel mode modules.

Test the IOCTL

The OAL IOCTL needs to be called via the kernel, which requires a processes running in kernel mode. The way to do that is from a stream driver running in kernel mode.

1. Create a new, simple stream driver using CEDriverWiz:

   ➤ Stream Name: TestMyIOCTL

   ➤ Stream Prefix: TMI

   ➤ Kernel Mode

   ➤ Retail or Debug Messages

   ➤ No IO functions, No Power, No Cancel

   ➤ No Shared memory & No Device Context

   ➤ No IOCTLs

2. Add the subproject to the OS project.

3. Set the stream driver to be included in the image and built in debug mode.

4. Implement the TMI_Init function as follows:

Available for download on Wrox.com

```
#include "stdafx.h"
#include "windows.h"
#include "vpc_ioctl.h"
#include "pkfuncs.h"

DWORD TMI_Init( LPCTSTR pContext, LPCVOID lpvBusContext )
{
    if (!KernelIoControl(x86_IOCTL_VPC_MY_FUNC,NULL,0,NULL,0,NULL))
    {
        RETAILMSG(1,(TEXT("KernelIoControl x86_IOCTL_VPC_MY_FUNC failed.\r\n")));
    }
    else
    {
        RETAILMSG(1,(TEXT("KernelIoControl x86_IOCTL_VPC_MY_FUNC worked.\r\n")));
    }
    return 1;
}
```

Code snippet is from the TMI_Init Function (as in chapter sample code TMI_Init.txt)

5. Add the following line to the bottom of the SubProject's sources as an extra include directory:

   ```
   $(_TGTPLAT)\src\inc  \
   ```

   Code snippet to be added to the test driver's sources file (as in chapter sample code TMI_Init.txt)

6. Build the subproject and then MakeImage.

7. Insert some breakpoints in the TMI_Init function above and BSPIoCtlMyFunc in the OAL code.

8. Start the OS and observe that the IOCTL is called.

9.   Shut down the OS.

10.   Reconfigure the test driver (TMI) to be loaded in user mode:

➤   `Flag=0x10` in the driver's registry file.

➤   Remove SHK flags in the driver's BIB file.

➤   (The registry and BIB files are listed under the project's parameter files)

11.   Rebuild the test driver subproject. Then do MakeImage.

12.   Start the OS and observe that the IOCTL call failed. It will fail because the call is from a process that is not running in kernel mode.

SUMMARY

This chapter covered the key concepts for understanding how a target Compact 7 system is configured to interact with the operating system through the Board Support (BSP) components. These are the Bootloader, which gets the image into memory, the OAL, which is responsible for the hardware-kernel interface, the board drivers, and configuration files. The role of KITL for a development system was also covered.

PART VI
Advanced Application Development

36

Introduction to Real-Time Applications

WHAT'S IN THIS CHAPTER?

➤ Using Real Time in an embedded system

➤ Understanding the impact of the operating systems on Real Time

➤ Generating Real Time with Windows Embedded Compact 7

A real-time application is an application with a critical timing requirement, in which the application must response to an event and process required tasks within a set minimal amount of time; otherwise, the system fails. The level of difficulty involved in real-time application development can vary greatly depending on a combination of the required response time, hardware processing resource, and available system memory.

This chapter provides an overview of real time in embedded systems and presents details on the Windows Embedded Compact 7 services available to develop real-time applications. The main objective is to give you an understanding of time determinism in Compact 7 at each level of the computing chain from hardware Interrupt level, to the operating system's internal mechanisms, to native or managed application runtime.

REAL-TIME APPLICATION OVERVIEW

Before entering the description of Windows Embedded Compact 7 real-time capabilities, you need a general presentation on time determinism in computer systems. The first section of this chapter introduces important notions such as notifications and latencies and the influence of hardware on computing delays.

Using a sophisticated operating system such as Compact 7 to build a real-time application is not mandatory; numerous real-time systems do not use an operating system. The operating system has an influence on time determinism and may prevent the developer from accessing low-level functionalities. The motivations to use an operating system in a real-time application may come from software engineering constraints such as code portability or functional constraints such as user interface. In such systems, the developer must know the deterministic services of the operating system to build the path to real-time processing.

Time Determinism in an Embedded System

As the term *embedded* suggests, an embedded system is not dedicated to the same usage as a general purpose computer such as a PC or a server. Most of the systems belonging to this category will never be noticed by the final user; they are inside metal boxes under the car's hood and react to driver actions, or they are installed in waterproof cabinets next to cell phone antennas to switch voice and data packets.

Embedded systems often interact with their environment; as a consequence they need to provide a known level of reliability. The use of a numeric computer with a correct electronic integration offers a good guarantee on the system's reliability for arithmetic and logic behavior, at least equal or better than a mechanical automaton, for example — and much more flexible. Arithmetic and logic are directly expressed in the programming language event down to machine code if it is required; therefore, this level of reliability is entirely in the hands of the developer.

For some embedded systems the constraints include time deadlines; this means that a perfectly correct computation may be considered wrong if it is not delivered on time. Typical embedded systems with such time-deterministic behavior provide the control logic between sensors and actuators in industrial processes or robots; more generally any system in which the output has a time constraint with the input is in the scope, and this includes devices in charge of communication protocols.

The capability for a system to handle time determinism is called *real time*; this notion is particularly sensitive when the system relies on a computer because this one has absolutely no notion of time. You need to consider two separate technical aspects:

➤ Notifications

➤ Latencies

Both aspects are delays; the difference is that a notification is programmatic information that **must be clearly expressed in the software, whereas latency comes from run-time. In other words,** notifications can be provided to the developer as a system service; latencies are a consequence of system design including hardware, system, and application development. The distinction is often made between *hard real time* systems that do not tolerate a single latency overrun and *soft real time* systems where a certain proportion of latency overrun is tolerated.

Handling Notifications

The instructions of the Von Neumann finite state machine care only about memory, registers, logic, and arithmetic; you won't find the following instructions in the assembly code:

```
JIN    label, 64H    ;jump to label in 100 milliseconds
WAIT   0AH           ;will resume execution in 10 milliseconds
```

These instructions don't make sense in a sequential automaton because they suppose the execution flow will stop for a while and resume. The HALT instruction, available as HLT in the x86 architecture, stops the flow of execution but requires an external source of interruption (and some time) to resume.

In this context, the developer can measure only instructions' execution time and use loops to handle delays. This development technique is valid on a simple system based on a low-end microcontroller and handling a few I/Os. It is extremely tedious or even impossible for a high-end embedded system handling multiple functions and responding to several devices.

The solution to overcome computer weaknesses in time management goes through an external circuitry; you need a dedicated peripheral to provide a hardware interrupt source and a time counter register. The basic function provided by such a circuit is to raise a hardware interrupt within a predefined delay; this somehow corresponds to the previously listed JIN instruction. The usual name for this mechanism is Watchdog, and in embedded systems, it is often used to reset the device if the software does not work properly. This implies that in the "proper mode" the software has to re-arm the delay to avoid a Watchdog bite; this is a perfect example of a true hard real-time constraint, and the consequence is quite severe.

The Watchdog approach is widely used to build deterministic software; its main drawback is the need for a dedicated hardware source for each delay, which leads to dedicated architectures and a lack of software portability. As companies need a software production process that protects their assets, portability is considered critical; therefore, developers should prefer standard operating system services to hardware-dependent solutions when applicable.

One solution consists of a combination of a periodic watchdog simply raising an interrupt and the corresponding software interrupt routine controlling multiple delays. This is the basic mechanism at the heart of a preemptive operating system in which the objective is to launch activities at predefined deadlines. With this service in place, developers can manipulate notifications on their own; no extra hardware is needed if some new periodic deadline is required, as long as the period is a multiple of the interrupt period. From a software development perspective, the periodic interrupt called *tick* represents the basic granularity for all software notifications.

Handling Latencies

As said earlier, latencies are not something the developer asks for; they are a consequence of the sequential nature of the CPU and of the choices made during hardware design. Latencies are one-out-of-many technical aspects the designer has to take into account; the objective is to obtain the best possible knowledge on latencies to calculate time determinism for the overall system. When you consider real-time constraints, the true enemy is not the latency by itself but its variation, often called *jitter*, which may be caused by variations at the hardware level such as an uneven flow of interrupts or a bus contention. Jitter may also come from variations at the software level such as thread competition, synchronization objects' contention, or differences in the critical code execution path. During the design phase of a system, you can use jitter information in two ways:

➤ Consider jitter average and design a system that is mostly performing on-time, also called *soft real time*.

➤ Consider maximum jitter (worst case) and design a system that is always performing on-time, also called *hard real time*.

CPU performance has a strong impact on computation latencies and less impact on hardware latencies. For example, time spent to compute in-memory data or to perform a context switch between threads will be shorter with a faster CPU, but this will have little impact on time to access a PCI bus or to write a GPIO. During the design phase of the system, all latencies with their corresponding variations must be considered to guarantee the real-time behavior.

Influence of the Operating System on Determinism

General purpose operating systems were not originally created to offer time-determinism but *time-sharing*, which is a completely different service. The main goal of time-sharing is to provide well-balanced execution of several programs in parallel; this means the operating system can take any measure at any time to ensure all programs execute equally. On a computer based on a general purpose operating system, anybody can install a new application and run it without changing the behavior of other applications; this is what is required for personal computers and servers. Time determinism, with its strong requirements for an execution path, is hardly compatible with the intrusive execution policy of a time-sharing system. Embedded systems designers have many reasons to avoid using a general purpose operating system like memory footprint, source control, or time determinism. This situation created a dedicated market for real-time operating systems.

To use an operating system in a time deterministic embedded device, you need to ensure the designers of this system did not work primarily for the time-sharing objective. This situation is obvious at the application level, but it is also true at the system level, in which a time sharing operating system may introduce delays because it must dispatch driver's activities. On a time-sharing operating system, writing code in a device driver is generally not a solution to determinism (unless you use the driver to install your own deterministic operating system).

The constraints on a real-time operating system design are in direct relationship with the notions described earlier: notifications and latencies. Notifications are provided as system services, and latencies are a consequence of system design choices.

Operating System and Notifications

System services providing notifications represent a small subset of the operating system services:

➤ Software timers

➤ Software watchdogs

These two services offer an abstraction of their hardware counterparts without the burden of low-level programming. The Software Timer calls a routine at predefined time intervals, and this routine is a standard callback with no restrictions on a system's API access. The Software Watchdog can cause the calling thread to simply resume execution after a predefined time delay has expired. In both cases the notification mechanism is based on the system's tick. These notification services are provided by most operating systems nowadays, both real time and non-real time. When considering the real-time constraints, you need to focus on tick precision and timer callback execution control.

Multithreading is another important service to facilitate notification handling; the programmer can use threads to create execution contexts dedicated to notification events and propagate notifications between threads using synchronization objects. Therefore, all operating system services providing thread synchronization can have an impact on final determinism; the next section comes back to this.

Operating System and Latencies

For an operating system offering real-time capabilities, two levels have to be considered concerning latency:

➤ Interface with the hardware

➤ Internal operating system mechanisms

Interface with the hardware covers all the techniques used by the operating system to set up a running environment. The critical areas for determinism include interrupt handling and device driver architecture, because they have a direct impact on data acquisition and processing latencies. Memory management is another area in which mechanisms such as cache or page pooling may have an impact on latencies.

Latencies of operating system mechanisms come from internal implementation strategies. An operating system must handle transactions on its internal structures; therefore, it contains unbreakable code sections. For a preemptive operating system, this also means sequences in which hardware interrupts are disabled. All these sequences impact the overall system's reactivity. Thread scheduling policy also has an impact on latencies because it may create situations in which a thread does not take control as expected after a notification. It is essential for the real-time developer to have a clear understanding and to be fully confident in scheduling policy. Time-sharing schedulers, for example, need to modify the thread priorities to balance execution, whereas real-time schedulers offer a *fixed priority* policy. Thread synchronization primitives represent the last area in which latencies need to be under control in a real-time operating system. These include synchronization objects used for mutual exclusion, transaction safe counters and flags, and other primitives that may cause a thread context switch.

WINDOWS EMBEDDED COMPACT 7 AND REAL TIME

Modern high-end embedded operating systems such as Windows Embedded Compact 7 offer a comprehensive set of services, covering almost the same functionalities as a general purpose operating system such as Windows 7:

➤ Multiprocess and multithreaded execution

➤ Virtual memory and page pooling

➤ Software timers and watchdogs

➤ Hardware abstraction through drivers

➤ Persistence with mountable file systems

➤ Standard communication protocols

➤ Component framework

➤ Integrated user interface services

➤ Multimedia framework

➤ Internet interface and browser

➤ Object-oriented framework

The first three services in this list offer a time deterministic behavior in Compact 7; other services such as memory allocation, file system primitives, or graphical user interface do not offer time-bounded behavior. Using Compact 7 as a foundation, you can combine several operating system services and keep the deterministic behavior of targeted modules exclusively based on time deterministic services (that is, threading, hardware drivers, and timers). During the architecture design stage, the separation between deterministic and nondeterministic modules will be based on thread priorities as they strictly guarantee the order of execution. Nondeterministic modules use low-priority levels and can even run in a Time Sharing scheme as Compact 7 offers on-demand quantum-based scheduling for threads at the same priority level. Deterministic modules use high-priority levels and must be carefully designed to avoid thread contention. The challenge in such an architecture design is to break synchronous dependencies between nondeterministic and deterministic modules. A classic error is to write deterministic code as a response to the WM_TIMER event, which belongs to the nondeterministic GUI service.

Designing embedded systems offering both high-end services and determinism on the same hardware is a great advantage as devices become more and more multifunctional. For example, a manufacturing device can perform real-time control on sensors and actuators while displaying a rich GUI and communicating through the network.

In a multifunctional embedded device performing real-time computing, the software architecture must be rigorously designed, and the final system will exclusively run software that has been originally designed and validated. If the system needs to receive updates, upgrades, or even new functionalities, these must be carefully validated before they are deployed on the field.

Hardware Interface Layer

As explained at the beginning of this chapter, notification comes from a dedicated circuit, and the OAL plays an important role in time determinism because it provides the tick. Microsoft requires that a one millisecond tick should be provided to the kernel by the OAL; this value may be different because it is an OEM decision.

Interrupt latencies also have an important impact on time determinism. Compact 7 provides a common infrastructure for interrupt handling spread over two levels:

➤ An Interrupt Service Routine (ISR) provided in the OAL and called by the kernel on interrupt notification

➤ An Interrupt Service Thread (IST) provided in the device driver and notified on an event after the ISR finishes

This infrastructure facilitates driver development because it restricts pure interrupt handling code to the kernel and OAL. The developer can concentrate on data input and output in the IST, which is a normal thread having access to all Compact 7 API. To make IST development even easier, the OAL provides helper functions to standardize IO access such as `READ_PORT_UCHAR` or `WRITE_PORT_UCHAR`.

The impact of this interrupt infrastructure on latencies mainly resides in the ISR to IST notification because thread context switching time is usually longer than hardware interrupt propagation time. For an x86 platform such as the eBox 3300 running at 933 MHz, ISR maximum latency is 6 microseconds, and IST maximum latency is 30 microseconds (figures given by the ILTiming tool). Compact 7 driver infrastructure is suitable to handle hardware interrupt response within 50 and 100 microseconds depending on hardware characteristics and system usage. If a latency of a few microseconds is required, you may consider writing code in an installable ISR (GIISR) to be called by the kernel before IST notification, but the run-time context of a GIISR does not enable access to a Compact 7 API or application memory.

Thread Scheduling and Synchronization

The fixed priority scheduling policy is an important aspect of the Compact 7 operating system for real-time development. This scheduling policy gives a guarantee of execution corresponding to priority level for threads that are not registered as Quantum-based. At any time during execution, a thread priority may be set to one of the 256 levels; this thread immediately executes before any other thread at a lower level. When threads compete at the same priority level, the execution depends on per-thread Quantum policy; threads with quantum share the CPU, and threads with no quantum run to completion. In a real-time embedded system, high-priority levels will be used for ISTs described earlier and will also be used for application threads sending and receiving notifications in the path of time deterministic processing. The Compact 7 scheduler does not apply its fixed priority scheduling policy in one specific situation in which a high-priority thread is delayed by a Mutex owned by a low-priority thread. To avoid this delay, the owner's priority will be raised to release the Mutex. This mechanism called *Priority Inversion* is coherent with the attribution of high priorities to real-time threads, as long as the targeted Mutex is always used with deterministic code, even in low-priority threads.

Under normal run-time conditions, thread context switch time has an upper bound in Compact 7; abnormal conditions include huge rate of hardware interrupts or memory shortage. Memory shortage is a problematic situation on a computer because memory is still required to run the code solving the problem. To avoid this dead-end situation, Compact 7 has a pre-reserved memory pool called *Page Pool* for system or application code with a cleanup mechanism to prevent saturation. The Compact 7 Page Pool size and threshold are set up in the OAL and have an impact on cleanup time. A real-time embedded system must be designed to avoid memory shortage at all times, but memory cleanup may happen before a shortage if the Page Pool parameters are set incorrectly.

Windows Embedded Compact 7 can run on multicore architectures; as a consequence threads can execute in parallel, and this enhances the throughput. Parallel libraries such as OpenMP are available to facilitate parallel code implementation and maintenance, but these are not useful for real-time development because they offer no or little control on priorities or synchronization. CPU parallelism is interesting in a multifunctional embedded device in which real-time modules have to share the CPU with user interface or communication modules. The new Compact 7 API has functions to set processor affinity to a process or a thread, which may be used in a real-time system to reduce thread contention and in fine context switch latencies. The processor affinity approach requires a complete control on all applications to isolate targeted threads; if the control is not complete, a thread with affinity may receive less processor time than a thread without.

Native Applications Runtime

The native application runtime — namely the Win32 API — is the unique way developers can use to access to operating system services. All mechanisms described previously in this chapter are in direct conjunction with this runtime. A small subset of the native runtime has bounded execution times, and this subset is the foundation for all Compact 7 real-time applications.

Native code can run in two different areas of the Compact 7 system: kernel space and user space. For the same code, this may have an impact on performances because system calls are not treated identically whether they come from kernel space or user space. Kernel code being considered safe, system calls are routed directly with no parameter control, whereas calls from user space are checked first and therefore delayed. The delay on user space calls to the runtime also has a remarkable impact on user-mode driver performances because IO functions parameters will be copied and checked. This delay does not change the deterministic nature of the function, but it can cause a bigger latency. The system designer may choose to put the real-time code in a kernel module and to avoid running time-critical drivers in User mode.

Managed Applications Runtime

The managed application runtime — namely the .NET Compact Framework — is built upon Compact 7 native services (the Compact Framework is a native DLL) but offers a dedicated runtime environment with its own internal mechanisms for code management, memory control, or threading. Developers using the Compact Framework can benefit from powerful object-oriented languages combined with rich services. The result is unprecedented productivity, and this creates a high rate of adoption for this technology.

The Compact Framework design objectives were not primarily targeted at time determinism; internal mechanisms such as Garbage Collection may cause delays at the managed application level because they have to block execution as they work. In a more general perspective, you may consider the compromise between "writing code faster" and "controlling the execution path." The Compact Framework is not systematically slow or uneven, but some programming techniques may cause delays, and these include normal techniques such as using the Garbage Collector.

You can use the Compact Framework as part of an embedded real-time system because it will not impact native code determinism:

➤ It has no impact on interrupts and driver architecture.

➤ It does not modify the fixed priority scheme of the scheduler.

➤ It does not block or modify Compact 7 kernel calls.

➤ It does not run at a high-priority level.

The software architecture of a real-time system using managed code must be designed carefully, and one rule of thumb is to exclude managed code from any time-critical execution path. In such a system the GUI may be developed in managed code, and the sensors' control code is native. This type of architecture already applies in a pure native development because GUI services are not time-deterministic.

SUMMARY

To design a real-time embedded application, you need to control time notifications and execution delays. Windows embedded Compact 7 services include timers, watchdogs, a fixed priority scheduler, and device driver architecture, which are suitable to build time deterministic software. During the design of a real-time system, you need to consider time determinism at the overall system level, including influences of both hardware and software layers. An embedded system designed with Compact 7 may combine real-time processing with other nondeterministic functionalities such as user interface or networking.

37

A Simple Real-Time Application

WHAT'S IN THIS CHAPTER?

➤ Controlling and measuring execution time

➤ Understanding real-time application architecture and code

➤ Using real-time execution and assessment

This chapter illustrates the notions introduced in Chapter 36 by describing an example of a real-time application based on Windows Embedded Compact 7. The chapter first exposes the purpose of the application and its architecture, and then in a more detailed section focused on application code, it provides explanations of Compact 7 services and their capability to be time-deterministic. Execution traces of this simple real-time application on a Compact 7 target illustrate the notions of latencies and jitter; you can also use them to demonstrate the influence of scheduling on time determinism.

DEVELOPING A SIMPLE REAL-TIME APPLICATION

Real-time constraints in embedded devices often come from external equipment such as sensors or actuators, which are accessible by the software through I/O registers. In this I/O-driven situation, designing a simple real-time application is a challenging task because I/Os are not standard. To develop a portable and yet useful application the approach is to work on a platform assessment tool rather than I/O control software. The objective of the application is to measure and display information on time determinism for targeted Compact 7 services; you may see it as a simplified version of some tools provided with Windows Embedded Compact 7 such as *ILTiming* or *OSBench*. The principle of these tools consists in calling dedicated Compact 7 primitives, which are known as deterministic, and measuring the actual time spent during the call by using a high-resolution chronometer.

The simple real-time application focuses on the *Periodic Notification* provided by the *Timer Driver* service of Compact 7. Using Timer Driver functions, the developer can request a function call or an event state modification to happen at predefined periodic instants as shown on the expected timeline at the top of Figure 37-1. Latencies coming from both hardware and software can impact these periodic instants and create uneven periods, as shown on the measured timeline at the bottom of Figure 37-1.

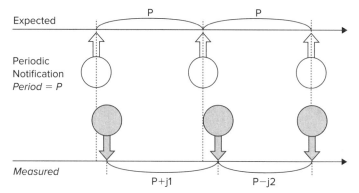

FIGURE 37-1

If latencies were perfectly stable, the measured period would always be exactly the expected period and, from a Period Generator perspective, the system could be considered perfectly deterministic. Remember from Chapter 36 that latency alone is not your enemy; you need to fear latency variations called *jitter*. On a real system you see variations in the measured periods; therefore, you can measure the jitter of the notification service. In the simple real-time application, these variations are collected during execution and displayed when you close the application.

How To: Measure Execution Time

Measurement of execution time requires a high-precision chronometer; in Windows Embedded Compact 7, you have a high-resolution time counter called *High Performance Counter* for this purpose, and the interface of this service is simple because it includes only two functions:

➤   QueryPerformanceFrequency

➤   QueryPerformanceCounter

Use these functions with care because their implementation is only partially provided by Microsoft; the heart of the high-precision measurement is provided by the card manufacturer in the Compact 7 Board Support Package. This situation is a consequence of the need for dedicated hardware when you want to deal with time in a computer; therefore, the behavior of these functions is platform-dependent, and you need to write code to take care of portability issues.

If the Board Support Package does not provide an implementation for the *High Performance Counter* the interface functions still return values for frequency and counter, but these values can use the system tick information, which is not a high-precision chronometer. Hardware simulation is a typical situation in which High Performance Counter is not implemented in the Board Support Package — the reason is obvious because timer circuitry cannot be simulated with accuracy. As a consequence you cannot make an accurate time measurement on a Virtual PC, and the simple real time application is not designed for this platform.

The QueryPerformanceFrequency function returns the frequency of the underlying timer circuit; this value can translate Performance Counter values into standard time values.

The QueryPerformanceCounter function returns the current value of the counter; this implies that for a transaction with a hardware register some delay may be introduced by the function itself, and this delay can create a perturbation in the time measurement. To eliminate or at least minimize the perturbation created by the function call, time measurements usually focus on counter differences.

The "Hello-Deterministic-World" Application

Knowing that you may not be perfectly time-deterministic with a computer program is an important step in real-time software development; the next step is to identify and measure the imperfections. The *Hello-Deterministic-World* application (called *HDWorld* in this chapter) measures the imperfections of Compact 7 Timer Driver service with the help of High Performance Counter. This application must run on real hardware to be representative; the figures provided in the chapter are from an ICOP-eBox3300-933MHz using the BSP available in the installation of Platform Builder 7.

The HDWorld application creates a periodic software timer and measures delays between consecutive timer occurrences; you can obtain the jitter values by subtracting the expected timer delay. To provide a report on determinism, jitter values are stacked in an array of time intervals; this array displays on the console when closing the application. Minimum and maximum values are also stored, and a message displays on the console when a new minimum or maximum value is reached. Figure 37-2 represents a screenshot of *HDWorld* output on a Compact 7 console.

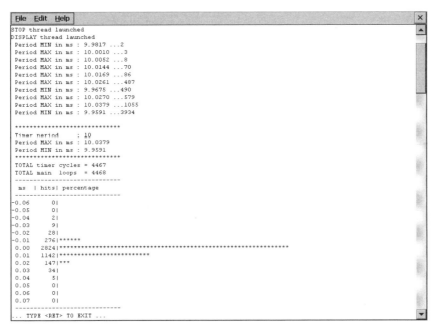

FIGURE 37-2

The first section of the output (before the first line of *star* characters) represents updated minimum or maximum values of the timer period in milliseconds, followed by the timer occurrence number. This section updates during the execution of HDWorld, whereas the second section displays when you stop the application by pressing the Return key. In the second section, you see the execution report with minimum and maximum values followed by a list of jitter occurrences and a simplified graphical representation of percentages. The representation of jitter occurrences gives a view of the deterministic behavior for the software timer.

The architecture of the application should minimize the impact of data processing on measured values. For this purpose, the different processing levels distribute among several threads with dedicated priorities and communication channels, as shown on Figure 37-3.

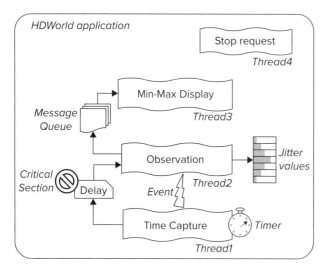

FIGURE 37-3

Thread1 in charge of Time Capture is created by the Compact 7 Time Driver service on timer initialization. Thread1 receives the System notification, and it performs time measurement to calculate the Delay value. This thread should have a high-priority level to minimize latency between notification and Delay measurement. You can control the priority of all Time Driver threads with a Registry key, and HDWorld demonstrates the impact of this modification on determinism.

```
[HKEY_LOCAL_MACHINE\System\MMTIMER]
"Priority256"=dword:10
```

Thread2 is in charge of observation and storage for jitter values; it is notified by Thread1 through an Event Object when a new Delay value is available. To avoid contention on shared variables, Thread2 makes its own copy of the Delay value using a CriticalSection Object. Thread2 runs the main function of HDWorld, which has three consecutive phases:

➤ Initialization of all objects and other threads

➤ Delay observation loop

➤ Display report on Min-Max and jitter distribution.

The observation loop must have a known level of determinism to receive all event notifications and to compute all Delay values; this is why no messages are printed by Thread2 during the loop. The priority level of Thread2 must also guarantee that all notification from Thread1 is handled; this is controlled by a loop counter in Thread2 and a timer counter in Thread1.

Thread3 is in charge of console display for new minimum or maximum values, which are noticed by Thread2 during the observation loop. Displaying messages on the console is not a deterministic activity; therefore, Thread3 priority is low. To avoid contention Thread2 uses a *Message Queue Object* to send print requests.

Thread4 is in charge of console input and simply waits for the user to press the Return key to stop the HDWorld application. Thread4 updates a global Boolean variable to inform Thread2 that the observation loop must be stopped and to display the report. Thread4 priority is low and access to the global Boolean variable does not require contention protection because it is a state transition with a unique writer.

As said earlier, Thread2 is the main thread of HDWorld and is in charge of all initializations for time measurement, Timer Driver service, synchronization objects, and other threads. The first action in Thread2 is the preparation of time measurement by obtaining the characteristics of the Performance Counter on your local hardware.

```
LARGE_INTEGER  Freq ;        // frequency measurement
double      PCount2ms ;      // conversion to milliseconds
if ( TRUE == QueryPerformanceFrequency(&Freq) )
{
       PCount2ms = 1E3 / (double)(Freq.LowPart);
       printf("Frequency: hi=%d-lo=%d\n",Freq.HighPart,Freq.LowPart);
}
```

Code Snippet is from performance counter frequency measurement in HDWorld.cpp

To set up a software timer, Thread2 uses four functions in the Compact 7 Timer Driver service interface. To link your application with the Timer Driver service, you must edit the properties of your project and add MMTIMER.LIB in the linker Additional Dependencies section.

➤ timeBeginPeriod

➤ timeEndPeriod

➤ timeSetEvent

➤ timeKillEvent

The two xxxPeriod functions control the capabilities of the Compact 7 Timer Driver service for the calling application or driver. timeBeginPeriod must be called before creating a software timer, and timeEndPeriod must be called after closing the software timer. The minimum timer resolution is provided as an argument in both functions and is used by the Timer Driver service to set up internal mechanisms to control all software timers initiated by the application at run-time, and return the code indicated if the timer resolution can be achieved by the service (TIMERR_NOERROR) or is out of range (TIMERR_NOCANDO). The HDWorld application uses the smallest timer resolution available, which is one millisecond.

```
// Timer Driver service
#define PERIOD_RESOLUTION  1      // period resolution in ms

// enter Timer Driver section
if ( timeBeginPeriod(PERIOD_RESOLUTION) != TIMERR_NOERROR )
    return 1;

        // ... create the software timer ...
        // ... use the software timer ...
        // ... close the software timer ...

// leave Timer Driver section
if ( timeEndPeriod(PERIOD_RESOLUTION) != TIMERR_NOERROR )
    return 1;
```

Code snippet is from Timer Driver capability setting in HDWorld.cpp

Use the `timeSetEvent` function to create a software timer. The first argument is a predefined period expressed in milliseconds, and the fifth argument is a flag setting the timer as one-shot or periodic and also the action taken on expiration. In HDWorld the timer is periodic, and the default action is a call to a specific function `TimerCallback` given as the third argument. This function receives the fourth argument `&CurrentCounter` as a parameter at runtime, which is used as a Performance Counter memory between calls. The second argument defines a constraint on timer precision; HDWorld sets the smallest resolution of one millisecond.

```
#define TIMER_RESOLUTION 1  // timer resolution in ms
UINT  TimerPeriod ;         // timer period
UINT  TimerId = 0 ;         // timer identifier
LARGE_INTEGER  CurrentCounter ; // Current Count

// create & start software timer
TimerId = (UINT) timeSetEvent(timerPeriod,
                              TIMER_RESOLUTION,
                              TimerCallback,
                              (DWORD) &CurrentCounter,
                              TIME_PERIODIC ) ;
if ( NULL == TimerId )
{
    timeEndPeriod(PERIOD_RESOLUTION);
    return 1;
}
```

Code snippet is from creation of the Software Timer in HDWorld.cpp

`TimerCallback` runs in the context of Thread1. It measures the actual timer period and updates the `PeriodInCounts` variable, which is shared with Thread2. Before returning, the `TimerCallback` function increments timer occurrences and notifies Thread2 using an Event object.

```
// -------------- Public Declarations ----------------
HANDLE    hEvent = NULL ;     // event object
CRITICAL_SECTION timerCS;     // mutual exclusion
```

```
DWORD       PeriodInCounts = 0; // timer period measured in counts

void CALLBACK TimerCallback (UINT uTimerID, UINT uMsg, DWORD_PTR dwUser,
                             DWORD_PTR dw1, DWORD_PTR dw2)
{
LPVOID counterValue = (LPVOID) dwUser;
LARGE_INTEGER PrevCount;

    // number of ticks since last call
    PrevCount.LowPart = ((LARGE_INTEGER*)counterValue)->LowPart;
    QueryPerformanceCounter((LARGE_INTEGER *)counterValue);

    // Updates period value
    EnterCriticalSection(&timerCS);
    PeriodInCounts = ((LARGE_INTEGER*)counterValue)->LowPart
                                      - PrevCount.LowPart;
    LeaveCriticalSection(&timerCS);

    if ( evtLoopCount > 0  && isRunning ) // timer occurrences
        timerCount++;

    SetEvent(hEvent) ;  // signals main thread
}
```

Code snippet is from Software Timer callback in HDWorld.cpp

The observation loop section in Thread2 synchronizes on the *Event object* and first makes a copy of the measured period to compute the jitter value. The incrementation of evtLoopCount unlatches incrementation of timerCount in TimerCallback, which in turn enables the first jitter measurement in Thread2.

```
double JitterValue = 0.0;  // Jitter value in milliseconds

// ------------- Event loop -----------------
while ( TRUE == isRunning )
{
    evtLoopCount++;  // loop occurrences

    // Wait for synchronization event from timer callback
    switch ( WaitForSingleObject(hEvent, INFINITE) )
    {
    case WAIT_OBJECT_0 :
        // first valid period is on second event occurrence
        if (timerCount < 2)
            continue;

        // get Period information with mutual exclusion
        EnterCriticalSection(&timerCS);
        localPeriodInTicks = PeriodInCounts;
```

```
        LeaveCriticalSection(&timerCS);

        PeriodInMilliSeconds = (double)(localPeriodInTicks)*PCount2ms;
        JitterValue = PeriodInMilliSeconds - (double)timerPeriod;

        // ... described later in the chapter ...
    }
```

Code snippet is from observation loop and jitter calculation in HDWorld.cpp

The jitter values measured during each cycle sort by time interval in a counter array to report jitter distribution at the end of the measure. The jitter counter array centers on zero, and the interval maximum is 70 microseconds.

```
// jitter measurement
#define TABJITTERMAX 7      // Zero centered interval
#define DELTAJITTER  0.01   // jitter gap in milliseconds

int     TabJitterCounters[2*TABJITTERMAX]; // Jitter counters
double  TabJitterValues[2*TABJITTERMAX];     // Jitter gap values

// initialize jitter counters and values
for (int i=0; i < 2*TABJITTERMAX; i++)
{
    TabJitterCounters[i] = 0;
    if (i < TABJITTERMAX-1)
        TabJitterValues[i]=(-1.0)*DELTAJITTER*(double)(TABJITTERMAX-
                                                    (i+1));
    else
        TabJitterValues[i]=DELTAJITTER*(double)((i+1)-TABJITTERMAX);
}
```

Code snippet is from structures to store jitter distribution in HDWorld.cpp

In the observation loop, each measured jitter value is counted by incrementing the corresponding `tabJitterCounter` array cell. Both ends of the `tabJitterCounter` collect jitter values which are larger than the predefined interval.

```
// Set jitter marker array value
for (int i=0; i < 2*TABJITTERMAX ; i++)
    if (JitterValue < TabJitterValues[i])
    {
        TabJitterCounters[i]++;
        break;
    }

// MAX index collects out-of-scope jitter values
if (JitterValue > TabJitterValues[2*TABJITTERMAX-1])
    TabJitterCounters[2*TABJITTERMAX-1]++;
```

Code snippet is from jitter information recording in HDWorld.cpp

The last information collected during the observation loop are jitter minimum and maximum values; these complement the `tabJitterCounter` information and are also useful to inform the user by displaying messages on the console. Thread3 is in charge of the console display, and a packet of information is sent by Thread2 on a dedicated Message Queue.

```
// Message Queue packet for display thread
typedef struct {
    BOOL    isMax ;     // TRUE for Max value, FALSE for Min value
    Double  Value ;
    DWORD   Counter ;
} _tinfoMinMax;
```

Code snippet is from message structure for Min-Max display in HDWorld.cpp

The Compact 7 Message Queue object may be created and used with an extended set of options. Thread2 uses a pre-allocated, nonblocking Message Queue with a capacity of ten messages.

```
TCHAR    MQname[]=_T("MQMINMAX");   // message queue name
MSGQUEUEOPTIONS  DisplayMQ;         // message queue options
HANDLE           hMQdisplay;        // message queue Handle

// Set parameters & Create Message Queue with Writer Handle
DisplayMQ.dwSize = sizeof(MSGQUEUEOPTIONS);
DisplayMQ.dwFlags = MSGQUEUE_ALLOW_BROKEN;
DisplayMQ.dwMaxMessages = 10;
DisplayMQ.cbMaxMessage = sizeof(_tinfoMinMax);
DisplayMQ.bReadAccess = FALSE; // write access

hMQdisplay = CreateMsgQueue( MQname, &DisplayMQ );
```

Code snippet is from writer side Message Queue initialization in HDWorld.cpp

Thread2 calls the `writeMsgQueue` function with a timeout parameter set to zero to avoid unexpected delays during the operation.

```
newMinMax.isMax = TRUE;
newMinMax.Value = PeriodMax;
newMinMax.Counter = evtLoopCount;

WriteMsgQueue(hMQdisplay,&newMinMax,sizeof(_tinfoMinMax),0,NULL)
```

Code snippet is from preparing and sending a display message in HDWorld.cpp

Thread3 creates a Message Queue object with the same characteristics except the `bReadAccess` field, which is set to TRUE.

```
MSGQUEUEOPTIONS readMQ;        // message queue options
HANDLE          hMQread;       // handle to read MQ
_tinfoMinMax    DisplayInfo;   // data from main thread
DWORD cbRead, dwFlags;         // ReadMQ parameters

//Set parameters & Create read Message Queue
readMQ.dwSize = sizeof(MSGQUEUEOPTIONS);
readMQ.dwFlags = MSGQUEUE_ALLOW_BROKEN;
```

```
readMQ.dwMaxMessages = 10;
readMQ.cbMaxMessage = sizeof(_tinfoMinMax);
readMQ.bReadAccess = TRUE;

hMQread = CreateMsgQueue( (LPCWSTR)lpParameter, &readMQ );
```

Code snippet is from reader-side Message Queue initialization in HDWorld.cpp

Thread3 calls the `readMsgQueue` function with a timeout parameter set to `INFINITE` to be synchronous with Thread2 transmissions.

Available for download on Wrox.com

```
// Message Queue read loop
while ( TRUE == isRunning )
{
    if (ReadMsgQueue(hMQread,&DisplayInfo,
                sizeof(_tinfoMinMax),&cbRead,INFINITE,&dwFlags))
```

Code snippet is from receiving a display message in HDWorld.cpp

Execution Time Assessment

The *jitter* measurement and classification inside the *HDWorld* application give a view on time determinism at the Software Timer Callback routine level because this is where the actual measurement is performed. The determinism at the observation loop level is measured only on a per-cycle basis; when you see that the timer counter is larger than the observation loop counter, you know that some event notifications from Thread1 did not reach Thread2 because the loop did not complete its processing during the timer period.

When you run HDWorld on a Windows Embedded Compact 7 system with standard Registry settings, you can notice important jitter values and a distribution showing high percentages at the limits of the interval, as displayed in Figure 37-4.

These important jitter values are caused by Thread1 having a low priority. The Remote Process Viewer in Figure 37-5 shows a default priority of 248 for Timer Driver threads, meaning that any thread with a higher priority preempts Thread1 and creates unexpected delays.

```
********************************
Timer period    : 10
Period MAX in ms : 10.9045
Period MIN in ms : 8.9802
********************************
TOTAL timer cycles = 16255
TOTAL main  loops = 16256
--------------------------------
 ms  | hits| percentage
--------------------------------
-0.06   227|*
-0.05    4|
-0.04    16|
-0.03    73|
-0.02   138|
-0.01  1693|**********
 0.00 10348|*************************************************
 0.01  2326|**************
 0.02   374|**
 0.03   706|****
 0.04   101|
 0.05    18|
 0.06    10|
 0.07   220|*
--------------------------------
```

FIGURE 37-4

FIGURE 37-5

To raise the priority of Thread1, you need to create a dedicated Registry key and set it to a high-priority level. You can do this during the OSDesign phase or with the Remote Registry Editor, as shown in Figure 37-6.

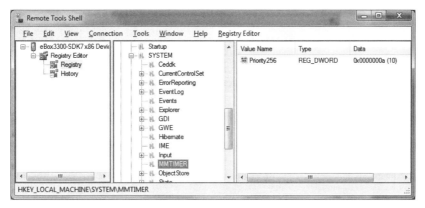

FIGURE 37-6

When the Timer thread runs at a high-priority level, it is subject to less preemption by other threads in the system and the jitter distribution is limited, as shown in Figure 37-7.

In this figure you notice that the limits of the measurement interval have accumulated no jitter values during the test; the maximum variation of the software timer was 52 microseconds.

```
*******************************
Timer period     : 10
Period MAX in ms : 10.0521
Period MIN in ms : 9.9591
*******************************
TOTAL timer cycles = 45687
TOTAL main  loops  = 45688
-------------------------------
  ms  | hits| percentage
-------------------------------
-0.06     0|
-0.05     0|
-0.04     1|
-0.03    14|
-0.02   294|
-0.01  4940|*********
 0.00 30568|**************************************************************+
 0.01  6774|**************
 0.02  1070|**
 0.03  1796|***
 0.04   180|
 0.05    49|
 0.06     1|
 0.07     0|
-------------------------------
```

FIGURE 37-7

SUMMARY

This chapter presented some of the deterministic mechanisms available in Windows Embedded Compact 7 and demonstrated their usage in the context of an application having time constraints. This simple real-time application has a multithreaded architecture and dedicated synchronization and communication channels to protect deterministic parts from perturbations from nondeterministic functions such as console display. You can use the Hello Deterministic World application to qualify the level of determinism for dedicated hardware platforms.

38

Extending Low-Level Access to Managed Code

WHAT'S IN THIS CHAPTER?

➤ Using native and managed code in embedded devices

➤ Gaining direct access to a driver from managed code

➤ Understanding driver interface parameters

Accessing low-level system resources and system hardware has been a challenging task to the managed code developer. This chapter shows what is needed to develop a wrapper to the low-level code and enable managed code developers to easily access and use low-level system resources and hardware.

THE NATIVE MANAGED INTERFACE

The previous chapters focused on application determinism from the execution time perspective. Managed code development may seem inappropriate in the context of a deterministic system because the .Net Compact Framework implements intrusive asynchronous mechanisms at the runtime level such as *garbage collection* or *boxing/unboxing*. Managed code developers can use techniques to gain some control on the Compact Framework behavior, but this may reduce productivity, which is one of the main motivations for using managed code. A mix of managed and native code is a good approach to optimize time constraints and development cost, as well as performances. In such a heterogeneous architecture, you need to organize the communication between the two worlds and, as always in software, many options are available.

Typical Native Code Modules

Production of time deterministic code requires a specific knowledge, and the correct approach is native code because, as said in Chapter 36, "Introduction to Real-Time Applications," it requires full control from hardware to application layers. Good-bye to managed code? No, because if you use a full-featured operating system such as Windows Embedded Compact 7 in your device, some parts of your software such as network exchange, database query, file system transactions or even user interface, may not be time deterministic. If you consider the example of a connected robot control system with a graphical user interface, the proportion of code implementing the time deterministic path may be less than 20 percent. Considering the productivity gap between native and managed code, the choice has a strong impact on your cost and deadline because it applies to 80 percent of your development effort. As a result, the best approach is to use the best language fit, which often leads to a mix of native and managed code.

In a general architectural representation of your system, one challenge is to draw the line between native and managed modules; another challenge is to build the interface because you cannot directly link a native module inside a managed application. Figure 38-1 gives an example of a heterogeneous architecture with the separation line and the resulting interfaces.

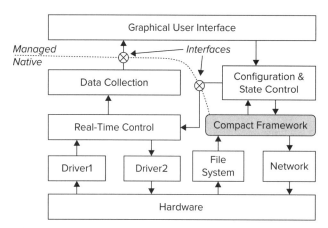

FIGURE 38-1

Some specific software modules such as device drivers cannot be in managed code, Windows Embedded Compact 7 loads only native code DLLs as kernel-mode drivers or user-mode drivers. The development of a specific device often includes *Stream Device Drivers* as described in Chapter 32, "Stream Interface Drivers"; these drivers offer a virtualized byte stream interface accessible through the standard Win32 file IO function set: `CreateFile`, `ReadFile`, `WriteFile`, and so on. These Stream Device Drivers are suitable for most dedicated hardware interfaces such as General Purpose Input Output (GPIO) or Watchdog Timers, even if these interfaces are not pure byte streams. The Watchdog Timer Device Driver can send and receive only base types for configuration and query. The GPIO Device Driver manipulates data in and out, but the unit of information is the bit and not the byte. As a consequence the GPIO registers which are bytes must include masking operations during read-and-write access and the `ReadFile` and `WriteFile` functions cannot be used with their standard semantics. (And it is not a good idea to modify the semantics by tweaking them.) The

XXX_IOcontrol stream driver entry point can help you implement all these dedicated operations on the hardware because it offers a bidirectional transaction model with no predefined semantics; it is accessible for the native developer through the DeviceIoControl Win32 function and all the following calls are valid for dedicated actions on the hardware:

```
// Simple action with no data input or output
ret=DeviceIoControl(hS,CTL_1,NULL,0,NULL,0,&cb,NULL);

// Simple write of a DWORD value to the driver
ret=DeviceIoControl(hS,CTL_3,&myDw,sizeof(DWORD),NULL,0,&cb,NULL);

// Simple read of a DWORD value from the driver
ret=DeviceIoControl(hS,CTL_2,NULL,0,&myDw,sizeof(DWORD),&cb,NULL);

// Complete transaction with an IN and an OUT structure
ret=DeviceIoControl(hS,CTL_4,&mydataIn,sizeof(dataIn),
,&mydataOut,sizeof(dataOut),&cb,NULL);
```

In all these examples, the second parameter dwControlCode gives the semantics of the operation, and the proprietary information resides in parameters 3 and 5. Using DeviceIoControl during the implementation of a device driver is like sitting on both sides of a tennis court — you send and you receive the balls — you choose which data formats are behind parameters 3 and 5.

In some cases a device driver may not be related to any hardware. You can choose to wrap some application code in a driver to have it run inside the kernel and avoid a process context switch with hardware-related device drivers. This is not a common situation and should be considered with care because kernel mode drivers have constraints. For example, any exception in their code is a kernel exception.

Such situations may include time deterministic modules, such as a control loop or filters, where you need to access only the deterministic native services inside the operating system, as described in Chapter 36, without any extra computation from the runtime environment, which would have a negative impact on *jitter*.

Even when they are not encapsulated inside device drivers, regulation loops, filters, or distributed middleware (field bus) represent situations in which a native code approach may be mandatory. When you plan to develop some parts of your architecture in managed code, the communication with these native code modules can require the development of corresponding DLL.

The generic architecture displayed in Figure 38-1 represents a typical situation where some device drivers connect to a real-time control loop. This would be 100% of the code if you used a microcontroller or a simple multitasking environment for a single purpose non-connected device. The architecture in Figure 38-1 is much larger than the pure control loop because Compact 7 is targeted at high-end devices with connectivity and rich user interface. This often implies a native code data collection module "on top" of the real-time part to create a transaction safe multi-access data exchange layer having the smallest impact possible on the real-time module. (A Message

Queue may be useful here to avoid contention, as described in Chapter 37 "A Simple Real-Time Application.") From these native code foundations, you can build configuration, state control, and user interface modules in managed code; one or several DLLs will be added to implement the interfaces between the two environments.

The Need for Managed Code Access

Native code may be the right choice to develop modules using dedicated device drivers and involving time constraints; on the contrary you may prefer managed code for modules using services available through the Compact Framework classes. In an embedded device based on Compact 7, the graphical user interface often represents an important part of the development, and the choice of a specific graphical library may have a huge impact on the project timeline. The actual choices in Compact 7 follow:

➤ Native Win32 C functions also called GDI

➤ Native C++ class libraries: MFC, ATL, and WTL

➤ Native Silverlight code using C++ and XAML

➤ Managed Compact Framework Forms

GDI development has long been the favorite choice in former Window CE projects, for multiple reasons, including memory footprint and average embedded developer's confidence in delivering as long as you program in C (and assembly). Nowadays, GDI has become one of the best ways to scare young developers; it always had a poor productivity ratio because its API combines C language and an awkward function set.

MFC is a class library offering an Object-Oriented Programming (OOP) model by encapsulating most of the Win32 API in C++ classes. Using MFC you can combine OOP productivity and keep control on performance. The MFC library footprint is ten times smaller than the .NET Compact Framework but still considered too big by some embedded developers. The opinions on MFC are highly contrasted; some developers who experienced it on the desktop appreciate it on Smart Device projects, and some developers consider it awkward. Microsoft supports MFC in Compact 7 but, as in Windows CE 6.0, it is not a catalog component; this has often been interpreted as a message to switch to something else. ATL and WTL are C++ template libraries dedicated to COM and Windows development; they are efficient for the embedded developer because using templates avoids including extra code in your target. All these C++ libraries require a high level of expertise, especially on an embedded device where resources are scarce, and productivity at the end is close to native Win32 coding.

Silverlight for Windows Embedded Compact 7 is dedicated to the user interface part of your project. It is based on a graphic engine that loads and renders objects' descriptions provided in XAML files; this approach is perfectly adapted for Rich User Interfaces with graphical effects and animations, but it requires high-end hardware acceleration, and its productivity ratio corresponds to C++ standards if you have skilled developers.

The .NET Compact Framework version 3.5 is available in Windows Embedded Compact 7; it offers a subset of the desktop .NET Framework and some specific features for embedded devices.

The reasons for a dedicated framework include memory footprint, power management, and a limited set of services in Compact 7 compared to the desktop OS. Due to these differences, it is recommended to develop Compact 7 managed code on the target platform rather than to port it from a desktop project. You may still use an emulator or a different device, but verify you have all required native services included in the platform because the Compact Framework is built upon them. For example `System.Net.Sockets` raises an exception if native sockets are not part of your target OS.

An important concern when using the Compact Framework for some modules in a real-time application is the potential impact of managed code runtime and services such as garbage collection on native code threads that would prohibit the capability to write time deterministic code as mentioned in Chapter 36. Internal mechanisms of the Compact Framework do not block the kernel for long periods or perform run-to-completion actions inside high-priority threads. They run a normal application priority level inside each managed code application; therefore, it is safe to build an architecture, as described in Figure 38-1, where some native real-time modules coexist with managed modules.

The consequence of building a heterogeneous architecture is the need for dedicated native code interfaces because you can't cross-compile native and managed code; special care is required when designing these interfaces. The next section focuses on the device driver interface, which raises most of the questions on P/Invoke interface design.

TECHNIQUES FOR LOW-LEVEL ACCESS TO MANAGED CODE

The interface between Compact Framework managed code and native code is based on synchronous function calls that you can achieve with two different techniques:

➤ Explicit Platform Invocation Service or *P/Invoke*

➤ Implicit binding of COM objects or *COM Interop*

You may notice that a third technique available on the desktop Framework called *It Just Works*, or IJW, is not listed here; this is because it requires managed C++, which is not available in the .NET Compact Framework.

In both cases, P/Invoke or COM Interop, the Compact Framework needs to perform specific operations on cross-frontier function calls for type checking and translation purposes; as a consequence some specific design is required when building the interface. The good news is that special helper classes exist in the Compact Framework to reduce the effort of the developer.

The next paragraphs present managed code interoperability to access the Compact 7 Watchdog Timer driver presented in Chapter 31, "Interrupts."

Using P/Invoke

To execute native code from a managed application, you simply need three elements:

➤ A native DLL exporting a function including this code.

➤ Declare usage of the .NET `InteropServices`.

➤ Declare a static managed method referencing the exported function.

All Win32 API calls are exposed by the Compact 7 system DLL `coredll.dll`; therefore a call to `CreateFile` requires only a single declaration. Your Smart Device application written in C# can open a driver and get a HANDLE. Following is the native prototype for the exported `CreateFile` function:

```
// -- native Win32 CreateFile prototype --
HANDLE WINAPI CreateFile(
    __in        LPCTSTR lpFileName,
    __in        DWORD dwDesiredAccess,
    __in        DWORD dwShareMode,
    __in_opt    LPSECURITY_ATTRIBUTES lpSecurityAttributes,
    __in        DWORD dwCreationDisposition,
    __in        DWORD dwFlagsAndAttributes,
    __in_opt    HANDLE hTemplateFile
);
```

Following is a managed method declaration for a P/Invoke call on the `CreateFile` function:

```
// -- a managed prototype for CreateFile --
using System.Runtime.InteropServices;

[DllImport("coredll.dll", EntryPoint="CreateFile",
                SetLastError=true,
                CharSet=CharSet.Auto)]
static extern IntPtr CreateFile(
                string lpFileName,
                int dwDesiredAccess,
                int dwShareMode,
                ref int lpSecurityAttributes,
                int dwCreationDisposition,
                int dwFlagsAndAttributes,
                int hTemplateFile
                );
```

Code snippet is from Program.cs (project WDT_Console)

The managed `CreateFile` method must reside within a class; it is declared *static* because it does not belong to an object's instance, and the *extern* keyword tells the compiler that you won't provide a code body for it. The `DllImport` attribute declaration between brackets acts as a constructor for the `CreateFile` managed method; it may contain several parameters: The first one is not optional and gives the name of the native DLL, and the other parameters are optional.

In the preceding example you see one optional parameter, `EntryPoint`, giving the name of the function in the export table of the DLL. This name may be different from the function name inside the code because the export table of a DLL contains information generated by the compiler. To implement method overloading, a C++ compiler "decorates" method names (also called *name mangling*); as a consequence you get strings such as "`?MyMethod@YA@Z`" inside the export table. All functions in `coredll.dll` are exported with their original names. When you create your own DLL using C++, you may decide to disable the name decoration with the *extern* "`C`" statement.

The optional parameter `SetLastError=true` tells the managed environment to retain the error value that will be set if the native call fails. You can get the error value in the managed application with a call to the `Marshal.GetLastWin32Error` method.

The optional parameter `CharSet=CharSet.Auto` tells the managed environment how to process character strings parameters; the `CreateFile` first parameter is a string. With the value `CharSet.Auto`, the managed environment can adapt its behavior to the conventions of the underlying OS (here Compact 7, which is Unicode); you could force the convention to `CharSet.Ansi` or `CharSet.Unicode`.

A tribute to pay for cross-environment interoperability is that no Compiler/Linker validates the consistency between your managed method declaration and what actually is in the DLL. An important issue here is to guarantee parameter handling consistency before the call (done by managed code) and during the call (done by your native code compiler). One common risk is that each side doesn't handle parameters identically because C/C++ compiler default behavior is not the same as managed code compilers. To avoid this problem, exported native functions should be declared with the `_stdcall` prefix, commonly found inside the WINAPI macro present in each Win32 function declaration. If you cannot declare a native function as `_stdcall`, a special `DllImport` attribute parameter called `CallingConvention` must be set to the value `CallingConvention.Cdecl`.

Marshaling P/Invoke Parameters

If you take a closer look at the managed `CreateFile` method declaration, you may notice that native parameter types have been translated to managed types. First see the managed call for the managed version of `CreateFile` exposed earlier:

Available for
download on
Wrox.com

```
public static int NULL = 0;
public IntPtr hWdt;

hWdt = CreateFile("WDT0:",
                  GENERIC_READ | GENERIC_WRITE,
                  0,
                  ref NULL,
                  OPEN_EXISTING,
                  0,
                  NULL);

if ( hWdt.Equals(INVALID_HANDLE_VALUE) )
{
    Console.WriteLine("Open WDT0 failed");
    return;
}
```

Code snippet is from Program.cs (project WDT_Console)

Several parameters are set to zero, and a constant int "NULL" was declared to set the null pointer value. Some parameters are bit-fields flags and control the behavior of `CreateFile`. To set these flags you need a substitute of `windows.h` in your managed code to compose predefined bit-fields.

Preprocessor macros do not exist in managed code; you need to create your flag values with consistent flag types, as shown here.

```
// value type flags
private const uint GENERIC_READ = 0x80000000;
private const uint GENERIC_WRITE = 0x40000000;
private const int OPEN_EXISTING = 3;
private const int INVALID_HANDLE_VALUE = -1;
```

Code snippet is from Program.cs (project WDT_Console)

The flag values may also be declared with an enumeration as shown here:

```
// enumerated flags
public enum MyFlags
{
    GENERIC_READ = 0x80000000,
    GENERIC_WRITE = 0x40000000,
    OPEN_EXISTING = 3,
    INVALID_HANDLE_VALUE = -1
}
```

When the call to `CreateFile` succeeds, you can control all Watchdog Timer operations with a unique function, which has the following native prototype:

```
// -- native Win32 DeviceIoControl prototype --
BOOL WINAPI DeviceIoControl(
    __in            HANDLE hDevice,
    __in            DWORD dwIoControlCode,
    __in_opt        LPVOID lpInBuffer,
    __in            DWORD nInBufferSize,
    __out_opt       LPVOID lpOutBuffer,
    __in            DWORD nOutBufferSize,
    __out_opt       LPDWORD lpBytesReturned,
    __inout_opt     LPOVERLAPPED lpOverlapped
);
```

The native `DeviceIoControl` Win32 function has an interesting set of parameters, and you may find various managed prototype declarations for it. Use this specific function to dig into parameter processing between managed and native environments; this domain is called `Marshaling` and it has its own `Marshal` class inside `InteropServices`. Using the `Marshal` class in your managed application, you can write explicit memory transactions on your parameters before and after the call to native code, to push and retrieve data from complex types.

The Compact Framework is a friendly environment, and to avoid the burden of manual marshaling, which leads to even more challenging cross-language debugging, the managed environment can achieve automatic marshaling on common types by simply matching native and managed types in the `DllImport` method declaration. Figure 38-2 provides a matching table with four columns from left to right: native C/C++, Win32 types, managed C#, and CLR types.

C/C++	Win32	C#	.Net
void*	HANDLE	void*	IntPtr
unsigned char	BYTE	byte	Byte
short	SHORT	short	Int16
unsigned short	WORD	ushort	UInt16
int	INT	int	Int32
unsigned int	UINT	uint	UInt32
unsigned long	DWORD	uint	UInt32
long	LONG	int	Int32
unsigned long	ULONG	uint	UInt32
long long	LONGLONG	long	Int64
long	BOOL	bool	Boolean
char	CHAR	char, sbyte	Char, SByte
char*	LPSTR	string	string
		stringBuilder	StringBuilder
float	FLOAT	float	Single
double	DOUBLE	Double	Double

FIGURE 38-2

From this table you can easily create a generic prototype for the `DeviceIoControl` managed method:

```
[DllImport("coredll.dll", EntryPoint="DeviceIoControl",
                          SetLastError=true)]
static extern bool DeviceIoControl(
                        IntPtr hDevice,
                        uint dwIoControlCode,
                        IntPtr pBuffIn,
                        uint dwLenIn,
                        [out] IntPtr pBuffOut,
                        uint dwLenOut,
                        ref uint pdwRetBytes,
                        IntPtr lpOverlapped
                        );
```

All native numeric types match managed value types. Marshaling can automatically copy these parameters to the stack, and the native function can see them as standard C/C++ `By Value` parameters. If the native function has pointer parameters to numeric types, like the seventh parameter in `DeviceIoControl`, the *ref* keyword indicates to the managed environment that the address should be copied to the stack, and the native function receives a standard C/C++ `By Reference` parameter. The `ref` or `out` keywords can also be used with a cell in an array or a field in a structure.

Automatic Marshaling for Pointers

Some pointer types listed in Figure 38-2, such as `void*` and `char*`, match specific managed types. These are special types where marshaling may be automatic or require some manual operations.

The C/C++ `char*` has no semantics, but the Win32 LPSTR tells you that a character string is required by the native function, and the managed environment does automatic marshaling on the `string` type when it is used as an `in` parameter (one way from native to managed environment). If the native function modifies the content of the string parameter, a dedicated `StringBuilder` type is available, and you can retrieve the modified `string` after the call by using the method `StringBuilder.Tostring()`.

The C/C++ `void*` has no semantics, and the Win32 LPVOID confirms that it is considered opaque in `DeviceIoControl`. This parameter can be considered as an unsigned 32-bit (Compact 7 has no 64-bit version) and you may use it to pass anything that fits into 32-bit like a `Byte`, an `Int16`, or an `Int32` and their unsigned versions. If all data going through `void*` `DeviceIoControl` parameters are numeric types, you may declare the managed parameter with the corresponding type. Following are simplified versions of `CreateFile` and `DeviceIoControl`:

```csharp
// --- managed CreateFile ---
[DllImport("coredll.dll", EntryPoint="CreateFile",
                          SetLastError=true,
                          CharSet=CharSet.Auto)]
static extern int CreateFile(
                string lpFileName,
                uint dwDesiredAccess,
                int dwShareMode,
                ref int lpSecurityAttributes, // always null
                int dwCreationDisposition,
                int dwFlagsAndAttributes,
                int hTemplateFile        // always null
                );

// --- DeviceIoControl #1 with int parameters ---
[DllImport("coredll.dll", EntryPoint="DeviceIoControl",
                          SetLastError=true)]
static extern bool DeviceIoControl(
                int hDevice,
                int dwIoControlCode,
                ref int pBuffIn,      // [in] int
                int dwLenIn,
                ref int pBuffOut,     // [out] int
                int dwLenOut,
                ref int pdwRetBytes,
                int lpOverlapped      // always null
                );
```

Code snippet is from Program.cs (project WDT_Console)

With these two declarations, C# code is easy to write because all parameters have basic types with automatic marshaling. Beware of parameters where you suppose an "always null" value. You have no way to control that a developer puts a non-null value, and this may cause a crash inside the native function.

If you suppose one specific `IOCTL_GIVE_STRING` uses the third parameter `pBuffin` to pass a string to the driver, a correct prototype for `DeviceIoControl` appears as follows:

```
// --- DeviceIoControl ---
[DllImport("coredll.dll", EntryPoint="DeviceIoControl",
                        SetLastError=true)]
static extern bool DeviceIoControl(
                        int hDevice,
                        int dwIoControlCode,
                        string pBuffIn,     // [in] string
                        int dwLenIn,
                        ref int pBuffOut,   // [out] int
                        int dwLenOut,
                        ref int pdwRetBytes,
                        int lpOverlapped    // always null
                         );
```

And if one other specific `IOCTL_GET_STRING` uses the fifth parameter `pBuffout` to get a string from the driver like the name of the message queue from the WDT driver, a correct prototype for `DeviceIoControl` appears as follows:

```
// --- DeviceIoControl #2 with int and StringBuilder ---
[DllImport("coredll.dll", EntryPoint="DeviceIoControl",
                        SetLastError=true)]
static extern bool DeviceIoControl(
                        int hDevice,
                        int dwIoControlCode,
                        ref int pBuffIn,         // [in] int
                        int dwLenIn,
                        StringBuilder pBuffOut,  // [out] string
                        int dwLenOut,
                        ref int pdwRetBytes,
                        int lpOverlapped         // always null
                         );
```

Code snippet is from Program.cs (project WDT_Console)

You now understand that the `DeviceIoControl` prototypes are imposed by the driver's interface designer. Inside the managed class you may declare as many `DeviceIoControl` prototypes as you need because the managed code compiler knows about method polymorphism, and it performs the correct calls based on parameter types, as follows:

```
int cBytes = 0;
int iValue = 0;

//set WDT Irq (prototype #1)
iValue = IRQ7;
DeviceIoControl(hWdt, IOCTL_SET_IRQ,
                ref iValue, Marshal.SizeOf(iValue),
                ref NULL, 0,
                ref cBytes,
                ref NULL);
Console.WriteLine("Irq set to: " + iValue.ToString());

//get WDT IRQ code (prototype #1)
DeviceIoControl(hWdt, IOCTL_GET_IRQ,
```

```
                    ref NULL, 0,
                    ref iValue, Marshal.SizeOf(iValue),
                    ref cBytes,
                    ref NULL);
    Console.WriteLine("Get encoded IRQ: " + iValue.ToString());

    // get Message Queue name from WDT (prototype #2)
    StringBuilder sbMQname = new StringBuilder("");
    DeviceIoControl(hWdt, IOCTL_GET_MSGQ_NAME,
                    ref NULL, 0,
                    sbMQname, MAX_MSGQ_NAME,
                    ref NULL,
                    ref NULL);
    Console.WriteLine("MQ name: " + sbMQname.ToString());
```

Code snippet is from Program.cs (project WDT_Console)

Polymorphism is an elegant technique to let the managed compiler and run-time do the job for you.

Manual Marshaling for Pointers

If you use opaque void* parameters in DeviceIoControl for complex types, or if they contain different data types for different IOCTL_CODE and you don't want to use polymorphism, you need to perform manual marshaling with the dedicated IntPtr type. The IntPtr managed type is intended to contain a pointer; it directly maps the native void* type and does not require the ref keyword. If you write ref IntPtr, it maps to a void** native parameter. The basic idea of manual marshaling is to drill a hole in the wall between managed and native environments to enable one environment to see (and manipulate) some space of the other environment. Be aware that you need to reseal the hole when you finish to avoid memory leaks. This hole is special because it works one-way — like a peephole — so you need to decide which direction is most suitable for your parameters:

➤ The managed environment sees the native data.

➤ The native environment sees the managed data.

When you want to expose native data to the managed environment, the special managed method Marshal.AllocHGlobal can allocate bytes in the native memory area of the application. Native memory is not subject to garbage collection and it will be locked; as a consequence you need to do your own household by calling Marshal.FreeHGlobal at some point. Inside the managed environment you can use Marshal.Copy to transfer content between the native memory and your managed variables; this method has many prototypes and can be used to copy in both directions. Following is an example of getting a byte array from the pBuffOut parameter when it is declared as IntPtr.

```
    // --- Manual marshaling with explicit allocation ---
    byte[] twoManagedBytes = { 0, 0 }
    uint nbRet = 0;

    // Allocate native memory
    IntPtr hNativeBytes = Marshal.AllocHGlobal(2);

    If ( DeviceIoControl(hWdt,
```

```
                          IOCTL_GET_TWOBYTES,
                          IntPtr.Zero,
                          0,
                          hNativeBytes,  // allocated native bytes
                          2,
                          ref nbRet,
                          IntPtr.Zero) )
{
    // copy from native memory to managed array
    Marshal.Copy(twoManagedBytes, 0, hNativeBytes, 2);
}

// Free the native memory
Marshal.FreeHGlobal(hNativeBytes);

// ... use the bytes in twoManagedBytes ...
```

When you want to expose managed data to the native environment, do not allocate memory but simply ask the garbage collection to enable access to a managed object by creating a GCHandle wrapper with the GCHandle.Alloc method. The first parameter of GCHandle.Alloc is the managed object you want to expose to unmanaged code. When passing parameters to a native function, you must forbid garbage collection and relocation of this object by giving GCHandleType.Pinned as the second parameter. An address can now be obtained from the GCHandle object by calling its AddrOfPinnedObject method. When you finish with the GCHandle object, just call its Free method. Following is an example of getting a byte array from the pBuffOut parameter when it is declared as IntPtr:

```
// --- Manual marshaling without explicit allocation ---
byte[] twoManagedBytes = new byte[2];
Uint nbRet = 0;

// Tell GC to lock the object and get a Handle
GCHandle pinnedBytes = GCHandle.Alloc(twoManagedBytes,
                                      GCHandleType.Pinned);

// Get object address from GCHandle
IntPtr hNativeBytes = pinnedBytes.AddrOfPinnedObject();

If ( DeviceIoControl(hwat,
                     IOCTL_GET_TWOBYTES,
                     IntPtr.Zero,
                     0,
                     hNativeBytes,  // exposed managed bytes
                     2,
                     ref nbRet,
                     IntPtr.Zero) )
{
    // Bytes are now in twoManagedBytes, no copy is required
}

// Free the pinned object
pinnedBytes.Free();
```

The .NET framework manages variables in two different ways depending on their type. There are value types and reference types. That distinction has an impact on memory management because value types variables (base types and structures) are copied when passed as parameter, whereas reference types variables (objects) only have their reference copied but not their content. The framework allows the direct assignment of a value type into a reference type, as in the example code below:

```
int MyInt = 33;
object MyObj = MyInt;   // MyInt is "boxed"
```

This implies the automatic allocation of a reference type associated to the value type. This operation is called "boxing," and a symmetric operation called "unboxing" happens when a reference type is assigned to a value type as in the example code below:

```
MyObj = 33;
MyInt = (int)MyObj;   // MyObj is "unboxed"
```

This management has an impact on manual marshaling because GCHandle.Alloc works on Object types. If you give it a struct which is a value type, this one is automatically boxed, and the native environment will access the boxed object and not the original struct.

Other Marshaling Techniques

If the opaque void* parameter is a pointer to a structure containing an inline fixed size character array, you cannot use automatic marshaling because the native environment gets a 4-byte pointer and not an inline character array. You can still perform automatic marshaling in this case by using a specific MarshalAs field attribute in the struct declaration:

```
// --- Native struct with in-line char array ---
#define MAXSZ 32

typedef struct MyNativeStruct
{
    DWORD dwField1;
    TCHAR szString[MAXSZ];
    DWORD dwField2


// --- Managed struct with automatic String marshaling ---
Const int MAXSZ = 32;

Public struct MYSTRUCT
{
    public int iField1;
    [MarshalAs(UnmanagedType.ByValTStr, SizeConst=MAXSZ)]
    public String cInlineString;
    public int iField2;
}
```

You can apply the MarshalAs attribute to a whole range of types including C-style arrays or function pointers. In some cases such as array marshaling, extra parameters are required to provide the array size at runtime. The MSDN documentation contains a comprehensive description of the `MarshalAs` attribute capabilities.

Another technique to manipulate pointers in managed code is to use the `unsafe` statement and to modify your project's properties to allow integration of `unsafe` code. In an `unsafe` block you can manipulate explicit pointers, and you may use these pointers as `P/Invoke` functions' parameters. Even when you write code in an `unsafe` block, remember that you are executing managed code. If you pass an `unsafe` pointer to a native DLL, you must take care of the garbage collector, which may relocate the managed pointer. To avoid relocation by the garbage collector, an `unsafe` pointer (that is, a pointer declared in an *unsafe* block) can be declared with the `fixed` statement. Following is an example of a very generic `unsafe` `DllImport` for the `DeviceIoControl` method:

```csharp
// --- managed unsafe DeviceIoControl ---
[DllImport("coredll.dll", EntryPoint="DeviceIoControl",
            SetLastError=true)]
public static extern unsafe bool DeviceIoControl(
    int hDevice,
    int dwIoControlCode,
    void* pBuffIn,    // [in] buffer
    int dwLenIn,
    void* pBuffOut,   // [out] buffer
    int dwLenOut,
    int* pdwRetBytes,
    int lpOverlapped
    );
```

Code snippet is from Program.cs (project WDT_Unsafe)

And following is an example of unsafe code using this `DeviceIoControl` method with pointer parameters:

```csharp
// --- Managed unsafe call to DeviceIoControl ---
static void Main(string[] args)
{
    unsafe
    {
        int hWdt;
        int cBytes = 0;
        int iValue = 0;
        int* NULL = (int*)0;

        hWdt = CreateFile("WDT0:", GENERIC_READ | GENERIC_WRITE,
                        0, 0, OPEN_EXISTING, 0, 0);
        if (INVALID_HANDLE_VALUE == hWdt)
        {
            Console.WriteLine("Open WDT0 failed");
            return;
        }
        else
        {
```

```
            iValue = 1000;
            DeviceIoControl(hWdt, IOCTL_SET_TIMER_REGISTER,
                        &iValue, Marshal.SizeOf(iValue),
                        NULL, 0,
                        &cBytes, NULL);

            Console.WriteLine("Timer set to: " + iValue.ToString());

            DeviceIoControl(hWdt, IOCTL_GET_TIMER_REGISTER,
                        NULL, 0,
                        &iValue, Marshal.SizeOf(iValue),
                        &cBytes, NULL);

            iValue /= 32;
            Console.WriteLine("Get timer: " + iValue.ToString());

            CloseHandle(hWdt);
        }
    }//end of unsafe block
}
```

Code snippet is from Program.cs (project WDT_Unsafe)

The unsafe technique may look nice to a C/C++ developer because old habits are hard to break. You should try to avoid this technique because it does not display a consistent syntax to the pure managed developer.

Wrapper DLLs and COM Components

For some drivers, the `DeviceIOControl` function has complex types for the `pBufIn` and `pBufOut` parameters. Instead of writing complex manual marshaling that may be hard to debug, you may decide to P/Invoke in a wrapper C/C++ DLL. The complex memory transactions can then happen in the native environment where you have much better access and debugging tools than in the managed world. The P/Invoke interface of your wrapper DLL should ideally use automatic marshaling for each parameter to simplify the work of the managed developer. One drawback of this technique is an extra layer of processing between the managed code application and the driver code, but remember that the `Marshal` class creates the same sort of interference. Another drawback could be the need to program in native C/C++; you may consider this as a brain training exercise. As you decide to make the move to native C/C++ coding, a new opportunity awaits you: Why simply create a wrapper DLL where you could produce a COM component?

The .NET managed environment came to life in the early 2000s; it provides an unprecedented object-oriented programming environment, but it also has a mighty ancestor: *Component Object Model (COM)*. Ancestor is the correct word because parts of the .NET runtime are still implemented inside COM objects. COM by itself is a native infrastructure, but it has a long history of interoperability with non-native runtimes such as Visual Basic. COM is totally focused on interoperability as it emerged during the early 90s in a world of heterogeneous computer systems, years before HTTP and XML began to rule the world. The interoperability in COM roots in an even older technology called *Remote Procedure Call (RPC)* and the circle is complete! Remote Procedure Call is all you've been doing since the beginning of this chapter.

The originality of a COM native DLL is that it does not directly expose its functions, therefore allowing for special parameter processing before and after the call . . . and yes, Marshaling is the name. Moreover a COM DLL may contain a detailed description of its interfaces in a language dedicated to interoperability, where each parameter has attributes for direction (in, out, and so on), type checking, and other cross-language concerns. You recognized the `MarshalAs` attribute and its whole `UnmanagedType` enumeration.

The connection between a managed application and a COM component does not require `DllImport` declarations because it is generated automatically by the managed compiler in a RCW for `Runtime-Callable Wrapper`. The RCW is a DLL generated by the development tool from the COM component interface description; you just need to add the component in the References of your managed project. A tool called TLBIMP can generate the interface description from a COM component having no internal metadata.

The following section shows the construction of a COM DLL encapsulating the WDT driver and its use by a managed application. The easiest technique to create a COM DLL is to open a native Smart Device project in Visual Studio 2008 and to choose the "ATL Smart Device Project" Template, as shown in Figure 38-3.

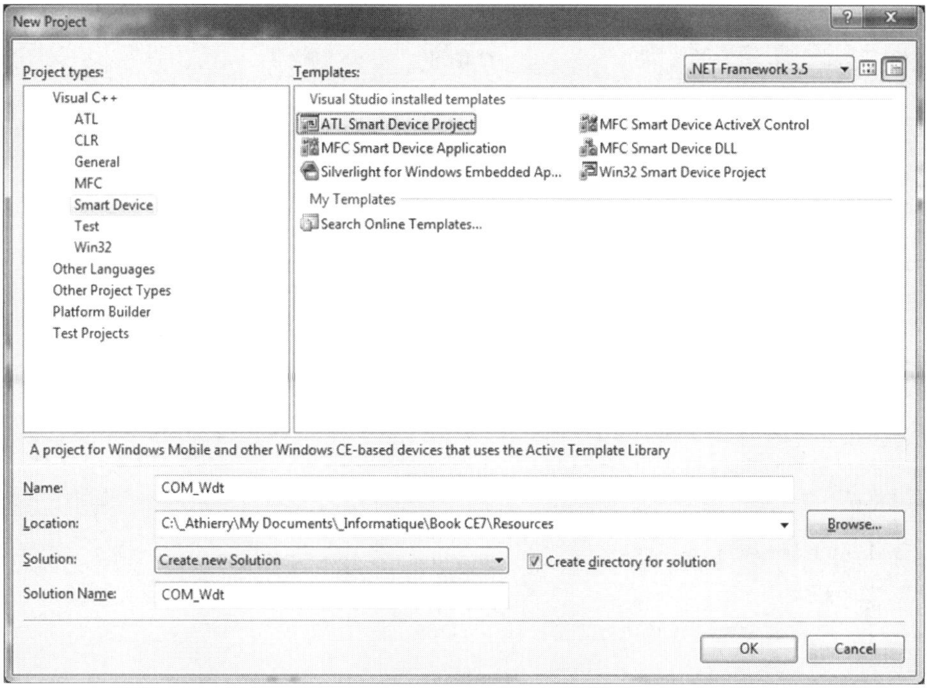

FIGURE 38-3

ATL stands for "Active Templates Library": this collection of C++ templates is very useful during the development of COM objects because it contains complex management code required by the COM framework. Inside your newly created COM DLL, using the "Add Class" menu as shown in Figure 38-4, you will be able to add your own personal COM interface (a collection of method prototypes — the concept is the same as in a C# interface but the code behind is different). Don't be disturbed by the term "Class": what you create in the following operations is both an interface and a class that provides an implementation.

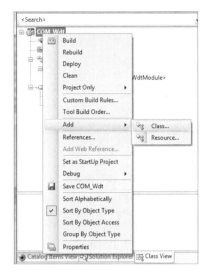

The class template to choose for your wrapper COM DLL is the ATL simple object, as shown in Figure 38-5.

FIGURE 38-4

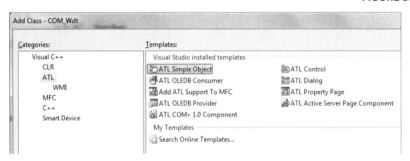

FIGURE 38-5

When creating the ATL Simple Object, the wizard asks for a "Short name," and it automatically populates the names for all the objects and source files created during this operation, as shown in Figure 38-6.

FIGURE 38-6

Several COM entities are created by the wizard and the C++ classes for implementation, as you can see in Figure 38-6.

➤ A COM interface for prototypes: `IWDT_interface`

➤ A COM Class for implementation: `WDT_interface`

➤ A C++ class containing the code: `CWDT_interface`

➤ A C++ source file for the class: `WDT_interface.cpp`

➤ A C++ header file for the class: `WDT_interface.h`

At this point the COM interface exists but it has no methods: you will create them with the "Add Method" menu, as shown in Figure 38-7.

For each added method the return type is fixed to HRESULT and you provide the name and parameters as shown in Figure 38-8 for the "Open" method, which has two parameters:

> ➤ An [in] long integer for WDT number.

> ➤ An [out, retval] boolean for error/success that will be seen as the return value in managed code.

To simplify the usage of the WDT wrapper interface for managed code developers, some specific watchdog information like IRQ number, Timer value, and Message Queue name are exposed as "properties," as shown in Figure 38-9.

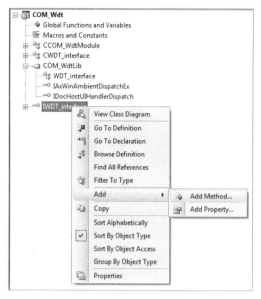

FIGURE 38-7

FIGURE 38-8

FIGURE 38-9

For each method or property exposed by WDT_interface the wizard generates one or two (get/put) methods in the CWDT_interface C++ class. You add the code inside these entries as follows:

```
STDMETHODIMP CWDT_interface::Open(LONG WdtNum, VARIANT_BOOL* Ret)
{
    // Open current WDT
    hWdt = CreateFile(_T("WDT0:"),GENERIC_READ | GENERIC_WRITE, 0, 0,
                      OPEN_EXISTING, 0, 0);
```

```cpp
    if ( INVALID_HANDLE_VALUE == hWdt)
    {
        hWdt = 0;
        *Ret = false;
    }
    else
        *Ret = true;

    return S_OK;
}

STDMETHODIMP CWDT_interface::get_Timer(LONG* pVal)
{
    DWORD dwBytes;
    // Get current WDT Timer value
    if (hWdt != 0)
        DeviceIoControl(hWdt, IOCTL_GET_TIMER_REGISTER, 0, 0,
                        pVal, sizeof(LONG), &dwBytes, 0);
    else
        *pVal = -1;

    return S_OK;
}

STDMETHODIMP CWDT_interface::put_Timer(LONG newVal)
{
    DWORD dwBytes;
    // Set current WDT Timer value
    if (hWdt != 0)
        DeviceIoControl(hWdt, IOCTL_SET_TIMER_REGISTER, (LPDWORD)&newVal,
                        sizeof(LONG), 0, 0, &dwBytes, 0);

    return S_OK;
}

STDMETHODIMP CWDT_interface::Close(void)
{
    // Close current WDT
    CloseHandle(hWdt);
    hWdt = 0;
    return S_OK;
}

STDMETHODIMP CWDT_interface::get_MQ_name(BSTR* pVal)
{
    DWORD dwBytes;
    // Get current WDT MQ Name
    if (hWdt != 0)
        DeviceIoControl(hWdt, IOCTL_GET_IRQ, 0, 0, pVal, 40, &dwBytes, 0);
    else
        *pVal = 0;

    return S_OK;
}
```

Code snippet is from WDT_interface.cpp (project COM_Wdt)

When you build the COM wrapper project, two important files are created for the managed code developer:

➤ COM_Wdt.dll that contains the code of the COM object.

➤ COM_Wdt.tlb that contains the meta-data of the COM object.

Using the meta-data, you can reference the COM object in a managed project and manipulate it as a managed class. The COM_Wdt.tlb file must first be transformed into a managed DLL with the tlbimp.exe command line tool:

```
TLBIMP COM_Wdt.tlb /out:COM_Wdt_tlb.dll
```

The COM_Wdt_tlb.dll file is the Runtime Callable Wrapper (RCW) that contains the marshaling code to translate managed calls to native implementation inside COM_Wdt.dll. You simply need to include this file as a reference in your managed code project to access a new COM_Wdt_Tlb.WDT_ interface type that encapsulates the wrapper DLL. This type makes writing managed code trivial:

```csharp
public partial class Form1 : Form
{
    COM_Wdt_Tlb.WDT_interface MyWDT;

    public Form1()
    {
        MyWDT = new COM_Wdt_Tlb.WDT_interface();
        InitializeComponent();
    }

    private void btn_Open_Click(object sender, EventArgs e)
    {
        MyWDT.Open(0);
    }

    private void btn_setTimer_Click(object sender, EventArgs e)
    {
        MyWDT.Timer = int.Parse(textBox1.Text);
    }

    private void btn_getTimer_Click(object sender, EventArgs e)
    {
        label_timer.Text = MyWDT.Timer.ToString();
    }

    private void btn_Close_Click(object sender, EventArgs e)
    {
        MyWDT.Close();
    }
}
```

Code snippet is from Form1.cs (project COM_CFuser)

You see in this example the MyWDT object representing the abstraction of the Watchdog, and how easy it is to modify its characteristics by using the C# assignment operator.

The `COM_Wdt_tlb.dll` file must be copied to the Compact7 target with the managed application EXE file. The `COM_Wdt.dll` file must also be copied to the target and registered there with the `regsvr32.exe` command line tool available in the Compact7 `PUBLIC` tree.

SUMMARY

Development of managed applications using the Compact Framework in Compact 7 may have an important impact on your productivity. You still need to develop specific modules such as drivers or real-time processing in native code, and this is consistent with managed code development because P/Invoke interoperability is available between the two environments. This chapter covered the constraints and techniques of the P/Invoke technologies that you can use on your embedded projects.

39

Extending Low-level Access to Managed Code with Messages

WHAT'S IN THIS CHAPTER?

➤ Understanding native code to managed code communication

➤ Using Windows Messages

➤ Using Synchronization Objects

➤ Synchronizing managed code with the Watchdog Driver

This chapter provides additional coverage from the previous chapter, showing the possibilities offered in native code to call or send notifications to managed code. You see details on these possibilities for a managed application receiving direct interrupt notifications from the Watchdog Driver.

COMMUNICATING FROM NATIVE TO MANAGED CODE

The .NET Compact Framework provided with Windows Embedded Compact 7 offers several techniques to call managed code from native code. If you compare with the desktop .NET Framework, some techniques are missing, some are the same, and you can even find one which is unique to the Compact Framework.

The structural difference between native and managed environments creates a huge difference when you have to make a direct call to a function inside the other. Native code Dynamic Link Libraries were introduced in the early days of Windows 1.0 to 3.0 to save memory; the library code was not included in the executable; and several programs shared the whole content of a DLL at runtime. Things haven't changed that much with 32-bit environments; the code inside a DLL is still shared between applications, but the data isn't shared anymore. Because it is meant to be used by a *linker* and a *loader*, the interface of a DLL is extremely simple — imagine a table of direct pointers to binary code. The export table of a DLL doesn't contain function prototypes, therefore no syntax check is possible during compilation or linking — everything depends on the prototype declared by the user of the DLL. For example you can compile and link a one parameter function call that ends up in a two parameter function code at runtime, thus creating an unstable situation. This extreme simplicity of the DLL interface combined with late binding provided unprecedented flexibility for the developers. Some unstable situations such as that described above, however, have interfered in the system. The resulting instability has been widely experienced by final users who have come to name this phenomenon "DLL Hell." The P/Invoke technique available in .NET takes advantage of this simplicity. As described in Chapter 38, "Extending Low-level Access to Managed Code," you just need to give an import name, and your managed application will do the call. Remember that in .NET, this call is resolved at runtime, and you are powerful enough to create your own "DLL Hell."

The .NET Framework and its little brother .NET Compact Framework came after the terrible days of "DLL Hell," a time when you wouldn't care about boundaries because there were simply no boundaries. In the managed environment, final binary code is compiled at runtime; it does not make sense to seek an address or a memory offset inside a managed DLL because it contains Intermediate Language. As a consequence a native application cannot operate late binding on a managed DLL by using simple statements such as *DllImport*. You need more sophisticated techniques to impact your native and managed code.

The techniques outlined next, to communicate from a native to a managed environment, focus on the Watchdog Driver interface. Depending on your application architecture or driver capabilities, you may choose one or a combination of them.

Using Windows Events

Windows messaging is one of the areas in which the .NET Compact Framework differs from the desktop Framework. It is based on a specific `MessageWindow` class exported by a namespace dedicated to device programming with the Compact Framework. You first need to add a reference to this namespace in your Smart Device project by opening the Project/ Add Reference dialog box in Visual Studio and selecting the namespace Microsoft. Windowce.Forms, as shown in Figure 39-1

The Microsoft.Windowce.Forms namespace contains an interesting set of classes dedicated to device development such as `SystemSettings` for screen orientation or `InputPanel` for Software Input Panel (SIP).

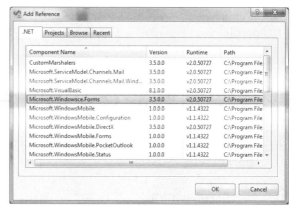

FIGURE 39-1

The `MessageWindow` class exposes the basic mechanism inside the Windows family of operating systems providing the magic of graphical user interface: "I click and it reacts." To create a connection between user-events such as mouse clicks and the applications controlling the pixels on the screen, some callback mechanism is required, and each Window has its own Window Procedure called when the user interacts with it (that is, inside its pixel for mouse events). When a user-event occurs within a window, the Window Procedure is not called directly but the system generates a message and sends it to the application owning the window. For each application event, messages are stored in a Message List and retrieved one at a time by an infinite loop containing basically two Win32 calls:

➤ `GetMessage` reads from the Message List

➤ `DispatchMessage` triggers the Window Procedure

This infinite loop transferring event messages to the Window Procedure is called the Message Pump, as illustrated in Figure 39-2. All applications must have one but it is visible only to the C developers using the Win32 library.

Each message transmitted to the Window Procedure is a structure containing the Window handle, an action code, and data parameters. **When you know a window handle (`hWnd`) you may** send Messages to the window by using one of two Win32 functions:

➤ `PostMessage` returns immediately and the message is processed through the Message Pump.

➤ `SendMessage` causes a direct call to the windows procedure.

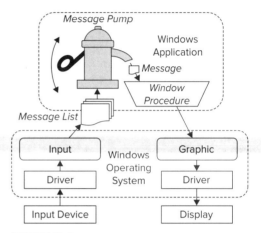

FIGURE 39-2

From native code you cannot send messages directly to a managed code `Form` but you can send messages to an instance of a `MessageWindow` class. Inside the managed code `Form`, this instance of `MessageWindow` can be used as an intermediary to receive messages and make calls to form methods. In the following code the `WDT_MessageWindow` class overrides the `MessageWindow` class and gets a reference to the main form instance through its constructor. The `WndProc` method is the Windows Procedure and calls the `RespondToIrqMessage` method of the main form. The message code `WM_WDT_IRQ` was created specifically for this purpose and its value lies in the range 0x0400-0x7FFF reserved for user messages (`WM_USER` to `WM_APP-1`).

```
public const int WM_WDT_IRQ = 0x5555;  // Driver Message code

// -- WDT_MessageWindow receives the IRQ message from the driver --
public class WDT_MessageWindow : MessageWindow
{
    //the main form where Irq must be handled
    private WDT_Form formWDT;

    public WDT_MessageWindow(WDT_Form FormWDT)
    {
        this.formWDT = FormWDT;
    }
```

```
// Windows procedure of the MessageWindow
protected override void WndProc(ref Message m)
{
    //if the message is from the driver, call main form IRQ method
    if ( WM_WDT_IRQ == m.Msg )
    {
        this.formWDT.RespondToIrqMessage();
    }
    base.WndProc(ref m);
}
}
```

Code snippet is from MyMessageWindow.cs (project WDT_FormTst)

In the main `Form` class you create an instance of the `MessageWindow` and transmit its window handle to the WDT driver by making a call to `DeviceIoControl` with the specific control code `IOCTL_SET_CALLBACK_HANDLE`, which causes the launch of an Interrupt Service Thread (IST) in charge of posting the messages.

```
public partial class WDT_Form : Form
{
    public static int hWdt;
    public WDT_MessageWindow MWindow;
    public const int IOCTL_SET_CALLBACK_HANDLE = 6;

    [DllImport("coredll.dll", EntryPoint = "DeviceIoControl")]
    public static extern int DeviceIoControl(
            int hDevice,
            int dwIoControlCode,
            ref int lpInBuffer,
            int nInBufferSize,
            ref int lpOutBuffer,
            int nOutBufferSize,
            ref int lpBytesReturned,
            ref int lpOverlapped );

    private void RegisterIrqMWHandle()
    {
        // Start MessageWindow and pass it to the WDT diver
        MWindow = new WDT_MessageWindow(this);

        int MWhandle = MWindow.Hwnd.ToInt32();
        DeviceIoControl(hWdt,
                    IOCTL_SET_CALLBACK_HANDLE,
                    ref MWhandle, Marshal.SizeOf(MWhandle),
                    ref NULL, 0,
                    ref NULL, ref NULL);
    }
}
```

Code snippet is from WDT_Form.cs (project WDT_FormTst)

Now you need to define the behavior of the `Main Form` class when a `WM_WDT_IRQ` message is posted by the WDT driver. In the code below a counter is incremented and displayed in a textbox control.

```csharp
public partial class WDT_Form : Form
{
    public int InterruptCount = 0;

    // This callback method responds to the Windows-based message.
    public void RespondToIrqMessage()
    {
        InterruptCount++;
        WDT_MW_count.Text = InterruptCount.ToString();
    }
}
```

Code snippet is from WDT_Form.cs (project WDT_FormTst)

Before you ask the WDT driver to post a message for each IRQ, you first need to open a handle to the Watchdog Driver with WDT_Open_Click and to initialize the time period and the interrupt number with WDT_Set_Click.

```csharp
public partial class WDT_Form : Form
{
    public int iWdtIrq = 0;
    public int iWdtTime = 0;

    // Open Timer Handle
    private void WDT_Open_Click(object sender, EventArgs e)
    {
        iWdtId = int.Parse(WDT_num.Text);
        Devname = "WDT" + iWdtId + ":";
        // open WDT
        PublicData.hWdt = CreateFile(Devname, GENERIC_READ | GENERIC_WRITE,
                                     0,
                                     0,
                                     OPEN_EXISTING,
                                     0,
                                     0);
        if (INVALID_HANDLE_VALUE == PublicData.hWdt)
        {
            MessageBox.Show("Open WDT failed");
            return;
        }
        else
        {
            DeviceIoControl(PublicData.hWdt, IOCTL_WDT_DISABLE,
                                     ref NULL, 0,
                                     ref NULL, 0,
                                     ref NULL, ref NULL);

            // ... Enabled buttons management ...

            return;
        }
    }
}
```

```
    // Set parameters
    private void WDT_Set_Click(object sender, EventArgs e)
    {
        //set WDT Irq
        iWdtIrq = int.Parse(WDT_irq.Text);
        DeviceIoControl(PublicData.hWdt, IOCTL_SET_IRQ,
                            ref iWdtIrq, Marshal.SizeOf(iWdtIrq),
                            ref NULL, 0,
                            ref NULL, ref NULL);

        //set WDT time
        iWdtTime = int.Parse(WDT_count.Text); ;
        DeviceIoControl(PublicData.hWdt, IOCTL_SET_TIMER_REGISTER,
                            ref iWdtTime, Marshal.SizeOf(iWdtTime),
                            ref NULL, 0,
                            ref NULL, ref NULL);

        // ... Enabled buttons management ...
    }
}
```

Code snippet is from WDT_Form.cs (project WDT_FormTst)

The last step is to start the WDT message queue operations with `WDT_MW_go_Click`:

```
// Start timer in Message Window mode
private void WDT_MW_go_Click(object sender, EventArgs e)
{
    // initialize MW counter
    PublicData.WdtMWcount = 0;

    // Start the receiving Window
    MWindow = new WDT_MessageWindow(this);

    Running = true;

    // Give the receiving window handle to the WDT driver
    int MWhandle = MWindow.Hwnd.ToInt32();
    DeviceIoControl(PublicData.hWdt, IOCTL_SET_CALLBACK_HANDLE,
                        ref MWhandle, Marshal.SizeOf(MWhandle),
                        ref NULL, 0,
                        ref NULL, ref NULL);

    // ... Enabled buttons management ...
}
```

Code snippet is from WDT_Form.cs (project WDT_FormTst)

The managed code is now complete. If you look at a highly simplified version of the WDT driver code, you notice the call to `PostMessage` in the Interrupt Service Thread when the driver has a valid HWND to signal.

```
DWORD WINAPI WdtIst(LPVOID lpv)
{
    // ...

    While(!pDevContext->bKillFlag)
    {
        // Synchronization between IRQ and IST
        Result = WaitForSingleObject(pDevContext->hEvent, INFINITE);

        if ( pDevContext->hWnd != (HWND)NULL )
        {
            PostMessage(pDevContext->hWnd, WM_WDT_IRQ, NULL, NULL);
        }
        // ...

        InterruptDone(pDevContext->SysIntr);
    }
}
```

Code snippet is from WDT_DRV.cpp (project WDT_DRV in Chapter 31)

Figure 39-3 gives an overview of all the actors in the chain.

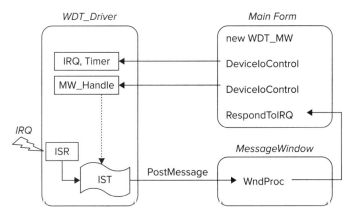

FIGURE 39-3

Note that the message receiver is not restricted to a managed code MessageWindow instance; it may be a native code Windows application.

Using Message Queues

The Watchdog Driver provides another notification channel than PostMessage in the form of a Message Queue, which is a native Win32 synchronization system object providing both data transport and notification. The Message Queue object is a specific resource only available on devices using Windows CE and Compact 7; it was presented in Chapter 37, "A Simple Real-Time Application," for communication between threads. The Watchdog Driver can send IRQ notifications through a dedicated Message Queue, and it provides the interrupt count in the message.

The Message Queue object has no dedicated interface in the managed environment. To read messages sent by the Watchdog Driver inside your managed form application, you need to use the P/Invoke mechanism and import the reader-oriented Win32 functions and structures for Message Queue.

➤ MSGQUEUEOPTIONS

➤ CreateMsgQueue

➤ ReadMsgQueue

➤ CloseMsgQueue

```csharp
public partial class WDT_Form : Form
{
    // MSGQ options structure
    public struct MSGQOPTIONS
    {
        public int dwSize;       // size of the MSGQOPTIONS structure
        public int dwFlags;      // MQ behavior
        public int dwMaxMessages; // maximum messages in the MQ
        public int cbMaxMessage;  // maximum size for a message
        public bool bReadAccess;  // Reader OR Writer
    }

    [DllImport("coredll.dll", EntryPoint = "CreateMsgQueue",
                        CharSet = CharSet.Auto)]
    public static extern int CreateMsgQueue(
            string lpFileName,
            ref MSGQOPTIONS options );

    [DllImport("coredll.dll", EntryPoint = "ReadMsgQueue",
                        SetLastError = true)]
    public static extern bool ReadMsgQueue(
            int hMsgQ,                      // MQ handle
            ref int lpBuffer,               // out buffer
            int cbBufferSize,               // size of lpBuffer
            ref int lpNumberOfBytesRead,    // byte returned in lpBuffer
            uint dwTimeout,                 // timeout in ms
            ref int pdwFlags );             // message flags

    [DllImport("coredll.dll", EntryPoint = "CloseMsgQueue",
                        SetLastError = true)]
    public static extern bool CloseMsgQueue(
            int hMsgQ );
}
```

Code snippet is from WDT_Form.cs (project WDT_FormTst)

Figure 39-4 gives an overview of all the actors in the chain when you use Watchdog Driver Message Queue notification.

You can see many commonalities between Figure 39-4 and Figure 39-3 in the previous section. The Watchdog Driver uses the same interrupt number and timer period variables, and it also uses the same ISR to IST construct to capture hardware interrupts and transform them into notifications.

The behavior of the Interrupt Service Thread is different because in Figure 39-4 it is writing a message to the `Message Queue` instead of posting a `Windows Message` in Figure 39-4. (Although they contain the term `Message` in their names, these two mechanisms have nothing in common.)

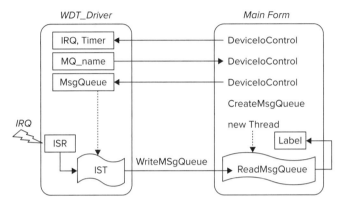

FIGURE 39-4

The managed form application also shows some commonalities with Figure 39-3. The initialization code for the interrupt number and timer period are identical, but the synchronization is completely different. As the `ReadMsgQueue` function is blocking, you must call it in a dedicated thread to keep the user interface of the application alive.

The construction of the receiver message queue uses a specific `DeviceIoControl` with the code `IOCTL_GET_MSGQ_NAME` to retrieve the `Message Queue` name from the Watchdog Driver. All `Message Queue` options are passed to the `CreateMsgQueue` function as a reference to a structure. You must take special care of the `bReadAccess` field, which determines the direction of the `Message Queue` handle you open (Read or Write). The message size and max number of messages are aligned with the driver's options.

```csharp
// Message Queue constants
private const int MSGQ_CBMSG = 4; // size of a message
private const int MSGQ_MAXMSG = 20;     // max messages

private bool OpenMessageQueue()
{

    //Create options structure
    MSGQOPTIONS WdtMQ_options;

    WdtMQ_options.dwSize = 0;              // for Marshal.SizeOf
    WdtMQ_options.bReadAccess = true;
    WdtMQ_options.cbMaxMessage = MSGQ_CBMSG;
    WdtMQ_options.dwFlags = MSGQUEUE_ALLOW_BROKEN;
    WdtMQ_options.dwMaxMessages = MSGQ_MAXMSG;
    WdtMQ_options.dwSize = Marshal.SizeOf(WdtMQ_options);

    // get MQ name from WDT
    StringBuilder sbMQname = new StringBuilder("");
```

```
        DeviceIoControl(hWdt, IOCTL_GET_MSGQ_NAME,
                        ref NULL, 0,
                        sbMQname, MAX_MSGQ_NAME,
                        ref NULL, ref NULL);

        string MQname = sbMQname.ToString();
        WDT_MQname.Text = MQname;

        // open Message Queue
        hMsgQ = CreateMsgQueue(MQname, ref WdtMQ_options);
        if (NULL == (uint)hMsgQ)
        {
            MessageBox.Show("Open Message Queue failed");
            return false;
        }
        return true;
    }
```

Code snippet is from WDT_Form.cs (project WDT_FormTst)

When the Message Queue is successfully opened, you can request the Watchdog Driver to send messages to the queue. This call can be done without prior opening of a Message Queue in reader mode; in this case another application may be launched to open and read the Message Queue.

```
    private void WDT_MQ_go_Click()
    {
        // Open message queue, start Thread and WDT MQ mode
        if (OpenMessageQueue())
        {
            // initialize MQ counter
            PublicData.WdtMQcount = 0;

            // launch the Message Queue reader thread
            Thread MqThread = new Thread(new ThreadStart(ThreadReadMQ));
            MqThread.IsBackground = true;
            MqThread.Start();

            Running = true;
            MQ_on = true;

            // Start WDT Message Queue
            DeviceIoControl(PublicData.hWdt, IOCTL_SET_CALLBACK_MSGQ,
                            ref NULL, 0,
                            ref NULL, 0,
                            ref NULL, ref NULL);

            // ... Enabled buttons management ...
        }
    }
```

Code snippet is from WDT_Form.cs (project WDT_FormTst)

A dedicated thread can read the Message Queue using the blocking function ReadMsgQueue. You may notice that the out parameters passed to ReadMsgQueue must be locked in memory during the call; the Garbage Collector can keep variables in memory from their declaration to a call to GC.KeepAlive. The interrupt counter in the Watchdog Driver is passed inside the message; the reader thread could check that it didn't lose notifications by comparing its counter and the driver counter.

```csharp
// Message Queue Reader thread
private void ThreadReadMQ()
{
    int IRQcount = 0;
    int cbRead = MSGQ_CBMSG;
    int iFlags = 0;

    while (Running)
    {
        if (ReadMsgQueue(hMsgQ,
                         ref IRQcount, MSGQ_CBMSG,
                         ref cbRead,
                         INFINITE,
                         ref iFlags))
        {
            // get count from MQ message
            PublicData.WdtMQcount = IRQcount;
            DisplayMQlabel();
        }
        else if (Running == true)
        {
            // get MsgQ Read Error code
            int Err = Marshal.GetLastWin32Error();
            // .. handle error ..
            return;
        }
    }
    GC.KeepAlive(IRQcount);
    GC.KeepAlive(cbRead);
    GC.KeepAlive(iFlags);
}
```

Code snippet is from WDT_Form.cs (project WDT_FormTst)

If you want to update a FORM control on a Watchdog Driver notification, you need to create a Delegate method because a thread may not be allowed to access the Form controls directly.

```csharp
// used for MQ Reader thread to access Form control
delegate void DelegateDisplayMQlabel();

// actual display method
private void DisplayMQcount()
{
    WDT_MQ_count.Text = PublicData.WdtMQcount.ToString();
}
```

```
// Thread display method with delegate invoking
private void DisplayMQlabel()
{
    if (WDT_MQ_count.InvokeRequired)
    {
        WDT_MQ_count.Invoke(new DelegateDisplayMQlabel(DisplayMQcount));
    }
    else
    {
        DisplayMQcount();
    }
}
```

Code snippet is from WDT_Form.cs (project WDT_FormTst)

The final step is to close the `Message Queue` and the driver handle when the reading process finishes.

```
// Close Handle
private void WDT_close_Click(object sender, EventArgs e)
{
    Running = false;
    if ( MQ_on )
        CloseMsgQueue(PublicData.hMsgQ);

    CloseHandle(PublicData.hWdt);

    // ... Enabled buttons management ...
}
```

Code snippet is from WDT_Form.cs (project WDT_FormTst)

The managed code is now complete. If you take a look at a highly simplified version of the WDT driver code, you may notice the call to `WriteMsgQueue` in the Interrupt Service Thread when the driver is in `Message Queue` mode.

```
DWORD WINAPI WdtIst(LPVOID lpv)
{
    // ...

    While(!pDevContext->bKillFlag)
    {
        // Synchronization between IRQ and IST
        Result = WaitForSingleObject(pDevContext->hEvent, INFINITE);

        if ( pDevContext->hMsgQ != (HANDLE)NULL )
        {
            DWORD buff = pDevContext->interruptCounter;
            BOOL res = WriteMsgQueue(pDevContext-> hMsgQ,
                                     &buff, sizeof(buff),
                                     0, MSGQUEUE_MSGALERT );
        }
        // ...
```

```
            InterruptDone(pDevContext->SysIntr);
        }
    }
```

Code snippet is from WDT_DRV.cpp (project WDT_DRV in Chapter 31)

Figure 39-5 shows the graphical interface of the WDT_FormTst application running in *Message Queue Mode,* with the interrupt count shown in a label next to the GO MQ button. In this mode you can use the Reset button to force the interrupt count back to 0.

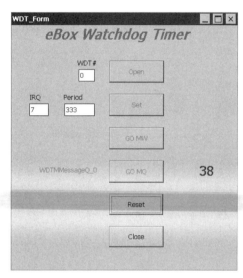

FIGURE 39-5

 If you need to use the Watchdog Driver as a notification provider in a real-time architecture, as presented in Chapter-36, "Introduction to Real-Time Application," the `Message Queue` mode is perfectly suitable. In this case you may not read the messages from a managed thread inside a managed code application but from a high-priority thread hosted in a native application. The `Message Window` mode is not suitable for a real-time architecture because notifications go through a `Message Pump` on which you do not have total control, even inside a native application.

Figure 39-6 shows an architecture combining real-time constraints and a managed application for the user interface where a native wrapper DLL is handling the `Message Queue` and notifies the managed application through by posting messages to a `Message Window`.

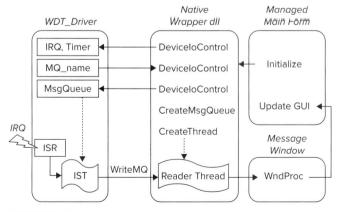

FIGURE 39-6

SUMMARY

Considering the development of .NET Compact Framework managed applications for your embedded devices, you now have a full perspective on the techniques available to communicate between managed and native environments — from managed to native by using the P/Invoke mechanism and from native to managed by using Message Windows or Message Queues. These different techniques are adapted to specific architecture designs and should be carefully planned because they imply a development effort.

40

A Web Server Application

WHAT'S IN THIS CHAPTER?

➤ Servicing embedded devices on the field

➤ Using the Internet Protocol

➤ Using a dedicated web server to explore the registry

For a headless device built without a user interface, a web server application provides an effective mechanism for the user to access the device to set up and configure settings needed for the device to operate.

This chapter works through an exercise showing the steps needed to develop a web server application that enables the user to access the device using a web browser remotely to explore the device's registry.

EMBEDDED WEB SERVER WITH COMPACT 7

Previous chapters describe the special characteristics of an embedded device from an internal perspective: You read about OS construction, device drivers and BSP development, real-time constraints, and heterogeneous application architectures. One other important aspect comes from an external perspective: How do I efficiently service my device when it is in the field?

Many devices are headless or their user interface cannot be used for service because it does not have the adapted input devices. Think of an ATM cash machine: You cannot easily navigate the file system or edit configuration files with a numeric keyboard and a few dedicated buttons. It is even worse when you know that the numeric keyboard does not belong to the embedded device by itself but to a specialized, secure microcontroller, which — for obvious security reasons — won't let the embedded computer interact with its keyboard.

Servicing Embedded Devices

The Visual Studio 2008 and Platform Builder 7 IDEs offer a large panel of possibilities to interact with a Compact 7 target; they are dedicated to different categories of situations:

➤   OS design and BSP development

➤   Smart device application development

➤   Factory tests and assessment

➤   Field tests and maintenance after shipment (with technologies like Error Reporting or Passive KITL mode)

The first three items in this list occur in a controlled environment, usually the OEM integration platform. They are dedicated technical situations where trained workers use dedicated workstations. The software installation on the computer of a smart device application developer requires licenses and a well-defined installation procedure.

Field tests and device maintenance do not necessarily occur in the same controlled environment. In these situations you can still offer servicing capabilities using what may be considered as a standard means of communication nowadays: HTTP transport protocol and HTML data description format. With such an approach every computer equipped with TCP/IP and a browser is usable as a service terminal.

Implementing a Dedicated Web Server

When you need an HTTP server running on your embedded device, you can include the server available as a catalog component in your OS design. However the Compact 7 HTTP server will require some HTML pages and your dedicated maintenance functions must be coded with a scripting language or placed inside an ISAPI DLL (a DLL that will be loader by the server). Developing your own HTTP server is an option if you know all the maintenance functions in advance; this has the advantage of a monolithic development using a single programming language. The following list gives important points that explain why such a development is possible:

➤   The HTTP transport protocol relies on the lower-level TCP/IP protocol for data delivery, so you do not need to implement a sophisticated transport layer.

➤   HTTP clients are everywhere, so you do not need to develop that part either. The browser is a much bigger development task than the server; it handles graphics, text representation, and user interaction for you.

➤   The HTTP service can be seen as a simplified file transfer protocol: Imagine an FTP server unable to list its content. The service protocol has two commands and can be used with one of them — GET — associated with a unique text argument as the requested filename.

HTML is a plain text format description with tags that allow the inclusion of interactive elements in the form of hyperlinks. From these points you understand that the development of an HTTP server may be extremely simple as long as you control the content of your HTML pages. The transport layer is provided by TCP sockets and the data exchange layer can use the HTTP-GET command sent by the browser when you click on hyperlinks. The information presented to the user must be formatted in a HTML page and a good technique to control this content is to create the pages on-the-fly.

A dedicated HTTP server that generates dynamic content has many advantages on an embedded device:

➤ Small footprint with maximum flexibility.

➤ Develop your service algorithms in C/C++.

➤ Few OS dependencies: TCP/IP and LIBC.

➤ Configuration is simplified as everything is inside an EXE file.

➤ Several servers may run on the same device if they use different port numbers.

If you already have the Compact Framework runtime on your target OS or if the footprint is not your biggest concern, you may even use managed code to develop the server.

The closest thing to a dedicated web server on Compact 7 could be an ISAPI DLL or an ASP COM object installed with the web server available as a Catalog component. A complete ISAPI sample is provided for remote web server configuration in the Compact 7 PUBLIC sources section:

➤ `%_WINCEROOT%\ public\servers\oak\samples\http\webadmin`

The web server is published in the PRIVATE section of the Compact 7 sources; this section will not be included in your Platform Builder installation if you do not accept the "Enterprise Source License":

➤ `%_WINCEROOT% \ private\servers\http`

The objective of this section is not to create a sophisticated web server with a file root directory, virtual folders, authentication, scripting, and logging. You can take advantage of HTML and HTTP browsers to provide an interactive registry display tool with a dedicated tiny reghttpc7 web server developed in less than 350 C-language statements.

The registry navigation and user interface modules inside reghttpc7 are specific and are described in a dedicated section. The HTTP transport layer is standard and can be reused for any specific web server because it is based on TCP/IP. The transport layer is implemented in the `NET_TOOL.CPP` source, and the functions exposed in the `NET_TOOL.H` header file:

```
extern short netServerTCPInit(short tcp_port);

extern short netServerTCPAccept(void);
extern short netCloseCli(void);

extern short netCloseSvr(void);

extern short netClean(void);

extern long netSend(char *sendbuf, long length);

extern long netReceive(char *readbuf, long length);
```

Code snippet is from TCP wrapper prototypes in NET_TOOL.H

The NET_TOOL transport is implemented as a static module, with one TCP socket exposed by the server to accept client connection, and another TCP socket to transmit packets between the server and the client. The static client TCP socket restricts the server to one client at a time (second parameter in *listen*); this is suitable here because HTML pages are simple and interaction is limited. The HTTP protocol opens a client socket for each GET request and closes it when the answer is received; therefore a unique static client socket inside the server can handle browser requests serially.

```cpp
// global variables
SOCKET sockSvr = -1;     // server TCP socket
SOCKET sock;             // client TCP socket

// TCP server initialization
short netServerTCPInit(short tcp_port)
{
    struct sockaddr_in sin;
    short version = MAKEWORD(1,1);
    WSADATA wsa_data;

    // Initialize WINSOCK.DLL
    if(WSAStartup(version, &wsa_data) != 0)
        return -1;

    // Open sockSrv TCP socket
    if ((sockSvr = socket(AF_INET, SOCK_STREAM, 0)) < 0)
    return -2;

    // Initialize address structure
    memset((char *) &sin, 0, sizeof(sin));
    sin.sin_family = AF_INET;
    sin.sin_addr.s_addr = INADDR_ANY;
    sin.sin_port = htons(tcp_port);

    // set address of TCP socket
    if ( bind(sockSvr, (struct sockaddr far*)&sin, sizeof(sin)) < 0)
    {
        closesocket(sockSvr);
        return -3;
    }
    // Set socket to listen mode (1 at a time)
    if ( listen(sockSvr , 1) == -1)
    {
        closesocket(sockSvr);
        return -4;
    }
    // TCP server socket ready
    return 0;
}
```

Code snippet is from TCP initialization in NET_TOOL.CPP

The server function is a simple wrapper of the TCP/IP accept function, which opens a dedicated socket for each connection request.

```
// TCP server wait for client connections
short netServerTCPAccept( void )
{
    // Wait for a client
    sock = accept(sockSvr, (struct sockaddr * )0, (int*)0);
    if (sock == -1)
    {
        closesocket(sockSvr);
        return -5;
    }
    // Client socket is ready
    return 0;
}
```

Code snippet is from TCP client accept in NET_TOOL.CPP

The data receive and send functions are wrappers of the TCP/IP recv and send functions.

```
// TCP receive data
long netReceive(char *readbuf, long length)
{
    int status;

    status = recv(sock, readbuf, length, 0);

    // add a string terminator
    if ( status >= 0 && status < length +1 )
        readbuf [status] = '\0';

    return( status );
}

// TCP send data
long netSend(char *sendbuf, long length)
{
    int status;

    status = send(sock, sendbuf, length, 0);
    return( status );
}
```

Code snippet is from TCP receive and send in NET_TOOL.CPP

The cleanup functions wrap the `closesocket` and `WSACleanup` functions. Remember that a client HTTP socket is used for one transaction only; it must be closed after the data has been sent by the server.

```
// close server socket
short netCloseSvr(void)
{
    if ( sockSvr != -1)
        closesocket(sockSvr);

    return 0;
```

```
    }

    // close client socket
    short netCloseCli(void)
    {
        if ( closesocket(sock)!=0)
            return -1;

        return 0;
    }

    // clean WINSOCK
    short netClean(void)
    {
        return WSACleanup();
    }
```

Code snippet is from TCP cleanup in NET_TOOL.CPP

Web Server Example: Accessing the Device Registry

Using the small set of functions described earlier, you can perform all the protocol steps required from an HTTP server. The example described in this section is a registry viewer, as shown in Figure 40-1.

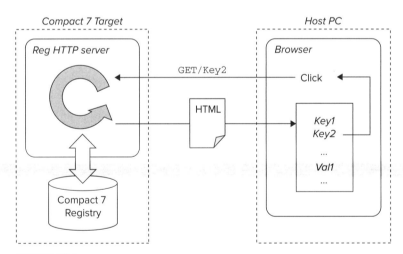

FIGURE 40-1

The HTML pages sent to the browser are not static files installed on the target storage like in a standard web server; they are built at run-time. One HTML page of the reghttpc7 server contains the subkeys and values of a specific registry key indicated by the browser in its GET request. The users can type registry keys in the address bar of their browser to get the list of subkeys and values returned by the server. Another possibility is to click on hyperlinks in the page as the reghttpc7 server implements a navigation paradigm corresponding to the natural tree structure of the registry.

The communication protocol uses the TCP helper functions described earlier to get the HTTP request from the browser.

```
#define MAX_RECV  2048  // TCP Socket reception
#define MAX_SEND 14336  // answer size
#define MAX_NAME   255  // key name length
#define MAX_CTX   2048  // context length

// ------- PUBLIC DECLARATIONS  -------
Char  AscKeyName[MAX_NAME];   // ASCII Key name
wchar_t UniKeyName[MAX_NAME]; // UNICODE Key name
char  htmlline[MAX_CTX];      // Html temporary buffer

char  CurrentCtx[MAX_CTX];    // current key context
int        level = 0;         // current depth level

int wmain(int argc, char* argv[])
{
    Short    port;           // TCP port numbert
    char*    bufferin;       // TCP receive buffer
    char*    bufferout;      // TCP send buffer
    bool     StopIt = false; // Server lifetime
    HKEY     hKey0;          // Key handle
    HKEY     hSubKey;        // SubKey Handle
    Int      DoHeader = 0;   // header request level

    port = 3303 ; // 0x0CE7

    if ( (bufferin = (char*)malloc(MAX_RECV)) == NULL )
        exit(1);
    if ( (bufferout = (char*)malloc(MAX_SEND)) == NULL )
        exit(1);

    // initialize TCP connection socket
    if ( netServerTCPInit(port) < 0 )
        exit(1);

    printf("Registry HTTP server on port %d\n", port);

    // client connections reception loop
    while ( !StopIt && netServerTCPAccept() >= 0 )
    {
        // receive the GET request from the browser
        if (netReceive(bufferin, MAX_RECV) == -1 )
            continue;

        // Parse the Get request
        GetHttpRequest(AscKeyName, bufferin);

        // ****** Handle the request ******
    }

    // End of server
```

```
        if (netCloseSvr() < 0)
            netError("netClose");

        // Close WinSock
        netClean() ;
        return 0;
    }
```

Code snippet is from TCP main loop in reghttpc7.cpp

The GET request received from the parser contains a description of the client machine, browser
identification, and accepted formats. Following is a typical HTTP GET request example:

```
GET /HARDWARE HTTP/1.1
Accept: text/html, application/xhtml+xml, */*
Referer: http://192.168.0.1:800/HKEY_LOCAL_MACHINE
Accept-Language: fr-FR
User-Agent: Mozilla/5.0 (compatible; MSIE 9.0; Windows NT 6.1; WOW64; Trident/5.0)
Accept-Encoding: gzip, deflate
Host: 192.168.0.1:800
Connection: Keep-Alive
```

The only information interesting for reghttpc7 is the second string, immediately after GET. This string,
as the whole GET request, is encoded ANSI, and some special characters like spaces may have an
escape sequence encoded with their hexadecimal value (%20 for space). The GET parser implemented
in reghttpc7 is basic but does the job:

```
void GetHttpRequest(char * name, char * cmd)
{
    while (*(cmd++) != ' ');
    while (*(++cmd) != ' ')
        // character %20 is space
        if (*cmd == '%' && *(cmd+1) == '2' && *(cmd+2) == '0')
        {
            cmd += 2;
            *name++ = ' ';
        }
        // character %7B is {
        else if (*cmd == '%' && *(cmd+1) == '7' && *(cmd+2) == 'B')
        {
        cmd += 2;
        *name++ = '{';
        }
        // character %7D is }
        else if (*cmd == '%' && *(cmd+1) == '7' && *(cmd+2) == 'D')
        {
            cmd += 2;
            *name++ = '}';
        }
        else
        {
```

```
            *name++ = *cmd;
        }
    *name = '\0';
}
```

Code snippet is from the function to parse HTTP GET requests in reghttpc7.cpp

The GET request may contain other information than a registry key name — either because the browser generates it or because it is a special command. These special requests must be handled first:

```
// ignore favicon
if (!strcmp(AscKeyName,"favicon.ico"))
{
    if (netCloseCli() < 0)
    netError("netCloseCli");
    continue;
}
// browser termination command
if (!strcmp(AscKeyName,"0xDEAD"))
{
    StopIt = true;
    sprintf(bufferout,"<html><body>Bye Bye...");
    CloseAndSend(bufferout);
    continue;
}
// create hive roots page on empty or Root request
if ( AscKeyName[0] == ' '
    || AscKeyName[0] == '\0'
    || !strcmp(AscKeyName,"Root") )
    level = 0;

sprintf(bufferout,"<html><body>%c%c",13,10);
```

Code snippet is from TCP main loop: special requests handling in reghttpc7.cpp

When reghttpc7 context level is zero, no valid key is available, and a special static page must be displayed proposing the different registry hives

```
switch (level)
{
    // --- Root level - build & send base page ---
    case 0:
        sprintf(htmlline,"<A HREF=\"HKEY_LOCAL_MACHINE\">HKEY_LOCAL_MACHINE
                        </A><br>%c%c",13,10);
        strcat(bufferout,htmlline);
        sprintf(htmlline,"<A HREF=\"HKEY_CLASSES_ROOT\">HKEY_CLASSES_ROOT
                        </A><br>%c%c",13,10);
        strcat(bufferout,htmlline);
        sprintf(htmlline,"<A HREF=\"HKEY_CURRENT_USER\">HKEY_CURRENT_USER
                        </A><br>%c%c",13,10);
        strcat(bufferout,htmlline);
        sprintf(htmlline,"<AHREF=\"HKEY_USERS\">HKEY_USERS
```

```
                          </A><br>%c%c",13,10);
        strcat(bufferout,htmlline);
        level++;
        CloseAndSend(bufferout);
        break;
```

The GET requests coming from this static hive page are not key names but hive names and they must be treated accordingly when using the registry API. Each hive has a predefined constant for its HKEY, and this constant must be initialized before opening the registry.

```
// --- Hive level - open hive ---
case 1:
    sprintf(htmlline,"<A HREF=\"Root\">>< Root</A><br>%c%c",13,10);
    strcat(bufferout,htmlline);
    hKey0 = GetHiveKeyFromName(AscKeyName);

    // open hive
    wcscpy(UniKeyName, L"");
    if (ERROR_SUCCESS == RegOpenKeyEx(hKey0 ,UniKeyName,0,0,&hSubKey))
    {
        level++;
        // save hive context
        strcpy(CurrentCtx,AscKeyName);
        strcat(CurrentCtx,"/");
        ProcessSubKey(hSubKey, bufferout);
    }
    else
    {
        // error message
        sprintf(htmlline,"Cannot open Hive %s<br>%c%c",
                        AscKeyName,13,10);
        strcat(bufferout,htmlline);
        CloseAndSend(bufferout);
    }
    break;
```

The translation from the hive name to the hive HKEY value is done by a dedicated function:

```
HKEY GetHiveKeyFromName(char * HiveName)
{
    HKEY hKey = 0;

    if ( !strcmp(HiveName,"HKEY_LOCAL_MACHINE") )
        hKey = HKEY_LOCAL_MACHINE;
    else if ( !strcmp(HiveName,"HKEY_CLASSES_ROOT") )
        hKey = HKEY_CLASSES_ROOT;
    else if ( !strcmp(HiveName,"HKEY_CURRENT_USER") )
        hKey = HKEY_CURRENT_USER;
```

```
        else if ( !strcmp(HiveName,"HKEY_USERS") )
            hKey = HKEY_USERS;

        return hKey;
}
```

Code snippet is from the function to get hive HKEY from hive name in reghttpc7.cpp

When the hive HKEY is available, a description page is generated by the ProcessSubKey function, as for any valid registry key. Figure 40-2 shows the page for the registry key HKLM/Drivers/BuildIn/Serial1 as it appears inside the browser:

The page displayed in Figure 40-2 contains three sections relative to the current key:

➤ A clickable header describing the **complete key path**

➤ A clickable section containing the subkeys

➤ A static section containing the Values names and contents

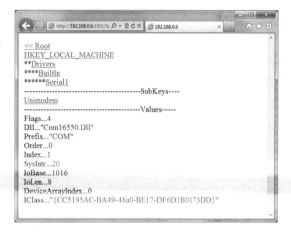

FIGURE 40-2

The header section is always present, and the first line << Root allows navigation back to the hive page. If you click a key in the header section, the page refreshes with the content of this key.

The SubKeys and Values sections may not be present, depending on the content of the current key. When you click a SubKey, the page refreshes with the content of this subkey as the current key.

The HTML source code generated by reghttpc7 for the Serial1 registry key contains all hyperlinks and text sections as follows:

```
<html><body>
<A HREF="Root"><< Root</A><br>
<A HREF="HKEY_LOCAL_MACHINE*">HKEY_LOCAL_MACHINE</A><br>
**<A HREF="**Drivers*">Drivers</A><br>
****<A HREF="****BuiltIn*">BuiltIn</A><br>
******<A HREF="******Serial1*">Serial1</A><br>
----------------------------------------SubKeys----<br>
<A HREF="Unimodem"> Unimodem </A><br>
----------------------------------------Values-----<br>
Flags...<font color="#990000">4</font><br>
Dll...<font color="#990000">"Com16550.Dll"</font><br>
Prefix...<font color="#990000">"COM"</font><br>
Order...<font color="#990000">0</font><br>
Index...<font color="#990000">1</font><br>
SysIntr...<font color="#990000">20</font><br>
IoBase...<font color="#990000">1016</font><br>
IoLen...<font color="#990000">8</font><br>
```

```
DeviceArrayIndex...<font color="#990000">0</font><br>
IClass...<font color="#990000">"{CC5195AC-BA49-48a0-BE17-DF6D1B0173DD}"</font><br>
</body></html>
```

You may notice that each hyperlink determined by a <A HREF...> </A> section generates a GET request with a single key name; reghttpc7 has a current context and it does not handle a complete key path. The hyperlinks in the header contain special * characters that reghttpc7 can recognize to step back in the current context.

The ProcessSubKey function generates the three sections in the HTML page:

```
void ProcessSubKey(HKEY sKey, char * answer)
{
    BuildHeader(answer);
    EnumKeysAndValues(sKey, answer);
    CloseAndSend(answer);
}
```

Code snippet is from the function to generate the description page for a HKEY in reghttpc7.cpp

The BuildHeader function creates the key header section from the current context stored as a path string in reghttpc7. The special characters * are included only in the hyperlink HREF but not in the name for a better display in the page.

```
void BuildHeader(char * answer)
{
    Char temphtml[MAX_NAME];
    int  ctxLevel = 1;

    while (ctxLevel < level)
    {
        GetKeyInCtx(AscKeyName, CurrentCtx, ctxLevel);

        // tabulate context
        strcpy(temphtml, "");
        for (int i = 1; i < ctxLevel && strcat(answer,"**"); i++);
        for (int i = 1; i < ctxLevel && strcat(temphtml,"**"); i++);
        strcat(temphtml,AscKeyName);
        strcat(temphtml,"*");

        sprintf(htmlline,"<A HREF=\"%s\">%s</A><br>%c%c",
                         temphtml,AscKeyName,13,10);
        strcat(answer, htmlline);
        ctxLevel++;
    }
}
```

Code snippet is from the function to generate the header section in reghttpc7.cpp

The EnumKeysAndValues function prepares the SubKeys and Values sections by obtaining the counts for each of these categories in the current opened registry key.

```
void EnumKeysAndValues(HKEY hKey, char * answer)
{
    DWORD cntSubKeys = 0;
    DWORD cntValues = 0;

    // Get the SubKey the Value counts
      RegQueryInfoKey(
         hKey,                    // key handle
         NULL,NULL,NULL,          // unused
         &cntSubKeys,             // number of subkeys
         NULL,NULL,               // unused
         &cntValues,              // number of values
         NULL,NULL,NULL,NULL);    // unused

    // enumerate Keys
    if (cntSubKeys > 0)
        EnumKeys(hKey, cntSubKeys, answer);

    // enumerate Values
    if (cntValues > 0)
        EnumValues(hKey, cntValues, answer);
}
```

Code snippet is from the function to count subKeys and values for an HKEY in reghttpc7.cpp

The last operation is to generate the SubKeys and Values sections; in these operations you face a common issue with character representation. The HTML page uses ANSI or 8-bit characters represented by the char type, and the stings returned by registry query functions use UNICODE or 16-bit characters represented by the wchar_t type. You need to convert these strings from one representation to the other in both directions with the functions MultiByteToWideChar and WideCharToMultiByte with MultiByte meaning 8-bit and WideChar meaning 16-bit.

The EnumKeys function uses RegEnumKeyEx to get all subKeys of the current key. This function receives an index and returns a specific constant ERROR_NO_MORE_ITEMS when the index exceeds the subKey count.

```
void EnumKeys(HKEY hKey, DWORD cKeys, char * answer)
{
    int idK = 0;
    DWORD   cbSKey = MAX_NAME;;  // SubKey size

    sprintf(htmlline,"-------------------------------------SubKeys---
                    <br>%c%c",13,10);    strcat(answer,htmlline);

    while ( ERROR_NO_MORE_ITEMS != RegEnumKeyEx(hKey,idK, UniKeyName,
                                    &cbSKey,NULL, NULL, NULL, NULL) )
    {
        WideCharToMultiByte(CP_ACP, 0, UniKeyName,-1,
                            AscKeyName, MAX_NAME, NULL, NULL);

        // Add subKey ref in HTML file
        sprintf(htmlline,"<A HREF=\"%s\"> %s
```

```
                          </A><br>%c%c",AscKeyName,AscKeyName,13,10);

            // do not break the limit of answer buffer
            if ( (strlen(answer) + strlen(htmlline))
                 < (MAX_SEND - MAX_NAME) )
            {
                strcat(answer, htmlline);
                idK++;
                cbSKey = MAX_NAME;
            }
            else
            {
                sprintf(htmlline,"... %d more SubKeys<br>%c%c",
                                                cKeys-idK,13,10);
                strcat(answer, htmlline);
                break;
            }
        }
    }
}
```

Code snippet is from the function to enumerate subKeys of an HKEY in reghttpc7.cpp

---

The `EnumValues` function uses `RegEnumValue` to get all Values of the current key. This function receives an index and returns a specific constant `ERROR_NO_MORE_ITEMS` when the index exceeds the Values count. The `EnumValues` function retrieves the Value name and content. All names are exposed, and the content is exposed for data types `REG_DWORD` and `REG_SZ`.

```
void EnumValues(HKEY hKey, DWORD cValues, char * answer)
{
    int idK = 0;
    DWORD cbSKey = MAX_NAME; // SubKey size
    DWORD dwType;
    DWORD cbData = MAX_NAME;
    BYTE  bData[MAX_NAME];
    char  szData[MAX_NAME];
    DWORD *pData,dwData;

    sprintf(htmlline, "-------------------------------------Values-----
                    <br>%c%c",13,10);
    strcat(answer,htmlline);

    while (ERROR_NO_MORE_ITEMS != RegEnumValue(hKey,idK,UniKeyName,
                            &cbSKey,NULL,&dwType,bData,&cbData))
    {
        WideCharToMultiByte(CP_ACP, 0, UniKeyName, -1,
                        AscKeyName, MAX_NAME, NULL, NULL);
        switch (dwType)
        {
        case REG_DWORD:
            pData = (DWORD*)bData;
            dwData = *pData;
            sprintf(htmlline,"%s...<font color=\"#990000\">%d
                        </font><br>%c%c",AscKeyName,dwData,13,10);
```

```
        break;
    case REG_SZ:
        WideCharToMultiByte(CP_ACP, 0, (wchar_t*)bData, -1,
                                       szData, MAX_NAME, NULL, NULL);
        //UniToAsc(szData,(wchar_t*)bData);
        sprintf(htmlline,"%s...<font color=\"#990000\">\"%s\"
                          </font><br>%c%c", AscKeyName,szData,13,10);
        break;
    default:
        sprintf(htmlline,"%s<br>%c%c",AscKeyName,13,10);
        break;
        }

        // do not break the limit of answer buffer
        if ( (strlen(answer) + strlen(htmlline))
            < (MAX_SEND - MAX_NAME) )
        {
            strcat(answer, htmlline);
            idK++;
            cbSKey = MAX_NAME;
            cbData = MAX_NAME;
        }
    else
    {
        sprintf(htmlline,"... %d more Values<br>%c%c",
                          cValues-idK,13,10);
        strcat(answer, htmlline);
        break;
    }
  }
}
```

Code snippet is from the function to enumerate Values of an HKEY in reghttpc7.cpp

The last element to handle is the opening of the registry key inside the *main* function; it may be a header key or a normal key:

```
default:
    sprintf(htmlline,"<A HREF=\"Root\"><< Root</A><br>%c%c",13,10);
    strcat(bufferout,htmlline);

    // --- Header key, reopen from current context ---
    DoHeader = IsHeader(AscKeyName);
    if (DoHeader > 0)
        ProcessHeaderKey(&hKey0, &hSubKey,DoHeader,bufferout);

    // --- normal key, open from current SubKey ---
    else
        ProcessNormalKey(&hKey0, &hSubKey,bufferout);
    break;
```

Code snippet is from the TCP main loop: static Hive page generation in reghttpc7.cpp

The ProcessHeaderKey function must re-open all registry keys using the current context. The first step is to find back the hive name and open the hive key; then the function enters a loop to open keys down to the required level.

```
void ProcessHeaderKey(HKEY* phKey, HKEY* phSubKey,
                               int doLevel, char* answer)
{
    char newCtx[MAX_CTX];

    level = 1;
    // get hive name and key
    GetKeyInCtx(AscKeyName, CurrentCtx, 1);
    RegCloseKey(*phKey);
    *phKey = GetHiveKeyFromName(AscKeyName);

    // open hive
    wcscpy(UniKeyName, L"");
    if (ERROR_SUCCESS == RegOpenKeyEx(*phKey,UniKeyName,0,0,phSubKey))
    {
        level++;
        // save hive context
        strcpy(newCtx,AscKeyName);
        strcat(newCtx,"/");
    }
    // error message
    else
    {
        sprintf(htmlline,"Cannot open Key %s<br>%c%c",
                                            AscKeyName,13,10);
        strcat(answer,htmlline);
        CloseAndSend(answer);
        return ;
    }

    // open keys down to DoHeader level
    while (level > 1 && level <= doLevel)
    {
        // get key name
        GetKeyInCtx(AscKeyName,CurrentCtx,level);
        MultiByteToWideChar(CP_ACP, MB_PRECOMPOSED,
                            AscKeyName, -1, UniKeyName, MAX_NAME);
        RegCloseKey(*phKey);
        *phKey = *phSubKey;

        if (ERROR_SUCCESS ==
                        RegOpenKeyEx(*phKey,UniKeyName,0,0,phSubKey))
        {
            // update context
            level++;
            strcat(newCtx,AscKeyName);
            strcat(newCtx,"/");
        }
        else
        {
```

```
                    // error message
                    sprintf(htmlline,"Cannot open Key %s<br>%c%c",
                                                AscKeyName,13,10);
                    strcat(answer,htmlline);
                    CloseAndSend(answer);
                    return ;
            }
        }
        // save context and process the subkey
          strcpy(CurrentCtx, newCtx);
        ProcessSubKey(*phSubKey, answer);
    }
```

Code snippet is from the TCP main loop: static Hive page generation in reghttpc7.cpp

The `ProcessNormalKey` function simply opens the chosen key and request for processing:

```
void ProcessNormalKey(HKEY* phKey, HKEY* phSubKey, char* answer)
{
    // prepare for RegOpen
    MultiByteToWideChar(CP_ACP, MB_PRECOMPOSED, AscKeyName,
                                        -1, UniKeyName, MAX_NAME);
    RegCloseKey(*phKey);
    *phKey = *phSubKey;

    // Open subkey from previous key
    if (ERROR_SUCCESS == RegOpenKeyEx(*phKey,UniKeyName,0,0,phSubKey))
    {
        level++;
        // update context and process subKey
        strcat(CurrentCtx,AscKeyName);
        strcat(CurrentCtx,"/");
        ProcessSubKey(*phSubKey, answer);
    }
    else
    {
        // error message
        sprintf(htmlline,"Cannot open Key %s<br>%c%c",
                                        AscKeyName,13,10);
        strcat(answer,htmlline);
        CloseAndSend(answer);
    }
}
```

Code snippet is from the TCP main loop: static Hive page generation in reghttpc7.cpp

When the rehttpc7 server runs on an embedded device, you simply need the IP address of this device and a browser on any connected host such as a Windows Phone 7 or a PC, and you can browse the device registry.

SUMMARY

Servicing your embedded devices on the field may be a challenging task because standard Windows Embedded Compact 7 tools are not available on the average host; they are not even available for smart phones or non-Microsoft platforms. HTTP and HTML are effective mechanisms to retrieve and display data from a Compact 7 device on any host computer. This chapter demonstrated how to use an HTTP server dedicated to specific needs with a minimal impact on your device footprint and configuration.

41

A USB Camera Application

WHAT'S IN THIS CHAPTER?

➤ Introducing the USB camera driver

➤ Building a CeWebCam in Compact 7

➤ Using an application to create snapshots with a USB camera

Due to the lack of device driver support for Windows Embedded Compact from the hardware manufactures, USB camera support is one of the most common how-to questions.

This chapter talks about an available open source USB camera driver and works through the steps to show how to utilize this driver to access a USB camera from a Windows Embedded Compact 7 application.

USING A USB CAMERA ON COMPACT 7

Embedded devices often have to interact with their environment with no specific user interaction or guidance. Sensors are key functionalities in such devices because they can transform real-world elements into data that will be computed by dedicated algorithms. Infrared or ultrasound sensors offer an inexpensive way to explore the closed environment for embedded devices, such as robots or on-board vehicle equipment, but they cannot help when you have to work with shapes or colors.

Obtaining images of the environment through a digital camera is a common way of interaction for numerous embedded devices; the images may simply be transmitted or recorded if the aim is monitoring, or they can go through shape, color, or motion detection. As Windows Embedded Compact 7 is targeted at 32-bit CPUs nowadays running at frequencies up to 1500MHz, the computing capabilities are sufficient to even integrate image processing in the deterministic computing path if the embedded system has to react to external events.

Like its predecessors Windows Embedded Compact 7 comes with a general multimedia infrastructure called DirectShow, which is an extensible software framework for media rendering. The basic elements of the DirectShow infrastructure are media filters ranking in three categories: Sources, Transforms, and Renderers. DirectShow filters are COM objects interconnected at runtime to organize a multimedia pipeline. You may use the DirectShow infrastructure to handle the video functionalities in your embedded devices, which requires some COM object programming capabilities. Helper projects are provided in the Compact 7 source tree in the following location:

```
%_WINCEROOT%\public\directx\sdk\samples.
```

The WebCamRead application presented in this chapter is based on a simpler architecture than DirectShow; it uses the Windows CE Webcam Project, an open source USB camera driver available in Codeplex:

```
http://cewebcam.codeplex.com
```

The CeWebCam driver exposes a simple Stream interface as presented in Chapter 32, "Stream Interface Drivers," where most transactions with the camera use dedicated IOCTL commands directly accessible through the `DeviceIOControl` Win32 function. The WebCamRead application was designed to have a minimal set of dependencies in the Compact 7 catalog; in addition to interfacing the CeWebCam driver it contains all the code to transform camera frames into standard image file formats BMP and JPG, hence avoiding the use of binary codecs.

Building CeWebCam in Compact 7

The interface and internal mechanisms of the CeWebCam driver are described in a white paper published by Doug Boling in the Codeplex project. This section focuses on the installation of the CeWebCam project inside your Windows Embedded Compact 7 OS design to add the Camera driver to your image.

The CeWebCam driver is a multiplatform driver targeted at Windows CE. The high level of compatibility between Windows CE 6.0 and Compact 7 enables a direct build of the unmodified project sources to obtain a USB Camera driver. However, the project you download from Codeplex cannot be imported directly in Compact 7 because some Windows CE makefile macros can cause build errors in Compact 7.

CeWebCam is provided as a Visual Studio workspace with an MDD library and a PDD dynamic link library, which is the driver file. Each PDD and MDD section contains a SOURCES files with specific macros designing pathnames. You may modify these SOURCES files to adapt them to Compact 7, but there is a faster way to build and test your CeWebCam driver.

The idea is to develop your driver as a subproject DLL inside your OS design; therefore, all macro definitions will be correct as they are generated by Platform Builder 7. When you have created an empty DLL subproject, you can copy the CeWebCam files to the project folder with or without modification depending on their nature:

➤   Source files (.CPP, .H) are unmodified.

➤   Parameter files (.BIB, .REG, .DEF) may require modifications.

You might also need to modify the SOURCES file of your subproject to add include and libraries dependencies. All these copies and modifications are described hereafter.

Figure 41-1 displays the content of the file `WebCam_100.zip` you can download from the CeWebCam project on Codeplex.

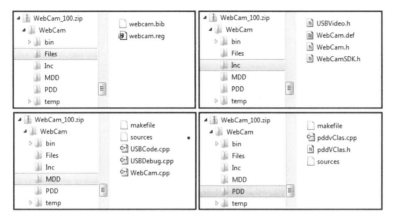

FIGURE 41-1

The `webcam.bib`, `webcam.reg`, and `WebCam.def` files contain the name of your final DLL; you may choose WebCam as the name of your subproject DLL to leave these files unchanged.

After creating the WebCam DLL empty subproject, copy the following files to the root of your subproject. Do not create the `Files`, `Inc`, `MDD`, and `PDD` subfolders — notice that two files are not copied:

➤ `Webcam.bib`

➤ `Webcam.reg`

➤ `USBVideo.h`

➤ `WebCam.def`

➤ `WebCam.h`

➤ `USBCode.cpp`

➤ `WebCam.cpp`

➤ `pddvClas.cpp`

➤ `pddvClas.h`

The next step is to incorporate the source files in your subproject by selecting Add ➪ Existing Item on all `.CPP` and `.H` in the previous list. You should get the subproject structure shown in Figure 41-2.

Before you build the subproject DLL you must specify the include pathnames for the compiler and additional libraries for the linker. This may be done by using

FIGURE 41-2

the subproject's Properties dialog box, but the Visual Studio team made this task extremely uncomfortable by proposing fixed-size tiny text boxes in the C/C++ and Link tabs. The most comfortable (and delightfully old-fashioned) technique is to open the SOURCES file of your subproject with a double-click (or right-click + Open) on the WebCam name at the top of the structure. The SOURCES file contains several macro definitions such as SOURCES or TARGETNAME. You must complete the TARGETLIBS macro with usbclient.lib and create the INCLUDES macro with ddk includes, as displayed hereafter:

```
TARGETLIBS= \
    $(SG_OUTPUT_ROOT)\sdk\lib\$(_CPUINDPATH)\coredll.lib \
    $(SG_OUTPUT_ROOT)\oak\lib\$(_CPUINDPATH)\usbclient.lib \


INCLUDES= \
    $(SG_OUTPUT_ROOT)\ddk\inc \
```

Code snippet is from Macro definitions in the WebCam SubProject SOURCES

As the build process uses the .BIB and .REG files of your subproject to incorporate the DLL in the Compact 7 image and to create the registry keys dedicated to driver loading, you may check the content of these files to avoid a successful but useless build.

The WebCam.bib file contains a unique line for the WebCam.dll executable file; the letter K at the end can incorporate WebCam.dll as a kernel driver.

```
webcam.dll      $(_FLATRELEASEDIR)\webcam.dll      NK      SHK
```

Code snippet is from Subproject file WebCam.bib

The WebCam.reg file contains USB Video_Class driver loading directives.

```
[HKEY_LOCAL_MACHINE\Drivers\USB\ClientDrivers\Video_Class]
    "Prefix"="CAM"
    "Dll"="Webcam.dll"

[HKEY_LOCAL_MACHINE\Drivers\USB\LoadClients\Default\Default\14\Video_Class]
    "DLL"="webcam.dll"
```

Code snippet is from Subproject file WebCam.reg

When your subproject builds successfully, the RELDIR and MAKEIMG steps of the OS build process can incorporate the driver in your image. Testing the compatibility of the WebCam driver with your camera is fairly straightforward. You just have to let the image boot on your target and then plug in your USB camera; the screen of the target should not display a pop-up asking for a USB driver name. Following are some USB cameras successfully tested with the CeWebCam driver:

```
USBCAMSTRUCT csCameras[] =
{
    {TEXT("Logitech QuickCam Pro5000"),VID_LOGITECH, PID_QUICKCAMPRO5000},
    {TEXT("Logitech QuickCam Fusion"), VID_LOGITECH, 0x08c1},
    {TEXT("Logitech QuickCam Orbit"),  VID_LOGITECH, 0x08c2},
    {TEXT("Logitech QuickCam Notebook Pro"), VID_LOGITECH, 0x08c3},
    {TEXT("Logitech WebCam C210"),      VID_LOGITECH, 0x0819},
    {TEXT("Logitech HD WebCam C270"),   VID_LOGITECH, 0x0825},
    {TEXT("Logitech Portable WebCam C905"), VID_LOGITECH, 0x080a},
    {TEXT("Logitech QuickCam Vision Pro"),  VID_LOGITECH, 0x09a6},
};
```

Code snippet is from updated USB camera list in USBCode.cpp

When the WebCam driver is loaded, you are ready to take pictures and save them in image files on the device.

Using the USB Camera Inside an Application

WebCamRead is a console application that uses the WebCam driver to take pictures; it first queries the WebCam driver to obtain the video formats supported by the connected USB camera. The available video formats display on the screen, and the user chooses one of them to take a snapshot. Depending on the image encoding of the video format, the snapshot is stored in a dedicated image file:

➤ Uncompressed RGB bitmap (.BMP)

➤ Compressed JPEG (.JPG)

➤ Raw camera output (.DAT)

All camera transactions inside WebCamRead require only three Win32 functions that call the driver interface:

➤ `CreateFile`   calls   `CAM_Open`

➤ `CloseHandle`   calls   `CAM_Close`

➤ `DeviceIOControl` calls   `CAM_IOControl`

The entry `CAM_Init` is called when the camera is connected to the system in and the driver is loaded by `device.dll`, and `CAM_Deinit` is called when the camera is disconnected from the system and the driver is unloaded. You may reinitialize the WebCam driver by simply using the plug-and-play capability of the USB bus.

All the structures and constants required to talk to the WebCam driver are in a dedicated file called `WebCamSDK.h`. The list of include files for WebCamRead clearly shows the minimal dependencies of this application.

```
#include <windows.h>        // Win32 API
#include <winioctl.h>       // Needed for CTLCODE macro
#include <stdio.h>          // ANSI C IO
#include "WebCamSDK.h"      // USB camera diver interface
```

Code snippet is from Include section in WebCamRead.cpp

To gain access to the camera, you need a valid handle from the WebCam driver with a call to `CreateFile`. When a Webcam is connected to the system, the driver is loaded as the first instance so you always open the name `"CAM1:"`

```cpp
HANDLE hCam;                     // driver handle

// Open WebCAM driver
hCam = CreateFile (_T("CAM1:"), GENERIC_WRITE | GENERIC_READ,
                   0, NULL, OPEN_EXISTING, 0, NULL);
if (INVALID_HANDLE_VALUE == hCam)
{
    _tprintf(_T("Cannot open Camera Driver\n"));
    return 0;
}
```

Code snippet is from USB camera initialization in WebCamRead.cpp

With a valid handle you can list the supported formats by using a dedicated IOCTL code. The characteristics of each format are described in a `FORMATPROPS` structure, and the `DeviceIOControl` function must provide the format index and frame index in a `VIDEOFORMAT` structure.

```cpp
// Camera Properties array
#define MAX_FORMATS 20
FORMATPROPS vFormats[MAX_FORMATS];

// Obtain video formats
for (int i = 0; i < MAX_FORMATS; i++)
{
    VIDFORMATSTRUCT videoFormat;
    DWORD dwQueryBytes = 0;

    // query structure preparation
    memset (&videoFormat, 0, sizeof(videoFormat));
    videoFormat.cbSize = sizeof(VIDFORMATSTRUCT);
    videoFormat.wFormatIndex = 1;
    videoFormat.wFrameIndex = i+1;

    // Get information about a given video format
    res = DeviceIoControl(hCam,
                    IOCTL_CAMERA_DEVICE_GETVIDEOFORMAT,
                    (LPVOID)&videoFormat, sizeof(VIDFORMATSTRUCT),
                    &vFormats[i], sizeof(FORMATPROPS),
                    &dwQueryBytes, NULL);

    if ( !res  || dwQueryBytes != sizeof(FORMATPROPS))
    {
        _tprintf(_T("Last VIDEOFORMAT at index= %d\n"), i);
        break;
    }
    dwBytes += dwQueryBytes;
}
```

Code snippet is from USB camera video formats query in WebCamRead.cpp

The video formats display on the target screen, and the user can select one of the formats to capture a snapshot. Figure 41-3 shows an example of the WebCamRead output screen.

```
File  Edit  Help
Last IOCTL_CAMERA_DEVICE_GETVIDEOFORMAT at index= 18

No    Resol.   Type  Index Frame    Bytes
-------------------------------------------------
0     640x480    5     1     1      614400
1     160x120    5     1     2       38400
2     176x144    5     1     3       50688
3     320x240    5     1     4      153600
4     352x288    5     1     5      202752
5     640x360    5     1     6      460800
6     640x400    5     1     7      512000
7     768x480    5     1     8      737280
8     800x456    5     1     9      729600
9     800x504    5     1    10      806400
10    800x600    5     1    11      960000
11    864x480    5     1    12      829440
12    960x720    5     1    13     1382400
13   1280x720    5     1    14     1843200
14   1280x800    5     1    15     2048000
15   1600x904    5     1    16     2892800
16   1600x1000   5     1    17     3200000
17   1600x1200   5     1    18     3840000
-------------------------------------------------
Do a snapshot for which No? 4
...Got frame, size= 202752 bytes

Image saved in \Temp\frame.bmp
```

FIGURE 41-3

The FORMATPROPS structure contains several fields in addition to those listed by WebCamRead, but the width, height, and type are the most important for image capture. One camera usually has a unique type for all its video formats; the types codes are defined in WebCamSDK.h.

```
// These video format IDs match the formats supported
// by the USB Video spec.
//
#define VIDFORMAT_UNCOMPRESSED              0x0005
#define VIDFORMAT_MJPEG                     0x0007
#define VIDFORMAT_MPEG2TS                   0x000A
#define VIDFORMAT_DV                        0x000C
```

Code snippet is from USB camera video types in WebCamSDK.cpp

The most common types supported by USB cameras are bitmap (0x0005) and JPEG (0x0007), corresponding respectively to uncompressed and compressed images. The buffer size in FORMATPROPS corresponds to the maximum image size; it is exactly the image size for the uncompressed type and maximum image size for the compressed type. The image type can be used to select the correct storage file format when WebCamRead can save the snapshot.

To capture a frame, WebCamRead starts a video acquisition sequence and grabs the first frame returned by the driver. A STARTVIDSTRUCT is passed to the driver in the DeviceIOControl to provide format identification and video acquisition characteristics.

```
// ------- start stream and get first frame ------------
STARTVIDSTRUCT svStruct;

// Parameters needed to start a stream
dwBytes = 0;
svStruct.cbSize = sizeof(STARTVIDSTRUCT);
svStruct.wFormatIndex = vFormats[formatIndex].wFormatIndex;
svStruct.wFrameIndex = vFormats[formatIndex].wFrameIndex;
svStruct.dwInterval = vFormats[formatIndex]
                        .dwInterval[vFormats[formatIndex]
                        .nNumInterval - 1];
svStruct.dwNumBuffs = NUMBUFFS;
svStruct.dwPreBuffSize = PREBUFFSIZE;
svStruct.dwPostBuffSize = 0;

// Start the video stream
res = DeviceIoControl(hCam,
                        IOCTL_CAMERA_DEVICE_STARTVIDEOSTREAM,
                        (LPVOID)&svStruct, sizeof(STARTVIDSTRUCT),
                        0, 0,
                        &dwBytes, NULL);
```

Code snippet is from video acquisition start sequence in WebCamRead.cpp

When the video stream starts, the application reads frames from the driver using a specific "get next frame" IOCTL, which requires two structures. One GETFRAMESTRUCT provides information about the operation, and the other GETFRAMESTRUCTOUT can be used to retrieve the frame. You may note that this IOCTL is also used when you read the camera output continuously. One constraint in that case is to give back the frame buffers to the driver by passing the (n-1) frame pointer in the GETFRAMESTRUCT typed parameter and by setting the GETFRAMEFLAG_FREEBUF_VALID flag.

```
// Call the driver for a frame
GETFRAMESTRUCT gfsIn;
GETFRAMESTRUCTOUT gfsOut;
int nbFrm = 0;

memset (&gfsIn, 0, sizeof(GETFRAMESTRUCT));
gfsIn.cbSize = sizeof(GETFRAMESTRUCT);
gfsIn.dwFlags = GETFRAMEFLAG_GET_LATESTFRAME;
gfsIn.dwFlags |= GETFRAMEFLAG_TIMEOUT_VALID;
gfsIn.dwTimeout = 10000;

memset (&gfsOut, 0, sizeof (GETFRAMESTRUCTOUT));
gfsOut.cbSize = sizeof (GETFRAMESTRUCTOUT);

// Get the next frame of video
res = DeviceIoControl (hCam,
                        IOCTL_CAMERA_DEVICE_GETNEXTVIDEOFRAME,
                        &gfsIn, sizeof(GETFRAMESTRUCT),
                        &gfsOut, sizeof(GETFRAMESTRUCTOUT),
                        &dwBytes, NULL);
```

Code snippet is from video frame acquisition in WebCamRead.cpp

The frame returned by the driver can be stored in an image file according to the video type. For types bitmap (0x0005) and JPEG (0x0007), to build valid BMP and JPG image files, WebCamRead has to modify the frame buffer and/or prepare a file header. This job is achieved by two dedicated functions: storeBMPfile and storeJPGfile.

Available for download on Wrox.com

```
// store frame according to format
switch (vFormats[formatIndex].wFormatType)
{
case VIDFORMAT_UNCOMPRESSED :
    storeBMPfile(TEXT("\\Temp\\frame.bmp"),
                (unsigned char*)gfsOut.pFrameData,
                vFormats[formatIndex].dwWidth,
                vFormats[formatIndex].dwHeight);
    break;

case VIDFORMAT_MJPEG :
    storeJPGfile(TEXT("\\Temp\\frame.jpg"),
                (unsigned char*)gfsOut.pFrameData,
                gfsOut.dwFrameSize);
    break;

default :
    storeframe(TEXT("\\Temp\\frame.dat"),
                (char*)gfsOut.pFrameData,
                gfsOut.dwFrameSize);
    break;
}
```

Code snippet is from video frame storage in WebCamRead.cpp

When the snapshot is saved in a file, WebCamRead closes the video stream with a last IOCTL and also closes the driver handle.

Available for download on Wrox.com

```
// close video stream
res = DeviceIoControl(hCam,
                    IOCTL_CAMERA_DEVICE_STOPVIDEOSTREAM,
                    0, 0, 0, 0, &dwBytes, NULL);
CloseHandle(hCam);
```

Code snippet is from video frame storage in WebCamRead.cpp

The compressed frame format is MJPEG and corresponds to the frame buffer description of a JPEG file. The only actions storeJPGfile has to perform is to add a constant JPG file header and to remove the existing AVI header at the beginning of the frame. This code is provided in the demo application of the CeWebCam Codeplex driver.

The uncompressed frame format of the USB cameras listed earlier contains pixels encoded in YCbCr-422. Y stands for luma Cb and Cr stand for chroma (respectively blue and red); 422 means that the luma information is twice the size of the chroma information. In the frame buffer pixels are encoded by pairs (pix0, pix1) on 4 bytes containing respectively (Y-pix0, Cb-pix0&pix1, Y-pix1, Cr-pix0&pix1); you notice that pixels in the pair share their chroma components.

To create a 24-bit BMP file, the YCbCr-422 encoding must be converted in RGB values by a dedicated YCbCrToRGB function.

```
// brief Saturate value between 0 and 255
inline unsigned char saturate_0_255(int val)
{   return ((val < 0) ? 0 : ((val > 255) ? 255 : val)); }
#define Y_MUL         1.164f
#define CR_MUL_RED    1.793f
#define CR_MUL_GREEN  0.534f
#define CB_MUL_GREEN  0.213f
#define CB_MUL_BLUE   2.115f


#define YCB422_TO_BGR_SCALEBITS 15
#define YCB422_TO_BGR_ONE_HALF (1 << (YCB422_TO_BGR_SCALEBITS - 1))
#define YCB422_TO_BGR_FIX(x)  ((int) ((x) *
                                (1<<YCB422_TO_BGR_SCALEBITS) + 0.5))

//    Translate 2-byte YCbCr to 3-byte RGB
inline void YCbCr422ToRGB(unsigned char* source, int width, int height,
                          unsigned char* dest)
{
static const int yMultiplier       = YCB422_TO_BGR_FIX(Y_MUL);
static const int crMultiplierRed    = YCB422_TO_BGR_FIX(CR_MUL_RED);
static const int crMultiplierGreen  = YCB422_TO_BGR_FIX(CR_MUL_GREEN);
static const int cbMultiplierGreen  = YCB422_TO_BGR_FIX(CB_MUL_GREEN);
static const int cbMultiplierBlue   = YCB422_TO_BGR_FIX(CB_MUL_BLUE);
static const int oneHalf            = YCB422_TO_BGR_ONE_HALF;

int i, j, w2 = width >> 1;
unsigned char* bmpdata;
int y0, y1, cb, cr, crcbGreen;

  // fill pixels from the end for BMP file
  bmpdata = dest + width*height*3 - 1;

  for(j=0; j<height; j++)
  {
    for(i=0; i<w2; i++)
    {
      y0 = *source++;
      cb = *source++;
      y1 = *source++;
      cr = *source++;

      cb -= 128;
      y0 = (y0 - 16) * yMultiplier;
      cr -= 128;
      y1 = (y1 - 16) * yMultiplier;
      crcbGreen = (crMultiplierGreen * cr) + (cbMultiplierGreen * cb);

      // fill pixel array, 3 bytes per pixel
```

```
        *bmpdata-- = saturate_0_255((y0+(crMultiplierRed*cr)+oneHalf) >>
                                    YCB422_TO_BGR_SCALEBITS); //R0
        *bmpdata-- = saturate_0_255((y0-crcbGreen+oneHalf) >>
                                    YCB422_TO_BGR_SCALEBITS); //G0
        *bmpdata-- = saturate_0_255((y0+(cbMultiplierBlue*cb)+oneHalf) >>
                                    YCB422_TO_BGR_SCALEBITS); //B0
        *bmpdata-- = saturate_0_255((y1+(crMultiplierRed*cr)+oneHalf) >>
                                    YCB422_TO_BGR_SCALEBITS); //R1
        *bmpdata-- = saturate_0_255((y1-crcbGreen+oneHalf) >>
                                    YCB422_TO_BGR_SCALEBITS); //G1
        *bmpdata-- = saturate_0_255((y1+(cbMultiplierBlue*cb)+oneHalf) >>
                                    YCB422_TO_BGR_SCALEBITS); //B1
    }
  }
}
```

Code snippet is from uncompressed format transformation in WebCamRead.cpp

The `storeBMPfile` now has a 24-bit RGB frame buffer; it has to create a BMP header with the corresponding image fields and write the snapshot file.

Available for download on Wrox.com

```
//    Save UNCOMPRESSED frame as BMP file
int storeBMPfile(LPCWSTR fname, unsigned char* pFrame, int width,
                 int height)
{
HANDLE hFile;
DWORD nbbytes;
unsigned char *rgb;
BMPHeader myH;
unsigned short magic;

    hFile = CreateFile(fname, GENERIC_READ | GENERIC_WRITE, 0,
                    NULL, CREATE_ALWAYS, FILE_ATTRIBUTE_NORMAL, NULL);

    if (INVALID_HANDLE_VALUE != hFile)
    {
        rgb = (unsigned char*)malloc(width * height * 3);

        // transform YCbCr values to RGB
        YCbCr422ToRGB(pFrame, width, height, rgb);

        // prepare BMP header (all 32 bits unless indicated)
        magic = 0x4D42;     //16 bit
        myH.filesize = width*height*3 + sizeof(myH) + sizeof(magic);
        myH.unused = 0;    // 2x16 bit reserved
        myH.start = sizeof(myH) + sizeof(magic);
        myH.leftbytes = sizeof(myH) + sizeof(magic) - 14;
        myH.width = width;
        myH.height = height;
        myH.planes = 1;     //16 bit
        myH.bppixel = 24;   //16 bit
        myH.compress = 0;
        myH.pixlsize = width*height*3;
```

```
        myH.hres = 2835;
        myH.vres = 2835;
        myH.palette = 0;
        myH.colors = 0;

        // write header
        WriteFile(hFile, (char*)&magic, sizeof(magic), &nbbytes, NULL);
        WriteFile(hFile, (char*)&myH, sizeof(myH), &nbbytes, NULL);
        // write pixels
        WriteFile(hFile, rgb, (width * height * 3), &nbbytes, NULL);

        CloseHandle(hFile);
        _tprintf(_T("Image saved in %s\n"),fname);
    }
    else
        _tprintf(_T("Cannot create file %s\n"),fname);

    return 0;
}
```

Code snippet is from Save frame as BMP file in WebCamRead.cpp

The WebCamRead application has now completed the process to capture an image and save it to a file. The series of actions taken during this operation are:

1. Open the driver.

2. Get the list of video formats for the connected camera.

3. Start a video stream for a given format.

4. Grab the first frame of the stream.

5. Convert and save the frame to a file.

6. Close the video stream.

7. Close the driver.

SUMMARY

By integrating a USB camera in your embedded devices, you open a wide field of possibilities; it can also enhance the interactivity and attractiveness of the equipment you design.

This chapter demonstrated how you can use the CeWebCam driver from Codeplex on a Compact 7 platform. This driver has a simple interface based on IOCTL commands and is suitable for embedded applications with strong constraints on component dependencies.

PART VII
Sample Projects

42

Develop a Windows Network Projector

- ➤ Developing a Compact 7 OS design using the Network Projector design template
- ➤ Customizing the Network Project OS design
- ➤ Deploying a Network Projector OS run-time image
- ➤ Using the Windows Network Projector

Whether delivering a presentation to a large audience in the auditorium, or small group in the business conference room, using a projector to show PowerPoint slides from the computer to a larger screen has been a common practice for years. As part of the presentation task, the presenter has to tangle with a bulky cable and adjust the computer's display settings to be compatible with the projector. Afterward, the presenter has to manually adjust the display settings back to the original settings. Sometimes, getting the projector to work with the computer can be problematic.

Using a Windows Network projector, built with Windows Embedded Compact technology, you can easily connect a Windows 7 or Vista notebook PC to the project through a wired or wireless network connection, using the Connect to Network Projector Wizard. This wizard is included as part of Windows 7 and Vista Home Premium or higher versions.

When connecting to the Windows Network Projector, the Windows 7 or Vista PC's Connect to Network Projector Wizard can detect the display resolution supported by the Windows Network Projector and automatically adjust the PC's display settings to work with the projector. Afterward, the wizard reverses the PC's display settings back to its original settings, as it disconnects the PC from the projector.

The Windows Network Project and the Connect to Network Projector Wizard greatly simplifies the tasks to establish connection between a computer and projector, without the need to install additional software or drivers.

Using hardware with quality BSP for Windows Embedded Compact, you can easily build a Windows Network Projector device with the design template provided as part of the Platform Builder development tool.

WINDOWS NETWORK PROJECTOR APPLICATION

The Network Projector OS design template is one of the templates provided as part of the Platform Builder for Compact 7 development tool. This template provides the starting point for OEM device makers to develop a Windows Network Projector device that works with the Connect to Network Projector Wizard, which comes as part of Windows 7 and Vista operating systems, Home Premium and higher versions. When developing a Compact 7 OS design using the Network Projector template, the Pictor application, Windows Network Projector application, is included in the OS design from the following directory:

```
$(_PUBLICROOT)\RDP\OAK\PICTOR
```

This directory provides source code for the Windows Network Projector application, which you can use as the starting point to customize and build a Windows Network Projector device.

DEVELOPING A WINDOWS NETWORK PROJECTOR

The exercise in this section goes through the steps to develop a Windows Network Project device using an eBox-3310A (eBox) as the target device.

After you complete the exercise, you can use the eBox, equipped with the Compact 7 OS run-time image from the exercise, to enable an existing projector to become a Windows Network Projector.

 The exercise in this section provides simplified steps to develop and customize an OS design. Refer to Chapter 7, "OS Design," for more detailed coverage of OS design development.

Create a Windows Network Projector OS Design

Launch VS2008 and work through the following steps to develop an OS design using the Network Projector template:

1. From the VS2008 File menu, select New, and click Project to bring up the New Project screen.

2. From the New Project screen's left pane, select Platform Builder.

3. From the right pane, select OS Design, enter **MyWNP** as the project name, and click OK to bring up the OS Design Wizard.

4. Click Next to bring up the Board Support Packages selection screen.

5. From the list of available BSPs, select ICOP_eBox3310A_70A: X86, and click Next to bring up the OS Design Templates selection screen.

6. Expand the Enterprise Device folder to select the Network Projector template, and click Finish.

7. At this point, the Catalog Item Notification screen displays to warn the NDIS User-mode I/O Protocol Driver, Web Server, and Web Services on Devices components, included in the OS design, may pose potential security issues. Click Acknowledge to close the screen.

With help from the OS Design Wizard, Network Projector OS design template and ICOP_eBox3310A_70A BSP, the above steps created the initial OS design project workspace for the exercise in this chapter.

Customize the Windows Network Projector OS Design

Continue from the previous section, and work through the following steps to customize the OS design:

8. From the VS2008 View menu, select Other Windows, and click Catalog Items View to bring up the Catalog Items View tab.

9. From the Catalog Items View tab, expand the ICOP_eBox3310A_70A: X86 BSP node, under the \Third Party\BSP folder.

10. Select and include the following components from the ICOP_eBox3310A_70A BSP in the OS design:

>   ➤   ATAPI (IDE) Storage driver

>   ➤   XGI Z9s Display driver

>   ➤   VGA-06 1024x768x16 @ 60Hz

>   ➤   R6040 Ethernet driver

>   ➤   256MB RAM

>   ➤   USB Audio driver

11. From the VS2008 Project menu, click MyWNP Properties to bring up the MyWNP Property Pages screen.

12. From the MyWNP Property Pages screen's left pane, expand the Configuration Properties node to select the Build Options node.

13. From the right pane, change the Enable KITL build option from Yes to No.

14. Click Apply and then click OK to close the MyWNP Property Pages screen.

At this point, the MyWNP OS design is configured with the necessary components and settings to generate a working Compact 7 OS image for the eBox, with a Windows Network Projector application included as part of the OS run-time image.

Generate an OS Run-Time Image

Continue from the previous section, work through the following step to generate an OS run-time image from the OS design:

15. From the VS2008 Build menu, click Build Solution to launch the process to build and generate an OS run-time image from the OS design.

Depending on the development station's processor speed, available system memory, and other factors, the build process may take from 10 minutes to more than 20 minutes.

After the build process completes, the Compact 7 OS run-time image, with Windows Network Application compiled as part of the image, is generated in the build release directory.

Deploy OS Run-time Image Using DiskPrep

In the previous section, a Compact 7 OS run-time image, `NK.BIN`, is generated in the following build release directory, for the MyWNP OS design project:

```
$(_OSDESIGNROOT)\RelDir\ICOP_eBox3310A_70A_x86_Release
```

Work through the following steps to deploy the OS run-time image to Compact Flash storage for the eBox, using a USB to Compact Flash adapter:

1. Create the following folder to use as the workspace for the exercise:

```
C:\WorkSpace
```

2. Copy the following files to the `WorkSpace` folder:

➤ The DiskPrep utility's executable, `DISKPREP.EXE`. This utility is available for download from `http://archive.msdn.microsoft.com/DiskPrep`.

➤ Compact 7 OS run-time image, `NK.BIN`, generated from the MyWNP OS design, in the build release directory.

 Chapter 28, "The DiskPrep Power Toy," provides more detailed information about the DiskPrep utility.

3. Attach the USB to Compact Flash adapter to one of the USB interfaces on the Development station.

4. After the system recognizes the Compact Flash, launch the DiskPrep utility, `DISKPREP.EXE`, to bring up the DiskPrep screen.

5. From the DiskPrep screen, select the Compact Flash from the Disk Selection drop-down list.

6. From the Use File System Format selection, select FAT32.

7. Select the Load Specific Image File Copied From option, and click Browse to bring up the Select File to Execute on Boot screen.

8. From the Select File to Execute on Boot screen, navigate to the MyWNP OS design's build release directory, select the NK.BIN file, and click Open. At this point, the DiskPrep screen should look like Figure 42-1.

9. From the DiskPrep screen, click OK to configure the Compact Flash. As you click OK, the Confirm Dangerous Action screen is shown to warn the process will destroy existing data in the Compact Flash.

10. Click OK to continue and bring up the DiskPrep Progress screen.

11. The DiskPrep Progress screen displays a series of messages, showing the activities and progress. After the task to configure the Compact Flash completes, the DiskPrep Progress screen, along with the main DiskPrep program screen, closes.

FIGURE 42-1

At the conclusion of this exercise, the Compact Flash for the eBox is configured to launch the Compact 7 OS run-time image generated from the MyWNP OS design. When you install this Compact Flash to the eBox, the OS run-time image boots up to the Windows Network Projector application, as shown in Figure 42-2.

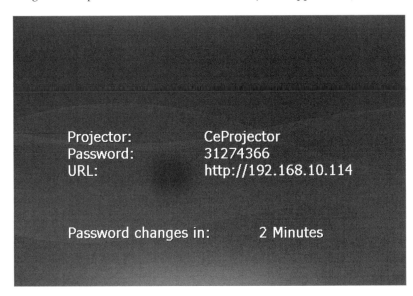

FIGURE 42-2

USING WINDOWS NETWORK PROJECTOR

Following are the steps to use the Windows Network Projector device:

1. Attach a projector to the eBox, and connect the eBox and notebook computer to the same Local Area Network, as shown in Figure 42-3.

2. Power on the projector and eBox.

3. After the projector displays the output from the eBox (refer to Figure 42-2), it's ready for use.

From the notebook computer, work through the following steps:

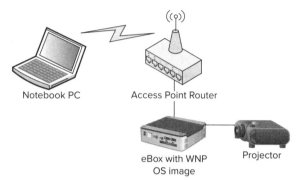

FIGURE 42-3

1. From the startup menu, select the Accessories group, and click Connect to a Network Projector to bring up the Connect to a Network Projector screen, as shown in Figure 42-4.

2. Click Search for a Projector. As Windows Network Projector is detected, the screen updates and lists the detected projector in the Available Projectors list, as shown in Figure 42-5.

FIGURE 42-4

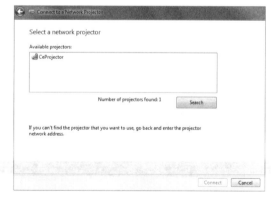

FIGURE 42-5

3. From the Available Projectors list, click the CeProjector, enter the password from the screen, as shown in Figure 42-6, and click Connect.

4. As the Connect to a Network Projector Wizard attempts to connect, the Network Projector screen displays to warn that connecting to the projector will change the computer's display resolution, as shown in Figure 42-7.

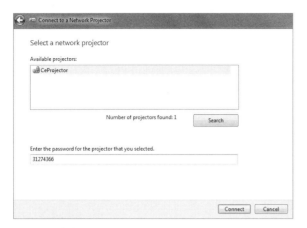

FIGURE 42-6

FIGURE 42-7

5. From the Network Projector screen, click Yes to continue.

6. At this point, the Network Projector - Display Settings screen displays, as shown in Figure 42-8. Click Yes to continue.

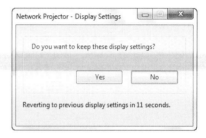

FIGURE 42-8

After the preceding step, the notebook computer's screen should display on the Windows Network Projector.

To disconnect, click the Network Project Program icon from the notebook computer's task bar to bring up the Projecting: CeProjector screen, as shown in Figure 42-9, and click Disconnect.

After disconnecting from the Windows Network Projector, the notebook computer automatically reverts back to its original display settings.

FIGURE 42-9

SUMMARY

Although the Windows Network Projector is a complex device to develop, the information provided in this chapter shows you can rapidly develop this device with the right hardware and tools.

Platform Builder for Compact 7 is an effective and efficient tool, with a large pool of resources, design templates, and sample code to help you rapidly develop a broad range of smart, connected, and service-oriented embedded devices.

43

Phidgets Devices

WHAT'S IN THIS CHAPTER?

➤ Using a Phidgets driver for Windows Embedded Compact 7

➤ **Developing an OS design with Phidgets support**

➤ Developing Compact 7 RFID reader application

In addition to the host controller, an embedded development project often needs to integrate with different peripherals to capture input and detect or sense system and environment status. These peripherals are typically built with a small microcontroller that provides a simple function and interfaces to the host controller through a USB, an RS-232, an RS-485, an I2C, an SPI, or a parallel or GPIO interface.

This chapter talks about interfacing external peripherals, using Phidgets devices, to a Windows Embedded Compact 7 device to add additional functionality to the Compact 7 device.

This chapter goes through the exercises to develop a custom Compact 7 OS design, integrate the necessary driver components to support the additional peripherals to the OS design, develop an application to access the device, and package everything into a compiled OS run-time image to deploy to the target device.

PHIDGETS DEVICES

A Phidgets device is a family of low-cost microcontroller-based modules with a USB interface. The Phidgets product family consists of different modules; each design serves a different purpose. Following is a list of different types of currently available Phidgets devices:

➤ Microcontroller module with GPIO

➤ Microcontroller with analog input and output

➤ Microcontroller module with relays

➤ Servos and motor controller

➤ Temperature sensor

➤ Light sensor

➤ Motion sensor

➤ IR distance sensor

➤ Pressure sensor

➤ RFID reader

These Phidgets devices are cost efficient and popular among the academic and hobbyist developer communities.

Device Driver Project on Codeplex

There is a community project to develop a Windows Embedded Compact device drivers for the Phidgets devices on the Codeplex site, initially created to support the previous version of Windows Embedded CE 6.0.

An updated device driver component designed to support Windows Embedded Compact 7 is now available from the project site. The URL to the Phidgets device driver project on the Codeplex site is:

```
http://phidgetswincedriver.codeplex.com
```

The exercise in the chapter is developed based on the driver component from this Codeplex project, using the following driver package:

➤ PhidgetsFrameWork v214 for Compact 7 (x86)

The source code for the Phidgets driver is available from the Codeplex site, for those of you interested to delve into the code.

Phidgets Driver Component

The Phidgets driver component used for the application project in this chapter is created as one of the Compact 7 third-party company components. When properly installed, it shows up on the Platform Builder for Compact 7 component catalog, which you can select and include as part of an OS design project, to be compiled as part of the OS run-time image.

The Phidgets driver component is installed in the development station in the following directory:

```
$(_WINCEROOT)\3rdParty\PhidgetFrameWork_v214_Compact7
```

When properly installed, the Phidgets driver component appears on the Platform Builder for Compact 7 component catalog, under the following folder:

```
\Third Party\Embedded101\
```

PHIDGETS DEVICES APPLICATION

In addition to supporting the native code environment, the Phidgets driver for the Compact 7 component package includes a library component to support managed code applications and uses a similar namespace structure as the .NET Compact Framework.

This chapter works through different exercises to develop the following:

➤ Configure a custom OS design to support the Phidgets device, using an eBox-3310A as the target device.

➤ Generate a SDK from the OS design project to support application development.

➤ Develop an RFID reader application using the Phidgets RFID reader module in managed code.

➤ Include the application to the OS design, and compile as part of the OS run-time image, configured to launch the application during startup.

Prerequisites

To develop an OS design for an eBox-3310A configured to support the Phidgets device and develop the RFID application for the exercises in this chapter, you need to have the following components installed in the development station:

➤ Compact 7 BSP for the eBox-3310A (ICOP_eBox3310A_70A)

➤ Phidgets driver for Compact 7 (PhidgetFramework_v214_Compact7)

➤ AutoLaunch component for Compact 7 (AutoLaunch_v200_Compact7)

➤ CoreCon component for Compact 7 (CoreCon_v200_Compact7)

In addition to the required software, you need the following hardware components:

➤ An eBox-3310A

➤ A PhidgetRFID reader

You can find more information about the eBox-3310A and PhidgetRFID reader from the following URLs:

```
http://www.embeddedpc.net/eBox3310AMSJK/
```

```
http://www.embeddedpc.net/PhidgetRFID/
```

Develop an OS Design with Phidgets Support

Work through the following steps to develop an OS design for an eBox-3310A that supports a Phidgets device:

1. From the VS2008 File menu, select New, and click Project to launch the New Project screen.

2. From the New Project screen's left pane, select Platform Builder. Select OS Design from the right pane, enter **MyRFID** as the project name, and click OK to bring up the OS Design Wizard.

3. From the OS Design Wizard screen, click Next to bring up the Board Support Packages selection screen.

4. Select the ICOP_eBox3310A_70A: X86 BSP, and click Next to bring up the Design Templates selection screen.

5. From the Design Templates selection screen's left pane, expand the Enterprise Device folder, select the Industrial Controller template, and click Next to bring up the Application and Media selection screen.

6. From the Application and Media selection screen, select the following component, and click Next to bring up the OS Design Wizard's Networking and Communication selection screen:

   ➤ .NET Compact Framework 3.5

7. For the Network and Communication selection step, keep the default selection, and click Next to continue and bring up the final OS Design Project Wizard step.

8. As you click Finish, security warning messages are raised, via the Catalog Item Notification screen, to notify one or more of the catalog items included that the OS design may compromise system security. Click Acknowledge to acknowledge the warning, and close the screen to complete the OS Design Wizard steps.

Customize and Build the MyRFID OS Design

After the OS Design Wizard completes, Platform Builder creates and configures the initial workspace for the MyRFID OS design project, using the selected OS design template, BSPs, and components.

Work through the following steps to customize and build the OS design:

1. To configure the OS design to include the component needed to support the RFID application, locate and include the following ICOP_eBox3310A BSP components in the OS design, from the Platform Builder component catalog:

   ➤ ATAPI – IDE Storage

   ➤ Hive-based registry support

   ➤ Z9s XGI Display driver

   ➤ VGA-00 640x480x16 l@ 60Hz

   ➤ R6040 Ethernet driver

   ➤ 256MB RAM

2. Locate and include the following Compact 7 OS component in the OS design, from the Platform Builder component catalog:

   ➤ CAB File Installer/Uninstaller

3. Locate and include the following third-party components in the OS design, from the Platform Builder component catalog:

> ➤ AutoLaunch_v200_Compact7

> ➤ CoreCon_v200_Compact7

> ➤ PhidgetFrameWork_v214_Compact7

4. From the VS2008 Solution Explorer tab, double-click the OSDesign.reg registry file to open the file for editing in the code editor window.

5. On the code editor window in the lower-left portion, click Source to view the OSDesign .reg file in source format, and append the following entries to the file:

```
; Registry for AutoLaunch
[HKEY_LOCAL_MACHINE\Startup]
    "Process0"="ConmanClient2.exe"
    "Process0Delay"=dword:00002710
```

Code snippet is from Chapter43_Snippet.txt

6. From the VS2008 Project menu, click MyRFID Properties to bring up the MyRFID Property Pages screen.

7. From the left pane, expand the Configuration Properties node, and select the Build Options node to bring up the Build Options screen.

8. From the right pane, disable KITL, and click OK to close the screen.

9. From the VS2008 Build menu, click Build Solution to build the OS design project.

Create an SDK from MyRFID OS Design

After the build process completes, continue and work through the following steps to create an SDK for the OS design to support application development:

1. From the VS2008 Project menu, click Add New SDK to bring up the SDK Property Pages.

2. Enter **MyRFID_SDK** as the SDK name and product name.

3. Enter the version number, company name, and company web site information, and click Apply.

4. On the left pane, click Install, and change the MSI File Name from SDK1.msi to **MyRFID_ SDK.msi**; click Apply.

5. On the left pane, select Development Languages.

6. On the right, select the Managed development support option and click OK to close the SDK Wizard.

7. From the VS2008 Build menu, click Build All SDKs to build the SDK.

Install SDK to the Development Station

The MyRFID_SDK generated from the MyRFID OS design in the previous section needs to be installed to the development station to support VS2008 application development.

Launch the following MSI file to install the SDK:

```
$(_OSDESIGNROOT)\SDKs\SDK\MSI\MyRFID_SDK.msi
```

Download an OS Run-time Image to a Target Device

With the SDK needed to support VS2008 application development generated and installed to the development station, download the OS run-time image generated from the MyRFID OS design to the eBox-3310A to support application development in the following section.

 For more information about developing an OS design, refer to Chapter 7, "OS Design."

Develop a Phidgets Application in Managed Code

With the OS run-time image from the previous section downloaded and launched on the target device, you have the necessary environment to support application development for the exercise in this section.

This section works through an exercise to develop an RFID reader application in managed code. Using Visual Basic to develop the application, it provides simple and easy-to-understand code to demonstrate some of the managed code environment's advantage.

Work through the following steps to develop the RFIDReader application:

1. Launch another instance of VS2008.

2. From the VS2008 File menu, select New and click Project to bring up the New Project Wizard screen.

3. From the Project types pane on left, expand the Other Languages node; follow by expanding the Visual Basic node, and click Smart Device.

4. From the Templates pane on the right, click Smart Device Project, enter **RFIDReader** as the project name, enter **c:\Lab** as the location for the project, and click OK to bring up the Add New Smart Device Project screen, as shown in Figure 43-1.

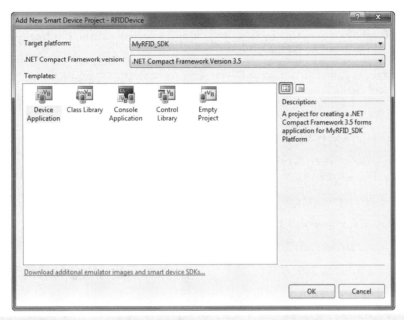

FIGURE 43-1

5. From the Target platform selection, select MyRFID_SDK.

6. From the .NET Compact Framework version selection, select .NET Compact Framework Version 3.5.

7. From the Templates selection pane, select Device Application, and click OK to create the new project.

8. At this point, VS2008 creates the initial workspace for the RFIDReader project and includes a blank form, Form1, with the `mainMenu1` control.

RFID Reader Application — Graphical User Interface

In the previous section, with help from the New Project Wizard, the initial project workspace for the RFID reader application was created. In this section, work through the following steps to assemble and configure the graphical user interface for the application:

1. Work through the following steps to remove the `mainMenu1` control, change Form1's caption, and resize Form1:

   a. Right-mouse-click the `mainMenu1` control, and click Delete to remove this control.

   b. Right-mouse-click Form1, and click Properties to show the properties listing for Form1.

   c. Change Form1's `Text` property to `Compact 7 - RFID Reader`.

   d. Change Form1's `Size` property to 360, 360.

2. From the VS2008 View menu, click Toolbox to bring up the Toolbox window. You can add controls from the Toolbox onto Form1 by double-clicking a selected control. Or drag the selected control from the Toolbox tab onto Form1.

3. From the Toolbox tab, expand the Common Device Controls category to add a `label` control to Form1, and change the following properties for the `label` control:

   a. Change `Location` property to 20, 25.

   b. Change the `Size` property to 150, 20.

4. From the Common Device Controls category, add a `TextBox` control to Form1, and change the following properties for the `TextBox` control:

   a. Change `ScrollBars` property to Vertical.

   b. Change `Multiline` property to True.

   c. Change `Location` property to 20, 50.

   d. Change `Size` property to 320, 200.

5. From the Common Device Controls category, add a `button` control to Form1, and change the following properties for the `button` control:

   a. Change `Text` property to Turn ON RFID.

   b. Change `Location` property to 220, 270.

   c. Change the `Size` property to 120, 20.

6. From the Toolbox tab, expand the Device Components category to add a `Timer` control to Form1. The `Timer` control does not have visual display element. At this point, all the controls are positioned on Form1, as shown in Figure 43-2.

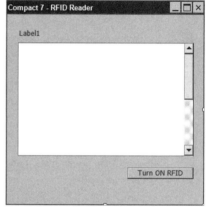

FIGURE 43-2

7. The preceding steps added the following controls onto Form1:

   a. `Label1`

   b. `TextBox1`

   c. `Button1`

   d. `Timer1`

RFID Reader Application — Code

The exercises in previous sections created the initial project workspace and assembled and configured the graphical user interface for the application. In this section, work through the following steps to add a library reference and application code to complete the project:

1. To access the Phidgets RFID reader, you need to add a reference to the required Phidgets library. From the VS2008 Project menu, click Add Reference to bring up the Add Reference screen, as shown in Figure 43-3.

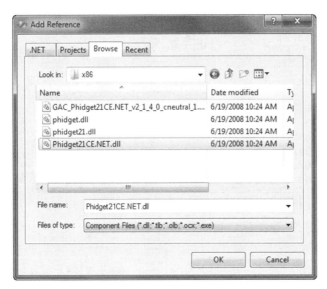

FIGURE 43-3

2. From the Add Reference screen, click the Browse tab. Navigate and select the `Phidget21CE`
`.NET.dll` file from the following directory, and click OK:

```
$(_WINCEROOT)\3rdParty\PhidgetFramework_v214_Compact7\Bin\x86
```

*Phidget Event Handler code runs on a separate thread from the Compact 7's
graphic user interface (GUI) code, which requires you to use the Invoke method
within the Phidget Event Handler to update the application's GUI.*

3. From the VS2008 Solution Explorer tab, right-mouse-click `Form1.vb`; click View Code to
launch the code editor window, and replace all the code, for `Public Class Form1`, with the
following:

Available for
download on
Wrox.com

```vb
Public Class Form1

    Dim WithEvents m_PhidgetRFID As Phidgets.RFID
    ' Variable to keep track whether the RFID reader is attached
    Dim bool_PhidgetRFIDAttached As Boolean

    Private Sub Form1_Load(ByVal sender As System.Object, _
                           ByVal e As System.EventArgs) _
                       Handles MyBase.Load
        '
        bool_PhidgetRFIDAttached = False

        m_PhidgetRFID = New Phidgets.RFID
        m_PhidgetRFID.open()

        Dim dt As Date = DateTime.Now
```

```vb
            Label1.Text = dt.ToString("G")

            TextBox1.Text = ""
            Button1.Text = "Turn On RFID"

            Timer1.Interval = 1000
            Timer1.Enabled = True
        '
    End Sub

    Private Sub Button1_Click(ByVal sender As System.Object, _
                         ByVal e As System.EventArgs) _
                         Handles Button1.Click
        '
        If Button1.Text = "Turn On RFID" Then
            If bool_PhidgetRFIDAttached Then
                m_PhidgetRFID.Antenna = True
                Button1.Text = "Turn OFF RFID"
            End If
        Else
            If bool_PhidgetRFIDAttached Then
                m_PhidgetRFID.Antenna = False
                Button1.Text = "Turn ON RFID"
            End If
        End If
        '
    End Sub

    Private Sub Timer1_Tick(ByVal sender As System.Object, _
                       ByVal e As System.EventArgs) Handles Timer1.Tick
        '
        Dim dt As Date = DateTime.Now
        Dim s As String
        '
        s = dt.ToString("G")
        Me.Invoke(New PrintGUI_delegate(AddressOf PrintGUI_labelTime), s)
        '
    End Sub

    Protected Delegate Sub PrintGUI_delegate(ByVal arg As String)

    Private Sub PrintGUI_labelTime(ByVal arg As String)
        Label1.Text = arg
    End Sub

    Private Sub PrintGUI_TextBox1(ByVal arg As String)
        TextBox1.Text = arg + vbNewLine + TextBox1.Text
    End Sub

    Private Sub PhidgetRFID_Attach(ByVal sender As Object, _
                            ByVal e As Phidgets.Events.AttachEventArgs) _
                            Handles m_PhidgetRFID.Attach
        '
        bool_PhidgetRFIDAttached = True

        Dim s As String = "Attached: " + e.Device.Name + " " + _
```

```
                        e.Device.SerialNumber.ToString()
        Me.Invoke(New PrintGUI_delegate(AddressOf PrintGUI_TextBox1), s)

    End Sub

    Private Sub PhidgetRFID_Detach(ByVal sender As Object, _
                                   ByVal e As Phidgets.Events.DetachEventArgs) _
                                   Handles m_PhidgetRFID.Detach
        '
        bool_PhidgetRFIDAttached = False

        Dim s As String = "Detached: " + e.Device.Name + " " + _
                            e.Device.SerialNumber.ToString()
        Me.Invoke(New PrintGUI_delegate(AddressOf PrintGUI_TextBox1), s)

    End Sub

    Private Sub PhidgetRFID_Tag(ByVal sender As Object, _
                                ByVal e As Phidgets.Events.TagEventArgs) _
                                Handles m_PhidgetRFID.Tag
        '
        Dim s As String = "RFID Read: [" + e.Tag + "]"
        Me.Invoke(New PrintGUI_delegate(AddressOf PrintGUI_TextBox1), s)
        '
    End Sub

End Class
```

Code snippet is from Chapter43_Snippet.txt

In the previous steps, the necessary library reference and code were added. Continue to work through the following steps to configure the project to build in release mode and build the project to generate the application executable:

4. From the VS2008 Build menu, click Configuration Manager to bring up the Configuration Manager screen.

5. From the Configuration Manager screen, select Release from the Active solution configuration selection combo box, and click Close.

6. From the VS2008 Build menu, click Build Solution to build the RFIDReader application project.

Deploy a RFIDReader Application to a Target Device

To deploy the RFIDReader application created in the previous exercise to the target device, you need to do the following:

➤ Install the MyRFID_SDK.msi generated from the MyRFID OS design project, earlier in this chapter.

➤ Download the OS run-time image, generated from the MyRFID OS design earlier in this chapter, to the target device.

➤ Attach a PhidgetRFID reader to the eBox-3310A.

Work through the following steps to deploy the RFIDReader application to the target device:

1. From the VS2008 Tools menu, click Options to bring up the Options screen.

2. From the Options screen's left pane, expand the Device Tools node, and click Devices, to show the Devices selection, as shown in Figure 43-4.

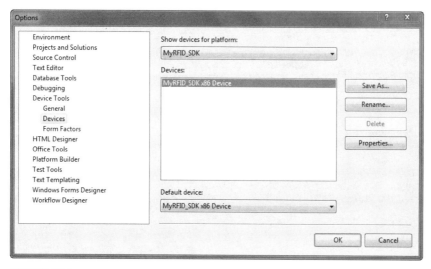

FIGURE 43-4

3. From the Options screen's right pane, select MyRFID_SDK x86 Device from the Devices selection list, and click Properties to bring up MyRFID_SDK x86 Device Properties screen, as shown in Figure 43-5.

4. From the MyRFID_SDK x86 Device Properties screen, click Configure to bring up the Configure TCP/IP Transport screen, as shown in Figure 43-6.

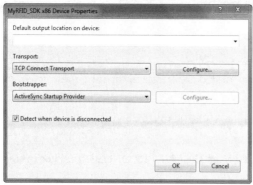

FIGURE 43-5

FIGURE 43-6

5. From the Configure TCP/IP Transport screen, select Use Specific IP Address, and enter the IP address for the target device. Click OK to save and close the screen.

6. Click OK to close the MyRFID_SDK x86 Device Properties screen and Options screen.

7. From the VS2008 Tools menu, click Connect to Device to bring up the Connect to Device screen, as shown in Figure 43-7.

8. From the Platform selection, select MyRFID_SDK, and click Connect. A Connection Succeeded message is shown on the Connecting screen to indicate the CoreCon connection is successfully established between the development station and target device, as shown in Figure 43-8.

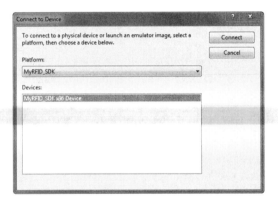

FIGURE 43-7

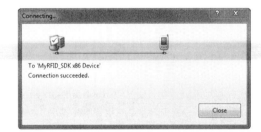

FIGURE 43-8

9. Click Close to close the Connecting screen.

10. From the VS2008 Debug menu, click Start Debugging to deploy the application to the target device, and bring up the Deploy RFIDReader screen, as shown in Figure 43-9.

11. From the Deploy RFIDReader screen, click Deploy to deploy the application.

12. At this point, the Microsoft Visual Studio screen is shown, indicating there are deployment errors, as shown in Figure 43-10.

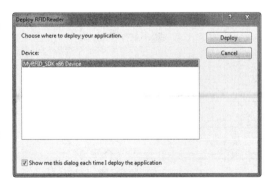

FIGURE 43-9

13. Click Yes to continue and deploy the RFIDReader application. The application should deploy and launch on the target device, as shown in Figure 43-11.

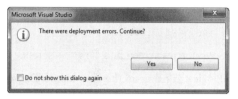

FIGURE 43-10

FIGURE 43-11

VS2008 Application Deployment Error

During the exercise in the previous section, in step 12, a Microsoft Visual Studio dialog was raised to indicate there were errors while deploying the RFIDReader application to the target device.

You can eliminate this error by changing the RFIDReader application project's device setting. Work through the following steps to change the setting:

1. From the VS2008 Solution Explorer tab, right-mouse-click RFIDReader, and click Properties to bring up the RFIDReader project properties.

2. From the RFIDReader properties windows, click Devices to show target device settings, and uncheck the following option, as shown in Figure 43-12:

   ➤ Deploy the Latest Version of .NET Compact Framework (Including Service Packs)

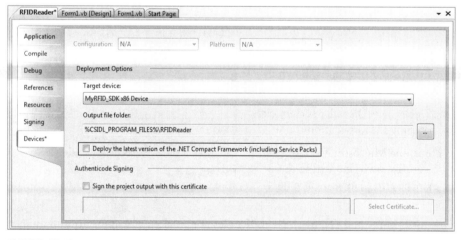

FIGURE 43-12

Include the RFIDReader Application in the OS Run-time Image

To complete the Compact 7 RFID Reader device project, you need to include the RFIDReader application in the OS design and compile the application as part of the OS run-time image. Then configure the OS design to launch the RFIDReader application during startup.

In the earlier exercise in this chapter, the RFIDReader application project was created in the `C:\Lab` folder. The `RFIDReader.exe` application executable for the project was configured to build a release mode executable in the following folder:

`C:\Lab\RFIDReader\RFIDReader\bin\Release`

Work through the following steps to include the RFIDReader application to the OS design and compile the application as part of the OS run-time image:

1. Create the following folder:

   `C:\RFID`

2. Copy the `RFIDReader.exe` executable to the `C:\RFID` folder, from the following directory:

   `C:\Lab\RFIDReader\RFIDReader\bin\Release`

3. Launch the MyRFID OS design project from the VS2008 IDE.

4. From the VS2008 Solution Explorer tab, double-click `OSDesign.bib` to open this file in the code editor window, and append the following entries to the file:

   ```
   FILES
   RFIDReader.exe  C:\RFID\RFIDReader.exe   NK
   ```

5. From the VS2008 Solution Explorer tab, double-click `OSDesign.reg` to open this file in the code editor window, and append the following entries to the file:

   ```
   [HKEY_LOCAL_MACHINE\Startup]
       "Process2"="RFIDReader.exe"
       "Process2Delay"=dword:00002710
   ```

6. From the VS2008 Build menu, click Build Solution to build and generate an OS run-time image compiled with the `RFIDReader.exe` executable and configured to launch during startup.

7. Download the OS run-time image to the target device. After the image is launched on the target device, the RFIDReader application should launch, after approximately a 10-second delay. The value for the Process2Delay registry entry, 00002710 is in hexadecimal. 2710 in hexadecimal is equal to 10000 in decimal, representing 10000 milliseconds, which is equal to 10 seconds.

This concludes the exercise for this chapter. For more information about deploying the Compact 7 OS run-time image to the target device's local storage, refer to Chapter 25, "Deploy OS Run-time Image."

SUMMARY

As you can see from the exercise in this chapter, using the eBox-3310A as the target device, that has a BSP to support Compact 7, and the Phidget RFID reader module, that has a device driver component to support Compact 7, developing Compact 7 RFID reader is a simple process.

Software development is not much different from other work environments that need tools to help the working professionals to perform their jobs efficiently.

The Visual Studio 2008 and Platform Builder for Compact 7 development environment provides an efficient and effective environment to help application developers to rapidly create a new generation of smart, connected, and service-oriented embedded devices.

44

FTDI Devices

WHAT'S IN THIS CHAPTER?

- ➤ Using FTDI USB to Serial devices
- ➤ Creating VCP and D2XX driver Catalog components
- ➤ Exploring FTDI system integration and modules
- ➤ Introducing the CEComponentWiz Wizard
- ➤ Developing a stream driver as a driver wrapper
- ➤ Using serial port access

Future Technology Devices International (FTDI) manufactures USB to serial integrated circuits (ICs) that can be integrated into a board design to give it USB to Serial capabilities. This chapter covers the integration of FTDI ICs with a board design. It also covers the use of some third-party modules that use the FTDI devices to give a system extra functionality such as GPIO, relays, and RFID. The FTDI driver is used as an example of how to integrate a binary driver into an image and for how to wrapper a driver to provide high-level functionality. Managed and native code access to a serial port is introduced. A wizard for creating components for Compact 7 that adds content to an image is introduced and used in integrating the FTDI driver as a Catalog component.

FTDI DEVICES

Future Technology Devices International (FTDI) is a semiconductor manufacturer based in Scotland, that is well known for its USB to serial integrated circuits. The main attraction for using its devices is that they come with royalty-free drivers, although not in source form. FTDI provides device drivers for Windows Embedded CE from CE 4.2. Because the Compact 7 architecture is largely unchanged from CE 6, the current CE 6 FDTI driver can work with Compact 7. Two drivers are available from FTDI for its devices: the Virtual COM Port (VCP) driver and the Direct (D2XX) driver.

A typical FTDI-integrated circuit is the FD232R, a USB to serial device, as illustrated in Figure 44-1. As outlined in Figure 44-2, it implements a USB device interface on one end with an RS232 serial asynchronous receiver and transmitter (UART) interface on the other. Internally it takes the serial signals and translates them to USB signals as the USB to Serial protocol.

FIGURE 44-1

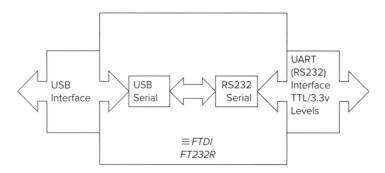

FIGURE 44-2

FTDI make available a range of these integrated circuits with varying functionality with various USB bit rates and RS232 BAUD rates. The FT232R supports fast USB (bit rate maximum of 10M bps) and BAUD rates up to 3M. Although this chip is only compatible with the faster USB 2 (480M bps), other FTDI devices can fully implement USB 2.

A number of FTDI development modules are available that facilitate a simple inclusion of USB functionality into a system that implements all ancillary USB circuitry. Also third-party modules can implement functions such as sensors, RFID, and CAN Bus, which use an FTDI-integrated circuit to implement the USB interface. These modules plug into a host that has the FTDI driver installed and provide their functionality to the host via serial or stream driver code.

FTDI HARDWARE INTERFACE

An FTDI-integrated circuit has the two interfaces (USB and UART) (as shown in Figure 44-2). As per typical UART devices, serial signals are only at TTL or 3.3v levels, not RS232 voltage levels. This means that the UART can directly interface with a microprocessor UART. An FDTI device such as the FT232R would typically integrate into a microcontroller system to implement a USB interface for the system. This would enable the target system to directly connect to a computer system via that system's USB host. The USB interface is implemented, as shown in Figure 44-3. The FT232B UART interface would be directly interfaced to the UART interface of a microcontroller, as shown in Figure 44-4.

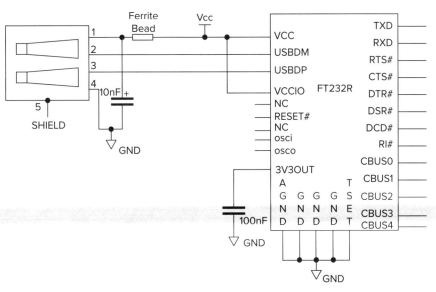

FIGURE 44-3

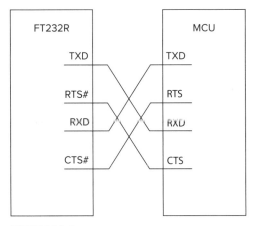

FIGURE 44-4

A USB to Serial cable can be implemented using the device. The FT232R UART signals would be level shifted to RS232 levels via a MAX232 device, as shown in Figure 44-5. The other RS232 modem signals, such as DTR, DSR, DCD, can be similarly implemented.

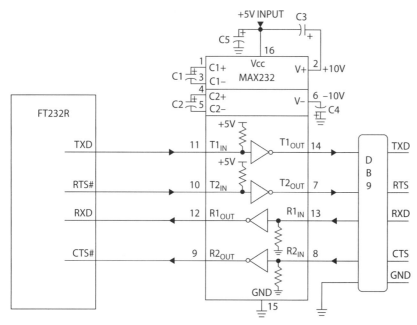

FIGURE 44-5

FTDI Usage

The simplest use of the FTDI technology is as a USB to Serial cable (refer to Figure 44-4). The EasySync Ltd USB-RS232 Adapter Cable is an example of such a cable. Install the FTDI driver and plug the USB end of the cable into the USB host port of the system. Now the system has a serial port. This is useful for systems that don't have serial ports, such as newer desktop PCs and laptops. Most Compact 7 development systems have serial ports though. FTDI markets a USB-USB cable that implements a null modem cable using USB at both ends. The advantage of a cable that uses an FTDI device with a Compact 7 system is that the driver is readily available.

The second usage scenario is where the FTDI is used as the USB interface to a target Compact 7 system. An FTDI device integrates into the target system via the system's microprocessor UART (refer to Figure 44-4). For such a configuration, the system can implement its functionality and provide a custom serial protocol than runs on top of the serial or stream layer. Other systems can connect this device via the USB interface and require an FTDI driver to be installed. End user applications then would action the target system's functionality as a serial or stream application using the custom protocol.

The third usage scenario is to use a third-party module that includes a FTDI chip as its interface. These plug into a computer or Compact 7 system through its USB host port and provide their functionality to the host over the FTDI driver's virtual serial port or via the FTDI stream. The host system requires an FTDI driver so that applications on it can interact with the module. These modules implement a specific set of functions and can simply extend the functionality of a Compact 7 system. There are modules for such things as temperature sensing, RFID, relays, GPIO, ADC, accelerometers, and ZigBee-embedded radios. The plus for using these modules is that the hardware is implemented simply by plugging the module into the system, and the driver is an FTDI driver.

FTDI AS THE USB INTERFACE TO A SYSTEM

As explained before, one usage scenario for the FTDI device was where the system microprocessor has a spare UART that can connect to the FTDI, as shown in Figure 44-6. Generally for development boards this is not an option because there are no spare UARTs because they are usually all fully implemented as RS232 ports. If developing a new board, then an FTDI integrated circuit could be included in the design. Why would you do so when many embedded microprocessors already have USB ports? The answer is because it saves having to develop a USB driver.

The FTDI driver is not part of the BSP because this is needed on the host end of the USB. A BSP driver would need to be developed that implements a serial protocol over the UART for interacting with the Compact 7 system.

The registry settings for the driver include a VendorID (VID) and a ProductID (PID). For systems that use an FTDI integrated circuit, although the VID must always identify FTDI in the driver's registry setting, FTDI can grant OEMs unique PIDs that identify its product. If this is the case, typically a system would use the D2XX driver and implement custom functionality.

For development purposes, there are development modules such as the UM232R. These modules implement the ancillary USB circuitry plus a USB connector. The UART connectivity is provided as some pins. That means that for a development system, a pin-out from the microprocessor's UART that matches the FTDI development module's pin-out is all that is needed to implement USB from a hardware perspective. For example, the UM232R shown in Figure 44-7 plugs into a standard 24-pin 0.6in wide DIP socket.

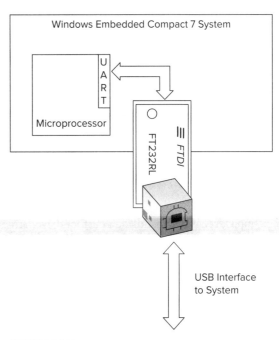

FIGURE 44-6

FIGURE 44-7

FTDI DEVICE DRIVERS

FTDI make available two drivers, the Virtual COM Port (VCP) driver and the Direct (D2XX) driver. The VCP is generally the simpler to use for applications, whereas the D2XX would be used where an FTDI device implements a board's USB interface.

Virtual COM Port Driver (VCP)

The VCP driver is used where a standalone microprocessor implements low-level functionality, such as temperature measurement, which a higher-level system uses. The VCP driver emulates a standard serial port such that the USB device may be communicated with as a standard RS232 device. With the VPC driver installed on a target system such as a PC or Compact 7 system, an FTDI module is plugged into the system's USB host socket via a USB cable. The module's functionality is then available to an application on the target system as a serial interface via a COM port. The module can implement a protocol for its configuration and status and data transfer as a textual protocol via the serial interface.

Direct Driver (D2XX)

The D2XX driver enables direct access by an end user application to an FTDI USB device via a DLL interface. When installed, a custom driver stream is installed. The download of this driver contains the driver DLL (`ftdi_d2xx.dll`), the registry file (`d2xx.reg` in the INF FILEs directory), and the FTDI stream API files that are used with an end-user application. `FTD2xx.h` is the include file that needs to be referenced by the application; `FTD2XX.lib` is linked with it; and `ftd2XX.dll` is the DLL that the application would load and use to interface to the stream and so is deployed with the built application. D2XX would typically be used where an FTDI is used as the USB "front-end" to a Compact 7 system because it facilitates greater end-user customization of the architecture.

For application development using the D2XX driver, refer to `www.ftdichip.com/Support/Documents/ProgramGuides/D2XX_Programmer's_Guide(FT_000071).pdf`.

FTDI USB to SerialRegistry Settings

Recapping from previous chapters, when a USB device is inserted into a USB host, it provides its Vendor ID and Product ID to the host, which then uses it to find the device's registry key for its driver installation. For the FTDI devices the Vendor ID is VID_0403. The default Product ID is PID_6001.

The VCP registry settings follow.

```
[HKEY_LOCAL_MACHINE\Drivers\USB\ClientDrivers\FTDI_DEVICE]
"Prefix"="COM"
"Dll"="ftdi_ser.dll"
"ConfigData"=hex:\
01,00,3f,3f,10,27,88,13,c4,09,e2,04,71,02,38,41,9c,80,4e,c0,34,00,1a,00,0d,\
    00,06,40,03,80,00,00,d0,80
"InitialIndex"=dword:00000000
"DeviceArrayIndex"=dword:00000000
"LatencyTimer"=dword:00000010

[HKEY_LOCAL_MACHINE\Drivers\USB\LoadClients\1027_24577\Default\Default\FTDI_DEVICE]
```

```
"DLL"="ftdi_ser.dll"

[HKEY_LOCAL_MACHINE\Drivers\USB\LoadClients\Default\Default\255\FTDI_DEVICE]
"DLL"="ftdi_ser.dll"
```

Code snippet is from VCP Driver Registry Settings in the driver download from FTDI

Note the 1027_24577 string in the USB LoadClients string. This string represents the decimal values for the VID and PID:

0x0403 = 1027

0x6001 = 24577

The FTDI device will be identified using this VID/PID string and will load using the `ftdi_ser.dll` driver using COM0:. FTDI devices that do not return that string can be identified through their Class ID 255\FTDI_DEVICE.

The D2XX registry settings follow.

```
[HKEY_LOCAL_MACHINE\Drivers\USB\ClientDrivers\FTDI_D2XX]
"Index"=dword:00000000
"Prefix"="FTD"
"Dll"="ftdi_d2xx.dll"

[HKEY_LOCAL_MACHINE\Drivers\USB\LoadClients\1027_24577]
[HKEY_LOCAL_MACHINE\Drivers\USB\LoadClients\1027_24577\Default]
[HKEY_LOCAL_MACHINE\Drivers\USB\LoadClients\1027_24577\Default\Default]
[HKEY_LOCAL_MACHINE\Drivers\USB\LoadClients\1027_24577\Default\Default\FTDI_D2XX]
"DLL"="ftdi_d2xx.dll"


[HKEY_LOCAL_MACHINE\Drivers\USB\LoadClients\Default]
[HKEY_LOCAL_MACHINE\Drivers\USB\LoadClients\Default\Default]
[HKEY_LOCAL_MACHINE\Drivers\USB\LoadClients\Default\Default\255]
[HKEY_LOCAL_MACHINE\Drivers\USB\LoadClients\Default\Default\255\FTDI_D2XX]
"DLL"="ftdi_d2xx.dll"
```

Code snippet is from D2XX Driver Registry Settings in the driver download from FTDI

The D2XX settings are incompatible with the VCP settings. You can configure the system only for one of the drivers; not both.

This loads the `ftdi_d2xx.dll` driver as the stream FDT0. Again, there is a default FTDI class specification.

CECOMPONENTWIZ: ADDING CONTENT TO AN IMAGE

In the following section, Catalog components are created for the drivers that add the driver DLL file and registry settings to an image as a subproject. Those activities make use of another Codeplex Wizard that integrates into Platform Builder in a manner similar to CEDriverWiz (see Chapter 33, "Developing a Stream Interface Driver"). First, look at using the CEComponentWiz Wizard. The form for the wizard is shown in Figure 44-8.

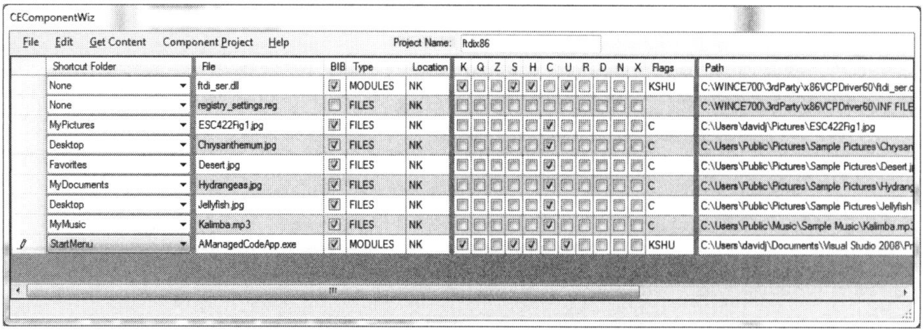

FIGURE 44-8

About

This wizard creates a subproject of a Compact 7 OS project that collects together resources as files and copies them to the release directory when the subproject is built. The user selects existing files on the development system for inclusion. The project generates a BIB file that is also copied that specifies the inclusion of those resource files in the image. Modules are by default included in the Modules section of the BIB file, whereas other files are in the Files section. The BIB flags and location section can be modified in the wizard after a file has been added. The wizard also facilitates the creation of shortcuts for resource files and the specification of which folder on the OS the shortcuts are to be placed. For a driver component, if a registry file is selected, then its content is copied into the subproject's registry file, which is also included in the image. A Catalog file is generated so that the subproject and its resources can be treated as Catalog components.

Installation

You can download the CEComponentWiz Wizard from `http://CEComponentWiz.codeplex.com`.

The installation instructions are in the downloaded zip file. As per the reasons discussed in Chapter 33 for CEDriverWiz, choose the PB Script option when installing Compact 7.

Starting the Wizard

CEComponentWiz runs in a manner similar to CEDriverWiz from the Tools/Platform Builder menu.

1. Load a Compact 7 OS project.

2. The first time you run the script, select Menu ➪ Tools ➪ Platform Builder ➪ Configure Scripts.

3. Choose the CEComponentWiz script and run it.

4. From then on it shows as the Active Script on that menu.

When in Configure Script, you can create a keyboard shortcut for the script. When it is open (running), it runs in the Build context, which prevents you from doing build actions.

Using the Wizard

When the wizard starts it determines the location of the OS project and generates a subproject under the OS project's Subprojects folder.

1. Run the Wizard as you did in the previous section.

2. From the Get Content menu choose existing content. Each submenu is for a specific class of files.

3. Resolve any issues that show the following:

> ➤ Duplicate names are not permitted.

> ➤ Filenames with spaces are not permitted.

4. Modify the BIB flags and Type if required.

5. Create shortcuts if needed. All files are actually deployed to \Windows. Shortcuts enable them to appear to be elsewhere.

6. Enter the component metadata.

7. Select Menu ⇨ Component Project ⇨ Component Details. Fill in the information for the following:

> ➤ Project Name

> ➤ Description

> ➤ Vendor

Vendor is the subtree of the Third Party Catalog under which the component appears in the Catalog.

You can generate the component in two ways. The first is for development within the current OS project only. The second is published for use in all OS projects on the development system.

8. Select Menu ⇨ Component Project ⇨ Generate Development Component

Or

Select Menu ⇨ Component Project ⇨ Publish Component to 3rd Party (and Catalog)

9. Select File ⇨ Save Workspace. You can reload the component later if it is saved and modify it.

10. Close the wizard.

11. Refresh the Catalog.

12. Find the component under Third Party in the Catalog and select it.

13. Go to Solution Explorer and examine the subproject. The selected files are included under the Resources folder, including any shortcuts.

14. Examine the .dat file under Parameter Files if you created any shortcuts.

15. Open postlink.bat for editing. You can see that it copies the files to the required locations.

16. Open the sources file by double-clicking the project. It doesn't actually build anything (NOTARGET). All the project does when it is built is copy the files.

FTDI DRIVERS AS CATALOG ITEMS

These two activities demonstrate using an existing driver binary DLL file with its registry settings. A VCP driver project and a D2XX driver project will be created. A Catalog file that can be included in the Catalog generates for both drivers. This will be accomplished using the CEContentWiz tool.

The drivers as downloaded are not installation packages and need to be added to a Compact 7 image as content. The required content is the driver DLL file and the associated registry settings. In the download package there are also some INF files that can be ignored.

Requirements

➤ A Compact 7 development system

➤ CEContentWiz installed

➤ Compact 7 System that has a USB host port

➤ Existing Compact 7 Retail image for that system with that USB host port driver enabled that has been built and tested

➤ FTDI Module and a USB cable

VCP Driver

In this activity you create a VCP driver project that can be added to an existing Compact 7 project. You test only that the driver loads at this stage.

1. Download the VCP zip folder for Windows CE for the system CPU from

    www.ftdichip.com/Drivers/VCP.htm

Get the Windows CE 6.0 driver for the same CPU in the target device.

2. Unzip the file into a temporary directory.

3. Copy `ftdi_ser.dll` to a working directory.

4. Open `INF/registry_settings.txt` in notepad.

5. Save it in the working directory as `ftdi.reg`.

6. Modify the file by removing the top five lines. The remaining top line should be blank.

It should have the same content as in the previous section in this chapter, "FTDI USB to Registry."

7. Save the file.

8. Run Visual Studio and load the OS project.

9. Run CEContentWiz from within Visual Studio.

10. Name the project **FTDI_VCP_x86.**

11. Add the two files in the working directory (the DLL and registry files) as previously done. The DLL is configured for Kernel space. The registry file is not going to be included as a separate file. (Its BIB it unchecked.) Its content will be copied into this project's registry file.

12. Set the driver Vendor to FTDI.

13. Select Project ⇨ MetaData ⇨ Vendor.

14. Add a description of the driver.

15. Generate the project:

    Select Component Project ⇨ Publish Components to 3rd Party

16. Save the component project and exit CEComponentWiz.

17. In PB Catalog View, refresh the Catalog.

18. Include the FTDI device driver in the image configuration. It will be located at Third Party/FTDI. Set the subproject to be included in the OS, to be built with it and not in Debug mode.

19. Build the operating system.

20. Open the image file (`nk.bin`) and check that `ftdi_ser.dll` is included. You may also want to check that its registry settings are included.

21. Close the image file.

22. Run the OS.

23. Run the Remote Registry Tool and check that the registry settings are in place.

24. Plug the FTDI device in and check that it loads. You should see a message in the Debug window such as the following:

```
PB Debugger Loaded 'C:\WINCE700\OSDESIGNS\MyOS\MYOS\RELDIR\
EBOX3300_X86_RELEASE\FTDI_SER.DLL',
 no matching symbolic information found.
```

25. Ignore the symbolic information note because the driver is not in Debug mode. (You don't have the source code for the driver.)

26. Search the registry `HKLM/Drivers/Active` for FTDI using the Remote Registry tool as in Chapter 34, "Stream Driver API and Device Driver Testing." Note that the driver's COM port. It should be zero.

If a dialog box pops up when you plug in the USB device asking for the driver, the OS couldn't find the driver. Check the build configuration.

 There is a sample Managed Code (VB) Serial Port program provided in the code for this chapter: VB2008_SerialPortApplication.

27. Launch a separate instance of Visual Studio, load this project, configure it for your system, and build it.

28. Run the application as a Managed Code application on the target system Compact 7 as described in earlier chapters.

29. Choose the serial port as per the driver's active key (COM0:).

30. Open the driver. If the driver is installed correctly and the module is functioning correctly, then the driver should open.

31. Trying pinging the module if it's one of the modules listed in this chapter. (See the "Third-Party FTDI Application Modules" section.)

D2XX Driver

In this activity you create a D2XX driver project that can be added to an existing WEC7 project. Again, you test only that the driver loads at this stage.

1. Uncheck the VCP driver from the project in the Catalog.

2. Download the D2XX version of the CE driver from `www.ftdichip.com/Drivers/D2XX.htm`.

Get the Windows CE 6.0 driver for the same CPU in the target device.

3. Again using the CEComponentWiz Wizard, create a separate driver project as was done for the VCP driver.

4. Call it **FTDI_D2XX**. The required files this time are `ftdi_d2xx.dll` and `d2xx.reg` in INF FOLDER. No modification is needed for the registry file.

5. Refresh the Catalog and add the D2XX driver from the Catalog as previous.

6. Set the subproject to be included in the OS, to be built with it and not in Debug mode.

7. Select Menu ⇨ Build/Copy Files to Release Directory.

8. Make the new subproject.

9. Select Menu ⇨ Build/Make Run-time Image.

10. Open the image file (`nk.bin`) and check that `ftdi_ser.dll` is included. Close the file.

11. Run the OS.

12. Plug the FTDI device into a USB host port on the Compact 7 device.

13. Check that the driver is loaded using the Remote Registry Tool, as in Chapter 34 "Stream Driver API and Device Driver Testing." It doesn't load as a serial device but as an FTD stream device (FTD0:). An application needs to open the stream to it to use it.

14. Try opening this with the stream Basic Test App as generated with CEDriverWiz Wizard in Chapter 33, "Developing a Stream Interface Driver," and Chapter 34, "Stream Driver API and Device Driver Testing."

THIRD-PARTY FTDI APPLICATION MODULES

As discussed previously, the FTDI Third-Party modules enable a system to extend its functionality. The module plugs into the system's USB host port and requires only an FTDI driver to be installed to programmatically access the module's functionality. A representative sample of modules is listed in Table 44-1 and display in Figures 44-9 through 44-12.

TABLE 44-1: Some Third-Party Modules

	FIGURE	MODULE	DESCRIPTION	SOURCE
1	44-9	DLP-IO8-G	USB-based data acquisition and control module with eight channels supporting digital I/O, analog in, and temperature measurement.	FTDI
2.	44-10	DLP-IOR4	USB-based module to control external relays. (Relays are included in the module.)	FTDI
3.	44-11	DLP-RF1-Z	USB-based ZigBee development module based on Freescale MC13193 RF transceiver.	FTDI
4.	44-12	Elexol USBIO2R	Digital I/O module providing 24 GPIO pins.	Dontronics

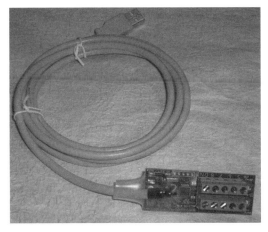

FIGURE 44-9

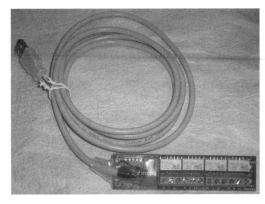

FIGURE 44-10

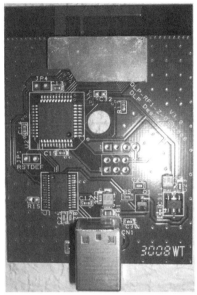

FIGURE 44-11

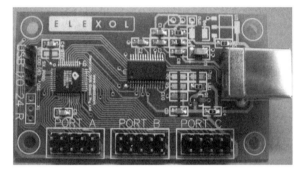

FIGURE 44-12

The data acquisition, relay, and Elexol modules all implement a simple textual command protocol as described in their datasheets. Datasheets for the DLP modules can be obtained from the FTDI web site. The Elexol datasheet URL is `www.elexol.com/Download/documents/USBIO24Rds1.pdf`.

Now look at the DLP-IOR4 Relay Module in some detail. It has four SPDT latching relays, which means that each relay can be switched (and stays there) to take one of two inputs (A or B) to its output. The relay terminals do not connect to the system and can be used to switch a device on and off, including main powered devices subject to safety considerations. The four relays are driven by 4 bits via the serial port. To switch a relay you send a character to the serial port. The API commands for this module are shown in Table 44-2.

TABLE 44-2: DLP-IOR4 Relay Commands

RELAY	CONNECT TO A	CONNECT TO B
1	'1'	'Q'
2	'2'	'W'
3	'3'	'E'
4	'4'	'R'
PING	An apostrophe	

The ping command returns 'R' if all is well.

To use this module you install the FTDI VCP driver (include it in the Compact 7 as described in the previous section) and plug the module into the system via its USB host port. A serial port application can then write those commands to COM0. You can use the sample Serial program to test its functionality. Start with the PING command. Try the others by listening for the clicks of the relays when they switch.

The DLP-IO8-G GPIO Module has a similar but more complex API. It has eight channels, each of which can be used in five modes. The commands for Channel 1 are shown in Table 44-3.

TABLE 44-3: DLP-IO8-G GPIO Module Commands

COMMAND	FUNCTION	RETURNED VALUES
'1'	Digital Out-High	Nothing
'Q'	Digital Out-Low	Nothing
'A'	Digital Input	Returns 0 or 1
'Z'	Analog In (ADC)	Voltage as an ASCII string, for example, "1.25V"
'9'	Temperature	Temperature as an ASCII string, for example, 78.2^0F
		Requires DS18B20 and 1.5K Ohm resistor (see Datasheet)
Apostrophe	Ping command	Returns 'Q'

The Elexol module implements 24 GPIO pins that are managed as three ports A, B, and C. It has a textual API, as shown in Table 44-4.

TABLE 44-4: USBIO24R Commands

COMMAND	FUNCTION	DATA
'?'	PING	Returns "USB I/O 24"
'A'	Write to Port A	1 byte
'B'	Write to Port B	1 byte
'C'	Write to Port C	1 byte
'a'	Read Port A	Responds with 1 byte
'b'	Read Port B	Responds with 1 byte
'c'	Read Port C	Responds with 1 byte
'!A'	Write Part DDR (1 = input)	1-byte bit pattern
"!B"	Write Part DDR (1 = input)	1-byte bit pattern
"!C"	Write Part DDR (1 = input)	1-byte bit pattern

For development activities, these modules can be mounted in a box and wired to the underside of a Breadboard. Figure 44-13 shows the Elexol module so mounted.

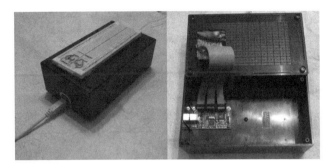

FIGURE 44-13

The ZigBee module requires more complex coding. It uses a packet structure consisting of a header and data. Each transceiver in the radio network needs a unique ID. The reader is referred to the datasheet for details. You need two modules on separate systems to test functionality, and one needs its ID reprogrammed from the default value.

SERIAL PORT ACCESS FROM A COMPACT 7 APPLICATION

For a native application to access a serial port, it uses the same API as for a stream driver. Through standard serial port IOCTLs (implemented by all serial class drivers), additional functions can be applied to a serial port such as configuring its BAUD rate, number of stop bits, and so on. Events can also be trapped by threads using `WaitForSingleObject` (or `WaitForMultipleObjects`) as used with the Watchdog Timer. These events include when the transmit buffer is empty, when data has been received, and when a modem control pin such as CTS changes state. The Compact Framework from Version 2 has provided a Serial Port class that implements similar functionality in managed code. This class is the basis of the VS2008_SerialPortApp introduced earlier in this chapter.

In the Custom FTDI stream driver in the next section of this chapter, the stream driver "wrappers" the serial port COM0 as loaded with the FTDI VCP driver. Because the driver is native code, it can use only the native interfaces to the serial stream. (Wouldn't it be nice to have drivers that could use managed code?) It needs to open and close the serial port, read and write with it, and configure the port. Table 44-5 shows a summary of the code. The stream as implemented does not need any event handlers.

TABLE 44-5: The Serial Port API for the Custom Stream Driver

ACTION	FUNCTION/DETAILS
Open serial port	CreateFile
Close serial port	CloseHandle
Write	WriteFile

ACTION	FUNCTION/DETAILS
Read	`ReadFile`
Header needed for following	`winbase.h`
Configuration structure	`DCB`
Get configuration	`GetCommState`
Set configuration	`SetCommState`
DCB properties	`.BaudRate=CBR_9600`
	`.Parity=NOPARITY`
	`.ByteSize=8`
	`.StopBits= ONESTOPBIT`

The port is configured after it is opened by getting the configuration data from the port into the DCB structure using `GetCommState`, modifying its properties, and then writing it back to the port using `SetCommState`.

For completeness, the Serial Port managed code class is outlined in Table 44-6 as used in VS2008_SerialPortApp:

TABLE 44-6: Compact Framework SerialPort Class

FEATURE	CLASS
Serial Port Class	`System.IO.Ports.SerialPort`
List of serial ports	`System.IO.Ports.SerialPort.GetPortNames`
	`(Not in Compact Framework 2)`
	SERIALPORT CLASS PROPERTY OR METHOD
Open method	`.Open()`
Close method	`.Close()`
OpenState property	`.IsOpen`
Properties (Config)	`.PortName="COM0:"`
	`.Parity=Parity.None`
	`.DataBits=8;`
	`.StopBits=StopBits.One`
Write method	`.Write(stringMessage)`

continues

TABLE 44-6 *(continued)*

FEATURE	CLASS
Read methods	`.ReadExisting()`
	`.ReadByte/Char/Line()`
Other properties	`.BytesToRead`
	`.Handshake=False`

Delegates can be added to handle serial port events for the `SerialPort` class.

A CUSTOM FTDI STREAM DRIVER

Starting with a Compact 7 system with the FTDI VCP driver installed and one of the modules 1, 2, or 4 (as in Table 44-1) connected, it would be simple enough to create an application that opens COM0: and reads and writes to it. These three modules all have a similar textual API. This could be done as a native application or as a managed code application. It would require writing code with a lot of magic numbers, or should I say magic characters, to implement the module's textual API. It would be neater though to have a set of commands across all three with some commonality. For example, the ping command would have a similar meaning across all these boards. In this section a stream driver is developed to wrapper the FTDI VCP driver specifically for these three modules.

Table 44-7 shows some common commands.

TABLE 44-7: Stream Driver Commands

INDEX	COMMAND	DLP GPIO	DLP RELAYS	USBIO24R
	Ping	Ping sent and get ping result if any		
	SetMode	0	1	2
0	Clear	Clear receive buffer, set circuit to known state, and initialize any data structures.		
1	SendByte	Send a byte.		
2	GetByte	Receive a byte.		
3	SetBit	Set GPIO bit.	Set relay 1 to A.	Set GPIO.
4	ClrrBit	Clear GPIO bit.	Set relay to B.	Set GPIO bit .
5	SetDDR	-	-	Set DDR.
6	GetBit	Get bit.	-	Get bit.
7	SendPort	-	-	Send byte data to port.
8	GetPort	-	-	Get byte data.

INDEX	COMMAND	DLP GPIO	DLP RELAYS	USBIO24R
9	SetPort0	-	-	Set to Port 0.
10	SetPort1	-	-	Set to Port 1.
11	SetPort2	-	-	Set to Port 2.

SetMode indicates which module is used and will be implemented as the Write stream function, sending 0, 1, or 2 as a parameter. Ping is implemented as the Read function with no parameters. The other commands will all be implemented as IOCTLs with an IOCTL code indexed from the Clear IOCTL code as per the Index column. All parameters are bytes except SendStr and GetStr, which use a string.

Creating the Stream Driver

➤ Start with an existing Compact 7 OS project for a board target that has a host USB port. Add the FTDI VCP driver to the project. Build and test the OS as previous.

➤ Specify a new stream driver project using CEDriverWiz Wizard:

  ➤ Name the driver **FTDIModules**

  ➤ Prefix: FDM

  ➤ Compact 7

  ➤ UserMode

  ➤ All IO functions except Seek, PreDeInit, and PreClose

  ➤ No Power functions and no Cancel

  ➤ Simple IOCTLs

  ➤ No Device Context

  ➤ No Shared Memory

  ➤ No Open Context

➤ Create all subprojects.

➤ Add all the projects via the common dirs. file. The file is in OS SubProjects/FTDIModules.

➤ Configure them to be excluded from the image and built as Debug.

➤ Build and test the subprojects with the OS.

➤ The stream driver header file needs to be modified to define an IOCTL for each function.

```
#define IOCTL_SIMPLEBASE                    1024
#define IOCTL_INC    1  /*SIMPLEBASE*/

#define IOCTL_FTDIModules_CLEAR             (0*IOCTL_INC+IOCTL_SIMPLEBASE)
#define IOCTL_FTDIModules_SENDBYTE          (1*IOCTL_INC+IOCTL_SIMPLEBASE)
```

```
#define IOCTL_FTDIModules_GETBYTE          (2*IOCTL_INC+IOCTL_SIMPLEBASE)
#define IOCTL_FTDIModules_SENDSTR          (3*IOCTL_INC+IOCTL_SIMPLEBASE)
#define IOCTL_FTDIModules_GETSTR           (4*IOCTL_INC+IOCTL_SIMPLEBASE)
#define IOCTL_FTDIModules_SETBIT           (5*IOCTL_INC+IOCTL_SIMPLEBASE)
#define IOCTL_FTDIModules_CLRBIT           (6*IOCTL_INC+IOCTL_SIMPLEBASE)
#define IOCTL_FTDIModules_SETDDR           (7*IOCTL_INC+IOCTL_SIMPLEBASE)
#define IOCTL_FTDIModules_GETBIT           (8*IOCTL_INC+IOCTL_SIMPLEBASE)
#define IOCTL_FTDIModules_SENDPORT         (9*IOCTL_INC+IOCTL_SIMPLEBASE)
#define IOCTL_FTDIModules_GETPORT          (10*IOCTL_INC+IOCTL_SIMPLEBASE)
#define IOCTL_FTDIModules_SETPORT0         (11*IOCTL_INC+IOCTL_SIMPLEBASE)
#define IOCTL_FTDIModules_SETPORT1         (12*IOCTL_INC+IOCTL_SIMPLEBASE)
#define IOCTL_FTDIModules_SETPORT2         (13*IOCTL_INC+IOCTL_SIMPLEBASE))

#define IOCTL_BASE  IOCTL_FTDIModules_Clear
#define IOCTL_NUM 14
```

Code snippet is from File: FTDIModules.h in FTDIModules Stream Driver subproject.

➤ Similarly, the source code for the driver needs to be modified for the `FDM_IOControl` function. In the `switch` statement create a case branch for each IOCTL, and remove the others. Implement all 14. Some examples follow.

Available for download on Wrox.com

```
switch (dwCode) {

    case IOCTL_FTDIModules_CLEAR:
RETAILMSG(1,(TEXT("FDM_IOControl  IOCTL_FTDIModules_CLEAR:\n")));
    bRet = true;
    break;

    case IOCTL_FTDIModules_SETMODE:
RETAILMSG(1,(TEXT("FDM_IOControl  IOCTL_FTDIModules_SETMODE:\n")));
    bRet = true;
    break;

    case IOCTL_FTDIModules_SETBIT:
RETAILMSG(1,(TEXT("FDM_IOControl  IOCTL_FTDIModules_SETBIT:\n")));
    bRet = true;
    break;

    case IOCTL_FTDIModules_CLRBIT:
RETAILMSG(1,(TEXT("FDM_IOControl  IOCTL_FTDIModules_CLRBIT:\n")));
    bRet = true;
    break;

. . . etc.
```

Code snippet is from the switch case branches from the stream IOControl function. File: FTDIModules.cpp, Project: FTDIModules Stream Driver.

The stream driver functions can read and write to the serial stream COM0: because that is what the VPC driver loads it as. This requires a stream handle variable. Another variable, Mode is required. This indicates which of the three modules is being used. This allows for code to be conditional upon the module to be driven. The Elexol device has three byte ports, and the driver can interact with one at a time. This needs a further variable. A reference to winbase.h is needed for the serial port configuration. Finally, a function prototype is needed for the configuration function that will be placed at the bottom of the driver's source file.

➤ In the global variable space for the stream source file (near top) include the following:

```
#include <winbase.h>
HANDLE hStr= INVALID_HANDLE_VALUE;
BYTE Mode=0;
BYTE ElexolPort=0;
BOOL SetComms();
```

➤ The stream Open function opens the serial stream:

```
LPCTSTR   wstream = _T("COM0:");
hStr = CreateFile(wstream, GENERIC_READ | GENERIC_WRITE, 0, NULL, OPEN_EXISTING, 0, 0);
```

Code snippet is from the function FDM_Open, File: FTDIModules.cpp, Project: FTDIModules Stream Driver.

The stream function Close will close the stream.

```
CloseHandle(hStr);
```

Code snippet is from the function FDM_Close code. File: FTDIModules.cpp, Project, FTDIModules Stream Driver.

➤ For those two functions you should include some error checking and handling on hStr. This is implemented in the sample code for this chapter.

➤ The stream Write function can set the mode of operation. That is, which module is used.

```
DWORD FDM_Write(DWORD hOpenContext, LPCVOID pSourceBytes, DWORD NumberOfBytes)
{
    Mode= * (BYTE *) pSourceBytes;
    DWORD dwRet = Mode+1;
    return dwRet
}
```

Code snippet is from the function FDM_Write, which implements SetMode. File: FTDIModules.cpp, Project: FTDIModules Stream Driver.

➤ The stream Read function can send the appropriate ping character to the serial stream and get the result:

```
DWORD FDM_Read(DWORD hOpenContext, LPVOID pBuffer, DWORD Count))
{
    char ping='\'';
    switch (Mode)
    {
```

```
    case 0:
        ping='\'';
        break;
    case 1:
        ping='\'';
        break;
    case 2:
        ping='?';
        break;
    }
    DWORD dwWritten;
    //Write the ping character to the module
    WriteFile(hStr, &ping , sizeof(char), &dwWritten, NULL);

    DWORD dwBytesRead;
    BOOL rs = ReadFile(hStr, pBuffer, Count, &dwBytesRead, NULL);
    return dwBytesRead;
}
```

Code snippet is from the function FDM_Read, which implements Ping. File:
FTDIModules.cpp, Project: FTDIModules Stream Driver.

Two things are left:

(a) Configure the serial port. This is done in the stream Init function.

(b) Implement the IOCTLs.

The serial configurations follow:

➤ Baud Rate

    ➤ Module 1: 115200

    ➤ Module 2: 9600

➤ Module 2 also requires the following:

    ➤ 1 start bit, no parity

    ➤ 8 data bits

    ➤ 1 stop bit

    ➤ No flow control (No hardware control)

No settings are required for module 3 because it always runs at full speed.

1. Add the following function to the bottom of the stream driver source file, and call it in the stream Open function after the stream has been opened.

Available for
download on
Wrox.com

```
BOOL SetComms()
{
    //If Elexol nothing to set
    if (Mode==2) return TRUE;

    //Get configuration block
```

```cpp
DCB dcb = {0};
dcb.DCBlength = sizeof(DCB);
if (!GetCommState (hStr,&dcb))
{
    return false;
}

//Set BAUD Rate
switch (Mode)
{
    case 0:
dcb.BaudRate=CBR_115200;
break;
case 1:
dcb.BaudRate=CBR_9600;


break;
}

//Set other config.
dcb.Parity=NOPARITY;
dcb.ByteSize=8;
dcb.StopBits= ONESTOPBIT;
dcb.fDtrControl=DTR_CONTROL_DISABLE;
dcb.fOutxCtsFlow=false;
dcb.fOutxDsrFlow=false;
dcb.fRtsControl=RTS_CONTROL_DISABLE;

//Configure serial port
if (!SetCommState (hStr,&dcb))
{
        return false;
}
}
```

Code snippet is SetComms functions. File: FTDIModules.cpp, Project: FTDIModules Stream Driver.

2. You should now build the stream driver subproject. Build the `BasicTestApp` and `LoadUserMode` and Unload applications as well.

3. Run the OS and test load the driver. Check for errors and resolve any issues.

4. Open the stream with the `BasicTestApp` and check for errors.

5. Close the stream and check for errors.

The Ping and Mode Commands

The mode command sets which module is connected. This is implemented as the stream driver's `write` function. The ping command which is implemented as the stream driver's read function, can then be used to check that it is properly and the communications are correctly configured. This section implements an application to call both functions in the driver.

1. Open the `FTDModulesApp` source file.

2. Modify the `WinMain` code to the following:

```
{
    //Open the stream
    HANDLE hStr =
    CreateFile(_T("FDM1:"), GENERIC_READ | GENERIC_WRITE, 0, NULL, OPEN_EXISTING, 0, 0);
    if (hStr == (HANDLE)-1)
    {
        RETAILMSG(1, (_T("FTDIModulesApp: Cannot open FDM1:")));
        return (int)hStr;
    }
    else
    {
        RETAILMSG(1, (_T("FTDIModulesApp: Openned FDM1:")));
    }

    DWORD dwWritten;
    DWORD dwBytesRead;

    //Set the mode
    BYTE mode = 1 ;   //or 0 or 2 depending upon which board you are using
    WriteFile(hStr, &mode, sizeof(BYTE), &dwWritten, NULL);

    // Ping the module.
    char pingStr[20];
    BOOL rs = ReadFile(hStr, &pingStr, 20*sizeof(char), &dwBytesRead, NULL);

    //Translate char * to LPWSTR for RETAILMSG
    wchar_t PingStr[20];
    mbstowcs(PingStr, pingStr, dwBytesRead);

    if (rs)
    {
        RETAILMSG(1, (_T("FTDIModulesApp: Ping message: %s"), PingStr));
    }
    else
    {
        RETAILMSG(1, (_T("FTDIModulesApp: Ping message failed")));
    }

    //Command tests here

    // Disconnect from driver.
    CloseHandle(hStr);
    return 0;
}
```

Code snippet is to call the Ping code command from an application. It is WinMain. File:
FTDModulesApp.cpp, Project: FTDModulesApp.

3. Remember to set the correct mode for the module being used.

4. Build and test the application with your module.

5. If you have more than one module, then modify.

The IOCTLs

Now implement three of the IOCTLs: `Clear`, `SetBit`, and `ClrBit`. It is left to you to implement the other IOCTLs or to download the completed driver and test applications.

1. Modify the `TestIOCTLs` application source file to test the 14 IOCTLs. Modify the following

```
for (i=IOCTL_BASE ; i<IOCTL_BASE +10*IOCTL_INC; i+=IOCTL_INC ) {
```

to

```
for (i=IOCTL_BASE ; i<IOCTL_BASE +14*IOCTL_INC; i+=IOCTL_INC ) {
```

2. Build and test this application. Check that the 12 IOCTLs don't return any errors. They won't do anything yet because they haven't had their switch case branches implemented.

3. Add the following arrays to the globals at the top of the file:

Available for download on Wrox.com

```
char DLPA[] = {'1','2','3','4','5','6','7','8'};
char DLPB[] = {'Q','W','E','R','T','Y','U','I'};
char DLPRead[] = {'A','B','C','D','E','F','G','H'};
char ElexolWrite[] = {'A','B','C'};
char ElexolRead[] = {'a','b','c'};
char * DDRA = "!A\0";
char * DDRB = "!B\0";
char * DDRC = "!C\0";
```

Code snippet is to implement command data structures. File: FTDIModules.cpp (At top), Project: FTDIModules Stream Driver.

4. And add the following lines of code at the start of the stream function `FDM_IOControl`.

Available for download on Wrox.com

```
DWORD numBytesWritten;
DWORD numBytesRead;
BYTE bit;
BYTE byte;
BYTE bitPattern;
char ch;
int i;
BOOL bRet = true;  //This line should already be there.
```

Code snippet is from the function FDM_IOControl. File: FTDIModules.cpp, Project: FTDIModules Stream Driver.

5. Implement the Clear IOCTL as follows in the stream `IOControl` function:

Available for download on Wrox.com

```
case IOCTL_FTDIModules_CLEAR:
    RETAILMSG(1,(TEXT("FTDIModules: FDM_IOControl  FTDIModules_CLEAR\n")));

    if (Mode < 2)  //DLP
```

```
        {
            for (i=0;i<8;i++)
            {
                if ((Mode==1) && (i>3) ) break;
                //Digital Lo for each GPIO varBit
                ch=DLPB[i];
                //or relay contact A for each relay
                if (Mode==1) ch = DLPA[i];
                WriteFile(hStr,&ch,sizeof(char),&numBytesWritten,NULL);
            }
        }
        else
        {   //Elexol

            //Write zero to the DDRs .. All output
            WriteFile(hStr,DDRA,3,&numBytesWritten,NULL);
            WriteFile(hStr,DDRB,3,&numBytesWritten,NULL);
            WriteFile(hStr,DDRC,3,&numBytesWritten,NULL);

            //Clear each port
            varByte=0;
            ch = ElexolWrite[0];
            WriteFile(hStr,&ch,sizeof(char),&numBytesWritten,NULL);
            WriteFile(hStr,&varByte,sizeof(BYTE),&numBytesWritten,NULL);
            ch = ElexolWrite[1];
            WriteFile(hStr,&ch,sizeof(char),&numBytesWritten,NULL);
            WriteFile(hStr,&varByte,sizeof(BYTE),&numBytesWritten,NULL);
            ch = ElexolWrite[2];
            WriteFile(hStr,&ch,sizeof(char),&numBytesWritten,NULL);
            WriteFile(hStr,&varByte,sizeof(BYTE),&numBytesWritten,NULL);

            ElexolPort=0;
        }

        *pdwActualOut=0;
        bRet = true;
        break;
```

Code snippet is to implement the Clear command as IOCTL_FTDIModules_CLEAR in FDM_IOControl. File:
FTDIModules.cpp, Project: FTDIModules Stream Driver.

6. Implement the `SetBit` IOCTL as follows:

```
case IOCTL_FTDIModules_SETBIT:
    //Check Input
    if (    ( dwLenIn >8) ) return false;

    varBit = (BYTE) dwLenIn;
    RETAILMSG(1,
(_T("FTDIModules: FDM_IOControl  IOCTL_FTDIModules_SETVITt Bit No: %d\n")
,varBit));

    switch (Mode)
    {
```

```
        case 0:  //DLP GPIO
            ch=DLPA[varBit];
            WriteFile(hStr,&ch,sizeof(char),&numBytesWritten,NULL);
            break;
        case 1:  //DLP Relay
            ch=DLPA[varBit];
            WriteFile(hStr,&ch,sizeof(char),&numBytesWritten,NULL);
            break;
        case 2:  //Elexol
            //Get the current port value
            ch= ElexolRead[ElexolPort];
            WriteFile(hStr,&ch,sizeof(char),&numBytesWritten,NULL);
            ReadFile(hStr,&varByte,1,&numBytesWritten,NULL);

            //Bit Mask to set
            bitPattern = 1<<varBit;
            varByte |= bitPattern;

            //Bit Mask to clear
            //bitPattern = 1<<varBit;
            //bitPattern = ~bitPattern;
            //varByte &= bitPattern;

            //Write to the port
            ch= ElexolWrite[ElexolPort];
            WriteFile(hStr,&ch,sizeof(char),&numBytesWritten,NULL);
            WriteFile(hStr,&varByte,sizeof(BYTE),&numBytesWritten,NULL);
            break;
    }
    *pdwActualOut=0;
    bRet = true;
```

Code snippet is to implement the SetBit command as IOCTL_FTDIModules_SETBIT in FDM_IOControl.
File: FTDIModules.cpp, Project: FTDIModules Stream Driver.

7. Implement the `ClrBit` IOCTL similar to `SetBit`.

8. Build and load the driver.

9. Open the `FTDIModulesApp` source file.

10. Add the following code to test the IOCTLs created after the ping command call and before the driver handle is closed.

```
//Set the module into cleared state.
BOOL  successIOCTL =
DeviceIoControl(hStr,IOCTL_FTDIModules_CLEAR,NULL,0,NULL, 0,&dwBytesRead,NULL);

BYTE Bit;
for (Bit=0;Bit<8;Bit++)
{
    if ((Bit>3) && (mode==1)) break;
    successIOCTL =
DeviceIoControl(hStr,IOCTL_FTDIModules_CLRBIT,NULL,Bit,NULL, 0,&dwWritten,NULL);
```

```
    Sleep(1000);
    successIOCTL =
DeviceIoControl(hStr,IOCTL_FTDIModules_SETBIT,NULL,Bit,NULL, 0,&dwWritten,NULL);
    Sleep(1000);
}
```

Code snippet is to test the commands from an application. It is WinMain. File:
FTDModulesApp.cpp, Project: FTDModulesApp.

11. Build and test run the application.

If the relays are used you should hear each one click in turn. With other devices you might need to set up some LEDs to indicate the state or use a multimeter to test the state.

The code for this chapter contains the fully implemented driver and test applications. You may also want to extend the DLP-108-G module functionality to include the ADC and temperature functions.

SUMMARY

This chapter introduced the use of the FTDI USB to Serial devices and modules. The FTDI driver was used to introduce a number of topics. You learned how to include a binary driver as a Catalog component and how to wrap a driver as a higher level stream driver. How to add content to an operating system project using the CEComponentWiz Wizard and accessing a serial port were also introduced in the chapter.

A Codeplex site has been established as a community activity to further develop the FTDI module driver and applications. The VCP and D2XX Catalog components are also available that site. The site is at:

```
http://FTDI4CE.codeplex.com
```

45

Integrating Managed Code Projects

WHAT'S IN THIS CHAPTER?

➤ Including a managed code application in the OS Image

➤ Deploying managed code applications over KITL

➤ Building a managed code application with the OS build

This is the last but not the least chapter of the book. There are some treats here to finish up with. In some of the previous chapters, you were shown how to develop a managed code application for a running Compact 7 system. For development purposes, this required two instances of Visual Studio: one for the OS and one for the application. This chapter shows you how to package a working managed code application using CEComponentWiz so that it can be included in the OS build. This chapter also demonstrates a few tricks of the trade with managed code development for Compact 7. You can deploy a .NET application directly to a running OS using KITL rather than deploying it over Connection Manager. It is also possible to include a .NET application in the OS build.

NATIVE CODE

A refresh: now we will recap some aspects of native code development in Platform Builder.

Native code can be a user mode application, a user mode application library (DLL), or a driver (user mode or kernel mode). A native code module is added to a Compact 7 OS project by adding the module's subproject to the OS project. Existing projects are added by browsing to the subproject folder and selecting its source file. New projects are added via Platform builder templates or third-party wizards such as CEDriverWiz (Chapter 35, "The Target System") and CEComponentWiz (Chapter 44, "FTDI Devices"). A subproject contains parameter files

(`.bib`, `.dat`, `.db`, and `.reg`) used in integrating the project into the Compact 7 OS project and two project files (the sources and `.pbxml`). If source code is to be built, then the project can contain one or more source files and optionally one or more header files. Content resources such as media files and configuration files may also be optionally added to the subproject. When the OS is built, subprojects can be configured to be built (or not built), and included (or not included) in the image. They can also be configured to be built in Debug mode (or not) (See Chapter 34). When subprojects are built, the built components are placed in the OS project's release directory (sometimes called The FlatRelease directory). These components include the parameter files for the subproject as well as the built module and resource files. If the subproject is configured to be included in the image, when the OS is built the contents of the parameter files are added to the system's parameters. Built modules and resources are then included if they are in the release directory and the concatenated system BIB file has them included.

There is no subproject option to create a managed code application directly as part of the Platform Builder. There has been a capability of the Build System to build C# applications using Platform Builder since CE 4.2 but it has lacked documentation. Note there is a managed code tab on the property dialog for a subproject. There are now some MSDN references with respect to C# code building in a CE 6 OS project:

➤ Using managed code in a Subproject

`http://msdn.microsoft.com/en-us/library/aa909768.aspx`

➤ Subprojects: managed code Settings

`http://msdn.microsoft.com/en-us/library/aa909464.aspx`

This chapter uses some less formal techniques.

Debugging Native Modules

A native module can be debugged when the operating system is launched from a suitable development workstation. The operating system must have both KITL enabled and Kernel Debug enabled (regardless of whether the OS is a Debug or Retail build). These are set in Solution Explorer, OS Project properties/Build Options. This requires that a Target Control Support Catalog component (Core OS/Core OS Services/Kernel) be included in the OS design. Also in the Connectivity Options/Core Service Settings, KITL needs to be enabled as well as Enable Access to desktop files. (These three items are typically included/enabled by default.)

If the target is an application or application DLL, then the OS needs to be only in retail mode. If a driver is the target for debugging and it is in user mode, then a Retail build is again suitable. If the driver is in kernel mode, then the OS has to be built in kernel mode to debug it.

If the target module is in user mode (application, DLL, or user mode driver) it is best to not include the subproject in the image. That way the subproject can be modified and rebuilt while the image runs.

➤ Subprojects so configured, when built are copied to the Release directory but not included in the image.

➤ They can be accessed from the running system under `\Release` in the file system.

> ➤ When an application runs from the Target Control window or Run Programs menu, it can be in either \Windows or \Release.

> > ➤ Hint: If the application has resources such as image files, then the application may have to access them via \Release.

A native code application then can be debugged using such techniques as inserting Breakpoints and Debug Macros (refer to Chapter 35). The Platform Builder Debug infrastructure works directly with the source code through the .pdb files it creates when it builds a Debug subproject. Program Database (.pdb) files are required for debugging, as they provide symbolic information to the debugger.

MANAGED CODE APPLICATIONS AND WINDOWS EMBEDDED COMPACT 7

A managed code application for a Windows Embedded Compact 7 system requires the .NET Compact Framework. The framework version 3.5 is available as a Catalog component. There is the standard version of this in the Catalog as well as a headless version. Managed code needs to be written in C# or VB. The Compact Framework does not support managed C++. When a managed code application is compiled, a Microsoft Intermediate Language (MSIL) file is created, not a binary executable or DLL. This code is CPU-independent. That is why a Compact Framework project can run on a variety of Compact 7/CE platforms and CPUs without rebuilding. The OS just needs the required version of the framework.

To create a managed code project in Visual Studio, you choose a Smart Device project, Windows CE Target Platform, and .NET CF Version 3.5 (can be version 2.0 as well), and then choose a template.

To develop the application you need two instances of Visual Studio: One for the OS and one for the managed code. The OS needs the Corecon component for Compact 7 (http://corecon4ce .codeplex.com). You then run the OS, run the two Corecon components (ConmanClient2 followed by CMAccept) on the target, build the application on the second instance, configure Options/DeviceTools/Devices for Platform Builder, connect to the device from this instance, deploy the application, test it...

It should be simpler than that and it can be!

Besides this "traditional" manner for developing a managed code application for Windows Embedded Compact/CE devices, there are three other options:

> ➤ Package a .NET application for inclusion in the OS image.

> ➤ Deploy a .NET application directly over KITL.

> ➤ Include the build of a managed code application in the OS build.

These approaches are discussed in the following sections.

PACKAGE A .NET APPLICATION FOR INCLUSION IN THE OS IMAGE

You can use CEComponentWiz to package a built managed code application as a Catalog component. You would do this after the application has been debugged. All resources such as image and configuration files would be packaged into the Catalog component. For example, the Serial Port application from the previous chapter is reused as the code for this chapter with the modification that an image is loaded from an image file when the application starts. If that image file, e101.jpg, isn't present, then an error is generated.

Including a Built Managed Code application in the OS image

In this activity, you can use CEComponentWiz to create a Catalog component for the Serial Port application. That way it can be included in any Compact 7 project.

1. Get the VB2008_SerialPortApplication project in the download for this chapter. Build and test the application in release mode in the traditional manner.

2. Open the project folder in Explorer and browse to the bin\Release folder.

The image file and the application file are both in this directory. Both are needed to be included in the Catalog component and hence in the image.

3. Run CEComponentWiz (refer to Chapter 44) for a Compact 7 project. Enter suitable metadata for the component (Menu-Component Project/Component Details).

4. Get Content (Menu):

   ➤ Modules — Browse to the bin/Release folder of the application and select the application.

   ➤ Images — Browse to the same directory and choose e101.jpg.

Managed code modules are not placed in the MODULES section of the BIB file because they don't run with the OS the same as native modules.

5. Change the application type from MODULES to FILES.

6. Remove its K, S, and H flags by clicking them. It won't run in kernel space.

When the image is deployed, both files will be in \Windows. It would be nice to have a shortcut for the application.

7. Add a shortcut for the application so that it appears on the Start menu.

8. From the drop-down list in the Shortcut column for the application entry, choose Start Menu/Programs. The subproject can now be generated.

9. Select Menu-Component Project/Generate Development Project.

Now create a Catalog File:

10. Select Menu-Component Project/Reference Development Project in Catalog.

You can save the workspace for this component so that you can fix any errors later or so that it can be modified later. When the component has been tested, you can reopen the project and publish it to the Third Party folder.

11. Select Menu-File/Save Workspace.

The dialog indicates that that a .ccw file has been saved in the SubProjects folder of the OS.

12. Close the wizard.

13. Either add the subproject via Solution Explorer, or refresh the Catalog and select from its Vendor tree of the third-party components.

14. View the subproject in Solution Explorer and observe all the files created.

➤ In particular note the three resource files, the application, the image file, and the shortcut (.lnk) file.

➤ Open the BIB file and note that three files are included in the image. Open the DAT file and note that the folder is created for the shortcut and will be placed in that folder.

➤ Open the sources file (double-click the project) and note that that there is nothing to build (**NOTARGET**).

➤ Finally open postlink.bat and note that it just copies all the files in the Resources directory.

15. Configure the project to be built with the image, included in the image and not debugged.

The whole OS doesn't need building for this.

16. Select Menu-Build/Copy Files to Release Directory.

17. Build the subproject.

18. Select Menu-Build/Make Run-time Image.

19. Check that the files are included in the image file (nk.bin) via Solution Explorer (Show Built Image).

20. Run the OS and test run the application from the Start Menu.

 Note that to modify the component, uncheck it from the Catalog, close Visual Studio, delete the subproject folder, restart VS, and reload the OS project. Then run the wizard and reload the .ccw file and modify from there.

This is how to formally include a debugged and built managed code application in an image.

DEPLOY A .NET APPLICATION DIRECTLY OVER KITL

As an alternative, the OS project's release directory can be set as the build target for the managed code application. This would allow some further development because the application is not part of the image but can be run from the Target Control Window and the Run Programs dialog. This works because .NET applications only need to be copied to a target system and also because the release directory is exposed to the running OS if it is configured as previous. The managed source code can't be stepped through though, as Platform Builder supports debugging of only native code. Also, the application would need to reference any resources its uses from the \Release directory.

This approach can avoid the need for a second instance of Visual Studio. The project can be added to the Solution of which the OS is a part, not as a subproject of the OS but as a subproject of the solution. It can then be built independent from the OS by right-clicking it in Solution Explorer.

Building to the Release Directory

This activity uses the same Serial Port Project. It will build directly to the Release directory where it can be run from the OS.

1. Shut the OS down.

2. The OS needs to be configured for KITL debugging as outlined in the native code debugging section of this chapter.

3. Uncheck the Serial program from the Catalog.

4. Perform a clean build of the OS.

5. You need to get rid of the subproject files from the image and release directory.

6. Run the OS and check that none of the subproject is in the image.

7. Open the Release Directory Build Window. Make a copy of the Release folder's path from the command prompt.

8. Go to the other Visual Studio and go to the Project Properties (the one with the Serial Port Project).

9. Paste the Release directory path into the project's Build Output Path, as shown in Figure 45-1.

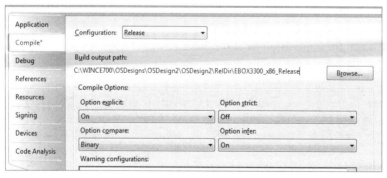

FIGURE 45-1

You cannot find the e101.jpg image file in \Windows. It is in \Release, which is available to the OS when it runs.

1. Open the source code, and find the image file reference at the end of Form_Load. Change:

   ➤ "\Windows\e101.jpg" to "\Release\e101.jpg"

2. Rebuild this project.

3. Return to the OS project and run the application.

4. Select Menu-Target/Run Programs.

5. Find the Application (VB2008_Serial_PortApplication) and run it.

If the application ran alright then the image issue was resolved. If it didn't run then the image was probably the issue, so rework that aspect.

6. Shut down the application after testing it.

7. On the device run File Explorer and browse to \Release.

8. Find the application there. Run it from there.

You are getting near the end of the book but there is more to come!

Now get rid of the second instance of Visual Studio.

1. Close the Serial Port Visual Studio instance.

2. Shut the image down.

3. Copy the serial port project to the OS SubProjects folder.

4. From Solution Explorer in the OS project, right-click the Solution, not the OS project, and choose Add Existing Project as in Figure 45-2. (Not as an existing SubProject.)

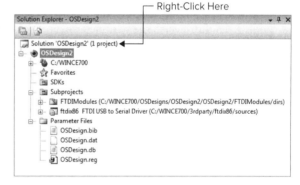

5. Browse to the Serial Port project.

6. Drill down until you get to the file VB2008_SerialPortApplication .vbproj and select it.

7. Check that its build path still points to the Release directory.

FIGURE 45-2

8. Rebuild it.

9. Run the OS and run the application again as in this section.

The project can be rebuilt while the OS runs. You can modify code, but you can't modify the form design with it running. Try this.

INCLUDE THE BUILD OF A MANAGED CODE APPLICATION IN THE OS BUILD

OK, so you have managed to simplify things so that only one instance of Visual Studio is needed for managed code building. Debugging is a different issue, though. Wouldn't it be even better if the

.NET CF application could be included in the OS project and get built with it? Especially after that project has been developed and tested?

The approach used in this section works only in Compact 7 because it has a unified build system. This means that subprojects and the operating system are built using the exact same build tools. Previously, subprojects were built using a slightly different set of tools than those used for the OS.

Including a Managed Code Application in the OS Build

In this section the managed code project is merged into the OS project as a subproject.

1. Shut the image down.

2. Add the existing SubProject. (Right-click SubProjects folder.)

3. Browse the serial project drill down, and select the same `.vbproj` file.

4. You will get a message as shown in Figure 45-3.

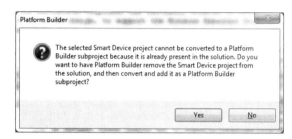

FIGURE 45-3

Finally, Platform Builder is doing something to assist with managed code! It can assist with merging the managed code project by automatically adding the things such the parameter files, a solution file and so on.

5. Choose Yes.

6. The serial port project is now a fully fledged member of the OS project!

7. Try rebuilding it. Note that it is built like a PB subproject now.

8. Note that it has parameter files. Open the BIB file.

9. The image file isn't included so you need to add that.

10. Add another entry in the BIB file (in the FILES section as well):

```
e101.jpg    $(_FLATRELEASEDIR)\e101.jpg          NK
```

Code snippet is from managedCodeInBuild.txt to be placed in the project BIB file

There is again an issue with the image file. (It was put into the project to demonstrate these issues and how to resolve them.) The configured build directory in the VB project's properties is ignored. It builds the application. The application and parameter files are copied to the Release directory. The image file isn't copied, though. A build event could be added to the managed code project to copy this file to the release directory after it is built. Alternatively a `postlink.bat` file could be used similar to the one generated by CEComponentWiz:

11. Add a new text file to the subproject and name it `postlink.bat`.

12. Add the following content:

```
copy "%BUILDROOT%\e101.jpg" "%SG_OUTPUT_ROOT%\oak\target\%_TGTCPU%\%WINCEDEBUG%"  /Y

copy "%BUILDROOT%\e101.jpg" %_FLATRELEASEDIR%  /Y
```

Code snippet is from managedCodeInBuild.txt to be copied to the project postlink.bat file

The sources file needs to be told to use this.

13. Explore the subproject and find its subproject. Open it and append a blank line and the following:

```
POSTLINK_PASS_CMD=postlink.bat
```

Code snippet is from managedCodeInBuild.txt to be added to the project sources file

14. Save the sources file and close it.

15. Open the subproject source file and change the image file reference back to `\Windows\e101.jpg`.

16. Set the subproject to be built with the image, included in the image and not debug.

17. Rebuild the OS.

18. Run the image.

19. Start the application from the Windows directory or from the Target-Run Programs dialog.

You have managed to build a managed code project as part of a Compact 7 image build.

WHAT NOW?

The resource file issue (the image file) is a bit messy. Also there are no shortcuts created.

The main drawback of these techniques is that you can't debug the managed code applications like you can for native code applications for the reasons stated previously in this chapter. It would be possible to platform invoke (PInvoke) some of the debug macros or do some printf/writeLine style of debugging (write messages) through the PB Debug Window. The Compact Framework doesn't provide any code metadata information, though. In the full .NET framework, you can get line numbers to feed into debugging macros, but this information is not available in the .NET compact framework.

There is a Codeplex community project being developed to resolve some of these integration issues with managed code in a Compact 7 OS project, including resource files, debugging macros, and shortcuts. More information is available at `http://managedcode4C7.codeplex.com`.

SUMMARY

Managed code is not far from being a first-class member of Platform Builder. A working managed code application can be included as a Catalog component using CEComponentWiz along with its resources. Alternatively, the project can be built to the OS Release directory and run via KITL from there. Finally, a managed code application can be integrated into a Platform Builder Compact 7 operating system project and built along with it.

Virtual PC Connectivity

When properly configured, a Virtual PC virtual machine (VM) behaves and functions similar to a real PC running current and legacy operating systems including DOS, Windows 95, 98, and 2000. Microsoft Virtual PC runs on Windows 7, XP, and Vista.

A Virtual PC BSP is provided as part of the Platform Builder for Windows Embedded Compact 7. With this BSP, you can create a Compact 7 OS run-time image that is able to run on a Virtual PC for Windows 7 and Virtual PC 2007 for Windows XP and Vista.

The Virtual PC BSP provides a convenient and cost-efficient means for a developer to establish a test target for Compact 7, using VM, without the associated hardware cost.

CONFIGURE VIRTUAL PC CONNECTIVITY

Although you can configure a Virtual PC to acquire an IP address dynamically from an attached DHCP server, when working with Windows Embedded Compact development using a standalone development station without access to DHCP, it's best to configure the Virtual PC machine and the host computer to use static IP addresses to establish connectivity, using the loopback adapter.

Loopback Adapter

To configure the Virtual PC machine and host computer to establish connectivity using the loopback adapter with static IP addresses, you need to install the Microsoft loopback adapter driver to the host PC first, prior to configuring the VM to use the loopback adapter.

Install the Loopback Adapter on a Windows 7 Development Station

Work through the following steps to configure the loopback adapter for a Windows 7 development station:

1. From the Windows 7 desktop's Start menu, execute the following command to launch the Device Manager:

   `mmc devmgmt.msc`

2. After the Device Manager launches, click the Computer node. (This action is needed to access the Action menu in the next step.)

3. From the Device Manager Action menu, click Add Legacy Hardware to bring up the Add Hardware Wizard; then click Next to continue.

4. Select the Install the Hardware That I Manually Select from a List (Advanced) option, and click Next to continue.

5. From the Common Hardware Types selection list, select Network adapters, and click Next.

6. From the Manufacturer pane on the left, select Microsoft.

7. From the Network Adapter selection pane on the right, select Microsoft Loopback Adapter, and click on Next.

8. At this point, the wizard is ready to install the Loopback adapter. Click Next to complete the installation process.

Configure the Loopback Adapter for a Virtual PC Machine

In addition to installing the Loopback adapter to the development station, you need to configure the Virtual PC machine to use the Loopback adapter.

A Virtual PC machine, `cevm.vmc`, preconfigured with Windows Embedded Compact bootloader is provided as part of the Virtual PC BSP.

Work through the following steps to configure the Loopback adapter for the `cevm.vmc` virtual machine:

1. Launch Windows Explorer; navigate to the following folder:

   `_PLATFORMROOT)\VirtualPC\VM`

2. Double-click `cevm.vmc` to launch this virtual machine.

3. From the cevm Windows Virtual PC's Tools menu, click Settings to bring up the Windows Virtual PC Settings screen, as shown in Figure A-1.

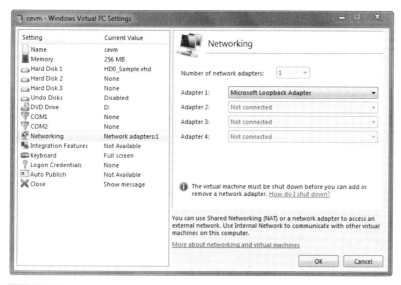

FIGURE A-1

4. From the left pane, select Networking.

5. For Adapter 1 on the right pane, select Microsoft Loopback Adapter, and click OK.

After the virtual machine restarts, the Loopback adapter takes effect.

Configure Static IP Addresses

In addition to installing the Loopback adapter, you need to configure the proper static IP address for it to function.

Static IP Address for Development Station

Work through the following steps to configure the static IP address for the Loopback adapter installed on the development station:

1. Launch Control Panel.

2. Click Network and Internet.

3. Click Network and Sharing Center.

4. From the left pane, click Change Adapter Settings.

5. There should multiple network device icons on this screen. Right-mouse-click the Microsoft Loopback Adapter network icon and click Properties to bring up the Local Area Connection Properties screen.

6.   From the Networking tab, select Internet Protocol Version 4 (TCP/IPv4) and click Properties to bring up the IP address configuration screen.

7.   Select the Use the Following IP Address option, enter an IP address, subnet masks, and click OK.

Static IP Address for the Virtual Machine

For the virtual machine, you need to configure the bootloader to launch with a static IP address. You need to separately configure the static IP address for the Compact 7 OS run-time image.

Work through the following steps to configure the static IP address for the virtual PC machine's bootloader:

1.   Launch Windows Explorer; navigate to the following folder:

    _PLATFORMROOT\VirtualPC\VM

2.   Double-click cevm.vmc to launch this virtual machine.

3.   After the virtual machine launches, press the space bar to enter the configuration.

4.   From the Main Menu, press 4 to enter the Network Settings.

5.   From the Network Settings menu, press 5 to set the IP address. Enter an IP address and press Enter.

6.   Press 4 and select the option to disable DHCP.

7.   Press 0 to exit the Network Settings menu.

8.   From the Main Menu, press 7 to save settings.

9.   Press 0 to exit the configuration.

After the preceding configuration, the virtual machine reboots, launches the bootloader and sends BOOTME messages.

 After the Compact 7 OS run-time image downloads and launches on the virtual machine, the IP address configured for the bootloader no longer is in effect. You need to separately configure the IP address for the Compact 7 OS runtime image. You can configure the OS design to generate an OS runtime image with a preconfigured IP address. Refer to Chapter 10, "The Registry," for more information about the registry entries to configure IP address.

VIRTUAL PC 2007

The preceding section talks about Virtual PC connectivity for a Windows 7 PC. When using a Windows XP or Vista PC as the development station, you need to use Virtual PC 2007, available for download from the following URL:

www.microsoft.com/download/en/details.aspx?displaylang=en&id=24439

The `cevm.vmc` Virtual PC provided as part of the Virtual PC BSP is able to function as a Virtual PC 2007 virtual machine.

VIRTUAL PC INFORMATION RESOURCES

You can find lots of useful information about Virtual PC from the Virtual PC Guy's Blog, at the following URL:

```
http://blogs.msdn.com/b/virtual_pc_guy
```

B

Microsoft Resources

You can find plenty of information related to Windows Embedded Compact from Microsoft web sites. Some of the resources from the previous versions may be applicable to Compact 7. You can search and locate these resources using the following product names and acronyms:

- ➤ CE 5.0
- ➤ CE 6.0
- ➤ Compact Framework
- ➤ .NET CF
- ➤ NETCF
- ➤ Windows CE
- ➤ Windows Embedded CE
- ➤ Windows Embedded Compact

EVALUATION SOFTWARE

Microsoft provides an evaluation version of Windows Embedded Compact 7, available for download from the following URL:

```
http://www.microsoft.com/windowsembedded/en-us/downloads/download-windows-
embedded-compact-ce.aspx
```

This URL provides links to download all the necessary software to evaluate Windows Embedded Compact 7, including Visual Studio 2008 Professional and Expression Blend 3.

From this URL, you can find links to other resources.

DRIVERS AND UTILITIES

This section lists the Windows Embedded Compact device drivers and utilities available from Microsoft web sites.

Windows Embedded CE 6.0 USB Camera Driver

This CE 6.0 driver, released with source code, supports a USB camera that meets the USB Video Class specification.

```
http://www.microsoft.com/downloads/en/details.aspx?FamilyID=2ef087c0-a4ae-42cc-
abd0-c466787c11f2
```

Windows Embedded CE DiskPrep Power Toy

The DiskPrep utility is used to format and configure flash storage with BIOSLoader to launch a Windows Embedded Compact OS runtime image.

```
http://archive.msdn.microsoft.com/DiskPrep
```

Windows Embedded CE 6.0 XML Web Services WSDL Generator

This utility automates the process to generate Web Service Definition Language (WSDL)/Web Service Modeling Language (WSML) files for Windows Embedded CE 6.0 XML web service projects.

```
http://archive.msdn.microsoft.com/cewsdlgen
```

PipeTerm for Windows Embedded CE 6.0 and Virtual PC 2007

You can use this utility to display serial debug message output from a Windows Embedded Compact OS runtime image running on a Virtual PC.

```
http://archive.msdn.microsoft.com/PipeTerm
```

Remote Tools for Smart Devices

This utility enables you to control running processes on a Windows Embedded Compact device and view the device's system information remotely.

```
http://archive.msdn.microsoft.com/RemoteTool
```

BusEnum2

BusEnum2 is an enhanced bus enumerator for Windows Embedded CE 6.0 that supports loading a device driver asynchronously.

```
http://archive.msdn.microsoft.com/BusEnum2
```

DevHealth60

DevHealth60 is a utility that you can use to monitor memory usage on a Windows Embedded Compact device, and it provides a starting point for investigating memory leaks and other memory usage issues.

```
http://archive.msdn.microsoft.com/DevHealth60
```

AppVerifier

AppVerifier is a tool to assess an application's stability. This tool can detect and pinpoint memory and handle leaks. This tool can also detect some forms of heap corruption.

```
http://archive.msdn.microsoft.com/compact7appverifier
```

WINDOWS EMBEDDED COMPACT FORUMS

As of this book's writing, there are three established Microsoft forums related to Windows Embedded Compact:

➤ Forum for Windows Embedded Compact managed application development

➤ Forum for Windows Embedded Compact native application development

➤ Forum for Windows Embedded Compact platform development

Following is the URL for the Windows Embedded Compact Forums landing page where you can access these forums:

```
http://social.msdn.microsoft.com/Forums/en-US/category/windowsembeddedcompact
```

Community Resources

WINDOWS EMBEDDED COMMUNITY

Developers independent of Microsoft contributed the community resources in this section.

www.Embedded101.com

The Embedded101 community portal provides information resources to help developers who are new to Windows Embedded and provides a platform for the developers in the community to share their knowledge and help others. You can find technical articles, blog posts, and other information resources related to Windows Embedded on this site.

www.we-dig.com

Windows Embedded Developer Interest Group (WE-DIG) is a user group based in Redmond, WA. The monthly user group meeting usually takes place on the Microsoft campus. If you happen to be in the Seattle area, check its schedule and drop by one of the meetings. There is a good chance that you can meet some of the Microsoft folks from the Windows Embedded product team.

COMMUNITY PROJECTS FOR COMPACT 7

This section lists the community projects with resources created to support Compact 7.

AutoLaunch for Windows Embedded Compact (CE)

The AutoLaunch utility is provided as Compact 7 and CE 6.0 components. After installation, it shows up as one of the components on the catalog, which you can include in an OS design and compile as part of the OS runtime image. With the AutoLaunch component added, the OS runtime image can be configured to launch multiple applications with command-line parameters during startup. Each application can be configured with an independent time delay to control the application startup sequence.

```
http://autolaunch4ce.codeplex.com
```

CEDriverWiz — Windows Embedded CE Stream Driver Wizard

This is a stream interface device driver wizard for Windows Embedded Compact. This wizard helps create the initial project workspace needed to develop a stream interface driver. It also provides the option to generate utilities, as subprojects to an OS design, to load, unload the driver, and test whether the driver is started.

```
http://CEDriverWiz.codeplex.com
```

CoreCon for Windows Embedded Compact (CE)

To establish connectivity between the VS2008 development station and a Compact 7 device to support application development, the necessary CoreCon files need to be accessible from the device file system or compiled as part of the OS runtime image.

The CoreCon4CE is a Compact 7 component. When included in an OS design, it contains the build command script needed to include the necessary CoreCon files in the OS runtime image.

```
http://corecon4ce.codeplex.com
```

FTDI Resources for Windows Embedded Compact/CE

As covered in Chapter 44, "FTDI Devices," FTDI provides a USB-to-Serial port hardware solution, to add a serial port to a Compact 7 device through an USB interface. The manufacturer released the driver for Compact 7 that requires you to manually add the driver binary and registry entries to the OS design.

This project packages the FTDI driver into a Compact 7 component to simplify the tasks needed to include the driver to an OS design.

```
http://FTDI4CE.codeplex.com
```

Managed Code4 Tools for Windows Embedded Compact

Although Platform Builder has support for building managed code applications, little documentation is available on how to include a managed code application as a subproject to an OS design with no documentation covering how to develop them over KITL.

This project provides the resources to include a managed code application project, as a subproject to an OS design, and to compile as part of the OS design's build process.

Chapter 45, "Integrating Managed Code Projects," is the starting point for this project.

```
http://ManagedCode4C7.codeplex.com
```

Windows CE Component Wizard

This wizard helps package software components into a Compact 7 component that installs and appears on the component catalog, which can be selected to be part of an OS design.

If you have software components that need to be distributed to other developers to be included as part of their OS design, or you need to package the software component to reuse in multiple OS design projects, this wizard helps simplify the process.

```
http://cecomponentwiz.codeplex.com
```

Windows CE Driver for Phidgets

This Codeplex project was initiated to create a Windows Embedded Compact driver to support the Phidgets devices. Phidgets is a family of devices that include different types of sensor, relay, and motor control modules that have a USB interface.

The exercise in Chapter 43, "Phidgets Devices," uses the Compact 7 Phidgets driver from this project.

```
http://phidgetswincedriver.codeplex.com
```

OTHER COMMUNITY PROJECTS

This section lists the community projects created for the previous versions of Windows Embedded Compact. It's likely that the application development frameworks created to support previous versions can support Compact 7.

32feet.NET

This Personal Area Networking for a .NET shared source project provides the library to make personal area networking such as Bluetooth and Infrared (IrDA) easily accessible from a managed code application.

```
http://32feet.codeplex.com
```

MobFx — Mobile Application Development Framework

This is a general purpose application development framework for Windows Embedded Compact and Windows Mobile.

```
http://MobFx.codeplex.com
```

MTConnect Managed SDK

MTConnect is a set of open, royalty-free standards intended to foster greater interoperability between controls, devices, and software applications by publishing data over networks using the Internet Protocol.

The MTConnect project on the Codeplex site is a managed SDK that provides Agent, Adapter, and Client object models to facilitate both exposing MTConnect data from the device as well as consuming data published by remote MTConnect Agents.

```
http://MTconnect.codeplex.com
```

OpenNETCF

OpenNETCF provides several software tools for Compact Framework developers, including the Smart Device Framework (SDF), which was initially developed to provide functions not available as part of the .NET Compact Framework 1.0. Although the version 3.5 of the .NET Compact Framework has gone through significant improvements and includes more features than the initial 1.0 release, the SDF still adds significant value by providing features that are not part of the .NET Compact Framework. There is a free community version available for personal and commercial use.

```
http://www.opennetcf.com
```

OpenNETCF Autorun Manager for CE

This project provides the code to automatically launch an application whenever a FAT storage volume is either mounted or dismounted on a Windows Embedded Compact device.

```
http://autorunmgr.codeplex.com
```

OpenNETCF MTConnect VirtualAgent

The OpenNETCF VirtualAgent is a cross-platform implementation of an MTConnect agent running on any platform that can execute code meeting the Common Language Interface (CLI) such as C# or VB.NET. The VirtualAgent adds several capabilities not included in a Standards-defined Agent by the MTConnect specification, including the ability to integrate models, custom controller logic, and data collection.

```
http://MTcAgent.codeplex.com
```

OpenNETCF.Telephony

This is a telephony application interface (TAPI) library for Windows CE and Windows Mobile devices.

```
http://TAPI.codeplex.com
```

OpenTimeCE

Windows CE does not support the full set of `time_t` functions in `time.h` from the C Standard Library. This project ports the ANSI C `time_t` functions to support Windows CE.

```
http://Time.codeplex.com
```

Smart Device Information and Remote Processes Tool

This Codeplex project provides a utility to manage processes on Windows CE and Windows Mobile devices from your desktop PC and display device information remotely.

```
http://RemoteDeviceManager.codeplex.com
```

TFTP Server for Windows CE

This is a Trivial File Transfer Protocol (TFTP) server for Windows CE, ported from a GPL Unix implementation of the TFTP protocol.

```
http://TFTPCE.codeplex.com
```

Windows CE Splash Generator

This is a Windows desktop utility that you can use to convert a graphic image file to a file in BMX image format, `splash.bmx`, to use as the splash screen for a Windows Embedded Compact device. This utility can convert BMP, PGN, GIF, or JPG files to BMX image files.

```
http://SplashCE.codeplex.com
```

Windows CE Utilities — LoadDriver

This is a command-line tool for loading and unloading a Windows CE device driver, useful for driver development.

```
http://bogong.codeplex.com
```

Windows CE Webcam Project

This project provides a Windows Embedded Compact device driver for a USB camera that meets the USB Video Class 1.1 specification. It was initially developed to support Windows CE 5.0 and was updated to support Windows Embedded CE 6.0.

The exercise in Chapter 41, "USB Camera Application," is based on this driver.

```
http://CEWebCam.codeplex.com
```

OTHER RESOURCES

www.Embeddedpc.net

The `Embeddedpc.net` portal was created initially to support students participating in the Windows Embedded Student Challenge competition, which became part of the Imagine Cup in 2007, Imagine Cup

Embedded Development Invitational. Imagine Cup is a worldwide student competition. In 2010, there were more than 300,000 students signed up to compete in different categories (`www.imaginecup.com`).

This portal provides Windows Embedded resources to the academic and hobbyist developer communities. You can find board support packages, SDKs, hardware information, learning references, and links to academic resources for Windows Embedded.

Embedded Hardware

Embedded development involves tinkering with hardware. Because Windows Embedded Compact is designed to support hardware based on the ARM, MIPS, and x86 processors, you have a broad range of hardware options to work with.

For developers new to the Windows Embedded Compact environment, to efficiently learn and engage with Windows Embedded Compact development, it's important to select hardware with appropriate Windows Embedded Compact 7 support.

EMBEDDED HARDWARE CONSIDERATIONS

A development environment good for learning the technology may not be the best for professional development. To minimize the time and unnecessary aggravation during the learning process, it's best to select a hardware platform with proper support for Compact 7.

Following are the basic requirements for the hardware needed to establish a proper Compact 7 development environment:

- ➤ Board support package for Compact 7 that includes all the required drivers
- ➤ Kernel Independent Transport Layer (KITL) driver needed to support debugging
- ➤ Bootloader to launch OS runtime image from local storage
- ➤ Bootloader to download OS runtime image from the Platform Builder development station

Device driver and OEM adaptation layer development are major tasks. If the necessary device driver and OEM adaptation layer are not provided by the hardware manufacture or Microsoft, these are challenging and difficult components to develop.

eBox-3310A

The eBox-3310A (eBox), the target device for the exercises in this book, is built with MSTI PDX-600 System-on-Chip (SoC), a derivative of the Vortex86DX SoC. There are Compact 7 BSP, device drivers, bootloader, SDK, and utilities available to support the eBox.

The eBox family of products has been used as a learning platform for Windows Embedded Compact within the academic community worldwide since 2005 and has been chosen by Microsoft as the hardware platform for the annual Imagine Cup Embedded Development competition since the inception of this global student competition, where participating students develop solutions, based on Windows Embedded Compact, to solve some of the toughest worldwide problems, as stated in the United Nation's Millennium goals:

http://www.un.org/millenniumgoals/

http://www.imaginecup.com

The eBox is also used as the target device for the "Introduction to Embedded Systems" curriculum developed by Professor James Hamblen at Georgia Institute of Technology. This is a full-semester embedded system curriculum initially released in 2007 with the second revision released in 2008. This curriculum has been translated to Chinese, German, Japanese, and Korean. Following are the URLs to this curriculum:

http://www.microsoft.com/education/facultyconnection/articles/articledetails
.aspx?cid=1814

http://users.ece.gatech.edu/~hamblen/

A low-cost Windows Embedded Compact jump start kit, based on the eBox-3310A, packaged with the necessary components, including memory, flash storage, and power supply is available to the academic and hobbyist community:

http://www.embeddedpc.net/eBox3310AMSJK

The eBox-3310A is a compact computing device built with the following:

➤ 1.0GHz MSTI PDX-600 SoC (Derivative of Vortex86DX)

➤ **512MB DDR2 RAM**

➤ 10/100 Mbps Ethernet

➤ XGI Z9s video and CM119 Audio

➤ Type I/II Compact Flash and Micro SD slots

➤ 2 RS-232 serial ports and 3 USB 2.0 host interface

➤ Dimensions: 115mm x 115mm x 35mm

➤ Power by +5VDC

With more than 7 years of cumulated support resources, and used by key universities worldwide as the reference hardware platform to teach embedded system curriculums, eBox is one of the best hardware platforms to learn Windows Embedded Compact.

x86 Embedded Hardware

Many legacy-embedded developers consider x86 processors to be designed for the desktop PC, notebook, and server and do not consider x86 hardware a good option for embedded devices.

As technology and the market evolve, things do change. The new generation of Vortex86DX System-on-Chip, based on X86 processor architecture, is designed to support embedded, industrial, and robotics applications. By integrating feature I/O peripherals as part of the chip, the Vortex86DX SoC enables embedded engineers to design powerful, smaller-footprint processor modules such as the RoBoard, as shown in Figure D-1, built with the following features:

➤ 1.0 GHz Vortex86DX SoC with 256MB DDR2 RAM

➤ Micro-SD slot

➤ 6 serial ports

➤ I²C Bus

➤ Mini-PCI expansion slot

➤ 10/100 Mbps Ethernet and 3 USB 2.0 host interfaces

➤ 16 channel PWM to control servos and brushless DC motors

➤ 8 channel A/D

➤ Power by +6 to +24VDC

➤ Dimensions: 96mm x 56mm

FIGURE D-1

More information about the RoBoard is available from the following URL:

http://www.roboard.com

Varieties of other embedded processor modules are built with the Vortex86DX SoC; to find them just search the Web.

Although embedded hardware based on the x86 processor is considered a late-comer to the embedded development domain, the x86 hardware's well-defined architecture, standardization, along with almost 30 years of cumulated application development resources from the desktop PC, makes it an attractive hardware option that should not be taken lightly.

ARM Processor

Embedded hardware based on the ARM processor has been around for awhile. Different flavors of ARM processors exist, with different features, designed to serve different vertical markets.

Although broad ranges of embedded hardware selections are based on the ARM processor architecture, processor modules based on the ARM processor lack standardization, making it difficult to use support resources from one processor module with another.

When selecting hardware based on the ARM processor for a project, you need to consider the added cost and development schedule needed to develop the required device drivers and BSP components.

SUMMARY

An abundance of embedded hardware is available, built with different features, for differing purposes. The technology landscape is evolving rapidly with new creations that can replicate existing technology with better features and more efficient use of energy at a lower cost.

Technology is expected to change rapidly. Just think about the mobile phone, gaming console, and portable media player in the market today, 3 years ago, and 5 years ago.

When selecting a hardware platform for an embedded development project, keep an open mind and chose a proper hardware platform based on an engineering perspective and not corporate culture.

INDEX

P

Y

Z

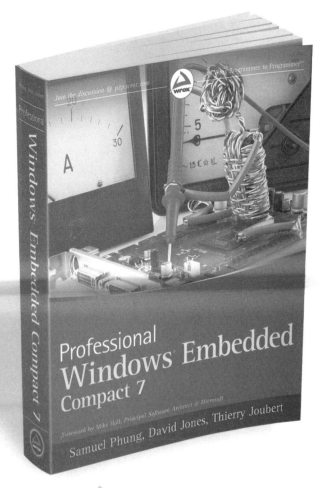